RELIGIOUS LIBERTY IN EASTERN EUROPE AND THE USSR

BEFORE AND AFTER THE GREAT TRANSFORMATION

Paul Mojzes

EAST EUROPEAN MONOGRAPHS, BOULDER
DISTRIBUTED BY COLUMBIA UNIVERSITY PRESS, NEW YORK

1992

EAST EUROPEAN MONOGRAPHS, NO. CCCXXXVII

Contents

Devoted to the memory of my father and mother as well as millions of others who suffered because of religious persecutions.

FOREWORD

Two vague intuitions which sprang slowly upon my consciousness in my middle age guided the writing of this book. Both of them focused originally on the Holocaust, but seemed appropriate as the scope of suffering and restrictions based on the Communist strategy of dealing with religion became obvious.[1]

The first one was the one that Edmund Burke verbalized clearly "the only thing necessary for the triumph of evil is for good men to do nothing." After it was reinforced by Elie Wiesel in his Nobel Peace Prize acceptance speech, it became a compelling reason for writing this book. A lot of well meaning people stood by doing nothing while religious liberties in many places around the world eroded or made no progress.

The second, regarding remembering the victims was stated by Paul Ricoeur, "we must remember because remembering is a *moral duty*. We owe a *debt* to the victims. And the tiniest way of paying our debt is to tell and to retell what happened . . ."[2]

My adult scholarly life, beginning with graduate school and doctoral dissertation, is marked by an intense concern and concentration on the developments in Eastern Europe and the USSR, which is the general region of my birth, childhood, and youth. Religious developments in particular became the focus ever since I migrated to the United States from Yugoslavia during my student years and was attracted to religion and the study of it. Nearly all phases of religious developments interested me, but I devoted particular attention to the history of religions of Eastern Europe, especially contemporary history and the Christian-Marxist dialogue, about which I wrote a book published in 1980 entitled *Christian-Marxist Dialogue in Eastern Europe* (Minneapolis: Augsburg Publishing House).

Since the publishing of that book I continued high intensity involvement in Christian-Marxist dialogues, attending and organizing conferences in Europe, East and West, and the U. S. I continued to write on various aspects of these issues and seeing that there is no journal in the U. S. that is devoted entirely to the broad range of religious issues in the USSR and Eastern Europe, I founded and still edit the *Occasional Papers on Religion in Eastern Europe*. The question of religious liberty was always of grave concern but as the decade of the eighties progresses, it increasingly came into focus for me. First, it was my colleague, Leonard Swidler, who asked me to write a paper on religious liberty in Yugoslavia for an international conference held in Havertown, PA focusing on the need for worldwide religious tolerance. Chapter 13 on Yugoslavia is a greatly revised and expanded version of "Religious Liberty in Yugoslavia A Study in Ambiguity," in *Religious Liberty and Human Rights in Nations and in Religions*, edited by Leonard Swidler (Philadelphia Ecumenical Press, 1986). Then I became involved in a series of conferences aimed to promote the 1981 United Nations Declaration on the Elimination of All Forms of Intolerance and of Discrimination Based on Religion or Belief.

What brought the issue into far sharper focus was not general awareness of suppression of religious liberties in Eastern Europe of which I already had first-hand knowledge and awareness since my childhood but that each time on my frequent trips to the Soviet Union or the various Eastern European countries I had occasions, planned as well as inadvertent, to meet people who were victims to various degrees of religious persecution and repression. Some of those meetings were so intense that they would drive me to anguish as I reflected on these people's experiences and predicaments and became even more aware of the blessings of a life fortunately sheltered from the need to give witness to my faith in such demanding manner. I observed how the pressures of a persecuting ideology and state apparatus made some people into heroes, others into cowards, some into compromisers, others into near psychotics. By 1987 I knew I wanted to write a book-length work on religious liberty. The bibliographical survey, *Church and State in Postwar Eastern Europe* (Westport, CT: Greenwood Press, 1987), which I wrote, made me aware that while most authors who wrote on religion in Eastern Europe dealt to some degree with the issue of religious liberty there were no scholarly studies focusing entirely on that issue. I decided to take on the task, but since Eastern Europe is so diverse, I did not know whether to restrict the theme to a few countries in the form of case studies or to look for other colleagues in the field who might become co-authors or to go it alone. The latter option was a challenge though the task was humbling and discouraging at times as after much arduous work the end of the tunnel was not to be seen. Unlike my work on the Christian-Marxist dialogue in Eastern Europe which had to be built from scratch because there had been a dearth of materials, and when I wrote the book, there simply was not much left that was not included in it, in this case I faced the opposite problem. Namely, such an enormous amount of material had been written touching on one aspect or another of the topic that I knew I could not digest it all. What I would need to do is to stress reliability and balance rather than comprehensiveness. Using original sources with such diverse countries as Albania and Poland or Romania and East Germany would be impossible. Greater reliance would have to be placed on a selection of published sources combined with interviews, first-hand experience, and selective reading of primary sources. Given the nature and scope of the area I am convinced that this is the best, though not ideal approach.

With about half of the first draft of the manuscript written the Great Transformation of 1989 took place which unsettled the original approach. The initial intention had been to explain the tension between two claims: one that religious liberty is completely suppressed in Eastern Europe and the other that religious liberty in socialist Eastern Europe excels above all previous social orders. The former was asserted by many who fled Eastern Europe during the darkest Stalinist destructions of all things religious: buildings, organizations, and people. Cold war propagandists and many who simply feared the advance of Communism came to believe and propagate the notion that no legitimate religion was practiced anywhere in Eastern Europe, except perhaps in the catacombs. The other view was fostered not only by official government spokespersons but also by many religious leaders from those countries in their public appearances at international gatherings, when visiting us or when we visited them. To most people it was obvious that neither picture was accurate, for at least occasionally, they saw evidence that religion not only survived but was lively in socialist circumstances (e.g the election of a Polish archbishop to the papacy) or else that the same religious leaders when they felt safe could in confidence detail difficulties that their government created for them or for others.

Thus my initial approach was going to be an attempt to describe the unprecedented restrictions of religious liberties, which, however, differed from country to country and even from village to village and to point out factors that worked for limitation and even termination of religious liberty. At the time many of these factors were not public knowledge and were certainly vigorously and angrily denied by Eastern European governmental and religious leaders.

But *perestroika* and *glasnost* changed all that. Trends, causes, and factors that I thought might be carefully drawn, inferential insights, and the occasional dramatic revelation suddenly were acknowledged, sometimes even by the culprits. For instance, as the security forces of East Germany and Romania collapsed and their files became available, it became a fact, rather than merely a reliable conclusion, that even clergy were drawn into the network of spies and reporters and that specific sections of the secret police had been formed to control and muzzle religious life in the country. There were public acknowledgements by Communists that religious liberty was, indeed, denied.

Revelations of the past misdeeds were significant, but even more so was the fact that suddenly the situation improved and that mechanisms of oppression were being dismantled hence making it possible for far greater religious liberty than before. What seemed in 1987 only an utopian, idealized model of religious liberty for Eastern Europe suddenly became real prospect.

One possible reaction was to restrict myself to deal with the periods up to the Great Transformation. The advantage would be that one could deal with a time period which is already largely over. But a more attractive possibility was to insert the subtitle "Before and After the Great Transformation" thus presenting the situation on both sides of the great watershed. The "before" covers an epoch in the history of humanity (or at least of Europe) which seems to have come to an end; the "after" is only in its inception. Where it is heading is not clear at all, except to know that it is rather distinct from the "before." That makes the work a bit more tentative but also more relevant. Fully aware that a greater distance from the events is useful for a proper historical perspective, it is evident to me that works closer to the events have a more dynamic possibility of influencing those who may yet have an impact on the events as they unfold. The risk is that one is liable to look somewhat silly in retrospect if events overtake the analysis.

Many people provided useful assistance at various stages of the project. First there were the large number of people whom I have interviewed or from whom I received insights in conversations or lectures. My way of expressing my gratitude to them is by footnoting their views at appropriate places. It does not mean that they would agree with my overall presentation of the material, but I trust that I reflected their views faithfully, and I certainly learned a great deal from them. Some of them were scholars, others were clergy, and still others were dissidents or simple believers.

Drafts of various chapters were read by many colleagues in the field. I wish to thank professors Dr. John Burgess of Doane College, NE, Dr. Waldemar Chrostowski of the Academy of Catholic Theology in Warsaw, Dr. Tamás Földesi of University of Budapest Law School, Dr. Finngeir Hiorth of University of Oslo, Dr. Leslie Laszlo of Concordia University in Toronto, Dr. Jan M. Lochman of University of Basel, Dr. Otto Luchterhandt of University of Cologne, Dr. Earl Pope of Lafayette College, PA, Dr. Joseph Pungur of the University of Alberta in Edmonton, Dr. Spas Raikin of East Stroudsburg University, PA, and Rev. Uldis Savaljevs of Riga, Latvia. Their critical comments, bibliographical assistance, corrections, and advice were helpful, though they bear no responsibility for the way I organized or presented the material. I have also profited from the discussion of the chapter on Yugoslavia presented at a conference in Havertown, PA. in 1985, chapter on Albania presented at a conference in Warsaw, Poland, in 1988 and the chapter on Theory (ch. 1) at an international conference on Human Rights in Washington, DC where I profited from the critique of professors Dr. Vladan Perišić of Belgrade, Yugoslavia, and Dr. Pál Bruno Turnay of Panonhalma, Hungary. The accuracy of the work benefited by the criticism of all of these colleagues, though, as always the author bears the responsibility for any flaws that may be found in the book. I am especially grateful to my colleague at Rosemont College, Dr. Jacqueline Murphy, who read all the chapters and corrected my sometimes tortured prose trying to make it into a more effective communication. She as well as numerous others encouraged me to stay with this project.

I wish to express my thanks to the Pew Charitable Trust which gave a Faculty Development grant to Rosemont College that enabled me to get a reduced teaching load during the Fall semester 1988 while I was working on chapters 2 and 5. Chapter 2 is a revised version of a paper presented at a Christian-Marxist Dialogue on Human Rights in Washington, DC in October 1988 and was published as "The Theory of Religious Liberty" in *Christian and Marxist Dialogue on Human Rights* edited by Leonard Swidler (New York: Paragon House, 1991).

Parts of chapter 12 on Yugoslavia are based on my chapter in *The Religious Liberty and Human Rights in Nations and Religions*, edited by Leonard Swidler (Philadelphia: Ecumenical Press and New York: Hippocrene Books, 1986), pp. 23–41.

A concern that haunts me in connection with this book was again well expressed by Ricoeur,

> Historians, sociologists, and economists may claim to explain the tragedy so thoroughly that it becomes merely one case of barbarism among others. Even worse, an alleged full explanation may make the event appear as necessary, to the extent that the causes–whether economical, political, psychological, or religious–would be held to exhaust the meaning of the event. The task of memory is to preserve the scandalous dimension of the event, to leave that which is monstrous inexhaustible by explanation.[3]

It is hoped that the lengthy treatment of this disturbing subject will not rob it of some of its unsettling and shameful dimension.

INTRODUCTION

Monumental changes have swept through the Soviet Union and Eastern Europe for the second time in the twentieth century. First came the Bolshevik revolution in the Soviet Union at the end of the first of the two world wars. It was followed by a series of revolutionary changes in the countries covered in this book that came to be known under a slight misnomer, Eastern Europe, after the second of those global conflagrations. A totalitarian system was imposed which had the appearance of permanence; some called it the wave of the future. But the permanence was illusory. By the end of the eighties of the same century when it began, totalitarian communism destructed more from within than from external pressure. Neither its demise nor the quickness of it could be anticipated. The low level of violence accompanying the changes, often called the "velvet" or "quiet" revolution, was also unexpected and there was good reason to be jubilant though not gleeful. By the time the book's first draft was finished one of the countries included in this study, the German Democratic Republic, disappeared from the map, having reunified with the Federal Republic of Germany on October 3, 1990. Two other countries could also change their present borders and perhaps be drastically remade by the time the readers get the book, namely the Soviet Union and Yugoslavia. Both are multi-national, multi-religious federal states that are straining under the impact of centripetal forces that threaten to break them up or at least contain some secessions. Estonia, Latvia, and Lithuania did secede and joined the family of independent nations. Most of the other countries were also radically remade during the Great Transformation of 1989/90. Not only were multi-party democratic processes introduced, but governments were changed; the parliaments were re-made; the prefixes "socialist" or "people's" were dropped from their official names; flags or emblems altered, and so forth. The changes taking place in the direction of democracy were as profound as the changes that had taken place previously in the direction of socialism. Needless to say, a great deal of dislocation took place, sometimes bordering on the chaotic, because two world wars and two revolutions in less than a century, in addition to other lesser upheavals, is surely more than enough. Many Eastern Europeans can agree with the sentiments of a proverbial Chinese saying, "may you live in interesting times"—they know it as a curse. Thus many of them do not share the enthusiasm and optimism experienced in the West about these changes but are far more cautious and even downright pessimistic. This was, in brief, the historical context of religious liberties investigated by the author.

The Approach and Method

The overwhelming majority of the literature on religious liberty in the USSR and Eastern Europe seems to emphasize the discontinuity between the practices under Communism and that of the previous period. It also contrasts it with the practices in Western countries or with the idealized picture of what religious liberties ought to be. Such discontinuity is duly noted also in this book since it was both real and pervasive. But what seems to be lacking was the recognition of some continuities. In order to be able to discern them it was necessary to provide a survey of each country's experience with religious liberty prior to the communist revolution or takeover. This approach helps the reader to note that certain historic patterns tended to be continuous even under the Communist regime, for example, patterns of Josephinism in Hungary, of Orthodox inclination to follow the lead of the state authorities even when they became inimical to the Church, patterns of ethnic identification with certain churches that contributed to church growth during the ethnic revival under and after communism, patterns of Catholic power in Poland, and so forth. Thus each chapter begins with a historical survey of religious liberty in the respective country, and these experiences tended to differ sharply from country to country and even in segments of the country.

What all of the countries under study had in common was the superimposition of a Marxist-Leninist interpretation of religion and religious liberty by the Communist party, usually in stages. In order to see what that tradition had to say about religious liberty two chapters are devoted to the two formative strands of the tradition, Marxian, i.e. that of Marx and Engels (chapter 2) and that of Lenin (chapter 3). No attention is paid to their theories of religion because that does not fit the scheme of the book while the exposition of Marx's and Lenin's view of nature and role of religion has been often described. Prior to surveying Marx's, Engels', and Lenin's view on religious liberty one needs to discuss the various ideas about religious liberty, those that had arisen in Eastern Europe as well as general notions. Chapter 1 provides the introductory discussion of various concepts of religious liberty and ends with the author's comprehensive notion of religious liberty. As the author explored different notions of religious liberty, it became obvious that several historical patterns of religious liberty were available and in use over the years. The author adopted a four-point typology applicable to religious freedom, discerning four distinct models, purer of course, in theory than in history. This typology was then implemented in each chapter showing how the models varied in each country from one epoch to another. Two of those models were absolutist, one ecclesiastic (Type A) and the other one secularist (Type C), while two models were tolerant, one providing religious tolerance (Type B) and the other complete religious liberty in a pluralistic society (Type D). The reader will note that in those countries where Type A had a more powerful hold Type C was more triumphalisticly implemented because the mentality and acceptance of the imposition of an intolerant absolutistic attitude was prevalent. Dominance of one view simply gave way to dominance of another, but the structural relationship did not need to change. In those countries where type B had prevailed over Type A and had been in practice for a longer time in those countries, Type C experienced greater resistance, and there was a tendency of features of Type B to persist along with features of Type C. It also seems that Type D could be more emphatically victorious in those countries where Type B had taken deeper roots.

Chapter 4 on the Soviet Union is by far the longest and should be read in conjunction with the chapter on Lenin (chapter 3). This is appropriate since the Soviet Union's experience with socialism is the longest. The Soviet Union was such a trendsetter, partially due to its own claim of "the first country of socialism" and "the older brother" and partially to the objective fact that the only place the neophyte Communist parties of other countries could learn was the Soviet Union. On top of that the imperial policies of the Soviet Union tended toward conformity, not just cooperation, and starting with the Comintern and the Informbureau and the Warsaw Pact and Comecon, instructions emanated from the center, and cooperation was compelled so that the Soviet patterns willy nilly were being applied at least for brief periods of time, especially during the Stalinist period in all Communist countries. Thus to understand the patterns in other countries one needs to read the segment on the Soviet Union. In it there are also some theoretical observations applicable to other countries and helpful in understanding their problematic.

Albania, Bulgaria, Czechoslovakia, East Germany, Hungary, Poland, Romania, and Yugoslavia each have a chapter devoted to the issue of religious liberty as it developed in each country. The chapters could be arranged in various orders or clusters, e.g. countries with one predominant religion over against plural religions or countries with Eastern Orthodox predominance over against western Catholicism and Protestantism. Still another way of clustering them would be along a north-south axis, namely East Germany, Poland, Czechoslovakia, and Hungary in one cluster and Romania, Yugoslavia, Bulgaria, and Albania. After much reflection, I see no advantage to any such clustering actually I think it is misleading, for it implies parallels that are not as significant as such clustering implies. Many readers may wonder about the wisdom of arranging them simply alphabetically behind the USSR, but I maintain that there is less harm in this ordering than reinforcing artificial clusters. There simply are no advantages to the other orderings.

The method is historical. The author is a historian of religion, and he has aimed here to provide a historical interpretation presenting the narrative of the developments of what affected religious liberty and as many factors influencing that development as possible. The author refrains from using approaches other than those that are historical; there are no attempts to use theories of governance, sociological analyses, or psycho-social analyses and patterns of dissent.

Scope and Limitations

The scope of this study is the European part of the USSR (with the greatest weight given to Russia consonant to the Soviet practice to make the Russian Federation's legislation and practices copied by the other republics) and the once socialist countries of Eastern Europe. Marx, Engels, and Lenin, and within the chapter on the Soviet Union, Stalin are the only thinkers and leaders to whom any significant attention is given. Other leaders have had some impact on church policies, Khrushchev did so in a restrictive, Gorbachev in a liberating, Rákossi in a restrictive, and Imre Poszgay in a liberating way. But it was impossible to provide within a general study such as this a closer analysis of the impact that individual government leaders of all these countries had on religious liberty.

Most books on religion in Eastern Europe dealt with church-state relations, Marxist analysis of religion, and the martyrdom or adaptation of religious people to the new circumstances. This book is definitely *not* dealing with these subject matters though occasionally issues of that type appear insofar as they are relevant to the study of religious liberty. This is *not* a history of religious developments in Eastern Europe; it is *not* an analysis of communist legislation on religion, *nor* is it an account of church state-relations, church in society, religion and politics, religion and ethnicity, ecumenical relations, or anything *except* an examination of religious liberty, its restrictions or expansions in the specified area during a specified period. This necessitated the omission of many fascinating issues that are of interest to the author and the reader, but the limits have been kept rigorously. To paraphrase Soren Kierkegaard, the reader who is not interested in this issue need not read further.

The author did try to shed some light on the role of certain mechanisms operating in the Communist system which had a bearing on religious liberty such as Communist patterns and strategies of rule over a society, with the specific role of the Communist party, patterns and mechanism of surveillance and control, modes of making believers into second-class citizens, national traditions in regard to church formations (e.g. *Volkskirche*, state church, national church, free church patterns). Attention has been given to some of the legal framework that affects religious liberty, but the author expresses his conviction that legal proclamations of religious liberty carried practically no weight in a society ruled primarily by administrative decrees, many of them secret and unwritten orders on how to implement general Communist Party principles of the harmful nature of religion from which the people need to be protected and religion itself forced into oblivion.

Specific cases of harassment, torture, imprisonment, and killing because of a person's religious convictions could not be itemized though each of these acts are a radical denial of religious liberty. I did try to draw attention to these as consisting of one of the darkest chapters in the twentieth century, a century otherwise famous for colossal atrocities. There has been a school of scholarship that tended to gloss over these, dealing with them, in a generalized euphemistic manner, describing them as "administrative measures," "security measures," "state repression," "brutalities of the police apparatus," "totalitarian enslavement," "purges," etc. This does not suffice. The horrors of the Communist rule, especially of the Stalinist period, were matched in horror only by the Holocaust and is entirely appropriate for scholars to express indignation, revulsion, moral judgment, and outrage at such repulsive deeds. I am far more concerned about becoming inhuman than being "unscholarly" when I write about these activities, though I do not delve into the gruesome details. There had been scholars who had concentrated only or primarily on these aspects of inhumanity. I do not wish to concentrate on it or to avoid it but rather place it into a larger picture. The qualities that I sought to accomplish are reliability, fairness, comprehensiveness, and balance. The reader will judge whether I have achieved this.

List of Abbreviations

AB – *AKSA Bulletin* (London)

AKSA – Catholic Press Agency [Association of Christian Contemporaneity Agency]

ALRC – Christian Committee for the Defense of Religious Freedom and Freedom of Conscience (Romania)

Art. – Article

CPC – Christian Peace Conference (Prague)

CDU – *Christian Demokratische Union*

CES - Conference on European Security

CPSU(B) – Communist Party of the Soviet Union (Bolshevik)

DRO – *Die Religionsfreiheit in Osteuropa* (Eugen Voss, editor)

ECCB – Evangelical Church of the Czech Brethren

EKD – Evangelical Church of Germany

GDR – German Democratic Republic

G2W – *Glaube in der 2.Welt* (Zollikon, Switzerland)

HDZ – Hrvatska Demokratska Zajednica [Croatian Democratic Union]

HSATPB – *A History of Soviet Atheism in Theory and Practice, and the Believer* by Dimitry V. Pospeilovsky

HSWP – Hungarian Socialist Workers' Party

HWP – Hungarian Workers' Party

KGB – Soviet State Security

Kis – *Kirche im Sozialismus* (West Berlin)

LCY – League of Communists of Yugoslavia

MFAC – Ministry of Foreign Affairs and Cults (Bulgaria)

NIN – *Nedeljne Informative Novine* (Belgrade magazine)

OARD – Office for the Affairs of Religious Denominations

OPREE – *Occasional Papers on Religion in Eastern Europe* (Rosemont, PA)

ORA – Office of Religious Affairs

par – paragraph

PUWP – Polish United Workers' Party

RCL – *Religion in Communist Lands* (Keston, England)
ROC – Russian Orthodox Church
RSFSR – Russian Soviet Federal Socialist Republic
SED - *Sozialistische Einheits Partei* (GDR)
SESWNII – *Soviet Evangelicals Since World War II* by Walter Sawatsky
SOCA – State Office for Church Affairs
U.D.B.A. – Yugoslav State Security
U.N. – United Nations
USSR – Union of Soviet Socialist Republics
YMCA – Young Men's Christian Association

Chapter 1

RELIGIOUS LIBERTY: DEFINITIONS AND THEORETICAL FRAMEWORK

Great diversity exists not only in regards to the extent to which religious liberty is observed and cherished but also how this term is understood. "Religious liberty" is generally used as if it were self-evident, needing no defining. Yet, the well-known Swiss ecumenical leader, Lukas Vischer, disagrees, stating, "Religious liberty is not a concept whose validity is evident in advance. It needed, like the Gospel, to be proclaimed. Certainly, the validity of the principle of religious liberty can be proven."[1]

Sometimes the same concrete situation is given contradictory assessments, one protesting the absence and the other asserting the full extent of religious freedom. The reasons for such discrepancy may be many but often it hinges on how one defines religious liberty. One interpretation is that religious liberty consists of the right to believe and worship according to one's own conscience with no government curbs except for such behavior that violates the freedom of others. Others say that religious liberty means that a religious community has legal rights of existence, i.e. there are legal provisions that permit communal worship under specific government regulations. At stake is a conflict of two philosophically opposite legal interpretation. The one, which corresponds to the first interpretation, states that everything is allowed which is not explicitly forbidden. The other, which corresponds to the second interpretation states that everything is forbidden which is not explicitly allowed. The first principle tends to be followed in democratic societies, the second in totalitarian.

Both of these two notions, which are so sharply at odds with each other, exist—albeit with great tension—in Eastern Europe. The former notion favors the religious communities and is generally espoused by those keen on promoting the classical human rights. The holders of the second view assert that the existence of constitutional or other legal statements which proclaim the freedom of conscience or freedom of religion prove the actual existence of such liberties in real life. When they point to the constitutional guarantees they are doing this not entirely cynically because they equate religious liberty with freedom to worship in a designated building. To them belief is an entirely private matter.[2] This was the official position of the theoreticians and defenders of the East European people's republics until the late 1980s.

Hence it is necessary to distinguish between tolerance toward religion and religious liberty as a human right. Tolerance is what the state practices at its discretion. Religious liberty as a human right is what the individual can claim as an inalienable right. If a state does not practice tolerance it will hardly be able to guarantee religious liberty. In most Eastern European countries religious liberty is equated with tolerance granted by the state to the citizen as a concession. Some Eastern Europeans, however, understand by tolerance a more positive and benevolent approach to all who differ, granting the dignity and rights of all.

A smaller but significant number of Eastern Europeans whose influence expanded first steadily and then dramatically in 1989 regard religious liberty as part of a more comprehensive expression of human rights. Scholars like Tamás Földesi,[4] Zdenko Roter[5] Esad Ćimić, and Srdjan Vrcan reject the notion of special socialist human rights with emphasis on social and economic rights gained at the expense of civil and political rights, including religious liberty. Rather, they favor the notion of universal human rights valid in all societies and favor the notion of rights not as granted from above but as attached to each person by virtue of their being human.

1. Theoretical Models Regarding Religious Liberty

There are those who argue that religious liberties are modified by various contextual particularities, and that, furthermore, this ought to be the case, over against any claim of universality for religious liberties. Thus for instance, Zambia, the German Democratic Republic, Brazil, and the Soviet Union attempted to modify the United Nations Declaration of the Right to Religious Liberty in order to neutralize claims to universality.[6] In this regard Eckehart Lorenz, a West German Lutheran theologian formerly working at the Lutheran World

Federation in Geneva, distinguished three types of postures by states toward religious liberty:

(1) totalitarian societies which do not give a person who thinks differently the legal right or equality to express her/his views,

(2) limited-freedom states, which make space for certain religious activities (e.g., worship) but not for others, and

(3) states which emphasize and practice freedom and pluralism.[7]

Most countries of Eastern Europe generally belonged until the end of the 1980s to the first type, namely, societies with a totalitarian outlook, and occasionally to the second group which permit limited freedom. None belong to the third category as yet, though by early 1990s several of them seem capable of moving to that level.

Professor Charles Davis of Concordia University, Montreal, Canada, provides another helpful theoretical approach to the relationship between religion and political society.[8] He discerned sacral, secular, and pluralist societies.

1. *Sacral* societies are those in which there is no differentiation between the religious and political realm, presenting a monolithic stance to issues and disallowing alternatives to the official viewpoint. "It is monolithic because it acknowledges and allows only one solution to the problem of order on the level of symbol, doctrine, practice, institution and history."[9] For those not embracing the particular sacral view there are no liberties; the only way to deal with those whose views differ is forcing them to change their views and submit to the official viewpoint, by violence if need be.

There are two kinds of sacral societies, traditional and reactive. The traditional sacral society is one in which religion is so intertwined with all other areas of life that it is impossible to separate them. Religion makes an absolute and total claim on person and society; separation of the two realms is unimaginable. The reactive sacral society is the one in which there is a strong reaction to attempts to separate the religious from the secular realm, a retreat due to the perception of a threat to the aspired role for religion in society.

One may say that nearly all Eastern European societies until the recent past belonged to the category of traditional sacral societies. Russia perceived itself to be Holy. The Eastern Orthodox Church's understanding, stemming from early Byzantine times, was that the state was in God's domain, and that the king or emperor and the patriarch were to harmoniously lead all God's people in carrying out

God's will. While the emperor and the patriarch each had a certain separate primary responsibility, these responsibilities intersected. The emperor had the ultimate responsibility for implementing God's commandments, as the emperor was Christ's vicar on earth.

The Roman Catholic approach was similarly sacral. The king would receive papal blessing to rule the realm and would closely cooperate with the hierarchy of the land. While the relationship between the pope and the kings oscillated, it was nevertheless an inseparable relationship. In Poland and Hungary, for instance, the kings were perceived as the defenders of the faith, while in times of dynastic crises, the episcopal primates assumed important political functions. In both countries the Virgin Mary was regarded as the "queen" of the realm.

The Islamic practice was likewise sacral. The Ottoman Turkish sultan was simultaneously the caliph. Islam never differentiated between religion and politics. The ultimate aim was the spreading of the *umma* over the entire world. Islamic *shariya* [law] was to be the law of the land, having full application among Muslims and limited application among other *villayet*, that is people of other faiths. In the Ottoman Empire the head of the religious community was at the same time also responsible for the political behavior of his people.

The Protestants were the only ones that showed some deviation from the sacral type. The Lutheran model was closest to it in the form of *Landeskirche* [church of the land] in which the prince of the state determined the religion of all his people and closely supervised the religious practices of the people. Yet the Lutheran doctrine of the "two kingdoms" made possible the separation of responsibilities between the sacred and secular. The Reformed or Calvinist tradition had in it the greater potential for the distinction between religion and politics. In Eastern Europe, especially in Hungary, it had the tendency to set the nobility against the emperor's centralizing tendencies, thus bringing a conflict between the emperor's Catholicism and the nobility's Protestantism. Much later, the presence of the "free church" approach became a strong impulse toward pluralism, but not so much because of the theory, which still aimed at incorporating the whole world into God's kingdom, but because in practice, their small size inclined them to strive for tolerance.

It is an open question whether a Marxist socialist society may also qualify as a reactive sacral society. A case could be made, if one accepts those analyses which have treated Marxism or Communism as a pseudo-religion or a religion (perhaps of the idolatrous kind in Paul Tillich's analysis) that at least certain stages of socialist societies, e.g., Stalinist types, are indeed sacral societies. However, we shall not press this issue here because the secular type of society offers a more natural locus for communist societies.

In conclusion, sacral society offers very limited freedom, namely, only to those who conform to its framework. Since there are no genuine options available it means that there is little genuine freedom.

2. *Secular* society emerges as a reaction to the sacral model. Davis points out how Christianity carried the seeds of secularism in its midst. Secularism attempts to eliminate the religious discourse and approach from all other arenas of life, arguing particularly for the total separation of societal life from the influence of religion. Religion is excluded from the public order and limited to private expression.

Secular society is by nature a reaction to sacral society. Davis does not differentiate in his essay between different secular societies. However, such differentiation is necessary. There are those secular societies that have gradually evolved away from sacral societies and in which over the years, with no particular outward violence, religion practically receded from public life. One may call this the modern liberal secular state. And there are reactive secular states that have resorted to drastic, violent measures to drive religion out of spheres of social, public life and, moreover, have sought to eliminate religion by propaganda or force from citizens' private lives.

The secular tendencies were first expressed and pursued in the West; there we find forms of the modern liberal secular state. But secularism had never been so militantly implemented as in the Soviet Union and Eastern Europe. Secular society in those countries did not result from evolution away from the stifling limitations of sacral society, but was, rather, an explosive reaction to the persistence and inflexibility of the sacral model. Impatient with the slow progress of secularization and the setting in of a reactive mood of sacral society which blocked the road to pluralism, the reactive secular model was established with the same kind of dogmatism as found in the reactive sacral type. Secular communism is monolithic and exclusive. It also "allows only one solution to the problem of order on the level of symbol, doctrine, practice, institution and history."[10] This is not surprising, because it is often the case that one dogmatism or extremism gives way to another. The content changes but not the form, because people have been accustomed to operating in the given form.

One authoritarianism gives way to another more easily than to power sharing. Thus the role of the tsar in determining the religion of the people in the sacral model was replaced by the role of the general secretary of the Communist Party in determining what the population believes and practices. The Communist secularist view is given the constitutional privilege of having a leading role in the nation, just as a specific church used to be proclaimed constitutionally privileged in sacral societies. The degree of freedom in the reactive secular state is as minimal as it was in the sacral state. The secular authorities fear that granting freedom to the religious sphere, especially in public life, will diminish the degree of its influence.

Protagonists of the secular, especially the reactive, model live with the conviction that they have already liberated people from the clutches of the sacral model and that this is what freedom means, and nothing more. To them granting freedom to express religious beliefs and practices appears to be a retreat into the sacral model, namely, an enslavement of people, and they experience it as a threat to their concept of what freedom means. Thus they perceive themselves as liberators, while the religious people are pictured as obscurantist reactionaries who want to regain the previous monopoly of control over the population.

3. The pluralist society is one in which there is the possibility for all views to contend. No special preference is given to either the religious or secular approaches each in their variety of expressions. Every view, whether one of the variant religious types or one of the variant secular types, is allowed public expression and advocacy. No group is given the constitutional, legal, political, economic, cultural, and social monopoly or primacy.

> Pluralism implies disagreement and dissention within the political community. But one cannot speak of pluralism unless there is one community. Pluralism, then, also implies unity, some consensus or agreement. The divergent groups form one community; they agree to live together and cooperate in action for common goals. Pluralism is not brute plurality. It means harmony amid discord, unity in social life and political action amid religious and valuational conflict.[11]

> There should be a public deliberation about values, through which the implications and consequences of divergent value judgment are comprehensively displayed. The

supposition is that open and adequate deliberation will favor the occurrence of correct value judgment on the part of men of good will and thus create a sound public consensus. A pluralist society allows dissent. It does not, however, exclude, but rather as a human society or community of meaning presupposes a consensus, created and maintained freely in open discussion. A public consensus will not eliminate dissent; indeed, as a freely created agreement, it presupposes and implies dissent. But dissent is identified as dissent with reference to the consensus, and a minimum of consensus is a condition for political agreement.[12]

No Eastern European society has experienced genuine pluralism except perhaps Czechoslovakia briefly in the period between the two world wars. In that case pluralism developed out of a sacral society. Until 1989 no genuine pluralism emerged out of a secular society, though there were strivings in that direction by followers of "socialism with a human face" not only in the brief interlude of the Prague Spring in 1968 but also in Hungary and Yugoslavia. Pluralism has now become a potential model for Eastern Europe which would greatly enhance all freedoms, including religious ones.

A four-fold typology of church-state relations regarding religious liberties is being proposed here instead of the one by Davis, developed by the author in part with the assistance of Professor Zdenko Roter, a sociologist from Ljubljana, Yugoslavia.[13]

1. Type A – Ecclesiastic Absolutism. This type could also be called Absolutist Sacral because of the exclusive power vested in a single religious option or Preferential/Discriminatory because one religious institution is given preferential treatment while others are discriminated against, but for conciseness Ecclesiastic Absolutism seems best. Ecclesiastic Absolutism means that only one religious organization is supported by the state. The government provides preferential treatment and extends freedom only to those who fully comply with the beliefs and practices of that "state church," but denies or sharply curtails freedoms to all those who do not believe or believe differently. This type is, by and large, a model of the past; yet in Eastern Europe it was not the too distant past when churches like the Russian Orthodox Church in the Russian Empire, Roman Catholic Church in Poland, the *Landeskirchen* in Germany, the Bulgarian Orthodox Church in Bulgaria and so forth, were, indeed, in a distinctly privileged position (one might call it an intimate relationship between a church and a state), while other churches and atheists suffered various degrees of unfreedom.

2. Type B – Religious Toleration. Another name for this model might be Preferentially Religious because religion as such is preferred and supported by the state. This means that theoretically the state is separated from the religious organizations, which are treated equally before the law; yet the state remains benign toward all religions. In reality, Roter sees such states as giving practical preferences to the stronger churches and discriminating against nonbelievers, either legally or by various manipulations of public opinion. The amount of religious liberties is much greater in Type B than in Type A and hence this is a definite advance in the right direction.

In history there are frequently situations which do not fit clearly given categories, often because states and religions were in transition. This seems to have been the case in a number of East European countries before socialism. For instance, in Hungary Roman Catholics, Hungarian Reformed, and Lutherans were given more opportunities and privileges than communities such as Baptist, Jews, and Methodists. In Yugoslavia the Serbian Orthodox Church in the eastern and southern regions of the country and the Catholic Church in the western regions of the country were established churches. Some religious communities, such as the Lutherans, Muslims, and Jews, had certain legal standing and protection, while groups like Baptists and Methodists were tolerated but with distinctly limited rights. Certain religious groups were outlawed; so were the Communists after a brief period of legality. These groups had few freedoms. These were countries in transition between Type A and Type B. Czechoslovakia may have been the only Type B country having granted a greater degree of religious liberty and yet the Roman Catholics were more influential than the others, despite the vigor of the Czechoslovak Church and the Church of the Czech Brethren.

3. Type C – Secularistic Absolutism. A different name for this model could be Obstructionist because it hinders all religious expressions and favors a single brand of secularist world view. Religion as such is rejected by the state. Seemingly diametrically opposed to Type A, all religions suffer various degrees of restrictions, while nonbelievers, especially militant atheists, often receive privileges. Not infrequently this alleged atheist state promotes the adoration of the state and its leadership which renders it a secular religion, thus making it actually a very close kin to Type A.[14] Type C arises as a result of dissatisfaction with Type A, but the exclusivist mentality remains the same. According to the Italian scholar Giovanni Codevilla, such a state "refuses to recognize that there can exist a difference between a nation and its official ideology and acts with force to create an absolute *religious (spiritual)* unity within the state."[15] In Type C religious liberties are drastically reduced, although in some formal ways all such states constitutionally declare the same freedoms as states of Type B. The need for drastic limitation of existing religions is because the Communist party advances an ideology which invades the realm of religion by defining itself

> as the center of truth for the realization in time and space of a universal *salus societatis*, both exclusive and definitive. . . . Indeed, among other goals, it assigns itself the task of seeing to the disappearance of religion because it finds in Marxism-Leninism, taken as a comprehensive or pseudo-religious doctrine, the justification for its existence. In other words, the Soviet State places itself in a position vis-à-vis the party and Marxism-Leninism equivalent to that of the European Absolutist state vis-à-vis the universal Church and religion. It finds precisely here the entity which justifies its own sovereignty.[16]

The famous Serbian novelist and social analyst, Dobrica Ćosić, a former Communist, points out correctly that Bolshevism and/or Stalinism is/are political religions.[17] Those who say that the religious policy of Bolshevism was primarily pragmatic need to explain why such severe repression and total alienation of the religious population followed after Bolshevism prevailed when the religious population could have been turned into allies. The pre-revolutionary rhetoric of Lenin and of all Communist parties conceding religious liberties mislead many people into thinking that only pragmatic considerations brought about the conflict between Communists and religious believers and institutions. Actually Lenin's Bolshevik approach was temporary. The attack on all religions was related to the distinctly religious belief of the Bolshevik/Stalinist type Communists that Marxism-Leninism *alone* gives the full understanding of the world and can promote human happiness.

The Communist revolutions established Secularistic Absolutism (Type C) in all countries where they were successful. This meant a sudden and dramatic loss of liberties for those who were before the revolution privileged or at least equally tolerated. Momentarily, as a matter of tactics, the state in Type C may improve the conditions of those religious groups that were being repressed in previous societies in order to publicly manifest that it is not discriminating against religion but only restricting abuses of formerly privileged churches. But both Marxist theory and practice show that such accommodations can only be temporary since no religion is seen as beneficent for the population. In later developments of Type C there are evident both some vestiges of Type A and B, as well as a tendency to tolerate some features of Type B or Type D.

4. Type D – Pluralistic Liberty. Other possible names could be Free Non-interventionist or Unhindered Libertarian, Enabling, or Tolerant Secular, but Pluralistic Liberty connotes the full exercise of freedom in a context of a variety of truth claims. The state is really indifferent and neutral toward religion or non-religion. According to Roter this type is a human possibility but not yet a historical achievement, but in my conviction this model has been and is being experienced at least in rudimentary form in some areas of the world. In such a state religious organizations and the government will be truly separated with no intention on part of either to dictate or mix into the affairs of the other. Roter sees it as somewhat utopian—in the sense of a hoped for—model of the future worth being aspired to. He believes that Type D will provide heretofore undreamed of human—including religious—liberties because the only limit upon the right of any one person or group will be the rights of others. There are evidences that features of this Type D are gradually appearing in various modern societies.

There is a close linkage between Types A and C on the one hand and Types B and D on the other. In their pure form Type A and C are both intolerant toward all except those whom the state decides to favor. Type C is currently more problematic because Type A is all but non-existent in modern Western societies (not so in the Islamic world), while Type C came into existence in the twentieth century when the totalitarian and manipulative power of the state has reached unprecedented scope. Hence the inquisitorial practices and religious wars which characterized Type A seem to pale into insignificance when Type C makes its brutal appearance.

Type B and Type D are very close in principle. Both not only proclaim but respect at least a *de facto* separation of church and state (certain Western European societies still contain *de jure* preferential treatment of certain churches but in real life make no efforts to suppress atheism or the work of other religious organizations). It is the practice of Type B which sometimes handicaps nonbelievers or adherents of new or minority religions. Yet there is a dynamic in societies of the B type which aims at extending in practice the freedoms granted in principle and therefore Type B can become gradually Type D. One of the major questions for the future will be whether it is possible to move from Type C to Type D. This would involve a major realignment of those Marxist tenets which see human development tied to the loss of religion or the abandonment of Marxism altogether. But separation of church and state are a Marxist aspiration which may be usefully affirmed and extended until conditions become ripe for a gradual transition from Type C to Type D. It appears as if in some countries of Eastern Europe there are forces which work in that direction.[18]

One possible scenario would be that the memory of a Type A with its absolute, total, monolithic claims, has two options in development. One is to develop gradually into Type B, pluralistic democratic society, or into Type C, which is the reactive counterpart of Type A, seeking to develop a secularist, atheist totalitarian claim/society, by dismantling religious institutions and persecuting religion. This society likewise seems to be destined to develop into a Type B or a Type D society, which is pluralistic. The necessity of that development is due to the historically evident inability to suppress religion effectively, so that there is practical pluralism even during periods of oppression. Such oppression is capable of giving way to toleration and then perhaps to genuine pluralism of religious and secular world views and practices within a society. Originally there seems to have been only freedom to believe, but not not to believe. On the one hand a tolerance toward non-believers in some contexts developed from this situation while in others freedom not to believe, but not the freedom to believe arose. Finally there may come a time of full freedom both to believe and not to believe, which,in its rudimentary form is already being achieved in a number of Western societies.

Thus the stages would be:

Type A: Monopoly of a religion society.

Type B: Social preference for religions. Religious toleration with religious views being at advantage and atheism at disadvantage.

Type C: Near-monopoly of state atheism. Decisive disadvantage for religion.

Type D. Pluralism and freedom for all views and practices, except those most patently destructive (e.g., it is hard to imagine that a cult wishing to sacrifice human beings would enjoy full freedom!)

2. Definitions and Descriptions of Religious Liberty

Religious liberty is both freedom to believe and freedom to act whatever a person chooses, and, *ipso facto* not to believe or act religiously. It is closely linked to freedom of conscience in the sense that freedom of conscience is the right not to be coerced by the state to do anything that would change that person's sense of identity and dignity. Religious liberty is a fundamental human right and not an entitlement, which means that each person has the right to it whether or not she or he deserves it in the eyes of the government. Ideally the government abstains from passing laws with the intention of restricting religious belief and activity by its citizens while safeguarding the free exercise of religion. The American constitutional separation of church and state with its subsequent history of benevolent non-intervention has provided a clear model of what religious liberty ought to be.[19]

However, this was generally not the case in Europe. In the past many churches colluded with their governments to suppress other people's religious beliefs and non-religions convictions. The concept *cuius regio, eius religio* served broadly as a principle of privileging some churches while discriminating against other religious beliefs and practices both legally and practically. Today that concept still has its secular expression in Eastern Europe as religious groups, both majorities and minorities, are not fully accepted, are discriminated against, and often clearly oppressed.[20] This led to the situation of churches not being always in a morally tenable position to demand religious liberties when they had denied such liberties to others. Only with self-criticism and repentance and only when they do not claim religious liberty solely for themselves but also for others will they be able to assert this right.

There seems to be a correlation between the degree of tolerance of religious practices with the degree of toleration which the religious institutions accorded to internal dissenters in the past. In those areas where the churches were too closely identified with the ruling classes or elites and where little tolerance was accorded to others in religious and non-religious matters, a strong anticlerical attitude developed that also came to permeate the Marxist approach to religion. It led to the sharp curailment of religious freedom by Marxists when they attained power.

That correlation *explains* the intolerance of most communist parties toward religion for a certain limited time-period after the takeover, but it does not *justify* the continued repression of religion. The equation of religious liberty with freedom to worship is closely connected to the Bolshevik experience and the primacy which this experience enjoyed in the world Communist movement. The major church that the Bolsheviks encountered was the Russian Orthodox Church. The essence of that church is expressed in liturgy. The prerevolutionary Russian Orthodox Church was also closely tied to the tsarist government. The Bolsheviks wanted to decisively sever that relationship and therefore they advocated the separation of church from the state and the schools and felt that if religious worship were allowed, this would be tantamount to religious liberty. This distinctly Soviet approach was later made by the hegemonistic Soviet Communists the model for all Communist Parties in Eastern Europe immediately after they came to power. Only recently did it become evident that the Bolshevik experience was not adequate for all countries and for all times.

Increasingly, there is general understanding that religious freedom goes beyond the freedom to worship according to one's conscience and includes the social expression of responsibility according to "certain ethical norms."[21] This has been agreed upon in the various consultations and conferences in the World Council of Churches and the Council of European Churches in which church representatives from East and West participated. It is not clear that the Eastern European communist governments actually support such statements, although there too, more and more openness developed toward expanding at least the level of toleration toward certain religious activities. Such openness was due both because of pressure from within and pressure from without. The pressure from within arose in the conflict with the churches and because of the government's need to obtain at least the passive cooperation of the churches. It is not surprising to see that the stronger the churches and the weaker the government, the more concessions were granted in the field of religious liberties and vice versa.

The pressure from without came not only in the criticism of antireligious practices by various observers, including emigrants, but also by international agreements. There are a number of international standards which affirm religious liberty, some of which have the force of law among signatory nations. These are:

1. The Universal Declaration of Human Rights (1948),

2. The International Covenant on Civil and Political Rights (1966),

3. The Principles of the Helsinki Final Act (1975), and

4. The Declaration on the Elimination of All Forms of Intolerance and of Discrimination Based on Religion or Belief (1981). The latter is not legally binding, which is regrettable, but, despite the lack of sanctions, it is increasingly adhered to and promoted.

These documents and all the discussion which preceded and succeeded them point to a most intimate link between religious liberty and other human rights. Three basic positions exist on this linkage.

One suggests that human rights are indivisible as all of them belong to human dignity and that religious liberty is a fundamental right, but not separable from others. This means that promoting religious liberty requires promoting all human rights.[22]

The second maintains that while religious liberty can be honored only within a complete respect for all human rights that it is the basic human right. Nothing is more important to the integrity of a person than to be able to believe or not believe and to be able to testify to one's convictions.[23]

The third alternative is to divide human rights into individual (among which religious liberty would be classified) and collective rights (primarily socio-economic) and to give the priority to collective right.

> The socialist interpretation of human rights postulates that even as individuals, people are determined by social circumstances. Socialist civil rights set the standard for personal freedom in relation to social necessities and needs: they are related to the state or society.[24]

To put it more bluntly, "one needs to differentiate between bourgeois and socialist democracy and freedom," according to Ivan Ocek[25] and the former is dismissed as a hoax. It is here that one of the most important misunderstandings occur in regard to religious liberty. Ricardo Antoncich, S.J. pointed out that:

> the Anglo-Saxon cultural tradition particularly emphasizes the political rights of the individual with regard to the arbitrariness of the state. In the socialist countries, on the other

hand, it is considered a bourgeois prejudice to limit the authority of the state when planning the economy or when the socialization of political life is at stake.[26]

What is common to all communist governments is the belief that religion has no place in a future communist society because religion is an expression of profound human alienation. Therefore, contrary to official separation of church and state the government to various degrees attempts to control the churches, discriminates toward believers and places various obstacles in the path of the individual and collective expressions of religious convictions. While there are some signs in the last decade of a certain number of Marxist intellectuals reappraising this negative evaluation of religion, such reappraisals still did not decisively eliminate restrictions upon religious life until the onset of the "Great Transformation" of 1989.

3. Eastern and Western Concepts of Human Rights

In response to a questionnaire sent out by the Churches Human Rights Programme office in Geneva to European member churches in 1980 the churches in Eastern Europe stated they were primarily interested in religious liberties and peace, while the churches in Western Europe were interested in social issues, though occasionally Western churches showed interest in religious liberty and human rights, while Eastern churches showed interest in Western-type social problems. Eastern European churches maintained that there was a close link between religious liberties, human rights and peace.[27]

Are there differences between Eastern and Western concepts of human rights? And are they compatible?

Two meetings of church leaders from East and West in Moscow (1984) and Eisenach, GDR (1984) answered that there are differences and that they may be incompatible.[28] However, one should add that the church members in the East were by no means unanimous in espousing a so-called "Eastern" human right position which gives priority to socio-economic human rights and relegates political and civil rights to a secondary place. The official representatives of churches from the East often saw no other alternative but to affirm what has become nearly a societal dogma, namely, that the interest of the collective or the community is greater than that of the individual and that the interest of certain individuals may have to be neglected or violated in order to preserve the community interests. As a general observation this is hardly contestable and there are few if any soci-

eties in which this principle is not upheld in one way or the other.
However, if the interests of the individuals are not simultaneously
very carefully protected, it is very easy and very tempting to trample
on the rights of a few or of many individuals in the presumed interest
of the community. There is some ambiguity as to what is in the best
interest of the individual, but that issue can be settled more easily
than what is in the interest of the community. The interest of the
community can be settled by the will of the majority, but that can
easily issue in the tyranny of the majority if there are no protections
of the rights of the minority. Worse yet, a small group often takes
the right to adjudicate what is in the best interest of the community and this *de facto* turns out to be the will of the elite of decision
makers. Eastern European societies manifest this kind of situation.
The decision-makers in Eastern Europe have been the Communists,
the party in general but more concretely its leadership. This is not
only so *de facto*, which has been corroborated by nearly all who write
about the political and legal system of socialist countries of Eastern
Europe, but it is also the case *de jure*. Namely, the hegemony of the
Communist Party, its leading or "avant-garde" role in all sectors of
social life is legally, even constitutionally, established. This is one of
the most decisive factors when it comes to human rights issues and
any other political issues. The real resolution of problems in any society depends on the existing distribution of power, which is capable
of changing and expanding during processes of democratization or
constricting during processes of monopolization of power.

In Western democratic societies, aside from the actual pluralistic distribution of power among various components of society there
is also the legal division between the legislative, executive, and judicial branches of government, which is a form of distributing power.
In Eastern European socialist countries, while there is on paper a
division between these three branches of government in fact such a
division of power does not exist because the power is lodged in the
Communist Party.[29] This is most simply illustrated by the fact that
until recently the Secretary General of the Communist Party was automatically the real leader of the Soviet Union who negotiated and
decided both on domestic and foreign matters without necessarily
even being formally a member of the government or its president; the
formal head of the government was mostly a ceremonial post. This
meant that the Communist Party is in control and gave impulses to all
three branches of government. Any democratization which would take

place in Eastern Europe would necessarily mean placing some limitation on the party's hegemony.[30] The crucial question was whether it is possible to restrict the monopoly of the Communist Party in politics; until the end of the 1980s that seemed not to be possible. But under the revolutionary popular pressures of the second half of 1989 and early 1990 the Communist Parties in most East European countries, including the USSR lost its monopoly position in the political and social life. It remains to be seen whether a real division of power among the three branches of government will take place. This is of utmost significance for these countries. Until recently the power was held monopolistically both legally and politically by the Communist Party.

The traditional socialist state was not a law state. Thus there was a problem of legality which led to a tremendous discrepancy between the laws and social practice. Of course, a good law may not elicit a good practice, and vice versa, a bad law may not mean necessarily a bad practice. Applied to religious liberty it means that there may be a progressive and good law which declares religious liberty but in real life the situation may be very bad and religious liberties may be all but non-existent. On the other hand, there may be restrictive laws about religious life, but in reality more freedom may be allowed to religious people. But often bad laws reflect a bad situation and good laws reflect a good situation.

An important insight in respect to socialist legality is that the written laws generally meant little. When the Communist Party made a decision, that decision was implemented no matter what the laws said. The party, for instance, relayed to a judge what the decision should be in a case to be tried; the judge, who was always a member of the Communist Party, was bound by party discipline to implement that decision; some way was found to legally condone the political decision. Thus the law was simply an instrument in the hands of the Party's political power and overall position in society in a given moment.

Another cardinal point is that contrary to what Marxist analysis asserts in respect to economic determinism, Communist Party rule was based on the monopoly of political power. After political power was captured in a revolution or in a military take-over, it was monopolized by means of creating a party bureaucracy or *nomenklatura*. *Nomenklatura* is a medieval-like system of promoting party cadres by the top of the leadership pyramid to whom the appointees were constantly beholden. A careful observation of the nature of this bureaucracy makes it possible to avoid a rigid understanding of the hegemonistic avant-gardist role of the party. Members of the Communist Party had unequal power. Those who held the power in the party lived in constant fear that they may lose their position at least in some if not in all sectors should the party's role in society diminish. The de-professionalization of the Party cadres is a prerequisite to the evolution of the separation of the Party from power monopoly. If the power of the Party were to recede, where will former Party leaders and bureaucrats go? Effectively they can only be retired because they generally have no adequate education for any other job. The party cadres were usually educated in special higher party schools. Graduates of the party educational system were, of course, trained exclusively for party jobs. This was the way to regenerate the bureaucracy. Such people have practically no other professional future and they therefore desperately tried to protect their jobs. They were threatened by any change. The more turbulent the political situation in a country—and struggle for human rights, including religious liberty can be a source of such turbulence—the more these specially trained cadres tried to make themselves indispensable. They would even sabotage general trends in liberalization from above in order to justify their positions and wield power. This explains why there are sometimes huge regional differences in the application of laws or higher party decisions; the local party bureaucrats were clinging to their prerogatives and tried to expand their job descriptions. If they were to lose their job, for instance, in supervising religious communities, they may be out of power entirely and thereby out of all of the perquisites which power brought with it.

This is not the only linkage of power and religious liberties. The general process of liberalization in a communist country may not drag with it, so to say, more freedom for religion. This was true, for instance, in the Khrushchev period in the Soviet Union (1959–1964) or in Yugoslavia from 1948–1953. The explanation lies in the resistance to the liberalization by the hard-line critics within the communist movement. In order to show to the critics that there is no abandonment of the path to communism the leaders who presided over the measures of relaxation tried to prove their "orthodoxy" by being inflexible and harsh in those areas which are least likely to cause delays for their project, areas such as religious liberties. We may call this the principle of uneven development. Many observers have misunderstood this principle. The development of socialism cannot be expiained by only a single factor. Religious liberties and human rights are only one factor. Hence one may not judge that Stalin—because he gave the churches some space after the Nazi invasion—was better than Khrushchev, who revitalized the antireligious campaign. The principle of uneven development would, indeed, suggest, that it is very likely that during major social changes the governments policies toward the churches are likely to be more rather than less severe for a while. At a later time the general relaxation or democratization may catch up also with the treatment of the religious institutions.

This insights does not invalidate the belief that human rights are inseparable, because the human being is one entity. It is, indeed, inconsistent to promote one kind of human freedom or right and be indifferent to others. But if one views the entire sphere of human rights and liberties, then one may say that with the enlargement of any liberty or right one obtains an increase in the entire sphere or sum total of liberties. The increase in the field of one liberty seems to bring pressure also in other fields. And while one may not agree with any specific ranking of human rights and liberties, it is certainly possible to espouse specially one or more types of liberties which the promoter may feel are particularly crucial, but with the understanding that progress or regress in one area does affect all other areas and, of course the entire sphere of liberties. In both the East and the West an exaggerated role has been given to the discussion of whether the bourgeois civil and political rights and liberties have primacy over the socialist social and economic rights and liberties or vice versa. This seems to me to be the wrong issue. It is sounder to affirm that all human rights are crucial and belong to the humanistic inheritance of our contemporary world. They are not achievable easily and without combat, nor are they without ambivalence and moral paradoxes. The struggle for these human rights are never in a vacuum, but are always waged in the context of each society and each historical period.

Recently Professor Tamás Földesi, former dean of the Law School of University of Budapest, provided a courageous and insightful analysis of the role of human rights theories in Eastern Europe.[31] He pointed out that the human rights situation in Eastern Europe was characterized by a duality, namely, the "official" acceptance of such rights in the form of international treaties and basic domestic legal principles, and yet simultaneously and contradictorily the limitation of them in practice, leading to juridical incoherence. The culprit is the Communist Party's assertion that human rights must practiced only in harmony with the interest of socialism; they disassociated themselves only from some of the excesses of the "cult of personality."

This contradiction, under fire from Western critics, was vigorously denied by the communist government, with the complicity of many Marxist scholars. Sometimes it was the complicity of silence, but in many cases Marxist social scientists developed, what Földesi calls, a monolithic theory of human rights. According to this theory it was only the socialist countries that first developed full human rights, at least in essence, but also in comprehensiveness (political, economic, and other rights). The denial and limitation of some of the classical "bourgeois" human rights was defended as being consistent with this socialist fruition of human right, a veritable sign of great progress. This claim was based on the notion of the discontinuity of human rights. The classical political human rights were declared not only in origin but in their very essence bourgeois, hence not applicable to socialism. Such civil rights were seen as being in conflict with the new society and the newly espoused rights.

Földesi notes the paradox of claiming that such rights in the East are more advanced than rights in the West and yet that their value is reduced since in the new society the opportunity for human emancipation and enhancement is so great that it is not necessary to defend the individual from the people's government that invariably promotes the interests of all their citizens. Hence no institutions which might help protect human rights, aside from the party, the state, and to a lesser degree, religious institutions, are allowed to operate. Human rights then becomes a "tabu" issue due to the governing elite's sensitivity and they tend to always be dealt with apologetically (with immediate counterattacks on the country from which the criticism emanated pointing to even greater human rights violations among the allies of that country) rather than critically. Not only bureaucrats but social scientists engaged in such false justification.

Földesi promotes the notion that a humanistic society must assert the cardinal role of human rights in a critical manner. Continuity of the classical civil and political human right must be affirmed by noting that human right are *universally human*. There is no need for separate "socialist human rights" but simply for HUMAN RIGHTS which would be implemented according to various historic conditions. The Marxist promotion of a one party state, is not an expression of the strength of the Communist Party but rather its weakness. Földesi states that while in the immediate post-revolutionary period one may understand this desire for monopoly, in the present it is an expression of insecurity and that political plurality would likely lead to development of more human rights and the elimination of the various limitations and denials. The monolithic concept restricts the development of human right as does the fear of Western and domestic criticism. Földesi feels it would be best for East European societies to acknowledge that the situation in regard to human rights is not good and seriously to get on with the task of affirming all human rights (except the right to private property) in principle, in law, and in life.

4. Religious Liberty: A Contemporary Description

Since the subject of this chapter is religious liberty, the author feels entitled to list some desiderata in respect to the concept of religious liberty, knowing full well that in each concrete country the actual struggle for religious liberty leads to different degrees of achievement of some of these desiderata. From experience, study and reflection, I would like to present what I consider the essential elements of religious liberty.

Religious liberty means that each person can chose to believe according to his or her conscience to express in private and in public by means of symbolic or social action, alone or in conjunction with others whatever that person holds. This freedom, of course, entitles each person also to reject any particular religious on non-religious belief.

Groups of people have the right to incorporate themselves for purposes of exercising their religious beliefs and actions and have the right to be recognized as such by the government, which is not entitled to withhold recognition of such incorporation. Groups not wishing to legally incorporate themselves into a normal religious body nevertheless have the right to exercise their religious or non-religious convictions and freely propagate such views. No one has the right to deny legal rights, benefits, and privileges of citizenship, employment, including government service, possibility of election to all offices in the land, and access to education to themselves and members of their family, because of religious or atheist or areligious convictions.

People have the right of access to the press and media to propagate their views and have the fight to publish their literature, including sacred books, catechetical books, textbooks, periodical literature, pamphlets, and books on religious or atheist topics and have the right to distribute them for pay or without charge. Taxation of religious enterprises should be equitabie, namely, either not taxed as a non-profit organization or taxed in a non-punitive way.

Each person has the right to educate their children while they are minors both at home and with the help of religious leaders and educators. In case of conflict of interest between parents or parents and children the case should be adjudicated by an independent judiciary, respecting the interest and the will of the children. Each religious institution is entitled to strive to build a sufficient financial base for its activities by means of contributions of members or other legal sources, including contributions from abroad.

Religious institutions may freely keep contact with other co-religionists and other religious bodies within the country and abroad and must be allowed to live up to the laws and regulations of their own religious community regardless where the headquarters of the community is. Religious institutions are allowed to form ecumenical or interreligious councils domestically or internationally.

People have the right to draw out implications of their faith by being critical of various aspects of the socio-economic and political system of their societies.[32] For instance, religious and other conscientious objection to military service is to be respected and alternate service to the country is to be provided for.

Members of a religious group also have rights and liberties to dissent from the official views of their churches and have the right to due process when in conflict with religious authorities. The document of the Second Vatican Council, "*Dignitatis humanae*" stated the concern for liberty which applies both within the religious community and in respect to the outside world, as

(a) a human being has the right to look for truth, to hold truth as she or he knows it and to regulate her or his life according to this truth, and

(b) respect for the integrity of the human being, including human social nature, which means that a person has the right to his or her opinion and is allowed to express it and act upon it.[33]

Is religious freedom an absolute right? Yes and no. It is an absolute right in the sense that every person absolutely is entitled to practice what they believe, but it is not absolute in the sense that a person has the right to act on each and every belief.

Obviously there is a limit to this freedom as there is to every freedom, namely, where it collides with the freedom of others. If there is a deliberate injury to the health and dignity of others, if certain reasonable standards of health and education are not met on account of religious convictions, if it leads to enslavement, perjury, theft, arson or other generally recognized criminal or mentally imbalanced action, the state has the right and responsibility to intervene and defend the victims. There are religious practices which are dangerously antisocial and every society has the right to protect persons and property from the abuse of religion, but the danger of the antisocial nature of the act must be obvious, rather than a mere excuse for harassing religious people. Here a clear theoretical line is hard to draw; usually case to case examination is a sounder approach.

Furthermore, the religious individuals or institutions have no right to expect or demand financial support from the government or ask them to collect dues, tithes, contributions, or fees, taxes, etc. Nor can religions expect to have *ex officio* representatives in the government (e.g. parliament), even where this has been the historical tradition, unless, of course, they have been properly elected. Nor do they have the right to actively and explicitly mix into purely political matters in their capacity as religious leaders rather than as citizens with religious convictions. What is "purely" political is not always easy to discern from the legitimate social and national concerns of the churches for the well-being of individuals, the community or humankind, but in theory at least it is possible to separate issues which have purely political or economic implications not of such nature that the religious authorities need to pontificate and instruct their members how to think or how to vote. In fact, it is a sign of our times that it generally weakens the authority of religious leaders to pretend to instruct their members what to think on all issues. Certainly it would be inappropriate of the religious leaders to approve or disapprove of certain candidates for office unless it is clearly evident that such persons are destructive for the community (e.g., oppose the rise of a potential dictator). In this respect laws which have been directed against the use (or misuse) of the pulpit for political purposes pose a serious dilemma. The dilemma consists of the effort to delineate clearly between politics and religion or secular and sacred. In real life these areas overlap and therefore one needs to say yes and no to such provisions. Here one may use the American experience of denying the use of non-profit moneys and status to advocate a clearly political agenda and candidate and yet protect religious approval or opposition to certain policies which affect the well-being of the people (e.g. support or opposition to a war, work on behalf of equality, justice, and freedom).

Religious communities have no right to demand governmental support for their theological or moral agenda, though it is legitimate for them to advocate government support of certain ethical policies without demanding, however, compliance by those who think differently (e.g. consider the problematic of abortion or divorce debates in many countries). Persuasion must be their goal. Religious people have no right to incite hatred and prejudice against those who are of different religion or no religion, though they have the right to demand certain criteria for membership in their institutions. Religious individuals and organizations have no right to be outside the pail of criticism, by the media or any group in society, except that the government per se does not have the right to show such partisanship. The religious people, of course, have the equal right to engage in criticism of other groups, including the government.

Religious people have equal obligations of citizenship and should expect to pay the price of disobedience, e.g. non-violent active disobedience, when they break the laws. They have the right to urge the change of laws which they deem objectionable.

There are definite restrictions upon the government in regard to religion. The foremost is that the government has no right to mix into the internal affairs of religious groups. It may not spy upon them, may not manipulate elections, may not have any say as to who is a suitable or nonsuitable candidate for a position of religious leadership. In respect to the latter the European tradition is particularly vulnerable because in many countries in Europe, both East and West, there is still the practice that certain government agencies have veto power over the candidates for a certain office, e.g. a bishop or patriarch or *reiss-ul-ullema*. The government has no right to certify clergy, decide on where they shall reside, in which churches they may officiate, and who may or may not be accepted for training for "clerical" offices. The government has no right to impose a *numerus clausus* on theological schools, as has often been the case in Eastern Europe. It has no right to pre-censor or censor sermons, pastoral letters or religious publications, although such public pronouncement are liable to the same legal provisions as every other person or institution in the state, including government or party officials. There is, in other words, no right by government officials to reduce religious persons to second-class citizenship. The government has no right to dictate to religious people (or any other) a preference for a certain social or political system (e.g. prefer capitalism, socialism, or some third way), though it is natural that advocacy of such preference is allowed, provided people's preferences are not coerced.

Not infrequently there is a real conflict in regard to specific cases of alleged religious repression in Eastern Europe. When some of the official representatives of Eastern European clergy were publicly questioned about religious persecution they would maintain that in their country there is perfect religious liberty, that no one is imprisoned on account of their religious convictions, but that such people are imprisoned for breaking the law of the country. On the other hand there are those in the West who assume that every prisoner or mental patient in Eastern Europe who is religious is a victim of religious persecutions. It seems that both of these views are wrong. Certainly there are among religious people in Eastern Europe those who are criminals and mentally ill and they ought to be institutionalized based on the merit of the case and the law of the land. However, it is also quite as evident that certain laws have been passed which limit religious freedom and which many religious people feel duty-bound to violate, e.g. provisions prohibiting them from providing religious education for their children or to evangelize.

There are other laws, perhaps even more destructive, which due to their deliberate vagueness (e.g. anti-state propaganda, harming the interest of the social system) can be turned against any person targeted for persecution. They victimize people for no other reason than to restrict their religious freedom or to terrorize the population. Here the culprit is the legal formulation as well as the administrative willingness to obliterate or restrict religion under the cloak of legality. In reality, in most of these cases, they are in fact, religious persecutions. It would seem that the burden of proof is on the authorities to demonstrate criminal or insane activity, rather than the burden of proof being on those concerned for the protection of human rights. In these times of massive government abuse–after having lived in and witnessed Stalinist brutalities, massacres and genocides (this also applies to Hitlerite and other tyrannical crimes)–it is the human rights and ecological activists who deserve more credibility than the oppressive governments. The governments possess enormous propaganda apparatus capable of misinformation about crimes against people. Fortunately, this is so obvious in Eastern Europe that it has produced

a negative credibility; people almost automatically distrusted whatever the government asserted, creating a situation of public paranoia
and distrust with a simultaneous willingness of the people to suffer
even the most outrageous and unbelievable claims.

After years of high powered propaganda many people in Eastern
Europe have come to accept at least some of the official interpretations
on religious liberty as being correct. Not having a chance to compare
first-hand what religious liberty is elsewhere, some concluded that the
situation is satisfactory, especially if there is no human rights tradition in the respective country.[34] The more privileges certain churches
enjoyed in countries which did not grant a broad range of liberties,
the more it became possible to curtail their rights, namely, the more
restrictions were imposed against religious freedom.

None of the Eastern European countries had a tradition of separation of church and state; the idea of a secular state did not exist.
Unlike the West the bourgeois revolution in the East did not create
an independent secular state authority. So in the East this separation
was accomplished by the socialist revolution which brought to an end
the hegemony or monopoly of a church or churches. In the beginning this separation had some significant positive consequences for
religious liberties but this, as we know from the Western experience,
is not necessarily the lasting outcome. Sudden reversals seemed unlikely but gradual improvements had taken place. Oscillation in the
degree of liberty were typical. The tendency of evolution in socialist countries, as pointed out above, was that an increase in a certain
field of liberties, e.g. economic freedom, often does not bring simultaneously an increase in religious freedom. When, for instance, Poland
experienced sharp economic problems, the role of the Roman Catholic
Church in the national life increased markedly.

Occasionally nearly all freedoms undergo simultaneous change.
This was the case in Czechoslovakia in 1968. During the "Prague
Spring" all liberties were increased; after the Soviet intervention in
August, 1968 all freedoms were sharply reduced or curtailed. This
makes it necessary to judge religious liberty and human rights issues
in the context of the history of each country. Likewise it necessi-
tates adjusting one's procedures for expanding religious liberties and
human rights according to each case. Another instance of simultaneous improvement of all liberties was the "Great Transformation" of
1989–1990.

One of the reasons why so many American and other Western

concerns for human rights in Eastern Europe tended to fail was the assumption that certain responses or pressures will work universally. We have witnessed sometimes the opposite results from those desired because there was a lack of understanding of the traditions, concerns, and needs both of different religions and of different countries. Not all religions have an equal need for Bibles, the right to emigrate, formal training for clergy, Sunday schools, etc. Not all countries respond in an equal manner to economic sanctions, public attack, or quiet diplomacy.

It is hoped that this study will provide some data and approaches for a more effective struggle for the expansion of religious freedom, although obviously in addition to knowledge of the specific religious liberty issues there is also the need for knowing the tradition and history of specific countries and individual religious groups, which an exploration like this cannot provide. No attempt has been made here to be comprehensive, although the issue was addressed in some detail, because theoretically there should be no limits on liberties. There may be eventually liberties which one may not even envision at this time. Therefore it is sounder to approach the issue legally by pointing out clearly the few restrictions needed at a particular time. Everything that is not explicitly prohibited ought to be permitted. The notion of what is decisively dangerous for the state is open to discussion, but this should be determined by a broad debate rather than a political party's platform. It would have been naive to expect, even before the dramatic Great Transformation of 1989, that such a change in Eastern Europe could happen without a profound change of the form of governing, but it was not farfetched to claim that even socialism can and ought to develop into a greater "domain of freedom," which Marx himself expected to happen under communism. This, indeed, was an aspiration of many Marxists, Christians, and other religious and non-religious people who lived in socialism—and outside of it.

Chapter 2

MARX AND ENGELS ON RELIGIOUS LIBERTY

To most Marxists it is of great, perhaps decisive influence what the classical authors of Marxism (Karl Marx, Friedrich Engels, and Vladimir Ilyich Ulyanov-Lenin) wrote and said about a given subject. Depending on the degree of sophistication and scholarly conscientiousness such going to the sources may either be simply quoting a text that appears appropriate or a careful placing of Marx's thoughts into the context of the time. Regretfully the former, the proof text method, is much more typical, not unlike Christian fundamentalism. A particular policy or view held by a Marxist person or group is likely to be supported by one or more citations, usually thought to clinch the argument. Bitter contentiousness among various Marxism are a result of the prevalence of this approach.

Here we wish to set out, with no claim to comprehensiveness, what Marx, Engels, and, (in the following chapter) Lenin thought of religious liberty.

Marx on Religious Liberty

Religious concerns were on the periphery of Karl Marx's thought,[1] and religious liberty was on the periphery of his thought on religion. Here discussion will be strictly limited to Marx's notions of freedom, especially as applied to religion.

In general Marx recognized the category of freedom stating that it is so much part of being human that one may deny it perhaps to someone else but certainly not to oneself. Yet Marx rejected the understanding of liberty proclaimed by the French Revolution because he felt that such freedoms do not bring people into a relationship with one another but rather separate them from each other.[2] For Marx, it is unthinkable to see the individual as a holder of legal human rights in opposition to society. Thus he saw civil liberties as a contradiction to the social nature of the human being. As Peter Ehlen, a German philosopher from Munich demonstrated, freedom as a category is unattainable prior to the achievement of the stage of societal development that Marx calls "Communism" because only in Communism is the "Kingdom of Necessity" reconcilable with the "Kingdom of Freedom." Prior to that stage "freedom" is an illusory, even alienating notion. Marx does not recognize any inherent human values in the individual. Therefore he does not designate the human being as being the source of freedom as a value.[3]

The core of Marx's attitude toward the question of freedom and religion was that he was far more concerned about freedom *from* religion than freedom *of* religion.[4] With respect to the notion of freedom, Marx, as Thomas Sowell, an American Marxologist, ably argued, advocated freedom *for* more than freedom *from*.[5] He felt that it was impossible to be free from constraints of others, and true freedom is possible only in community; individual freedoms are a delusion. For Marx real freedom was only "environmental freedom," namely not only freedom from constraints but the availability of real choices and options.[6] "Only in community with others has each individual the means of cultivating his gifts in all directions; only in the community is personal freedom possible," wrote Marx.[7] Thus, what is often perceived as individual freedom is in fact a form of slavery.

> Indeed, the individual considers as his *own* freedom the movement, no longer curved or fettered by a common tie or by man, the movement of his alienated life elements, like property, industry, religion, etc.; in reality, this is the perfection of his slavery and his inhumanity.[8]

For Marx human rights would only make full sense when people are radically changed; currently people are too selfish and they take human rights to be rights to own, believe, and exploit.[9] Arthur McGovern, S.J., an American philosopher who studied Marx extensively, concluded that Marx believed that human rights are a sign of egoism.[10] When human potentialities do not develop freely, they appear in warped forms, where people do not recognize them as their own essence, such as religious self-alienation. When conditions in which human needs can be satisfied come about, then there will be no more need for things like money and gods to dominate people.[11] In socialism the entire question of religious liberty should become moot because socialism will not contribute positively to the creation of religious consciousness nor will there then any reason for atheism as the antithesis of religion.[12] Thus, for Marx, liberty of religion in pre-socialist formations is not a value since it would lead to alienation from one's authentic being, while in socialism it will become superfluous since religion will have become obsolete.

The presence of religion in a society shows that people are still unfree. In *On the Jewish Question*, the writing most relevant to the issue of freedom, Marx himself stated:

> But since the existence of religion is the existence of a defect, the source of this defect can only be sought in the nature of the state itself. . . . We do not insist that they must abolish their religious limitation in order to abolish secular limitations. We insist that they abolish their religious limitations as soon as they abolish their secular limitations.[13]

Simple separation of church from the state would not lead to the desired liberation of people from religion as was evident from the example of the United States where such separation was accomplished, yet people remained largely religious. Thus Marx wanted more than the political emancipation of the state from the church. As David McLellan, a British expert on Marx, pointed out, for Marx "religion was metaphysically and sociologically misguided and that its disappearance is the necessary precondition for any radical amelioration of social conditions."[14] To put it in Marx's words:

> to abolish religion as the illusory happiness of the people is to demand their real happiness; the demand to give up illusions about the existing state of affairs is the demand to give up a state of affairs that needs illusions.[15]

The reason for the ambivalence as to whether the criticism of religion is the premise of all other criticism[16] of whether secular emancipation preceded religious emancipation is linked closely to Marx's ambivalence about human nature, which in Marx is closely linked with the notion of freedom.

> If man is unfree in the materialist sense, i.e. free not through the negative power to avoid this or that, but through the positive power to assert his true individuality, crime must not be punished in the individual, but the anti-social source of crime must be destroyed, and each man must be given social scope for the vital manifestation of his being. If man is shaped by his surroundings, his surroundings must be made

human. If man is social by nature, he will develop his true nature only in society, and the power of his nature must be measured not by the power of separate individuals but by the power of society.[17]

One may presume that what applies to crime would also apply to religion and that hence the primary struggle should not be against religion *per se* but against alienating and exploitative conditions which give rise to religion, a question which Marx addressed, but which need no special treatment in this chapter.

During the Paris Commune in 1870 Marx advocated freedom of religion and separation of church and state saying, ". . . the pay of the priest, instead of being extorted by the tax gatherer, should only depend on the spontaneous action of the parishioners' religious instincts."[18] He praised the Parisians for attempting "to break the spiritual force of repression, the 'parson power,' by disestablishment and disendowment of all churches as proprietary bodies."[19] Thereby priests and religion were forced into a private sphere, where Marx felt they belonged, something he had advocated already in 1842 from a somewhat different perspective. "Once a state includes several confessions with equal right it cannot be a religious state without violating particular confessions."[20]

Marx's analysis of the failure of the Paris Commune had a far more important impact on later communists both prior to their taking of power and after they took control than his remarks about their treatment of religion. He assessed that the Paris commune failed because of the lack of decisiveness of those who took the power; still burdened with bourgeois attitudes they were unwilling to use ruthlessly all the necessary power. This lesson the Communists were not likely to forget; party training manuals underlined the need to strike out against all that could potentially threaten the proletarian revolution.[21] Religion certainly belonged in that category.

In the *German Ideology* Marx wrote about individual people being able to control their life and work in a future communist society, yet he believed that society determines human nature and that by changing social conditions human nature also changes.[22] He did not endorse attempts to forcibly eliminate religious practices, but he was not in favor of freedom of conscience, which is closely linked with freedom of religion. In his *Critique of the Gotha Program* in 1875 the mature Marx wrote:

. . . "Freedom of Conscience!" If one had desired at the time of the *Kulturkampf* to remind liberalism of its old catchwords, it surely could have been done only in the following form: Everyone should be able to attend to his religious as well as bodily needs without the police sticking their noses in. But the workers' party ought at any rate in this connection to have expressed its awareness of the fact that bourgeois 'freedom of conscience' is nothing but toleration of all possible kinds of *religious freedom of conscience,* and that for its part it endeavours rather to liberate the conscience from the witchery of religion. But one chooses not to overstep the "bourgeois" level . . .[23]

From this it is evident that Marx was not a defender of religious liberty but favored liberation from religion, an idea which was to be latched on by his followers. It seems unlikely, if not impossible, to use Marx as a basis for the building of a principled human rights policy. He was so concerned about substantive equality that he neglected any juridical defenses of human rights since he thought that they would be affirmed in completely unmediated ways in the future communist society that no politics, political parties, state organs, police or army, and of course, no laws would be needed for the full exercise of human rights and potentials.

Engels on Religious Liberty

Engels examined concrete historical religious developments more extensively than Marx did, especially in the period when Marx turned his attention predominantly to political economy. He tended to see certain stages in religious history as being progressive rather than reactionary. Like Marx he did not directly espouse religious liberty, but he was distinctly opposed to religious persecution and militant atheism. In his opinion the working class of France and the socialist oriented workers of Germany were beyond any significant influence of religion. Hence a vigorous atheist propaganda may only serve the reawakening or reenforcing of religious convictions, which was, according to Engels, attempted by some leaders of the Paris Commune. He leveled this criticism at the Blanquists and Bakuninists:

This much is sure: the only service that can be rendered to God today is to declare atheism a compulsory article of faith and to outdo Bismarck's *Kirchenkulturkampf* laws by prohibiting religion generally . . . .[24]

Religion will vanish gradually and naturally when economic forces which subdue human beings become so profoundly changed that the religious reflection of these forces vanish. Therefore he wrote this in his polemic against Dühring:

> . . . when therefore man no longer merely proposes, but also disposes—only then will the last alien force which is still reflected in religion vanish; and with it will also vanish the religious reflection itself, for the simple reason that there will be nothing left to reflect.
>
> Herr Duehring, however, cannot wait until religion dies this, its natural death. He proceeds in more deep-rooted fashion. He out-Bismarcks Bismarck; he decrees sharper May laws not merely against Catholicism, but against all religion whatsoever; he incites his gendarmes of the future against religion, and thereby helps it to martyrdom and a prolonged lease on life.[25]

This turned out to be a prophetic warning of Engels, disregarded by his own followers at the peril of many religious people, who were, indeed, martyred by the communist movement. Engels merely proposed not to mistreat religion; lacking is a positive statement as to how religion should be dealt with in socialism, i.e. how much liberty should be accorded to religion. Apparently he thought it to be a non-issue; there is little need to make provisions for a phenomenon that will soon naturally expire. When the masses become educated in the sciences, they will have the tool which heretofore religion provided in order to deal with the problems and fears of life.

Implications and Impact of Marx's and Engels' Views

Marx and Engels neglected issues such as justice[26] and seldom explicitly dealt with human rights; though viewed from another perspective many of their writings dealt with analyzing conditions which create injustice and violate human dignity. Since later Marxists tended to be so dependent on the words of the founders rather than the overall thrust of their writings, socialist societies tended to neglect justice and human rights. The presence of strong critical remarks about the abuses of justice and rights in capitalism and the absence of explicit positive endorsements of justice, human right, and liberties contributed to the massive devaluing of these concepts in socialist practice. Krystyna Gorniak-Kocikowska, a Polish philosopher from University of Poznan, pointed out that Marx was not an heir of the emphasis upon individual salvation but rather shared an Augustinian or early medieval notion of the individual being bound up in society which makes her/him a citizen of the world.[27] This would play a role in Marx's interest in liberating all the people from enslaving conditions and his disinterest in freedom of the individual from societal coercion. This probably played a role in the lesser appeal of Marxism in societies where the Reformation, Protestant and Catholic, stimulated concern for the individual but had greater response in societies which were unaffected by individualism. This was certainly the case in Russia, Poland, and on the Balkans where the content of Marxism may not have become popular, but the basic terms of his concern for societal transformation would be acceptable even to the foes of Marxism.

One source of potential problems for future followers of Marx was Marx's way of presenting his material. Trevor Ling assesses this problem by noting that "Marx had a mordant, journalistic style and decorated his pages with many a clever and satirical turn of phrase." Much of his writing "is good vigorous pamphleteering, intended no doubt to stir the blood, but it has little to offer by way of useful sociological analysis."[28] The problem is that Marx painted with big brush strokes, involving generalities such as "religion," "species-being," "Christianity," "Judaism," and so forth which have little correspondence to real life, and yet he presented them in such a way as if these were, indeed, most concrete historical realities the world over.

Perhaps unwittingly Marx and Engels likewise contributed to the problem of liberty in socialism by means of the notion of the withering away of the state. In a polemic against those socialists and anarchists who favored the abolishing of the state Engels wrote:

> So long as the proletariat still *uses* the state, it does not use it in the interest of freedom but in order to hold down its adversaries and as soon as it becomes possible to speak of freedom the state as such ceases to exist.[29]

On the one hand this belief can easily be construed to mean that during the transitional stage the socialist state need not be concerned with freedom because it needs the state apparatus to hold down its enemies, who remain broadly undefined and could apply to any group or person who is allegedly a vestige of bourgeois interest. On the other hand the utopia of the withering away of the state made it unnecessary for proponents of a socialist revolution to prepare any mechanisms which would protect freedoms from abuse and encroachment either by the state in the period in which the state "still" exists or in the afterward. Perhaps the most misleading idea was to posit the possibility that there would be a time when the state would not exist because in practical terms it makes the important need to fortify human rights in face of its possible denials by the state into a non-concern to the visionaries, revolutionaries, and bureaucrats. Still it would be erroneous to blame Engels for the lack of civil liberties and democracy in the USSR. and most countries of Eastern Europe because, as will be seen later, they did not have them beforehand.

It is clear that neither Marx nor Engels proposed the prohibition of religion. The reason for this is that they both considered religion to be an expression of an alienated need and longing which can disappear only when social conditions which create such a need have been basically altered. The predecessors of Marx and Engels, the mechanistic materialists, worked for the abolishment of religion; the dialectical materialism of Marx and Engels had some space for free will and for political liberties.[30] Thomas Sowell provided a well targeted critique of Marx's notion of freedom with which I agree. He stated that Marx's belief in progress meant ignoring of the need for constraints. Marx felt that all limits would vanish once people actually became "free."[31] Since he did not speculate what such a free society would be like, it became possible for his followers to use this notion as a *carte blanche* to experiment at will for the alleged purpose of creating freedom *for* the people rather than freedom from the abuses of power, thus:

> trampling their 'freedom from' authorities in hopes of promoting their 'freedom to' achieve various anticipated social and economic benefits. But the much despised bourgeois 'freedom from' authorities owed its evolution precisely to the awareness of the need to protect people from their 'betters' or their saviors.[32]

Marx felt that he knew how to provide real freedom from alienation to the masses, saving them from illusory happiness. According to Sowell:

> [w]hatever Marx intended, the actual effect of the doctrine of historical justification was to provide wide latitude for the

most sweeping violations of every moral principle and every sense of decency and humanity.[33]

The Marxist propensity to judge an idea by its origin, as a part of the social environment, made it unnecessary for many Marxists to intellectually confront it, and this became a politically efficacious way of maintaining power without limits.[34]

According to Arthur McGovern, Marx's and Engels' belief that it is possible to shape human nature influenced many Marxist elites to decide to do just that in an aggressive way unanticipated by the founders, by means of education, propaganda, and repression. This notion of the malleability of human beings, McGovern perceives as standing in conflict with Christian teachings on human nature[35] and, I believe, also leads to conflict in regard to religious liberty. Religious persons or groups may decide to express their convictions or teach their progeny, while a Marxist local or national government may decide that such belief is not in the interest of those individuals or of society and will undertake efforts to reeducate the believers in one way or another. Even when religion did not directly endanger the socialist society and even when a limited recognition was given to religious liberty, especially legally, nevertheless, historically Marxists have always found new ways to restrict religious freedom in practice.

Finally there is another emphasis of Marx and Engels which has had serious implications for the Marxist problematic track record on certain human rights, especially for religious liberty. It was the imbalance of attention to society and individual. Marx and Engels were interested in the major implications for society. Social well-being takes precedence over individual well-being, though they did think that eventually the individuals comprising the group would come for their due as sharers in the general well-being. I believe that the founders did not have sufficient appreciation of "the tensions between freedom, justice, and equality inherent in moral man and moral society."[36] They cut through this ambiguity by giving clear preference to the interest of the community. And this turns out to be the source of the problem. An individual can decide what is in his or her interest, even if it may not turn out to be their best long-range interest in retrospect. But who decides what is the best interest of society? In Marxist socialist societies this has generally been a small group of revolutionaries who believe that Marxism as an objective social science provides them with the understanding of what is in the best interest of society, even against people's own will.

Marx's emphasis on the community over the individual fell on particularly fertile ground in Eastern Europe where traditional societies habitually gave preference to the community. The individual's worth was always judged in terms of the benefit to the larger group, be it nation, region, church, or whatever. Even the three most powerful religious groups, Eastern Orthodoxy, Roman Catholicism, and Islam put the stress on the community. Only Protestantism provided a relatively greater emphasis upon the individual, but Protestantism played a relatively minor role in Eastern Europe. Thus the emphasis on the community was seen as selfevident, and this had some ominous implications not only for individual religious freedom but even religious liberties of ecclesiastical groups when they were judged to be against social interest by the Marxist decision-makers.

Thus it may be concluded that while Marx and Engels would most likely not have endorsed the cruel repressions of religion (and other forms of repression), they were, nevertheless, direct contributors of ideas which could be easily adopted for justifying repression, and therefore they are to a significant extent responsible for what happened in their name by their followers.

Until the Great Transformation of 1989 their thought was dogma among Communists in Eastern Europe (and elsewhere); only rarely did humanistic Marxists dare to challenge some precept of Marx and Engels. However with the crisis and seeming collapse of Eastern European Communism, Marx and Engels are sharply diminished in the esteem of many of their present and former followers. Their ideas on religious liberty appear to rapidly fade in impact, reduced from the utterances of demi-gods to the radical and often dangerous (in terms of consequences) ruminations of two nineteenth-century visionaries.

Chapter 3

LENIN'S IMPACT ON RELIGIOUS LIBERTY

Lenin's Theory and Practice of Religious Liberty

No single person is as determinative of the Communist approach to religious liberty as Vladimir Ilyich Ulyanov-Lenin (1870–1924). Not even Marx or Engels. Lenin saw himself as an "orthodox" follower of Marx and Engels and liked to project the image of a faithful disciple and promoter of true Marxism. He took the helm of the revolutionary forces in Russia at a decisive time, shaped the most important policies, including religious one's of the new revolutionary government and remained the most important theoretician and practitioner of the revolution sufficiently long prior to his untimely death to see its victory assured.

Some picture Lenin as a hero, a demi-god, who decisively brightened human history leading it to a new stage of happiness and enlightenment. Others see him as the villain who inflicted immeasurable misery for religious people of every ilk. Even sixty years after his death it is not easy to establish his actual historical portrait. Nor will this be attempted here as it exceeds the self-imposed limits of this study. Among those who are his heirs, there are today some who see the problems which he caused with some of his theories and practices vis-à-vis religion. Among his opponents there are those who recognize the great significance of his historical role and who see that he was more nuanced in his religious policies than were some of his followers, especially Stalin.

In some ways Lenin continued the *tsarist* attitude toward religion, and in other ways he drastically altered them. He continued the practice draconically applied by Peter the Great in which the state tries to completely dominate over religious institutions. But he discontinued favoring religion. Thereby he reversed, put upside down the previous policies—and that, indeed, was revolutionary—thus establishing the first Secularistic Absolutist or Type C (see chapter 1) country in history. Now religion was viewed negatively. Lenin established, with means as ruthless as those of Peter the Great, policies to stamp upon society his notion of the role of religion in society. He envisioned himself as the liberator of the varied people of his land from the oppression of religion. Part of his assessment, that religion is oppressive, he got from Marx. Part of it he got from the indigenous Russian experience (see chapter 4). It is not easy to determine whether the Russian Orthodox Church and the other religious institutions were as oppressive as the Bolsheviks pictured them or whether the religious institutions were the benevolent protectors of the valuable national and religious traditions as the followers of these religions tend to portray. The truth is likely to be neither as positive as believers would like to think nor as diabolical as Lenin and the Bolsheviks portrayed them. But the real situation is in any case not nearly as important as perceptions of it.

Lenin perceived religion to be oppressive, but of even greater importance to him was that he felt that the old regime had the loyalty of the churches, especially the Russian Orthodox Church. Even though many a believer may have favored some or many of the changes that the revolution promised and participated in the revolution[1] and even though reforms were on the mind of even the higher clergy, Lenin felt that at the moment of decision the religious loyalties, particularly of the influential higher clergy, will be anti-Bolshevik. In that he was probably right, although his own anti-religious views and orders for violent actions had much to do with shaping such negative attitudes by many of the religious leaders and people.

Although his parents were religious, Lenin broke with religion already at the age of sixteen. He got his irreconcilable views toward religion from Georgi Plekhanov, who believed that "absolute disagreement with religion" was the only consistent socialist approach.[2] Plekhanov felt that religion was not even a private matter but that everything should be done to destroy religion in a person who joins the party or at a minimum prevent that person from spreading religious prejudices among workers.

Lenin selected an even a narrower focus than Plekhanov because he saw only the political role of the church—always meaning only the Russian Orthodox Church—which was, in his opinion, too closely associated with the imperial regime and was pacifying the masses with its other-worldliness. Although he was a theoretical atheist, McLellan rightly points out that he was primarily anti-religious and anti-clerical.[3] It seems to have been mainly a tactical move when in 1903 he proclaimed:

> . . . the Social Democrats . . . demand that everyone shall have full and unrestricted right to profess any religion he pleases. . . . No official should have the right even to ask anyone about his religion; this is a matter for each person's conscience and no one has the right to interfere. All religions and all churches have equal status in law.[4]

Had this become more than a tactic, namely a basic principle, cherished and promoted there would have been a chance that socialist societies could change from Secularistic Absolutism (Type c) to Pluralist Liberty (Type D). But such was not the case. Already in 1905 in his single article dealing with the topic, "Socialism and Religion" Lenin stated that religion primarily justifies oppression by making the masses meek and the exploiters gain satisfaction by giving a little charity. Socialism should use science to fight religion which dulls the people's will to fight for political change. He introduced the famous formula which is often repeated by his followers, namely that from the perspective of the state religion ought to be a private affair of every citizen, but from the perspective of the Communist Party religion must be fought. The party, said he, cannot be "indifferent to lack of class-consciousness, ignorance, or obscurantism in the shape of religious belief."[5]

This could work in principle as long as the Communist Party (Bolshevik) was not in power and the government would commit itself to non-intervention in religious matters. But once the Bolshevik Party took power and for all practical purposes became fully identified with the government then the Leninist lines of separation become completely blurred in practice, as will be obvious in the following chapter. Foremost among Lenin's convictions were that party propaganda must be anti-religious because it is scientific, but that religion should not be fought abstractly. Rather it should have a distinctly political orientation.

The two-pronged Leninist emphasis was also evident after the Revolution. Although the Constitution of 1918 guaranteed freedom of conscience and freedom of both religious and atheist propaganda, in 1919 Lenin wrote into the Bolshevik Party Program,

With regard to religion, it is the policy of the Russian Communist Party (Bolshevik) not to content itself with the already decreed separation of the Church from the State and of the School from the Church. . . . The party strives for the complete dissolution of the ties between the exploiting classes and the organization of religious propaganda, as well as for the real emancipation for the toiling masses from religious prejudices; to this end, the party organizes the widest possible scientific, educational, and anti-religious propaganda.[6]

The beginning and the end of that paragraph constitute the seed of untold problems with regard to religious liberties. First of all Lenin explicitly admitted that the Constitutional guarantees were not the ultimate commitment of the Communist Party but that one should move further in a direction of changing these guarantees. As a party in the midst of a revolution and civil war it makes sense for it to commit itself to strive for a separation between religion and the 'exploiting classes,' but this is followed by the intention to emancipate not only party members but 'the toiling masses,' meaning nearly everyone, from religious 'prejudices.' Lest a reader imagines that Lenin differentiated between religious prejudices and what one may consider sound religion, it is clearly evident that Lenin simply believed that religion equals prejudice. As the party and government increasingly overlapped, for all practical purposes the government simply did not respect its own constitution but became actively antireligious.

In a heated condemnation of another Bolshevik, Anatoliy Lunacharsky, who at one point advocated the creation of a secular religion of "god-building" with humanity being deified, Lenin wrote:

Those who toil and live in want all their lives are taught by religion to be submissive and patient here on earth, and to take comfort in the hope of a heavenly reward. But those who live by labour of others are taught by religion to practice charity whilst on earth, thus offering them a very cheap way of justifying their existence as exploiters and selling them at a very modest price tickets to well-being in Heaven. Religion is opium for the people. Religion is a sort of spiritual booze, in which the slaves of capital drown their human image, their demand for a life more or less worthy of man.[7]

One should note that Lenin misused Marx's phrase, "opium *of* the people," calling it now "opium *for* the people," [italics added] a change of emphasis not at all slight. This was reinforced in 1909 when he wrote:

> Religion is the opium for the people—this dictum of Marx's is the cornerstone of the whole Marxist view on religion. Marxism has regarded all modern churches and all religious organizations as instruments of bourgeois reaction that serve to defend exploitation and to drug the working class. . . . Marxism is materialism. As such it is relentlessly hostile to religion . . . . We must combat religion–that is the rudiment of *all* materialism, and consequently of Marxism.[8]

Arthur McGovern has pointed out the shift in emphasis here from Marx's assessment of a drug generated by the workers themselves to escape the cruelties of their life to Lenin's notion of the drug being administered to the workers by the capitalists.[9] Lenin did not doubt that combatting religion was very important although it was to be subjugated to the central Marxist task of spearheading the class struggle to free the exploited workers. If the struggle against religion was tactically impeding the class struggle because some workers were still attached to religion, Lenin was willing to soften the approach to religion. When this was not the case, then the struggle against religion can be hardened. This must be done if the church allies itself with re-actionary forces. In the struggle against religion Lenin believed that it was more advantageous if the clergy were stereotypically reactionary, stupid, drunkards, cheats, authoritarian, immoral, and so forth. Such clergy would present far less problems than the progressive, intelli-gent, creative, spiritual, democratic, and honest ones. Uneducated workers who retained their religiosity could be allowed to join the party, provided they did not propagate their religious views among members. But this did not apply to religious intellectuals whom he perceived as dangerous. Lest one think that he opposed only the powerful Russian Orthodox Church, he stated emphatically, even in regard to the pseudo-religious God-builders of such progressives as the writer Maxim Gorki and the previously mentioned Lunacharsky,

> Every religious idea, every idea of God, even every flirtation with the idea of god is unutterable vileness; . . . it is vileness of the most dangerous kind, "contagion" of the most abominable kind.[10]

It should be noted that no attempt was made by Lenin to study and understand religion or to refute it on rational grounds; only emotional name-calling is used. In his defense one must say that many of his writings and utterances were made in very turbulent, revolutionary situations, but there is no evidence that he modified his views in the relative quiet of emigration or during the times when he could write analytically and sharply on other issues. It is clear that, like Marx, he did not assign a very prominent place to religion in his intellectual scheme or overall revolutionary strategy, except to see religion as a serious impediment which must be removed, regardless of methods. Thus it is difficult to find positive assessment of religion by Lenin.[11]

Another factor is crucial in understanding Lenin. That was his attitude toward democracy and democratic liberties. In the undemocratic conditions of the Russian Empire, the Communists were forced into a clandestine, secretive existence in order to conceal their activities. "In these circumstances democracy could be—and was—dismissed by Lenin as a 'useless and harmful toy.' "[12] Jacobinism and Peter Tkachev's attitude toward imposing ideas upon the masses from above influenced Lenin's views on central controls. He saw no reason why to change his views on democracy in the period of the revolution or afterwards. Sowel's remark is pertinent, "Once dictatorial power was centralized by necessity in the hands of the revolutionary leaders, they had every incentive to hold on to it long after the revolution . . ."[13]

Perhaps more important than the explicit statements of Lenin about religion and democratic freedoms were his views of the role of the Communist Party as the avant garde of the proletariat and his notion of democratic centralism. Both of these notions were not passing tactical moves but major strategic concepts of how a proletarian revolution can take place under conditions of barely developed capitalism ("the chain snaps at its weakest link," according to Lenin). Lenin did not want a debating club or open discussions about various revolutionary projects; he wanted a disciplined group of activists totally dedicated to the toppling of the old order, for which, he recognized most of the Russian proletariat—for whose benefit this revolution would be carried out and the new order built—was not necessarily prepared despite their dissatisfactions and unrest. So he formed the Bolshevik Party as the striking force, which would hit hard and efficiently, benefiting by popular unrest and fomenting it for the achievement of goals for which the party alone would not be capable. While publicly lauding the "revolutionary masses of peasants and workers" there was ultimately little trust in the masses, but there was a trust in a certain elitist concentration of power and decision-making in the party. This became particularly obvious in the early twenties when the party struck against some of the *soviets*, (councils) when they demanded more autonomy.

This is led directly to two notions:

(1) that only the Communist Party, armed with the absolute certainty of "scientific materialism," knows what people really need— more so than the people themselves, and

(2) that all alternate world views must be eliminated as they are "unscientific" and, incidentally, threaten the monopoly of Party in shaping people's opinions.

Within the Party, and *only* within the Party, Lenin advocated "democratic centralism." According to this principle before a decision is made, every party member may have his or her say and contribute to the shaping of policy. But once the decision is made, presumably by the majority of those voting, no Party member, whether present or not, could deviate in any way, by continued discussion or action. From that moment on all party members must show enthusiastic support and implementation of the task. Many analysts have noted that the word which was emphasized was not the "democratic" but the "*centralism.*" It is true that in retrospect Lenin's time seems to shine with freedom of discussion, of which, indeed, there were many exciting one's during the immediate postrevolutionary period. Stalin eliminated such free discussion, and it was the leadership that imposed decisions which were unanimously supported without any possible dissent. But even though Lenin was much more supportive of a degree of free discussion in the Party, and even though the times were uncertain, brutal, and the fate of the revolution was at stake, one may still say that despite all these excuses and justifications, it was Lenin's policy of democratic centralism which is the ultimate cause of the totalitarian direction of subsequent communist generations in the Soviet Union (and elsewhere). More accurately, it was the deification of Lenin, the canonization of his works, and the slavish emulation, the unwillingness to apply critical, even Marxist critical thinking to Lenin, which is responsible for the perpetuation of this strategy. This was recognized ever more widely by many in the Soviet Union since the introduction of *perestroika* and great rage is directed both against the assessment of Lenin and his cult that flourished under state auspices.

Many observers, even Marxists, feel that without a significant shift away from centralism to democracy, the space for all freedoms will remain limited in a communist society. A good first step may be simply to shift the emphasis to "*democratic* centralism," but this needs to be followed by some fundamental steps of democratizing in which the disagreement even prior to a decision is not quickly labeled as "dissent." And in which, after the decision is made, dissent is not only tolerated but encouraged because only thus can there be continuous checking whether it is the right decision.

Another obstacle for freedom created by Lenin, which continued to grow after him was the process of turning "scientific" materialism into a doctrine, an undisputed orthodoxy. This move stripped it immediately from its claim of being scientific. The change would fail to give it a scientific character, namely that of a hypothesis—or even theory—which is constantly challengeable, correctable, and debatable. The nineteenth century notion of scientific laws has been retained almost exclusively among dogmatic Marxists. As Marxism presents itself as a scientific law of social development, it surely provides no room for alternate, religious or non-religious worldviews: these must be wrong by definition. But if Marxism is an interpretation and methodology of action for social change, then, indeed, other alternatives are not only possible but even desirable, because only in complex interaction of interpretations can a better way be found. Liberties increase with the stripping away of false pretenses which were built for Marxist historical materialism as a "science" and when Marxists reach for the more authentically Marxian "critique of all existent realities"— which, of course, also includes socialism (not only capitalism, especially the outlived capitalism of the nineteenth century) in all its manifestations.[14]

In the field of legislation Lenin took away with one hand what he gave with the other. While, as noted above, many classical liberties were granted in the Constitution of 1918, which was in force until 1936, it must be noted that Lenin limited these right and liberties to members of the working class alone. This means, for instance, that clergy (even the terribly poor ones), remnants of the other classes, and with some clever interpretation nearly every potential opponent of the leadership could be and were denied all civil and economic rights.[15] In the principles and precedents established by Lenin, one can discern the root of the ruthless power-struggle among the successors of Lenin in which they denied even to each other not only rights but even their very lives.

The single most destructive view for religious liberty was Lenin's notion of who is the class enemy and how to deal with the class enemy in order to hold on to power. The class enemy are political opponents from the ruling classes and all their allies, their military forces no matter how people were conscripted into these forces, and those in one's own ranks that are undependable.[16] Religions were certainly viewed as being a part of the first category. The Leninist line, followed subsequently by all Communist parties of Eastern Europe, for they certainly defined themselves as Leninist, was to liquidate the class enemy by any means necessary, even the most brutal. This was something well understood by both Communist leaders and members. Lenin's cruelty toward the "reactionary clergy" was not easily surpassed as his secret instructions written in 1922 to Vyacheslav Molotov about the confiscations of church property and treasures indicate.[17] Once a decision was made by the party leadership individual units or even members of communist units did not need a special approval in liquidating class enemies or else the instructions were communicated orally and covertly. This seems to have been the single most important factor in explaining why the churches, particularly their religious leaders were dealth with so brutally across the board, except that in East Germany and Poland milder forms of dealing with the class enemy were resorted to for tactical reasons.

The last but not the least formative stance of Lenin which made an enormous impact on his followers was his praxiological ethic that 'the end justifies the means.' Nikola Milošević ably traced Lenin's fundamental dictatorial position which quickly evolved to tyranny (which would culminate in Stalin). Milošević pointed out that Lenin himself stated that dictatorship is the unlimited governing, unrestricted by any law or rules based on direct brute force. He apparently believed that any means may be used in order to take and retain power. Furthermore he urged uncompromising hostility toward the 'enemy' saying, "The larger the number of members of the bourgeoisie and clergy whom we can kill at this time that much the better. Just now we must give those people such a lesson that for decades they will not think to resist us."[18] Later this attitude resulted in the inability of Communism to achieve the liberating ideals that Lenin claimed to espouse.[19]

From all the above it would appear that Lenin's role in delineating a very narrow space for many political and civil liberties, including religious liberties, was, indeed, very large. Dogmatic Marxists, who idolized Lenin, justified and defended it by raising the perennial claim that civil and political, including religious liberties are meaningless until all economic and social liberties are satisfied, no matter how long it may take. Therefore no public criticism of Lenin was allowed in the Soviet Union, and the same held in other socialist countries where Lenin was regarded as the infallible founder of the real socialist order. Even in Yugoslavia, where individuals have published critical remarks on Lenin, the Communist Party was unwilling to distance itself from Leninism the way the Spanish and Italian Communist Parties have done.

The hard-liners are not the only ones who idolized Lenin. Gorbachev and the promoters of *perestroika* also tend to go "back to Lenin" and Leninist principles and practices as they tried to reform vestiges of Stalinism and Brezhnevite "stagnation." They selected those moments in Lenin's work in which he was a hard-nosed realist willing to compromise or make concession and urged some of his more ardent followers to moderate their fanaticism. Thus Lenin can also be an idol to the "new thinkers," who still found it a useful oratorical weapon to summon Lenin to the defense of this or that position which they espouse.

With both the hard-liners and reformist Marxist appealing to Lenin's authority it comes as a surprise when finally under the policy of *glasnost* the long overdue public criticism of Lenin himself is finally taking place in the Soviet Union. Vasily Grossman's posthumously published "Forever Flowing" in *Oktyabr* (June 1989) contains the following statements: "Lenin—all victories of the party and the state are linked with the name of Lenin. But all cruelty committed in the country has become the tragic burden of Vladimir Ilyich."[20] Grossman pointed out that the terror and dictatorship commenced not with Stalin but with Lenin. He wrote:

> Lenin's intolerance, unshakable aspiration to achieve a goal, contempt for freedom and cruelty to those who thought differently, his ability to remove from the earth whole regions, areas. which did not comply with his orthodox rightness— all those features were not added to Lenin's character by the revolution, they go much deeper, into Lenin's youth. . . . Lenin didn't try to find the truth in discussions, but to win. When debates were transferred from the pages of newspapers and magazines into the streets, battlefields and

wheatfields, it was realized that all cruel means were useful and good.[21]

Grossman, who died in 1964, also wrote that:

> Bolsheviks did not believe in the value of personal freedom, freedom of speech and press. They, like Lenin himself, considered those freedoms which were the dream for many revolutionary workers and intelligentsia as . . . insignificant.[22]

The conclusion to which Grossman arrived was that:

> [t]hings inherited from Lenin, like revolutionary dictatorship, terror and the struggle against bourgeois freedoms, which Lenin viewed as temporary, were used by Stalin for building a foundation . . . [and] became a whole with the traditional national lack of freedom in Russia.[23]

At first there were not many in the Soviet Union who agreed with this assessment, but, as *glasnost* endured, an increasing number of thoughtful observers were forced to a reappraisal of Lenin which brought it more in line with those who have noted the tragic legacy which Lenin left to the Communist movement which threatens to overshadow his positive contributions to the workers' movement. One wonders how different socialism may have been and how different its respect for human rights, including religious liberty, might have been had a man with different values and personality climbed to the helm of the revolution. It seems that in Russia the most propitious leader for a radical revolution in such chaotic times would be one who had uncompromising hostility toward political and civil rights—Lenin. The result will be analyzed in subsequent chapters.

Chapter 4

U S S R: THE TREND SETTER IN REPRESSION

It is tempting to write an up-beat chapter on the issue of religious liberty in the Union of Soviet Socialist Republics based on the improvements in this area which are taking place under Mikhail Gorbachev's "new thinking." However, commitment to truth demands that the situation be viewed neither from the present perspective alone nor only from the perspective of Stalinist purges, but that the entire Bolshevik and post-Bolshevik periods be carefully presented in a nuanced a way, a task nearly impossible.

The impact of the Soviet Union, the country first to implement socialism, upon other socialist countries is hard to overestimate. The consequences for the theory and practice of religious liberty in other socialist countries of Eastern Europe turned out to be decisive. As a comparative exploration makes quickly evident, the religious conditions in the pre-revolutionary Russian Empire as well as during and after the revolution in the USSR were rather unique. The attempt to project the Soviet problems and solutions upon other countries created manifold difficulties and may have been one of the most tragic decisions made within the international socialist movement. Due to that ill-conceived scheme, it is impossible to understand the problem of religious liberties in any East European country without first understanding the Soviet model although nearly all Eastern European countries later made adjustments due to their historical peculiarities which made them diverge more or less from the Soviet model.

First the tradition of religious liberties in *tsarist* Russia will be described. The theoretical and practical work of Lenin was already presented in the previous chapter; the reader should recall at this point the Leninist legacy. The Soviet policies and practices in regard to religious liberty will follow, arranged according to the major historical stages.

Religious Liberty in the Russian Empire

The Russian Empire prior to the Bolshevik Revolution considered itself an Orthodox Christian land despite the fact that the population was both multireligious and multinational. The Russian Empire was a Type A–Ecclesiastic Absolutist society (see chapter 1),
namely church-state relations in it were such that the state not only
endorsed religion as such, but in particular promoted, defended, and
gave privileges to one religion, namely the Russian Orthodox Church.
Yet since it was not the only religion and since some of the other
religious institutions were receiving grudging legal recognition and
a degree of tolerance, elements of Type B–Religious Tolerance were
asserting themselves contributing to the complexity of the situation.
Clearly the Russian Orthodox Church was the established religion, i.e.
the religion of the *tsar* and the entire court and government and of
the largest and dominant ethnic group, the Slavic Russians, as well as
among the Ukrainians, and Byelorussians. A similar established role
was played by the Georgian Orthodox Church among the Georgians
and the Armenian Apostolic Church among Armenians. The Russian
Empire saw itself as the protector of all Orthodox lands in the world
because so many of them had been for centuries under hostile non-
Orthodox occupation. This does not mean that there was no legal
existence for others, such as Catholics and Uniates, Old Believers,
Muslims, Jews, Protestants, Buddhists, and indigenous "sectarians"
and tribal religionists. The degree of toleration toward them varied
significantly.

An underlying Eastern Orthodox notion is of harmony between
the head of the state and the church. The emperor, as the vicar of
Christ, was responsible for the worldly well-being of citizens-believers
while the patriarch was responsible for their spiritual well-being. The
two spheres, church and state, were seen to be in an organic, indivisible unity. To be Russian meant to be Eastern Orthodox; nationhood
carried with it the spiritual element of holiness, generally associated
with the term "Holy Mother Russia."

The geographical position of Russia and the Mongol (Tartar)
overlordship (1240–1480) had isolated Russia from the rest of Europe. The many invasions which Russians had to fight against were all
by non-Orthodox. The Muslim Mongols/Tartars, the Catholic Teutonic Knights, Poland-Lithuania, and Napoleonic France and Protestant Sweden and Prussia all presented not only national but religious

threat as well. In the Crimean War Russians faced Protestants and Muslims. All this contributed to the notion that Orthodoxy needed the protection of the rulers, while the rulers needed the blessing and encouragement by the Orthodox Church. Those of other religions were intrinsically linked with that which is foreign and dangerous.

There were several historical turning points which shaped the Russian church-state relations determining the degree of religious liberty. Mostly these turning points seemed to narrow rather than broaden religious liberty.

First was the controversy between the Non-Possessors (epitomized by Nils Sorskiy, 1433–1508) and Possessors, (led by St. Joseph of Volokolamsk). The Non-Possessors argued that the church should hold no lands, own no peasant serfs, and that the state should not intervene in religious matters as there must be no coercion in religion. The elevation of Joseph into sainthood is telling of who won this conflict; the victory of the Possessors sanctioned large land and serf owning, and the intrusion of the state into church matters, approving the legitimacy of coercion in religious matters. Many people were imprisoned, forcibly held in monasteries, exiled, and executed because of religious convictions.

The second turning point was occasioned by the seventeenth century schism between the Old Believers and the Orthodox. The monk Avvakum (1620–1682) and his followers insisted on no change in the ancient Russian liturgy while patriarch Nikon (1605–1681) demanded liturgical revisions which he deemed (incorrectly as is now evident) to be more ancient and apostolic. The Old Believers were severely repressed, had undergone a number of additional schisms and were treated by the church and the government as "sectarian"—hence a denial of many liberties and intense persecution of these groups and the government's strong preference of the official Church. Later Nikon struggled for power against emperor Alexei, which Nikon lost. This confirmed the supremacy of the emperor over the church.

The supremacy was further reinforced by Peter the Great (1682–1725) who, in another major turning point, decisively subjected the Russian Orthodox Church to the interests of the state, making the church virtually a department of the state. Peter abolished the Patriarchate, established a Holy Synod which was manipulated by an appointed layman who was the Procurator of the Holy Synod and forcibly introduced some reforms patterned on the prevailing German Lutheran model of the supremacy of the princes in the affairs of their *Landeskirche*. These reforms were generally alien to the Russian Orthodox Church, and there was much passive resistance by the Church until the Revolution of 1917, yet the Church basically complied with this subservience in the hope, as it has and still continues to do, that the civil and religious authorities must act harmoniously (based upon the ancient Byzantine concept of *symphonia*) for the long range benefit of the people. From now on the "paternalistic" role of the emperor, which had already been frequently violated by some cruel tsars like Ivan the Terrible, had been wedded to the centralized absolutistic and often arbitrary role of the ruler justified by tradition and violence. The church was unable to show decisive disagreement with the policies of the leader of the state. Such a role of the ruler fostered in the people patience and conformity, a very limited understanding and need for freedom, a willingness to comply with and support the autocratic will with whatever justification was offered. The Russian Orthodox Church's promotion of the adoration of God, other-worldliness, submissiveness to authority (the church's and others'), and the virtue of suffering became convenient props for such a regime.

Fundamentally these attitudes existed both before and after the Revolution. They have not changed much until the present, though the concrete content given to this attitude differs.

Formally there was little space for liberty unless it was officially sanctioned. Thus people found ways to extend it in a manner that would be less liable to provoke the wrath of the authorities. Space for freedom was found in the interiorization of spiritual life expressed in the well-known Russian mysticism, seen not only in saints but also in writers and in common people. Others found space for freedom in certain monastic forms, especially in the phenomenon of *startsi* [elders]. Many monasteries were built in remote places where pressures from the center were less evident. Some of the monks retreated entirely into the vast expanses of Russia practicing a simple, rigorous lifestyle. Such individuals tended to become famous not only for their alleged miraculous powers but also for their advice and compassion. Among the masses such a *starets* would be vastly more influential than the village priests or even the patriarch or emperor. Pilgrimages to the isolated dwellings of *startsi* was a characteristic of Russian spirituality which led to personal transformation and the creation of more freedom from within.

In the immediate pre-Revolutionary period, namely the later part of the nineteenth and the first few years of the twentieth century two things characterized Russia. One was a slightly expanded toleration and increase of religious liberty to the non-Russian Orthodox population, especially around the time of the 1905 Revolution and an increasing presence of atheists. The atheists (not only of the Marxist type) became more militant as repression and censorship grew. For the atheists it was easy to identify as common enemies both the state and the church (and for most Russians the word church automatically meant the Russian Orthodox Church) since the repressions by the state of all non-Orthodox alternatives was not protested by the church except by an occasional theologian with a greater ecumenical vision (e.g., Vladimir Soloviev). The increase in toleration to the non-Orthodox was due largely to the increasingly European orientation, by intermarriage, trade, and foreign policy, of the imperial family and nobility, some of whom actually became imbued with Western religious ideas, resulting, for instance, in the creation of Russian Bible societies.

There is another heritage which needs to be highlighted and which was not inherited by the Bolsheviks from their own land, namely, radical anticlericalism which was fairly common at the turn of the century not only among some radical elements but which was also expressed in a number of revolutionary movements around the world.

For instance, in 1903 the church-state issue was explosive in France. In 1905 the Law of Separation of church and state was adopted in France that abolished the Concordat with the Papacy, suppressed the annual revenue of the churches, and administered all church buildings by the government (the law *Associations Cultuelles*).[1] During the Portuguese Revolution of 1911 there was looting of convents, imprisonments of nuns and priests, and the expulsion of bishops from their dioceses. The Mexican Revolutions of 1911 and in the 1920s were likewise radically anti-clerical, leading often to the imprisonment and murder of priests. Evidently resentment and hostility toward the church and religion were by no means unique to the lands of the Russian Empire.

Thus in the Russian empire there co-existed both the traditions of intense religiosity and radical anticlericalism—a feature which persists until today.

The analysis of the Soviet Union's experience with religious liberty will be divided into two sections. The first will be a historical narrative, presenting the oscillations of the Soviet approaches to religious liberty. The situation of the Jews will be treated separately, followed by theoretical considerations exploring various factors which shaped the policies. Religious liberties after the Great Transformation will be analyzed in a separate section.

RELIGIOUS LIBERTY DURING THE BOLSHEVIK PERIOD

Periodization

Despite the persistence of Communist anti-religious strategy regarding the ultimate goal of eradicating religion there have been tactical changes of considerable complexity since the October Revolution of 1917. Therefore, it is not a simple matter to discern clearly defined periods in respect to religious liberties.

Dimitry Pospielovsky, a Russian Orthodox historian residing in Canada, who has done very extensive studies of Marxist-Leninist atheism and Soviet anti-religious policies both in theory and practice, provides separate and differing periodizations for atheist propaganda and for anti-religious policies.[2] In respect to anti-religious policies he stipulates a period from 1917 to 1941 with three phases, 1917–1920, 1921–1928, and 1929–1940, then skipping World War II he periodizes from the War to Khrushchev, the Khrushchev rule, and policies after Khrushchev.[3]

The other periodization which Pospielovsky provides is from 1917–1921, from 1919–1939 (in respect to anti-religious propaganda) and 1921–1941, from 1941–1953 (which he calls "an interlude"), then 1958–1985 as renewal of sharp anti-religious propaganda, while in respect to persecution he simply divides them into persecution under Khrushchev and after Khrushchev.

In this book a simpler, and hopefully clearer and more consistent periodization will be presented.

First Period, 1917–1929. Vacillating denial of religious liberties.

   Phase I: 1917–1922

   Phase II: 1922–1928

Second Period, 1928–1942. All-out war on religion.

Third Period, 1942–1958. Easing of pressure, yet continued hostility.

Fourth Period, 1958–1987. Restrictions on religious liberty.

   Phase I: 1958–1961

   Phase II: 1961–1962

Phase III: 1963–1965

Phase IV: 1966–1970

Phase V: 1970–1975

Phase VI: 1976–1987

Fifth Period, 1988–1989. New policies toward religions leading to increase in liberties.

Religious Liberties After the Great Transformation, 1989–1990, will be treated separately at the end of the chapter.

Vacillating Denial of Religious Liberties: 1917–1928

When the Bolsheviks came into power they faced an entirely novel experiment. The protracted civil war which ensued only made it more difficult to figure out what policies to implement. As they struggled for survival from 1917 to 1923 they necessarily followed a pragmatic and sometimes contradictory course. Bohdan Bociurkiw, a Canadian-Ukrainian scholar specializing in Soviet religious policies, discerns two tendencies among the Soviet Communists. One, "the leftist" in Bolshevik parlance, i.e. ideological and fundamentalist, advocated the use of "administrative measures," namely using all conceivable means, including violence to destroy religion. The other, "rightist" in the same circles, more practical and pragmatic, "mechanistic" advocated the creation of opportunities for suppression of religion mostly by means of creating those socio-economic, cultural, educational, and recreational conditions which would lead people to abandon their religion.[4]

The leftists, among whom the most prominent were leaders of the *Komsomol* [Communist youth organization] and the League of Militant Atheists, favored an all-out struggle against all religions. The practical group, consisting mostly of government and police officials favored a more discriminating policy, namely rewarding those religious groups and individuals who did not resist them or who had sympathies for some of the Bolshevik programs, while attacking especially those groups which were the greatest threat to them in their resistance to the new Soviet power.

Bociurkiw points out that neither of these two trends prevailed completely since neither the ideological framework nor their concrete historical experience equipped them with "a ready-made, tested solution to the church probiem."[5] In real life, even the Bolshevik leaders (e.g. Lenin, Trotsky, Lunacharsky, and Yaroslavsky) shifted between these positions. Sometimes those who were perceived as more moderate would engage in extreme words and actions and vice versa. It is difficult to pinpoint where the various leaders stood on the issue of persecuting religion and atheist propaganda not only because policies shifted according to the exigencies of the moment but also because many of their secret orders differed from their public pronouncements.

a. First Phase: 1917–1922

In the period of "Red Terror of the War Communism Era" (1917–1921) the main motivating factor was the need to survive, i.e. to win the civil war. Pospielovsky pointed out four major factors which guided the Bolshevik attitude toward religion: (1) suspicion of collaborating with the enemy prior to the revolution or during the civil war, (2) blaming the Bolsheviks for the civil war and attacking Marxism-Leninism, (3) resisting the decree on separation of church and state and confiscation of church properties (February 5, 1918) and (4) supporting Patriarch Tikhon's anathema and excommunication of Bolsheviks for desecrating churches (February 1, 1918).[6]

For all practical purposes the major target of suppression and persecution was the Russian Orthodox Church, especially those Orthodox who were royalists.[7] The number of those clergy and laity who were killed and tortured, churches and monasteries closed or destroyed amidst general carnage, is difficult to comprehend. Just in regard to Russian Orthodox Bishops it is estimated that between 1918 and 1943 292 of them disappeared and were presumed dead, i.e. killed; another estimates 271 episcopal martyrs.[8] While in many instances these were willful deeds of Red Guard detachments and spontaneous local outbursts of unspeakable cruelties, it is also clear that the Bolshevik leaders never denounced it and probably secretly ordered it by means of oral commands. One may surmise that it went along with their belief that the Russian Orthodox Church must be hit so hard that it would be cowed into submission not only in the short run, but for decades.[9] Hence from 1917 the imprisonment of clergy and believers was not for the purpose of re-education as was claimed but for terrorizing and annihilating the church (see below for some of the post-Great Transformation disclosures).

Public debates between some Marxist atheist theoreticians and Russian Orthodox theologians which evoked lively interest indicate that during this period there were still ambiguities of how to handle the Orthodox Church. However, these debates were suspended when

it became apparent that they did not result in the rout of the Orthodox debater but often elicited interest and support by the assembled
audience. Some noticed that a number of the former nominal church
members renewed their interest in the church during the difficult times
and persecutions, so much so that Lenin ordered an easing of the persecutions lest they fanaticize the believers. It was during this period
that he coined the phrase in reference to religion, "the harder you hit
a nail the deeper you drive it in." Some Bolsheviks realized the folly
of antagonizing the majority of the people; though some, like Trotsky,
believed that the Russians were basically an atheistic people with few
real ties to the church.

On the other hand, many of the other churches and religious institutions were unhampered in their work. Some of them experienced
a veritable renaissance. Lenin considered anti-Semitism a punishable
crime, and many Jewish religious and cultural activities flourished,
though from time to time there were attacks on Jews, allegedly not
because of their religion but because their bourgeois activities (the
problem of religious liberties for Jews will be discussed below in a
separate section of this chapter). The well-known Mennonite historian Walter Sawatsky, pointed out that the Protestants enthusiastically welcomed the decree separating church and state and for them
a twelve-year of unprecedented expansion took place.[10] For a while
the Ukrainian Churches, both Catholic and Orthodox, received good
treatment, and so did the Muslims for whom even a special government department for Islamic affairs was created with a Muslim *hodzha*
heading it. One may say that all non-Orthodox, except for random
violence against individuals resulting from the chaos and meanness
of the time, experienced greater freedom than they did during *tsarist*
times, when they were discriminated against. But even these religious
groups which harbored resentment against the Orthodox expressed
consternation at the vicious treatment accorded to the Orthodox.

One may ask whether the Russian Orthodox Church contributed
to the violence of the conflict. The answer is positive, though it is
not as easy to establish the degree of guilt. Surely most of the higher
clergy and many of the lower clergy as well as lay people remained
loyal to the royal family and sided with the Whites against the Reds.
The White military units considered themselves Orthodox, and many
priests fought in them. In fact "Jesus regiments" composed entirely
of clergy were created.[11] In the midst of combat the Reds were hardly
interested whether such regiments received explicit Patriarchal sup-

port or not. But it would be inaccurate to conclude that the entire Orthodox Church was opposed to the revolution; had that been the case the Revolution would hardly become successful, for after all, the vast majority of the Russian people were at least nominally Orthodox. But that fact did not prevent the Bolsheviks from twisting the truth. It is true that in the early years of the civil war they would contrast in their propaganda the cooperation of some of the poor village priests in turning over church treasures with the opposition given by the Patriarch. Later the attack on the church became frontal, depicting the entire Russian Orthodox community as the enemy, because the Bolsheviks perceived the world in simple, sharply contrasting terms. The former Italian Communist Ignazio Silone, who spent considerable time in the Soviet Union from 1921 to 1927 gave the following testimony,

> What struck me most about the Russian Communists, even in such really exceptional personalities as Lenin and Trotsky, was their utter incapacity to be fair in discussing opinions that conflicted with their own. The adversary simply for daring to contradict became a traitor, an opportunist, a hireling. *An adversary in good faith* is inconceivable to the Russian Communists.
>
> . . . how difficult it was to reach an understanding with a Russian Communist on the simplest, and for us the most obvious questions; how difficult, I don't say agree, but at least to understand each other, when talking of what liberty means for a man of the West, even for a worker . . . . "Liberty"—I had to give examples—"is the possibility of doubting, the possibility of making a mistake, the possibility of searching and experimenting, the possibility of saying 'no' to any authority—literary, artistic, philosophic, religious, social, and even political." "But that," murmured this eminent functionary of Soviet culture in horror, "that is counter-revolution." Then she added, to get a little of her own back, "We're glad we haven't got your liberty, but we've got the sanatoria in exchange."[12]

If such rabid intolerance existed toward people within the same ideological movement, one may imagine the degree of intolerance toward others, especially those conceived as the ideological enemy. Violence against the churches would have occurred in any case, but the systemic nature, the duration, and the growing scope of it, was due to the ideoiological underpinnings that emanated from the Communist leaders who incited them.

b. Second Phase: 1922–1928

Violence against Orthodox clergy and laity and confiscation of property continued. A new element was added, that of the government's support of a schismatic movement, the so-called Renovationist-Living Church in order to internally weaken the Russian Orthodox Church. Those who opposed the schism were openly persecuted.

While in the area of economy any measure of relaxation leading to limited free enterprise was introduced (known as the New Economic Policy), this did not lead to ideological compromise or cessation of attack upon the Russian Orthodox Church. Anti-religious propaganda, of course, with state support, became more extensive and more sophisticated. A large number of anti-religious periodicals and even more extensive lectures were the main means of this propaganda. The forcible confiscation of church treasures was intensified for the purpose of purchasing food during the period of famine, though it is alleged that much of the confiscated material ended in the coffers of the Che-Ka (predecessor of the KGB) for promotion of Communism. Those who resisted the confiscation were tried at prominently publicized trials and many were executed. Numerous clashes, about 1,500 of them bloody, were reported between believers and armed units. Some Jewish and Roman Catholic leaders were also tried.

In the Ukraine a shift occurred from toleration to intense pressure as the Soviet regime faced the problem of Ukrainian nationalism. While the Ukrainian Autocephalous Orthodox Church was initially promoted as a means of weakening the Russian Orthodox Church, attempts were made in this period to weaken the Ukrainian Autocephalous Orthodox Church both by promoting the same schismatic Renovationist-Living Church movement and by declaring illegal in 1923 the All-Ukrainian Orthodox Church Council.[13]

Toward the end of the period the Soviet government succeeded in obtaining declarations of loyalty from all churches. After the arrest of Patriarch Tikhon, the Patriarch *locum tenens*, Metropolitan Sergiy, signed the declaration. Metropolitan Mykolai Boretskiy of the Ukrainain Autocephalous Orthodox Church did likewise. Those clergy who refused to recognize such declarations were imprisoned, murdered, or otherwise removed from influence. By 1930 that church was forced to liquidate itself.

By 1923 the Soviet government turned also against the Protestant communities, primarily because of their pacifist attitude. They forced them to repudiate pacifism; some of their leaders now actively urged their members to carry out their military obligations.[14] Even though a number of the leaders were Christian socialists and formed a fairly large number of successful communes, the government not only withdrew the promised support but forced their disbanding and mounted the pressures against the Protestants. Some Jewish and Roman Catholic leaders were also tried.

Pospielovsky estimates that during this period about 8,100 Orthodox clergy were murdered (2691 married priests, 1962 monks, 3,447 nuns).[15] As previously noted, many of the leading bishops also lost their lives. Other churches also experienced large losses of life.

The schools, beginning in 1926, changed from being a-religious to anti-religious and teachers from that point on to 1991 had to conceal their faith if they were religious.[16]

c. Legal Provisions from 1917 to 1928

Nearly all the laws governing religious behavior during this period were passed in 1917 or 1918. In 1917 the Act of the Commissar of Education of December 11, 1917, handed over control of all educational institutions, including theological seminaries with all their property, to the Commistariat on Education. Lenin signed on December 18, 1917, the Decree on Dissolution of Marriage which ordered the turning over of records and the invalidation of religious courts' decisions regarding dissolution of marriage and handing this task over to secular courts. On the same day a Decree recognizing only civil marriages was signed by Lenin.

On January 6, 1918, the Order of the People's Commissariat of Military Affairs curtailed military chaplaincy, except in units that explicitly demanded it and were willing to support it. Subsidies to churches and religious orders were halted by the Order of the People's Commissar of Welfare on January 20, 1918.

The most significant and comprehensive was the Decree of the Soviet of People's Commissars of January 21, 1918. Its full text is:

1. The Church is separated from the state.

2. Within the territory of the Republic, it is forbidden to pass any local laws or regulations which would restrain or limit freedom

of conscience or which would grant special rights or privileges on the basis of the religious confession of citizens.

3. Every citizen may confess any religion or profess none at all. Every legal restriction connected with the profession of no faith is now revoked.

   Note: In all official documents every mention of citizen's religious affiliation or non-affiliation shall be removed.

4. The actions of the government or other organizations of public law may not be accompanied by any religious rites or ceremonies.

5. The free performance of religious rites is granted as long as it does not disturb the public order or infringe upon the rights of citizens of the Soviet Republic. In such cases the local authorities are entitled to take the necessary measures to secure public order and safety.

6. No one may refuse to carry out his citizen's duties on the ground of his religious views.

7. Religious vows or oaths are abolished. In necessary situations a ceremonial promise will suffice.

8. The acts of civil status are registered exclusively by the civil authorities at the departments for the registration of marriages and births.

9. The school is separated from the church. The teaching of religious doctrines in all state and public schools, or in private educational institutions where general subjects are taught, is prohibited. Citizens may receive and give religious instructions privately.

10 All ecclesiastic and religious associations are subject to the same general regulations to [sic] private associations and unions, and shall not enjoy any benefits, nor any subsidies either from the Government, nor from any of its autonomous or self-governing institutions.

11. Religious organizations are prohibited from calling obligatory gatherings for its members, from establishing membership dues, and from disciplining any of its members in any way.

12. No church or religious organization are permitted to own property. They do not have the rights of a legal person.

13. Any and all property that any church or religious organization may have in Russia is hereby declared to be public property.

Buildings and objects required specifically for religious ceremonies, are to be given only by special decrees by either local or central governmental powers, for the free use for the appropriate religous organization. (Chairman of the Council of People's Commissars, V. I. Lenin)[17]

While provisions 1–5 seem very appropriate for a Type D–Pluralistic Liberty society, the later provisions (particularly 12 and 13) provide basis for a type C–Secularistic Absolutist society's dealing with religion which ultimately override the earlier provisions.

The People's Commissar of Public Property ordered on January 14, 1918, that all Imperial Court clergy be released and all the churches and properties which belonged to the Imperial Court were to be turned over to various government institutions with the churches being able to use such church buildings only if they paid for all the costs. By February 17, 1918, under a decree of the People's Commissar of Education all teachers of religion, regardless of their denomination, were released, retroactively to January 1, 1918. One of the most far reaching decisions were incorporated in the Declaration of the People's Commissar of Justice of August 24, 1918. In it a minimum of twenty local citizens (called the *dvatsatka*), forming a religious association, is required to receive permission to use religious property. They are obligated to relinquish such property at once upon the demand of government institutions. All local citizens (i.e. even those antagonistic to religion) have equal rights to participate in the administration of such property as do the founders of the religious association. No religious ceremonies or functions or displaying any religious paraphernalia are allowed in any government or publicly administered buildings. Written governmental permissions, obtained for each separate occasion are required for any religious procession or function held outside the church buildings.[18]

From the above it seems clear that the notion of separation of church and state, declared in one provision is effectively contradicted by other legislation which gave the state thoroughgoing regulatory powers over religious activities, limiting the free exercise thereof severely. Such contradictions persisted throughout the history of the Soviet state. One might say that the church was separated from the state but not the state from the church because the state continued a very active interventionist role in the internal affairs of the church, following the Peter the Great model of governmental dictates to the church, but increasing the intervention to the absurd level of involvement in order to destroy. While the legislation does not reflect the degree of commitment to destroy religion, one can read from the writings of Lenin and Trotsky that there was to be no mercy toward those not like-minded to the Bolshevik leaders.[19]

It is by no means clear that had men such as Lenin and Trotsky ruled the Soviet Union for a more extended times that the evils of Stalinism might have been avoided, for these leaders displayed a self-admitted ruthlessness and terror toward any opposition, which may have matched Stalin's. But here we move in the realm of the speculative; Stalin provided the "real thing."

Second Period: 1928–1942

a. Stalin's Genocide

Yosif Visarionovich Djugashvili-Stalin (1879–1953) may stand on the pinnacle of the greatest mass murderers of all times, with Hitler running a close second.[20] Recent Soviet sources estimate "that 15 million had died because of the dictator" while "[d]issident historian Roy Medvedev gave the 40 million figure . . ."[21] Previous Western estimates were at 20 million. Most of the people died in the famine of the 1930s for which Stalin's policies were largely responsible, but the Great Purge of 1933–1939 took an even greater toll. Mass graves with thousands of Soviet citizens shot in the back of the head are still being discovered, matching in horror that of the thousands of Polish officers killed in the Katyn forest. No one was safe. Outstanding old Bolshevik revolutionaries, friends of Lenin and Stalin were killed as were foreign revolutionaries such as the Hungarian Bela Kuhn or the entire Politburo of the Polish Communist Party. The creme of the crop of Soviet generals were shot on the eve of World War II, as were scientists, writers, peasants, workers, etc. The destruction was not specifically aimed at religious people—Communists died (often lauding Stalin while dying at his orders) in equally large numbers. If those loyal to the Communist cause died en masse, why spare the ideological opposition?

By the outbreak of World War II nearly all religious leaders and uncounted religious people perished cruelly, mercilessly in the greatest orgy of blood the world has ever experienced.[22] It is impossible to exaggerate the extent of destruction and the degree to which it warped Soviet life for generations to come. Philip Walters accurately applied

the term "Holocaust" to Stalin's terror over the general population
and the churches in the 1930s.[23]

While the details of the destruction are either unavailable or,
paradoxically, too great to be enumerated here, one must stress that
Stalin and Stalinism are responsible for this genocide. Stalin may
very well have been a deranged, psychotic individual, but that does
not suffice as an explanatory hypothesis for the horrors of his reign.
Clearly Stalin alone could not have implemented this without the
cooperation of large numbers of others and the preceding terror during the Revolution and Civil War and the imperial despotic tradition
provided the milieu in which Stalinism could flourish. There was
also an ideological link between Lenin and Stalin. As Milovan Djilas, the author of *The New Class* analyzed it in another book of his,
Lenin, who operated in a hostile environment, saw science as an ally
that would support his *a priori* truths and encouraged intellectuals
to attempt to reconcile science and Marxism. Stalin was secure in
power and rejected *everything* that disagreed with his dogmas which
were accepted by generations of Marxists both in the Soviet Union
and elsewhere as absolute truth; intellectuals either perished or conformed and expounded Stalin's own interpretation of Marxism. Yet,
basically, Lenin and Stalin shared the view that Marxism is capable
of predicting everything that happens to society and individuals.[24]

Stalin's personal responsibility cannot be diminished. Surely
Stalinism is the major traffic accident of socialism. Some believe
that the vehicle was totalled. Others think that even major repairs
could never make the vehicle the same. But terror and propaganda
were so effective that many pretended not to see the damage; some
even deceived themselves into denying it or justifying it. For purposes of illustration rather than documentation one may mention the
execution in the 1930s of about 6,000 nuns and monks in the political
prison camp in the Mordovian region of Borashevo. The Ukrainian
human rights activist, Mykola Rudenko, who was interned in the same
prison camp was told this by surviving eyewitnesses from surrounding
villages, which moved him to write the following poem:

Six thousand—wooded Mordovia stands witness—
Shot, lifted onto blades
Swallowed in the lifeless earth
Where today the birches proudly grow.

They screamed into the night, into the threatening clouds
About the Judgment Day, these raped young nuns,

For a long time you could find
Little copper crosses and shoes in the grass.

Mordovia, your woods woven with barbed wire,
You were then just a child . . .
Live, Mordovia, watch out over these camps,
You will live for centuries God's witness.[25]

Jane Ellis, a British church historian specializing in Russian Orthodox Church affairs, pointed out that by 1939 only four of the Russian Orthodox bishops were still carrying out their responsibilities and only a few churches remained open. Gerhard Simon, a German scholar with similar expertise, estimates seven bishops and a few hundred churches and clergy remaining just prior to the outbreak of World War II. The major cathedral church of the Assumption in Moscow was dynamited and in its place a swimming pool was built.[26] Robert Tobias, an American expert on churches under Communism in Eastern Europe estimates that in this effort to obliterate the churches 45,000 priests and nearly as many church buildings were destroyed,[27] but it is not clear whether this figure covers only the Orthodox Churches or also others. "Clergymen were charged with espionage, sabotage, arson, terrorism, immorality and similar crimes, ang were 'liquidated' or given severe sentences."[28] By 1936 only one of the six Evangelical-Baptist congregations in Moscow remained functioning. Already in 1930 nationwide 60 percent of the Evangelical-Baptist churches were closed—and they tended to be more tenacious about meeting despite persecutions—and 40 percent of the leadership was arrested or fled.[29]

One can imagine the degree of devastation after the years of terror. The length of this processes testifies that these were not sporadic or spontaneous outbreaks of violence but a systematic approach to all real or presumed enemies. Its origins can be discovered already in the legistation of 1929.

b. Stalinist Legislation

In 1929 a number of laws were passed that severely limited the rights of clergy and churches. Clergy and their families were deprived of voting and had to pay 5–10 times greater taxes than workers. They were not permitted to live in municipally owned housing and were not permitted to own even small gardens. Since they were not permitted to serve in the armed forces they were to serve in alternate services and were additionally assessed a special military tax.[30]

The Law on Religious Associations was passed on April 8, 1929. Its provisions clearly indicate Stalin's intention to destroy religion. The law establishes the *dvatsatka*, namely a minimum of 20 adult members of the same religious cult (art. 5), who may apply for registration to the city or *raion* (district) committee on religious matters (art. 6). Such application may be refused without the reasons being specified (art. 7). These associations were to be monitored by the Permanent Committee for Religious Matters of the Council of Ministers (art. 8). Buildings and objects for worship may not be owned by the religious group but may be leased free of charge by the district or city soviet (art. 10) which the believers are to maintain on their personal responsibility and the premises must pass technical and sanitary inspections. Religious communities are prohibited from renting presses to print religious or moral books (art. 11). General assemblies of believers may be held only upon receiving governmental permissions (art. 12). Organization of Biblical and literary meetings, clubs, and groups to study religion as well as to open libraries and readings rooms is prohibited. Only liturgical books are allowed in churches (art. 17). Teaching of religion in schools is prohibited. Teaching religion is permitted in special schools for the training of leaders established only if permitted (art. 18). Clergy may carry out their ministries only within the territory of the association that employs them (art. 19). All-Russian or All-Union associations of religious societies may be organized, but only upon permission by the appropriate Committee for Religious Matters (art. 20). All property, even newly donated, for carrying out religious rites is nationalized (art. 25). Detailed instructions are provided on recording and administering such properties and for discontinuing such leases (art. 27–53). Collection of money for payment to the clergy and maintenance of the building is allowed within the building but only among those who belong to the respective religious group (art. 54). For services taking place within the designated building local government organs need not be informed but advance permission must be obtained if a service is to take place elsewhere (art. 57) and no religious symbols may be displayed in any public institution. Except for funerals a two-week advance registration is necessary for outdoor services or processions: (art. 59–61).[31]

The churches were not allowed to provide financial or material assistance to their own members, nor was any other charitable, social or educational work allowed. It was forbidden to organize special meetings for children, young people or women, for prayer or other purposes, likewise general Bible, literary or handiwork meetings, gatherings for common work, religious instruction or other ends . . . also to arrange excursions and children's playgrounds, to open libraries and reading rooms, to organize sanatoria or medical assistance. (art. 17).[32]

The government authorities had sweeping authorization to control the churches by registering the churches and clergy (art. 4-8) and being able to exclude individuals from the administrative body (art. 14) and they had the ability to determine on ground of any excuse whatsoever that a church could be closed.

This law was amended on June 23, 1975, in a manner which updates and details the law of 1929 but did not liberalize it.[33] The 1929 Law was not repealed formally until 1990 so that even when concessions have been made at later times the possibility always existed that the valid laws of 1929 could be invoked again, creating constant tensions in the lives of believers. Since copies of that law were not generally available the vague possibility of having one of the many unknown clauses invoked always hang over the churches as a distinct possibility.

By 1929 the provision of the 1925 Constitution was changed henceforth disallowing religious propaganda and allowing only atheist propaganda. This was later incorporated into the Constitution of 1936.[34] Article 124 stated:

> With the aim of securing freedom of conscience for citizens, the Church in the USSR is separated from the State and the school from the Church. Freedom of religious worship and freedom of anti-religious propaganda is recognised for all citizens.[35]

The constitution took away *de jure* the right to religious propaganda which had been *de facto* abolished years ago. There were those in the constitutional commission who argued that freedom of religion should be denied outright, but Stalin insisted, probably sarcastically, on its inclusion in order to be consistent with the spirit of the document.[36] The positive feature of the 1936 Constitution was that it re-enfranchised the clergy (they had been disenfranchised in the 1918 Constitution).

In 1939 and 1940 Stalin obtained a chance to broaden the attack against religion when the Soviet Union incorporated into its territory Moldavia, Lithuania, Estonia, Latvia, the eastern half of Poland, as well as parts of Finland. Though at the time already aware of the possible confrontation with Hitler and the chance that Hitler may manipulate the issue of religious persecutions against the Soviet Union, Stalin ordered massive restrictions and persecutions in the newly incorporated areas of the USSR.[37] Feeble attempts were made to provide a veneer of civility toward religious institutions, but even in the short period between the Soviet take-over of these territories and their German occupation in 1942 the damage inflicted upon religion was so great that in the beginning the Nazis were perceived as saviors by the occupied people.

The Stalinist period from 1929 to 1942 represents the purest Type C model in Soviet and East European history. It epitomizes, along with Albania, the most thorough attempt at abolishing all organized religion and in suppressing even the minutest religious sentiments which surfaced in public. Here religion was, indeed, restricted to the private sphere—the innermost secret of a person's mind—though legally Stalin did not go as far as his pupil Enver Hoxha of Albania. In real life the difference was negligible. Hoxha learned his lesson well from the master of obliteration of religion.

Third Period: 1942–1958

One of the great ironies of history is that the great enemy of the Soviet Union and a persecutor of religion, Adolf Hitler and his governmental and military apparatus, prevented the total annihilation of religion in the USSR. The Nazis were welcomed as liberators not only in the territories freshly occupied by the USSR but also in the Ukraine and Byelorussia and even parts of Russia.[38] Church life suddenly flourished in these territories. Wassilij Alexeev and Theophanis G. Stavrou presented a carefully documented study of this phenomenon, focusing particularly on the Russian Orthodox Church in German occupied territories from 1941 to 1944. They wrote:

> Both Soviet Communism and German Fascism, struggling on Russian territory during these years, were equally hostile to Christianity in general and to the Russian Orthodox Church in particular. Still, their confrontation, leading to the German occupation of a significant portion of the USSR with approximately one-third of the country's population, created peculiar conditions affecting significantly the

fate of the Russian Orthodox Church. In the beginning, the National Socialist Government of Germany did not clearly formulate its religious policy on occupied territory. In general, German forces were sympathetic toward the religious revival which greeted them as they were establishing their rule among the population of the USSR who at first, partly through misunderstanding, accepted Hitler's attack as a crusade against communism. Even after the populace realized the objective of this "crusade," they continued to utilize this opportunity of relative religious toleration in order to reestablish the Orthodox Church which had been persecuted by the Communists since the Bolshevik Revolution. On the whole, in scope and intensity this religious revival on the territory occupied by the Germans can be called the second baptism of Russia.[39]

The epithet "second baptism" may be exaggerated, but it hints at the radical difference in the degree of religious toleration by the enemies of the Soviet Union and by its own government. What was true of the Russian Orthodox Church was even more true of the Ukrainian Catholic, Roman Catholic, Lutheran, and other religions, except, of course, Judaism.

When one contrasts this experience of greater religious freedom under the Nazis with the courageous act of Metropolitan Sergiy of Moscow, who went to the streets the very first day of the German invasion and urged the populace to come to the defense of the motherland it becomes clear why Stalin changed his strategy after 1942. Even he recognized that the people were willing to defend their homeland when they were not eager to defend the ruling ideology and government. It is for good reason that the Soviets call World War II the "Great Patriotic War," rather than the defense of Bolshevism. Out of necessity, not good will, did Stalin, somewhat belatedly, accept the willingness of the churches to come to the aid of the beleaguered nation. Monies were collected to arm the tank division "Donskoi" and other sacrifices were made by the pitiful remnants of the religious communities. Soon after the Nazi attack it became clear that Hitler did not wage the war only against Bolshevism, but that his racist ideals led to the massacre of Slavic and Jewish population regardless of their ideological sympathies. Hence it was more reasonable to work with a domestic dictator than a foreign one.

From 1942 onward Stalin started gradually granting concessions to religious organizations, including the re-opening of many churches. In 1943 Stalin summoned three Russian Orthodox hierarchs to an unprecedented meeting. Three days later the Russian Orthodox Church was allowed to elevate Metropolitan Sergiy who was the patriarchal *locum tenens* to the rank of Patriarch on September 4, 1943. Upon Sergiy's death Aleksiy was promptly elected, and thereafter gradually the church hierarchy was rebuilt, so that by 1949 there were seventy–four Orthodox bishops and two theological academies and eight seminaries were operating. Church life was limited but "normalized." Stalin made sure that the government controlled strictly all aspects of church life and that religious leaders and members be coopted. The official church repeatedly pledged its loyalty to the government and promised to obey all the laws. Non-cooperative clergy continued to be persecuted and harassed, mostly on charges that had little to do with religion, e.g. tax evasion, but often no formal pretext was needed for a person to disappear or to be exiled. Few dared to oppose governmental orders. Those who did were imprisoned or exiled to remote portions of the country. The government cleverly used the church for purposes of its foreign and domestic policy and the leaders had to proclaim abroad that the fullest degree of religious liberty obtains in the USSR.

The period of 1942 to 1958 is characterized by unequal treatment of churches; some were dealt with more harshly than others. Many church leaders still languished in labor camps and exile. All ethnic German people (the so-called Volga Germans) had been exiled far into the interior of the Soviet Union (Kazakhstan and Siberia) and so had the Crimean Tartars. Anti-Semitism was revived and reached unprecedented proportions with many Jews simply being killed.[40]

The conclusion is that Stalin should not be given much credit for permitting a somewhat greater living space for the churches, particularly the Russian and Georgian Orthodox Churches, because it was not out of benevolence but out of sheer necessity and political advantage that made him alter the policies of the genocidal period of 1929–1942. Only in comparison with the previous period can one judge the period from 1942 to 1958 as being good. In absolute terms the status of the churches was still abominal.

The first few years after Stalin's death there was no appreciable change in policies toward the churches. His successors continued Stalin's measures to control the churches and to make use of them as supporters of Soviet policies at home and abroad.

Fourth Period. 1958–1987

With the ascent of Nikita Khrushchev to the leadership a sudden re-introduction of repressive measures became evident, especially between 1959–1964. Part of the reason may have been ideological, namely that atheist propagators felt that they had slackened in their work. More important was probably Khrushchev's need to mollify his more dogmatic opponents. Khrushchev denounced Stalin and Stalinism during the XXII Congress of the CPSU(B) and undertook a process of liberalization and reforms in many areas of life. When he was challenged by the hard-liners who questioned his ideological purity, he commenced with a persecution of religion which was to prove his doctrinal orthodoxy.[41] The change was symbolized by the replacement in 1960 of G.G. Karpov who had presided over the Council for Russian Orthodox Affairs since 1943 by Vladimir A. Kuroyedov who was more bent on repression, only to mellow his approach after 1965.[42]

It is estimated that over one thousand Orthodox churches and many others, particularly intensely in westernmost regions of the USSR, were closed between 1959 and 1964.[43] Individual clergy were harassed and imprisoned. The unexpected retirement and death on December 13, 1961, of Metropolitan Nikolay Yarushevich who headed the department of Foreign Affairs of the Russian Orthodox Church was widely interpreted by many of his admirers as a murder.[44] Archbishops Iov Kresovich and Andrei Sukhenko were imprisoned. The estimated 30,000 priests were cut by 50 percent. Many had been accused of illegal religious propaganda just for visiting the home of some believers. Many had been arrested for tax evasion and non-religious offenses. A large number of monasteries were closed, including the famous Kievsko-Pecherskaya Lavra (Monastery of the Caves). Those monasteries which were permitted to function were forced to drastically reduce the number of their monks and nuns and novices were not allowed to join. Seminarians were not allowed to defer military service as had been the case previously and many of these priestly candidates were pressured in the army to abandon their goals.

Particularly stunning to the Orthodox Church were the regulations which their Synod of Bishops was forced to adopt on July 18, 1961, which in the opinion of many Orthodox were uncanonical. In an extremely hastily convened council of the bishops and without a clue of the agenda the assembled bishops adopted on the urging of

Patriarch Aleksiy, measures about the local parishes which stripped the priests and even the bishops of any financial decision-making, placing that privilege entirely in the hands of the parish executive committee, on which sometimes even non-believers were placed. The explanation given was that such a move would curb the many alleged abuses of the funds by the clergy to which the Council of Ministers of the USSR has pointed out and requested the Council of Bishops to adjust church legislation to fit secular legislation.[45] It is evident that such a hasty departure from Orthodox canon law could have been made only under duress and that the bishops well understood what could happen to the Church should they not comply with the government's request. This was one of many instances of government meddling into internal affairs of the church.

The precarious legal position of priests and other religious leaders from the revolution onward needs to be pointed out. Essentially they were stripped of civil rights, taxed exorbitantly, could not receive appointments without the permission of the Council on Religious Affairs or local councils, could not get apartments in state owned buildings or have additional jobs in state institutions, were not allowed to catechize children and youth while their own children were usually deprived of higher education, and often lost even the ability to administer the congregations to which they were appointed. In a sense they were an outlaw profession, caught in a terrible paradox of being highly revered by the common believers and yet being discriminated against and held in contempt by the authorities and the secular world. Religious leaders had even more reason than the average believer to realize that they enjoyed no religious freedom.

Nearly all researchers dealing with the period note the end of the period of relative relaxation which took place around 1959 and lasted until the end of the Khrushchev period in 1964.[46] Walter Sawatsky provided the most detailed, nuanced, and accurate periodization and explanation of the motivation for the policies from 1959 to 1987, which will be utilized with modifictions by this author.[47]

Phase I: Leninist Legality. 1959–1961

While the 1929 laws had never been rescinded, Stalin and his successors allowed from 1941–1959 certain practical relaxations and non-implementations of the laws. Now under Khrushchev under the guise of a return to respect for Leninist legality the provisions of the law began to be implemented 'by hook and by crook.' Preceded by a massive antireligious propaganda which maintained that the precondition for the announced transition from socialism and communism is the removal of religious vestiges, sharp legislative and administrative actions were taken which resulted in a decimation of religious leadership and institutions. In a matter of months thousands of buildings of all religious groups were closed under various pretexts, the number of clergy reduced by more than half , some by denial of registration others by imprisonment, monasteries were interfered with and then closed by resorting to *pogrom* tactics. In distinction from the Stalin's purges of the 1930s, there was a greater subtlety in these persecutions, because the propaganda stressed that educational approaches are preferable to administrative intervention, yet in fact, without much fanfare cruel administrative measures were implemented for the purpose of eradicating religion. Michael Rowe, a British specialist on religious persecutions points out that the most frequently utilized laws of the Russian Federation Criminal Code (with appropriate parallels in the criminal laws of the other republics) by which religious offenders were prosecuted were Articles 70 ("anti-Soviet agitation and propaganda"), 142 ("violations of the laws on separation of church and state"), 227 ("infringement of the person and rights of citizens under the guise of performing religious rituals"), 190–191 ("dissemination of deliberately false fabrications slandering the Soviet state and social system"), 80 and 249 (refusing military duty), 190–193 (disrupting public order and resisting the militia), 205 (hooliganism), 209 (parasitism), 162 (prohibited trade) as well as fabricated charges of malicious disobedience, embezzlement, and even attempted murder.[48] Commitment to psychiatric hospitals was another means to punish an uncooperative religious person.

Phase II: Resistance and Toughened Legislation. 1961–1962

Such repressions signaled the resistance by the small dissident movement, consisting to a lesser degree of the Orthodox intelligentsia, and to a larger degree by the *Initsiativniki* or Reform Evangelical Baptists who refused to register.[49] The government had made registration of churches increasingly difficult by asking that the registration application be signed by all members of a local church. The discretionary power of the government agencies controlling religion, the most important of which was the KGB,[50] increased during this period so that much persecution resulted from secret laws, decrees, and even verbal

orders. Some of the practices were approved in 1962 by formal legislation, which Sawatsky proclaimed as being tougher than the 1929
laws against religious communities.[51] Official religious agencies, institutions, and leaders saw no alternative to obedience to such government policies and gave formal support to the official claim, especially
to the outside world, that religious liberties were fully observed.

Phase III: A Differentiated Policy and Reevaluation. 1963–1965

The antireligious campaign increased but became more sophisticated. The government made certain concessions to the embattled
official church hierarchies in order to more effectively attack the dissidents. While at the top there was talk of more educational antireligious propaganda at the local level this was perceived as the go-ahead
for a get rough policy against believers and many were imprisoned,
tortured, and some even martyred. Evidence exists of some horribly cruel torture, physical and drug-induced, some of which ended
in known deaths, others in disappearances. By 1964 there seems
to be an attempt to halt the most blatant abuses, while even some
state commissions confirmed the claims of the dissidents. The antireligious propaganda, however, increased and became mandatory
in educational institutions, among professionals, and, especially the
Communist Party cadres.[52] Emphasis was placed on denying parents the right to determine the religious orientation of their children.
Andrey Bessmertniy-Anzimirov, a Russian Orthodox dissident from
Moscow, wrote about it thus:

> . . . in our land, any organized form of children's reli-
> gious education is not only prohibited but are punished in
> accordance with a special article of the Criminal Code . . .
> Article 142 of the Criminal Code of the Russian Soviet Fed-
> erative Socialist Republic (and the corresponding articles in
> other republics) warns that:
>
> organizing and systematically educating minors on the sub-
> ject of religion is punishable by correctional labor for a pe-
> riod of up to one year or by a fine of up to fifty rubles.
>
> Repeated actions as well as organizational activity directed
> toward the completion of these deeds are punishable by the
> disenfranchisement of the personal rights to freedom for a

period of up to three years. (Decree of the Presidium of the Supreme Soviet of the RSFSR, March 18, 1966).[53]

With the ouster of Khrushchev there were some improvements in 1965, such as fewer arrests and a decisive toning down of anti-religious propaganda, including the dissolution of the ideological commission of the CPSU(b). There were pleas by propapandists to abandon administrative measures against believers. While high level party discussion may have taken place, no clear policy emerged. Interference in local affairs of churches continued. Bishops were being transferred from one eparchy to another every few years by the Council for Religious Affairs and those bishops and clergy who succeeded in reinvigorating the spiritual life of their eparchies or parishes were soon harassed and re-assigned to distant and nearly uninhabited localities.[54] Religious bodies and individual leaders responded, according to Philip Walters, the research director of Keston College in England, in five different responses to the pressure, (a) uncritical allegiance; (b) accommodation with discretion, (c) critical accommodation, (d) dissent, and (e) emigration.[55]

Phase IV: Resumption of Pressure. 1966–1970

The two councils for religious affairs, the Council for Russian Orthodox Church Affairs and the Council for Religious Cults were merged in 1966 into the Council for Religious Affairs headed by VIadimir A. Kuroyegov.[56] This represented greater centralization and greater discretionary powers for the council. Along with it came a resumption of "administrative measures" [read: persecution] especially of dissidents. The estimates of the number of imprisoned dissidents during this period, particularly of the *Initsiativniki*, unregistered Evangelical-Baptists, varied from 202 to 240.[57] This, however, did not deter the dissident movement but soon spread to other church groups particularly the Russian Orthodox and Lithuanian Roman Catholic, all of which published *samizdat* [self-published] clandestine publications often providing the most detailed particulars about the persecutions and arrests available up until then.

The dissidents tended to criticize the timidity and acquiescence of the officialdom of their religious organizations as well as to protest to the government authorities about the restriction of religious activities and to publicize official abuses both at home and abroad. This meant that they generally could not expect support from their religious leaders; sometimes they would be disciplined and publicly criticized by them. Also the government, the press, and the party ideologists attacked them by various means, including the spreading of lies about their private lives and accusing them of mercenary motives and financial misconduct. Not infrequently were both their faith and patriotism questioned; allegations of foreign financing and patronage were made.[58]

The Criminal Code of March 18, 1966, seems to have been aimed particularly at dissidents, proclaiming the following to be violations:

Refusal by religious leaders of communities to register them with state organs;

Violating the legally established rules for organizing and conducting religious gatherings, processions and other cult ceremonies;

The organizing and conducting, by servants of the cult and members of religious communities, of special children and youth meetings, and also of workers, literary and similar circles and groups, not related to cultic activities . . .[59]

Article 142 of the code specified the following violations which would be punished with up to three years incarceration,

. . . requiring compulsory collections and taxes for the use of religious organizations and cult servants;

the preparing for the purpose of mass distribution plus the actual mass distribution of statements, letters, leaflets and similar documents, which call on people not to observe the legislation on religious cults;

Carrying out deceitful acts with the purpose of awakening religious superstition in the population;

Organizing and carrying out religious meetings, processions and other cult ceremonies which violate social order;

Organizing and systematically conducting activities for teaching religion to underage children in violation of established legislative rules. . . .[60]

Phase V: Stalemate. 1970–1974

Sawatsky described this period as "a search for normalcy"[61] meaning that gradually religious activities were allowed to resume under the usual controls and restrictions. Some concessions were made, such as allowing the unregistered Council of Churches of Evangelical Christians-Baptists[62] to meet only later to crack down on its leaders and members. Generally the government was willing to make concessions to the official leadership provided they were willing to comply with the controls and restrictions and to proclaim during their sojourns in the West that religious liberties were steadfastly observed by the Soviet authorities.[63]

For many of the dissidents these were actually very difficult years as they were frequently harassed, intimidated, forced to go underground, and then hunted, arrested, tortured, and sometimes even killed. The children of some of them were forcibly removed from the families. Some of the dissidents were exiled against their own will. The fate of the dissidents became public knowledge in the West and created a strong expression of sympathy and support for them. Soviet authorities tended to be more reluctant in persecuting those whose identity was well known in the West, though in a number of instances they were not reluctant to impose stiff sentences even against those on whose behalf campaigns were being organized.

Phase VI: "Normalization." 1975–1985

In the year 1975 yet another revision of the 1929 laws came out which was more restrictive than the original 1929 legislation but more moderate than the 1962 version. On the whole the revision of the law changed practically nothing but the advance was that "the near equivalent of the right to juridical personhood" was granted to church headquarters and local congregations making it easier to function.[65] Yet the Council on Religious Affairs was strengthened again, which generally meant bad news for freedom of the religious communities, though, ironically, the Council liked to represent itself as defending the religious communities from local abuse and misunderstanding.

The situation was paradoxical. On the one hand certain concessions made it possible for the religious communities to experience a resurgence and renewed popular interest. As an eyewitness of that period the author can vouch that many of the churches were crowded, with young people and children and even a few uniformed soldiers in attendance in nearly all religious denominations. On the other hand the heavy harassment of many leaders continued and even increased.

The Soviet leaders have found themselves in an unenviable position. They had signed the Helsinki Agreement of 1975 which contained an affirmation of human rights, including religious liberty.[66]

This brought a great increase of hope for the religious communities and a not so great increase in actual concessions. Great deal of pressure was brought to bear upon the Soviet Union by various Western government and non-government groups which pointed to the basic violations of Basket One.[67] The Soviets became defensive and then went into counterattack. This defensiveness was manifested in the harsh treatment of those who recorded abuses (e.g. the Helsinki Watchdog Committee) as well as those who were asking for adherence to the stipulations of the Helsinki Accords. At least in some cases which were communicated to this author, some Pentecostals in the Ukraine were gassed to death by the KGB or imprisoned as they were told that the Helsinki Accords were intended for foreign consumption and not for internal application.[68] Western inquiries about violations of religious liberty were treated as interference in domestic affairs of a sovereign nation. Counterattacks were mounted targeting human rights violations, especially of religious persons, in the Western orbit. The language of human rights was being gradually adopted, but originally not in order to value it and implement it but to find ways to turn its cutting edge away from the socialist countries directing it elsewhere.[69]

By 1979 the dissident movement began to decline due to the very energetic handling of it by the KGB. Some of the dissidents were exiled. Many have been intimidated so effectively that they issued public, often televised recantations and apologies and turned witnesses against their friends and co-dissidents. Some were placed in psychiatric wards. Others were sent to the Gulag for many years to be followed by internal exile. Sentences were long and often at the end of one term another one would be added for the same crime. Most often the accusation was that the dissident broke Article 70 of the Criminal Code, being guilty of "anti-Soviet agitation and propaganda," an absurdly vague charge left to interpretation of the authorities and thus a most useful tool for suppression of dissent. Originally the sentence for "anti-Soviet agitation and propaganda" was deprivation of liberty for a maximum of seven years and five years of internal exile. In 1984 the maximum sentence was extended to ten years imprisonment plus seven years internal exile. A clause was added that the use of money or material goods from Western persons or organizations for anti-Soviet purposes was also a violation.

From personal conversations with five dissidents[70] who had suffered imprisonment in the Gulag, a sad picture of barbarous treatment emerges. Torture and threats may be applied already in jail, often by fellow inmates, criminals, who seem to have been promised advantages if they break their cell-mates determination to plead non-guilty or turn witness against him/her. The judge may smile sardonically and knowingly saying that they would be sent back to the cell to reconsider their plea. That night the criminal cell-mate attempted to strangle the accused with a wet towel causing him to faint.

In prison the three great enemies by which the religious convictions of the imprisoned would be tested to the extreme were time, hunger and cold, with the occasional mistreatment by the criminal prisoners who were used by the guards to do their dirty work. By time is meant that the exact length of the sentence cannot be calculated because the authorities may unilaterally extend the duration of imprisonment with or without another trial. Also the conditions of imprisonment may be worsened by placement in solitary confinement or punitive cells. This is often done when the prisoner asks for a Bible or shows evidence of religious behavior. Humane acts are dreadfully punished. Hunger and cold are often used in combination. In the bitter cold of the Gulag, if one prisoner has an overcoat and another does not, the one who owns the coat may have it taken away if she/he shares it with the cell-mate. When punished the prisoner is fed a single portion of bread soaked in water every second day, alternating the day in which each prisoner receives it. Should one of the prisoners wish to share the portion of food with the other, the guard will spill it. Clothing is entirely inadequate for the climatic conditions. In punitive cells only the scant prison "pajamas" are allowed. The punitive cell has been described as a cement coffin-like structure half-in-ground, half-above. There the prisoner is confined to five, ten, fifteen, or twenty days, nearly freezing to death, often losing consciousness, and being fed only once every two days of the above-mentioned *kasha*. Sometimes other prisoners may beat or even break a limb of the prisoner of conscience. Medical facilities, of course, were inadequate.

The prison authorities often reminded the prisoner that no one knew their whereabouts or cares what happens to them. One of their great fears was that they may suffer in vain. Sometimes the prison commander or investigator showed the prisoner statements by visiting Western religious leaders in which it is said that there is religious freedom in the Soviet Union. A statement by Billy Graham of this sort, for instance, infuriated one of the narrators, since it was rubbed in during her incarceration as the authorities attempted to make her look foolish. Generally they are promised quick release from their suffering should they be willing to sign a confession and retraction. The victims felt that somehow their suffering was at least as bad as during Stalin's time because the methods of torture had become even more refined.

Amazingly the victims seemed to harbor no ill will toward their tormentors and narrated their account with little display of emotion, even showing reticence to tell about their suffering. All were convinced that not even the Gulag can prevail over their convictions and the love of God.

The government policy toward the churches was deliberately paradoxical. For a limited number of church leaders who were deemed "safe" from the government's viewpoint much greater liberties were granted in their foreign dealings, for instance with the World Council of Churches, Council of European Churches, Christian Peace Conference, and so on. The Soviet government skillfully exploited their activities for foreign propaganda purposes.[71] On the other hand the government methodically oppressed, exiled, and persecuted the churches domestically as was reported in the so-called "Furov report" and by Kharchev, both chairmen of the Council on Religious Affairs.[72]

Brezhnev and his inner circle displayed no interest in religion, but were content to continue the general direction of his predecessors, though his regime tried damage control in regard to the dissidents by trying to outwardly adhere more strictly to "socialist legality" without creating any significant new legislation. Yet simultaneously during the Brezhnev era as 'stagnation' strict political control over the leaders of the churches was maintained by controlling clerical appointments and their travel abroad, categorizing them according to their cooperativeness with the regime, censoring religious publications, and keeping religious education under careful supervision.[73]

It is said that the night is darkest just before dawn. Certainly for the about 450 dissidents who were in the Gulag in 1985[74] there was no sign that the hardships inflicted by the regimes of the Leonid Brezhnev, Yuri Andropov, and Konstantin Chernenko era would be succeeded by the "dawn" that came with the leadership of Mikhail Gorbachev.

Fifth Period: 1985–1989

The Stalinist totalitarian perversion of socialism and Brezhnev's period of "stagnation" is blamed by the reform-minded Communists for the profound crisis of the system which Mikhail Gorbachev inherited from the Soviet gerontocracy. Others have predicted that the system may even collapse due to deep-seated contradictions and maladies in the economy, ideology, and politics of the Soviet Union. Gorbachev and his circle came to the conviction that the crisis is so profound that a thoroughgoing change, named *perestroika*, is the last chance for socialism to survive in the USSR (and consequently elsewhere).

Perestroika is the attempt at profound restructuring of the system; more than reform, less than revolution, though the changes have sometimes been declared by its admirers and promoters as nothing less than revolutionary. The changes were to affect mostly the economy—but related fields could not avoid being profoundly affected—though the Soviet economy has shown untractability and resistance to change which the Gorbachev team seems unable to solve.

Another word that entered many non-Russian languages, *glasnost* is a facet of *perestroika* rather than an autonomous development. In order to carry out *perestroika* Gorbachev and his followers judged that *glasnost* was needed. *Glasnost* means openness, publicity, public discussion and scrutiny of decisions which have heretofore been made in secret and by a very limited number of people. Many tabu topics surfaced and one could criticize former and current decisions. Gorbachev himself exposed to sharp criticism Stalin, Stalinism, and the period of "stagnation" caused by Brezhnev.

This is not the place to recount the many startling changes in the Soviet Union since 1985. Gorbachev's charisma, flexibility, suave diplomacy, and courage are well known; it has made him the most popular politician of the 1980s. He has shown such daring and imagination that many feared that the hard-liners would remove him from his position but he has shown himself a deft political player able to use the political process to his advantage, though the degree of resistance to his policies within the USSR is considerable, particularly because the political and ideological changes have not been followed by economic improvement. But he has dared the Communist Party and the people of the Soviet Union to engage in "new thinking," a sweeping notion that was at first, and is still by many people in the country accepted cautiously and skeptically because many have had experiences in the past that policies were reversed and those who embraced changes too readily suffered undesired consequences. One of the "new thoughts" was a actually not such a novel thought, namely to create a law state, i.e. striving toward "legality." Of course, for the Soviet Union it would, indeed, be a radical novelty to make the country into a country of laws and not autocratic decrees and administrative arbitrariness, which it has been for ages.

The press and media made their contribution by becoming the vehicles of *glasnost* by publishing reports about the past and the present which had been previously hidden from the Soviet public, at times to the chagrin not only of those whose misdeeds were exposed but even of the protected Soviet public that had been indoctrinated on some issues so successfully that it was difficult for them to face the truth.

At first many in the country and outside of it nurtured suspicions as to the seriousness, reality and extent of these changes, but by now the seriousness and reality of the changes are readily apparent; the extent is still questionable. Not only are not all areas of life equally affected by *perestroika*, but in effect are very unevenly implemented through this enormously large territory. One of the most serious questions was whether it will affect religious liberties.

At first religion was relatively unaffected. In the first years of his rule Gorbachev did not mention religion much and when he did it was fairly routine Communist jargon about the dangers of religion and the need to deal with it resolutely. This led many people to speculate that Gorbachev may follow Khrushchev's line, namely to persecute religion in order to mollify his ideological opponents. Certainly, one could assume that religion was sufficiently unprotected so that another wave of suppression would hardly exact a great price on its implementors. But happily such anxieties were put aside fairly dramatically during the celebration of the Millennium of the Baptism of Rus', 1988.

The preparations for the celebration of the millennium took many years, primarily by the Russian Orthodox Church, but even in late 1987 no clear plans for the festivities were announced, and there were questions as to how much cooperation, if any, they would receive by the government, the tourist agency, and so forth. Soviet bureaucracy could have easily grinded the preparations to a standstill. But, indicators pointed to the possibility of a fairly substantial change on part of the government. Already in the 1970s the Soviet government allowed, perhaps even encouraged some very large ecclesiastical conferences. One of them was the June 6–10, 1977, World Conference "Religious Leaders for Lasting Peace, Disarmament and Just Relations Among Nations" held in Moscow at the invitation of Patriarch Pimen. While one may argue that such a conference was of some benefit to the Soviet government's foreign policies, the conference did give a visibility to clergy and religious activities to which the Soviet public was unaccustomed.

Of greater significance was the appointment of Konstantin M. Kharchev as the new president of the Council on Religious Affairs in 1984. He admitted that his earlier views of religious people had negative effects, but he developed a new mentality, though in some parts of the Soviet Union, for instance in the Baltic republics, he continued to be regarded by church people as an enemy of the churches.[75] His predecessors were known for their repressive policies and their vehement defensiveness in regard to religious policies.[76] Both in his conversations with religious leaders from the Soviet Union and his travels abroad Kharchev surprised people by admitting to mistakes which have been made by the Communist Party and the government in regard to religion.[77] He promised that religious prisoners would be released. He rejected as false an emphasis on the incompatibility between socialism and religion and pointed out that religion is likely to survive for a long time and that therefore there is a need to find a positive place for religion in Soviet society. He also promised that new laws would be written because the 1929 Stalinist laws were unsuitable for the current regulation of religious life. Kharchev was removed from his position in May 1989 allegedly for his move toward liberalism too quickly, though formally it was made to look as if he stepped down in order to accept an ambassadorship in Africa.[78]

Kharchev's critical comment about former dealing with religion did not remain isolated; they were repeated at the highest level, namely by Gorbachev himself. At a reception for Patriarch Pimen and other Russian Orthodox dignitaries on April 29, 1988, Gorbachev expressed his hope for support by Christians for *perestroika* and admitted that the Soviet regime has perpetrated abuses upon the religious population in the past. In June, 1988, at the XIXth Communist Party Conference Gorbachev stated that human rights are not a gift by the government but are rather inalianable to socialism.[79]

Showing an understanding for symbolism and being able to seize the right moment Gorbachev allowed the Russian Orthodox Church to celebrate in style. All foreign guests were admitted without a hitch. To the great surprise of most observers the key celebration was held in the Bolshoi Theater, with both seminary/church and secular choirs performing a concert of sacred music lasting six hours. Seated next to Patriarch Pimen was Raisa Gorbachev, Mikhail's wife, seen amiably chatting with the aged hierarch. And all of this was televised by Soviet TV!

This was showmanship at its best. Was there also substance? The answer is an unqualified yes. Several nationalized monasteries; including Optina Pustyn and parts of Kievsko-Pecherskaya Lavra (the latter undoubtedly the most important religio-cultural monument in the country) were returned to the Church, along with the previously returned and for the millennium completed showcase of the Russian Orthodox Church in Moscow, the Danilov Monastery. Other churches have been reopened; a few new ones built. More publishing was allowed. The government claimed that it had released all religious prisoners. Some clergy appeared in TV shows and in other media interviews.

Other religious groups would also profit from the relaxations of the Millennium. Religious books could be more freely imported, both large gifts to denominations and packages to individual believers. These included holy scriptures of all religions, liturgical implements, and other religious materials.[80] The Evangelical-Baptists were allowed to import a large number of a Russian translation of Barclay's Bible Commentaries. Additional theological schools were allowed to be open; the Seventh-Day Adventists opened one, while the Evangelical Christians-Baptists negotiated with the government about opening one in Moscow. The number of emigrants who were permitted to leave for religious purposes (mostly Jews, Pentecostals, and Armenians) have dramatically increased. Even more surprising was the permission for religious communities to perform acts of charity and social action. Thus Russian Orthodox were allowed to volunteer at a hospital, Evangelical Christians-Baptists to work in a mental hospital and with the aged, and Mother Theresa's Sisters of Charity were allowed to start working near Chernobyl, in Tbilisi, and Yerevan. In a measure probably intended to dramatize the government's tolerance of religion the Russian Orthodox Church was allowed for the first time since 1918 to hold worship services in October 1989 celebrating the 400th anniversary of the establishment of the Russian Patriarchate in the Uspensky Cathedral within the Kremlin walls.[81] The bells chimed from St. Basil's Church in January of 1990 for the first time since 1922 with about 100,000 gathered to hear them.

Perhaps of greatest importance was the decision to come out with

new legislation on religious communities. That project has been un-
derway for several years, but regretfully the preparations for the law
have been shrouded in secrecy. Religious dissidents who expressed the
desire for input have been turned away with vague promises for later
hearings. A nationwide debate on the new law on religious communities seemed unlikely despite some calls for it. It is not clear whether
the leadership of the religious communities have been consulted, although Kharchev is said to have urged them to come up with a long
range wish list.

When one couples these concessions with the great spiritual revival taking place in the USSR with both institutional and non-
institutional ramifications, but most evident in the increased church
attendance by intellectuals and young people, then it is clear that
substantial changes for the better in respect to religious liberties took
place under *perestroika*.

But, one should not jump to the conclusion that full religious
liberty was instituted under *perestroika*.[82] There were still political
and religious prisoners of conscience even under *perestroika*. In 1988
many of the known prisoners of conscience were released, reducing
the number to 230, while in the Spring of 1990 the number fell to
67 religious prisoners of conscience.[83] Religious education was still
forbidden, though in a number of places the authorities allowed it
to take place. Article 52 of the Constitution which gave atheists the
right of propaganda but the religious people only the right to worship
still appeared not slated for change. The assignment of clergy was
still controlled by the government, the more active being transferred
from places where they were more effective, and some applicants for
monasteries were denied residence permits. The legal status of some
of the religious communities, such as the Ukrainian Catholic Church,
was left in a limbo until it was finally approved after Gorbachev's
well publicized meeting with Pope John Paul II at the Vatican which
meant that the Soviet government retreated from its long held claim
to decide which religion will be permitted and which not on Soviet
soil. Many Soviet citizens continued to fear reprisals if they are religiously active despite the real gains in religious liberty. Therefore
many people continued to shy away from public display of their religious practices or may take part in religious rites in a church in a
community where people do not know them.

The situation in 1989 can best be described as one of struggle, particularly on the local level. The various *samizdats* and other

sources, including Soviet newspapers point to numerous conflicts and abuses on the local level. There has always been a discrepancy between the local application of the law and the official line of the central authorities in the Soviet Union. The size and diversity of the country makes communication difficult. But even when communication was clear the manner of thinking of those in the center may be light years removed from those in the provinces. One should not forget that certain isolated regions of the USSR may be far larger than an European country and the local leaders in those provinces see no good reason why their way of doing things is in need for correction from some distant capital.[84] This is particularly true during *perestroika* where the more enlightened approaches of "new thinking" meet with resistance by the not so new local bureaucrats who are more comfortable with the old approaches, since *perestroika* would force them to serious readjustments.

The discrepancy in local conditions in regard to religious liberty were a constant feature of Soviet society. While, for instance, in Armenia or Georgia the main church of the area was obviously respected and admired and still carried a lot of prestige both in the population and even the officialdom, or where in Western Ukraine and the Baltic states, especially Lithuania, religion played a greater role, in some of the eastern regions (e.g Siberia) one cannot find a single church building or religious leader in most communities.

The discrepancy also existed from town to town or village to village. Often local authorities exercised enormous discretionary powers and created huge obstacles to religious leaders while in a neighboring place religious services were relatively unobstructed. "Indications that little has really changed for believers are still overwhelming, however,"—noted Sawatsky and added "that the situation of the churches changes as much by what they are able to do about it (that is, earning good will of society) as by what the state chooses to grant them."[85] The improvement in regard to religious liberties in 1988 was relative; great in comparison to the Stalinist period and restrictive when compared to the universal charter of human right.

Scholarship on religion has become more objective and sympathetic to religion during this period.[86] While in the past the scholars tended to be at the same time religious propagandists and therefore wrote about religion in uncomplimentary terms[87] changed attitudes were in evidence which did not automatically equate religion with superstition and reaction. The director of the Institute of Scientific Atheism of the Academy of Social Sciences of USSR, Viktor Garadzha, shocked many of the doctrinaire atheists when he attempted to introduce the principles of *perestroika* to atheist propaganda, causing a vigorous debate on that issue.[88] As a result of the Great Transformation the Institute changed its name into the Institute for the Study of Religion and Atheism, in which many, particularly younger scholars were sincerely striving to learn scholarly methods for the study of religion.

Anti-Semitism and the Problems of Religious Liberty for Jews

In regard to no other religion is the continuity between pre-Revolutionary and post-Revolutionary policies toward religion evident as it is in the case of Judaism. The reason why a separate section in this book is devoted to Judaism, but not to any other Soviet religion, is that the position of Jews in the Soviet Union as well as nearly all other areas of Eastern European life is unique. The problem which is endemic and persistent is usually summed up under the term "anti-Semitism." Since the eighteenth century Jews were geographically restricted in the Russian Empire, with few exceptions, to the Pale of Settlement, a territory roughly comprising the Ukraine, Byelorussia, the Baltic states, and parts of Poland under Russian control. The non-Jewish population in this area was infected with poisonous anti-Semitism which erupted every so often into massacres for which the Russian language contributed a word to the international vocabulary, *pogrom*. The situation of the Jews did not improve with the establishment of the Soviet Union. If anything, the Marxist animosity toward religion in general was fueled by ancient hatreds creating a particularly violent form of anti-Semitism which was rivaled perhaps only by the Nazi hatred for Jews. It created a gruesome situation for Jews to which the only reasonable response is the massive desire for emigration on the part of a large segment of the Soviet Jewish population and a frantic effort to assimilate by others.

Lenin initially condemned anti-Semitism and favored the complete assimilation of Jews. What complicated the Jewish question was that Jews were not merely a religion but also a nation, and unlike most other nationalities of the Soviet Union, they were a nation without a homeland, but with a burning desire for a homeland in view of the constant persecution everywhere. The Criminal Code of 1918 forbade anti-Semitism yet throughout the existence of the Soviet state anti-Semitism was one of the discernible threads of Soviet life, official and unofficial. Immediately after the Revolution the Bolsheviks did not oppose Zionist desires for a homeland in Palestine but that was quickly altered into a notion that Jews should be given their own territory in the Pale of Settlement or in Crimea and finally in Birobidzhan in the Far East, which, indeed, for a short time was constituted as a Jewish Autonomous Region, though Jews never made up even half of the region's population. Most recently even that concession was withdrawn so that presently there is no Jewish territory in the USSR, though the practice of identifying Jews as a nationality continues.

According to Bohdan Bociurkiw the oscillations in the treatment of Judaism roughly coincided with the overall policies against all religions.[89] Bociurkiw describes the first period from 1917–1929 as a period of pragmatism of the Bolshevik regime toward religions, the second period from 1929–1939 as the period of overall attack on all religions leading to a near complete destruction of organized religion, the third period from 1940–1953 as a return to pragmatism, a fourth period from 1954–1964 as an accelerated anti-religious campaign, and from 1965–1970 (the time of the writing of his article) as a relaxation of anti-religious measures and a transfer to more "scientific atheist education."[90] So Bociurkiw in regard to Judaism describes the first period as undermining the influence of Judaism among Jews by means of secularization and assimilation, the second period as mass closing of synagogues and the almost complete destruction of institutional Judaism except among the Transcaucasian and Central Asian Jews, in the third period Jews were allowed to resume some of their religious activities, were placed under the control of the Council for the Affairs of Religious Cults but were atomized by not being permitted to organize a central admistration. Many synagogues were closed again from 1948 onward as Stalin turned against "Zionism and cosmopolitanism." The Khruschevite religious repressions of 1954 onward did not spare the Jewish community and organized Judaism was reduced to about one-half million religious Jews served by only about sixty active synagogues and a few old rabbis. Bociurkiw admits that in comparison with other religions communities

> Judaism has been discriminated against in a number of respects, but it has not been alone in being denied some rights enjoyed by these denominations, and some religious groups in the USSR which had been banned for political reasons

(in particular the Uniates, the Pentecostal, and the Jehovah's Witnesses) have been placed in a worse position than Judaism.[91]

Bociurkiw's assessment is basically correct, but he seems to underestimate the special position of Jews in the USSR.[92] The full force of the comprehensive viciousness of the Soviet attitude toward the Jews has been demonstrated in Nora Levin's definitive two-volume work, *The Jews in the Soviet Union Since 1917: Paradox of Survival*.[93] She characterizes Soviet policy as sharply oscillating, leading to many reversals of policies due to many factors of internal and external Soviet needs, occasionally encouraging Jewish awareness and then radically crushing it. People were often jailed and killed for doing what was only yesterday promoted by the government.

Nora Levin described the destructive upheavals in the Pale of Settlement, the famine, the expropriation of property, and the fight for the meaning of being Jewish as the Bolshevik Revolution destroyed the traditional Jewish life style. For many the only thing that was left of their Jewishness was the use of the Yiddish language and even that was later on taken away from them. Jewish schools were destroyed, and there was an attempt to change the occupation of many Jews into "productive labor," (farmers and industrial workers) according to Marxist notions of class consciousness. Thus a very large number of Jews became *lishentsy*, namely de-classed and for many years stripped of all citizenship rights and privileges. Particularly destructive was the role of *Yevsektsiya*, the Jewish department in the Bolshevik party supported by Jewish communist zealots who narrowly saw everything in terms of class struggle and viciously turned against their own people, labeling their opponents "nationalists."

What hurt the Jewish ability to defend themselves was the absence of a territory of their own or even a compact population area. Jewish hopes were fueled by the seeming willingness on part of some Bolshevik leaders to grant them settlement rights and self-government either in the Ukraine or in the Crimea or finally in the unsettled Soviet East, namely Birobidzhan. In 1929 Stalin undertook the forced collectivization and industrialization and the purge of "nationalism" (along with other purges) which further disrupted the traditional Jewish existence especially in the *shtetl* [small towns] so that in Stalin's time Jewish life was completely stripped of its institutional framework. Stalin, who personally harbored strong anti-Semitic feelings despite his occasional public condemnation of it, fueled both the efforts at assimilation of Jews and the increase of anti-Semitism by accusing Jews of rootless cosmopolitanism and lack of patriotism.

When Stalin began the fierce anti-religious campaign in the fall of 1929, first against the Russian Orthodox Church but then against all religions, the "Evsektsiya outpaced the party in some of these repressions."[95] In 1930 the regime stopped its efforts to curb anti-Semitism and a sharp rise in anti-Semitism was noticeable during the purges as most of the Jewish old Bolsheviks had been exterminated. By 1931 not a single synagogue was left open in Kiev and only one was allowed to be reopened in Moscow. No Jewish institution survived the "Great Purges" of 1936–1938 as Stalin's crude anti-Semitism continued its sway.[96] Jews were further confounded when Stalin formed a pact with Hitler and sharply decreased anti-Nazi propaganda. Many additional Jews came under Soviet jurisdiction when eastern Poland, the Baltic states, and parts of Romania were occupied by the Soviets and were immediately subjected to intense Sovietization and anti-religions campaigns.[97] The anti-religious campaign was carried out under the ostensible demand by Jews themselves to stop all religions activities, yet on the other hand the government did not fail to train "red rabbis" in order to control the more staunchly devoted members. It should be noted that the anti-Semitic part of the population understood the message of the pact with the Nazis as encouragement for their actions.

With the outbreak of World War II Stalin needed Jews as allies in the war effort against the Nazis but did little beyond propaganda and drafting some Jews in the army. Jews were killed during the war not only by the Nazis and their allies but by Ukrainians, Poles, Byelorussians, Lithuanians, Latvians, and even by the Soviet partisan units. Yet when the war ended the Soviet Union systematically overlooked the specifically Jewish suffering. This should not be surprising because at that very time the Red Army still continued killings and outrages over some Jews who survived the Nazi destruction.[98]

From 1948 onward there was a wave of arrest of Jews probably due to the enthusiasm for the establishment of Israel, which was originally supported by the USSR. The severe persecution lasted to 1953 with 1948 and 1953 being the worst years as Stalin's feelings changed "from political hatred to racial aversion for all Jews."[99] There was a wave of arrests and destruction of all Yiddish and other cultural and religious books and artifacts. Most who were arrested perished in labor camps; some, even those from far away Birobidzhan, were shot as U. S. spies.[100] Ironically at the height of the persecution of Jews the government conspicuously allowed appearances both at home and abroad by some Jewish religions leaders in which they claimed that there were no problems for Jews in the USSR. Many rabbis compromised themselves. No new rabbis were being trained during this period and hardly any devotional literature was available.

After Stalin's death the situation of Jews improved relatively. Some religious activity was permitted but they were not allowed to form any regional or national body and thus each individual synagogue had to fight for its survival alone.[101] No restoration of Jewish cultural institutions were allowed under Khrushchev either so that the synagogues continued to be the sole locus for things Jewish. Then in 1957 Khrushchev mounted an attack against religion, which included Judaism. Among attacks on Judaism one could find that "Jews are a chosen people who hate others and deify money."[102] Some press articles accused Judaism of calling for the genocide of all people except for Jews.[103] In official propaganda Judaism was equated with Zionism because of Jewish interest in the Holy Land. Contact with Jews from abroad was not allowed. Students at the few *yeshivas* [religious schools] were harassed; the rabbis were isolated and dispersed. Khrushchev feared secular Jewish strength more than the religious Jewish strength and made rare concessions to the latter even though his general policies were repressive.[104]

In the 1960s there was a resumption of the attack on Judaism. Particularly nasty were some anti-Semitic and anti-Judaic publications which match in viciousness the publications of the Nazi regime.[105] Levin concluded:

> Institutionally, Judaism remained and remains as it had been—condemned, vilified, scarcely surviving. Without a center, it has no official standing; rabbis have no official contact with the government or outside religious bodies and cannot attend religious congresses or meetings of other Jews. It cannot issue publications or devotional literature or articles such as *talisim* [prayer shawls] or *tefilin* [phylacteries].
>
> Soviet authorities exercise complete control over the synagogues and other religious institutions through laws, decrees, arbitrary decisions, and control of the religious and lay leadership. When it is expedient, rabbis are pressured

to publicly denounce religion before a synagogue is closed, to affirm the rightness and justice of Soviet policy, and to attack the West, Zionism, and Israel. Executive boards can be dissolved and accommodating replacements appointed.[106]

With such policies it is hardly surprising that many people were fearful to attend their synagogue which deteriorated and/or were closed by the government and not allowed to re-open. House synagogues, to which Jews occasionally resorted, were against the law. Jews were even occasionally forced to instigate anti-religious activity. In 1962 it was banned to make *matzo* [unleavened bread] except in the Oriental provinces. No Bibles or Talmuds had been published since the Revolution and no prayer books or calendars since the middle 1920s. The government also tried to link synagogues with economic crimes and use those as pretext for synagogue closing. Informers and agents sowed anxiety and suspicion into the congregations.[107] Discriminatory measures were applied against Jews in education, professional life, and political institutions.[108]

However, there was also a movement which infused hope by offering resistance to the atrocious treatment of Jews. In the 1960s the dissident movement began which published *samizdats* and/or openly requested to emigrate. Both were harshly suppressed by the government. Since most applications for emigration were denied such applicants were named "refuseniks." They were, of course, harassed, lost their jobs, were imprisoned, placed into insane asylums, and even killed. Only occasionally were some of them allowed to leave or were even forcibly exiled. A new Jewish pride and self-awareness arose particularly among the younger people. Only after Gorbachev came to power, especially since 1988, has the number of immigrants substantially increased so that in 1989 Jewish emigration was made possible by the Soviet government[109] to nearly all who applied. Now the problem was that an insufficient number of American visas were available.

The fate of Judaism in the USSR since *perestroika* has improved although many ambiguities continue to exist.[110] A religious resurgence was in evidence coupled with greater freedoms to express Jewishness or to emigrate. Many Jews were apprehensive lest a change takes place regarding the possibility to emigrate. The number emigrating rose steeply to about 100,000 in 1989 and twice or thrice as large in 1990, leaving about 2 million of the formerly 3 million Jews still living in the USSR. After restrictions were experienced due to limitations in immigration quotas in the U.S. and other Western countries very large numbers of Jews emigrated to Israel. Those remaining in the Soviet Union were encouraged by the greater cultural and political freedoms of *glasnost* and started using it for a renaissance of some Jewish cultural and religious institutions, such as teaching of Hebrew and Judaism to children and opening of a Jewish museum.

Anti-Semitism has not yet been attacked vigoruosly. A Russian nationalist movement, *"Pamyat,"* has exhibited pronounced anti-Semitic features, raising concerns among Jews in the Soviet Union and abroad.[111] *Pravda* reported an "alarming" pace of the spread of public expression of hatred for Jews. As in the case of Nazi Germany, conversion to Christianity will not protect a Jew from anti-Semitism. One of the most dynamic Orthodox priests, Aleksandr Men', a Jewish convert, was brutally murdered with an ax on September 9, 1990, on the way to conduct the liturgy. Previous death threats and anonymous letters point to anti-Semitic motives leading to his death.[112] Anti-Semitism, instead of being confined mostly to some extremist segments of the population has become popular among some intellectuals and literary circles. *Molodaya Gvardiya* accused that the killers of the tsar's family were Jews.[113]

Despite vigorous denials by leaders of the Russian Orthodox Church anti-Semitism is also deeply imbedded in that church.[114] Father Alexei, a leading intellectual and spiritual force within the "catacomb" community who works as an electrician in a local hospital, explained the reason why the ROC has not more successfully dealt with this painful issue as follows:

> Our inability to confront the legacy of anti-Judaism reflects a failure to work through the agony in which the church has been caught. We have not yet found adequate ways to bring our own suffering to consciousness. We are still emerging from the cataclysm of the last war and the trauma of the purges. But you must understand that more was lost than lives. Our sense of values died. Our tradition broke down. We found ourselves living among former Christians, folks who had become barbarians. When we looked in the mirror, we were terrified by the beasts that stared back. How does one come to terms with such a monumental collapse? A living faith was reduced to a religious artifice. We drifted into an ideology with a set of self-serving allegiances. In the process, our church found itself in a passionate rivalry with Armenians, Protestants, Roman Catholics, Muslims, and of

course Jews. We live in an unacknowledged fear. Were we to acknowledge the suffering of others we would diminish the claims of our own community.[115]

Regretfully many other denominations, e.g. Ukrainian Catholics, likewise harbor anti-Semitism. With the increase in nationalism by the Lithuanians, Latvians, Estonians, Moldavians, Ukrainians, Armenians, Azerbeidzhanis, Georgians, Uzbekstanis, some of which have had anti-Semitic ingredients in the past, anti-Semitism may be fueled by such nationalistic passions, which for the moment are directed primarily toward the Russians or toward each other. Anti-Semitism does appear to be a perennial problem with which the Soviet government did not successfully come to grips. The question whether Jews in the Soviet Union will all emigrate, and the emigrants numbered in the hundreds of thousands in 1990 or assimilate or revive their religious and cultural identity is still not entirely clear. By and large the answer will be given in a hostile atmosphere which compounds the difficulty of a normal settlement of difficult issues. The Soviet example of treating Judaism cannot be a good precedent for other East European governments, yet, regretfully, it had been followed in several instances.

Theoretical Considerations on the Situation Before the Great Transformation

Winston Churchill once characterized the Soviet Union as a puzzle wrapped into an enigma. The suddenness of the changes and the secretiveness which has prevailed over the years tend to support Churchill's adage. While it may be true that all of life is full of ambivalence Soviet life is more so than most. There have been many sharp reversals of policies. The only constant was the desire of the Bolshevik leaders to monopolize power. Since in the Bolshevik ethics the end justifies the means[116] *everything* became possible if and when it was done in the name of the victory of the proletariat and the future of communism. Kosta Čavoški, a contemporary Yugoslav legal expert, named it "revolutionary Machiavellianism" arguing that Lenin was a consistent pupil of Machiavelli who instead of the interest of the state used the interest of the revolution for the justification of every imaginable evil deed.[117] Čavoški also provided a plausible explanation for the many shifts in Soviet policies. Namely, the basic goal was to establish their rule and make it invincible and only then figure out the utopian goals for which the monopoly of power was established.[118] The terror which the Bolsheviks used was sometimes justified by utopian revolutionary goals which are to be realized in the distant future while at other times it was their current interest in preserving power which were determinative. Hence the meandering in policies that were accentuated by the power struggles within the party for control by different individuals.

We have observed earlier (chapter 2) that Marx had a low appreciation of religion and believed that it had no place in a future society and that he had an equally low opinion of civil rights. His ideas were embraced by Lenin (chapter 3) who radicalized them. One reason for Lenin's hatred of religion was his conviction that religion, particularly the Russian Orthodox Church, was unalterably tied to the *tsarist* regime which he sought to overturn. Both the old regime and religion had to go. But there was another element. Bertrand Russell once said that of all the people he had ever met Lenin was the most evil.[119] It is known that Bertrand Russell was not an admirer of religion and was friendly toward the Soviet Union; his words should not be taken lightly. The founder of the Soviet State implemented terror both outside and inside the party and the Soviet Union was already well on its way toward totalitarianism in Lenin's lifetime. Though there is a vehement scholarly discussion about the issue this author concluded that Stalin is not in discontinuity with Leninist Communism but further evolved the system of violence founded by Lenin to an undreamed of extent. Lenin was a more educated person with an international experience, while Stalin was a man of more limited intellectual capacities who had a rather parochial view of the world. His rule was more crude and his capacity for self-aggrandizement unlimited. On top of that it is claimed that he was paranoid.[120] Both Lenin and Stalin did not avoid the use of terror to establish and maintain the rule of the Bolshevik party and their personal rule. Thus they are the co-creators of modern totalitarianism.

Totalitarianism is a system which tolerates no rivalry in any field, even in private thought. Hence there can be no freedom of thought, assembly, speech, press, etc. in totalitarianism. There can also be no freedom of religion but here an exception of sorts was made. The only institutions with an alternate world outlook which the Bolsheviks allowed were religious. Of course, they were not going to encourage them or leave them alone. Rather they tried different means of suppression, and Stalin in the 1930s came close to virtually eliminate them, thus taking totalitarianism to its purest level. Religion, though damaged and mutilated in all possible manners, became a refuge for all those who sought an alternative to Communist totalitarianism. Thus Communism itself became a source of religiosity and religion sometimes gained a reputation for its ability to survive despite the cruelest indignities perpetrated against it. It grew in moral authority, despite the ambiguous behavior of many religious leaders. On the one hand, it is indisputable that the prestige of religion and its outward successes have been greatly damaged by Communist repression and atheist propaganda as well as other secularizing trends. On the other hand, remarkably, it survived and showed at least periodic resurgence.

According to our typology (chapter 1) what happened in the Soviet Union is that from a Type A Society (Ecclesiastical Absolutism Society) in *tsarist* time it changed to a Type C Society (Secularistic Absolutism, or Monopoly Atheism Society or more accurately Atheism Privileged Society). The Russian Orthodox Church had a position of dominance and privilege in the Russian lands. Since the Russian Empire was a multinational state there were parts of the empire where other religions or churches were the national church. Thus the Roman Catholic Church, Armenian Apostolic Church, Georgian Orthodox Church, Lutheran Church and Islam held dominant positions (also of Type A variety) in their respective areas despite efforts of russification. There were some rudimentary features of a Type B (Religious Tolerance) society more so in certain areas of the empire than in others but the Type A concepts held sway. There was no question, however, which religion was the most influential at the court: Russian Orthodoxy.

In a remarkably short time, namely the duration of the Revolution and the Civil War, the Soviet Union became a Type C society. The rudimentary features of Type B society were given lip-service mostly in some legal formulations, but there is little evidence that those in power who adopted such formulations ever believed in them. They were nurtured in the atmosphere of privilege or monopoly. All that needed to be done is to turn things upside down. Instead of monopoly religion one would establish and maintain monopoly irreligion or atheism. The analysis of all the factors which made it possible to have this radical shift would be the subject of a monograph. Here only the most important factors will be presented, not ranked in any particular order.

1. The change from Type A to Type C was accomplished by a small but fanaticized group of revolutionary adherents to a rigid version of Marxism who desperately and by all means sought to destroy the old regime. Their animosity to all things associated with the old regime lead them to adhere to a *principle of radical discontinuity*—all features of the previous society were to be abolished. Values of the previous social system were declared disvalues. Hence all forms of religion were rejected and were to be stamped out by using all possible means ranging from the right to persuade others about the correctness of atheism to mass murder.

2. Another reason for the success of the drastic change is the lack of a political culture and civil libertarianism in the Soviet lands. Nearly all cultures of the present day Soviet Union nurtured a *tradition of authoritarianism and a hierarchy of power*, starting from patriarchal families, to the rule of aristocrats over serfs, to the rule of religious hierarchies over the believers, to the autocracy of the tsar as the "little father" of the people. There was little in that tradition that guaranteed the individual or groups the right to dissent. Differences in concepts were sought to be resolved by secession, establishment of independent nation-states, wars (political and religious) between groups, revolts, and so forth. Order was more important than freedom; freedom could lead to anarchy. The Bolsheviks accepted and improved the tradition of authoritarianism and a hierarchical structure. The established order, looked at from the bottom up, was the people, the proletariat, the Communist Party, the Central Committee, the Politbureau, and the General Secretary.[121] Even the most cruel dictator, with some help from the propaganda machinery, was regarded by the masses as their "father" and willingly obeyed. There is a lack of a democratic tradition of selecting and deposing leaders depending on the perceived quality of their service to the people. Contrary to the democratic notion that the government serves the people, what is prevalent in the Soviet as well as other bureaucratic systems is that the people are there to serve those in power.

3. A third reason was *collectivism*. The social value of the collective are seen as vastly more important than the value of the individual. In this respect the Soviet Union is a very traditional society. It seems self-evident to them that an individual should voluntarily sacrifice her or his freedom, abilities, and even life for the sake of the larger social unit. If people do not voluntarily subject themselves to the interest of the larger unit there is little doubt that the group has the right to

force them. What is nebulous in collectivist societies is the manner in which the collective decides. Generally those who are in leadership position mask their own individual agendas as being identical to the wish of the group. Dissent is squelched in the name of solidarity when, in fact, the leader destroys dissent since it threatens the leader's concept of how to rule the group. The social cohesion of the group is maintained by the leader presumably for the good of the group, which may or may not be so, but most importantly social cohesion becomes an instrument of manipulation by the leader over all members of the group. The leader clothes himself (there has not yet been a female leader) with an aura of selfless service for the benefit of the collective. Marxism became a useful tool as an ideology of collectivism and thus gave traditional collectivism a modern "scientific" formulation.

4. A fourth and decisive reason is *terror and the social pathology* which results from terror. Soviet leaders from Lenin onward (with the partial exception of Gorbachev) unhesitatingly resorted to terror for the implementation of their goals. Soviet society was (and continues to be to a lesser degree) a society of fear, anxiety, and suspicion. Under such conditions resistance can be broken either by physical elimination or by real or apparent agreement with those in power. Czeslaw Milosz, a Polish author and Nikola Milošević, a Yugoslav author, along with others, have noted the tremendous personality changes in those subjected to such terror. Milosz's book *The Captive Mind* points out that what is at stake is not a simple defense mechanism of the person who needs to survive terror but the basic human need for inner harmony and happiness. Thus Stalinist social pathology results not merely due to terror but also other forms of coercion. Milosz explains it by means of the Iranian Muslim notion of *ketman*, namely the practice of not divulging one's real convictions and making it a moral and religious duty to falsify data and even to self-incriminate in order to serve the right goal and to deceive the enemy. Thus the Stalinist social pathology creates a 'double-think' where people's devotion and acceptance of the official interpretation is at least acted out. But sometimes, due to effective propaganda and manipulation a "genuine interiorization of official ideology occurs."[122] Applied to religion this means that when those in power say that religion is bad one should at least act as if this is so. Many people are actually convinced that this is so without having to have empirical or rational evidence.

5. The fifth factor is that *Marxism became a quasi-religion* thus

replacing for many people the other religions. Atheism in the Soviet Union is not like Western secular atheism. It is a passionate, militant commitment to irreligion which becomes intolerant anti-theism. In spite of all protestations that Marxism is simply a non-religious humanism, reality is rather different. Marxist atheism in the USSR behaves like a crusading religion on a collision course with rival religions. In order to combat more effectively other religions atheism took on all the trappings of a religion, including saviors, apostles and saints, holy scriptures and a literalist interpretation of them, religious processions, confession of sins and absolutions, iconography, infallibility, etc. Often when people lose one faith, they search for meaning in another faith structure. While official Soviet parlance often refers to 'believers and non-believers' it would be more accurate to discern simply between different believers who have not advanced beyond intolerance in their relations to other believers.

6. A sixth issue was the need of the Communist Party to deal with the nationalities question which burdened the Russian Empire and remains unsolved in the Soviet Union. The intimate linking between nationality and religion in the eastern parts of Europe are common knowledge. As Ramet, an American political scientist specializing in Eastern European religious matters, has pointed out, the linkage between the nationalities factor and Soviet religious policy is extremely close.[123] An attack on a national religion is perceived as an attack upon that nation's consciousness. The rise of nationalism tends to be correlated to the rise of religiosity and vice versa. From the perspective of the Bolsheviks both nationalism and religion were vestiges of a class society which need to be controlled. Since national feelings cannot be eradicated at least they need to be linked with a healthier, more real association than religion. To the Soviet Communists religion was never an end in itself but always a part of a larger issue. As they sought to get rid of remnants of the pre-Revolutionary culture in their attempt to create the "New Soviet Man," they also felt the compulsion to eradicate or limit religion.[124] In the Soviet Union when one touches religion (except for the free churches), one touches nationality. The reverse also holds true. Therefore the religious and nationalities policies developed would tend to waver, but always lean in the direction of suppression and privatization. The aim was to supplement religion as the bulwark of national consciousness with atheism as the foundation for a larger Soviet loyalty. Then the question of nationalities might be more manageable—a rather desir-

able situation. Hence the need to change from Type A to Type C society. The developments during the Gorbachev era, however, indicate that a nationalism is capable of even more explosive forms after being pent-up for a long time, threatening to wreck the union.

Can the situation of religious liberties change enough to generate a shift from Type C to Type B or D? That has been the aspiration for many people in the USSR, though there are some who would like to see the return to Type A. The power constellation in the late 1980s was such as to preserve the Type C model, but there were visible stirring in the direction of more genuine guarantees for religious liberties. The forces working in that direction were:

• the example of those countries that guarantee genuine religious liberty,

• pressure of the United Nations, other governments and world public opinion,

• pressure from religious institutions and individuals abroad,

• pressure coming from the Soviet dissident communities of all persuasion, religious as well as non-religious,

• pressure from all the religious communities in the USSR for whom it would mean a drastic improvement in status,

• pressure from humanistic and critical Marxists who realized that the practice up until now has been at variance with the theory and with the laws,

• a call for the establishment of a state of law, in which the aggrieved would have recourse to an independent judiciary applying at least the present laws and probably more liberal future laws on religious freedom,

• demand to respect the pluralism of views within the Soviet Union rather than coercing people into a false uniformity.

These were significant factors that had the ability to shift the models from C to D, but historical developments did not lead in that direction.

Implications for Other East European Countries

It is hard to overestimate the importance of the Soviet experience in the determination of the policies toward religions in other Eastern European countries. Despite enormous differences in religious histories the Soviet experience was used as a model no matter how inappropriate it might be. The reason is rather simple. The

Soviet Union made much out of the notion of being the "first land of socialism." Soviet leaders believed that other Communist countries ought to make use of the Soviet experiences. Many Communist leaders from around the world were nurtured on the ideals of the Bolshevik experience and many of them lived in the Soviet Union, were educated there, visited on numerous occasions, sometimes married there, and altogether looked up with admiration to the Soviet experience. Stalin, however, did not leave it simply up to the spontaneous admiration for things Soviet. He created structures, the Comintern and the Informbureau, which would impose and inculcate the Soviet interpretation into the thinking and practice of Communists of other countries. Communist leaders of different countries were often so alienated from their own societies that the Soviet experience for them was far more real than the empirical reality of their own countries. When they came to power they tried to implement what to them seemed the only right way of doing things.

Soviet Marxism developed in such a manner that only one interpretation or version of Marxism was considered right. Fractional fights between Marxists in the nineteenth century were severe, but in the Soviet Union they had become bloody to the extreme (e.g. the cases of Trotsky, Zinovev, Kamenev, Bukharin, and others) and out of that struggle came Stalinist orthodoxy which, since it was mandatory in the Soviet Union was also going to be mandatory among those Communists leaders of Eastern Europe who survived the Great Purge.[125]

The Communists of Eastern Europe who relied so heavily upon the ideological and political and even economic support from Moscow usually started out emulating the Soviet approach to religion, especially in the first period after the take-over. Later, mostly due to the force of circumstance, some of them had to deviate from the model, though it is evident that for some of them such deviation was politically and psychologically extremely difficult, especially when the Soviet pressure to follow the model was paramount. This led to a rather unimaginative copying of the Soviet model under very different experiences thus doing violence to the national histories of the quite diverse East European peoples.

AFTER THE GREAT TRANSFORMATION

The Great Transformation in the Soviet Union took place slower and over a longer period than in most Eastern European countries. It also proceeded unevenly. i.e. quicker and more dramatically in some republics, like Lithuania, and slower in others. After the Eastern European countries went through their own Great Transformation the Soviet Union ceased to have the role of precedence and model that it had until that time. Dr. Ramet showed that for religion the Great Transformation did not occur with the inauguration of *perestroika.* Slowly did signs of improvement show up in 1986–87, with a qualitative jump in 1988 during the Millennium of the Baptism of Rus' which brought marked improvement to all religious denominations, most of all the Russian Orthodox Church, but not to the unregistered churches.[126] It manifested itself first in more open discussion about the values of religion and in a stricter adherence of the laws, i.e. less arbitrariness in dealing with the religious organizations. Yet the late 1989 and 1990 is the proper dating of the Great Transformation for religion in the Soviet Union. Only then did the changes become decisive and massive.

Religious liberty was gradually being restored first in practice and only then in law, confirming my previous conclusion that laws did not determine practice in the USSR and other socialist countries. Religious liberty evolved first by neglect and then the abolition of the revised 1929 religious legislation followed by the passing of a new law on religion. Even before the actual passing of the law there were obvious signs that freedom of religion was restored to such a degree that *Time* could entitle an article, "No Longer Godless Communism."[127] The sharp diminishment of oppression brought about increased social and political prestige to nearly all religions as intellectuals, cultural and artistic figures, and political leaders joined religious organizations. No longer was religion only for the marginalized. A quick survey of practical advances of religious liberty prior to the passing of new legislation follows.

The meeting of Gorbachev with the Vatican Secretary of State Agostino Cardinal Casaroli in June 1988 brought dramatic changes in Lithuania. The last two imprisoned priests, Svarinskas and Tamkevicius were released, Bishop Vincent Sladkevicius was made a cardinal,[128] Bishop Steponavicius was released from internal exile, and the Vilnius Cathedral and St. Casimir's Church were returned to the Church. Roman Catholic hierarchs met with the Communist Party and government representatives and when in October 1989 the Lithuanian popular front *"Sajudis"* took control the Lithuanian Supreme Soviet amended the Lithuanian constitutions giving religious organizations the status of juridical persons and introduced religious education into the public schools and bringing Lithuanian legislation into conformity with the Helsinki Final Act.[129] A Catholic youth organization was allowed to be organized and the first legal Roman Catholic journal in the USSR after the Bolshevik revolution, *Kataliku pasaulis* [Catholic Word], was published. The Franciscans and Jesuits resumed their work.[130] Similar freedoms were granted to the religious institutions in Latvia and Estonia where state control over religion was also abolished.[131]

Religious awakening and sharply increased church attendance were reported throughout the USSR and specifically in Armenia, Georgia and Moldavia. The Georgian Orthodox leader, Ilia II, "was raised in rank from Catholikos to Patriarch as his church was recognized as autocephalous by the Patriarch of Constantinople.[132] The churches of the various republics aligned themselves with the movements for greater autonomy and even independence and secession from the union.[133] A large number of theological schools were being opened by all denominations throughout the land from Byelorussia to Siberia.

In Russia the situation also improved. An animated discussion took place on the validity of the strategy for survival followed by the Russian Orthodox Church.[134] Kharchev revealed at a seminar that the Council of Religious Affairs consisted of KGB officers and Communist Party Bureaucrats, while Gleb Yakunin, the dissident priest who got elected to the Supreme Soviet of the Russian Federation revealed that the KGB officers who supervised the churches in the country belonged to Section 5 (Ideological Section) and those who dealt with Russian Orthodox Churches abroad belonged to Section 1 (Espionage).[135] The ailing and incapacitated Patriarch Pimen presented a problem for an adequate response of the Church to the new opportunities but he died on May 3, 1990. A lengthy search for a successor was predicted by those who knew and various candidates were mentioned but to everyone's surprise on June 8, 1990, Alexiy II (Alexei Ridiger), the former metropolitan of Leningrad, an Estonian of German ethnic background, a moderate with strong ecumenical leanings and with general sympathy and appreciation of Gorbachev's reforms, emerged as the new Patriarch. Apparently this was the first election without government manipulation.[136]

The Evangelical-Baptists Council chose a new leadership with the surprise election of Hrihoriy Kommendant of Kiev and nearly withdrew from the World Council of Churches, tabling the decision for the time being. It was obvious that when the churches received freedom to chose their leaders the choice was different from the earlier times when the government interfered in such elections. A Russian Bible Society was organized and many new periodicals and other publications appeared, including the Baptist *Protestant* and *The Christian Word*. A law on religion for the Russian Federation, characterized by Gleb Yakunin as the first democratic law in decades was discussed during the fall in the Russian legislature. It had more liberal provisions than the union law, as it allowed religious instructions in schools, proclaimed religious holy days as state holidays, and forbade state interference and control into the activities of the churches.[137]

The change in the Ukraine and Byelorussia did not occur as rapidly as in the Baltic, but nationalism gained strength and the Ukrainian "Rukh" soon became a leading political force aiming toward independence. In the Western Ukraine, especially Lviv and vicinity, religion, particularly the Ukrainian Catholic Church, played a great role. It brought a very serious Ukrainian reaction to the Russian Orthodox Church resulting in a significant defection of clergy and laity and an eventual loss of church property of the Russian Orthodox Church, including sixteen of the nineteen churches (as well as St. George's Cathedral Church) of Lviv. In Eastern Ukraine this process was slower because of a greater degree of Russification and intermingling with Russians but there, too, a reaction against the Russian Orthodox Church set in and resulted in the creation of an Ukrainian Autocephalous Orthodox Church (see below).

The Law Concerning Freedom of Conscience and Religious Organization of October 1, 1990, passed by a vote 341 for, one against, and one abstention and was signed by President Gorbachev.[138] The law has been in preparation since 1988 when it was announced that a commission would be working on the draft of the new law. Dissidents complained that no input by believers was sought;[139] only a very small group of the old, sometimes compromised religious leadership were consulted in regard to some of the last drafts. Two drafts of the law appeared in 1989.[140] The final, adopted version of the Law contains the following provisions:

Art. 1 guarantees that citizens have the right to determine and express their own relationship toward religion and without hindrance to conduct religious services, stating that all, regardless of their relationship toward religion, enjoy the same rights.[141]

Art. 2 and 3 specify the right to freedom of conscience stating that individually and collectively citizens have the right to profess or not to profess a religion and disseminate their convictions, "subject only to those restrictions which are necessary for the maintenance of public safety and order." Parents are given the unrestricted right to determine the upbringing of their children in regard to their own relationship to religion.

Art. 4 guarantees equality of citizens in all areas of life regardless of their relationship to religion. Restrictions or advantages based on religion or fostering of hostility toward people based on their relationship toward religion is forbidden. Citizenship obligations may not be refused because of religious convictions.

Art. 5 states that all religious institutions are equal before the law. Religious institutions may not be entrusted with carrying out state functions. The state does not finance religious or atheist activities. Agreement or nonagreement with religion or atheism may not be used as criterion for scholarly, educational, or publishing work. Religious organizations have the right of access to media and social life along with public associations, but may not be involved in the work of political parties or finance them. Individual believers and cleric have the right to participate in political life on an equal footing with all citizens. The state promotes mutual toleration and respect among all religions and those of no religions.

Art. 6 proclaims the separation of the secular school system from religious institutions. Religious doctrine may be taught according to free choice. Religious institutions may establish educational institutions for children and adults.

Arts. 7 to 16 deal with religious organizations. Religious organizations and associations may be established according to their own charters. Religious societies do not have to notify the state of their establishment. Those religions that wish to operate public institutions (e.g. monasteries and schools) need to register their charter "in order to receive the legal capacity of juridical person" based on an application of at least ten persons who would submit their charter to the local society. Religious societies may be directed from abroad. The law specifies the length of the waiting period for such registration of charters and the conditions or refusal of registration and appeals against local decisions.

The property of religious organizations is covered in arts. 17–20. Religious institutions may lease state properties. The state may also transfer ownership of state properties to religious organizations. Religious organizations have the right to own or use land according to established legislation. They may also own financial and manufacturing means to satisfy their religious needs, may solicit tax-exempt financial and other contributions and may own property abroad. Publishing, educational, manufacturing, agricultural, and charitable institutions may be organized all of which have the rights of a juridical person. Income from commercial enterprises owned by religious institutions are subject to the same taxes as those of other public organizations.

Articles 21-24 deal with the rights of religious citizens and organizations connected with freedom of religion. It gives religious organizations the right to establish and maintain worship and meeting places as well pilgrimage sites. Worship is to be conducted without any outside interference in the above places, cemeteries, funeral establishments, and homes. Military personnel may attend worship in their free time. Worship and rituals may be organized in hospitals, military infirmaries, homes for the elderly and veterans, and pennitentiaries either by request of the authorities who administer such institutions or by their own proposal. Religious literature and ceremonial object may be acquired, manufactured, distributed, exported, and imported by individuals and religious institutions. Religious institutions have the "the exclusive right of forming enterprises for the production of worship books and items for religious uses." Charitable work may be conducted by a great variety of religious and charitable associations, is tax free, and may use their own or state contributed funds. All religious organizations and citizens have the right to communicate and travel internationally, may study abroad at religious educational institutions, and receive foreign students.

The labor activities of religious institutions is covered in arts. 25-28. It gives religious organizations the right to employ workers and gives such workers the same right enjoyed by other workers as well as equal rights to social security, insurance, and taxation.

Art. 29 stipulates the existence of a state agency organized by the Council of Ministers of the USSR for religious affairs of the USSR which is described "as informational, consultative, and expert center." It is to maintain contacts and cooperation in the country, its constituent parts and abroad, provide a source of information on religious organizations and legislation on freedom of conscience and religious organizations, create a council of scholarly experts and representatives of denominations that may give counsel and advice to the judicial, executive, and legislative branches of government, facilitate understanding and cooperation among churches at home and abroad, and assists religious organizations in their dealing with state agencies. Similar agencies may be established by the autonomous republics.

Art. 30 provides for criminal responsibility for those who violate the legislation on freedom of conscience and religious organizations as established by the union and republican laws. In art. 31 the international agreements signed by the USSR on freedom of conscience and religious organizations take precedence over national laws if there is discrepancy.

The Law was followed by a resolution of the Supreme Soviet of the USSR on the implementation of the above law.

While there are some in the Soviet Union (e.g. Old Believers and Pentecostals) who questioned the need and wisdom of a special law on religion, the Law of October 1, 1990, is undoubtedly an immense improvement over the previous legislation. It certainly opens the road to far greater liberty for religious communities than they had at any time since 1917, though the question more important than the passage of the law is whether and how it will be implemented. Many of the previously forbidden activities are explicitly permitted by this law, which, indeed, provides greater freedom. More importantly, atheism was disestablished which provides a qualitative change: the abandonment of the Type C-Secularistic Absolutism. The provision that stipulates that international religious liberty agreements have precedence over domestic law is of great importance for the institutionalization of religious liberty according to Otto Luchterhandt.[142]

There are still some restrictive elements in the law. One of them is not providing for the possibility of optional religious education in schools. This is more in line with the American separation of public education from confessional religious education than it is with West European practice. Taking into account the diversity of Soviet population, which is more in line with the American diversity than that of more cohesive European countries, the avoidance to introduce religious education in public schools may be an advantage as long as atheism is equally denied propagation. Instruction on the history, development, and ideas of various religions and atheism does not seem to be precluded by this law. Educational institutions need to be regulated in a manner consistent to the passing of this Law.

The second one is the continued existence of a state agency to deal with religions. For the time being it was envisioned as meeting annually to compare notes and methods but in the future it could be abused for continued control and manipulation by the government, especially if some of the very unsavory characters who worked in such agencies heretofore continue to believe that it is their task to frustrate religions. For that reason the abolishment of the whole network of federal and local offices for religious affairs by the parliaments of the Russian Federation, the Baltic republics, and the Caucasus[143] are a much more significant contribution to religious liberty.

The third one is the ambiguity regarding registration of churches. The law is unclear as to what are the procedures for registration and why may the council refuse registration to a religious organization. This seems to open the doors to arbitrariness although the provision is modified by the possibility of organizing without registration provided an organization wishes to forego the status of a juridical person. Although implicitly the rights of clergy and hierarchs in deciding property and financial dealings of their denominations is granted by the concession that each church can organize itself according to its own rules, it is not entirely clear from this legislation whether the ten (rather than the former twenty) who are granted the charter for a religious association have the right to exclude their clergy and denominational leaders from making decisions regarding the property and the workings of a local organization. According to the previous legislation, for instance, only lay people but not the church leaders could petition the state authorities for the return of a church building.[144]

The practice of religious liberty after the Great Transformations seems to be highly checkered. Many of the deformations in the activities of both the religions and the government are the results of oppression, according to Rev. Kishkovsky, and may be of passing nature. Nearly all religious communities reported greater liberties, though in the more remote areas of the country the winds of change have not brought the desired thaw. A very large number of formerly confiscated churches were returned to the churches; the Russian Orthodox Church alone received between 4,000–6,000 such buildings between 1980 and 1990.[145] However, not all the confiscated churches were returned. Usually those in greatest need of repair were returned; others that have been put to other use (e.g. museums, concert and youth halls) were being delayed sometimes arbitrarily by local authorities. Sometimes the building ownership was contested by several churches, e.g. by the Russian and Ukrainian Orthodox and Ukrainian Catholics, and initially, before the legalizlation of the Ukrainian Catholics, the government returned many of their former church buildings to the Russian Orthodox, thus increasing the conflict between the two.

The official Russian Orthodox Church categorically opposed the revival of the "Uniates," but Orthodox dissidents and human right activists, including Andrey Sakharov, pressed for their rights. The Ukrainian Catholics were gradually allowed to surface beginning in 1988 but their legal recognition was granted only on December 1, 1989, when the announcement of legalization was made in Kiev on the same day when Gorbachev visited Pope John Paul II. This happened only after numerous demands for the return of church property to the Ukrainian Catholics and mass demonstrations on behalf of this church in Lviv and elsewhere. In Lviv the town council returned the Cathedral Church among the fifteen out of nineteen former Orthodox Churches to the Ukrainian Catholics after popular unrest, but at other times the local authorities and Russian Orthodox Church leaders would cooperate in denying the return of the churches to the Ukrainian Catholics.[146] Sometimes violence would break out between the Orthodox and Catholic inhabitants over the ownership of a church. The claims could be highly complex and problematic; no solution satisfactory to all could ever be found even if one had the proverbial wisdom of Solomon. Unlike the two alleged mothers in the tale of Solomon, sometimes the churches would rather destroy the building than cede it to the other church the mutual bitterness was so great.

Other important extensions of religious freedom took place. Religious activists and leaders were elected to the Supreme Soviet and other legislative bodies. This included not only the rather carefully orchestrated election of Patriarch Pimen as the representative of the Soviet Peace Committee, but also that of the dissident priest Gleb Yakunin. The dissidents have emerged from forced internal obscurity into public attention with their reputation uncompromised, probably because previously the state, with the sometimes involuntary complicity of the official church, tried to blacken their image. Former dissidents need not be labeled thus any longer but can now be rather called independent church activists. They still find themselves frequently in conflict with the official church, though complex relationships developed ranging from alliance to opposition. The conflict did open greater freedom within the church.[147] Some of the independent religious activists organized independent, religiously based political parties, such as the Christian Democratic Union organized by

Aleksandr Ogorodnikov and his circle (who complained of continued surveillance by the KGB) and Gleb Yakunin's Christian Democratic Movement. Other religious political parties were also organized in various parts of the USSR.

Another positive feature is that religious communities may now rent public facilities such as sports or municipal halls, auditoria, or stadiums for their gatherings. Both Western and local evangelists have used such opportunities. A number of religious organizations from abroad opened offices in the Soviet Union and many set up relief work and food assistance.[149] Congresses of various denominations were held, including Buddhists and Muslims. Thus, for instance, the Old Believers, organized a congress in Novosibirsk at which scholars from the Academy of Sciences participated and openly discussed religious persecutions since 1917.[150] Even Christian labor unions were organized.

The media present frequent and sympathetic portrayals of religious activities and by means of investigative reporting uncover many of the persecutions of the past. Thus, for instance, Soviet film showed the Solovyetsky monastery that was turned into a concentration camp in 1917 and documented that from the very beginning under Lenin it was turned into a death camp. Originally it was claimed that it was a re-education camp that turned into a death camp due to Stalinist deformations, but it has now been documented that the camp was intended to terrorize and kill. The killing was accomplished either by wetting and then freezing the clergy to death or by pushing them from the ledges of the monastic walls to their deaths. It is clear that this was not an exception but the prevalent pattern in the entire country from the outset of the revolution. Now the Solovyetsky monastery has been turned into a memorial. The struggle for humanity is, indeed, the struggle of memory against forgetfulness.[151]

One of the more surprising governmental decisions was the donation to the Russian Orthodox Church the parcel of land where the tsar and his family were executed by the Bolsheviks to build a memorial chapel.[152] Another important achievement is the recognition that the Council of Lviv by which the Ukrainian Catholic Church was terminated in March 1946 was illegitimate; it is now recognized simply as Stalin's intrusion into religious issues.

How religion will intertwine with nationalism is still unclear. The degree of religious liberty will depend from the way that interaction plays itself out. The Russian Orthodox Church's involvement with resurgent Russian nationalism is illustrated by the flourishing of a nationalist wing of the church, by the return of a part of the army's officer corps to the ROC, and by the presence of Boris Yeltsin and the mayor of Leningrad, Anatoliy Sobchak, at the patriarchal liturgy in the St. Isaac's Cathedral, returned to the Church in 1990 or the rebuilding of the Kazan Church on the Red Square in Moscow.[153]

Inhibitions of religious liberty are still many. Until August 1991 the KGB was still a significant presence in Soviet society and continued to observe and control behind the scenes. Entrenched bureaucrats and other Communist hard-liners continued their efforts to roll back the freedoms already achieved as they believe that these will lead to anarchy and chaos. Some of them continued their restrictive activities over the religious population by sheer inertia. After all, they have not been educated to see anything positive in religion; new thinking has not produced a reeducation. Even with the best intentions there are simply neither enough clerical personnel nor scholarly expertise to facilitate such reeducation. It will be decades before any significant dent can be made in the widely shared misperceptions about religion, even though religion as a phenomenon has gained acceptance, even popularity.

Another problem that restricts religious liberty are the intense rivalries between churches and within churches. Ecumenism which was officially promoted both by the state and the church officials has come into disrepute because of the suspicions that the former denominational leaders promoted it on state orders enhancing thereby government control over the churches.[154] The officially correct relationships between denominations was and continues to be often strained since no real dialogue but only superficial courtesy characterized those relationships. The Pentecostals decided to leave the Evangelical-Baptist Union into which they were forced by Stalin. The relationships between the Russian Orthodox Church and the Ukrainian Catholics are practically war-like. There is massive pressure in nearly all churches to ditch their world-wide ecumenical involvements.

Within denominations tension arose for two reasons. One is the well-based suspicion that many clergy and hierarachs cooperated with and reported to the KGB voluntarily or involuntarily. This, if unchecked, may lead to witch-hunts against the guilty and innocent. Patriarch Alexiy II wisely stated that "every case must be investigated individually and where priests or bishops are found to have had a connection to the KGB they will be punished and separated from the body of the Orthodox Church."[155]

The other strain is the creation of schism within the ROC and other churches.[156] In order to respond to Ukrainian demands the Moscow Patriarchate created the Autonomous Ukrainian Orthodox Church and the Autonomous Orthodox Church in Byelorussia, both in communion with Moscow. But a group of Ukrainian clergy and believers created the Autocephalous Ukrainian Orthodox Church which left the jurisdiction of Moscow. The émigré Russian Orthodox Church Abroad, a radically conservative body, established a network of churches in the Soviet Union. The "Church in the Catacombs" or the True Orthodox Church, consisting of a group of Orthodox believers who did not accept the 1929 agreement between church and state, has also emerged above ground.[157]

One of most positive evidences that religious liberty has been increased substantially is the greater freedom and openness by which all the above problems are discussed in 1990, not merely by courageous dissidents but also by the formerly cautious and timid church leaders.[158] The dissidents and exiles continued to be the more outspoken elements and they were joined by secular scholars and journalists who often wondered whether the church leaders who had been nurtured in fear and compromise will be able to transcend this reluctance to boldly seize new opportunities. After all, the church has been brutalized and debased even more than the rest of society and uncommon courage is as hard to find as water in the desert. The deeply inbred caution based on the wisdom of ages that those who raise their heads have them lopped off in times of authoritarian retrenchment and backlash will continue to instruct the behavior of the leadership. The policies of Gorbachev in the late 1990 and early 1991, indeed, indicate a distinct possibility of a roll back or even termination of *perestroika* under his own rule or that of a successor. The church leaders, especially of the Russian Orthodox Church, themselves not reformists, would not want to be caught overcommited to the "new thinking." Dimitry Pospielovsky correctly concludes:

> For seventy years the country has been ruled by decrees and secret instructions, not by laws, and as long as the old apparatus system remains in fact even if not in name, no radical improvement should be expected although there are gaps in it now, so that much depends upon the attitudes of local authorities.

Neither should the KGB be ignored. According to priests and seminary students, the KGB continues to threaten, harass and try to recruit them as before. . . . at the moment it cannot follow up on its threats if the seminarian or priest refuses to cooperate. But so many of them are still unsure whether the current freedom is to last, or whether one day the KGB will come down on them with vengeance as so many times in the past decades? This fear can be felt more on the periphery, which is at least one or two years behind Moscow or Leningrad in terms of *glasnost*, and where the KGB threats are still occasionally followed up by mysterious road accident beatings by 'hoodlums' who are never located, and even 'accidental' deaths.[159]

At this point the safest avenue to the various churches seems to be a steadfast clinging to traditionalism and national interests though this is likely to pit the churches as well as nations against each other, perhaps even more bitterly than in the past.[160]

Conclusion

The situation in the Soviet Union is so complex that those who think they understand it simply do not know what is going on, according to Kishkovsky. It has been said that Yugoslavia is a despair for tidy minds, and the same is applicable, but on a grander scale to the Soviet Union. It is clear that Secularistic Absolutism, Type C social model has crashed, but it is not clear what is replacing it. Type D, Pluralistic Liberty, though a possibility according to the recent legislation on religion is not the likely alternative because religious triumphalism, caused by the emergence and survival of religion after over seven decades of the greatest known religious persecution, may result in the suppression of the right of the atheists and other religionists. Likewise the relationships between various denominations and within the denominations is so embittered and estranged that attempts to suppress and manipulate which have already taken place will inevitably continue for an unforeseeable time. Excesses and distortions will occur for a while as the pent-up nationalism and religion, usually combined, seek to gain recognition and affirmation in both healthy and unhealthy forms. The most one may dare to hope for would be an uneasy establishment of Religious Toleration, Type B model, though the threat is that peace, toleration, and liberty will be continually endangered by elements of warring Type A absolutistic claims or "state churches" in which one religious community or the government may try to deprive other communities of their liberty.

The worst of all possible scenarios, but one quite realistic, is the disintegration of the union not peacefully but by a civil war. The best scenarios would be either

(a) the success of Gorbachev's attempt to redefine the union with a gradual development of democratic relationships or

(b) the success of the aspiration of many of the republics in the union, symbolized by Boris Yeltsin and the Baltic states, for an orderly dissolution of the unpopular empire after which each component state would seek to benefit from European integration and gradual transition to a more generally acceptable Religious Tolerance with growing features of Pluralistic Liberty. This would, naturally, transpire at different rates of speed and upheaval.

If it is true that no real understanding of the complexities of the Soviet developments is possible then it is even more true that no real forecast of the developments of religious liberty is possible.

Chapter 5

A L B A N I A: RELIGION OUTLAWED

How can Europe's most traditional society also be Europe's most secularist and the world's first atheist state? How can a Communist Party which was organized only in 1941 so completely dominate Albania that it can claim no political or religious competition or alternative by 1976, that is in about thirty years from non-existence into monopoly? Such questions cannot be answered easily, especially since the process took place outside of the scope of the scrutiny not only of scholars but even of the more normal channels of journalists, diplomats, tourists, and others who could report on this rather self-imposed secluded and secretive society. The sources are few and generally biased information in them is scant. There are very limited possibilities of going to Albania for first-hand research. Thus this presentation per force will be limited. Nevertheless a plausible explanation for not merely the diminishment but radical cessation of all religious liberties can be provided.

Pre-Communist Religious Situation

The Albanians are the remnants of ancient Illyrian native people of the Balkan Peninsula. Christianity came to some of the regions of present day Albania as early as the first, or more likely second century. With the increasing rivalry between the Pope of Rome and the Patriarch of Constantinople, their influence over Albanian Christians shifted back and forth. When the schism between these two branches of Christendom finally occurred, Albanians in the northern territories came under the papal jurisdiction and became Roman Catholics, while those in central and southern portions of the land became Eastern Orthodox, with strong Greek links. In the fifteenth century the Ottoman Turkish Empire conquered the land and a process of Islamization began at once which increased sharply in the sixteenth and seventeenth centuries to the point that over two–thirds of the population became Muslim. The Muslims were also divided among themselves, with the majority belonging to the Sunnis, while a minority were attracted to the various Sufi, i.e. Dervish Orders, mostly the Bektashis, who were Shi'a.[1]

The last religious cencus took place in 1938 and determined that about 70 percent of the population was Muslim, 55 percent of which were Sunni and 15 percent Bektashis, 20 percent were Eastern Orthodox, and 10 percent Roman Catholics. This means that the Albanians were sharply divided by their religious allegiance. The Muslims were bearers of Turkish influence to such a degree that the Muslim population was often regarded as "Turks." Arabic was the language of worship. The Orthodox Church was under strong Greek religious and cultural influence, with Greek language used in the liturgy, which made the Orthodox being called "Greeks." The Roman Catholics were the bearers of a Latin, namely Italian influence, and were labeled as "Latins." Thus the Turkish, Greek, and Italian influences were experiences as coming through the religious communities. The *Rilinja* movement of Albanian national awakening in the nineteenth century often regarded this religious division as an obstacle to Albanian nationalism and, perhaps in an outburst of lyrical enthusiasm, declared that "The Religion of the Albanian people is Albania."[2]

Although Albanians belonged to four different religious persuasions, it was far from being pluralist rather, there were sharply rival, contending sacral or ecclesiastic absolutist (type A) societies. Individual Albanians did not experience the freedom to chose their religion but did so by birth, each person being tightly drawn in the orbit of their religion and generally experiencing other religions as their enemies. But it would be oversimplified to say that the religious communities only detracted from the national identity of the Albanians. The situation was much more ambiguous because it was the Orthodox and Catholic clergy who were also the preservers of the national language, and the Catholics and the Bektashis were strong proponents of modernization of Albania, particularly after Albania gained independence from Turkey in 1912. The Orthodox also were not eager to remain under Greek influence. Though the ravages of World War I were barely over, in 1923 the Orthodox Church of Albania proclaimed its autocephaly, for which it still stands under anathema by the ecumenical patriarch of Istanbul, because it did so unilaterally, over Greek opposition.[3]

One of the questions which has some bearing on why it was that religion could be suppressed so easily has something to do with how deeply ingrained had Islam, Orthodoxy, and Catholicism become among the Albanians. There are those, among them both non-Communist and Communist Albanians, who say that the great historical religion never took very deep roots among the Albanians but that ancient tribal indigenous religion and customs of the Geg, Tosk, Gruda, Hoti, and Skreli tribes, including the oral customary law were the main undercurrent of Albanian life. Peter Prifti pointed out this role of this "pagan" undercurrent by saying;

> To this day one hears people in Albania swear "by this earth," or by the sun, or the bread they eat. . . . Indicative of this light-hearted approach to religion is the fact that the priest in the Albanian village was often the but of jokes and anecdotes. Indeed the favourite comic character in Albanian folklore is none other than Nastradin Hoxha, a bungling, often roguish and rather irreverent Muslim priest.[4]

The persistence of ancient indegenous tribal customs which survive to this day among the very tradition-bound Albanian clannish social structure is a factor which must be taken into account, but it would be a distortion to say that Christianity and Islam did not take deep roots among the Albanians. It is evident that among Albanians who live outside of Albania and who are not pressured to abandon their religious preference that religion plays a very significant role in their lives. This is the case among the Arbëresh, namely Albanians who live in Italy who are Roman Catholics, the Albanians in Kosovo and other regions in Yugoslavia, who are mostly Muslims or Roman Catholic, and those in the U. S. or other Western countries who belong to all three religious communities. It is most accurate to say that pre-Christian and pre-Islamic primal religious practices can be discerned in fairly large doses among the Christian and Muslim religious beliefs and practices.

The major clue for the rapid success in destroying institutional religion in Albania would seem to be discord among religions and, more importantly, Communist terror. While the latter will be described below, we need to reftect briefly on discord. The three great religions did not cooperate but each had the aspiration of becoming the religion of all Albanians. From historical experience it was evident that Islam aimed at converting all Albanians to Islam and that the Sunnis tended to be more intolerant than the Bektashis. After the Balkan Wars Christians were hoping for a re-Christianization of Muslims. The Catholics have traditionally aspired worldwide for the Orthodox to be brought back into the fold of the church universal by accepting papal primacy, while the Orthodox equally ardently hoped to see Catholics return to the true faith and practice. Thus all three major faiths had designs one upon the other leading to distrust and discord. These designs would not be simple because conversion would not be of individuals alone. Among Albanians, even more so than elsewhere on the Balkans, the extended family and tribal unit were associated with the religious identity. This is most evident not only in surnames, but even more in first names which tend to be distinctly Islamic or Christian, namely Catholic or Orthodox. Anyone who wanted to mold all Albanians into a more tightly unified nation would need to deal with the power of the religious traditions and the presence of religious discord.

Approaches different from the Ecclesiastic Absolutism also took place, showing some inclination to model B, Religious Toleration. Gjon Sinishta of University of San Francisco wrote, "Between the World Wars, both Christians and Muslims were free to practice their religion in a spirit of mutual trust and ecumenical relations."[5] This seems a bit idyllic since even after Vatican II there is a great deal of reluctance to enter into genuine ecumenical relations by Catholics and Orthodox on the Balkan peninsula, but regardless of whether Sinishta's observation is accurate or wishfully optimistic, the fact is that the Communist take-over of Albania in 1944 turned out to be the option for the radically Secularist Absolutistic model.

We need to stress that Albania had a very brief experience of independence before the Communist take-over. For a while they were ruled by King Zog, and then during World War II they were under Italian and later direct German occupation and tutelage, though ostensibly operating as "Great Albania," with extended borders. Thus Albania never experienced democratic political liberties, although there were attempts in the inter-war period to create a more modern society. Religious liberties were circumscribed by the context of one's own religious community.

POST-WAR PROHIBITION OF RELIGIOUS LIBERTY

1. Persecution of Religion: The Period from 1944 to 1967

The Albanian partisans, the liberation movement under the leadership of the Communist Enver Hoxha, fought against the Italian fascist and other occupying forces which cooperated to some degree with Tito's Yugoslavian partisans. The Communists of Albania were completely imbued with uncompromising Stalinism. In November 1944 they came into power albeit without Soviet military assistance and established a one-party government of the Party of Labor of Albania. It is estimated that prior to their take-over the Sunni Muslims had 1,127 mosques, 17 educational mosques and 1,306 clergy. The Bektashis had 260 Tekke cloisters with 65 Baba abbeys, 468 celibate dervishes, and 128 burial shrines of famous sheiks. The number of novices is unknown. There were also 844 Orthodox and 147 Catholic churches, of which 70 were monasteries. The combined clergy count was 9 archbishops and 638 priests, some of whom were foreigners.[6]

The ruthless persecution of religion began almost at once. This may be regarded as a continuation of some of the war-time hostilities toward those religious leaders who sided with the old regime. The terror was not frontal, against all religions, but rather against individuals who were accused, some rightly and some wrongly, of having been fascist collaborationist. Thus, for instance, the Franciscan priest Anton Harapi, who had formed a regency along with one representative of the other three religious communities during the Nazi occupation, was condemned to death at a show trial of "collaboration with the enemy" and executed.[7] In many instances the disguise of court procedure was completely dispensed with and many religious leaders were simply murdered, allegedly spontaneously by mob action. Priests of foreign extraction were summarily expelled as threats to the state. Most religious institutions were searched and many properties, such as schools, kindergartens and orphanages, were confiscated. What impresses the observer is the excessive cruelty which characterized this terror, a legacy of the age old practices of the Balkan peninsula where the conquerors perennially imposed their rule by unspeakable torture and where the brutalized populace responded in the same measure thus exacting a rough degree of justice. Milovan Djilas, when describing neighboring Montenegro, where many of the same attitudes prevail, described it aptly in the title of a book of his as "A Land Without Justice." A label like this would not be lost on Albania.

The settling of accounts takes place brutally, swiftly, and mercilessly. We shall get back to detailing some of these persecutions.

The initial laws which were passed are comparable with the Western liberal tradition. The Constitution of March 14, 1946, declares freedom of conscience and of faith and separation of church and state (article 18, which appears unchanged even after 1967), freedom of speech, press, organization, meetings, public assembly and manifestation (article 20). Article 15 states:

> All citizens are equal with no differences of nationality, race or religion. Any act which brings about privileges in favor of citizens or limits their rights on account of differences of nationality, race or religion is contrary to the Constitution and incurs punishment foreseen by law. Any attempt to sow hatred and cause dissention among nationalities, races and religions is contrary to the Constitution and liable to punishment according to law.[8]

It is worth mentioning that these legal provisions greatly resemble Yugoslavia's Constitution of January of 1946 and that both of them are modelled after Stalin's Soviet Constitution of 1936. In fact there are many parallels between the Yugoslav and Albanian approach to religion up to 1948 not only due to both of their dependence on the Soviet example but because of the close collaboration between the two Communist parties, which was, on Stalin's orders, to first lead to the absorption of Albania into the Yugoslav federation and thereafter to proceed to the creation of a Balkan federation with the addition of Bulgaria.[9] An illustration of this close link is the torture to death of an Albanian Franciscan priest, Lek Luli, and two other friars on the territory of Kosovo toward the end of 1944 by the Yugoslav secret police, UDBA, which is but an indication of the similarity of approaches, if not downright cooperation on how to deal with the churches.

The government, contradicting its own Constitutional principle, did not deal with all religions equally, which is again a parallel with Yugoslavia. Gjon Sinishta describes the three approaches as follows:

> 1. Toleration, within limits, of Islam. Generally, with a few exceptions of high clergy, the Muslim religion was not a great obstacle to the new regime. By applying cunning leniency, the government wished to use it as a propaganda tool toward the Muslim world.

> 2. Although the regime considered Eastern Orthodoxy

in general an enemy, they nevertheless attempted to use the Orthodox Church, because of her traditional patriotism, as an instrument for mobilizing Albania's Orthodox population behind its policies.

    3. Complete elimination of Catholicism because of its strong spiritual, cultural, and organizational power. For centuries the clergy and adherents of this Church were the frontrunners of Albania's national, cultural and religious renewal. The vast majority of Catholics were unsympathetic towardg the new (Communist) regime.[10]

The next step was to create specific regulations dealing with religious communities. The government issued:

    1. Decree No. 743 of January 26, 1949, "On Religious Communities."

    2. The "Statute of the Albanian Muslim Community," Decree No. 1064 of May 4, 1950,

    3. The "Statute of the Autocephalous Orthodox Church of Albania," Decree No. 1065 of May 4, 1950.

    4. The "Statute of the Albanian Bektashi Community," Decree 1066 of May 4, 1950.

    5. The "Statute of the Catholic Church of Albania," Decree No. 1322 of July 30, 1951.

It should be noted that these are not laws but governmental decrees. The general decree of January 26, 1950, repeats many of the Constitutional guarantees and in addition sets penalties for violations. Then all religious communities were given a three month period to draw up their statutes. Since none of them could meet this deadline the Statues were ordered by the Council of Ministers and issued in the form of decrees simultaneously for all religions except the Catholic. The reason for the longer time needed for the Catholic statutes was that the Catholic Church's canonical relationship with the pope had to be curtailed as the Albanian government wanted to create a national Catholic Church and could find no Roman Catholic who would endorse such a plan. Indeed, in the end the Catholic Church was not allowed to "maintain any organizational, economic or political relations with the pope."[11] The Orthodox Church's statute mandated that it must

> report connections and cooperation with the Orthodox sister-churches who practice the high principles of the Gospel with

regard to peace and true brotherhood, and every activity
and attempt to destroy peace, love and brotherhood among
nations of the whole world.[12]

Here intrusion by state authorities is distinctly written into governmental decrees, though intrusion occurred even when not mandated
by law. The religious groups resisted to varying degrees; this was
admitted by the Tirana weekly *Drita,*

> The reactionary Bektashi said stubbornly, "The Statute we
> made should not come into effect because it does not give us
> the rights we would like to have." The heads of Catholicism
> did not, under any circumstances, want to sign the church
> Statute and continue to operate as a national Church. They
> put up political resistance in order to keep the schools in
> the clutches of the clergy, they demanded from the Gov-
> ernment the recognition of the "right" to connections and
> co-operation with the Vatican under the pretext that "rebel-
> lion against the Pope was synonymous with rebellion against
> Catholicism," that "nobody was Catholic without the con-
> nection with the Pope," etc.—all kinds of demands which, if
> granted, would have resulted in the clergy not only working
> as spiritual oppressors of the working masses but also as a
> legal political tool of that centre of world reaction.[13]

Should one wonder why the four religious communities in Albania accepted these very restrictive statutes, one should be reminded
that the terror against the individual religious leaders soon escalated
into a furious extermination of the majority of the religious leaders
and brought enormous suffering to all who practiced their religion.
Proportionate to the size of the population the terror in Albania may
have exceeded that of Stalin during the "Great Purge." It will be impossible to detail vastness of the perpetrated cruelty, but for a stark
summary one can observe that:

> Taking the Roman Catholic Church as an example, in 1939
> there were 141 native and 62 foreign priests, 16 native and
> 16 foreign monks, as well as 73 native and 60 foreign nuns.
> In the Spring of 1971, only 14 Catholic priests were known
> of in Albania, 12 in prison camps and two in hiding. This
> number has since [written in 1975] been reduced further by
> one execution . . . and a suspected additional imprisonment.
> The entire Orthodox hierarchy and most of its clergy are in

prison. Little is known of the fate of the Islamic hierarchy.[14]

Whether the Muslims fared better or whether we simply know less about their suffering is unclear, but the following attests to their casualties. The three leaders of the Bektashis who were in 1946 elected as deputies to the People's Assembly, Baba Faja, Baba Fejzo, and Sheh Karbunara, were assassinated. The entire Muslim leadership was tortured, imprisoned and executed. Many simply never returned from prison camps.[15] Muslim lawyer, Muzafer Pipa, was executed for defending a Roman Catholic priest, Anton Harapi, OFM. No one has ventured to estimate the number of other Muslims who died in these conflict. One may grant that a certain number of these people died due to primarily political conflicts, but when one takes into account the Muslim inseparability of religion from other aspects of life, one can safely estimate that the majority of the casualties resulted from the government's attempt to make the Muslim community leaderless, or at least without independent minded leadership.

The Orthodox Church of Albania was likewise deprived of its leadership by exscuting Rev. Josif Papamihaili (1946), Archbishop Kristofor Kisi (1949), Archbishop Visarion Xhuvani (1951), Bishop Irine of Korca and Gjirokastra (1953), Bishop Irine of Pojan (1936), Bishop Agathangjel Cance (1958), and Bishop Damien Konessi (1973).[1] Archbishop Kristofor Kisi, the head of the Orthodox Church was replaced by a married priest (a canonical obstacle), Pais Vodica, a reputed Communist agitator, who closely cooperated with the Moscow Patriarchate during the period of Albania's friendship with the USSR.

The Roman Catholics fared worst. Martyred were Archbishop Gasper Thaci, the Primate of the Church (1946), Archbishop Vincenc Prendushi (1949), Bishops Luigj Bumci (1945), Gjergjj Volaj (1948), Fran Gjini (1948), Pjeter Dema (1955), Bernardin Shllaku (1973), Antonin Fishta (1973), and Ernest Coba (1979). In addition four monsignors, 53 parish priests, 31 Franciscans, 14 Jesuits, 10 seminarians, and 8 sisters are estimated to have been exterminated.[17] Some went through mock trials, others simply disappeared, some were imprisoned for many years, horribly tortured and mistreated. Bishop Coba, the Apostolic Administrator of Shkodër, for instance, after many years of internment in a labor camp died in April 1979 after he was severely beaten for having secretly baptized a child of a woman inmate.[18] The number of Catholic lay people who perished is unknown. One woman was, for instance, sentenced to eight years of imprisonment for having her twin babies secretly baptized by a Jesuit. No one can estimate the fear and suffering which such repressive measures cost the Albanian religious population. Sinishta described these onslaughts by periodizing them from 1944 to 1948, from 1949 to 1967, and from 1967 to the present.[19]

The losses in property were also significant, but these were mainly losses of church and mosque buildings, schools, and similar. Prior to the Communist take-over the religious institutions owned only 1.26 percent of the land; by 1947 this was reduced to 0.2 percent.[20] This simply means that the religious institutions were not large landholders and that some of the attack against them as being oppressors and exploiters fail to convince. From the Marxist perspective the clergy were exploiters by definition because they have not engaged in useful production but had lived off the working people's labor. Enver Hoxha's writings reflect that he based his intolerance of religion on the general Enlightenment rationalist critique of religion, the specifically Marxist and even more Leninist and Stalinist objectives of eliminating religion, and lastly a specifically Albanian xenophobia of foreign imports which the religions of Orthodoxy, Catholicism, and Islam represented to him.[21]

2. Abolition of Religion: Period from 1967 to 1990

If by the middle of the 1960s it seemed that religion would be exterminated in Albania, the perception would be right although the Albanian Marxist authorities would have asserted that all religious liberties were impeccably respected. All this changed in 1966 and 1967 with the implementation of a Chinese-inspired cultural revolution, when the Albanian Communist leadership decided for a consistent implementation of their Marxist vision of a religionless society. Originally the international Marxist vision was that the religionless society was near. In the face of the stubborn survival of religion in the Soviet Union and other Communist countries the date of the demise of religion was being revised, now expected to take place in the distant future. But the Albanian Marxists decided that the future is now!

The break with Yugoslavia in 1948 enhanced Stalinism in Albania. Even though Stalin died in 1953 Enver Hoxha's sympathies for Stalin's personality and method never subsided.[22] Thus they started quarrelling with the Soviet Union and other Eastern European countries over de-Stalinization, which lead to the breaking of diplomatic relations in 1961. Then Albania increasingly drifted toward Maoism.

Following China's example the Party of Labor of Albania declared in 1966 the beginning of the "ideological and cultural revolution." It first started on February 6, 1967, with a speech by Enver Hoxha, "The Revolutionization of the Party and the Government." In it the "puritanically" of oriented Hoxha[23] declared that Albania should be "the first atheist state in the world," and this was printed in the largest daily, *Zëri i popullit.* The sequel was disastrous for religion.

An alleged spontaneous demonstration by pupils and teachers in Durrës took place in which they closed all religious institutions in town. The idea appeared so attractive that church, mosque, and *tekiye* closing became rampant. Even older people were supposedly caught up in the leap to abolish religion. In three to four months all 2,169 religious buildings were demolished, boarded up or otherwise closed or altered for other purposes.[24] According to Peter Prifti, religious institutiom were

> hailed before the popular courts of reason, names of parents who gave religious names to children were placed on wall newspapers, children of clergy denounced them as deceivers, articles, pamphlets and books were published ridiculing religion, people pledged never to become involved with religion, etc.[25]

With the closing of places of worship there was no more need for the Decree on Religion, so it was revoked on November 13, 1967, whereby religion became illegal. This would need to be only confirmed in the Constitution, and, indeed, a new Constitution was promulgated in 1976 which declared:

> The state does not recognize any religion at all and supports and develops atheistic propaganda in order to implant in mankind the scientific-materialistic world view. [Article 37]

> The formation of any organization of a fascist, anti-democratic, religious, or anti-socialist nature is forbidden. Fascist, religious, warmongerish, anti-socialist activity and propaganda are forbidden, as is the incitement to hatred between people and races. [Article 55][26]

The Constitutional provision were then protected by the Penal Code of June 15, 1977:

> Fascist, anti-democratic, religious, warmongerish and anti-socialist agitation and propaganda, and also the production,

distribution or and propaganda, and also the production, distribution or storage with a view to distribution of literature of this kind, aimed at undermining or weakening the rule of the proletariat, will be punished with imprisonment of between three and ten years. If these actions occur in time of war or if they have caused particularly serious consequences, they will be punished with imprisonment of not less than ten years, or with death. [Clause 55][27]

Albanian leaders did not want the letter of the law to be out of step with reality. Nor did they wish to be hypocritical. Albania neither participated in the Helsinki Conference nor did it sign the Helsinki Agreement, thus not being bound by any international convention which stipulates religious toleration save those stipulated by United Nations membership.[28] The Minnesota Lawyers International Human Rights Committee carried out a thorough examination of the case of Albania and wrote that:

[t]he evidence overwhelmingly shows that the Albanian government has violated and continues to violate international norms concerning the freedom of religion, as enunciated in Article 18 of the Universal Declaration of Human Rights and the 1981 U.N. Declaration on the Elimination of All Forms of Intolerance and of Discrimination Based on Religion or Belief.[29]

Thus, in word and in spirit Albania, though a member of the U.N., is a country which provided no religious freedom whatsoever, because its leadership was convinced that religion is bad for its people. Just as a government could be proud of protecting its populace from a deadly pestilence, so the Albanian government was proud to have freed its people from the religious plague. No cases of formal religious observances have surfaced to the open; the few foreign visitors have not been able to detect the contagion, though some, at least wishfully, tried to deny the total victory to the government by insisting that somewhere, somehow, clandestinely there have to be some religious germs left, at least in the elderly and the dying.[30] But for over two decades religion has either been obliterated or at least effectively driven into the deepest recesses of the individual soul, where it survived in disorganized forms.

There are currently two views of what direction the communist party's attitude is toward religion. An Austrian observer, Heinz

Gstrein, maintained that religion was on the upswing.[31] According to Gstrein with the execution of Mehmet Shehu in 1981 the "ex-Islamic" militantly antireligious wing in the party declined in power and an "ex-Orthodox" more tolerant group lead by the Deputy Minister of Culture and Education, Anastas Kondo, undertook a change in direction from a most militant to a relatively more tolerant attitude toward religion as part of the national heritage. Books, though critical of religion, nevertheless depict it a bit more sympathetically and names of former religious figures which were not used for a decade or so, reappeared in print. He described even Enver Hoxha's later years, especially since 1983 as having re-evaluated his attitude toward Islam and supporting both Khomeini and the Afghan Islamic guerrillas, though this seems to be grounded in Hoxha's anti-Sovietism more than in appreciation of Islamic fundamentalism. Reportedly he avoided visiting those sections of Albania in which the greater conservatism in women's dress seems to reflect sympathies with Muslim traditionalism. In 1989 the Roman Catholic Bishop Nikoll Troshani and priests Mikel Koliqi and Simon Jubani were released by the authorities (another priests, the eighty-seven year old Jesuit Pjeter Meshkalla died in a prison camp in July 1988).[32] These data were taken as indications that the pressure was relaxing.

A rather different picture emerged in the writing of the Albanian communist Hulusi Hako in 1986. It was his conviction that religious or spiritual servitude has been removed along with economic and social exploitation. According to Hako:

> our people scored new gains toward greater freedom from religious ideology, and the deepening of the materialistic, atheistic-scientific world outlook. The fact is that even today we encounter in our life certain manifestations and remnants of religious preconceptions and practices and related superstitions and backward customs. The thrust and forms of these manifestations are much more limited than they were twenty or twenty-five years ago, and the number of people they affect is steadily smaller. But they are still sufficiently extensive and harmful and dangerous to merit the attention of the Party . . .[33]

Hako pointed out that while the institutional and outward appearances of religion have been removed, religion still affects not only the weaklings and deformed characters, ex-priests, remnants of old classes as well as "recent degenerates" and

> with these political and ideological ruffians, these cosmopoli-
> tans who are devoid of every patriotic sentiment, who have
> sold out to foreigners, these former agents of theirs who con-
> tinue their hostile activity, we are in an antgonistic contra-
> diction to this day. Toward them we sharpen our vigilance,
> and we punish them according to their guilt, from unmask-
> ing them in social courts and all the way to handing out
> penal sentences.[34]

However, religion affected subtly the very character of people,
and therefore the party must summon all its resources to continue to
re-educate people. Hako pointed out that religion hid in the recesses
of family life, in certain metaphysical thinking by individuals, in giving traditional religious names to children, in funeral and mourning
customs, in reluctance to enter into marriages across former religious
lines of division, and similar customs. Hako insisted that Hoxha's
successor in the leadership of the PLA, Ramiz Alia, stood on the
same firm lines of opposition to religion as his predecessor and that
the even more difficult task must be undertaken to drive out the vestiges of religion from the innermost recesses of people's consciousness
in order to build a happy and healthy citizenry. The schools should
be the institution of most insistent atheist education so that children
would not become tolerant of vestiges of religious sentiments in the
family, which is "the last fortress harboring religious remnants that
has to be occupied."[35] National names should be insisted upon instead of religious and foreign names. New funeral practices "that are
free of every religious influence"[36] should be instituted, and educators
should be educated how to pursue antireligious activities.

It would appear that Hako's strident antireligious bugle call was
the actual direction in which Albania's policies would go rather than
the anticipation of Gstrein, though the two are not altogether exclusive. Namely, Albanian nationalism is the most evident motivation and substance for all that takes place in Albania today, while its
own brand of Marxism-Leninism-Stalinism-Hoxhaism is only the form
which this nationalism takes. Hence it is not contradictory that some
appreciation may be shown toward the nationalistic expressions of religion in the past, such as Skenderbeg's ' rebellion, and, on the other
hand continue a relentless drive to accomplish a fully atheist society.
After all that would make Albania completely unique and would sep-

arate it from "revisionist" Titoist Yugoslavia and post-Stalin Soviet Union and post-Maoist China. In the opinion of the Albanian communist leadership mere separation of church and state coupled with antireligious propaganda as practiced in other communist countries is insufficient. It does not eradicate religion. Albanians, on the other hand, have identified religion as an irremediable evil and have decided to up-root it in the name of a happier future.

In terms of specific incidents, a Jesuit priest Ndoc Luli who had been in prison from 1946 to 1961, and upon release worked on a collective farm in his native village of Jushit was given a life sentence in 1980 for secretly baptizing twins while the mother was given an eight-year sentence.[37] The Albanian Orthodox continued secretly to celebrate their holy days and to hide icons.[38] Youth brigades were sent throughout the country in 1987 to combat "backward customs, superstitions, and recalcitrant religious practices."[39] In September, 1989, Ramiz Alia delivered a speech to the Central Committee of the Communist Party in which he reiterated that no concession will be made to any religious ideology, as it had been in the USSR, Hungary, and Poland, and that nothing will deter the unity of the people achieved under socialism.[40] Nexhmije Hoxha, Enver's widow and the chairperson of the Democratic Front declared in June 1989:

> The Democratic Front has always been in the front lines to free the people from the chains of religion and the savage laws of the unwritten code of the mountains. But this does not mean that we have eradicated all traces of patriarchal, conservative and religious rule.[41]

Yet in August of the same year the same Nexhmije Hoxha received Mother Theresa, an ethnic Albanian, who was finally allowed to visit the grave of her parents and her visit was given publicity.[42] This was in line with the permissions given since 1986 but intensified since 1988 for certain Albanian and non-Albanian clergy who had ties to the country to visit the coungy relatively unhindered and brought news of certain relaxation in regard to religion.[43]

As late as February 1990, the Albanian Minister of Interior claimed in the newspaper *Zëri i Popullit* that there were no prisoners of conscience in Albania despite evidence to the contrary gathered by the British Keston College and Amnesty International. It is said also that among the Greek minority there had been gatherings in abandoned churches asking for religious freedom which were dispersed by the police and that among Roman Catholics papal appeals and the proximity of Catholics among Kosovo Albanians religious interest has increased.[44]

3. Religion Permitted Again: 1990 Onward

While in the rest of Eastern Europe the Great Transformation affected the political, socio-economic, and religious structure, Albania appeared to be wedded to Stalinism with only the tiniest cracks appearing in the wall of isolation. For that reason the announcement made on May 9, 1990, that certain reforms in the area of human rights and legality, including the removal of the prohibition to worship privately,[45] came as a welcome surprise. That the announcement was made two days before the official visit to the country of the U. N. General Secretary, Javier Perez de Cuellar after serious accusations against Albania in the U. N. as one of the worst abusers of human rights, is perhaps not surprising.[46] Albania had consistently refused to even answer official charges and inquiries by governments and churches[47] about its religious policies, but in recent years there were acknowledgements of these charges both in the speeches of Albanian government leaders and in the press.[48] It appears that the bad publicity did have an impact despite the protestations to the contrary.

In July 1990 the first sign of popular dissatisfaction with the government manifested itself in the defection of several hundred people to foreign embassies in Tirana. Subsequently the government permitted these people to be shipped to countries of their choice. At that time the government announced certain additional liberalizing actions but there were no signs that this softening would result in the permission to resume public worship and even less assurance that it would eventually lead to religious liberty. However, a number of clergy who had been imprisoned previously or believed to have been killed had been released and a spontaneous public worship was held in the northern Albanian town of Lac on June 13, 1990.[49] Albania's interest in finally joining the Conference on European Security and Cooperation, having been the sole holdout, placed additional pressure to improve its human rights record, a part of the Helsinki Accords. It was that desire to become integreated into the European processes that explains the announcement by Ramiz Alia at an Albanian Party of Labor on November 8, 1990, that religious freedom and the rule of law would be respected and that the 1976 Constitutional prohibition of religion would be removed.[50] Such announcement, while welcome, need to be treated with scepticism, because as seen in the pre-1967 Albanian practice as well as the practice of other East European countries legal guarantees amount to practically nothing until there is a practical committment to human rights.

In the meantime, despite all the talk of progress and happiness Albania remains the poorest and most backward country of Europe. Some visitors who compared descriptions of certain Albanian cities concluded that they were thriving more early in the twentieth century than presently, while others report economic progress.[51] Certainly the population is more isolated from the world than in its previous history. Until 1989 most did not seem to know even about the work of their compatriot, the Nobel Peace prize winner, Mother Theresa.[52] Surely some progress has been made, especially in advancing literacy and bringing greater emancipation of women. These are laudable. But as to the near complete absence of religion, the opinions would depend on one's perspective. The Albanian Communists would say that the complete absence of religion means the full presence of freedom from religion, which they see as a scourge of the people. Others would say that currently there is a complete absence of freedom of religion and conscience. There is an equal absence of other civil rights, e.g. assembly, press and political opinion. The announced aim of the Albanian Party of Labor is complete uniformity in attitudes toward politics, economics, ideology, and religion. This appears to have been achieved at least outwardly. The price has been enormous. Thousands have been murdered, maimed, and otherwise tortured. Someone called Albania aptly, "a small country with a large Gulag." The land of the Shquiptares [Eagles, the Albanian name for themselves] is not a place where the Eagles can fly free. They are caged. Its true that they were caged before. Perhaps the advantage of the present order is that they are not caged by despised foreigners. The captors have changed; now they are from among their own. One wonders whether this is a great consolation. The country has gone from a pure Ecclesiastic Absolutism (Type A) to a pure and militant Secularistic Absolutism (Type C) with practically no intervening stages. There is a logic to this development because it is easier to move from one type of Absolutism to another than to tolerance and pluralism. In the past there was at least some freedom though the choices between Orthodoxy, Catholicism, and Islam may have been made under duress; nascent Type B. But with the monopolization of power by the Communists the choice was eliminated altogether. From unfreedom the country has moved to even greater unfreedom at least when it comes to practicing a religion. Though dim the hope may not be abandoned that some day all citizens of Albania will be free to follow the dictates of their conscience in matters of religion and belief in general rather than being dictated by others how to perceive themselves in the larger order of things. But at the time of writing Albania was the only country in Eastern Europe that has not experienced the Great Transformation and the sole country where the model of Secularistic Absolutism was yielding to Religious Toleration very slowly and reluctantly.

Chapter 6

B U L G A R I A: STEADY REPRESSION

Demonstrations demanding the repeal of restored religious rights for ethnic Turks and other Muslims in January 1990 are one of the most vivid evidences that policies regarding religious liberty reflect a country's historical tradition. Bulgaria is as homogeneous a country from the ethnic and religious perspective as one can find and forces supporting such homogeneity which sharply limits the freedom of minorities are deeply rooted in the past. The dogmatic Communist regimes of the post-World War II period reflected this potent national factor and their more liberal heirs must wrestle with the legacy of the past. Government willingness to grant greater religious freedom are not always enthusiastically received by the majority unless it applies only to themselves.

I. Historical Factors

Bulgaria is a country with one vastly predominant religion, Bulgarian Orthodoxy. Converted to Christianity in the ninth Century, after some skillful exploitation of the ambitions of Rome and Constantinople to expand their jurisdiction to the Balkan peninsula, Bulgarian kings accepted the Eastern Orthodox religion for their people and subsequently claimed autocephaly which the patriarch of Constantinople only reluctantly granted, thereby establishing the nearly always accurate equation that a Bulgarian is an Orthodox Christian.[1] According to the typology from chapter 2 Bulgaria was a classical Eccesiastic Absolutist, Type A society. This claim was not without challenge, mostly by other Type A claimants.

One of them was the Greek Orthodox hierarchy which over the centuries into the present one, owing to the proximity and intertwining of historical developments, sought to Hellenize the Orthodox

Church. The use of the old Slavonic liturgy and the nationalism of the lower clergy preserved the Bulgarian character of the church, despite continuous attempts of Greek spiritual and cultural dominance, especially during the Turkish rule.

The second were the occasional efforts, especially during the early years of Christianity by the pope to establish Roman Catholicism. The Bulgarian kings quickly realized that Rome was unwilling to grant the type of nationat control over the church that they desired, and thus the Roman card was used only to obtain greater concessions from Byzantium.

The third, the most traumatic challenge came with the Ottoman Turkish conquest in 1393 which lasted until 1878 when, with Russian Emperial diplomatic and military assistance, the Turks relinquished their control. During the Turkish occupation many Turks inhabited the area and on top of that succeeded in converting a smaller portion of the population to Islam (the converted Bulgarians are usually called the Pomaks). The political control and oppression by the Turks and the Turkish policy to place all the Orthodox population in their empire under the jurisdiction of the ecumenical patriarch in Constantinople nearly destroyed Bulgarian nationhood. The bitterness of the Bulgarians against the Turks (which also manifests itself among the other Balkan nations) is a powerful ingredient in all policies toward the Muslims from 1878 onward. In the West, Bulgarians were so little known that American Protestant missionaries in Istanbul in the middle of the nineteenth century expressed surprise upon discovering this ethnic group. It was the American Protestant missionaries, Congregational, Methodist, later Baptists and Pentecostals, who introduced Protestantism much to the chagrin of the Orthodox Church who perceived this as raiding of their membership. Bulgarian nationalists often perceived Protestant religious activity as a weakening of nationalism since the ethnic and religious link was so strong. Only after the Congregationalists and Methodists opened schools and colleges (e.g. the American College in Sofia) which provided a good education for some of the first Bulgarian government leaders, was some good will created toward the Protestants. But not before a good deal of harassment and violence broke out both against the missionaries and the converts, that subsided only gradually. Yet Protestant missionaries became ardent Bulgarophiles and lobbied strenuously with the United States government and among churches to help the cause of Bulgarian independence.[2]

The Treaty of Berlin in 1878 stipulated that Bulgaria guarantee equality to its citizens regardless of their religious affiliation and the freedom for each denomination to organize itself according to its own priciples. The supervision of religious affairs by the govemment was carried out through the Ministry of Foreign Affairs because so many of the denominations had headquarters outside of Bulgaria, a phenomenon that characterizes Bulgarian church policies to the present. The Bulgarian Orthodox Church was given a special legal position, called "dominant," in recognition of its historic role among the Bulgarian people, including state financing of the Orthodox Church down to priests' salaries. The other religious communities were also given legal rights and some received financial subsidies while others did not. In 1934 out of the six million population slightly over five million were Bulgarian Orthodox, 820,000 were Muslim, 48,000 Jews, 46,000 Roman Catholic (of which about 6,000 were of the Eastern Rite), and 8,000 Protestants. There was also an Armenian Apostolic Church.

In the period between the two wars the relationship between the religious communities was basically good, and one could classify Bulgaria at that time as a country with features of both Type A and Type B or Religious Toleration societies. Politically, however, there was great instability, as the country with no previous democratic experience struggled to get used to a multi-party system. The brief experience with elections gave way to a series of coups which was capped off by a coup by King Boris who proclaimed a royal dictatorship in 1935.

Hoping to gain Macedonian territories that Bulgarians regarded as part of a "Great Bulgaria" the king, whose family ties were German, entered Bulgaria into World War II on the side of the Axis which rewarded Bulgaria with annexation of sizeable Macedonian territories from Yugoslavia and Greece. The war did not bring considerable changes in regard to religious liberties except to the Jews and those Christian missions that had personnel from the Allied countries. An anti-Jewish legislation was adopted in January 1941 in the form of a "Law in defense of the Nation."[3] The Jewish population from the annexed Yugoslav and Greek territories suffered deportation by the Nazis to the death camps, but the Jewish population of Bulgaria proper was protected from that fate. They were exiled from the cities to the countryside. When in 1948/49 Bulgaria allowed free Jewish emigration to Israel all but around 6,000 secularized Jews emigrated, reducing the Jewish religious presence practically to nill.[4] As to the lands gained in World War II, they were lost again as a result of the Allied victory that also placed Bulgaria firmly into the Soviet orbit.

BEFORE THE GREAT TRANSFORMATION

II. Period of the Fatherland Front. 1944–1947

After the Soviet invasion of Bulgaria the country was placed under the Allied Control Commission, but was *de facto* ruled by the Soviets. Georgi Dimitrov, an internationally known Bulgarian communist who had been living in the USSR returned to Bulgaria and was named Prime Minister in a provisional government consisting of representatives of various political parties, united in the pro-Communist "Fatherland Front." In the period from the fall 1944 to fall 1947 the Communists increasingly took over the controls of the country until the complete take-over was effected by December 1947. Corresponding to the gradual take-over by the Communists there was a gradual intervention in the religious sphere, although the churches welcomed the end of the war and the re-alignment of the government with the Allies. Historically there had been much pro-Russian sentiment, which was to become a dominant feature in the country's life.

As early as September 1944, that is a few days after the Soviet occupation, the murder, disappearance, execution or imprisonment without trial of high Orthodox clergy took place.[5] These were omens of the onset of a government policy that intended the crushing or full domination of the churches. This happened despite the signing of the Armistice Agreement of Bulgaria with Great Britain, U. S. and USSR that guaranteed human rights and religious freedom. The attacks on clergy and believers was generally justified by real and imaginary collaboration with the Germans during the war. They took place despite the almost instantenous pro-Russian orientation by the Bulgarian Orthodox Church.

By January 1946 the Department of Religious Affairs of the Ministry of Foreign Affairs (hereafter Ministry of Foreign Affairs and Cults or MFAC) abolished by decree prayer and religious education in all schools and in the army, and pastoral appointments and dismissals were made by the same MFAC, despite protests by the Orthodox Church. Dimitrov announced the intention to separate church and state, to which the Orthodox Church objected but which the Protestants welcomed as they saw it as giving them equal rights with the Orthodox. In order to embarrass the Orthodox Church, Prime Minister Georgi Dimitrov characterized the Bulgarian hierarchy as "old men with fossilized brains" in their presence during a reception for Patriarch Alexei of Moscow at the Rila monastery in May 1946. The government also vigorously promoted a Union of Orthodox Clergy which was, in Spas Raikin's words, "hysterically pro-government"[7] in order to sow internal weakness in the church. Further obstructions were placed toward the work of religious education in the church and religious publishing.

When a Peace Treaty was signed on September 16, 1947, between Bulgaria and the Allies the Bulgarian government again guaranteed human rights and religious liberty.[8] This was a smokescreen as was the Constitution; the Communists had already decided to crush or deny any autonomy to the churches.

III. The Communist Reign of Terror, 1948–1953

A. General Trends

By the end of 1947 the Bulgarian Communist Party was firmly in power having practically eliminated all the other parties.[9] On December 4, 1947, a Constitution was adopted which was so remarkably like the Soviet Constitution of 1936 that it is unnecessary to present the pertinent text. It suffices to say that Article 76 separates church and state and guarantees freedom of conscience, religion, and the performing of religious rituals and prohibiting the misuse of religion for political purposes. The Constitution states that the activities of religious communities will be regulated by a separate law but that they are self-regulated.[10] In a separate communication to the Synod of the Bulgarian Orthodox Church it was forbidden to criticize the government but rather pressured to embrace the principle of the domination of the state over the church and to support government measures from the pulpit, yet stay out of active politics.[11]

One of the most brutal periods of terror in the history of Communist Eastern Europe began to be instituted which affected all political, cultural, economic, and religious aspects of life, including many Communists, even those from the very top of the leadership.[12] The strategy is clear in retrospect. In order to frighten the majority Bulgarian Orthodox Church into full submission the government first inflicted enormous suffering upon the leadership of the Protestant Churches, nearly destroying them, and then soon after unleashed a persecution of the somewhat larger Roman Catholic Church. It turned out to be a most effective strategy in gaining nearly complete control and subservience of practically all religious groups. Since unique evidence became available of the brutal persecution of the Protestants, a lengthier account of the strategy and methods of repression will be presented here.[13] Since similar methods were used in Romania, Hungary, and Czechoslovakia against some religious leaders, it will not be necessary to repeat the details in the corresponding chapters.

The gradual process of taking control over the Protestant churches commenced in 1947 with the issuance of the "Regulations for the Organization and Administration of the Evangelical Churches in the People's Republic of Bulgaria."[14] According to the regulations the Congregational, Baptist, Pentecostal, and Methodist Churches were to be recognized by the government as forming the Union of the Allied Evangelical Churches in Bulgaria under the administration of the MFAC with which they were to communicate through the Evangelical Religious Representative, elected by the denominations and approved by the DRA. The churches would have the right to confess their creeds and carry out their worship and religious services, if those did not infringe upon the laws and public ofder as well as "good customs" of Bulgaria.

An evangelical local church could be organized by at least twenty believers and could not be organized by a foreign citizen. A church was to be ruled by a Spiritual Council and a Board of Trustees to which only Bulgarian citizens and nationals could be elected, not less than twenty–one years old and not having been deprived of political and civil rights. The budget of the evangelical churches consisting of voluntary gifts, membership fees and similar income, would have to be submitted to the DRA and would be examined by MFAC and the Ministry of Finance. The annual report of the churches would also have to be submitted to the same authority.

Each evangelical church would be restricted to only one pastor, with exceptions granted only in emergency cases by the MFAC. All pastors would have to be confirmed by this Ministry on pain of criminal prosecution. Pastoral requirements were: (1) to be Bulgarian citizens of Bulgarian origin, (2) to be over twenty–five years of age, (3) to have regulated their military service, (4) to have at least secondary education, (5) not to have been under legal inquest or have been condemned to imprisonment nor deprived of political and civil rights, and (6) to have good repuhtion in the community. In addition they were forbidden to do anything inconsistent with their vocation and to perform any services to evangelicals of other denominations. Religious worship in the open was to be permitted only in exceptional cases by the local administrative authorities. Violators of the Regulations could be punished by reprimand, temporary dismissal from service for a year, and by permanent dismissal. The individual statutes of each denomination would have to comply with the regulations and would have to eliminate all that is contrary to these regulations and to be obliged to be elaborated where necessary to include the provisions of the Regulations. The statutes would then be considered for approval by the Ministry.

Such flagrant and open intrusion in the internal affairs of the churches by the state, which simultaneously proclaimed separation of church and state and prohibited the mixing of churches in state affairs, could not go without protest by the Protestants. It is likely that all denominations registered displeasure and protest. The pastors of the Methodist Church met in Sofia on May 29, 1947, under the leadership of Superintendent Yanko Ivanov and discussed the Regulations and agreed unanimously to a common resolution.[15]

In the resolution the Methodist pastors stated that they were glad that the recognition of evangelical churches was placed on the agenda, but that the Regulations were an unacceptable solution of the mutual relation of the Protestants and the government.

> This question could be resolved only when, above all other things, the Honorable Ministry shall recognize the Discipline, i.e. the fundamental statutes of the Methodist Church, and eventually the corresponding statutes of the separate evangelical denominations.[16]

The pastors stated that the administration and creeds of a church is the outcome of an historical and religious process and could not be changed by a law passed by the government. The Discipline of the Methodist Church, the regulations of a world-wide church, obligatory to each national branch of that church, could not be amended by the Mission Conference but only by the General Conference. The pastors stated that the historical services of the Methodists to the Bulgarian nation entitled them to the approval of their Discipline. They considered this moment as the most opportune moment for such approval. They requested the Supreme Council of the People's Republic of Bulgaria to withdraw the Regulations as they represented "an inaccurate forestalling and unjustifiable treatment of a matter already considered by the project of the Constitution.[17]

The Communist government did not allow any group, especially not a religious group, to oppose its measures. The pastors acted with the supposition that Bulgaria was a democratic country. Only later did they learn that opposition is not tolerated by the Communists.

B. The New State-Church Relations

When the short-lived government of Constantin Muraviev was ousted at the end of the war, the new provisional Communist-dominated government, established by the Soviet Union, declared on September 21, 1944, that it hoped to separate Church and State and to provide toleration and religious liberty. This was welcomed by Methodists and Congregationalists because they would be placed on equal footing with the Orthodox Church, formerly the state church, to which they were historically rivals. They struggled for religious toleration and equality since their beginnings in Bulgaria. The armistice between the Allies and Bulgaria, concluded on October 28, 1944, guaranteed such human right and religious liberties.[18]

During the year 1945 the approach of the pro-Communist *Otechestven Front* ("Fatherland Front") and the Communist Party toward the churches was cautious but not unfriendly. There was only a minimal persecution of churches and clergy in the mass trials against alleged and real war criminals,[19] but the churches and pastors were little involved, and did not raise their voices against these purges. Two Bulgarian Methodist pastors were imprisoned in 1944 because they had accepted employment with German commercial agencies during the war, and one of them was given a life sentence, later commutted to seven years, while the other was acquitted.[20]

Gradually restrictions were imposed. A decree issued in January 1946 banned religious education in schools, permitting private religious instructions upon parental requests. The MFAC was to approve pastoral appointment.[21] The schools soon became the center of antireligious propaganda under orders not to teach Christian virtues of love, forgiveness, and humility, which were held to be signs of weaknesses. The printing of religious publications became increasingly difficult as the church leaders were allowed to print only pre-censored articles. Premier Georgi Dimitrov made it known that religious leaders would not be persecuted but that the government did not want any "nests of reaction"; they therefore should stick to "spiritual" work.[22]

But in direct contradiction to this demand Protestants were asked to write a statement of propaganda value for Bulgaria for the Paris Peace Conference in 1947. The government knew that they had good Western connections. But the statement was written without Protestant participation, proclaiming that they were completely satisfied with the degree of religious liberties in Bulgaria.[23] Vasil Ziapkov, the religious representative of the Union of Allied Evangelical Churches was sent as a delegate to this Conference to negotiate in the best interest of Bulgaria.[24] He was considered as the pastor most cooperative with the Communist regime, known by conservative elements as "Red Ziapkov."[25] He was not a Communist, but he believed that Protestant churches would be recognized as progressive and permitted to enjoy the favor and prosperity, or at least be able to function. He therefore sought to participate in the affairs of the state. Ziapkov said that the govaernment looked with favor upon the Protestants and that no harm would befall them. In a written report to the Ministry of Foreign Affairs under the title "The Fatherland and the Evangelical Churches," he acclaimed the government for granting the evangelicals rights equal to those of other churches and for assisting them in rebuilding some of their churches as well as aiding them in their religious publications.[26] Ziapkov established good relations with the Director of MFAC, Dimitr Iliev, and was even invited by Premier Georgi Dimitrov to go with him to the grave of the communist Premier's mother who had been a Protestant from Samokov.[27]

After 1946 or before, secret agents were sent to make stenographic records of all sermons and the Ministry of Interior demanded church records and lists of the leadership and membership.[28] However, the Constitution of December 4, 1947, still proclaimed religious equality and prohibited religious hatred. The use of churches for political purposes was indeed prohibited, but the "freedom of conscience and religion and of performing religious rites" was guaranteed.[29] Despite this and efforts to gain support, the Protestants soon became an object of displeasure of the government. Secret instructions were sent to local and provincial Fatherland Front organizations, in which the alleged Western imperialistic war efforts were linked with the Protestant churches, whose pastors were branded as spies and saboteurs of the new social order, who allegedly demoralized the people by preaching about human impotence and God's omnipotence. The demand was that these local organizations expose as many pastors as possible as reactionaries and Western agents.[30]

Behind this action was, of course, the aim of the Communists to control all strata of society. Beside the Catholics the Evangelicals were the sole organized group outside the Fatherland Front. They adhered to an ideology different from the Communist, and there were cases when the church membership had criticized the pastor if he approved even of some moderate communist ideas.[31] It was the churches which held out the longest against Communist ideas. They were led by men of stature who could become potential leaders of the opposition after the Bulgarian intelligentsia was dispersed and all other political opposition ruthlessly destroyed.[32]

Before the war the Bulgarians evangelicals had been largely apolitical.[33] Later they remained in essence the same, but the increasing government hostility put them on the defensive. Their traditional ecclesiastical connections with the West, and activities that were previously regarded as permissible in Bulgaria, and still regarded in democratic countries as exercises of normal right, became the target of hatred by the Communists. In their religious and in cultural activities, the Bulgarian Protestants kept close relations with the West. The visits of western Church leaders representing the individual denominations or officials of the World Council of Churches and its agencies, were disliked by the Communists, despite their make-believe interest and cordiality.[34] Material aid from the West both for relief purposes and for support of evangelistic work, increased the hostility of the Communist. The Communists could not believe that this aid was given without political strings attached with evil intentions against Bulgaria; they had been used to receiving aid from the Soviet Union for their own revolutionary activities and secret plots and therefore assumed that all other groups supported from abroad were engaging in the same kind of shady operations.[35] The Communists were also opposed to religion in general and did not want to allow the financial support to extend the existence of churches. Only the Congregationalists had been more or less self-supporting for the past twenty years. The others were dependent on foreign support and the pastoral salaries were dependent on this aid. The churches were grateful for this aid as they were for the relief. They were permitted to distribute a part of the money sent by the World Council of Churches or other groups to their members in order that no American religious propaganda would be made among other Bulgarians,[36] while the government distributed most of the aid through the Red Cross, without the people knowing the benefactor.

As time passed, pressure on the Churches was stepped up. In June 1948 the church leaders received instructions from minister Iliev not to criticize the government, to support the process of nationalization, to counteract all anti-Communist and anti-Russian propaganda from the pulpit and in the religious press, to display portraits of the state leaders in churches and admonish their parishioners to love and obey them, to join the Fatherland Front and acknowledge the supremacy of the state over the church.[37]

In July 1948 the editors of the Protestant periodical *Zornitsa* were advised as to what might be published. A new drive was organized by the government to induce the pastors to join the Fatherland Front or the Communist Party under the threat of arrest,[38] but the pastors held themselves aloof from this proposal. The edict of August 3, 1948, forbidding all foreign schools,[39] affected also the Methodist-sponsored American Girls' School in Lovech.

The end of 1948 saw the climax of religious persecutions in most East European countries. The Bulgarian Communists were no exception. They wanted to demonstrate their firmness in dealing with churches. The Protestants were politically and numerically the weakest and thus the best target for "the iron heel." Such treatment was intended to silence political opposition and frighten Protestants and others into compliance.

A blueprint of Communist planning is discernible in the events of these months. First, ideological and propaganda "power levers" were applied, then a score of Protestant ministers and prominent laymen were imprisoned. By unrestricted coercion confessions of various alleged crimes were extracted. The official aim was to adopt a stiff law against churches after getting public support through a great public show-trial. The leaderless Protestants and the scared leaders of the other churches would then accept the law which subjected them to the state.

Such a law was passed on February 24, 1949, to govern church and state relations.[40] Vasil Kolarov, the Vice-President of the Council of Minister stated one of its aims:

> Our law on religious Creeds is aimed at preventing the Bulgarian servants of the church from becoming agents, who, under the veil of religion, can supply foreign political centers with information which, according to the law of all countries is considered a state secret.[41]

Under the new law freedom of religion and conscience, separation of church and state, and freedom of worship were still provided within the legal framework. The guidance of each church was still to be by its own statutes, provided these were not contrary to the law and were approved by the Minister of Foreign Affairs. It was confirmed that the churches could be built, and services held in them, but open air services and local or national church congresses or conferences were to be held only with police permission.[42]

The law further said that the leadership of the churches was to be responsible to the state and that it must be registered with the state authorities. Those who had been appointed from abroad for canonical or organizational reasons, must be confirmed by the Minister of Foreign Affairs. The churches were to be voluntarily supported by their own members but they might also be subsidized by the state provided they "loyally collaborate with the People's Government."[43] Church budgets must be submitted to the Ministry of Foreign Affairs, and are under the supervision of the state financial organs as all public organizations. Theological schools fell also under the control of the MFAC, who had the right to censor pastoral letters. Educational, welfare, and social work formerly carried on by churches were now no longer permitted and were to be expropriated. Foreign conacts and correspondence were not permitted unless specifically allowed by the MFAC. Missions from abroad were to be closed within a month, while material support from abroad might be received again only with government permission. Only ministers who had not been imprisoned and those with full civil rights might serve.

C. The Trial of the Fifteen Protestant Pastors

A wave of imprisonment of Bulgarian Protestant leaders was quietly begun early in 1948 when several provincial pastors were detained for "traveling without permit." Director Iliev of the MFAC, with whom a protest was lodged, explained that this did not concern his office since these were only local incidents.[44] Some evangelicals had been questioned by secret police agents in 1946 and 1947. Dimitr Nedelyakov of the YMCA was sentenced to ten years in prison because of his connection with the sons of former missionaries. These people and their parents, especially Floyd Black, former president of the American College in Sofia, were assailed as sinister agents of imperialism, together with military personnel of the Allied Control Commission, ecclesiastical functionaries, and various British and

American embassy diplomatic and military personnel, were branded as international spies. Any social contact of a Bulgarian with them was regarded later as traitorous, as were any contacts with the church leaders from abroad, whether from denominational, ecumenical or relief purposes. Opposition to Communism was interpreted as opposition to Bulgaria. The limited aid which various politicians and church members gave to the Allied Control Commission was also later interpreted as traitorous. Meanwhile the close co-operation of Bulgarian Communists with Soviet representatives, to whom no state secret was unknown and who gave instructions to them as to how to run their country,[45] was praised as a friendly act of a friendly government. Bulgarian Communist agents had gathered information as to the relations between the denominations, their means of support and ideology, the peculiarities of each denomination, their internal dissensions, and the careers of outstanding persons.[46]

A full scale attack started in April 1948, when Mitko Mateev, a Baptist pastor, was arrested for alleged black-marketing. Then he was released but visited every night by persons, probably secret agents.[47] In June he was again arrested. Of the fifteen pastors[48] tried in a body in February 1949, Mateev was the longest in prison. His will more broken than that of the others, he allegedly turned into a tool of the secret agents.[49]

The program of psychological pressure was applied in several (six) stages.

The first stage was the detailed study of the character of the accused, his reactions, and strength of his conviction.[50] Interest was displayed by the investigators in character flaws or past mistakes of the accused.

The second stage was the cross-examination under all kinds of physical and mental stresses, and complete isolation, and anxiety about the fate of one's family. Hope is offered only if the accused signs a confession. At least one evangelical was taken out of town at night and was told to dig his own grave, as if they were going to shoot him. They took him back, but the next night, after he refused again to sign a prepared confession, he was again taken to the same spot and was told to dig additional graves for his wife and child; this time he broke down and agreed to sign, but he had a mental breakdown and was declared insane.[51] During this process strange concepts were gradually impressed on the victim's tired mind, and things which he is known to cherish were represented as obstacles of "progressive" humankind. In time his will broke down, and new concepts were accepted.

In the third stage came an investigation of the activities of the accused, in great detail, and giving the normal activities hostile connotations. The state security then prepared the case, and constantly changed the charges according to continuous reinterpretations of testimonies. Testimonies of those who had given in were used to induce those more stubborn to make admissions. The accused having lost his own volition did not realize the extent of his incrimination, while those of weaker character started to believe what they are told to admit. Small facts were given absurd interpretations, and new "facts" were invented. Thus conversations with foreigners in which some well-known difficulties of Bulgaria were informally mentioned were taken to mean traitorous activity; the receiving of relief from abroad was taken to mean receiving of money for espionage; the study in a seminary abroad was interpreted as the process of being drafted for foreign intelligence; a private conversation between two friends about Bulgarian internal matters became plotting against the government or inciting to unrest, and so on.

Seemingly pastor Ziapkov was the primary target of this stage, for he was in the past sympathetic to socialism and to the government, and therefore, it was difficult to find any grounds against him. Because of his weak nervous system and his near-blindness, the pressure upon him was difficult to bear. His despair and disappointment seem to have caused nervous shocks during which he cried much.[52]

After this "basic work" was done, in the period of three to eight months, the individual entered a fourth stage lasting up to three months more in which he was isolated and left to contemplate what he did, or placed in a cell with a provocator, who tried to get out from him some additional information. They were often left without food and left under the impression of being abandoned by the family and friends. Told repeatedly to write about his misdeeds by the end of this stage he started to accept them as true.

A stage followed which differs entirely from the previous ones. After months of solitude the accused met a new set of investigators who, without abuse told him of the possibility of his being incorporated in the process of building a new society if he repents and becomes a new man, of the possibility of a light sentence, and the like. They told him that it is unbelievable that he had been tortured and that they will punish any investigators who did such things. Occasional visits with the members of the family may be arranged; better food and good cells might be provided; sleep was allowed; the investigators became polite—all this building up unjustified hope in the accused that if he goes along he will be spared.

The final stage consisted of the declaration by the accused of his willingness to live a new life. The "good inspectors" do not let him forget that he depended upon their mercy, giving him hope of being released soon, if he were to correct his mistakes by publicly repenting. He was made to realize the terrible alternatives, concentration camps, or death for him and his family.

The Bulgarian Communists denied the truth of coercive acquisition of confessions labelling them as being slanderous of Bulgaria, as if the attack on their inquisitional method had anything whatsoever to do with the people of Bulgaria. They said that the accused had talked for periods up to six hours at the trial, certainly not a likely achievement for tortured people and that the accused were "clean shaved, with pomaded hair and neatly pressed pants."[53] Testimonies of the accused Pentecostal pastor Haralan Popov and Western church leaders implicated in the trial stand diametrically opposed to this denial. Pastor Haralan Popov provided detailed accounts of the dreadful tortures that he had to undergo before his trial and during the prison term. The four leaders of the denominations were given life imprisonment, another four were given 15 year sentences, three were sentenced to 10 years, one to 8 years and 8 months, one to 5, and two received a suspended sentence of one year.

Ten months after the great public trial a smaller trial was held unannounced by the press. Ten Protestant pastors were hurriedly tried and sentenced from one to ten years in prison. Many other pastors were never tried but spent as many as five years in prison and concentration camps. A number of those died very soon after their release. More cooperative pastors were placed in leadership positions and the church membership declined rapidly amidst fear and suspicion.

That all these measures were taken in order to destroy religion and bring churches under Communist control is evident from the attempt to break the Roman Catholic Church in 1952 by a very similar public trial of twenty-eight priests, at least one of whom, the Bishop of Nikopolis, Evgenii Bosilkov was executed.[54] The Catholic leaders were accused of spying for the Vatican, concealing weapons, and anti-Communist propaganda. For all practical purposes the activities of the Catholic Church were halted as effectively as were the Protestant. The only religious communities that were not openly persecuted were the Jews and the Armenians, the members of both having largely emigrated to Israel and Soviet Armenia respectively.

Having crushed the potential opposition by Protestants and Roman Catholics who had possible support from abroad the Bulgarian Orthodox Church that had no such connections was sufficiently intimidated and caved in. To be sure they did not escape the general terror either. Many village priests as well as archimandrites Paladi of Vidin, Iriney of Sofia, and Nahum of Ruse were simply murdered while metropolitans Paisi of Vratsa and Kiril of Plovdiv (the future patriarch) were imprisoned and tortured. Imprisoned were hundreds of clergy, high and low, some with and some without trials.[55] Hierarchs were placed in office and removed by political intervention. Particularly puzzling is the case of Metropolitan Stefan of Sofia who had been elevated to the position of Exarchs[56] of the Bulgarian Orthodox Church in 1945 with government support. Mysteriously he resigned in September 1948 and without a trial was placed in life-long house arrest in the village of Banya. The official explanation was that the resignation was due to exclusively internal church affairs, but Spas Raikin, having explored the issue carefully, indicates that the real reason for Exarch Stefan's removal was the government's distrust.[57] Raikin concludes that:

> [g]radually the church was transformed into an obedient and useful tool in the hands of the government. In exchange, it was allowed to register some ostensibly important but in practice hollov gains, among them the restoration of the patriarchate in 1953.[58]

The national shrine and holiest place, the Rila Monastery was taken away from the Church and converted into a museum, many of its treasures were stolen, and activities sometimes bordering on desecration were conducted there.[59]

Thus the government fully controlled the much weakened churches by 1953, and religious freedom was reduced to a minimum, i.e. to a status comparable to the status of churches in the Soviet Union, whom the Bulgarian government consciously emulated.

In 1950 the government also moved harshly against the Muslim Turks by exiling about one-third of the most religiously oriented one's to Turkey. The rest were to be assimilated and atheized.[60]

IV. Stagnation. 1953–1989

From 1953 until 1989 a very stable period ensued, one due to stagnation in church-state relationship. The government, having assumed full control over the religious institutions by terror and infiltration, saw no reason to alter the situation. In comparison to the previous period the terror lessened, and the government in due time released some of the clergy whose prison terms came to an end. But the religious institutions continued their life in isolation; only minor contacts with international religious agencies, primarily the Prague centered Christian Peace Conference and Soviet-based religious activities and the World Council of Churches were attended by a small, selected group of clergy. The formal connections of the churches that had headquarters outside of the country were not allowed,[61] though some of the Catholic Bishops were permitted to attend the sessions of the Second Vatican Council.

The 1971 Constitution brought no legal changes in the status of the churches. Generally the legislation had no appreciable effect on actual policies. Article 39 makes the Communist education of youth the responsibility of the entire society. Article 20 of the Constitution stating that the training and education of the youth is the exclusive prerogative of the state was interpreted in such a way as to prohibit all religious education of children under sixteen years of age,[62] bringing Bulgaria completely in line with Soviet practice. The government skillfully used the churches, especially the Bulgarian Orthodox Church, for the promotion of its own foreign policy agenda, namely to portray itself and the Soviet Union as peace-loving nations, to attack the West as warmongering, to proclaim that Bulgaria offers full religious liberty to all its citizens, and to promote Bulgarian patriotism at home and abroad among the emigrants, including claims that all Macedonians are Bulgarians. Spas Raikin pointed out that for the leadership of the Bulgarian Orthodox Church Bulgarian nationalism was more important than the gospel.[63] He stated that the millennia long service of the Orthodox Church to Bulgarian nationalism was a "service that it had agreed to perform for the present Communist regime in Bulgaria with enthusiasm and without reservations."[64] The Orthodox Church was also a strong promoter of Russophilism, which also coincided with the interests of the Communist Party.

While in Bulgaria the Orthodox Church rarely received public acknowledgement except when it was useful in promoting nationalism the publications intended for consumptions by Bulgarian emigrants were replete with pictures and statements of church figures. Bulgarian hierarchs frequently travelled West where they succeeded in rallying the Bulgarian Orthodox Churches to support or at least not to politically oppose the regime. The Bulgarian Orthodox Church was particularly helpful in bolstering Bulgarian claims to Macedonia and in endorsing the notion that the non-Orthodox population was somehow nationalistically alienated people who need to return to the unity of all Bulgarians. This the Orthodox Church could do in good conscience and enthusiasm because Bulgarian nationalism was, indeed, a shared faith and the Orthodox Church would stand to gain with this emphasis on the unity of all Bulgarians.

The Bulgarian Orthodox Church, basically a poor church in the past and in the present, continued to be dependent on state subsidies that were skillfully used by the govenment to bring the hierarchs into complete obedience. The Bulgarian Orthodox Church found itself in an asymmetrical relationship with the government in which on the one hand it became a close handmaiden of the government in promoting patriotism yet being hard-pressed by the government's virulent atheist propaganda and control.[65] Raikin concluded: "The communist state has reduced the Orthodox church to a state of absolute impotence. . . . This policy has been carried to the point of total annihilation of religious freedom."[66]

The only strong rejection of this process of assimilation came from the Muslims. The Turks live generally isolated from the mainstream of Bulgarian life in compact areas, and already in 1950–1951 there was a deliberate attempt to thin them out by exiling as many as 250,000 of them to Turkey, until Turkey closed its borders.[67] The government of Todor Zhivkov promoted the notion that all or nearly all Muslims in Bulgaria are ethnic Bulgarians whose ancestors have been forcefully converted to Islam and that they now present a population really and potentially disloyal.[68] In 1984 he commenced a campaign to reclaim them for the Bulgarian nation by changing their Muslim names to Bulgarian ones, to stop using the Turkish language and symbols (including the flag) and to stop all Muslim religious and cultural practices, such as circumcision.[69] The number of their hodjas and imams was drastically reduced and their contacts with Mulims other the Soviet one's was nearly eliminated. Amnesty International and other organizations, Western and Muslim, and, of course, Turkey itself, pointed to the harassment, persecution and even murder of Muslims who refused the process of Bulgarization. To rebuff these charges Bulgaria mounted a propaganda barrage which included testimonies by Syrian and South Yemeni Muslim leaders, as well as Bulgarian academics and other figures all maintaining that this is a matter of internal affairs of Bulgaria and that these Bulgarian Muslims are granted full religious freedom.[70] The seven *muftis*, including the grand *mufti* of Bulgaria also claimed that there were no barriers to their freedom.[71] Many Bulgarians were convinced that it was only right that Bulgaria be a country with one homogeneous nation and that the descendants of those allegedly Turkicized Bulgarians return to their original nationality. The Turkish population protested that they were not Bulgarians but to no avail. Bulgarians generally blamed the entire international incident to hostile military intentions of Turkey toward Bulgaria.

While prior to 1988 the Turks had great difficulties leaving Bulgaria, suddenly the policy was reversed so that those who are unwilling to Bulgarize were forced to leave for Turkey on a short notice, often without the right to take their belongings. About 300,000 out of the approximately one million Turkish Muslims were expatriated.[72] Those who returned to Bulgaria, after unsuccessful attempts to find jobs in Turkey, were paraded as proofs of the correctness of Todor Zhivkov's policies. But, in fact, such policies were implemented ruthlessly and with much violence, repeated incarceration, beatings, and attempts to hide and flee on part of the Turks.[73] After Zhivkov was removed from office by a 'palace revolution' on November 10, 1989, the government of Premier Georgi Atanassov declared that it will abandon attempts of forcible Bulgarization of the Turks upon which a number of large spontaneous street demonstratiom took place against that decision. Slogans such as "Bulgaria—a one-nationality country" were carried by protesters.[74] Later the government representatives and opposition groups sought to establish a policy which would guarantee each person to freely chose their name and practice their own religion.[75]

"The Bulgarian connection" in the attempted papal assassination[76] and the treatment of the Muslim minority created a lot of negative world public opinion which prompted Lyubomir Popov, the deputy foreign minister and chief of the "Committee for the Affairs of the Bulgarian Orthodox Church and of the Religious Denominations" to write a rather positive evaluation of the role and future of the churches, particularly the Bulgarian Orthodox in the newspaper

Otechestven front [Fatherland Front].[77] However, control and harassment over the internal life of the churches, especially the unregistered charismatic "Church of God,"[78] the imprisonment and internal exile of those clergy who seemed to the regime unreliable continued until the fall of 1989.[79] Thus a Sofia Methodist pastor, Petar Hristov, in whose church Bulgarian and foreign visitors could mingle was punished by a life-long prohibition to practice his profession when he refused to be transferred from the Sofia church by his "bishop" Ivan Nozharov.[80] The ban was lifted in October 1989.[81]

The policies of Secularist Absolutism, Type D, were quite successful in Bulgaria. The Bulgarian Orthodox Church was passive and collaborated with the government. The Roman Catholics and Protestants were effectively supressed, except that some of the Pentecontalists increased their tiny membership living on the fringes of society. The Muslims were likewise oppressed but were a serious problem to the government as they resisted assimilation and atheization. The Jews and Armenians moved out. The religious communities were unable to offer any serious dissent to the effective policies of denial of religious liberties.

AFTER THE GREAT TRANSFORMATION

The Upheaval of 1989

Occasionally the government of Todor Zhivkov would pay lip-service to *perestroika* and *glasnost*, but in fact continued its Stalinist practices until the Fall of 1989. Prior to 1988 there were no organized dissident activities. But under the impact of Gorbachev's *perestroika* and changes in other East European countries and the opportunity for international attention created by an ecological conference that took place in Sofia there were increasing signs of small-scale dissident activities. The first one was the Independent Association for the Defence of Human Rights in Bulgaria founded in January 1988 which had some Christian and Muslim members.[82] Some of the groups were religious, such as the Independent Committee for the Defence of Religious Rights, Freedom of Conscience and Spiritual Values, a primarily Bulgarian Orthodox group headed by the hieromonk, Hristofor Shubev, a former scientist, founded in October 1989.[83] They were all quickly repressed by exile, imprisonment or psychiatric confinement. Hristofor Shubev, who was also one of the founders of the independent underground labor organization *Podkrepa*, was first exiled to a monastery in early 1989 then imprisoned in June and released in September, 1989.[84] He had supported not only Orthodox rights but also those of Muslims. The Holy Synod of the Bulgarian Orthodox Church fiercely condemned Shubev and his colleagues. An unholy aliance was formed between the Council on Religious Affairs and the church authorities to silence the dissent.[85] The official church authorities declared that there was no need for any one to defend the right of believers since there was religious freedom in the country, and Patriarch Maxim sent a request to Lyubomir Popov of the Council for Religious Affairs not to register the Independent Committee. Upon his release Shubev organized prayers in the St. Dimitr Cathedral in Sofia for those who were persecuted and denied their rights and for the opposition.[86] After Shubev's release and just five weeks prior to Todor Zhivkov's fall the Independent Committee sent a petition to the National Assembly asking for changes in legislation on religion in order to make the Bulgarian laws consistent with the Universal Declaration of Human Rights and the Helsinki Accords. This petition was signed also by Zhelyu Zhelev, who was to become President of the Republic in the Summer of 1990. But the leadership of the Orthodox Church did not seem to be moved by the signs of change, as evident from their rejection of Shubev.

November 10, 1989, will long be remebered as the pivotal point of the Great Tranformation. Upon the fall of Zhivkov, Petar Mladenov, a more reformist minded Communist, became briefly the new head of the government. Encouraged by the political changes thousands Orthodox, Catholics, and Protestants protested in Sofia asking for greater religious liberties.[87] The Union of Democratic Forces, a coalition of groups which included the Independent Committee, requested in December a constitutional guarantee of equality of believers and unbelievers and a new non-restrictive law on religion as well as the abolishment of the Committee for the Affairs of the Bulgarian Orthodox Church and the Religious Denominations.[88] The representatives of the Protestant churches (Baptist, Church of God, Congregationalists, Methodist, Pentecostalist) met on December 24 and organized the "Initiative Committee for Contacts Between Evangelical Christians in Bulgaria" consisting of Baptist, Congregationalist, Methodist, Pentecostal, and the Church of God representatives and passed the following resolution:

1. Evangelical Christians in Bulgaria support *"perestroika"* which is now taking place in our country.

2. We demand that the new law of religious freedom be enacted and it is the wish of the believers that all restrictions on work with children and youth be discarded.

3. For decades there were many house searches and actions of the secret police. Thousands of Bibles and Christian literature were seized. Also thousands of *"leva"* [currency of Bulgaria] of church money, as well as video and audio cassettes with spiritual music and films were confiscated. We demand as a small compensation that we officially be permitted to import within the country for church purposes, 10,000 Bibles, 10,000 hymnals, as well as Christian literature.

4. We demand the organization of a new evangelical Christian youth association.

5. We demand permission to print a new edition of the evangelical newspaper named *Zornitsa*–[Morning Star].

6. We support the organization of an Evangelical Alliance of Bulgaria.

7. We demand that Christmas and Easter be celebrated in Bulgaria as official holidays.

By the end of December of 1989 and January 1990 political pluralism was declared as the operating principle in Bulgaria, leading to a multi-party system, free elections in June 1990, and presumably, as a result, potentially to the freeing of the churches from slavery to the state. Bulgarian Orthodox and Muslim leaders noticed that they did not have to remain subservient to the government and started raising their own demands. The Grand *Mufti*, Nedyo Gendzhev declared that there was discrimination and restrictions of religious activities of the Muslims, that Muslims be allowed their Islamic names and that they needed a theological school.[89] The Movement for the Rights and Freedoms of Turks and Muslims was created early in 1990 and so did a Christian Democratic Party and a Christian Republican Party. On December 18, 1989, the Holy Synod of the Bulgarian Orthodox Church sent to the National Assembly a list of 28 proposals seeking return of church property, permission to build new churches, availability of religious literature and, most importantly, constitutional and legal guarantees for complete religious liberties. Prominent Orthodox could acknowledge "the desparate situation in which the churches in Eastern Europe [were] during the totalitarian system."[90] Due to the freer atmosphere the Protestant churches were able to remove their government imposed leaders and freely elect new leaders. The Pentecostals elected Viktor Virchev, the Baptists Yordan Gospodinov, and the government formally recognized Heinrich Bolleter of Zurich, Switzerland, the episcopal leader of Bulgarian Methodists consistent to Methodist polity instead of the irregular "Bulgarian bishop." The Methodists were also able to reclaim properties nationalized by the government including a school in Lovech.[91] The Roman Catholics, who had not been legally recognized, complained that for them not much had changed.[92]

At the June 10, 1990, election the former Communist Party, now named Socialist Party won handily the free election with about 48 percent majority while the Union of Democratic Forces gained 34 percent.[93] But the Socialist Party's President of the Republic did not last long as political pressures continued against the former Communist and the independent intellectual former dissident. Zhelyu Zhelev, was elected to head the state on August 4, 1990. Student and other demonstrations against the domination by the former Communists continued into November when 70,000 protested in Sofia.

Perhaps more slowly than most other East European countries, Bulgaria is moving from Type C–Secularist Absolutism into which it decisively moved in 1948 to a Type B, Religious Tolerance society. All religious organizations will be legal but one may expect that the domination of the Bulgarian Orthodox Church will continue due to its far greater size than any other religious community and that religious tensions, particularly between the Bulgarian Orthodox and the Muslims will continue.[94] The non-Orthodox religious population will be at a disadvantage as the Balkan ethnic conflicts continue to flare up and the bonding between Bulgarian nationalism (ethnicity) and the Orthodox religion continue to be strong. The Bulgarian non-Orthodox religious people will continue to be suspected for being de-nationalized while the Muslims, even the Bulgarian ethnic one's will tend to be identified with Turkish interests. The rising Macedonian nationalism in Yugoslavia will increasingly make demands on the claim that Macedonians are in actuality Bulgarians and will cause as much stress in Bulgaria as the Bulgarian claims make in Yugoslavia. Thus the return to Religious Toleration, Type B society does not spell a fundamental shift in the dynamics of the relationship between the groups but it does connote far less repressive governmental intrusion in religious affairs—a definite improvement over the pre-Great Transformation time.

Chapter 7

CZECHOSLOVAKIA: A STATE WITH DEMOCRATIC TRADITIONS

Of all the countries in Eastern Europe only Czechoslovakia experienced a period of genuine democracy prior to becoming socialist. While some rudimentary forms of religious tolerance were experienced already while Czech and Slovak lands were still a part of the Austro-Hungarian Hapsburg monarchy, it found its full expression during the period between the two world wars, when Czechoslovakia was an independent multiparty parliamentary democracy. The rapid and profound democratization was due to a long-standing tradition going back to the Middle Ages.

Historical Roots

Already in the fourteenth century, when all of Europe, except perhaps Poland, was in the midst of Type A, Ecclesiastic Absolutism condition a reform movement grew in the Czech land of Bohemia, sprouted by Jan Milič of Kromeriz (1325–1375), blossomed through Jan Hus (1372–1415) and bore fruit in Bishop Jan Amos Comenius (1592–1670). The Czech Reformation was among the first movements to demand freedom for a religious quest different from the official church.[1] The two rival branches of the Hussite movement, the Utraquists and the Taborites spread in both Bohemia and Moravia and presented an alternative church that was officially recognized by the Council of Basel in 1432. The German and Swiss Reformation did not strengthen the Hussites but created more strife. The minority within the Hussite movement created the *Unitas Fratrum* (The Unity of Brethren) that was opposed and persecuted not only by the Roman Catholic Church but also by the Utraquists. By 1575 the Hussites and other Protestants succeeded to achieve sufficient unity to issue the "Czech Confession," common to all of them. Early in the sixteenth century Protestants were an overwhelming majority among the Czechs.

The Counter-Reformation organized by the Hapsburgs was repressive and violent and had a germanizing character. The emperor, Rudolf II, granted in 1609 a "Majestic Charter" by which the non-Catholic religions were given a high degree of toleration, but this toleration lasted only eleven years, and the Unity of Brethren was nearly destroyed in 1620 in the Battle of the White Mountain,[2] whereupon the Counter-Reformation ruthlessly re-established Catholicism by the Austrian Hapsburgs. Many continued to be Hussites and Protestants secretly, and there are those who say that the Hussite heritage is somehow in every Czech's make-up. Many Protestants were forced into exile. From that time onward the perception in Bohemia and Moravia was that Catholicism is anti-Czech nationalist because the Counter-Reformation was imposed by a foreign power to which initially only the Czech aristocracy acceded.[3] Thus the Hapsburgs and Roman Catholics were frequently perceived as two forms of a common enemy. Among the Czechs in particular the aversion to Hapsburg domination resulted in a sense of alienation from Catholicism, and therefore the Roman Catholic Church, to which paradoxically the vast majority of the population now belonged, was 'naturally' distrusted since for too long it had combined its interests with the Hapsburgs.

It was not until October 13, 1781, that the Hapsburg Emperor, Joseph II, issued his enlightened Edict of Toleration, that made it possible for the underground Protestant communities to be afforded limited toleration. Despite their desire to express their religious convictions in the form inherited from the Czech Reformation, this was not allowed and the 70,000 or so followers of the reformed movement had to chose between Lutheran and Reformed Churches because only they were officially tolerated but not equal by the Edict.[4]

Slovakia had an almost entirely different experience due to the fact that they were mostly under direct Hungarian domination. There Roman Catholicism never became perceived as anti-Slovak. The Protestants were not targeted for the kind of re-Catholicizing in Slovakia as they had been in the Czech lands because they were being protected by the Hungarian Protestant aristocracy. Empress Maria Theresa persecuted Slovak Protestants, but her son Joseph II changed that into a policy of religious toleration although Slovaks complained of ethnic, political, and cultural discriminations by

Hungarians.[5] In Slovakia the Protestant Slovaks tended to gather in the Lutheran Church while the Hungarians tended to gather in the Reformed Church since there were also German and Hungarian Lutherans.

In 1861 Emperor Franz Joseph I passed the Protestant Patent that gave non-Catholics personal equality before the law but not to their churches. Toleration did not mean truly equal rights; those were to be granted only upon the establishment of the independent Republic of Czechoslovakia in 1918.[6]

In the period after the creation of the Czechoslovak Republic there was such a degree of liberty for believers of all religions and unbelievers that the situation can be described as minimally Type B (Religious Toleration) and approaching Type D (Pluralistic Liberty). The lack of separation of church and state made it impossible to achieve the Pluralistic Liberty stage. The federal government passed the "Interconfessional Bill" that guaranteed completely free exercise of religion to every denomination. Proselytizing was regulated by another bill according to which a county commissioner was to examine whether the intended change of affiliation was voluntary and then issued a written notification to the respective clergy affecting an orderly transfer.[7] But laws did not stipulate discrimination at all, yet in the villages Roman Catholicism was so strongly entrenched that if one got into trouble with the Roman Catholic Church (or in other locations with the Orthodox Church) one could get in trouble socially, especially in school, where religion was being taught.[8]

Many new churches were organized. The Evangelical and Reformed Churches united into the Evangelical Church of the Czech Brethren. A fairly large movement away from Rome led to a large Catholic exodus into the Evangelical Church of the Church Brethren. An even larger schism resulted in the creation of the Czechoslovak Church in 1920 that renamed itself in 1971 as the Czechoslovak Hussite Church. The Evangelical Lutheran Church of the Augsburg Confession in Slovakia was organized in 1918 while the Silesian Lutheran Church was organized independently of other Lutheran confessions. Other religious communities, including the various "free Churches," all received full equality according to the law but did not enjoy some of the privileges of the historic churches.

The excesses of the Counter-Reformation resulted in a large-scale drift toward secularization by significant portions of the Czech population (but not the Slovak) while among church-goers it tended to promote liberalism. Among Roman Catholics there was a pronounced drift away from Rome and an internal struggle, but the Roman Catholic Church continued to remain by far the most influential religious community. Among Protestants it promoted openness toward various theological trends from the West. There was, however, a profound rift between Roman Catholics, the majority of the population, and the strong Protestant minority. The Roman Catholics anchored themselves into a priestly. i.e. institutionally hierarchical mold that would later set them up more decisively and even rigidly into a conflict with the Communists after the latter came into power. The Protestants, on the other hand, were more comfortable in taking on the prophetic posture that made it later possible to look at the Communist regime as a potential blessing, as a harsh and painful judgment of God, leading perhaps into a hopeful tomorrow. Thus the two main branches would react differently to the Communist takeover due to their mutual relationships.

Czechoslovakia was the only country in Eastern Europe in which there was a bourgeois revolution and which has a significant tradition of bourgeois liberties that no amount of repression can erase from the minds of the people. This explains why, whenever pockets of freedom appeared, such as the "Prague Spring," all freedoms re-emerged parallelly. It seems that the main factor that kept the Czechs and Slovaks from practicing and developing human rights including religious liberty at certain periods of their history were foreign interventions by the Austro-Hungarian Empire, Nazi Germany, and Stalinist Soviet Union.

Czechoslovak democracy was established by its first president, Thomas G. Masaryk (1850–1937), a man deeply committed to the promotion and development of far-reaching liberties, so that the country became the purest epitome of Type B (Religious Tolerance) in all of Eastern Europe and since people "without denomination" also received constitutional status and support[9] Czechoslovakia between the two world wars contained elements of a Type D society. The set-back was that the relationships between churches, particularly the Roman Catholic and the Protestants, were fairly strained and many conflicts occurred. No genuine separation of church and state followed despite Czech anti-clericalism and the government financed religious institutions. Church regulations when adopted by the federal parliament became the law of the land enforced by the state administration. The experience of that period as well as the spirit of the Czech Reformation left an indelibly positive imprint not only on the Protestant but also on the Roman Catholic and Eastern Orthodox population.

Among the Slovaks the adherence to Roman Catholicism was more intense though there the hierarchy's pro-Hungarian stance alienated it from the Slovak nationalism. However, among Slovak Catholics a leadership arose that accomplished "de-Magyarization" and culminated in an independent Slovak state during World War II lead by the Nazi puppet government of Monsignor Jozef Tiso. Thus in Slovakia Catholicism remained much more closely tied to the Slovak nation than the corresponding affiliation in Bohemia and Moravia.[10]

These freedoms of the interwar Czechoslovak Republic were not formally curtailed during the Nazi occupation of Czechoslovakia, except for their radical denial to the Jews. However, the entire nation was enslaved. The degree of religious tolerance depended upon the occupational authorities in Bohemia and Moravia and on the Nazi puppet government of Monsignor Tiso in Slovakia, as the country was partitioned. Certain Roman Catholic politicians succeeded to establish Roman Catholicism as the dominant political and cultural element, especially in Slovakia, severely restricting Protestantism.

In the post-war period there would be no ability for any significant Roman Catholic-Protestant cooperation or common action in respect to religious liberties because the non-Roman Catholics were suspicious that such moves may lead again to Catholic hegemony.

The fact that Western countries acceded to Hitler's conquest of Czechoslovakia through the Munich Agreement (the famous policy of appeasement) left the Czechoslovaks' trust in Western 'Christian' democracies deeply shaken and brought about a conviction that they must rely on their own powers. That led to some disillusionment with Christianity and turning to atheism. The absence of any concrete Western assistance when the Soviets and other Warsaw Pact countries crushed the "Prague Spring" in August of 1968, made the feeling of being left to their own devices even more pronounced.

FROM THE END OF WORLD WAR II TO THE GREAT TRANSFORMATION

In 1945 Czechoslovakia was re-established after the liberation by Soviet and American armed forces. It was the Soviets who made their "liberation" stick and Czechoslovakia found itself in the Soviet orbit although the multi-party democratic system in which the Communist Party played an increasing role was restored for a period of three years. After clever maneuvering with the help of Soviet authorities, the Communists carried out a *coup d'etat* in February 1948 making Czechoslovakia the last of the East European countries to become a "people's democracy." In the minds of most inhabitants their country was now deeply lodged in the East, where Soviet hegemony would dictate the course of events. Large numbers of the population regarded the Communist take-over as a national tragedy. Others accepted it more readily as they saw that the Communist Party had emerged as the largest vote-getter in the free elections of 1946.

In regard to religious liberties three periods are discernible: from 1948–1968, the "Prague Spring" of 1968, and from 1968–1989.

A. The Imposition of Stalinist Repressions, 1948–1968

Jan Milič Lochman points out that in regard to religious liberties, despite some variations,

> national religious politics has a uniform tendency in all of Eastern Europe. It arises out of a common official commitment to Marxist-Leninism. In its prevailing orthodox setting this governmental ideology includes atheism as an integral component; the attempt is consistently made to bring it to bear on all areas of life. The constitutions of most of the East European countries contain articles guaranteeing freedom of conscience and religious liberty. Yet the actual situation is different. This is not only because, as in other regions of the world, programme and reality are not in total agreement, but also because the principle of the "proportionality of freedom" is put into practice. Consequently, those who subscribe to Marxist "scientific philosophy" and those who follow "religious superstition" are not granted the same amount of freedom. The former are to be promoted, the latter are to be discouraged.[11]

That summarizes in a very mild form the situation since 1948 with a notable departure toward a more liberal vision during the "Prague Spring."

Czechoslovakia was rather suddenly plunged into full-blown Stalinism with the leaders of the Communist Party, Klement Gottwald, Antonin Zapotocky, and Antonin Novotny, all being submissive followers of the Soviet line.[12] Although among many Czechoslovak Communists there was an expectation of a "Czechoslovak path into socialism" that would follow a somewhat more social democratic path, the Soviet model of socialism was brutally imposed in the period from 1948 to 1954.[13]

The context which explains Czechoslovakia's abandonment of the Religious Toleration (Type B) and Pluralistic Liberty (Type D) models and plunging into Secularistic Absolutism (Type C)[14] is the utter victory of the Soviet Stalinist wing in the Czechoslovak Communist party over other alternatives. Karel Kaplan points out the dependence and frequent consultation of the Czechoslovak Communists with the Soviets.[15] Fred Eidlin claims that the rigidity of the Czechoslovak ideological institutional structure is due to Stalinism encountering a mass, deeply rooted democratic tradition which was asserting itself in 1945–1948, 1968, and, we may add, since 1989. In order to Stalinize, which was a distinctly foreign import, they had to impose Stalinism with the entire power of the Communist Party apparatus that made it from 1948–1968 and from 1969–1989 among the most rigidly repressive regimes in the socialist world.[16] This, indeed, seems to be the most reasonable explanation for the single-mindedness by which the Secular Absolutist model was being implemented after a successful experience with the far more permissive and enabling models of religious liberty of the more recent past. The disillusionment of many citizens with religions and the West made for a certain receptivity to look toward the East and follow the example of the USSR.[17] Indeed, Czechoslovaks voted for Communist candidates freely in large numbers (with a number of Christians joining the Communist party which was allowed until 1952) which facilitated the transition to socialism although it seems equally evident from the example of other countries that the very presence of the Soviet army would have secured a victory of the pro-Soviet forces in any case.

In the context of the victory of Stalinism a gigantic conflict took place between the Communist government and the churches, particularly the Roman Catholic Church. While the long-range strategy of the Communist government was the destruction of all religious activity, the short-range tactic, seen in retrospect, seems fairly clear, namely to clearly favor the Czechoslovak National Church and the Orthodox Church, to be flexible toward the Evangelical Church of the Czech Brethren and other main Protestant Churches and to crack down on the largest as well as the smallest churches, namely the giant Roman Catholic Church and the Greek-Catholic (Uniate) to which about two–thirds of the population belonged and the small 'sectarian' denominations, such as Salvation Army, the Mormons, Jehovah's Witnesses, and the Blue Cross. That tactic makes sense in view of the far more powerfully entrenched Roman Catholicism with strong ties to the Vatican and the Western links of the small "sects" over against which the other churches seemed more closely loyal to Czechoslovakia, i.e. more flexibly contextualized within the society that the Communist Party was trying to dominate.

Yet the attack was fundamentally against all religions as all were seen as ideological enemies, binding every Communist to the ultimate policy of liquidating the churches. On the way to liquidation the churches were to be reduced both directly and indirectly to increasingly limited activities.[18]

The Roman Catholic Church in particular found itself in a conflictual relationship with the Communist government practically from the outset and experienced the brunt of repressions, though formally it declared itself neutral and promised not to engage in outright political activity.[19] It was not only those Catholics who had collaborated with the Nazis, but even those who, like Archbishop Josef Beran, were in Nazi concentration camps, who were being arrested and placed into prison or concentration camps by the communists. As both Karel Kaplan[20] and Alexander Tomsky[21] amply demonstrate, the Communist Party even when it bargained with the Catholic Church did not bargain in good faith but had from the outset decided to attempt to crush that church. Kaplan, a former Communist, states that the Communists made promises that they never intended on keeping while the Catholic hierarchy negotiated in good faith attempting to protect the rights of the church as best they could.[22] Though outwardly displaying neutrality toward various forms of socio-political systems, it was nevertheless clear that the Catholic Church did not prefer the new system. Hence the creation of a church independent of the Vatican and subservient to the state became the ultimate goal of the Communist Party leadership as such a church could be more effectively controlled. The methods which they used to pursue this was by sowing internal strife in the church by creating mistrust, setting some of the clergy and laity against the hierarchy, portraying the church leadership as antagonistic and disloyal to the state and unwilling to come to terms with the new government, and taking over as many of the church's property and functions as possible.[23] Gottwald summarized it thus, "Our task is to provoke a political crisis among clergy, and thus create hostility and conflict among them."[24]

The attack upon the Roman Catholic and other churches took place on many fronts, namely by:

(A) passing restrictive regulations and laws that would all but immobilize the normal activities of churches,

(B) establishing an office for the control of the churches,

(C) splitting the leadership by driving a wedge between the higher and lower clergy,

(D) limiting or preventing contact between the Church and the Vatican,

(E) intimidating, arresting, exiling, imprisoning, etc. as many bishops, priests, and prominent lay people as possible, and

(F) closing down the monastic orders.

To briefly elaborate on each of these points, starting with the general measures:

(A) Unlike most of the other socialist countries the government of Czechoslovakia did not pass any laws separating state and church. The Constitution of 1948 remains mute on that question though in its preamble it acknowledges the role of Christianity and the values of the Hussite revolution.[25] Other Constitutional provisions declare equality before the law regardless of religious affiliation or absence thereof. Then follow the customary guarantees of the freedom of conscience, religion, and expression (articles 15–18). The act most directly affecting churches was the declaration of article 13 that all schools shall be state schools which affected most adversely those churches that had a number of schools. Later, even more damagingly, all schools for the training of clergy, including the determination of the curriculae, faculty, and student admissions, were placed into state hands.

Law No. 218 "For the Economic Security of the Churches and Religious Societies" was passed on July 15, 1949.[26] Having carried out a wide-ranging restructuring of social and economic conditions, having nationalized schools and property, the government 'offered' a compensation for the loss of properties by a short-range payment of salaries to clergy. On the surface this law deceptively hints at the government's concern for clerical and ecclesiastical welfare, but the law turns out to be an instrument of enslavement, despite some evident financial benefits to clergy.

(1) The state pays salaries to clergy who thereby become civil servants. Such clergy must function, and here is the hitch, only with the

consent of the government upon having taken an oath of loyalty and must be Czechoslovak citizens "politically reliable and blameless."[27] All appointments must be made by proper ecclesiastical authorities only with government approval. The clergy has rights to fulfill their responsibilities but only in the approved location. Without the appropriate clerical license no religious officiating may take place. The licencing of only those who appear reliable, the refusal to fill positions with candidates not to their liking, and the revocation of such licenses for supposed "attack upon the socialist order" or "abuse of clerical authority" gave the federal and regional councils on church affairs a most powerful tool to control the clergy and the churches. Should a position be vacated and not filled by the proper ecclesiastical authorities the government can decide whom to appoint. The government may withhold consent to appointment.

(2) All church property is henceforth supervised and owned by the state and each religious institution must submit their annual budgets for approval.

(3) Schools for the training of clergy are "kept up entirely by the state."[28]

(B) Another Law of October 14, 1949, establishes the State Office for Church Affairs, headed by a state official with the rank of cabinet minister with an additional state office for Slovakia, and local offices in every county.[29] Prior to that date Alexei Clepicka, the General Secretary of the National Front was in charge of church affairs. By March 18, 1948, the Commission for Religious Affairs was established, not as an arm of the government but of the National Front.[30] On October 14, 1949, the Commission was turned over to the government as the State Office for Church Affairs (hereafter SOCA). One should add that there was another crucial body dealing with the problem of the churches, called the "Church Six." This was an influential advisory committee subordinated to the Presidium of the Central Committee of the Communist Party.[31] In addition, the secret police had a department that was responsible to control and spy on the churches, bringing the number of departments dealing with the churches to three.

The SOCA and its regional and local branches were not liaison offices between the churches and the government but were established to *de facto* control the churches and was generally headed by officials negatively inclined toward the churches (this was especially true of Karel Hruza) except for the brief period of Dr. Erika Kadle-

cová's tenure during the "Prague Spring."[32] The SOCA, in addition
to the aforementioned control over theological schools and appointments of clergy and theological professors, also took over the control
of all remaining religious publications[33] (exercising strict censorship
and self-censorship) and charitable institutions. SOCA's representatives participated in the meetings of church leaders and without
their explicit permission no decision of an ecclesiastic leader could
be communicated to the people. Who was allowed to enter and stay
in theological schools and who would ultimately be ordained and appointed rested with the Regional State Secretary for Church Affairs.[34]
The fact that clergy salaries were paid by the state gave the pretext of
handling the clergy as civil servants whom the state could employ and
let go at will. Cooperation by clergy and laity in the Christian Peace
Conference (hereafter CPC) and in Christian-Marxist dialogues were
also regulated by these government agencies.[35] It was the exceptional
interference of these offices into the internal questions of the clerical profession that forced the secret ordination of some clergy and
bishops, especially by Roman Catholics.

(C) To weaken the Roman Catholic Church structure the government promoted a movement by left-wing priests to form in 1949
the "Peace Committee of the Catholic Clergy in Czechoslovakia," (an
alleged successor of the former "Catholic Action" that was disbanded
by the government). It renamed itelf in 1966 "The Peace Movement
of the Catholic Clergy." It was originally founded by Josef Plojhar,
a Catholic priest with close connection to the Communists, who participated in the Communist government despite the prohibition by
his ecclesiastical superiors. The priests' union was designed to be
a thorn in the Catholic ranks aimed at weakening the influence of
the bishops.[36] The government sought to portray the hierarchy as
the enemy of Czechoslovakia and the unionized priests as progressive
and patriotic. The general membership did not accept this portrayal
and the "peace clergy" were regarded largely as government stooges.
Enormous resources were spent by the government to organize a conference in Velehrad in 1950 and in Prague in 1951 of clergy for peace,
but with limited displays of enthusiasm by Catholic clerics. It is not
surprising that during the "Prague Spring" the union disbanded itelf.
Later, after the Soviet intervention, it was reestablished under the
name "Pacem in Terris" and continued to be held in low esteem and
suspicion.

(D) Knowing the anti-Vatican tendencies among many Czechoslovak Catholics the government attempted to make the Catholic Church into a national Catholic Church that would sever all of its ties with the Pope, but this was resolutely rejected. The Communist government then attempted to disrupt communication between the Catholic hierarchy in Czechoslovakia and Rome and to make it well nigh impossible for the pope to appoint archbishops and bishops. Historically such consent of the government was required but at the time the government was positively inclined to religion although it may have been at conflict with particular church leaders. Now when the government turned against any and all religion it was able to withhold recognition of leaders for years. Instead of the canonically appointed bishops empty episcopal areas were governed from the chanceries by priests from "The Peace Movement Catholic Clergy" or later the "Pacem in Terris" who were appointed by the SOCA and beholden, and sympathetic to the communists.[37] Moreover, quite bluntly, "commissars were placed in the consistories."[38] Many decisions and laws were made contrary to canon law.

The diplomatic relations between the Vatican and Czechoslovakia rapidly deteriorated from the middle of 1949 to the first half of 1950, and the papal nuncio and diplomats were either expelled or left the country.[39] No diplomatic relations were resumed until 1990. Travel by Czechoslovak hierarchs to the Vatican were prevented, and in many instances communication between the Roman Catholic hierarchy and Rome were monitored and disrupted through government action.

(E) The government moved forcefully against clergy, including the higher clergy. At first the alleged offenses were either collaboration with the wartime occupying authorities or the refusal to take the oath of loyalty required by the new law or who read pastoral letters in the churches despite the objections of the government. The State Security drew up plans for shadowing prelates, singling out those whom they were to arrest. A trial against some of the superiors of the monastic orders took place in Prague, March 30–April 5, 1950, only a few days after they had been imprisoned. They received sentences ranging from life to two years.[40] Many bishops and other administrators were placed under house arrest and forced to live away from their official residences and a large number of them (including six archbishops) were imprisoned or placed into forced labor or concentration camps.[41] Archbishop Josef Beran was under house-arrest and then forbidden to return to the country after a visit to the Vatican. From the government's viewpoint, acute isolation and house arrest was preferable to illegal arrests and many priests and bishops were consigned to it. Two monasteries, one in Pezinok, near Bratislava, and the other at Jašov, near Košice, both in Slovakia, were designated as the involuntary residence for most of the members of the religious orders although many of them languished in other labor camps.[42] Violence, perhaps even drugs, were used to obtain confessions prior to trials. Some were interned without trials. A number died in prisons and camps. Ludvik Nemec estimated that over 3,000 priests had been arrested of whom over 2,000 were placed in labor camps and 70 percent of the parish rectories were abandoned.[43] According to Norbert Zeman, O. Praem., 60,000 people were sentenced and 173 killed between 1950 and 1953.[44] The arrest of clergy continued until 1989 with some of them receiving very lengthy prison sentences for even a single infraction of rules, such as holding a mass without permission in the home of their parents.[45] Symptomatic was that a seventy-year-old archbishop, Vojtašák, received a twenty-four-year sentence![46] For all practical purposes the episcopate of the Roman Catholic Church had been *de facto* immobilized by elimination and subordination.

(F) Monastic orders, both male and female, became the target of severe measures that involved closing the majority of the monastic institutions. The action against the monastic orders was well coordinated and took place April 13–14, 1950 (Maundy Thursday!). The police and military surrounded the monasteries in a well-coordinated action (in Slovakia alone there were about 200 monasteries), confiscated them, relocated the members of the orders to the two "concentration monasteries" where they were to be re-educated. The charge against them was that they harbored enemies of the state, spies, and even assassins, and it was declared that the measure was taken to reinstate the original purpose of monasticism. A few months later the same fate befell the female orders with 13,000 nuns being dispersed to various factories and farms.[47] Only some very elderly nuns were permitted to take care of a few charitable institutions. As late as 1981 the police raided one such Caritas home run by Dominican nuns in Kadan, confiscating liturgical books and searching for illicit literature.[48]

That the conflict between the state and the Roman Catholic Church was particularly sharp is not surprising because the Catholic Church was indeed powerful and privileged and was able to summon remarkable resources, material, political, diplomatic, and religious (to which excommunications of those cooperating with the Communists were frequently resorted). The Roman Catholic Church claimed more privileges than a secular state is normally willing to concede and that other denominations may see as threatening to their own interests, but here the Roman Catholic Church was not being merely deprived of its privileges but also of its rights.

The intense historic rivalry between the Catholics and non-Catholics and the suspicion harbored particularly by the Protestants who were ill-disposed toward institutional Catholicism resulted in no clear solidarity action by the other churches when the attack against the Catholics occurred. In fairness one must point out that the other churches were also under attack, and the Stalinist practices of the regime left no one, not even Communists, actually not even high ranking communists, ultimately safe and willing to risk their safety on behalf of others. Archbishop Beran admitted at the Second Vatican Council during the discussion on religious liberty that the Roman Catholic Church of Czechoslovakia reaped the harvest of bitterness and intolerance sown during the Hussite Reformation.[49]

During a visit of Soviet Minister of Foreign Affairs, Andrey Vishinsky, to Karlove Vary in 1948, the Czechoslovak government agreed to liquidate the Eastern Rite Catholic Church (Uniate) which had about 320,000 believers and 330 priests. As in the Soviet Union they were forcefully converted to Eastern Orthodoxy by April 1950 after the Orthodox Church had been removed from the jurisdiction of the Serbian Orthodox Church and placed under the Moscow Patriarchate of the Russian Orthodox Church.[50] The two Eastern Rite bishops, Pavlo Goidych and Vasyl Hopko, and a large number of clergy were imprisoned for non-cooperation. Latin-Rite priests were not allowed to minister to those who used to belong to Eastern Rite churches. In 1968 during the brief period of freedom over two–thirds of these local chuches became legally Eastern Rite Catholic with a significant increase in their religious activity especially among children.[51] Pressure was again applied on them after 1969 to become Orthodox but most of them did not succumb to the pressure. Internal strife among the several ethnic groups of the Eastern Rite Catholics complicated matters but did not result in turning to Orthodoxy which was perceived to be under control of Moscow, even though the Moscow Patriarchate had granted autocephaly to the Orthodox Exarchate of Czechoslovakia in 1951. This Church tended to show its general loyalty to the regime and attempted to be as apolitical as possible.

The general government measures were directed against all

churches although they did not affect the others as profoundly as the Catholic Church because they did own as much property, schools, publications, and so forth. The Protestant churches were considerably more 'secularized' and sympathized with a number of the measures undertaken by the government. Whether with joy or with regret or resignation they had come to see themselves as part of the "Eastern" world—for which they blamed the Western democratic sell-out of Czechoslovakia to Hitler at Munich in 1939 and tried to make the best of a difficult situation.

The Czech National Church (later Czechoslovak Church or the Czechoslovak Hussite Church), which is strictly speaking neither Catholic nor Orthodox, nor Protestant, declared itself willing to support fully the new government.[52] Under the leadership of Patriarch Miroslav Novak it tended to be docile and cooperative with whatever trend became dominant in the government.

The position of the Protestant churches was greatly affected by the return of the most well-known theologian, Josef L. Hromádka,[53] from the U. S. Hromádka interpreted the changes that were taking place as an indigenous social revolution that was part of the larger wave of a world-wide revolutionary transformation from a decadent moribund capitalism to a vibrant though rough-hewn socialism.[54] Seeing that socialism may divorce itself entirely from Christianity, Hromádka felt that Christianity should give its critical approval to the emerging new social order so that it may contribute to its shaping and humanizing.[55] He believed that a Christian or the Church should give a general support (namely say "yes") to most communist policies, even if one were not in complete agreement with them, so that in case of a massive disagreement with the Communists one could then say a decisive "no." Hromádka's influence was decisive among Protestants and their leadership generally gave qualified support to the Communists. One must note that the vast majority of church members practiced the "theology of martyrdom"—namely the silent suffering from forces vastly superior to their own powers, hoping, sometimes against hope, that God's timely intervention will bring about God's reign in God's own good time. Hromádka himself may have set the tone for a preference to quiet intervention on behalf of some of the people who were unjustly suffering due to the excesses of the Stalinist government—a manner of action compatible with the traditional Czech response to power—but there were, indeed, some among the Protestants who chaffed at the lack of any more public display of protest.[56]

Of significance for religious liberty is the founding of the Christian Peace Conference with headquarters in Prague in 1961. In itself the Christian Peace Conference was both a reflection of how little religious freedom there was and the possibility of eking out some areas of freedom in the midst of unfreedom.

Realizing how deeply World War II and the Cold War had rent Europe and the world asunder a group of Protestant and Czechoslovak Church theologians and church leaders, with the assistance of some German (East and West) theologians sought to perform the service of reconciliation. After a series of meetings they institutionalized it to form the Christian Peace Conference that operated by means of major assemblies, commissions, committees, regional and state branches, and meetings throughout the world.[57] As it expanded, the CPC included as institutional members nearly all Eastern Orthodox and Protestant churches with the exception of Albania and Yugoslavia. Many Christians throughout Eastern Europe, including some Roman Catholics worked with the CPC, though the majority remained uninterested or suspicious, an attitude also prevalent in the West. The Roman Catholic Church did not join nor did the Protestant Churches of the GDR. When the Russian Orthodox Church joined it became immediately a decisive factor in the CPC, though the Czechoslovak origins and location of the headquarters were respected.

The CPC showed the degree of the captivity of the churches in the East by the degree to which many of their pronouncements reflected the stated policies of their governments.[58] While the pronounced pro-socialist stance reflected the personal convictions of some of the activists of the CPC there is good reason to suspect that such harmony of views was not the result of free convictions of the church members with their government but that rather a more interventionist role was played by the government.[59] It is fair to say that the institutional membership of entire churches from Eastern Europe was not placed for discussion by the membership. Many observers from the West, including most of those who involved themselves with the CPC, were aware of the limitations faced by East European Christians. The degree of 'captivity' differed from time to time and from country to country. The churches were being used by the government for certain purposes along the well-known peace agenda of the USSR and its allies. Basically the CPC attacked American and Western positions in the cold war as 'imperialist' while the Soviet and Warsaw pact views were considered peaceful.

But that was not the whole story. The churches and Christians who participated in the CPC also stood to gain from this enterprise and found ways to provide more elbow room for themselves while at the same time they worked on an agenda of great importance for the survival of the world. The CPC provided contacts with Christians from the West and the Third World at the time when such contacts were impossible through other channels. They could travel (those cleared for such travel)—and receive visitors (the latter were generally not screened and provided for many Westerners a useful first-hand experience). It gave the Christians of Eastern Europe occasion to meet one another and cooperate, an opportunity not previously practiced. And as harsh Stalinism gave way to modified milder Stalinism and moments of openness as the "Prague Spring," the Churches could address the world situation in a more balanced way than previously, for instance, appealing to both superpowers to halt the arms race. These were not positions completely contrary to their government's positions, but they were broader than their governments' positions.[60]

The period of servitude under Stalinism cast a deep shadow over life of the Czechs and Slovaks. The year 1952 stands out as the year of greatest Stalinist repressions. When in 1956 the Hungarians and Poles pressed for reforms, there were some in Czechoslovakia who thought that relaxation of the severe repression should also follow in Czechoslovakia. However as the Hungarian and Polish events turned to revolts the Czechoslovak Communists quickly condemned those events as counter-revolutionary and continued their own gloomy supremacy unabated so that the overwhelming impression as late as 1967 was greyness, resignation, fear, and servility.[61] There was little overt evidence of what was brewing underneath since 1961, namely "an increasingly intensified criticism,"[62] that rapidly and dramatically changed the face of Czechoslovakia from a socialism with a distinctly inhuman face to a hope and clamoring for a "socialism with a human face."

B.   The "Prague Spring": 1968

During the first half of 1968 in a wave of rejection of the Stalinist heritage and a search for a "socialism with a human face" alternative a period of rapid liberalization took place. While the primary thrust of the changes were in the political, economic, and ethnic domain, religious liberties were affected as well.[63] A change of personnel took place in the State Office for Religious Affairs where the feared head of that department, Karel Hruza, was replaced by the liberal Dr. Erika Kadlecová, who discontinued the government's meddling into the internal affairs of the churches and who communicated to the churches a much greater degree of openness. During that time it had become obvious to what degree the churches had been "infiltrated and manipulated by the pre-Dubček regime . . . ."[64] While most of the imprisoned clergy had been released already in the early 1960 some were not released from prison as late as seven months into Dubček's regime. The administrative stranglehold upon the churches was removed in 1967 and 1968, but none of the restrictive legislation had been removed; it was only less rigorously applied.[65] Processes of rehabilitation took place to clear the reputation of many falsely accused religious (and non-religious) citizens and those forcibly removed from their leadership positions were allowed to resume their responsibilities. It was made public that out of 13,000 regular Catholic clergy, about 10,000 remained faithful to the monastic vocations and that they had served cumulatively 42,000 years in prison.[66]

The religious institutions gained the respect of the population as it learned of the suffering, indignities, and even executions perpetrated upon the innocent leaders. To the credit of the churches there was no demand for retribution against the persecutors but only an attempt to tell the truth of the previous period. Religious life, such as youth activities, education, and religious publication that was previously hindered was now reinvigorated.[67] Clergy were reassigned to once empty parishes. Public meetings, including spontaneous Christian-Marxist dialogues took place in discussing the role of religion in a socialist society from a non-dogmatic perspective.[68] Some of the Communist-promoted organizations such as "The Peace Movement of the Catholic Clergy" were being dissolved of its own accord. Instead, the Roman Catholic bishops attempted to organize the "Force for Conciliar Renewal," but for reasons unclear it failed to receive official recognition.

What doomed the "socialism with a human face" experiment in August 1968 to a failure in addition to the brutal invasion of the Warsaw Pact forces (naturally under Soviet orders)? A most perceptive analysis for the failure of the "Prague Spring" was provided by Ludek Pachman.

The same persons in the Central Committee of the Party voted (almost always unanimously) in September 1967 for persecution of rebellious writers, in January 1968 for the fall of Novotny, in April for the party program of action, in May for putting brakes on it, in November for liquidating the program, in April 1969 for the fall of Dubček, and in September for a new wave of terror. There are few periods in world history that so perfectly reveal the true face of a movement, its inability to grow, the violence of its decline.[69]

The same author expresses the conviction, shared by many citizens of Czechoslovakia and by this author, that:

the "Prague Spring" is by no means merely a thing of the past. Only its events have become historical, but its underlying ideals—the principle of man's individual freedom—point imperiously toward the future. In our country these ideals can never again be extirpated.[70]

Another impressive conclusion:

It is foolish to think that it is possible to secure lasting freedom for some nations while withholding it from others. Freedom is indivisible, while its opposite is by nature aggressive. Unfreedom tends always toward expansion, which is why freedom must do the same—this is its only chance.[71]

This statement, does not apply to Czechoslovakia alone but to all times, places, and nations. It points to the invincibility of truth; hidden misdeeds are uncovered by later generation, as one can see in the case of Stalin and others who enacted reigns of terror.

C. Reintroduced Repression: 1969–1989

Using "salami tactics," namely the gradual erosion of freedoms which were gained during the "Prague Spring" as one may slice a salami, the Soviet puppet government of Gustav Husák reintroduced all the repressions and limitations upon religious life that existed before.[72] The government did not shrink away from acts of extreme violence, including murder.[73]

Symbolizing the reversion to the earlier practices was the return of the previous secretary for church affairs, Karel Hruza, known for his Stalinist grip on churches. He continued to do what he knew best: control and restrain religious activities. One thing changed dramatically; the previous idealistic slogans about the nature of socialism were now replaced with slogans that emphasized socialist reality and material values although still embroidered with lies about attempts at counterrevolution, eternal solidarity of the Soviet Union, peace coming from the East, and other slogans that no one took seriously. What was taken seriously was the presence of Soviet power and the sure knowledge that no reform undertaken in Czechoslovakia has a chance unless it is permitted by Moscow.

> No longer is a discrepancy between personal views and public behavior thought of as a moral dilemma. The believer is therefore caught in a situation where obeying the demands of his religion makes him appear an extremist, undermining the tacit agreement between the citizens and the totalitarian government.[74]

Until about 1972 some of the church leadership, for instance that of the Evangelical Church of the Czech Brethren, attempted to defend its independence by passing resolutions that could not have pleased the government. Slowly the leadership of the Synod was replaced and the subsequent resolutions urged the clergy not to criticize the authorities and implicitly condemned those who did get into conflict.[75] Increasingly the church structures buckled under state pressures, and in many instances people felt that the church leadership restrained religious renewal. For many the major concern became institutional survival for which they were willing to sacrifice the well-being of those individuals who seem to rock the boat of the compromise that had been reached between church and state. The Czech Protestant pastor Jan Šimsa reflected on the lack of support by his church leadership of him and other dissident pastors as the temptation by Satan not to take sides in the conflict between the government and the dissidents. Contrasted to that was the far more courageous stand by František Cardinal Tomašek who clearly stood by believers of all denominations who were persecuted by the government.[76] A number of prominent Protestant and Catholic clergy and theological professors who remained critical had their licenses revoked and were forced to support themselves by menial labor. The Ministry of Culture declared in 1971 that all legislation on religion passed since 1968 was invalid thereby making it possible for the government to increase the administrative suppression of religious activities and organizations. Particularly harmful was article 178 of the Penal Code making it a crime to "obstruct the state supervision of the church."[77]

Even the small Jewish community was affected by the tightening of the screws. The year 1969 was the millennium of Jews living in Czechoslovakian lands, but no millennial celebrations except some cultural one's were allowed.[78] They have no overtly religious publications or activities.

The signing of the Helsinki Accord in August 1975 which was adopted by the National Assembly on November 11, 1975, became a powerful incentive to resume the internal criticism of the regime's continually abysmal record on human rights.[79] On January 1, 1977, the famous human rights group "Charter 77" announced that three hundred people (among them six Protestant—and later seventeen Protestant and three Catholic clergy) signed a document in which they stated:

> Freedom of thought, conscience, and religious conviction, emphatically guaranteed by Article 18 of the International Covenant on Civil and Political Rights which had been signed by Czechoslovakia in 1968 and [which became effective Czechoslovak law on March 23, 1976—author's remark] is systematically curtailed by despotic arbitrariness; by restrictions imposed on the activities of clergymen, who are under constant threat of revocation or loss of the state permission to perform their functions; by reprisals affecting the livelihood and others aspects of life of those persons who express their religious convictions by word or deed; by suppression of religious instructions in schools, etc.[80]

The writers of the document pointed out that the restrictions and suppression are not done by means of legal norms but "behind the scene, often in oral form only" and that "the authorities are responsible only to themselves and their own hierarchy."[81]

The Synod Council of the Church of the Czech Brethren and the Roman Catholic Church stated that they did not sign the "Charter 77" statement but did not explicitly condemn it, while some of the other churches issued more condemnatory responses and stated that "Charter 77" meddled into their affairs.[82] Falsely the newspaper *Rude Pravo* stated that the Synod of the Evangelical Church of the Czech Brethren condemned Charter 77 although its members at the time had not even seen a copy of the Charter.[83] The church authorities came under very severe pressure and incessant interrogation in order to expel from membership those who signed the charter. Some of the clergy who distributed the text of Charter 77 were imprisoned, lost their jobs, and none received the support of their church. The Synod Council had become by 1977 an acquiescing tool in the hands of the government, according to Dr. Božena Komarkova.[84] Only rarely did the Synodal Council afterwards intervene on behalf of pastors who were losing their licenses.[85]

A Protestant clergy group called "Nova Orientace" [New Orientation], inspired by Bonhoeffer, although mostly former Hromádka's students, became rather reproachful of Hromádka's approach to socialism and his willingness to cooperate with the government.[86] Their state approval was withdrawn and ten of their members had to find menial jobs. Some of them (e.g. Rev. Svatopluk Korásek) were tried and imprisoned because of alleged subversive activity. Some members of this group stated during the "Prague Spring" that the government had previously tried to recruit them to spy on other clergy and when they refused they were persecuted. The seven clergy signatories of "Charter 77" wrote a statement, "Our position on Charter 77," in January 1977, in which they gave a theological analysis of Charter 77, seeing it as a prophetic document on behalf of the oppressed and lashing out against sinful structures.[87]

There was another style of action engaged in by many Christians which seemed to eschew confrontation with the state. Such people looked for quiet ways to work for improvement. For instance, during a visit to Switzerland, Miloš Lešikar, lay presbyter of the Synod in Lanškroun, when asked whether children of clergy are hindered from getting an education, pointed out that there are problems, but they are ususally worked out satisfactorily with responsible officials.[88] There are, of course, vocations which Christians could not enter, where ideological criteria were required, e.g. political cadres, army, and education. Hence one had to make a decision to be a Christian or not; then one was free to carry out the consequences of such a decision. He stated that in the last twenty years no new church buildings were allowed. To the question of whether one can speak freely, he suggested that instead the cliche of a persecuted and martyred church one should offer the notion of a smart and courageous church which uses whatever opportunities that the political system allows. Naturally one cannot go against the state, but one may defend one's rights. He also stated that the small, unregistered denominations cause a lot of difficulties.[89]

Such people generally avoided mentioning that continued imprisonments of clergy and active lay people took place in the 1980s mostly for a sizeable publishing activity in the form of *samizdats*. Curiously most of the *samizdats* were not dealing with material overtly critical of the government but mostly liturgical materials and news of the activities of the pope and comparable material that in other countries would be easily found in the official press. Another form of *samizdat* were literary, philosophical, and theological explorations of the meaning of life and analysis of Czechoslovak culture "to challenge not only the official socialist ideology of the State but also the traditional humanist 'orthodoxy' of the Czech intelligentsia."[90] In Czechoslovakia the religious press was so preoccupied with heavily censored peace proclamations (even the papal religious peace pronouncements where carefully doctored so that the statements would appear to be specifically endorsing the official East European line) so that the task of the *samizdat* publisher was to publish the accurate texts. Such innocuous publishing activity was vigorously prosecuted and severely punished because it challenged the monopoly of the government to decide what the citizens would be allowed to read.

The secular press declared that the relations between the churches and the state were without conflicts, stable and friendly and that all of the rights of believers were respected. Yet often they presented inaccurate and hostile report about the churches. The Roman Catholic Bishop Ján Chryzostom Korec of Bratislava, Slovakia, wrote a fourteen-page letter to *Rudé pravo* and *Pravda* in which he bitterly complained about such inaccuracies and presented a history of persecutions of the Catholic and Eastern Rite Catholic Church in Slovakia since 1948.[91]

The report of Dr. Vincent Mácovsk, deputy minister of culture of the Slovak Socialist Republic, is a fine indication of the ways in which the government limited religious freedom. Among the methods he mentioned were the revocation of clergy licenses from the critical spirits among the clergy, denial of permission to travel abroad to those church leaders who are uncooperative, placement of spies into church structures, spreading of disinformation, limitation placed on pilgrimages, quality youth work, religious education for the young, Western influence and media, elimination of all political overtones, and no promotion for certain religious leaders who are not suitable to the government.[92]

In the 1980s there were gradual evidences of the religious population's unwillingness to endure such repressive conditions forever.

František Cardinal Tomášek continued his inspiring leadership of the Roman Catholic Church, unwilling to accept a servile attitude toward the government, despite continued harassment. In Slovakia youth activities under the influence of the Polish "Oasis" movement took place despite government persecution. Over a hundred Catholic theological students in Bratislava protested some seminars that were organized by "Pacem in Terris."[93] The Synodal Council of the ECCB urged the government to provide to conscientious objectors alternatives to military service. Individuals continued to chide the leadership of the Protestant churches for their timidity in seeking to expand religious liberties.[94] The continuous harassment and imprisonment of well-known Charter 77 dissidents such as Václav Hável, Jan Patočka, Václav Benda, Václav Malý, Ján Duš, Josef Zverina, Vladislav Hejdánek, Jakub Trojan, Jan Šimsa, and Alfred Kocáb showed that they cannot be intimidated into abandoning their positions of integrity. An examination of documents from Eastern European countries shows that throughout 1987–1989 only the USSR has a comparable number of arrests, trials, detentions, and deaths of dissidents and clergy caused by the security police.[95] Some of the arrested received unusually lengthy terms of 8–10 years in prison. Also many people were threatened with death; others were confined to psychiatric hospitals. Out of the 45,000 prisoners it was estimated by Charter 77 observers that 5,000 were political prisoners, many of whom for religious offenses.[96]

Some of these dissident Protestant clergy wrote a critical letter to the World Council of Churches and the Lutheran World Federation accusing it of a double standard, namely being interested in human rights violations in some parts of the world but completely ignoring similar repression in Marxist countries. They accused the East European church leaders of lying to the World Council of Churches and no one among the other delegations opposing such lies.[97] In the meantime by 1989 over 600,000 signatures were collected in Czechoslovakia in a 31–point petition originally written by a group of Moravian Roman Catholics but signed by a great variety of persons directed to the Council for European Security claiming the human rights and religious liberties were being suppressed. The petition requests those religious rights that were in reality suppressed hence it is instructive to present the most important of these 31 points.

Request separation of church and state.

No state hindrance in naming of new bishops.

No intervention by the state in appointment of pastors or the selection of theology students nor restrictions as to their number.

Permission for all Catholic religious orders to commence their activities including the enlistment of novices.

The right to organize lay religious organizations.

The right to organize religious education in churches.

Permit pastoral visit to prisons and hospitals.

Permission to organize parish councils to assist the clergy in their tasks.

Permission to keep contacts with religious organizations throughout the world.

Permit unrestricted participation in pilgrimages abroad.

Freedom of the religious press under the leadership of church officials, the permission to import religious literature from abroad and the right to religious programs in the media.

The cessation of disturbances of religious programs from the Vatican and Radio Free Europe.

Allow not only atheist propaganda but religious evangelization and the right to criticize the teachings of Marx and Lenin without the threat of an inescapable punishment by the state.

The return of the confiscated religious buildings and permission to build new churches. Also the non-removal of old religious monuments from their original location.

To remove the power of control by the officials of the office for church affairs over clerical activity.

The rehabilitation of the unjustly persecuted religious activists.

The cessation of discrimination against believers in the work place and schools.

The right of believers to petition on issues in which they feel a moral obligation to take an alternate position.

To remove legislation that restricts the activity of the churches.

The removal or modification of Articles 16, 20, 24, 28, and 32 of the Constitution.[98] All religious legislation should be in line with international human rights agreements and conventions.

The appeal ends with a request for a mixed church-state commission that would pursue the implementation of these requests.[99]

The Evangelical Church of the Czech Brethren proposed in September 1989 in its periodical, *Kostnicke jiskry*, the following changes for the Czechoslovak Constitution:

Article 16, par. 1. that the entire cultural policy and educational philosophy be directed consonant with the development of science and related to the development of the life and work of the people.

Article 20. instead of par. 1–3, All citizens are equal and have the same rights and duties regardless of gender, nationality, race, origin, and religious affiliation.

Article 21. (1) All citizens have the right to select their own occupation; (2) the right to practice one's profession can only be limited by the courts.

Article 24. The entire educational and instructional process will be done in line with the development of science and the relationship of the school to the life and work of the people.

Article 30, par. 4. (1) No capital punishment is permitted; (2) the following constitutionally guaranteed rights may not be denied to any citizen because they were sentenced by a court: the right to equality, the right to protection of their health, the right to religious freedom, as well as the rights derived out of the law on nationalities.

Article 32. (1) Everyone has the right of thought, conscience, and religious freedom. This freedom includes the right to belong or to join a religion or world view of their own choice, the freedom to exercise one's faith alone or with others, publicly or privately by worship, observance of religious customs and instruction.

(2) No one may force the limitation of another's freedom to have or to join a religion or worldview.

(3) Religious faith may not be used as a cause to limit one's right to education, profession or employment.

(4) Parents have the right to decide freely about the religious and moral education of their children.

(5) The religious citizens have the right to join churches and religious communities; these are juridical persons whose establishment and organization is regulated by law. Churches and religious communities may carry out activities useful to the community.

(6) The dissemination of enmity and hatred in relation to belief or non-belief is forbidden.

(7) Religious faith or a worldview may not be used as an excuse to not follow the legal duties of citizens. Should the civil obligations contradict religious convictions, alternate service should be provided.

Article 37. (1) Those who object on grounds of conscience to service in the armed forces may carry out alternate useful services outside the army. Details will be regulated by law.

(2) Service in the army may apply to men eighteen years old.

(3) The government of Czechoslovakia is empowered to change service in the armed forces on a volunteer basis when the international situation and the security of the state permit.[100]

The Czechoslovak Hussite Church urged the free use of the Bible and religious literature as well as access by clergy to social institutions, the army, and prisons and the permission to hold worship services in these institutions. Also they advocated religious education for the youth movement.[101]

During the celebration of St. Methodius, the apostle to the Slavs in Veléhrad on July 7, 1985, a crowd of between 200,000 and 250,000 gathered, despite the usual attempts to limit attendance. Though the government tried to give the gathering a nationalistic character, particularly through the speech of the Minister of Culture, Klusk (who was booed by the crowd) the gathering took on a distinctly religious character. Interrogations and even arrests of two priests followed[102] but the entire event was interpreted by the religious community as clear evidence that even in the Czech lands religion is still deeply imbedded in the population giving concern to the government that religion is not as subdued as they were hoping. In 1987 in Slovakia three pilgrimages took place, one to Šastin with 40,000 people in attendance, another to Levoča had 230,000 pilgrims and a third to Gaboltov with 100,000 participants.[103] Most of the pilgrims had to go on foot for no public transportation was made available; rather roadblocks by the police hindered people, especially the large number of young people's arrival, while the government press attacked the pilgrimages. According to *Spisške Hlasy* the participation of young people is a concern because for a socialist society it is of concern how young people spend their free time.[104] The leadership of the pilgrimages was declared to be "clerofaschist" and antagonistic to the successful building of socialism and the unity of the Czehoslovakian people. In 1988 a pilgrimage to Nitra involved 120,000 people, while a Greek Catholic pilgrimage to Lutina involved 50,000 people. One might say that these pilgrimages were the staging of an increasingly public confrontation with the government being concerned about the continued public acceptance of the official religious leadership but also the effective campaigning and activity of the "secret church," that is the work of informal Christian circles who were being monitored by a vast secret police apparatus[105] who were nevertheless not able to suppress such devoted activity.

While in the neighboring Communist countries the situation was gradually becoming better, in Czechoslovakia it seemed that the state only strengthened its resolve to continue its rigid antireligious policy with practically no concessions. The Committee for the Defense of Unjustly Persecuted (VON), a human rights organization, estimated that between December 1987 to December 1988 497 citizens were unjustly persecuted.[106]

AFTER THE GREAT TRANSFORMATION OF 1989

The Velvet Revolution: November 1989

The precondition to the remarkable "Velvet Revolution" was Mikhail Gorbachev's *perestroika* and his announced and practiced non-interference in the attendant changes in Eastern Europe and the example of changes taking place in other East European countries, particularly in Hungary, Poland, and East Germany under popular pressure. (There is something to the 'domino theory!') Many people, including people in the churches saw themselves entering the process of *perestroika* and *glasnost* though this has not become the Government Policy—to the contrary the government desperately opposed it and prevented any constitutional, legal, or practical change. A new generation of Marxists started saying that a new attitude needs to prevail that would admit the contribution of Christians.[107] As Jakub Trojan pointed out, "the development in the late 1980s culminating in November 1989 and the following months cannot be understood properly unless the dialectic between the spectacular events and the hidden network of spiritual and political strivings underneath is recognized."[108] Trojan and other former dissidents realized by the 1950s, but even more decisively by 1968, that the socialist project in Czechoslovakia and other East European countries self-destructed because it handled the problem of power by undemocratic means, leading to unchecked abuse of power.[109]

On November 17, 1989, an approved student demonstration on the fiftieth anniversary of the death of Ján Opletal, a student killed by the Nazis, was brutally dispersed by the police when the students turned to go downtown. This event mobilized other students, citizens, and even the fairly apathetic workers, and within a few days, apparently without a single casualty, the governments of Gustav Husák and Miloš Jakeš toppled.[110] By November 29, 1989, the parliament revoked the legal formulation of the "leading role of the Communist Party" in governing the country. Within days revolutionary changes swept the country under the leadership of the "Citizens Forum" shedding its title "socialist," electing the playwright Václav Hável as its president and bringing Alexander Dubček out of ignominious non-personhood and elevating him to the post of the speaker of the parliament. Many of the dissidents went in short order from prison to the top government leadership positions (e.g. Ján Čarnogurský) for which they may not have had the expertise and training but for which they were suited because of their moral character, a characteristic apparently sadly lacking in the governments since Thomas Masaryk and Eduard Beneš. The heretofore rejected legacy of Masaryk and Beneš and the first republic was explicitly adopted and the country took off on the road to democracy, pluralism, freedom, and independence.

Not the least important is the almost immediate reappropriation of religious freedom. All provisions that limited human rights were struck down, particularly para. 178 "hindering the supervision of the churches by the state."

The Roman Catholic Church emerged out of the purgatory of the previous forty years with a completely new image of patriotism and moral courage, especially its ninety–year old primate, František Tomašek. "Pacem in Terris" was dissolved, ceasing to be a thorn in the administration of the Catholic Church. Many priests and bishops who had been ordained secretly surfaced and took their rightful position thereby terminating the impossible situation of a large number of bishoprics being without a bishop for decades. Catholic religious orders were permitted to reemerge after the long prohibition of their functioning and some of their nationalized properties were being returned and new abbots were installed. Theological training was opened to all. Those priests and ministers whose licenses had been revoked were now able to seek church appointments. The repair of churches and the resumption of charitable work that had been denied for such a long time could not be resumed. The remaining imprisoned clergy were freed. The principle of separating church and state was raised for discussion though it was obvious that the long financial dependence of the churches upon the state, especially clerical salaries, could not be immediately terminated.

The Synod of the ECCB that coincidentally met during the student demonstrations quickly sided with the students thereby also gaining in respect. Nearly all church bodies sided with the democratic upheaval. Hável, a Roman Catholic layman, quickly proclaimed the return of religion to public life by celebrating the taking of the office of Presidency with a mass and inviting Pope John Paul II and the Dalai Lama to visit Czechoslovakia. Among the new government leaders were also clergy, notably Josef Hromádka,[111] the Synodal President of the Evangelical Church of the Czech Brethren, who became Deputy Prime Minister for culture, education, and church affairs from November 1989 to June 1990. He abolished the Office for Church Affairs and fired its previous head, Vladimir Janků. The supervision of church life by local secretaries for church affairs was practically abolished.[112] According to Hromádka there was no serious movement among the public or the new government officials to separate church and state as this is not a local historical tradition. Freedom can be maintained without such separation; the churches as public institutions promoting the common good deserve continued and even improved government support, financial, and other. One may expect that the churches will pursue educational and charitable activities on a fairly large scale.

This time it was obvious that 1989 is not a rerun of 1968. There were no loud requests for "socialism with a human face" or "democratic socialism" but only for democracy. "Socialism" for all its European tradition has been so perverted by "real socialism" that, especially among the young, it had no support.

Without delay the churches submitted suggestions for the change in the constitution and the laws regarding religion, some of which preceded the November Transformation.[113] It is estimated that the work on a new constitution will last a couple of years, a period shorter than normal, due to the strength of the democratic tradition of the country.

At the first free election on June 9 and 10, 1990, Civic Forum (Czech) and Public Against Violence (Slovak) parties gained 169 out of 300 seats in the Federal Assembly and a similar proportion in the Czech and Slovak assemblies. The Communists won 48 seats and the Christian Democrats 40, with other smaller parties winning considerably smaller electoral support.[114] The Roman Catholic Church was at once allowed to replenish all their vacant episcopacies and received a boost from the papal visit that encouraged Catholic spirituality in a church that had won new credibility through suffering. The increase in church attendance witnessed in the few years before the Great Transformation, did not last very long as people, particularly the young, found outlets for their political aspirations in the free political activities.

Jan Lochman reports of a dramatic happiness of democracy that enveloped most citizens of the land as he visited his native land for the first time since 1968.[115] Though the "Babylonian Captivity" had ended, Joseph Hromádka, warned against euphoria as the country enters the stage of a pluralistic society. "In such a country the church loses the advantage of an 'oppressed' organization or group."[116] No longer are churches the only alternative to a single party and it will be necessary to find a suitable mode of contributing to the transformation of society, nor should it claim special priveleges on account of its sheer numbers and the burden of their past suffering. Hromádka warned against the temptation of churches trying to achieve power and covering society with a Christian, instead of a Marxist ideology. The churches can participate in the moral renewal of the nation but only if they are willing to morally renew themselves because the churches, too, were tainted in the distant and recent past by failures and abuses. The churches also must face that the range of responses to the former totalitarian regime ranged from loyalty (or collaboration) to critical opposition with many being caught in simple inactivity. The time of pure ideologies and pure religious doctrines is over, according to Hromádka. The involvement of religious people in social transformation will be valued only if it results in responsible actions toward God and the world.[117]

Jakub Trojan, the former Charter 77 dissident whose license to preach had been revoked from 1974 to 1989 and who had then become dean of the Comenius Theological School in Prague pointed out that the moral malady that had infected the church leaders, the churches, and society at large, was far from over. One of them was the exclusion of the public from processes of decision-making in society and the churches as only the final decision would be communicated.[118] The churches had been pushed outside of the domain of public life into the societal margins and they had come to acquiesce and even theologically to justify it. Now the task is to rediscover how to enter the public arena in a relevant and effective way.

If there is such a thing as a "national trait," the historic experience of the Czechs and Slovaks made them a patient, gentle, and flexible people who will suffer silently for long periods but who hold tenaciously to their desire for freedom, waiting for the moment when it can be asserted without national suicide, i.e. perfectly without violence. The flip side of the coin was a timidity and overcautiousness, looking out for one's own material interest and safety, and willingness to live oppressed by lies for too long, a feature strongly criticized by the dissident community, especially by the playright Václav Hável. The "Velvet Revolution" has shown that the manipulated people under totalitarianism did not lose their hope for freedom and democracy. Secularistic Absolutism (Type C) was decisively rejected by a non-violent surge in favor of a democratic aspiration for Pluralistic Liberty (Type D) although the reluctance to separate church and state for the historic churches is likely to bring back the pre-World War II condition of Religious Toleration (Type B) with tendencies to grow gradually into a full-fledged Pluralistic Liberty.

Chapter 8

EAST   GERMANY: RELIGIOUS LIBERTY IN A PROTESTANT LAND

The Heritage

The heritage of religious liberties prior to the formation of the German Democratic Republic [hereafter GDR or its more popular American equivalent, East Germany] in 1949 consisted of several strands.[1] Prior to 1919 there was no separation of church and state. The churches which were established by the principle *cuius regio eius religio*, stemming from the religious wars of the Reformation era, were basically the *Landeskirchen*, or establishment churches of the various German lands out of which the German Reich was made up. In the regions that were later to become the GDR the *Landeskirchen* were Protestant. This meant that the Lutheran teaching of the "two kingdoms," i.e. the temporal and the spiritual, was maintained engendering mutual respect but also a degree of autonomy of each realm. The *Landeskirchen* and their members enjoyed a position of privilege, though the spirit of the Enlightenment had permeated these German lands leading in practice to considerable tolerance and freedom for those who were not members, namely the Roman Catholics, "Free Church" Christians, and Jews.

At the end of 1919 the pressures to end this system of established Protestantism resulted in the formation of a Commission for Separation of Church and State headed by the very respectable scholar of sociology of religion, Ernst Troeltsch. The impulse for the separation came from the Social Democrats and from some church members. Initially, the opposition from the churches was furious. During the Revolution of 1918/1919 religious education was cancelled in schools, but later in a plebiscite the citizens voted it back into the school curriculum. Only a very small group of theologians shared the view that there should be a separation of church and state, among whom were

Emil Fuchs and Fritz Dehn. The majority opposed it. Additional support for the separation came from the "dialectical theologians," namely the Barthians (Karl Barth himself was a Social Democrat). The churches did not want to accept the abdication of the Kaiser [emperor] and the end of the empire and were basically unfavorable to democracy. The relationship between the churches and the Communists became very polarized at this time, and the churches tended to support political right-wingers.

The Constitution of the Weimar Republic separated church and state, thereby establishing a new stage in regard to religious liberties. The churches, however, received the status of a public society (*die Körperschaft des öffentliches Rechtes*), i.e. a legally recognized "public person," with a status higher than an association. Some privileges were still attached to the *Landeskirchen*, such as the right to receive church taxes collected on their behalf by the government. This, of course, only applied to the historic Protestant and Catholic Churches but not to the so-called "Free Churches" such as the Methodists and Baptists. The churches supported a large number of social and charitable causes: hospitals, old people's homes, orphanages, and various child care and educational enterprises, both church owned and private. In order to strengthen the intensity of church life *Gemeinschaften* (communities) were created by both those who stayed inside and those who left the historic churches. In the 1920s this movement was very strong and promoted a pietistic orientation. Religious life, institutions, and activities during this period were considered a natural, established order of things which not only had a place in the past and present of German history but also had an assured place in its future.

January 30, 1933, was the date of the rise of Adolf Hitler to power. He gradually succeeded in obtaining the passage of emergency laws which gave him dictatorial powers. The Nazi government established in 1935 the *Reichskirchenministerium* [Ministry for Churches] which was to regulate church affairs and oversee pastoral appointments. The Nazis made government support much more tenuous and dependent on the degree of cooperation by the given churches. Church lands were administered by the government.[2]

The most significant aid to the Nazi government's effort to control and use the churches was the "*Deutsche Christen*" [German Christians] movement, which began in the 1920s and was prominent in Thüringia. Renowned among its leaders were Leutheuser and Hossenfelder. It consisted of small nationalistic groups, with considerable public support, that sometimes stepped out of the bounds of Christianity, had a strong right wing political agenda, and wanted to promote the struggle against Bolshevism. They favored Hitler's measures even when it meant restriction or elimination of some of the churches' social and educational services. Religious education was made voluntary. In 1933 the Protestant and Catholic church youth movements and Scouts were abolished; the only youth organization functioning was the *Hitler Jugend* [Hitler's Youth]. Youth work in the churches had to be incorporated into congregational activities, rather than be a separate outlet.

A great struggle developed inside the churches. On the one hand the *Deutsche Christen* (the anti-church movement promoted by General Ludendorff and his wife) pushed for a Jew-free church in terms of liturgy, songs, scripture, and books, promoting racial and social theories akin to those of the Nazis. On the other hand the *Bekennende Kirche* [Confessing Church] movement opposed this *Deutsche Christen* anti-Semitic movement within the church, though not all were in opposition to the National Socialist government. The Nazis originally responded by saying that the church can do what it will; the Nazis are able to proceed alone. Only a smaller group of the Confessing Church gathered around Karl Barth also opposed the *Führer* principle and the Nazi movement and ideology, thus becoming a genuine Christian resistance movement. Most church members found themselves between these two groups, unsure of how to live their Christianity authentically. Some resisted, others cooperated, and still others tried to be bystanders.

The Nazis passed the Nürnberg laws in 1935. Among restrictions placed upon Jews was that they could not hold public office or jobs. The Christian churches were also marginally affected as a small number (5–6) pastors were born of Jewish parents. A struggle took place in which those who favored the acceptance of the Nürnberg laws won, thereby causing the expulsion of ethnic Jewish pastors and organists. This led to the criticism by the Confessing Church. Rudolf Bultmann stated that every baptized Christian has equal right. The problem was that most theologians spoke out only on behalf of baptized Jews. Dietrich Bonhoeffer was an exception, he pleaded for both baptized and unbaptized Jews. First on the Nazi target were *voll-Juden*, those of pure Jewish stock. Then later, during the war, the *halb-Juden*, i.e. those of mixed marriage, were also affected by Hitler's plan for the "final solution."

Jews were not the only target of the Nazis. Jehovah's Witnesses were also prohibited in 1933, then jailed and killed because they were considered unpatriotic. Gypsies were also annihilated. Free Masons were prohibited in 1933 and lost their position as a "humanistic religion."

The Germans practiced no separation of church and school. The state operated primary schools either for Protestant or for Catholic children, according to the principle *cuius regio eius religio*. There were even special state schools for Jewish children, but this was not true everywhere. For example, Jews were allowed to live in Mecklenburg but not to have Jewish schools; they had to send their children to Hamburg or Frankfurt. In the higher grades the children were not segregated by religious adherence; the Nazis considered them *Deutsch gläubig* [German believers]. Prussia had the reputation of being one of the most tolerant states, while Bavaria one of the most intolerant in the German Reich.

BEFORE THE GREAT TRANSFORMATION

A. After the War

After the war Germany was partitioned into four zones of occupation, with Berlin similarly divided. The Soviet occupational zone eventually established its own statehood, the German Democratic Republic.

A number of factors contributed to the fashioning of the policies in regard to religious liberties in the GDR.

The first factor was the heritage, which was described above. Anti-Communism and animosity toward the Soviets, stemming from both the war propaganda and experience and from the post-war experience with Soviet troops was another factor. Anti-Communism had been vigorously promoted by the Nazis and it remained ingrained in a considerable portion of the population.

Yet a third factor which weighed heavily was the experience of guilt and the discouragement of having lost another major war. Many knew that they had been personally implicated in the moral atrocities of the Reich. Collective guilt for the omissions and commissions of the Nazi era was also experienced.

One of the foremost tasks of the Soviet occupational authorities was de-Nazification. Surprisingly, the Soviets did not carry out an outright de-Nazification of the churches even though certainly there had been Nazis in them, but declared that the churches had been "organizations of resistance" to the Nazis.[3] Church services were allowed to continue; hence, there was no direct conflict between the Soviets and the churches. Many pastors, however, were nationalists and spoke out against the brutality of the Soviet armed forces. Even so, the Soviets left it to the churches to carry out their own de-Nazification. All the organizations of the *Deutsche Christen* and of the *Deutsch Gläubig* were prohibited.

Some groups benefitted immediately from the new order. Jehovah's Witnesses and Jews—those who survived—were again allowed to worship. Later in the 1950s the Jehovah's Witnesses were again prohibited as they had been accused as being instruments of the Americans, since their publication, *Watchtower*, came from the West.[4]

In regard to religious liberties, one can discern four periods. The first one was from 1945–1949, the second from 1949–1978, the third from 1978–1989, and the fourth from 1990 to 1991.

1. Attempted Cooperation Between the Communists and Churches in the Soviet Zone: 1945–1949

The Soviet occupational authority's policy toward the churches was originally one of friendliness and non-interference and many East German Christians and Communists were on good terms because of their joint concentration camp suffering. According to Richard Solberg, "until 1950 one cannot speak of a real church struggle in East Germany, except against the physical and spiritual privations which came as a result of Nazism and the war."[5]

This period contained the struggles between members of the Confessing Church and the majority of the nationalists and traditionalists. Only the most pro-Nazi element had to leave the church; most of the middle ranks stayed. The leadership of the churches was occupied, however, by people who did not need to be ashamed by their engagement with the Nazis. One of these leaders was the bishop of Berlin, Otto Dibelius, who had been both a nationalist and one of the leaders of the Confessing Church in Prussia. He became the leader of a strong anti-Communist approach in the churches. This prompted another internal struggle in the church between the *"Dibelianer"* (the nationalists and others) and those theologians of the Confessing Church who had organized in the *Bruderschaft* [Brotherhood] in Saxony. The

Confessing Church was not established as an organization after the war, but it inspired a series of confessions. First came the Stuttgart Confession of Guilt in 1945, which was fairly vague, followed by the much more powerful Darmstadt *Bruderwort* [Confession] in 1947. In Stuttgart Dibelius was in solidarity with Martin Niemoeller, the best known leader of the Confessional Church. The East German theologians had some difficulty in being allowed to attend the Stuttgart and Darmstadt conferences, but that was more the result of the general chaos of the post-war period rather than deliberate policy.

The church organization went through an institutional change from the federalistic *Deutscher Evangelischer Kirchenbund* [German Evangelical Church Federation] to the more centralistic *Deutsche Evangelische Kirche* (DEK) [German Evangelical Church] in 1933. The DEK was dissolved and in 1945 the *Evangelische Kirche in Deutschland* (EKD) [Evangelical Church in Germany] was organized in Treysa.[6] The EKD considered itself as a forerunner of German unity, but in 1969 the churches conceded the reality of the borders dividing the two Germanies, and the churches in the East left the EKD and formed the *Bund der Evangelischen Kirchen in der DDR* [The Federation of Evangelical Churches in the GDR].

In the period from 1945 to 1949 no serious restrictions on religious liberties were experienced, as there was still hope on the Soviet side that the re-unification of Germany might take place and they wanted to project an image of religious toleration. There were still many opportunities for significant church work. Some tensions were experienced in Saxony due to a plebiscite on the agrarian reform. The big landlords were expropriated, but the question of small landowners hung in suspension. Some churches were in favor of the land reform; others were not. The churches did not give up their land holdings, and the government continued to collect church taxes and support the churches, thus making separation of church and state more of a theory than a reality. Confessional schools were not abolished until 1947 (1948 in East Berlin).[7] The curriculum in public schools did not include religious education but the churches were allowed to organize one to two hours of religious education per week at their own expense. Though most health and social agencies were placed under government control, the needs were so great that the churches were allowed to continue some of their institutional charitable work. No systematic persecutions were carried out, although overly eager local administrators sometimes harassed or confiscated church agencies.

On June 26, 1945, the Christian Democratic Union [hereafter CDU] was formed, which in mid-July 1945, joined the Democratic Bloc which consisted of nine organizations.[8] Originally, this Christian political party had some aspirations to participate in governing the country. However, the role of this party was soon reduced to becoming a transmission belt for the decisions of the Socialist Unity Party [hereafter SED, for *Sozialistische Einheitspartai Deutschlands*]. The CDU was forced to admit that the SED was the controlling party on behalf of the proletariat, since it was armed with the scientific principles of Marxist dialectical materialism whereby it was able to make the right decision for the people of the GDR. The party had fifty–two deputies in the *Volkskammer* [People's Chamber of Deputies] which was fixed so that elections have no bearing on the number of deputies to which each party is entitled. Until 1989 the CDU became a docile tool in the hands of the SED, sometimes even exceeding the SED in its overtly zealous support of official policies.

It was already at this point that the church membership and leadership in the GDR could be divided into three main strands. One strand, among whom were many CDU members, but always a distinct minority among Christians, were vociferous supporters of the new socialist order. Many of them were highly ideologized and proceeded to provide theoretical justification of the new regime regardless of the real conditions of life, because of a proclaimed principle of *Parteilichkeit* [partisanship]. According to this principle there is no third way between imperialism and socialism; hence a Christian could in good conscience support only socialism.

Another group staunchly resisted socialism, hoping that the anticipated reunion with West Germany would eliminate the experience with socialism as one would eliminate a nightmare by waking up on a bright morning. Some have called them "internal emigrants," because they lived in body, but not in spirit in the GDR. A large number of them did succeed in emigrating. In the early post-war years the majority of the church people probably belonged in this group.

The third, and in the last decade or two by far the largest group, consisted of individuals who opted to find their role in a new society that was not of their own making, but was nonetheless subject to God's sovereignty. This group practiced "critical solidarity," discriminately offering support to a regime they regarded as permanent when they felt it offered positive programs, and distancing itself from policies they believed to be contrary to the interest of the people. It was leaders of this group who later coined the term, "the church in socialism," in contrast to the notions of a church for or against socialism. It was this centrist majority, blessed with strong leadership of integrity, which shaped the course of the church-state relations in the GDR. Theirs was probably the most creative adjustment to socialism by a church in Eastern Europe. The strength, courage, vitality, and integrity of this group, plus the GDR's precarious position in the Soviet bloc, has made the GDR the country in which the fewest brutalities against religious people occurred and in which there was a great deal of institutional liberty.

2. Sharp Limitations of Religious Liberties Followed by Gradual Abatement of Pressures: 1949–1978

This period begins with the formation of the GDR and coincides with the establishment of a socialist system. Horst Dähn has divided this period into stages of confrontation (1949–1958), decrease of confrontation (1958–1968) and gradual relaxation of tension between church and state (1969–1980).[9] The crucial meeting between top state and church leaders in March 1978 seems like a more decisive demarcation point between periods than the one suggested by Dähn and has been adopted here.

The 1949 Constitution, like the somewhat earlier promulgated constitutions of the *Länder*, guaranteed the freedom of religion and conscience and separated church and state very much along the lines of the 1919 Weimar Constitution.[10] Articles 40 to 48 dealt with religion and are here reproduced in full.

IV. Education

Art. 40. Religious teaching is a matter for religious communions. Free exercise of this right is guaranteed.

V. Religion and Religious Communions

Art. 41. Each citizen is given full freedom of faith and conscience. The undisturbed exercise of these religious rights is under the protection of the Republic.

Institutions of religious communions, religious rites, and religious teaching may not be used for unconstitutional or party-political purposes. However, the right of religious communions to take stand concerning vital issues of the people is undisputed.

Art. 42. Private or civic rights and duties are neither dependent on nor restricted through exercise of religion. Exercise of private rights and admission to public services are independent of religious confessions.

No one can be forced to manifest his religious convictions. Administrative organs have the right to inquire as to one's adherence to a religious communion only inasfar as rights and duties depend on it or is made necessary for statistical recording under the constitution.

No one can be compelled to join in any religious rite or celebration, to participate in religious activities or to use a religious oath.

Art. 43. There is no State Church. The freedom to establish religious communions is guaranteed.

Each religious communion arranges and administers its own affairs in accordance with the commonly valid laws.

Religious communions are recognized by public law, as heretofore, as juridical bodies. Other religious communions are given equal rights at their request, on the condition that their constitution and number of members provide some guarantee of continuation. In the case of association of several such public and legal religious communions, such an association will equally be regarded a public and legal body.

Public and legal religious communions are authorized to levy taxes on their members on the basis of official taxation lists in accordance with general and public instructions. Associations which have a common concern and ideology are considered equal to religious communions.

Art. 44. The right of the Church to give religious teaching on school premises is guaranteed. Religious teaching is given by persons chosen by the Church. No one can be forced or prevented from giving religious instruction. Guardians decide on participation in religious classes.

Art. 45. Public contributions to religious communions under previous law, treaties, or special titles are replaced by the present law. The right to hold properties and other rights of religious communions and religious associations in connection with their institutions, foundations or funds for cultural, educational and welfare purposes are guaranteed.

Art. 46. Insofar as there is demand for divine service and pastoral care in hospitals, prisons, or other public institutions, religious communions are permitted to perform their religious activities therein. No one can be forced to participate in such rites.

Art. 47. Whoever desires to give up membership in a public and juridical religious communion has to make a declaration before court or an individual statement in publicly recognizable terms.

Art. 48. Decision on affiliation of children to a religious communion, until they are fourteen years of age, is made by the guardian, thereafter the child decides on his or her affiliation to a religious or ideological organization.[11]

Of all the laws passed under a socialist government in Eastern Europe these provisions were the most advantageous. The explanation given by one of the few East German commentators on religious issues, Erwin Jacobi, was that East Germany in 1949 was by no means a socialist state and that the constitution reflected other ideologies as well as the Marxist-Leninist line.[12] It is likely that the special and clouded status of the new state required a liberal law in continuation with the democratic traditions of the Weimar Republic for purposes of satisfying the international public opinion. A few departures from the text of the Weimar Constitution can be found particularly in Art. 40, which separates church and education based on the Soviet model and in Art. 46, which does not allow churches the right to organize worship and pastoral care in the military.[13]

The Potsdam Agreement of October 7, 1949, guaranteed religious liberty to Roman Catholics. In addition to the right to gather for worship without police surveillance they were also given the right to gather for charitable and religious-cultural functions.[14]

A few legal provisions passed later were reminiscent of some of the Soviet legislation which could and would be used against those religious persons who proved to be an obstacle in carrying out the state's objectives. One of the most important was "The Act Amending the Penal Code" of December 11, 1957,

Art. 19. Propaganda and Instigation Endangering the State.

(1) Whoever:

1. glorifies or propagates fascism or militarism, or instigates people against other nations or races,
2. instigates against the Workers' and Peasant's Power, or instigates against its organs, against social organizations, or a citizen because of his membership in a State institution or a social organization, shall be punished by imprisonment for not less than three months. The attempt to commit any such crimes shall be punishable.

(2) The same penalty shall be inflicted upon anybody who produces writings, or other objects, with the above content, or who imports or circulates them with the intention to instigate.

(3) In severe cases the penalty shall be penal servitude, especially when the act was committed on the order of authorities or persons named in Art. 14, or act was committed according to a plan.[15]

In the period between the promulgation of the 1949 and the 1968 Constitutions came the greatest pressures upon the Churches, especially from 1949 to 1958. Richard Solberg points out that "all of the devices of hampering, interfering, and restricting the work of the Church—the cynical weapons of the slow war of attrition"[16] were being used by the government. In the beginning it seemed to be an excessive zeal by various local German Marxists and recourse could be usually obtained by complaining to the Russian occupational authorities who seemed to be more willing to make concessions to churches than the GDR leaders. Later the pressures became widespread. While no full-fledged persecution of religion ever developed in the GDR political violence and even imprisonment did occur, and religious people were relegated to second class citizenship. The churches were forced into another *Kirchenkampf*, i.e. struggle for the direction and identity of the church. While this struggle between church and state can be explained in terms of the issue of the church resistance to state-sponsored atheism (especially in the schools and in youth work), this is too simplistic an explanation. One needs to point out other political and ideological reasons, in particular the anxiety of the GDR government which favored a permanent division of Germany but contained a Church which was still in union with its counterpart in the Federal Republic of Germany [FRG]. Hence the church was perceived as a danger, both political and ideological, and the Marxist party undertook to force it into separating from the Church in FRG and to make an ideological adjustment with regard to socialism.

The 1968 Constitution did not radically alter the legislation of the 1949 Constitution, except in regard to the abolition of religious education in schools. Noteworthy is that religion received less attention in the 1968 constitution and that the leadership of the Protestant churches limited their responses to the draft of the constitution to the draft article 38 (later numbered 39 in the Constitution) according to which "the churches and other religious communities must order themselves and carry out their activities in accord with the Constitution and other legal provisions of the GDR."[17] The bishops, except Moritz Mitzenheim, proposed instead the following wording:

> The activities of the churches and other religious communities according to their religious profession, especially pastoral care, the instruction and for public utility are guaranteed. The churches and other religious communities order their affairs independently according to laws applicable to them. Their legal abilities, their property and their right to summon [*heranzuziehen*] their members to ordered tasks and offerings are guaranteed.[18]

The bishop's proposal would have expanded constitutionally guaranteed religious liberties but it was not accepted. Rather, Bishop Mitzenheim apparently influenced the expansion of article 20 to its final form,

> Every citizen of the German Democratic Republic, regardless of race, creed, social station or background has the same rights and responsibilities. Freedom of conscience and religion are guaranteed. Every citizen is equal in the eyes of the law.
> Article 6 prohibits manifestation of hatred against various creeds.

> Article 39 states,
> Every citizen of the German Democratic Republic shall have the right to profess a religious creed and to carry out acts of worship.

> The Churches and other religious communities shall conduct their affairs and carry out their activities in accordance with the Constitution and legal regulations of the German Democratic Republic. Further concerns can be regulated by means of additional agreements.[19]

Article 21 specified the central *right* and *duty* of the citizens to co-produce the socialist society. This means that the citizen should carry out the directives of the party and the government, but has no right to work against or even parallel to the party.[20] One should note that the legal concept of *duty* has priority over the concept of *right.* and that many rights hinge on prior exercise of duty. This conception is illustrated by a book title, *Bürgerpflicht und Christenpflicht.*[21]

The Penal Code of the GDR of January 12, 1968, prohibits persecution, expulsion, or destruction of religious groups (Art. 91). Hindering or forcing someone to take part in religious activities or disturbing acts of worship or behaving blasphemously within a place of worship is punishable by imprisonment, fine or reprimand (Art. 133). The Code of Criminal Procedure of the GDR of the same date allows clergy, according to Art. 27, to refuse to testify about information confided to them in their pastoral duties. The Punishment and Rehabilitation Law of April 7, 1977, allows prisoners to engage in religious activity upon request (Art. 34) and request food in accordance to religious customs (Art. 43).[22]

There were also some separate laws dealing with religion, but the key issue, of course, is that the SED was not bound by the Constitution. Otto Luchterhandt, a legal expert in West Germany, who studies GDR legislation, maintains that "there is no ground for doubt, that the GDR is a *legibus absoluta*, i.e. as sovereign it is basically free to dispose with the law and that it is capable to break its own laws, in *toto* as well as individually."[23] For instance, the Constitution guarantees equal access to all posts in the state, but the SED said that in the army and the government, the SED has more power. The state is under the party. In normal circumstances some unclear situations occur. These situations are regulated by the SED which tends to oscillate between a hard-line and moderation. On the other hand the SED attempts to impose a similar distinction among Christians saying that they are either moderate or pro-Western.

Another important notion for understanding the legal situation is that Marxist-Leninists perceive the law as a tool for social change in the hands of the proletarian government. The law is not so much for protection of certain rights but it is for the achievements of certain policy goals of the SED.

The GDR, like other socialist countries, signed an International Agreement on Civil and Political Rights on December 16, 1966. Art. 18 of that agreement defines religious freedom, which means that the socialist countries bound themselves to the same judicial definition of religious liberty as Western and other countries the result of which is that discrimination against religious citizens in education, employment, and politics and pressures toward atheization can be viewed as a clear violation of Art. 18.[24] The document was adopted by the GDR in 1973 but came to force only in 1976.

The great confrontation between the government and the churches took place in the 1950s and 1960s, climaxing in 1953, because the SED undertook to oppose the churches.[25] Among the measures against the churches was the creation in 1953 of the Office for Church Affairs (*Staatssekretariat für Kirchenfragen*) was created with the purpose of controlling and muzzling the churches. The Berlin Bishop Otto Dibelius came to symbolize the church's resistance to such pressure. The SED discriminated particularly against the church youth movement for being allegedly pro-Western and supported by the West German Chancellor Konrad Adenauer. A group of students and church workers were accused of being American spies and were imprisoned. One of the publications of the Evangelical Church describes the church's struggle in clearly defined arenas

- for the youth
- for charitable work
- for public spiritual care
- to rebuild destroyed church buildings
- for the freedom to proclaim
- for the independence from the state
- for financial security
- for unity.[26]

A similar Roman Catholic publication focuses on the Church's struggle against atheism in the state, government, and education, a struggle for the family, and trials against clergy. The government, unlike in the Nazi era, avoided trials against priests; those who were tried were always accused of nonreligious offenses. Lay people were sentenced more harshly, mostly for possession of religious literature and anti-state propaganda.[27] Roman Catholics, who were mostly emigrants from former German territories in the East, had to face problems of an insufficient number of priests and church buildings. Originally priests from West Germany were allowed to move to East Germany but in 1951 this was disallowed by the East German government. Then the Roman Catholics attempted to expand theological education by establishing a seminar in Berlin-Biesdorf but that was thwarted by the authorities. Only in 1952 were they allowed to establish the Philosophical Theological Study Center in Erfurt. The problem of insufficient church buildings was partially alleviated by the Protestants who offered to share their church facilities. Permission to build Roman Catholic Churches came reluctantly and by 1966 over 50 percent of all Roman Catholic masses were still being served in Protestant churches that allowed joint usage.[28]

Stalin died in March 1953. Though one may have expected a reprieve in repression, the opposite happened during the uncertain months following Stalin's death. However, the SED started slowly adjusting its policies and by June 11, 1953, Prime Minister Otto Grotewohl, in a meeting with the Council of the Protestant Church, stated that some of the government church policies (in particular the attack of the Party against the Christian youth) had been wrong and that freedom would be granted to the church youth movement.[29] Soon thereafter the event of June 16–17, 1953, took place—a short episode of rebellion against the Soviets.

The 1950s and 1960s were characterized by many tensions, and uncertainty developed between church and state with regard to education. Since atheism was strongly promoted in the schools, religious persons were considered non-socialists. Hence, being religious was regarded as not being on the right road to becoming a good citizen. Often children of religious parents or those who themselves were religious were denied access to higher education. In some areas absenting oneself from *Jugendweihe*[30] became a hurdle toward educational and vocational advancement.

Tensions increased especially on the issue of *Jugenweihe*, a state promoted ceremony of youth dedication which was perceived as a replacement of the traditional church confirmation of the youth. The Church was not sure how to react to this. Dibelius urged that people should resist *Jugendweihe*; Niemoeller, privately, said they did not have to. No clear winner emerged from this confrontation and in time most Christian young people participated in both confirmation and *Jugenweihe*, the latter of which has become nearly universal among fourteen-year olds, with about 97 percent participating in this rite either after or more or less simultaneously with confirmation.[31]

A number of clergy was arrested in the 1950s. For instance Schmuzler, director of a church-run educational center, was imprisoned having been accused that he had connections with the CIA and other western agencies. In 1952 *Neues Deutchland*, the official party organ, wrote that the *Kirchliche Hochschule* in West Berlin, from which many East German pastors graduated, was a center of American spies. Then it even became dangerous to write a letter to that school. The congregations reacted by praying *Fürbitten* [petitionary prayer] for those who were in jail—about 15–16 names. Since the late 1960s there have been no pastors in jail.

Bishop Moritz Mitzenheim[32] of Thüringia was credited with having coined the term "the Church in Socialism" (rather than against, beside, or for socialism) in 1968. (The Roman Catholic Church did not embrace this terminology.) The next year, on June 10, 1969, the eight provincial Protestant churches took the decisive step of separating themselves from the West German churches and the *Bund der Evangelischer Kirchen in der DDR* [Federation of Protestant Churches in the GDR] was organized.[33] This, perhaps more than any other factor contributed to a change of attitude among the SED leaders to grant greater liberties to the religious population and institutions in the GDR. For a while many of the stumbling blocks were resolved by negotiations between prominent church leaders who were trusted by the government (e.g. Bishops Mitzenheim and Albrecht Schoenherr and Emil Fuchs) and certain more flexible government personalities (Paul Verner and Hans Seigewasser), serving as mediators between church and state. This was to lead in 1978 to a top level meeting between the leaders of the government and the Protestant Churches.

Membership in churches dwindled from nearly 100 percent to something like a third of the population, but actual church membership is no real measure of the interest in religion (which had risen) as the church became a place where discussion could be held and dissenters protected. Thus the unusual happened that the churches became a greater haven of freedom than any other institution of society. It is unclear whether there was only interest in the "free space" provided by the churches or also an increased interest in religion.

The official leadership of the churches resisted successfully cooption and control by the government. Solberg concluded in 1960 that:

> no government-sponsored bishops preside over any of the eight provincial churches within the German Democratic Republic. No subservient synods have mouthed government-dictated resolutions. No hand-picked "church inspectors" sit on the Church councils. The Evangelical Church in East Germany still speaks with a clear voice and a free conscience.[34]

The well-known pastor, Johannes Hamel, made a statement that summarizes the problems of this period, stating that the churches are "engaged in a difficult struggle for the freedom of the gospel on two fronts: against our own evil, lazy, and loveless heart; and against a massive outside attack on faith, witness, and obedience."[35]

The role of the Conference on Security and Cooperation in Europe, the so-called Helsinki Accords which were accepted by thirty-five governments on August 1, 1975, for promotion of religious liberty in Eastern Europe is ambiguous, but in East Germany it seems to have had the most positive impact. Prior to the acceptance of the Final Acts, namely in the early 1970s as human rights were increasingly propelled onto the world stage, the Protestant theologians and bishops engaged in the discussion. East German Marxists, like their colleagues from other socialist countries habitually divided human rights into bourgeois (civil and political, mostly individual) and socialist (social and economic, mostly community) and accentuated the latter without verbally denying the former but made the former the subject of the prior implementation of the latter. This division was generally accepted by the theologians. For instance Bishop Hans-Joachim Fränkel of the Görlitz diocese acknowledged this two-fold division but pointed out that individual liberties, including freedom of religion and conscience, are only then respected when they are guaranteed to people without being subject to certain convictions.[36] These rights cannot be granted but are inherent and are based either on natural law (as in the U. N. Declaration of Universal Human Rights of December 10, 1948) or biblically and theologically grounded as part of divine creation and revelation. Fränkel pointed out that in a socialist society like the GDR, human rights had been linked to one's contribution to the building of socialism and that this was particularly so in the educational system. A plurality of values and norms were regarded as unnecessary to the socialist system and are inhibited. Only when pressure to implement a particular worldview by administrative methods or liabilities ceases may one speak of true tolerance. Human rights can be adequately guarded only from a liberal-democratic position, stated Fränkel and asserted that the catalogue of human rights must include not only social rights but also individual rights, including freedom of religion.[37]

A different emphasis was chosen by the Theological Study Department of the East German Committee of the Lutheran World Federation where the leading theologian Günther Krusche distinguished between human rights understanding of the First World which has certain individualistic aspects, the Second World in which social aspects dominate, and the Third World where structural aspects are emphasized. Krusche argued that each of these understandings included elements of the other two. In the case of the GDR Krusche pointed out that a socialist society does care about the welfare of the individual, who, in distinction from the Western model, is viewed as part of a social setting.[38] The theologians of the Study Department of LWF favored an open-ended list of human rights so that new ones could be added. They perceived the task of theologians not so much to list human rights or find their grounding but rather to articulate the co-responsibility in this struggle for societal progress.

The Final Act of the Helsinki Accords included Basket I in which human rights were recognized (principle VII specifies freedom of thought, conscience, religion and belief) and to which the signatories pledged themselves to adhere. But the document did not only address governments; it urged also non-governmental organizations, which includes churches, to work for the implementation of these agreements.

The Helsinki Accords played a three-fold role in East Germany and, also, to a lesser degree, in other East European countries. First, as the government signed the Final Act, though this did not become international law but a declaration of intent, nevertheless it gave these principles a *de jure* status. Second, it had a significant political and moral impact as people realized that one may appeal and even pressure the government to adhere to its internationally stated intentions. Third, the religious organizations, as non-governmental agencies, could legitimately study the situation and push for more adequate implementation of the principles, including religious liberty. One of the problems that the churches encountered was the tension between the human rights basket and the principle of non-intervention in the internal affairs of others. It was generally understood that this tension may not be misused for the purpose of denying human rights.

The World Council of Churches and the Council of European Churches quickly urged member churches to report on the situation in respective countries and what are the churches doing to promote the Helsinki Accord. In response to this the leader of the Secretariat of the Federation of Protestant Churches, Manfred Stolpe, reported that a meeting was convened in Buckow on October 27–31, 1973. At the meeting, a dossier of information was created for the use of church leaders. Also, additional activities were being planned to include discussions of the relevance of the CES Helsinki Accords for Christian teachers, youth, lay people, and clergy. The Helsinki Declaration was to be studied and explained and work was to be done on implementing it, particularly in respect to freedom of thought, religion, and belief.[39]

It would appear that the Helsinki Accords and the resulting discussion contributed to the significant normalization of the role of religious people in society in the subsequent period.

3. Normalization and Broadening of Religious Liberties; 1978–1989

This period saw a great improvement over the preceding period. After 1971 the SED attempted to set a more clear religious policy. The meeting on March 6, 1978, between the leadership of the Federation of Protestant Churches and a state delegation headed by Erich Honecker, is regarded as the crucial turning point in church-state relations.[40] One may say that from that year onward religion in its institutionalized form selectively re-entered the structures of society.

This meeting, which produced the equivalent to an Edict of Tolerance or a Declaration of Co-existence, has been carefully analyzed by one of its main participants, Bishop Albrecht Schoenherr. In his observations,[41] Schoenherr pointed out that Erich Honecker emphasized his commitment to the Constitutional guarantees of religious freedom to the individual, but asserted that the churches must order their inner life not by their own independent decision but consonant with the Constitution. Art. 1 of the Constitution defined the GDR "as the political organization of workers in city and village, which jointly under the leadership of the working class and its Marxist-Leninist Party brings socialism into realization." Clearly, the Church was not required to attach itself to this leadership, but was seen as an autonomous [*eigenständig*] organization. It originally appeared that the Church was to be viewed as a private matter, not part of public life, but the church leaders argued that churches deal openly with matters of public interest or else contradict the obligation of the Gospel. Hence, it was agreed that the churches are, indeed, relevant to society. Perhaps most significantly the state approved the building of new church buildings even in the newly erected industrial cities which heretofore lacked them. The Federation of Protestant Churches also got access to television four times a year with their own choice of speakers. The importation of religious books from West Germany was legitimated. The government promised money for the church to run clinics and homes for the handicapped. The joint communique of the meeting declared, "Openness and frankness are the barometer of trust. The relationship of church and state is as good as the experience with it of each individual Christian citizen in his or her local situation."[42]

At this meeting, at subsequent meetings between church and state officials, and at meetings in the church the church leadership spoke with unusual candor and courage. The most difficult alternative was selected by the church representatives, namely to say a cooperative "yes" to positive achievements and programs of the state and to utter a concretely critical "no" when the church felt the interest of people to be threatened. The church did not place itself above society as an arbiter but rather wished to suffer in the midst of the people and speak out on behalf of those who are hurt and alienated. Thus the Protestant Church declared itself, in the words of the former East Berlin Consistory President Manfred Stolpe, "neither the Trojan horse of counter-revolution" nor "the disseminator of ideas of the SED." The one thing seemed clear in these conversations and subsequently, that for all the issues raised by the term "church in socialism," the state would not request nor the church allow itself to become a "socialist church" or a church in favor of socialism. This set the church and the state on a path of mutual learning and normalization of relations rather than mere tolerance. The March 6, 1978, agreement was reaffirmed by Erich Honecker at a meeting with the chairman of the Conference of the Evangelical Church Leadership.[43]

The then Secretary for Church Affairs of the GDR, Klaus Gysi, declared often, for example in Geneva in 1981, that religious liberty was almost ideally realized in the GDR.[44] On the other hand Christians and church leaders of the GDR continued to complain about repeated hindrances and discriminations on account of religion. Even when the abuses by local or regional authorities were later corrected by intervention by central authorities, such misuses continued. At the least they prove that there was wide discrepancy in interpreting the meaning of religious liberty.[45] The *practical* reason for being concerned with religious liberty is that it would give churches more space to organize their activities. The *intrinsic* reason was that the message of Judaism and Christianity is closely tied with religious liberty, freedom of conscience, and human rights. Party theoreticians maintained that Marxists and Christians can coexist but that correspondingly there should be an increase in the ideological struggle, which, of course, had implications not only for the political sphere but also for the issue, so important to Marxists, namely of becoming partisans of the Marxist world view. Some church leaders wondered whether this did not signify that in the future Christianity would not be able to survive.[46]

The outstanding issue of the last period prior to the Great Transformation was whether the churches should be allowed to concern themselves with social issues: i.e. should people be allowed to discuss political and economic issues, including human rights and release of those who had been charged with political crimes inside and outside the church buildings?[47] No barriers existed any longer about the right to go to church; this issue was settled in favor of freedom to attend worship services. However, there was no right to proselytize or comment on political issues and organize cultural affairs.[48] The main question was the social discussion about (1) foreign policy (peace and disarmament)[49], (2) military draft, training and pre-military education, (3) environmental issues, (4) school (not forcing people to profess atheism and materialism), (5) all questions regarding foreign travel (e.g. visiting West Germany), and 6) other issues, including morality. These were, in the words of Professor Helmut Fritzsche, "neuralgic points,"[50] which were discussed in the churches and between church and government leaders although the state did not really want them discussed in the churches. The editors of church papers were warned not to discuss these issues too frankly in their publications because they were perceived as governmental prerogatives. Freedom of the press was understood by the government to be only that which promotes socialism. While freedom of religion included the church's right to publish periodicals, the state was, however, allowed to limit the supply of paper and could censor or confiscate offensive issues.[51] The government maintained that religion and church life are *not* cultural life but belong in the narrower sphere of religious life. The churches on the other hand said that they want to contribute to cultural life.[52]

Since the signing of the Helsinki Agreements in 1975 the churches involved themselves more explicitly with the study of human rights issues. A number of church leaders, including Günther Krusche, have maintained that a one-sided emphasis on individual liberties is not in the interest of people who live in socialism.[53] He maintained that personal freedom is related to social and state needs, and that rather than being opposed to one another they are subordinated to each other. Thus human rights are neither only an individual's private concern nor only a concession by the state. "In the well-adjusted system of socialist civil rights, economic, cultural-ideological, and political rights are combined."[54] For many church leaders, to strive for human rights meant to work for the rights of others.[55] The churches often engaged in such advocacy and defense of human rights, not only for their own members but also for the general population, especially the young people. The churches acknowledged the considerable achievements of the GDR in the field of full employment, stable prices, health care, day care centers, and women's employment. But they criticized restrictions in the freedom of information, pressure on critics of the regime and freedom of movement, both in respect to travel and to emigration.[56] Churches also spoke up (successfully) on behalf of alternative military service (the so-called *Bausoldaten*), against pre-military education in high school (unsuccessfully), and creating enemy images on which to raise the youth, and other peace and disarmament issues.

A Canadian church group observed in 1985:

> There have also been numerous arrests of young people engaged in peace activity in the German Democratic Republic. In that situation, resolutions have been somewhat easier to come by because of the relative lack of antagonism on the part of the state to a role for the church within society . . . while some have been arrested in the independent peace movement, there have also been massive gatherings of young people in the churches of that country to discuss race questions . . . they have gone on largely without interference from the State.[57]

The church protected small "dissenting" groups, especially of young people whose behavior was not sanctioned by the government and unofficial peace and ecology movements—namely those people who find no other gathering place for their activity but the church. Some were alienated by the discrepancies between the promised ideals of socialism and the reality.[58] The Church defended these movements arguing that their situation has been aggravated by the government's suppression of information and espousal of one-sided peace proposals. Such stances contributed greatly to the church's reputation for concern and integrity, even by those splinter groups which were harshly critical of the theology, liturgy, and organization of the church. The Protestant Churches offered the possibility of finding pockets of freedom in their midst to groups, mostly of young people, from within and on the margins of the church.[59] These included groups of homosexuals, punks, feminists, ecologists, peaceniks, and others. According to John Burgess, "In contrast to a state that encouraged outward conformity, the church offered a sense of freedom and acceptance that they did not find elsewhere in society."[60] The churches often envisioned themselves as having the task to serve all people of the GDR society, and even those in other countries, particularly the Third World, thereby asserting their freedom from the confinements to which Marxist theory and Communist practice relegated them. While sometimes the churches succumbed to the restrictions imposed upon them, nevertheless, they preserved a sufficiently distinct profile that they were clearly perceived as an alternative to the stifling Stalinist atmosphere.

Bishop Schoenherr maintained that the government fundamentally renounced interference in internal church affairs, so that church officials including bishops, were elected without state permission. No further constitutional privileges were sought, but there was need for the extension of existing possibilities in order to maintain a stronger Christian identity. Tension, however, was a persistent feature of this relationship.[61] For instance, rather lengthy negotiations were necessary in order to hold the 1987 Protestant *Kirchentag* and the "Meeting of Catholics."[62]

There were some fields at the universities, (e.g. medicine) where the discrimination against religious people persisted for a long time because the number of applicants were three times as large as the number of accepted, and it was difficult to know which criteria were used for selection. In some fields, such as regional studies of Latin America and Asia, one did not find children of clergy because many of the graduates were expected to enter diplomatic service. Yet, strangely, the children of higher clergy had a somewhat more easy access to some departments because their parents had good connections with the government through the Secretariat for Church Questions and because the government wanted to appear undiscriminating. Some unease was felt about such manipulations.

Some Christians reached high state positions. Töplitz was the head of the supreme court and Gerald Götting was president of the *Volkskammer*, but in general, very few Christians were in leadership positions. Götting's standing among Christians was very low, hence no upheaval was created when he abruptly lost his position to a SED party person, except, of course, a blow to him personally for the cavalier manner in which it was done. In 1988 only one Christian, Schulze, was the head of a Ministry (Post, Telephone, and Telegraph). In the district governments there were some CDU members who were in high positions but none were heading a district government. The CDU continued to have few independent ideas.

How did East Germans perceive their status in regard to religious freedom? The older and lower ranked members by and large felt they had religious freedom. Others on the middle level were uneasy because of the atheist propaganda and restrictions. Younger people felt that religious freedom should include the freedom to choose social systems and that option seemed absent. In any case, the thinking of the young people may have "opened up opportunities that the church would have been afraid to explore on its own."[63] Second-class citizenship was part of the religious reality. Many SED members considered it normal for non-party members to have some restrictions, particularly in education, because they felt that their own party membership entailed some privileges and restrictions. They said that religious people may be more independent from certain strictures and that some can become materially better off than party members because there were lesser controls on their behavior.

At the April 1985 synod of the Berlin-Brandenburg Evangelical Church a pastor from Potsdam reported that some young church members, both high school and student age, had been approached by the members of the state security seeking their cooperation in return for admission to a university. Similarly, it was reported that state security organs applied pressure on those attending church services by sometimes very visibly taking down car registration plate numbers of those seen to enter the church.[64]

The state has harassed some people who, upon applying to emigrate, met in churches to discuss their problems. On March 6, 1988, some of them were stopped by the police from attending church services at the *Sophienkirche* in East Berlin.

The religious institutions published many publications. The *Evangelische Verlagsanstalt* was, of course, not free in the Western sense. Every book had to be censored in previous years; by this time self-censorship was exercised, as the publishers had a sense of what could be published. For instance, they could criticize moral decline. Several times in 1988 the church newspapers were prohibited or appeared with white-outs. *Die Kirche* alone was forbidden circulation five times that year. The September 25, 1988, issue was to contain reports of the annual Synod of the Federation of the Evangelical Churches in the GDR, which took place in August at which comments were made about the status of church-state relations, urging "understanding, tolerance, and legal certainty" and pointing out that frank criticism is not to be equated with hostility to the government. Apparently the government was not eager to have such comments communicated with readers of a paper with a circulation of 42,500.[65] Similar censoring occurred in *Der Sontag, Potsdamer Kirche, Glaube und Heimat,* and *Mecklenburgische Kirchenzeitung.* The professional publications *Zeichen der Zeit, Theologische Literaturzeitung,* and *Die Christenlehre* were significant, but the most important was the work of the *Theologische Studienabteilungen,* in which young staff members were engaged to organize thought-provoking programs which attracted wide audiences.

One of the fascinating developments was the ardent embracing of Gorbachev's policies, especially *perestroika* and *glasnost,* on the part of many church members and those who attend churches, particularly since Honecker's government had steadfastly avoided to give support to those policies. Thus there was the paradox that the religious population was among the more fervent followers of the policies of the Secretary General of the Communist Party of the Soviet Union while the leadership of the SED was cautiously avoiding such support. Provost Heino Falcke bitingly reformulated a party slogan of the past, "*Von der Sowjetunion zu lernen, heisst siegen lernen,*" into "*Von der Sowjetunion zu lernen, heisst denken lernen.*"[66] The problem for the proponents of *perestroika* in the leadership was how not to encourage support of too radical and too quick changes which the government, and even East German allies, may not be able to handle without repression. Thus Manfred Stolpe argued the importance not of speed but of a discernible direction for restructuring, saying that even a snail's pace change will suffice as long as the party leaders make it clear in which direction such changes will go.[67] He urged the government and the media not to avoid pointing out a discernible path of reforms. Nor should "New Thinking" become an empty phrase, as supposedly an editorial in *Pravda* ironically urged its readers "to accept new thinking and not to change it!"

There were, however, those for whom this did not suffice. On November 25, 1987, the police arrested some people who were publishing unofficial anti-government publications in an annex to the Zion Church in East Berlin. Likewise many were arrested in Berlin when on

January 17, 1988, about 120 members of independent groups joined an official commemoration of the murder of Rosa Luxembourg and Karl Liebknecht as they carried placards with Rosa Luxembourg's quote, "Freedom is always also the freedom of those who think differently." The Ecumenical Gathering in Dresden on February 12–15, 1988, brought to light a document of profound alienation, in which the signers stated that they are estranged from the rest of the world by the existence of the Berlin Wall and from the holders of might inside their country. They complained that as citizens of the GDR they experienced inferiority complexes, helplessness, fear, inability to communicate, injustice, retreat from responsibility, lack of orientation, etc. which creates people with inauthentic, double lives.

> Therefore the delimit goes right through us. It was implanted in us already in school. Thus was achieved, that in our vocations we are what we are supposed to be. At home we attempt to be who we want to be. This forced double existence makes us and society ill.[68] Bishop Werner Leich of Thüringia acknowledges the increase in tensions, because, many citizens see in our church the only institution, which is not clearly bound and answerable to the state and they use therefore, this free space, to, openly express what, in their opinion, is wrong with the GDR. We take here to some degree a function of a representative, which is not actually an original task of the church. But we cannot retreat from this task.[69]

Often church leaders and church people did not support concrete protest actions by the independent groups, yet were willing to defend them even if it jeopardized the relatively good relations with government officials. Thus the church publications have repeatedly been censored for their willingness to publicize both what the issues were and the statement of the Protestant leaders on behalf of those who were antagonizing the state.[70]

The Roman Catholic Church's stance to many of the above issues was different from the Protestant. The formula "church in socialism" had not been accepted. Instead, a distancing from the government was typical of the attitude of that Church, with only unofficial meetings between the Catholic and government leadership taking place behind closed doors. The size and different historical role of the Catholic Church and the tension between the two churches in north-east German lands was responsible for that difference. However, on September 8, 1986, a pastoral letter of the bishops to all the clergy indicated a change in orientation. It consisted of a greater degree of acceptance of life in the GDR as a "common, habitable house" rather than living in a "foreign house." The letter contained the statement that [Catholic] Christians do wish to live in the GDR as equal citizens but do not wish to be manipulated for the building of an atheist, religionless society. For the Catholic bishops the major problems were the discrimination against Christians in job opportunities, armed services, and education. The bishops resolutely rejected any possible role of becoming an arm of the state. They were willing to see and undertake steps of encouragement in order to overcome the rising level of resignation and express their willingness to enter into official discussions with the government.[71]

The Jewish community kept a very low profile in the GDR until 1987. While allowed to operate community centers, the government treated the Jews coldly and by-and-large kept the population poorly informed about Jews and Judaism except, of course, that it harshly attacked Zionism. In 1987 for the first time in over thirty years, a rabbi resided in East Germany. Hopeful signs were that the GDR state, which steadfastly rejected the idea of any complicity in anti-Semitic activities of the Nazi state, finally made some positive overtures in that direction.[72] Official meetings between the highest state authorities and Jewish leadership took place. It seems that no special restrictions or concessions characterized the Jewish religious liberties.

The same may be said of the Free Churches. The government allowed the establishment of entirely new churches on the territory of the country, the building of new church buildings, the education of their clergy, and other activities. While not having the same stature as the Federation of the Protestant Churches, the Association of Christian Churches in the GDR (including observer churches) and the individual churches enjoyed a good relationship with the government. The exception were the Jehovah's Witnesses and, at least in the past, Christian Scientists whose activities were still viewed with reservation by the government.

What was still needed to be accomplished to have true religious liberties in East Germany?

1. True freedom for church publications, needed to be instituted without censorship or self-censorship. Thus far they were forced to concentrate on religious questions in a narrower sense and were not

able to satisfy their desire to address larger issues. It was not clear whether there was a need for more publications, but there was a need for increased circulation.

2. Deal with all problems of a human being.

3. No restrictions to be placed on religious persons with regard to holding jobs in the public sphere, including higher government and army positions.

4. The placement of no restriction in education, both in applying to be admitted and later in the classroom.

5. Allowing the church to discuss social issues.

6. Providing a genuine alternative military service. The *Bausoldaten* were still perceived as aiding the military effort. Many would prefer work in hospitals and social service organizations.

7. Permission to travel freely, including to emigrate. The church wrestled with the issue. Despite significant liberalization of travel there were still many who were not allowed to travel or, paradoxically, were forced to emigrate.

8. How might one find an alternative to socialism? What could it be? First, people hoped for more freedom in thinking and talking. But it became evident that this was not enough. With a mismanaged economy there is no real freedom, so there was a need for broader notions of freedom. But it was not clear how the "real socialist" system, including the alliance with the Soviet Union and other socialist countries, would permit that. The stability in the GDR made it possible for Poland and the Soviet Union to dare to experiment with "Solidarity," or *perestroika* and *glasnost* respectively. For a while the relationship between the church and the state in East Germany, in contrast to many other Eastern European states, stood out "as an exceptional experiment in state tolerance of a growing social role for the church and for believers."[73]

Two additional reasons existed for the increase in religious freedom. The first was related to the continuing decline in church membership. As stated earlier only a minority of citizens considered themselves church members. It was easier for the government to be more tolerant of a declining rather than growing church. The second was that the government might have deliberately provided religious liberty as a vent for other types of social frustration. This frustration could be expressed in church buildings where the church leadership might attempt to exercise control over them in order to preserve some of the church's privileges. Thus, the state could experiment with *glasnost* within the churches.[74]

That experimentation did not go on without police repression, however. Dissenters were frequently arrested and most were imprisoned and/or exiled (including the leader of the Protestant "Church from Below," Vera Wollenburger).[75] When the arrests became known, dissenters in increasing numbers (sometimes reaching 2,000 persons) flocked to the churches in all the major cities to show their solidarity. Bishop Gottfried Forck and the lawyer Manfred Stolpe effectively represented the arrested dissidents while the churches also established "Advice and Counseling Centers." The Protestants were joined by the Roman Catholic Joachim Cardinal Meisner of Berlin who urged support of the Protestant effort.[76] These efforts yielded positive results and already at the subsequent Olaf Palme Peace March church groups were allowed to carry their slogans.[77] The Protestant churches then again became the locus of criticism of the government during the mass exodus of primarily young East Germans in 1989 in which the church leaders pleaded with the government to pay heed to the social problems causing such a flight. When mass demonstrations took place in October 1989 in Leipzig, Dresden, East Berlin, and elsewhere, they often commenced inside and around churches. Pastors and bishops became spokespersons for the disaffected masses urging the demonstrators to maintain order and avoid violence and the government to undertake urgent reforms.[78]

B. Assessment

Germany may be classified as a former representative of a Type A (monopoly of a state church) society that gradually developed into a Type B (religious toleration with the state favoring certain churches) during the Weimar Republic. During the Nazi period there had been an attempt to revive the Type A situation with the *Deutsches Christentum* seeking monopoly. However, the Confessing Church courageously fought this attempt in the ensuing *Kirchenkampf*. With the establishment of the GDR, there was an attempt to move into Type C society, which is what the SED preferred. However, another *Kirchenkampf* took place, led by church leaders and church members nurtured in the spirit of the Confessing Church. The result was that Type C, following the Soviet model, was carried out only briefly and incompletely in the early 1950s. Type C never took deep roots and there were evidences that East Germany, albeit ambiguously, was showing traces of Type D society qualities along with remnants of Type C mentality espoused by the conservatives among the SED membership who prefer "a system of antagonistic separation of church and state,"[79] with attempts to limit the influence of the religious institutions upon society, especially the youth, by means of limitations, prohibitions, and propaganda. Those democratically oriented in society and the church were finding allies among the pro-*perestroika* members of the SED. On the whole there was a preference among Marxists for transcending religion gradually, over a long period of time, mostly by means of secularization and integration of religious people into the process of building socialism. The Marxists of this orientation argued that tolerance is an important aspect of humanism which may not be simply pushed to the side in a socialist society which aspires to be humanistic.[80] This was to be done, among others, by means of a dialogue between Christians and Marxists, which until the middle 1980s was explicitly rejected as an unnecessary exercise since presumably they had advanced beyond the dialogue stage.[81] The dialogue between Christians and Marxists in particular, began to be sought and promoted.

This is not the place to examine the Christian-Marxist dialogue in East Germany *per se* but a few words that have a bearing on religious liberties are appropriate. Dialogue became possible around 1983 during the Luther celebrations when Christian and Marxist historians engaged in a fruitful give-and-take. Such dialogues have continued and have been particularly promoted by theologians such as Fritzsche and Jens Langer of University of Rostock where in April 1989 an Institute for Peace and Understanding has been established by Christian and Marxist faculty members.[82] But many of the "mainline" theologians have not been included and thus it was always an important issue in East Germany as to who dialogues with whom. It is notable that the call for dialogue at the top has not always been translated into actual dialogue at the lower levels. Still there were indicators of readiness for dialogue in the greater willingness of media to give exposure to the views of younger Christians and afford some opportunities of interactions with young Marxists.

Thus just prior to the Great Transformation the situation in East Germany was fraught with ambiguities. In some respects the Christians there had more freedom than in many other East European countries. Yet on the other hand they faced a determined, highly ideologized orthodox Marxist government with a very efficient apparatus of repression headed by a very well informed secret police.

AFTER THE GREAT TRANSFORMATION

The Great Transformation (in the GDR the term used was *Wende*, i.e. Turning or the Gentle Revolution) and then the dissolution of the GDR happened with lightning speed. As noted above, changes had been taking place which testify that the Transformation was actually being prepared for many years, without awareness that it could succeed; most of the church leadership was convinced that the socialist system and the division of Germany was here to stay. During the late summer 1989 one could at best hope for gradual relaxation of the Stalinist Communist regime's approach, though Honecker expressed admiration for the unyielding Chinese Tianamen Square solution when confronted by pressure to reform. As recently as May 1989 the SED blatantly falsified the returns of a municipal election arousing sharp criticism from church leaders who called for political liberalization.[84] The SED thereby lost whatever moral authority it may have had. The churches likewise opposed the renewed effort of the SED to emphasize Communist and atheist education at a congress held in the summer of 1989.

The snowball that caused the avalanche was the exodus of many East Germans to West Germany when the Hungarians opened their border to Austria in September 1989. When the Czechoslovak-Hungarian border was sealed off to East Germans they rushed in large numbers to the West German embassies in Prague and Warsaw so that the GDR either had to decide to isolate itelf from all of its neighbors or allow these refugees to reach West Germany. The pressure increased quickly with the rapidly growing demonstrations within the country, first in Berlin and even more massive ones in Leipzig (especially the Nikolai church) and then quickly throughout the country. Typically the pattern was that from small prayer circles in churches the number of attenders increased daily as the authorities increased their surveillance and intimidation of the growing crowd. Before too long the number of people was so great that they could not fit into the church and then the mass moved from the churches to the public square making demands for changes. The SED folded quickly under such pressure first forcing Honecker to resign, and then in quick order getting rid even of the reformist minded Egon Krenz and Hans Modrow. The opposition first crystallized around the New Forum and then formed numerous other political parties. The multi-party pluralism prevailed as the SED reformed itself into the Party of

Democratic Socialism. In addition to the creation of a large number of new political parties, a metamorphosis took place within the four political parties, including the Christian Democratic Union, that had been obedient tools of the SED since 1948.

By far the most dramatic symbol of the Great Transformation in all of Eastern Europe happened on November 9, 1989. Upon the GDR's decision to open its borders completely, a spontaneous jubilation erupted on the Berlin Wall, resulting in the wall's subsequent dismantling. The whole world celebrated the removal of the most notorious symbol of the Cold War; a decisive forecast that the Cold War was over.

Suddenly the re-unification of Germany, an old topic, took on renewed vitality and urgency. In less than a year the reunification was accomplished—on October 3, 1990—and the GDR no longer existed, confined to the dustbin of history. In the intervening period free elections took place on March 18, 1990, in which the Alliance for Germany, a coalition lead by the revamped Christian Democratic Union (that had purged its old compromised leadership) under the new leadership of Lothar de Maizière won 48 percent of the vote, a decisive electoral victory that brought de Maizière the premiership.[84] The CDU decisively opted for reunification cooperating closely with its sister party in West Germany resulting in reunification and the subsequent nationwide electoral victory on December 2, 1990, by Helmut Kohl and the CDU. While in retrospect the process of "Turning" was forceful and proceeded without any great setbacks, it was fraught with anxieties that something may happen to restore Stalinism and later by new anxieties as to how the institutions and people will function in the radically altered environment.

On the whole the churches claimed no political mandate and did not instruct their members how and for whom to vote but did help educate the electorate to the importance of their choices.[85] Thus, for instance, Bishop Georg Sterzinsky, the Chairman of the Berlin Catholic Bishops Conference pointed out that according to Marxist ideology people have human rights only in so far as they function for the social good. Christians, however, cannot support this as they believe that human rights originate in one's being human.[86]

The role of the churches in the revolutionary events was enormous and accomplished literally overnight a complete religious liberty for all citizens and religious organizations. The State Secretariat for Religious Affairs was sharply reduced in staff in November 1989 and its functions were taken over temporarily by de Maizière as deputy chairman of the Council of Ministers and Minister for Church Affairs[87] before he was destined for an even greater role. He severely criticized the former SED approach to the religious institutions as they created the State Secretariat for Church Affairs as a location where the churches had to beg for permissions to carry out their activities and where they were manipulated to praise the regime and carry out the state's policies.[88] The Secretariat was abolished on September 30, 1990.

The SED quickly lost its dominant position in society and even more importantly the hated "*Stasis*" [*Staatssicherheit,* i.e. the state security forces) were disbanded. The Stasi records showed the pervasive nature of the Communist control system in which a very large number citizens, including many church leaders and activists, were involved in some sort of spying or reporting. After October 1989 nearly everyone, including many of the former collaborators, claimed that they were in the forefront of the revolution, but the files of the *Stasis* were likely to reveal the complicity of people and institutions. It will take a most massive research effort lasting years to unravel the real truth of the ambiguous Stalinist legacy of the GDR.[89]

The church was the "midwife, rather than mother" of the revolution, in the picturesque phrase of Superintendent Christoph Richter of Leipzig.[90] Protestant and Catholic clergy and activists served as moderators at the "Round Tables" between the SED and the opposition groups during the early stages of the Transformation. As the revolution proceeded, according to some analysts, the Protestant Churches were the single most important facilitators of the Transformation along with the small groups that functioned within that church space.[91] According to that argument, Protestant social ethics did not only provide an alternative during the years of "real existing socialism" but provided also the basis for a vision to re-capitalize East Germany, linking it with the modern European societal model. The General Superintendent of the Evangelical Church Berlin-Brandenburg, Günther Krusche, however, assessed the situation a little differently.

> In all honesty it must be said that the Evangelical Church was only one factor among others in bringing about the change that happened. Without the framework of the Helsinki process, which gave a charismatic personality like Gorbachev room to work, without the many activities of groups which

took the text of the concluding act of Helsinki as their charter, and without the self-caused breakdown of "real existing socialism," due to its bad public relations and inefficient economy (to name only the basic elements) the "Turning" would never had happened. In the last heated phase in the autumn of 1989, the church did indeed play a decisive role.[92]

The leadership of the opposition was recruited from the churches, including a large number of clergymen. In Pomeranian local elections on May 6, 1990, for instance, an astounding 42 percent of all clergy (!) were given mandate; some of them such major posts that they had to go on leave of absence from their churches in order to fulfill these political obligations.[93] Three Protestant clergy became GDR government ministers, including Rev. Rainer Eppelmann, a noted pacifist of the Berlin Church of the Samaritan, who became the Minister for Disarmament and Defense. Twenty-one theologians (among whom were nineteen ordained pastors) were elected members of the parliament. The reason for this was three-fold. First, people generally trusted clergymen as honest, an important virtue in the aftermath of shocking discoveries of corruption in the highest places. Second, pastors provided wise leadership during the demonstrations helping them to be carried out in an orderly and peaceful manner. Third, the churches were the only institutions that had any democratic tradition and the spirit of reconciliation permeated the process.[94] Sometimes people perceived that the pastors were a little too reconciling, for instance when pastor Uwe Holmer gave shelter to the disgraced Honecker couple after they were evicted from the government residence. Similarly, the churches counseled many former *Stasis* and distraught Marxists and ex-Marxists who suffered severe dislocations.[95] But this was evidence that at least a part of the clergy and the church was consistent in providing shelter for those who were not in political graces of the government; it had not been mere political sympathy.[96] Robert Goeckel, an American political scientist who studied the role of the churches in the East German Transformation or "the Turning" as it is more popularly called, concluded, "As a key element of civil society the institutional church provided leadership and mediation among the political forces in the revolutionary context."[97]

The problems of religious liberties facing religious institutions and members in the interim between the removal of the Berlin Wall and reunification were many. The basic one was the redefined church-state relationship in which the state ceased to restrict and control religion.[98] Other issues confronted were whether to be state-churches or voluntary membership churches,[99] whether to re-introduce religious education in schools, whether to revert to a church taxation system akin to the West German model,[100] and whether to restrict the liberal abortion laws. Generally the *Landeskirchen* quickly opted to follow the West German model and introduced both religious education in schools as of Fall 1991 and church taxation (which led to a rush of inactive people—70,000 in Berlin alone—to formally drop their membership in order to avoid taxes) while the free churches, such as the Evangelical Methodist Church, protested both measures.[101] Protestant and Catholic holy days were declared state holidays. The Salvation Army was allowed to function again. *Jugendweihe*, the youth dedication that had been so damaging to the religious orientation of the youth and so strenuously opposed by the churches, did not disappear at once as many hoped but changed into a rite of passage.[102] Compulsory Marxist and atheist education was discontinued; almost overnight the large battery of educators in Marxism at all levels had to seek other jobs. Entire university departments of Marxism were disbanded and the long road to building more classic philosophy departments began. The Communist children and youth organizations and pre-military education were eliminated from the schools. Churches did not need to have permission from the government for most of their activities. A number of organizations and journals that had been too cooperative with the former regime, e.g. the Christian Peace Conference, *Standpunkt*, and *Begegnung*, collapsed rapidly while other church publications expanded and were sold freely at newspaper stands.[103] Nearly all churches established those organizations they felt were useful for the political, financial, educational, and cultural welfare of their members and broader social work for all citizens in need. The Catholic Church also spoke up strongly in favor of human rights and especially the right of parents to be involved in decision-making in regard to the education of their children.[104]

Negotiations between churches in both parts of Germany toward reunion started at once,[105] but ecumenical relations were also improved, as for instance for the first time Protestant and Catholic Bishops of East Germany met to discuss common problems. On the whole the Catholic leadership tended to place the events of the past forty years behind and look for reconciliation between groups in conflict while the Protestants also favored reconciliation but also urged repentance saying that a healthy national life in the future requires facing the truth. A number of outstanding Protestant leaders expressed such repentance in their own behalf and that of the churches for mistakes they made prior to the Great Transformation.[105]

The result of the "Turning" was that each religious institution followed its own traditions and impulses in their religious and societal activities. All of them agreed that religious institutions must have the freedom to act as organizations with civic responsibilities in an unabashedly open manner, and not relegated to the sanctuary to which the Marxists wanted to confine them. The country was suddenly opened to evangelists of various sorts, Christian and non-Christian. Perhaps the most clear threat to religious liberty came not from the state but from within the historical churches as they attempted to put obstacles in the path of the "sectarian" proselytizers in a manner not entirely consistent with true religious liberty.[107]

On the whole the religious institutions were not guided by mere political expediency and were not dispensers of cheap grace but led the societal debate about the desirability and speed of reunification, raising helpful critical questions about the momentary euphoria, which would naturally wane in the ensuing period when real economic and political problems would emerge. Yet on the whole the churches were unprepared for the sudden change from a "church in socialism" to a church without socialism and needed to assess what they learned in their experience of the past forty years when they were distanced from the state and renounced power.[108] Now the Church needs to exercise its freedom in order to learn, according to G. Krusche, how to provide prophetic service to its new society, how to do pastoral service under conditions of new social needs, and how to be a moral agent to a society that has a very different post-socialist orientation.

Concluding Remarks

During the short period of its existence after the Great Transformation the GDR quickly threw off the hated Type C–Secular Absolutistic society model and resumed almost immediately the Type B–Religious Toleration pattern in which the historic Protestant and Catholic Churches, reunited in a reunited state, would have a somewhat privileged position and be enmeshed with the state but in which all other religions and ideologies, collectively and individually would be tolerated, though one suspects that Marxists would experience considerable public pressure. Such Type B arrangement contains a measure of Type D–Pluralistic Liberty characteristics because for all practical purposes in the reunited Germany individuals can freely choose to practice or not to practice any given religion. Yet some social stigma would be attached to the religions of the sectarians and certain foreign workers (e.g. Muslim Turks), as well as Marxists. Social privilege and status are granted to the historic churches despite resistance by free churches and liberal individuals from the historic churches.[109] Some of them complain that the ideologized Marxist world view is now being replaced by the historic churches' interpretations which are not acceptable to those with alternate concepts of reality. This indicates that Type D will not likely be implemented harmoniously.

With the full reunification of Germany on October 3, 1990, the German Democratic Republic disappeared as a separate unit and thus ceased to be a part of Eastern Europe. The sequel to these developments are then automatically exempt from further examination in this study.

Chapter 9

H U N G A R Y: CONCESSIONS BY
CHURCH AND STATE

While Hungarian self-consciousness can be traced back to the legendary Attila the Hun and the Arpád chieftains who settled the Carpathian Basin after migrating there from Asia, the Hungarians trace their nation and culture more closely to the conversion to Christianity in the tenth and eleventh century and the crowning of St. Stephen (997–1038) as king of Hungary in the year 1000 A.D. While at first the influence came from both Rome and Constantinople, the Western Roman Catholic influence soon prevailed and the Hungarian kings fought crusades against the Bogumils in Bosnia at the request of the pope. Originally an independent kingdom the Hungarian royalty extended its domain to Croatia, Bosnia, Transylvania, parts of Great Moravia (now Slovakia), and maintained excellent relationships and dynastic ties with Poland-Lithuania. According to the scheme adopted in chapter 1, Hungary was then a Type A–Ecclesiastic Absolutist society.

The Roman Catholic nature of the kingdom was threatened and nearly terminated on two fronts in the sixteenth and seventeenth centuries.

The first was the Turkish Muslim conquest in 1526 to which the larger middle parts of the country yielded for about a hundred fifty years. Very few Hungarians converted to Islam as Hungarians saw themselves, similarly to other Christians of that part of Europe, as the last bastion of Christendom, though some Hungarian cities had mosques that stand until the present. Most of them were used again as churches with the Christian cross symbolically superimposed over the Muslim crescent atop the church.

More serious was the second, the Protestant challenge to which at first the majority of Hungarians yielded. The Austrian Hapsburg dynasty incorporated all of the Hungarian domains after the death of the last Hungarian King Lajos II on the battlefield of Mohács fighting against the Turks (1526). They ruled Hungary until 1918 and faced opposition by the powerful Hungarian nobles. Since the Hapsburgs were staunch Catholics, it was natural for many Hungarian nobles to favor Protestantism, and so during the Reformation in the Western Hungarian lands, particularly Transylvania, the Calvinist Reformed tradition prevailed while in Eastern Hungary the Lutherans became predominant.[1] Only about one out of ten remained Catholic during the Protestant Reformation by the end of the sixteenth century.[2] The intensity of the Reformed and Lutheran struggle against anti-Trinitarians and Catholics indicate that the Protestants would have liked to replace Roman Catholics in the saddle of a Type A–Ecclesiastic Absolutist society except that the Hungarian Reformed had to co-exist with the Lutherans and vice versa and therefore practiced limited religious toleration among Protestants, which also included the Unitarians.

The Counter-Reformation, signifying an attempt to return to the Ecclesiastic Absolutist–Type A model, brought the Hungarian authorities and the Catholic Church into a very close relationship according to which bishops had the same rank as the higher nobility while in return they preached obedience to the crown. Though no religious wars *per se* were fought, Jesuits, accompanied by soldiers, forcibly converted people, imprisoned Protestant ministers, and confiscated Protestant lands.[3] Hence there was a period of the "bloody counter-Reformation" causing a lasting bitterness between Catholics and Protestants. Not before the eighteenth century did the Counter-Reformation, "bloodless" in its later stages, reclaim most Hungarians to Roman Catholicism forming a ratio of three–fourths Roman Catholics and one–fourth Protestant (20 percent Hungarian Reformed and 4 percent Lutheran) which, roughly speaking, persists to this day. The combat between Christians and Muslims and between Roman Catholics and Protestant during the sixteenth and seventeenth centuries created a strong undercurrent of religious intolerance which had an ill-effect on all attempts toward tolerance and religious liberty.

Several milestones of tolerance, however, did take place. The first was the Treaty of Vienna in 1606 by which Prince István Bocskai obtained recognition and religious liberty for the Protestants. The Transylvanian Protestant princes, Gábor Bethlen and György Rákoczi I, fought the Hapsburgs to defend religious freedoms for the

Protestants. Until the eighteenth century the Hapsburg monarchs did not provide any significant degree of religious liberty, but Emperor Joseph II (1780–1790) restored the legal status of the Protestant Churches by his "Edict of Toleration" in 1781 which provided some controlled freedom for the historic Protestant Churches. Joseph II subjected the Roman Catholic Church to rather strict control by the state, even expelling some of the monastic orders, often using the churches to promote his policies. This arrangement is generally referred to as Josephinism, and it represents the attempt to replace the Ecclesiastic Absolutism, Type A arrangements with a Religious Toleration, Type B model. Elements of Josephinism were retained during the historical changes which were to follow and seems to have been rather vigorously applied during the Communist period after World War II. Josephinism in Hungary was not of a general type but of a specifically Hungarian type. Namely the Hungarian churches became willing to give their loyalty and service to a Hungarian state but not to other states in which they were citizens. Until 1848 the Roman Catholic Church was the established church, though Joseph II Edict of Toleration of 1781 did allow individual Roman Catholics to convert to Protestantism and legally recognized the Reformed and the Lutheran churches. Act XXVI of 1790–1791 eliminated the most discriminatory practices against Protestants.[4]

During the Hungarian Revolution of 1848/49 a close cooperation of most Hungarians against the Hapsburgs resulted in a remarkable religious law according to which all religions were granted equality and the Catholic Church was disestablished.[5] With the defeat of the Hungarian Revolution Austrian laws were reimposed, but by 1855 the emperor Franz Joseph had signed a concordat with the Vatican according to which the Roman Catholic Church received much greater privileges. In 1867 Hungarians reached an agreement, called the Compromise, with the Austrian emperor by which they were equalized with the Austrians and the dual Austro-Hungarian monarchy was proclaimed, giving the Hungarians a much greater autonomy. Between the years 1865 and 1868 most of the provisions of the religious laws of 1848 were reenacted stipulating equality among the historic churches. These laws remained in force until 1948. The most salient features of this legislation affecting religious liberties[6] were that:

- Religions were divided into "accepted" (Roman and Greek Rite Catholics, Eastern Orthodox, Lutheran, Reformed, Unitarian, and Jewish), "tolerated" (Baptist, Methodist, and Muslim), while the other religions were not recognized as religions but as associations whose basic regulations had to be approved by the Ministry of the Interior, but their members were registered as being "without religion." The majority Roman Catholic Church was treated as an established church despite equal rights of the other "accepted" religions.

- The state guaranteed full freedom of worship, administration, and organization.
- The state controlled changes in church membership.
- Civil ceremony was required prior to church weddings.
- Religious education in schools was obligatory.
- Children of non-church going families still had to be educated in one of the "accepted" religions.
- Church taxes were obligatory and collected either by the churches or by the state for the benefit of "accepted" churches. Those who stopped attending churches had to pay the obligatory church taxes for six years.

A legislation that introduced a novelty, namely that the state will supplement the salaries of clergy, was passed in 1898 and was to affect church-state relation into the Communist period. It seems that a reason for this was the desire by some clergy to be more independent of parish support or episcopal supervision, and they clamored for state support to gain greater ecclesiastic independence.[7]

It is evident from the above that while some religious people enjoyed full freedoms and privileges, there was a lack of true religious equality, and a number of people felt legally and socially constrained to contribute or participate in religious activities not of their free choice and the state enforced this system. Only at the turn of the twentieth century did it become possible, due to an intense quarrel between Catholics and Protestants about children of mixed marriages, to be "without religious affiliation." Smaller church bodies encountered discrimination by the historic or "accepted" churches and persecution by the state. For instance children of 'sectarians' could not attend those worship services but had to attend a historic church until the age eighteen.[8] Baptists, Brethren, Methodists, Nazarenes, and Seventh-Day Adventists all experienced one form of persecution or another, including police surveillance. Intolerance toward "sectarians" can be sensed in the literature of the historical churches into the present era. There was, then no separation of church and state, though people belonged to varied religions.

Thus for a hundred years, from 1848 to 1948, Hungary became

legally a classical Type B Religious Toleration society with a few remnants of Type A Ecclesiastic Absolutist society. Socially and theologically resentment and tensions continued to be nurtured about the Reformation-Counter-reformation issues. Pedro Ramet maintains that despite the Roman Catholic 'quasi-establishment' according to which the government had to approve all Catholic ecclesiastical appointments, the government favored the Protestants by paying subsidies to them but not to the Catholics, but he disregards the fact that the Roman Catholic Church was a uniquely large feudal landholder (owning over a million acres of land). The government started paying subsidies to church-related educational institutions which were far more numerous than the state institutions and naturally brought additional state involvement beyond mere financial support. More significant from the perspective of religious liberties is what Leslie Laszlo calls "Hungarian self-assertion that, after the 1880s manifested itself in an unbridled chauvinism and a determination to 'Magyarize' the non-Magyar half of the population, by force if necessary."[9] While the non-Roman Catholic and non-Protestant churches became the bulwark of their respective nationalities due to the proximity of religion and nationality in Eastern Europe, Magyarization was experienced as an attack on human rights and indirectly on one's religious affiliation and liberties.

At the end of World War I Hungary emerged as an independent country, but with the territory which it regarded as its own whittled down by the Treaty of Trianon to about one–third. Prior to World War I Hungarian realms were multinational (Croats, Germans, Gypsies, Hungarians, Romanians, Ruthenians, Serbs, Slovaks), and multireligious (Roman and Byzantine Catholic, Reformed, Lutheran, Unitarian, Orthodox of several types, and Jews). Over three million Hungarians found themselves living in the newly established neighboring countries of Czechoslovakia, Romania, and Yugoslavia, while Hungary itself became rather homogeneous with only Jews and Gypsies and tiny German and Slavic minorities. The national trauma of the lost war was exacerbated in 1919 by the Hungarian Soviet (Bolshevik) Republic under the leadership of the Communist Béla Kun which lasted one hundred thirty–three days. Originally this experiment in socialism was lead and supported by social-democratically minded Protestants, but under Kun's manipulation it soon turned into "red terror" aimed at many traditional religious and societal values, slighted religious freedoms in favor of state-supported atheism,

and included torturing and executing of opponents. The "red terror"
did not have the time to develop as it had in the Soviet Union because the Communist Republic was crushed by internal opposition
with the assistance of Romanian troops and Western support. Instead came "white terror"—a conservative nationalist generally pro-
Catholic backlash which later moderated under the regent, Admiral
Miklos Horthy, himself a member of the Hungarian Reformed Church,
who ruled from 1918 to 1944 a country that was formally a kingdom
without a king. Few Communists remained in the land; most fled to
the Soviet Union.

The strong support which the Hungarian churches have already
given Hungarian nationalism now increased. Catholics, Protestants,
and even Jews continued to compete who is more Hungarian.[10] According to Leslie Laszlo, Hungarian nationalism became assertively
irredentist seeking the reclamation of disputed territories as well as
of Hungarians abroad. The churches passionately shared these national goals, though they continued to find reasons for mutual accusations in regard to perceived advantages with the government.
Despite Jewish loyalties to Hungarianism, anti-Semitic feelings increased leading to two discriminatory laws passed, one in 1939 and
the other in 1941.[11] Highly placed clergy were members of the senate
that passed these laws. Only some of the clergy who were not in the
parliament protested against the persecution of Jews, just as later
during World War II a number of church people tried to assist the
Jewish population.

Of the two great international alignments which would clash in
World War II Hungary could not be offered reclamation of former
borders by the Allied nations who determined the post-World War I
borders but only by the Axis powers who sought to change the map
of Europe and so Hungary sided with Hitler, i.e. the losing side. At
first it seemed that this alliance paid off because along with German victories Hungary reclaimed parts of it claimed territories from
Czechoslovakia, Romania, and Yugoslavia. For a period of several
wartime years the Hungarian nationals, especially from the reclaimed
territories, experienced greater national and religious liberties. Even
the Hungarian Jews at first seemed immune from the Holocaust as
they received a greater protection from mass destruction but not from
persecution and increasing anti-Semitism in Hungary up to 1944. As
it became obvious that the Axis powers would lose the war the Hungarian government sought to sign a separate peace treaty but before

it succeeded it was invaded by German troops on March 19, 1944, and the extermination of Hungarian Jews began in earnest under the supervision of the ill-famed Adolph Eichman. When Horthy indecisively tried to negotiate with the Allies, the Germans supported a *coup d'état* by the fascist "Arrow Cross" party in October 1944. The Ferenc Szálasi fascist government exploded in bestiality against all enemies, particularly the Jews.[12] Too few church leaders warned against the pro-fascist alliance or the persecution of the Jews. As a Hungarian Reformed publication admits, the "protest was at first too uncertain and when it became powerful, then it was too late."[13]

Liberties tend to be restricted in wartime and so it was that at the outset of the war recognition had been withdrawn from the Baptists, Nazarenes, and Seventh-Day Adventists. The Jews, of course, suffered infinitely more for it was much more than their religious liberties that was taken away.

Except for a very small minority of religious leaders and members the religious organizations were far too uncritical and supportive of the governments between the wars and during World War II as the arrangement by the major churches was entirely too cozy. This would prove to be very costly when the government fell into the hands of anti-religious forces after the war.

Though fighting in Hungary did not cease until April 1945 a Provisional Government was formed, made up of representatives of the Small-Holders Party, the National Peasant Party, the Socialists, and the Communists which then signed an armistice in Moscow on January 21, 1945. The Red Army was in complete control by the middle of April though the provisional government and provisional assembly were in place.

BEFORE THE GREAT TRANSFORMATION: COMMUNIST CONTROL FROM 1945–1989

The period from 1945, namely the end of the war, to 1989, the first free election formally marking the Great Transformation may be divided into the following periods:

(1) Increasing Restrictions During the Period of the Coalition Government, 1945–1948

(2) Stalinist Reign of Terror over Religions, 1949–1956

(3) Brief Liberation during the Hungarian Revolution, 1956

(4) Reimposition of Controls Through a Reign of Terror, 1957–1963 and

(5) Working out a *Modus Vivendi*, 1963–1989.

This is to be followed by a discussion of the restoration of religious liberties after the Great Transformation. Relatively more attention will be devoted to the earlier periods because they brought the loss of religious freedoms.

1. Increasing Restrictions During the Period of the Coalition Government, 1945–1948

Devastated by war, Hungary was wrenched away from a close association with the totalitarian Nazi German regime and fell under the tight control of the totalitarian Soviet regime for which the vast majority of the Hungarians had not the slightest sympathies or affinities. While the official terminology was that the Soviets "liberated" Hungary, in fact they occupied it as one does a belligerent country (Hungarian forces participated in the war against the Soviet Union). In retrospect it is obvious that Soviets would not relinquish their grip upon the country until many decades later but this was not immediately obvious though the anxieties ran to apocalyptic heights. As in other countries the Soviets took over by means of a coalition government in which the Communists, mostly returnees from the Soviet Union, of whom there were quite a few, were a junior partner. The Soviet occupational forces, of course, intervened where the actions of the Hungarian communists did not suffice. The tactic used was the gradual erosion of democratic approaches, later aptly described by the Communist leader Mátyás Rákosi as "salami tactics." The Provisional Government and Parliament, as well as the governments and parliaments set up after the 1945 and 1947 election,[14] contained a large number of clergy and religious activists (including the office of the President of the Republic), and at the outset it did not seem that the place of religion will be threatened in the light of frequent Soviet assurances and the statements of political leaders.[15] It should be pointed out that there were a number of positive accomplishments, such as the agrarian reform and democratic trends in society. Even the Stalinists tried to show they are "democratic" and they helped organize other political parties. The churches generally realized that a major adjustment would have to be made and most of them were ready, though reluctant to make such adjustments but they had not the slightest idea just how radical these changes would be. Hungarian politics of this period were very turbulent and violent as the

Communists manipulated and coerced a large number of governmental and political purges and changes, yet it showed some promise of being able to extract Hungary from the effects of its associations with Nazi totalitarianism were it not invisibly yet powerfully drawn into the Communist totalitarian orbit. Thus the picture was mixed, and therefore there was popular legitimation for the coalition governments. Since the economy was slowly recuperating from the wartime devastation, the people were not massively against the processes going on especially since democracy rather than socialization was put in the foreground.

Additional instabilities were created with the expulsion of about 200,000 Hungarians from Czechoslovakia and their forcible resettlement in Hungary and the Hungarian government's expulsion of about 250,000 of its German minority. Hungarian borders were returned to the demarcations set by the Treaty of Trianon with the additional loss of a small segment of the territory to the Soviet Union and Czechoslovakia. Again many Hungarians found themselves living outside of the borders, namely in Romania, Czechoslovakia, and Yugoslavia. All these changes created a great shift of church membership. Yet all of the churches were full to the brim because people had suffered and were fearful and sought hope and solace in the churches.

A small number of clergy and laity, especially of German nationality, had fled the country in the wake of the advancing Soviet forces. Soon some of those who had been in close cooperation with the Nazis became imprisoned and some were killed or disappeared,[16] though one should state that the number of clergy who resisted the Nazis was larger than those who cooperated. The first threat to the churches, particularly the Roman Catholic, which owned 86 percent of church-owned land, namely over a million acres, was a land-reform that was carried out hastily and without compensations. Only about 15 percent of the former holdings were kept by the churches.[17] The churches did not object to the promised distribution of the land to the peasants but complained, particularly the Roman Catholic, that the schools (over 60 percent of all the schools were church-related, the majority Catholic) that were supported by these land-holdings would collapse. The suspicion that one of the main aims of the increasingly Communist-dominated government was to take away the schools from the churches, it turned out, was well founded.

The majority Roman Catholic Church was fairly solidly conservative and this was enhanced in the fall of 1945 when bishop József

Mindszenty was elevated by the pope as the archbishop of Esztergom, the Primate of Hungary, and promoted him into a cardinal. Mindszenty was a highly politicized prelate with an autocratic, stubborn streak, holding a vision rather more like a feudal prince of the Ecclesiastic Absolutist–Type A church than a man of the twentieth century who saw himself as the bulwark against Communism, about which he had no illusions and in some way was more clear eyed about Stalinism than were many of his contemporaries. Mindszenty's notion of Catholicism was in some ways similar though completely opposite of the Stalinist Type C–Secularist Absolutism. These two were bound to collide. Mindszenty, however, claimed to support the notion of democracy and included freedom of conscience and the right of parents to determine the education of their children as hallmarks of democracy, while judging the governments that ruled Hungary as a series of totalitarianism.[18] He became a symbol of resistance and martyrdom for anti-Communists and villain for Communists. No accommodations with Communists was his policy which he pursued with single-mindedness, no matter how deviously or viciously his opponents were willing to play.[19] Under his leadership the Roman Catholic Church, until his imprisonment, was unwilling to make many accommodations and he fought the imposition of Communism with all his considerable talents and powers. There is no doubt that he was ably asserting rights and freedoms for his own group, but he was less inclined to be a spokesman for the rights of others.

With regard to the Roman Catholic Church the Hungarian Communists pursued the same tactic as the Communist government elsewhere, surely by coordination from Moscow, namely they attempted to drive a wedge between the Church and the Vatican, trying to establish a Hungarian national Catholic church. This was effectively resisted by both clergy and laity, except that the government succeeded in forming a group of cooperative "peace priests" who were greatly favored by the government and eventually placed into important chancery positions thereby gradually succeeding to neutralize the brunt of Catholic resistance. According to Steven Polgar,

> Once the peace-priests were strategically placed in positions of influence and power, they could be used both as informers and as "enforcers" of the State's wishes in the ranks of the clergy and as "representatives of the progressive elements within the Church." No one can gauge the exact extent of their activities, especially not in the 1950s, since it was

not and still is not in their interest or in the interest of the powers they serve that their identities be known.[20]

Among the Reformed and Lutheran clergy and membership there were conservative, moderate, and liberal clergy and a great internal struggle came to be waged in these denominations about the posture which the churches should take toward the radical social changes. A Reformed theologian, Albert Bereczky, emerged as the main proponent of the need for the churches to repent for their past sins and respond to the new constellation of forces in prophetic silence accepting it as God's punishment. Bereczky named his theology "the theology of the narrow way" because he was convinced that God left few options to the church and the task was to utilize whatever opening for the church was left, though it meant controlled existence within the Communist sphere. Bereczky's following included also some pastors who, with the help of the Communists, would eventually take over the leadership of these two churches but were less pure in their ideals than Bereczky, having more opportunist, careerist designs (e.g. the Reformed János Péter[21], and Imre Kádár, and Lutherans László Dezséri, and Lajos Vetö). In a period of three to four years the leaders who favored adaptation won a clear victory over the clergy who had deep suspicions about the ultimate design of the Communists and sought to defend the rights of the churches and believers (e.g. Lutheran bishop Lajos Ordass, Reformed Bishop László Ravasz). Many of the Reformed and Lutheran church leaders courageously resisted the onslaught against the churches, though there were also among them leaders, such as Baron Albert Radvánszky, General-Inspector of the Lutheran Church, who felt that at least his church had nothing to repent about because it had not sinned. There were certainly among leaders those who simply wanted to take the churches back to the pre-war situation, which, of course, was an impossibility.

The church struggle did not take place only among clergy but also among influential laity. The Reformed and Lutheran Churches had a history of distribution of power among the bishops and a balancing of the bishops' power by elected lay synodal leaders. The government, especially when the Communists got into firm control, preferred a system by which the power in both churches confluenced in the person of the senior bishop whom the government could more effectively and simply control.

The other religious communities did not exert a great influence. Unitarians, though a Reformation church and treated as a historic church which had to sign an agreement with the state, was too small to make an impact. The "free churches" were hoping for the affirmation of the pattern of "free church in a free society" and seem to have experienced a better treatment than they expected. They were forced to establish the "Alliance of Free Churches" (Baptists, Methodists, Seventh-Day Adventists as well as some smaller splinter groups) in order to be more easily supervised by the state. The involuntary nature of the Alliance is evident from its split-up in 1990 when the churches were free to make their own decisions. The Eastern Orthodox appreciated the increased relationships with other Orthodox churches, particularly the Russian and Serbian. The Jewish religious community came out more intact after the Holocaust than other East European Jewish Communities. It had better facilities and more trained rabbis and intellectuals, while Communist Jews played a significant role in the Communist ranks. Anti-Semitism was being condemned vigorously. On the whole, however, the role of these small religious communities was negligible; the great drama played itself out between the Communists on one side and the Roman Catholics, Reformed, and Lutherans on the other.

An increasing number of church leaders became interested in the separation of church and state by 1946. The battle on religious liberty was permeated with ambiguity as it was fought on two fronts. On the one hand there were grave violations of rights of religious people and organizations by the government as it forced the nationalization of schools, dissolution of the religious orders, and numerous imprisonments of clergy. On the other hand the government succeeded in making religious education in schools optional rather than obligatory, which was an increase in freedom for those who did not wish to receive confessional religious education.

The government started the repressions by not allowing some of the traditional public processions, such as the Corpus Christi procession, to take place. More importantly the battle was shaping up about the church-related schools, which the churches had increasing difficulty to financially maintain and were willing to accept state support but had to fend off state interference and the more obvious ultimate desire by the state to exclude the churches from the educational scene altogether. Most church people felt very strongly about the prospective loss of the schools and fought against it, ultimately unsuccessfully. The Communists achieved their victory by first getting the two Protestant churches to turn over their schools and then crushing the Catholic opposition. The Protestants were skillfully manipulated by having their divergences in theology and social views (one can discern a conservative, reformist, and leftist orientation among the pastors and theologians) exploited until the minority "leftist" were in the position to take over the leadership. Among these new leaders were some who were crypto-communists, some were even secretly members of the Communist Party[22] and others who were careerists, while some collaborated out of idealism or the opinion that this was the best way to protect the church from destruction. Dr. Nils Ehrenstrgm, a well-known Swedish Lutheran ecumenical leader who was an eye witness to many of these struggles, described the take-over as "very sophisticated."[23] The method used was to deal with one church at a time, slowly discredit its freely elected leadership and favor the opposition group, which at one point hints at breaking away from the institution if reforms are not instituted. After the "leftist" opposition was placed in power, the church government was centralized and by showing government benevolence toward it, use it for propaganda purposes.

Already in 1946 the government placed all religious association under the supervision of the Ministry of the Interior (Bill 7330/1946)[24] which was soon given to the Communists. After the Communists lost the first election they blamed the churches for the loss and asked that church groups who were in opposition be disbanded by the Ministry of Interior. The government also suspended temporarily radio broadcasting of sermons when the churches refused to submit in advance their programs for censorship. Yet the government also provided salaries to bishops and clergy and paid for the rebuilding of some of the cathedrals. The minority churches were officially recognized not any longer as associations but as churches. The attack upon the Roman Catholic Church increased in 1947 with the government labeling it oppositionist.

When the peace treaty was signed with Hungary in Paris in February 1947 the Allied Control Commission, except the Russians, withdrew. Now the road was open for a more decisive bid for power. The strategy was not derived by the Hungarian Communists in isolation but in consultation with all the other Communist countries at a meeting in Karlovy Váry, Czechoslovakia, in which it was decided that the governments would grant some rights to their churches negotiating exclusively with the hierarchies of the respective church within the country, cutting them off from whatever international denominational links they might have.[25] That strategy was implemented by means of a fierce attack carried out by combining antireligious propaganda, intimidations, and destruction of church properties by volunteer Communist squads, particularly of the Hungarian Democratic Youth Association,[26] the state security organs (AVO which later changed its name to AVH), and legislation.

The strategy was to take general education out of the hands of the churches and to make religious education optional. A bill to change religious education in schools from compulsory to optional was defeated in the parliament due to Mindszenty's vigorous opposition. Since it was obvious that the churches would not yield easily, it was decided to break their resistance by either changing the leadership of the churches and placing it in the hands of more cooperative persons or break them by force or use a combination of the two.

Since the Roman Catholic Church was the most powerful and most unbending, it was decided to first "pacify," or more bluntly control, the more malleable and manipulable Reformed and Lutheran Churches and then when these cave in, break the Roman Catholic resistance. This was planned in accordance with the "salami tactic" of Mátyás Rákosi, the Communist leader. Thus in March 1948 the Minister of Education and Cults, Gyula Ortutay, proposed a four-point program for the elimination of religious influence in church schools, including nationalization. The leadership of the churches immediately realized what this would mean. Bishop Lajos Ordass of the Lutheran Church became the strong spokesman for those who saw religious freedom eroding and he publicly responded by stating that the tension between church and state increased and he staunchly demanded freedom of religion.[27] The surrender of the schools was unthinkable because it would mean that children would be subjected to Communist indoctrination. Since the traditional leadership of the Protestant churches would not yield to the demand to nationalize church-schools, the Minister of Interior blatantly pressured the resignation of the Reformed Bishop Lázló Ravasz, a highly esteemed ecumenical figure, with threats against him and his family and equally insistently promoted the election of Albert Bereczky as his replacement.[28] When this was accomplished events moved speedily. In June the Reformed Synod took a more conciliatory attitude under the influence of Bereczky and during the same month the Parliament passed a bill to nationalize all confessional schools, except the theological seminaries. Teachers became state employees. The Reformed General Synod approved the draft of the agreement two days earlier, named the "Twenty Year Concordat" which was formally concluded on October 7, 1948. During the decisive meeting on which government officials, foreign visitors, delegates and police spies were present, the delegates fought bitterly.[29] The atmosphere was emotional; many wept and were hysterical charging that this would be a betrayal of Christianity, though they knew that all of their words would be reported. Bereczky's proposal was finally approved by a bare majority, which set the stage for a policy of cooperation with, and some would say cooperation by the state. This broke the Reformed Church and set the stage for similar surrender of the Lutherans and Catholics on December 14, 1948, and August 30, 1950, respectively.

The text of the agreements does not seem disastrous for the churches. The churches were promised the freedom for a fairly wide range of religious and charitable activities, required religious education in schools, and state financial subsidies of the churches first at the level of the year when the agreement was signed with a declining twenty-year scale.[30] In return the churches had to promise that they would, as in times past, celebrate appropriately state holidays and make intercessions for the country and its government as the God-given authority.

The problem with the agreement was two-fold. The churches did not embrace the agreement freely, a proof of which was that in 1990, when there was freedom to do so, the agreements were declared null and void. Nor did the government intend to stick to the agreement but changed a number of provisions without ever renegotiating the agreements.

To get the Lutherans to surrender the government had to remove the opposition of Bishop Lajos Ordass, then one of the vice presidents of the Lutheran World Federation. Since he was unwilling to back away on matters of principle he and the Lutheran lay leader were arrested on December 8, 1948, on fake foreign currency charges and Ordass was sentenced to two years in prison, to be released only in May 1950. In his absence the state forced the Lutherans to combine their four dioceses into two, leaving them with only two bishops.

By late 1948 it was evident that the Type C model of Secularist Absolutism which was the Communist option was making strong inroads upon the Type B, Religious Tolerance model. It would take a complete Communist take-over for the Type C, Secularist Absolutism to win the struggle in order to expand the uniformity being imposed on Eastern Europe by the Soviets.[31] By the end of 1948 the Communist Party had taken control by breaking down the opposition parties and uniting with the Social Democratic Party creating the Hungarian Workers' Party (hereafter HWP, later Hungarian Socialist Workers' Party, HSWP), which, in fact was the Communist Party. In the Spring of 1949 the parliament was dissolved and at the new election there was only one list, which won by a plurality of 90 percent. From this time onward to 1989 the country followed *de facto* a one party system.

2. Stalinist Reign of Terror Over Religions, 1949–1956

Though the process of take-over and imposition of control over religions started in the previous period, this period signifies the unrestrained effort to impose Type C, Secularist Absolutism. The ultimate goal of the HWP after it took control of the state would be to eliminate religion altogether, but prior to achieving this goal the Party would attempt to control the churches and make them very dependent upon the government. For that purpose, as in other Communist countries, the government set up first a provisional State Office for Church Affairs (hereafter SOCA) in 1949 and then made it a permanent office in 1951 which was used to control the churches (see similar narratives in other chapters.) The Hungarian Reformed, Evangelical Lutheran, and Unitarian Churches and the Jewish Religious Community had already been shackled by the concordats or agreements they were forced to sign in 1948.[32]

The last serious opposition that needed to be crushed was the Roman Catholic Church epitomized by its charismatic leader József Cardinal Mindszenty. To that task the government turned its attention. The government requested that the Bench of Bishops pledge allegiance to the government of the People's Republic of Hungary, support the agrarian reform, and accept the nationalization of schools. The Roman Catholic bishops, standing united behind Mindszenty hedged on the recognition, but most adamantly requested the return of the schools, the restoration of Catholic youth associations that had been disbanded, and the publication of a Catholic daily newspaper. The mass media were instructed to attack Mindszenty. A delegation was sent to negotiate with him yet attempts were made to turn some of the Catholic leadership against him. Directors and teachers in Catholic schools were pressured to turn against Mindszenty, and if they did not, they lost their teaching jobs and were relocated from good to very poor housing.[33] When none of that intimidated him, Mátyás Rákosi, the Communist leader, unleashed against Mindszenty the full fury of a police state. Mindszenty was arrested December 26, 1948; his trial took place in February 1949.[34] Mindszenty's *Memoirs* provide the gruesome details of the arrest, imprisonment, interrogation, beatings, drugging of his food, throwing him naked into the cell with other prisoners to humiliate him, depriving him of food, sleep, and communication with the outside world—a modern horror tale, unfortunately not restricted to this famous man. His secretary had been imprisoned several days before Mindszenty; Mindszenty declared that he will sign no confession or agreement of his own free will. The charges were high treason, espionage, and foreign currency dealings. Out of legal oppositionary activities the prosecutor fabricated illegal activities, plans to overthrow the government, and produced fake correspondence with the American ambassador alleging espionage and invitation of a military intervention. The prosecutor asked for the death sentence; he was given life imprisonment. Other co-defendants, such as Prof. Justin Baranyi, professor of canon law who had no public influence, was given a life-sentence. According to Joseph Pungur, a Canadian Protestant scholar who emigrated from Hungary, fear descended upon Hungary after the Mindszenty trial because if they could do it to him they could do it to anybody.[35]

Now that Mindszenty was crushed the regime moved against the churches with impunity. Decree 4288 of the Council of Ministers required an oath of allegiance of all clergy. Decree 5/1949 replaced compulsory with voluntary religious education. By 1950, presumably to counter the bishops prohibition for Catholic clergy to join the "Priestly Peace Movement," an event took place in Hungary that is similar to the mass action against the monastics in Czechoslovakia earlier in the same year. In the nights of June 7–9, 1950, 700 nuns and 300 monks were deported and another thousand followed June 18–19; others sources estimate the number at 3,000 monks and 12,000 nuns.[36] The deportations were mostly for purposes of forced labor to small villages or newly planned 'socialist towns,' but sometimes to the concentration camp at Recsk at the Mátra stone quarries. With these dramatic events Archbishop József Grösz, who chaired the Bench of Bishops in Mindszenty's ' absence, was forced to seek negotiations with the government and on August 30, 1950, the Agreement was signed.

The stipulations of the agreement were similar to that of the

Protestants, namely that Roman Catholic bishops and the clergy acknowledge the P.R. of Hungary, the new social order, to promote
loyalty to the state on part of the believers and to condemn all anti-
state activity. All schools were to be nationalized except for eight
high schools (gymnasia) at which a limited number of members of
four teaching orders would teach, and that the Catholic theological
school be separated from the university. The Catholic Church, like
the other churches, would receive a substantial government subsidy,
which was to be gradually phased out in a period of twenty years (for
the Catholics eighteen) as the churches would be able to increasingly
provide their own financing.[37] A number of Catholic orders were denied permission to operate in Hungary. In episcopal chanceries state
commissars were placed (often called "mustachioed bishops") in order
to carry out direct control.[38]

The first post-war constitution was adopted in August 1949. Article 54 declared:

> 1. The Hungarian People's Republic assureres freedom of
> conscience for the citizens and the right to freely exercise
> religion.
>
> 2. In the interest of freedom of conscience, the Hungarian
> People's Republic separates the Church from the State.[39]

One is tempted to quip that, indeed, the churches were separated
from the state as their influence upon the government was being reduced to nil, but the state was not separated from the church for
the state provided financial support of the churches and increasingly
controlled and dominated the churches either through outright interventions, to the degree of placing government agents into church
structures, to being able to forcibly move clergy from one appointment
to another or even to prohibit further pastoral work, to incarcerate
and physically harm clergy and lay people, send them for lengthy periods to concentration camps or internal exile, while many were also
forced to flee the country.[40]

Joseph Pungur provides a very useful analysis of the processes
of Stalinist control of the churches which shows the unusual degree
to which both the strategy and tactics of Communist governments
throughout Eastern Europe conformed (see other chapters). He points
out that the steps included:

(a) favoring a theological movement that is able to accommodate to
Communist control,

(b) promoting into leadership those clergy who have a servile attitude toward the state which then exercised strict control over the church, and

(c) creating state organs of supervision and control over the churches. These will now be examined more thoroughly.

(a) The new theologies were a form of self-control of liberties. In the Protestant churches a series of theological positions were developed, first Bishop Albert Bereczky's "Theology of the Narrow Way," and later in the period after 1958 Reformed Bishop Tibor Bartha's "Theology of Service," and Lutheran Bishop Zoltán Káldy's "Theology of Diaconia" (see below, subtopic #5). In the Roman Catholic Church the "Priestly Peace Movement" emerged which favored a particular interpretation of peace that was favorable to the government and critical of the Vatican and the episcopacy. A somewhat similar pro-socialist peace and justice interpretation was favored by the top Protestant church leadership which enrolled the entire churches in the Prague-based Christian Peace Conference (see chapter on Czechoslovakia). Without going into a discussion of these theologies, it is sufficient to state that they were, indeed, Christian and quite attractive to the modern ear but they were very partial, even slanted, i.e. they overemphasized one aspect of Christian thought and action and drastically neglected other aspects.[41] On top of that they were made into obligatory theologies among Protestants. Aspects of these theologies lauded the social justice work of the state in terms generally reserved to the glorification of the Reign of God. They definitely saw in socialism a system superior to all other systems and gave enthusiastic support to the socialist option. On the other hand these theologies were blind to the oppression by the regime. It is not surprising that before too long many church-going people as well as other observers saw these theologians as "court theologians" who lost much of their integrity and respect. That this is not just a subjective evaluation of the author can be seen from the empirical evidence that both in 1956 and in 1989 onward the proponents of these theologies as well as the theologies themselves were jettisoned at the first opportunity.[43]

(b) Promotion of clergy positively inclined toward the state by the government was a distinct interference and limitation of religious autonomy and freedom. The government, using mostly the SOCA, actively sought to discredit and eliminate those church leaders who were not pliant enough to their control and replace them with leaders receptive to government initiatives. Pungur points out several categories of people who were groomed for leadership positions. The first category was exceptionally gifted, bright, and "idealistic" clergy whose convictions were that the churches needed to adapt themselves to the new situation and who responded out of a sense of responsibilty coupled with the government's promises of greater freedom of action (e.g. Albert Berczky). The second group were people who were being blackmailed, namely who had been discovered to have a moral failing and the government forced them into reporting and carrying out their orders in order to keep their secret from reaching the church membership. The third group were the careerists who sought higher ecclesiastical or state appointments in line with their personal ambitions (e.g. János Péter, Ernö Mihályi, and Róland Kiss). Lastly after theological students became liable to military service, from which they were initially excused, the observation about their cooperativeness in the army was used for promotional purposes.[43] András Szennay, the Benedictine abbot of Pannohalma, pointed out that such bishops and church leaders were not trusted. They tried to save what was savable and had some successes here and there, but on the whole they settled for the conviction that the churches had become a foreign body in their own country and were confined to a ghetto existence, practically bleeding to death.[44] Such bishops would often persecute groups (e.g. basis communities) and individuals within their churches that troubled the state and were often much too ready to surrender to the state even when the pressure became milder.[45]

(c) Government supervision was carried out on three levels.

The first level were the church leaders whom the government placed into responsible positions. Zoltán Dóka[46] and Joseph Pungur both point out that the totalitarian governmental system promoted autocratism in church polity once the trusted leaders were in place, especially among Protestants. The government preferred to deal with one top person in each denomination (and for the free churches the president of the Council of Free Churches) and that this person would then transmit the government orders, often willfully through a church hierarchy where the key persons were appointed from among the trusted entourage of the leader. While such a system was not out of line with Roman Catholics, it departed sharply from the Protestant tradition and engendered much strife among them. On the whole the government preferred to keep order in this manner.

The second level was SOCA. Regular reports about domestic and foreign activities, written and oral, had to be made to SOCA headquarters and branch offices by the hierarchy and clergy. Depending on the head of SOCA the churches were dealt with either more brutally or more civilly (e.g. the last head of SOCA prior to its dissolution in 1989, Imre Miklós, had a humane and conciliatory attitude).

The third supervisory organ was the secret police, which, like in Poland and other countries, had a special department that created an "independent network of informers planted among the clergy and laity."[47] They sprang into action when someone could not be persuaded to be cooperative by usage of other channels.

A fourth level was set up in the HWP which had people responsible for ideological and (anti)religious concerns.

These four levels were an efficient apparatus of state supervision of religious activities.

With the Protestant churches subdued, the Roman Catholic Church continued to be persecuted and then polarized. After the perhaps most famous of the public trials against clergy, namely the Mindszenty trial, with the Primate safely disposed of in prison, the next target was the very archbishop who signed the agreement between the Roman Catholic Church and the government, namely József Cardinal Grösz. He and eight others were tried in 1951 for allegedly planning a *coup d'état* in order to restore royal rule, spying for the Americans and Tito,[48] and hinted of involvement in a murder. Grösz was sentenced to fifteen years.[49] Other clergy and bishops were exiled to remote villages or in some instances placed in a concentration camp. People felt unsafe to attend the church services; if they went at all, they would go to a church in a place where they would not be likely recognized. In theory the Communist Party differentiated between "reactionary clergy" and the "religious population"but in reality they fused the two concepts and thus everyone associated in any way with the church was suspect to the government. These were then truly years of a reign of terror which culminated with the decision that all higher ecclesiastical appointments be made subject to governmental approval and that episcopal chanceries and other lesser hierarchical positions had to be filled from the ranks of the peace priests.[50]

The churches were turned into a tool of propaganda for measures of socialization (e.g. clergy had to vigorously promote work ethics and collectivization of the land that only a few years ago was distributed to the peasants with much fanfare and now forcibly collectivized) and other HWP measures at home and Soviet peace proposals and foreign policy goals of the country abroad. The churches were brought to their knees by 1953 when Stalin died. Stalin's and Rákosi's cult of personality had to be duly fanned by cooperative clergy, some of whom went way beyond what the agreements stipulated.

After Stalin's death there was a brief liberalization by the government of Imre Nagy which was followed by a re-Stalinization in 1955. Changes in the government were reflected in corresponding liberalizations and rigidifications in the treatment of the churches but the church leadership was too intimidated to respond to these changes. In 1954 thousands of people were released from concentration camps and prisons, among them many clergy, members of religious orders, and others imprisoned for religious reasons. While this did not mean that religious liberty was obtained, hope emerged that some day it might be gained.[51] There were signs of renewal among younger Protestant clergy critical of the church leadership who published "The Confessing Church in Hungary 1976" echoing the protest against Hitler by the "Confessing Church" of Germany. Lutheran Bishop Ordass was released from jail and returned to his episcopal office. There were voices asking for the resignation of Reformed bishop János Péter and Prof. Imre Kádár for their undisguised communist sympathies, though Péter attempted to maneuver at the last moment to a more reformist position.[52] But in 1955 the reigns were tightened.

3. Brief Liberation During the Hungarian Revolution of 1956

The year 1956 was a year of unrest in Eastern Europe but nowhere did it explode as it did in Hungary from October 23 to November 4. During the tumultuous and heady days prior to the Soviet crushing of the Revolution, the churches experienced brief bursts of liberation. Cardinal Mindszenty was liberated by revolutionary military units. Mindszenty dissolved the "Priestly Peace Movement," cleaned the chanceries of all 'collaborators; and restored the old administrators to their posts. Mindszenty, the recalled traditional leadership of the Protestant Churches, such as bishops Ordass, Türoczy, and Ravasz as well as one of the new leaders to emerge during this period, László, Pap, the dean of the Reformed School of Theology in Budapest, became eloquent spokesmen for the church that lived underneath the surface, the church that in fact was followed by the majority of members. They addressed the people on "Radio Free Kossuth" encouraging them and counseling wisdom. Of the 225 major demands that were made by the revolutionaries over the Hungarian radios seven of them (3 percent) were for religious liberty.[53]

The tainted leadership of the Protestant churches all resigned. Instead of them the "Confessing Church" group (later renamed "Renewal Movement") emerged in order to prepare for free processes of determining the church leadership. Although this process was interrupted by the Soviet army the "Confessing Church" only started its heroic period. The Executive Committee of the Renewal Movement of the Reformed Church sent a letter to all congregations repeating former demands for religious freedom and new elections. Conferences in districts and seniorates supported this demand in face of the growing terror, showing that the reformers had popular backing.

4. Reimposition of Controls Through a Reign of Terror, 1957–1963

The process of "normalization," of what the government called "counter-revolution," a very complex and contradictory process, had two distinct stages. The first was the crushing of opposition by the newly appointed government of János Kádár and the Soviet occupational forces, which will be covered in this section, while the second was a gradual process of liberalization, which over the years brought to Hungary many of the things the revolutionaries asked for and lifted Hungary to relatively greater freedom than most of the Soviet bloc countries, which is to be covered in the next section. Features of the two stages, however, overlapped as the two processes sometimes proceeded simultaneously, as János Kádár publicized the approach of "who is not against us is for us."

The period from 1957 to 1963 was bloody. It was a veritable reign of terror, particularly against the less well known religious sympathizers of the revolution.[54] Controls started tightening even beyond the pre-revolutionary days. Torture, trials, executions (including that of several clergy), mass graves, secret deportations to the Soviet Union, a flood of refugees to the West, rewriting of history and propaganda— all were measures to which the government resorted in order to victimize its opponents. Prof. Földesi estimates that 350–400 people were executed as political prisoners and that many thousands were imprisoned. The population was unaware of the extent of the terror. In the immediate aftermath the Kádár government felt insecure and sought to attract the population by a better living standard and staying out of people's private lives, but by the middle of 1957 it could vent the full fury on the opponents.

The churches were affected dramatically. József Cardinal Mindszenty found political asylum in the U. S. embassy in which he was to stay for the next fifteen years, eventually becoming a block to resumption of more normal inter-governmental and ecclesiastical relations. In the Protestant churches the government quickly removed the leadership which emerged during the revolution and reimposed the pre-1956 leaders. The SOCA was briefly dissolved (1957–1959 with the Ministry of Education picking up SOCA's responsibilities) as a concession by the Kádár government but was reinstituted with vengeance so that SOCA permission had to be obtained even for typing and duplicating for church purposes.[55]

Ravasz, Ordass, Pap, and other pro-revolutionary leaders were forced to retire. Pap was first transferred to a remote village as assistant pastor but by 1963 he was sent into early retirement and placed under house arrest in his home in Budapest being forbidden to write or to preach.[56] Zoltán Dóka was given a choice of internment or a pastorate in a small village in the province and, naturally, selected the village pastorate.[57] Ordass was for the second time deprived of episcopacy and attended quietly every Sunday the services of a local Budapest church, while the pastor of that church, László Csengödy was regularly pressured by the authorities to ban Ordass from attending the worship services.

The churches were forced to re-invite the pre-revolutionary leaders in a humiliating manner. Only some of them accepted to return. In the reshuffling of leadership two new Protestant leaders emerged, Bishop Tibor Bartha of the Reformed and Bishop Zoltàn Kàldy of the Lutheran Church, who were to epitomize servility to the government and arbitrary domineering in their own churches. To justify the subservience of the churches the twin "theology of service" and "theology of diaconia" were promoted by Bartha and Kàldy respectively and uniformly imposed on all pastors and theologians. Going beyond acceptance of socialism, these ideologized theologies fostered the socialist system. The Roman Catholic Church was placed into a limbo since its head, Mindszenty, was not allowed to communicate to them out of his asylum. Bishops sympathetic to Mindszenty were gradually replaced with more accommodating ones.

The president of SOCA, János Horváth, intimidated the churches by turning the clock back to pre-revolutionary days, invalidating all the decisions made during the revolution and forced statements from churches and theological seminaries supporting the official theory of counter-revolution in which the churches also shared the guilt and repudiating the church actions that transpired during the revolution.[5?] Now SOCA openly intervened in internal ecclesiastical issues, making it clear that it intended to deal with the churches in a centralized manner through an acceptable leader who would curtail many local initiatives by simply asking the question, "don't you know that this will not be approved by the head of SOCA?" This would soon lead to a crisis of confidence not only in dealings not primarily in church-state relations but in relations between the church leaders and those whom they led.[59] Warnings were issued that the churches must obey the laws of the land and that they may not harbor enemies of the regime. The state intervention into church life was made into law in 1957 whereby the government tightened the controls by stipulating some novelties about state appointments. Before the war only Roman Catholic bishops had to be approved by the state. Now not only did all candidates for bishoprics in all churches need approval but even the deaneries, i.e. the more local ecclesiastical supervisory positions and the lay leadership had to be approved in advance as well by the Presidium of the People's Republic.[60] Professors of theological schools and principals of high schools had to be approved by the Minister of Education. Seminarians were thoroughly screened. In 1959 the government decreed that if a church does not fill a vacant post in two months, the government would step in and appoint someone. The press resumed attacking religion. Anti-religious propaganda and promotion of atheism increased.[61] In 1959 name-giving ceremonies were introduced as a substitute for infant baptism. Members of the HWP were often expelled and even lost their job if they attended religious services or permitted their children to be confirmed.[62] Licenses to practice the priestly profession were revoked to 225 Catholic priests in 1962 and 1963.

One of the bitter results of this period was the publication of a very servile report by the Lutheran Church in 1964 in which the socialist system was declared to be the best and the socialist ethics the highest of all ethics. This caused a considerable scandal both in and out of the church.[62] It was the way in which some pro-regime clergy promoted the adjustment of the church to the government in order to promote better cooperation.

5. Working Out a *Modus Vivendi*, 1964–1989

The period from 1964 to 1989 brought about the search for a *modus vivendi* and a certain domestication of the churches based on measures of liberalization by both government and church.

A general amnesty in 1963 for most political prisoners by the Kádár government precipitated the period as it indicated the government's willingness for a new, more tolerant and relaxed way of governing. Later the Helsinki Agreements provided an even more conducive context for the downplaying of harsh repressive measures. Also, by 1963, with the papacy of John XXIII, the Second Vatican Council and a new "Ostpolitik" of the Vatican negotiations took place between SOCA and the Vatican. This resulted in a limited agreement signed in 1964 involving the appointments of the hierarchy and the oath taking of clergy.[64] The Catholic Church was obligated to operate within the framework of the Patriotic People's Front. Part of the Church's mission in exchange for greater freedoms and a "policy of alliance" was now perceived as the building of socialism and working toward certain state-approved social goals including the support of government domestic policies in the parliament, Patriotic People's Front, and other forums and internationally to support the peace agenda of the socialist countries.[65] János Wildmann stated, perhaps too harshly, that the Catholic leadership from 1975 onward

> praises the measures of the communist government without any deviations in its public policy statements. It rejoices in the realisation of an ideal model of socialism, which places "the whole society in an ever more perfect humanitarian and democratic state of well-being and good health." It does not speak about social problems, human rights violations and restrictions on religious freedom.[66]

The positive achievements of such policy could already be felt in the permission for several Hungarian bishops to attend concluding sessions of Vatican II as well as to replenish the badly depleted episcopal ranks. The younger appointees were more willing to cooperate with the government. After a good deal of international wrangling Mindszenty was persuaded to leave the country and the see of Esztergom was proclaimed vacant. In 1975 László Lékai, the man to be known for his policy of "small steps," was installed as the new Hungarian Catholic Primate.[67] In regard to improvement of Catholic relations with the government nothing played as crucial a role as the removal of Cardinal Mindszenty from Hungary and the situation for the Clergy improved significantly though less formal, unofficial methods of intimidation against religious people, particularly for sending children or participating in religious education were continued.[68]

The 1968 economic reforms were not accompanied by political reforms. The impact of the economic reform only gradually made itself felt in the political realm by causing an erosion of monopolized power by the political elite. In 1972 Hungary adopted a new constitution in which article 63 retains the identical wording regarding religious liberty and separation of church and state as article 54 of the 1949 Constitution. Yet despite considerable social liberalization the constitution actually imposes some drastic limits on human rights stating in article 54:

> The People's Republic of Hungary respects human rights. In the PR of Hungary the civil rights of citizens must be exercised in harmony with the interests of socialist society; the exercise of rights is inseparable from the fulfillment of the citizens's duties.[69]

Article 61 disallows discrimination based on religion. Article 64 states that freedom of speech, press, and assembly are ensured "in accordance with the interests of the workers." No internal objections against such formulations of religious liberty and human rights were officially voiced by the churches.

In 1989 Tamás Földesi, then dean of the Law School of Eötvös Loránd University in Budapest, a non-religious scholar sharply criticized the shortcomings and discrepancies in such official policies and pointed out the large-scale limitations of freedom of conscience and religion.[70] He pointed out that the opportunities which religions had for dissemination of their convictions were minute in comparison to the opportunities of the official Marxist ideology, the churches were not autonomous but were obligated to report to SOCA "all their more significant actions, plans, and ideas."[71] The limitations, Földesi pointed out, are not occasional but widespread. Official Marxistdom considered religion as a "necessary evil" and linked it with bourgeois societal forms which in the long run "must . . . succumb in a conflict of values."[72] He reviewed the various conservative and reformist Marxist evaluations of religion but found that all of them relegated religion to being eventually eliminated. Contrary to the assertions made both by official government and Marxist ideological spokspersons as well as the officialdom of the major Protestant churches, Földesi wrote:

> I do not agree that the situation in regard to the freedom of conscience and religion was satisfactory in Hungary although I do not reject the partial results and relative successes, especially when compared to certain other countries of Eastern Europe.[73]

He argued for a real implementation, not only declaration of equality of chances. In an article published written a year earlier Földesi had exposed the fallacy of distinguishing between bourgeois civil and political rights and socialist social and economic rights and the assertion that the latter are more important and superior to the former, occasionally even necessitating the limitation of the former allegedly for more effective pursuit of the superior socialist human rights. He concluded that human rights are human rights in all societies.[74]

While such radical criticism of formerly held postulates were not heard until 1988 there had been significant improvement in the position of the churches in Hungary since the middle 1970s, so much so that Hungarians claimed to be a model for state-church harmony. A number of church leaders, including bishops were *ex officio* members of the parliament, while a few others were 'elected' on the one slate ballots. Such church leaders were given VIP status[75] and received all the perks that went with high officialdom.

Unquestionably the church-state relations became much friendlier since the middle 1960s and even more so a decade later. The government continued to finance the churches, allowed the students of the church-related schools to go on to the universities (this had not always been the case), the press treated the churches and church leaders more sympathetically, some religious architecture had been repaired with state aid, dialogues between Marxists and Christian intellectuals about ways to improve cooperation for the benefit of the country had taken place on several occasions both during the Paulus-Gesellschaft international dialogues just prior to 1968 and later in the 1970s and 1980s both domestically and internationally. Imre Miklós, the dynamic head of the SOCA from the 1970s to its abolition in 1989 impressed foreigners by his seemingly frank and up-beat treatment of the religious situation in Hungary. All of this was a testimony that there had been a substantial change since the oppressive Stalinist days prior and after the 1956 events.

But underneath there was a bundle of trouble. In 1963 a Jesuit was arrested for giving religious instructions, being charged with conspiracy against the state. Raids were carried out leading to imprisonment of twelve priests and confiscation of religious literature in 1964.[76] The government continued to employ priests (estimated 10–15 in the Roman Catholic "Priests for Peace Movement" and probably similar number in the other major churches) to collaborate and to inform on other clergy. Clergy who were not at least superficially showing that they were not oppositionist could be dismissed from their active service and end up doing menial labor or if engaged in youth work, face imprisonment or sometimes morals charges.[77] The "Priests for Peace Movement" was dissolved as it had not episcopal or papal blessing. The "Opus Pacis" was formed in 1957 but the membership simply shifted from one organization to another, now with Vatican approval![78] Roman Catholic analysts bitterly complained about the insufficient number of permissions to study theology and an aging priestly corps. A rather bizzare requirement that had been instituted in the 1950s, namely that all scholarly work must be based on scientific materialism was applicable also to theological schools. As of the 1970s this requirement was not always applied fastidiously. This oddity was on the books until it was formally removed for all institutions of learning in 1989.[79]

Police surveillance of church attendance ceased in most cases by the mid–1960s and freedom to attend services increased dramatically.[80] These were definite improvements. But religious education continued to be restricted. Instructors had to have a state permit. Audiovisuals were forbidden. Registration was inconvenient and parents were sometimes pressured against registering their children. Those who took religious education often faced problems with admittance to the university. Internal conflicts were created in the lives of children who were being simultaneously exposed to a religious and atheistic education. Religious instruction at home, unless by a family member, was illegal.[81] The church presses were severely limited, thus often limiting the information about religious developments abroad, though gradually a wider range of publication was permitted. Those who were dissidents to the official line were unable to get access to disseminate their views except by *samizdats*.

Several dilemmas faced the religious institutions and individuals.

The first was the question "politicizing religion." On the one hand the clergy and churches were forbidden by the state authorities to use religion for political ends, but on the other hand the state frequently prodded them to provide support and an "actively positive attitide" toward many political domestic and international goals of the government. This in reality meant that they were expected to be politically engaged on behalf of the political aims of the HWP but prohibited from opposing any such policies. The very dependence of the religious institutions on SOCA, i.e. a political agency, for all their activities structurally led to a significant "politicization of religion." SOCA determined whether a clergyperson met their expectations and if they did not sanctions would be imposed, ranging from a warning, to transfer to a more remote and difficult locality, or revocation of the permission to carry out any pastoral activity. In 1968 it was estimated that there were a thousand Roman Catholic clergy, counting former members of religious orders, who were disallowed to practice their vocation.[82] In a smaller number of cases legal charges were brought against clergy, such as plotting to overthrow the government, undermining the state, and incitement against the political system and the Constitution, (Penal Code articles 116, 117, and 127).

Another dilemma was whether to cooperate with the Marxists and engage in dialogues with them. Many of the liberal Marxists urged a more constructive cooperation and dialogue which would incorporate the believers in the societal process of building socialism. But most of the Marxists were unwilling to relinquish the ideological battle between Marxism and religion and felt that the ultimate aim ought to be the dissuasion of the believers to abandon their religious ideas. In a sense that would make the Christian participants of the dialogue into contributors of their own demise. Fortunately the dialogue was much more complex than cast in the form of this dilemma and many benefits emerged from the dialogue,[83] including a much better understanding of religion on the part of the Marxists as well as urging by the Marxist proponents of the dialogue to grant greater religious liberty. Particularly the Marxist professor József Lukács (and upon his death, Tamás Földesi) increasingly provided a theoretical framework for a more positive Marxist attitude toward religion which shaped the views not only of their students but also of SOCA.[84] A series of well publicized dialogues between György Aczél, deputy prime minister and chief ideologist of the HWP and Bishop József Cserháti of Pécs in which both wrote openly about the pluses and minuses of cooperation at the present stage also contributed to the improved circumstances.[85] One should note that the dialogue took place in the context of increasing intellectual and economic freedoms as Hungary slowly became a showcase of flexibility in the Communist world.

A third dilemma arose out of the government's practice of "Communist Josephinism," namely the claim of being the supreme patron of the churches, harking back to the Austro-Hungarian empire times. While on the one hand the state did everything it could to restrict religion to the sphere of a private matter (though far more liberal than in the Soviet Union) on the other hand the government, being the supreme patron of the churches interfered with both pastoral appointments, transfer and removal, and pastoral activities of the clergy.[86] Even retirement requests had to be approved and were sometimes delayed by SOCA, and in some instances made irrelevant by the applicant's death. Some appointees of the Vatican to the episcopacy were not approved nor allowed to go to their dioceses as late as 1975. Younger clergy, who had not experienced the harsh repressions felt "that the Church's leadership sometimes adheres more than necessary to external pressures rather than inner convictions, without admitting that such is the case."[87] Efforts were made to lower the age of the leadership.

In 1975 a New Regulation of Religious Instructions was passed which permitted voluntary religious instructions both in schools and in church buildings for ages six to fourteen and opened more opportunities for the evangelization of youth. Teachers were allowed a wider range of teaching approaches. Problems regarding registration were eased. Religious education may be offered no more than twice weekly for an hour. Clergy were unpaid for religious education in churches. The authorities had to be informed where and when religious instructions would take place.[88] Originally these New Regulations appeared advantageous to the churches but it was soon noted that the local authorities often had a way of interpreting them as new opportunities to restrict church activities by mandating sometimes inconvenient hours and places for religious instructions, having the local school principal present for registration, requesting lists of registered students and following other "methods of intimidation and chicanery which had been tried and proven successful in discouraging religious instruction in the schools. . . ."[89]

Gradually, however, such intimidations diminished and more flexibility and authority were handed over to the church leadership. Access to the mass media remained sharply limited, namely only one radio program offered a half-hour religion program on Sunday morn-

ings from 7:00–7:30 which had to be alternated by the religious denominations, which meant that annually only about nine hours were
available per major denomination on combined media.[90] However, religious leaders in some of the neighboring countries would have been
envious at such opportunity.

The leaders of all major religious communities had openly pro-
ciaimed their loyalty to the government and stressed that good relationships existed between church and state. Cardinal Lékai stated
in 1976, that "[t]he faithful can thus rest assured . . . that they
will be allowed to exercise their religion freely and without concern
about reprisals."[91] The state reduced the number of administrative
interventions against church officials, became more subtle in dealing
with the churches, and began to use dialogue as a means of relating;
a "new type of relation" in the words of Imre Miklós of SOCA. This
resulted in the visit of the general secretary of the Socialist Workers
Party of Hungary, János Kádár, to Pope Paul VI in 1977.

The exception to the pattern of toleration were dissenting groups,
such as Father György Bulányi's "Bush" and *Regnum Marianum* who
also had strong independent peace and conscientious objection agenda
and which the government at the outset harassed directly. Priestly
advisors to the young people involved in the basis communities were
often imprisoned for anti-state activities.[92] But as of 1976 the state
avoided trials and imprisonments of religious activists and preferred
to move against them indirectly by exerting pressure upon the hierarchy to discipline and restrain them.[93] Such groups often criticized
the church leadership for compromising with an atheist government
and advocating democracy both in society and the church and thus
became a thorn in both the state's and church's side. Cardinal Lékai
sought to brand such groups accusing them of schism and heresy
but it took years before such censure was supported by the Vatican. The government had been particularly troubled by the Roman
Catholic "Bulányists" who claimed to be conscientious objectors. As
of 1977 alternative service options were given to members of the historic peace churches, namely the Nazarenes, Jehovah's Witnesses and
Seventh-Day Adventists but the threat of Roman Catholics requesting a conscientious objector status was taken seriously and many of
the Bulányists ended in jail.[94] A lively *samizdat* literature emerged
around the pacifist question and a number of the *samizdats* started
enumerating restrictions in religious liberties which lingered on, such
as ending the distinction between "recognized" and "unrecognized"

religions, permitting teachers to worship, and the state's inconsistent application of the separation of church and state.[95]

Although SOCA became gradually less obstructionist nevertheless it continued to be an obstacle to the work of the churches because of the bureaucratic supervision. They had to approve everything issued by the churches from pastoral letters to parish bulletins, from parish seats to rebuilding the church, from minor expenditures above 20,000 forints[96] to filling even minor, assistant pastor positions. Theology students had to be approved for a work permit otherwise there was no point in ordaining them since they could not be assigned to a position. SOCA also disbursed the financial subsidy of the government to supplement the salaries of those employed by the church.

It also approved or denied foreign travel. In the case of the latter there were mostly the same clergy who could be seen at one conference after another, practically always representing the Hungarian churches, while others were repeatedly denied passports even for private visits or vacations. Such discrepancies created a lot of ill will and dissension among clergy. When in 1988 this author asked Imre Miklós why there was a need for SOCA, seeing that in countries where there is a tradition of religious freedom there is generally no office for "liaison" between the churches and the government, Miklós answered that the churches themselves requested such an office to assist them. It is ironic that the office was actually abolished on July 1, 1989, much to the relief of the churches.

Imre Miklós himself raised the issue of religious freedom maintaining that there was a lack of clarity in this regard. He maintained that his office's view that religious liberty means the free activity of religious groups and the "social prerequisites" for such activity is the correct interpretation over against those who maintain that "all kinds of other social rights" are also part of the concept.[97] He claimed, "Liberty of conscience and freedom of religion in Hungary are unlimited."[98] It includes not only freedom to participate in religious ceremonies but that it entails the religious education in schools, work with youth, offering of correspondence course by theological schools, and to publish religious literature. The only obstacles to greater religious freedom, he thought, was the endeavor to use religion for anti-socialist political aims. He conceded that there are among Marxists those who disagree with SOCA's policies and assert that one should not be lenient with religion but confine administratively and politically such work as much as possible. Such Communists sometimes

seek to restrict religious liberty, though this was not official government policy, according to Miklós.[99] Miklós stressed that socialist circumstances are so different from capitalist ones that capitalist notions
of religious liberty are simply inapplicable and therefore attacks upon
Hungary with charges that religious liberty is guaranteed on paper
but not in life are misguided. He felt that there was agreement by the
government and the churches that the situation in regard to religious
liberty in the Hungarian socialist society is quite satisfactory.

Although Miklós was a positive factor in providing greater fred-
doms to religious expression, he was neverthless in favor of the government controlling the churches. His claims about the degree of
religious liberties are rather excessive. Emeric András, the leader of
the Hungarian Institute for the Sociology of Religion in Vienna and
a Roman Catholic Hungarian priest correctly points out that Miklós
overlooks the absence of court protection of those who feel that their
religious liberty has been limited and that the religious press was subject to both censorship and self-censorship. In addition, the degree
to which religious liberty is available varies greatly from one place
to another, depending largely on the very unstable basis of personal
relationships. According to András:

> the degree of freedom is the result of a continual trial of
> strength, i.e. in accordance with the developments at any
> given time in the relations between local Church and State,
> or Party, representatives, or between the pastor and the
> council chairman or Party secretary. . . . in reality Hun-
> gary's Church leaders (the partners in the Church-State di-
> alogue) find themselves in a relationship of dependence, in
> a position of constrainment.[100]

The local conditions may differ from the national conditions, one
village may be more or less advantageous than the next. Political
pragmatism overrides the principle of human rights. And while the
churches often came to settle for the present arrangement far too
many of the arrangements were imposed upon the churches by government force and were decided by one or another public or secret decree.
While it was admitted by later more flexible governmental leaders that
the present arrangement was the result of "historical development,"
which meant concretely Stalinistic brutalities and surveillance, little
had been done to actually abolish the arrangement which was created
at such disadvantageous time for religious institutions.

András also pointed out the problem that arose for the churches by all activities being divided into "legal," "not legal," and "illegal" the differences between which were often minute and yet of decisive importance.[101] Some of the "legal" or "regulated" activities were the product of agreement between church and state at one of the historical junctures, but some of these regulations have never been made public, hence local religious people or officials could break them unaware of their existence.[102]

A discussion on church support or opposition of the government took place. Protestant church leaders were for support and cooperation. For example, Dr. Károly Tóth, bishop of the Hungarian Reformed Church described and supported a "new quality" relationship of partnership, relations "not only good, but friendly."[103] He wrote that "'believers can participate in the cooperation of this partnership without conflict of conscience, because we are all concerned with a new kind of society for all, which we are building together."[104] Some difficulties may continue to exist, but they were rarely, if ever, publicly itemized or specified. Most Protestant bishops followed this approach until the late 1980s. In all fairness, it was difficult for a man like Tóth to critically distance himself from the government when he was not only a member of the parliament but also of the Presidential Council in 1988 just as Bishop Tibor Bartha had been previously. Lékai, and his successor László Paskai, favored the approach of "small steps," following both alliance and opposition, but increasingly following both alliance and opposition, but increasingly stressing alliance. Then there was a minority in the churches, usually not in top leadership positions, who privately[105] or publicly complained of the restrictions and "captivity" of the churches and their leadership. Most notable among these were the Bulányist among the Roman Catholics, already mentioned above, and the Lutheran pastor Zoltán Dóka and his circle.[106] Most of the Hungarian émigrés felt that opposition was more appropriate than uncritical alliance by which they felt the leadership of the churches compromised themselves.

When passing judgment about who was compromised and who was not it is important to note that in an authoritarian society, such as Hungary was until 1988, nearly everyone was forced to compromise to one degree or another. The question, which cannot be answered in general but only by careful individual examination, was whether the compromise was good or not, for the benefit of the religious community's liberty.

It is ironic that the suffering of Hungarians in Romania contributed to the expansion of religious liberty and freedom in general in Hungary in the second half of the 1980s. In Nicolae Ceausescu's totalitarianism they could reject a pattern of Stalinism that not so long ago was prevalent in Hungary, but it is always easier to see the faults of a system elsewhere. With the rejection of Ceausescuist dictatorship the Hungarians could more decisively opt for the opposite tendency, namely democratization. Thus the aging János Kádár, who provided space for gradual but limited democratization, could finally be pushed out of power and replaced by reform-minded Communists who would eventually open the door to multi-party democracy and free elections that would lead to the Communist Party's loss of control over the country. As Hungary argued for more open borders on part of the Romanians, it became soon apparent that they could not sustain the closed borders with Austria and this eventually lead not only to completely open travel opportunities by Hungarians but a window of opportunity for the escape of East Germans leading ultimately to the toppling of the Berlin wall and German unification.

For the churches the ever larger influx of refugees from Romania, mostly Hungarians but also of others, provided an opportunity based on acute need for relief work among the refugees, to offer social services and be appreciated by all, including the government, for selfless service to the refugees. The church leadership then found the courage which it lacked in previous upheavals in the communist world, to speak out on behalf of the refugees in international forums such as the World Council of Churches, the World Reformed Alliance, Lutheran World Federation, etc. and accuse Romania of violating human rights, including ethnic and religious oppression, thus creating a massive conflict with Romanian church leaders.[107]

Among the liberties gained by the late 1980s one should list the opportunity to send missionaries abroad, to keep good contacts with the Hungarian émigré churches, to establish church associations (e.g the Reformed Bethesda Brotherhood Alliance and a Catholic female religious association), retreat houses, and expanded social services were made possible.[108] Hungarian theological studeng were sent to study abroad and foreign students studied in Hungary. Meeting in private for religious purposes was no longer obstructed and there was an increasing study of the Bible. Elections for church leadership became more open, with more than one candidate for an office. Greater access to churches was given to mass media and there was a vastly more sympathetic coverage in the media. The Christian heritage of Hungary was now openly acknowledged and many of the suppressed historical persons and events were resuscitated. A number of national and international Christian-Marxist dialogues took place at which a rather open atomosphere prevailed.[109]

Between 1985 and 1987 a number of discussions on the role of religion at conferences and in periodical literature took place, with an increasing number of Marxist and non-Marxist scholars showing appreciation for the contribution of religion and urging more freedom for believers.[110] The Central Committee of the HSWP[111] and the National Assembly had a fairly dynamic discussion of the government's religious policy and the role of SOCA in 1987 and in 1988 the Prime Minister Károly Grósz met with the leaders of the churches for lengthy conversations in which he announced the preparation of new church legislation which would not be restrictive but regulative in character.[112] The Catholic leaders, particularly bishop József Szendi, made demands for the restoration of religious orders, youth organizations and greater equality, the right to pastoral visitations of schools, hospitals, and prisons, recognition of Catholic conscientious objectors, and the right to public reply to anti-religious assertions. A sharp exchange in 1988 between Roman Catholic Bishop Endre Gyulay and Imre Miklós regarding the need for the government to end discrimination and acknowledge all of the past wrongdoings points out that in the new atmosphere of greater freedoms a few church leaders gained the courage to speak up and that, in the words of Bishop Gyulay "the era of blind subservience toward the authorities" is over.[113]

Coincidentally with the increasing demands for religious liberties by the *samizdats* and certain church leaders, Imre Poszgay, the reformist general secretary of the Patriotic People's Front spoke out in 1988 in favor of dropping restrictive religious legislation. In June 1988 a new law allowing unofficial organizations, including religious, to function legally without government approval was passed by the parliament and presented a gigantic step toward greater and more concrete human rights and religious liberty.[114] It is interesting to note that the leadership of all churches asked the government not to allow informal associations to use a denominational name unless it has been approved by the leadership, which indicates that one may expect some pressures to restrict religious freedom even by the churches themselves. Dr. Kálmán Kulcsár, then Justice Minister, pointed out that "almost every church in Hungary wants to preserve its own special status in relation to the state and wishes to think of itself as a public body with special rights."[115] Kulcsár also pointed out that it is not clear whether all churches want real separation of church and state because that would mean the cessation of financial aid by the state (only those churches whose lands were confiscated received financial help) and pointed out the obvious, that if the government provides finances, the churches must expect some government interference.

The government informed the churches in the fall of 1989 by letter of the contents of the new law on church policy. The letter states that all discriminatory practices on account of belief, including teachers, will be removed, that the churches will be granted full autonomy. Religious education will not be hampered by any of the restrictive measures such as the annual reapplication for teachers, restrictions as to place and time of meeting, of the number of students and nor would their names have to be reported to the government. The government also invited the churches to work actively on drafting the new law.[116]

In evaluating the developments of this period it should be noted that the religious institutions found themselves in a position between loyalty and opposition. The question why the Hungarian Churches, especially the Roman Catholic, did not follow the same pattern as the Polish opposition, an issue raised by the Polish Catholic Episcopate when they implied that if the Hungarians were more forthright in their demands over/against the state it would be easier for the Polish Church to make its own, requires some attention to the specificity of the Hungarian situation. First, Hungary is multi-confessional and the Catholic-Protestant relations were so aggravated that the churches were unwilling to provide any kind of common posture toward the government. Protestants were not unhappy if the Catholic Church weakened as a result of government interference. Second, Hungarians were far more secularized than the Poles and did not give their churches the kind of support that the Poles did; the Hungarian population could stand on the side-lines and observe the oppression of the churches without getting too worked up about it. Third, the Hungarian population expected a close cooperation between church and state, as it had been a tradition, while in Poland (see chapter on Poland) the interests of the church and state were not viewed as identical by the populace and if there was a conflict the population would rather side with the church. The Hungarian population had come to expect that the churches would depend upon the state.

Thus in Hungary between 1945 and 1989 the conflicts between

the Type B–Religious Toleratation and Type C–Secularist Absolutism model, while very violent at times, were masked and modified by some remnants of Type A–Ecclesiastic Absolutism expectations, namely that the government would work out some harmonious relations with the churches. It would seem that this was the ultimate downfall of the Type C approach. The fact that religion could not be rooted out quickly played in hand to the Type B pattern because the government had to make allowances for the continued existence of certain kinds of religious freedom. One might say that as of the middle 1960s the Type B model was assured survival in what was called "the Hungarian way" of regulating church-state relations. By the late 1980s the country found itself on the threshold of a new era—it was palpable to both secular and religious people—an era with a promise of greater human rights and liberties but also of new challenges, especially for the religious people and institutions which had been marginalized for so long that they could no more easily envision what their role was in a public life.[117]

AFTER THE GREAT TRANSFORMATION

Hungary experienced the Great Transformation or as they tend to call it the "quiet revolution" earlier and more gradually than most other East European countries. The trends were already seen in "goulash communism" or "the Hungarian way" of economy, travel, intellectual flexibility, liberty and greater openness to the outside world apart from the bloc. Gorbachev's *perestroika* did not cause the transformation in Hungary because Hungary's reforms preceded Gorbachev's. One might even argue that the changes in Yugoslavia, Poland, and Hungary (and perhaps the memory of the Prague Spring) provided a ready made model of more humanistic socialism for Gorbachev's attempts to restructure the Soviet Union. What was crucial about the role of Soviet *perestroika* in Hungary and in all other East European countries is that Gorbachev pledged himself to noninterference in the internal matters of East European countries and thus the changes could proceed without the imminent threat of Soviet military intervention. Instead the reformers had an ally in the Kremlin. What greater argument could a reform-minded Communist in Eastern Europe have than to point to the relentless push for change in the colossus to the east who had in the past been the epitome of intransigence and Communist orthodoxy!

The Hungarian Socialist Workers' Party went through an exciting power-struggle between the reformists and the traditionalists. The party split with the orthodox Communists retaining the name, HSWP, while the reformists changed the name of their branch to the Hungarian Socialist Party.[118] The reform Communists should be credited with facilitating many dramatic relaxations of state controls and the advancement of human rights. Other political parties emerged further escalating the demands for greater freedoms. Among these parties the more significant are the Hungarian Democratic Forum, the Alliance of Free Democrats, the Small-Holders Party, Alliance of Young Democrats, and even some religious parties like the Christian Democratic People's Party. For a while there was real danger that the middle level Communist bureaucrats would slow down or sabotage the reforms or even that the hardliners might try a coup. The landslide, it turned out, could not be stopped. It resulted in the first free elections in the Spring of 1990 in which for the first time since 1949 a non-communist parliament, government, and head of government was elected, József Antall.

A great role in this process of democratic change, revolutionary change one might say, was played in the reappraisal of the 1956 events which heretofore where judged as counter-revolutionary but which the population cherished. The decision was made to recognize the revolutionary character of the 1956 events as well as to rehabilitate and publicly re-bury Imre Nagy and other leaders (with 200,000 people in attendance at the re-burial). Laszlo points out that the religious leadership came out with rather timid statements at this occasion. Likewise it was not the leadership of the religious institutions that demanded the rehabilitation of those who suffered most during the years of religious persecution but it was the political opposition, Hungarian Democratic Forum.[119] Introduction of the multi-party system and complete freedom of speech, press, association, assembly, and other human rights to which the Hungarian government now pledged itself in earnest internationally and domestically, brought also breakthroughs in religious liberty. In the new parliament there were no more bishops or denominational leaders *ex officio* or clergy elected by virtue of the Communists promoting their candidacy in nonfree elections. Instead eight clergymen were elected, some of whom have handily defeated their electoral rivals. Hungary sought a new security arrangement instead of the Warsaw Pact and declared major steps of demilitarization, including also provisions for alternate service for conscientious objectors of any religious background.

An important task was to unlink the churches from their un-healthy "cordial" relationship with the state. The curious thing was that while in politics and economics enormous changes took place, including personnel changes there was initially little change in the churches.[120] The reaction of the church leaders in office was cautious, for, after all, they had all been originally scrutinized and approved by SOCA. Opportunities for declaring independence and freedom of action continued to be missed; the church leadership was generally either against reforms in church and society or silent. Gyula Bárczay maintains that this anti-reformist mood was true for the Hungarian Reformed Church leaders.[121] He points out that while in society there were severe criticisms not only of Stalinism but also of the period between 1958 and 1989 the church leadership was critical only of Stalinism. It was without the Reformed church leadership that in February 1989 the Protestant Alliance for General Education, forbidden since 1948, re-emerged. Likewise, on March 18, 1989, the Reformed Youth Organization, in April the Movement for Church Renewal, and in September the Reformed Ministerial Alliance, independent of the church leadership.

But not all church leaders were equally implicated. Some were much more actively associated with the state than others. It is not a black and white situation, but mostly shades of gray. One needs to especially point out the partial exception of the Lutheran Bishop Béla Harmati who was elected much more freely in late 1987, but still with government permission which was necessary at the time. Several candidates were permitted to run[122] and far greater internal freedom was permitted in the process of selecting Harmati.[123] He had been perceived as independent-minded though acceptable to the government. The lay curator of the Lutheran Church was also elected in much greater freedom. Bishop Gyula Nagy was criticized for collaborationism and was forced to retire. Instead of him the Lutherans selected in 1990 Imre Szebik under conditions of greater freedom. [124] In the ensuing freedom strong criticism and pressure for replacement of those also implicated in the "excessive collaboration" emerged in the churches against those who were perceived as tools in the hands of the government. A number of leadership changes took place. The Reformed Church Synod of June 1990 decided that all church leaders will have to go through a secret re-election in 1991. Only one of the four previously elected bishops, Elemér Kocsis, survived the re-election.[125]

Former leaders such as Mindszenty, Grösz, Ravasz, and Ordass and professors László Pap, István Török and many other clergy (e.g. Dóka and Nemeth) were rehabilitated (by the church authorities or the government) or amnestied.[126] The Council of Free Churches was dissolved amidst much searching by the "free churches" how to proceed after being shackled for so long. Reformed and Lutheran theologians felt free to remove the shackles of the near-mandatory theology of service and theology of diaconia and search for new theologies. Pungur points out that among the Protestant churches there is a call for an official confession of sins committed by the church during the Communist period by collaborating with oppressors and assisting in oppression.[127] There have been calls for a pull out of the Protestant churches from the Christian Peace Conference (The Hungarian Reformed Church tabled the motion for six months) and in June 1990 Bishop Károly Tóth resigned as the president of the CPC as this organization confronts the issue whether to change or to collapse.

In the Roman Catholic Church both the "Peace Committee of Roman Catholic Priests" and "Opus Pacis" (and their newspaper, *Katolikus Szó*) had been disbanded and instead chapters of the international Catholic "Justitia et Pax" are being established. Already in 1988 the government beset with an economic crisis which also affected education, offered some of the nationalized high schools back to the churches, and, indeed, the churches took on the heavy financial burden to sponsor such schools. Obligatory education in Marxist-Leninism vanished from all schools. Religious education will be offered wherever it is feasible, but attendance is optional and the courses will not be registered on school transcripts. For those who do not attend a course in ethics or history of religions will be offered. The entire issue was hotly debated, including who is going to pay the teachers, will they be on the school staffs, where will it fit in the curriculum, etc. In the field of higher education some theologians were invited to joint philosophy departments of the universities. The Roman Catholic Theological School, "Peter Pázmány" was given university status. The Reformed Theological School in Debrecen was re-incorporated by the Debrecen University.

In July 1989 the Catholic Bishops' Conference issued a statement, "On the Renewal of Church Life and Society" which unlike the previous years did not claim religious liberty and church-state harmony as achievements but rather provided a sober assessment of the situation over the years and urged the membership to join in an effort toward renewal. The Church, they said, would not recommend any particular social or political system but present Catholic social teachings to help Catholic citizens make responsible choices. The Catholic Bishop's Conference became emboldened and without waiting for the new law on religion called for the reorganization of the formerly banned religious orders (the government had been consulted and gave its consent).

As mentioned previously, *de facto* in April but *de jure* on July 1, 1989, SOCA was abolished. A minimum of its former tasks was passed on to a newly organized Secretariat for Church Policy of the Council of Ministers headed by Barna Sarkadi Nagy. There was some concern that this Secretariat may continue the functions of SOCA under an altered name. A consultative body, called the National Religious Council presided by the prime minister and representatives of all churches, was formed. Each ministry would deal on its own with each specific church as the need arises.[128] While pastoral ministry and worship service in hospitals was allowed there was lack of clarity about such ministry in the army and prisons.

The most important change was that all of the agreements between the government and the churches which, as seen above, were brought about by coercion, were declared null and void, thereby lifting a heavy burden off the religious communities. Instead of the old church laws a new church law was passed in the summer of 1990. A forum on liberty of conscience and religion was organized in January 1989 at the Political College of the Hungarian Socialist Workers Party consisting of Marxists and religious specialist and functionaries which contributed to the shaping of the new law.[129]

On January 24, 1990, the parliament, shortly before adjournment passed a new law on religions which immediately drew fire by critics who pointed out that this was still a parliament that had not been elected freely and that its predecessors had passed oppressive church laws. Hence many felt that the freely elected parliament would need to make at least some amendments if not replace it. But this criticism is of limited validity because the situation has changed so dramatically that the reformed communist and other parliamentarians had changed their views so decisively that the new law passed with a vote 304–1–11 (for-against-abstentions).

The law declares that no one must interfere in the practice of religion.[130] Freedom of religion, conscience, and thought are every-

one's rights, explicitly stating that Hungary had been a signatory
of a number of international conventions, such as the International
Pact for Civic and Political Rights (1966) and the Helsinki Final Act
(1971).[131] This included the right to practice religion alone or with
others or not to practice a religion. Church and state are separated.
The preamble contains appreciative evaluations of the role of religion
in public life. Religious liberty is granted by virtue of birth and cannot
be denied or withdrawn by the state. World views, such as the Marxist, are also protected by this formulation, but unlike in previous years
it is not specially promoted or protected by the government. Religion
may be expressed by any means of communication, which includes the
right to propagate it. Religious freedom is not unlimited. It may be
limited because of (a) equal rights of others, (b) constitutional limits,
(c) in the interest of common security, order, health and morality,
(d) non-discriminatory clauses, (e) certain general civic obligations.
(f) legally approved authorities, e.g. parents (the principle that children be educated in the socialist spirit has been revoked.) A further
limitation applies to the army in which private worship is allowed
but no public or institutional chaplaincy is provided. However, for
other social institutions (hospitals, prisons, children and youth institutions) there are no legal limitations. The churches are granted full
autonomy. All religious communities with over 100 members may be
registered provided they are not anti-constitutional or work against
the laws. Already recognized churches do not need to be re-registered.
The churches received the status of juridical persons, but not the more
desirable status as corporations of public law. Church associations are
allowed but must be approved by the leadership of their respective
denominations. Most importantly, no government approval is needed
for the election to any church post. The state is completely neutral to
all religions and ideologies and may not be antagonistic toward religions. All churches have legal parity. The state may not use force for
implementation of religious laws but only the court system. The law
forbids the creation of a state organ to supervise churches. Church-
state issues should be guided by a Council consisting of 13 Roman
Catholic, 8 Reformed, 5 Lutheran, 2 Jews, and one each of all the
other religious communities chaired by the Prime Minister. All other
matters between the individual churches and the governments should
be regulated by agreements. Religious communities are permitted to
raise funds for their own financing with no government approval or
supervision and may engage in commercial activities in order to raise

money for their activities. These commercial activities are tax free if they are for educational, publishing, social, or charitable purposes. The government would no longer finance the churches, though the parliament may provide subsidies. State support may be given to churches only for their educational, social, and charitable work but not to exceed the support to state institutions. Churches may run schools and their theological schools are granted university status and may be re-incorporated into the universities to which they once belonged. No government approval is needed for any of the church appointment, meetings, decisions, or laws.

It should be noted that some of the provisions of the new law had already been put into practice both before and after the passing of the law. For instance many educational institutions formerly belonging to churches were returned as were some other properties though there is a great deal of complexity what to do with properties that had obtained new owners or where great changes were made. Generally the churches did not make unreasonable demands for the return of problematic property. Religious education is being instituted on a voluntary basis in all schools.

The new law on religion provides the legal framework for Hungary's adoption of the Type D–Pluralistic Liberty society in regard to religious liberties, though in the meantime Type B–Religious Toleration model seems to be assured. Pluralistic Liberty, Type D is a distinct possibility in the not so distant future, though time is needed to see how the legal framework gets implemented in practice.

Everywhere there seems to be searching as to how to function in a post-communist society. Catholics and Protestants are searching for spiritual renewal and finding a niche in the new society. Some of the churches have gone through soul searching and written declarations of guilt and repentance for their collaborationism and lack of courage in opposing the evils of Stalinism and other victimizations of the populace without the churches having become a defender of their rights.[132]

Most Marxists seem to be willing to radically change their attitude toward religion because they seem to realize that the former policies toward religion and other mistakes lead to deep moral crisis. In the opinion of the author, one of the major factors for the dramatic transformations was not the pressure of the religious population for greater freedoms including religious liberty, but actually the libertarian strivings of humanist Marxist and non-Marxist intellectuals, youth activists, and dissidents who over the years kept eroding Communist orthodoxies. When the humanist Marxists started the process, they could not have envisioned the actual disintegration of the Marxist theoretical and practical hold over the country, but the more this process of de-communization became a reality the more the most reformist among them pushed to bring it to a logical conclusion, namely the emergence of democracy. Many of them may have preferred a social or socialist democracy, but they became so wedded to the notion of democracy that they would settle for whatever the people democratically agreed upon. Many of them admitted past mistakes in regard to restrictions on religious liberties and urged the complete unshackling of such restrictions.

Among certain religious persons there are those who wish to return to pre-1945 establishment positions, but that option does not seem to be realistic. In fact the churches seem to be considerably weakened, according to Leslie Laszlo, in regard to a leadership which has a preponderance of older clergy, a spirit of timidity acquired by the leaders through years of oppression, lack of creativity and vigor especially in religious education because of weaker links with the rest of their denominational connections, and the ignorance about religion by the general population and a tendency to equate religion with superstition and anti-scientism, even by church members. The offsetting factor is that there is a significantly greater interest in religion among younger people.

The churches are facing the task of reversing nearly forty years of ceaseless privatization of religion. At first even the private faith was going to be rooted out but then the Communists became satisfied to restrict religion to the sphere of worship. Religion was driven out of the public domain. In order to keep the peace the churches agreed with this privatization and even fostered this notion.[133] Now enormous ignorance prevails in matters of religion and the churches have too few intellectuals in their ranks because they had been deprived of effective educational possibilities.

Most Hungarians are looking forward to joining the European community with its strong commitment to human rights, including religious liberties. Freedom of speech, press, association, and assembly were realities of Hungary of 1990.

It seems that Hungary is facing two options, Type B–Religious Tolerance or Type D–Pluralistic Liberty, with good chances for the establishment of a genuinely free society with equality for the religious and non-religious segment of the population in an "open market" of ideas. The greatest obstacle seems to be the legacy of Catholic-Protestant enmity. The common experience of suffering and oppression by a secular state would seem to provide some hope that ecumenism between the two may have a chance for serious reconciliation, but there are too many parochialism or clinging to historic or, more accurately, legendary memory which prevents many from looking toward future reconciliation when they can rather live in the world of past grudges. It will take serious effort to reverse the legacy of mistrust.

A positive sign is that there is a desire in Hungary to look courageously to the past and tell the whole truth. Such process is painful and can lead to blood-letting but the inclination seems to be to bring to the open what was heretofore hidden. Here the Hungarians seem more inclined to go the path of the Yugoslavs and East Germans than the Poles.

The country has a history of vigor and a generally well educated population with a well defined sense of identity, especially national, which could serve it well in its aspiration to become a modern, free European society. There will be no more need to declare that limited religious liberty is full religious liberty, for full religious liberty will be secured.

Chapter 10

P 0 L A N D: UNIQUE RELIGIOUS STRENGTH

Nearly all observers and protagonists of the Polish religious phenomenon agree that it is unique in Eastern Europe. The position of
the Roman Catholic Church in Polish society is astonishingly powerful, nearly monopolous, and in recent years, amidst the general decline
of religiosity everywhere around it, it seems to have increased rather
than decreased in power and influence. It seems that no other Eastern European country has a single religion playing such a dominant
role. While in other Eastern European countries churches have been
frequently so marginalized that it practically does not matter what
they say, this is not the case in Poland. Nearly every pronouncement
of the Roman Catholic Church hierarchy has an effect upon society.[1]

Poles also pride themselves on an unusually high degree of tolerance that has made Poland over the centuries a realm in which diverse
religious people sought refuge from intolerance and persecution elsewhere. A clue to this unusual combination of power and tolerance
lies in the Roman Catholic Church being a national but not a state
church. Namely, while displaying some of the characteristics of the
Ecclesiastic Absolutism (Type A) model in terms of influence Poland
actually functioned as a Religiously Tolerant (Type B) model in terms
of the treatment of variety of religions.

Having been converted to Roman Catholicism and becoming an
electoral kingdom with a multinational population, the country subsequently lost its independence. The ultimate homogeneity of the
Polish population and the equation of being Polish with being Roman
Catholic is a result of being controlled by nations in which different
religion were dominant as well as the vagaries of twentieth century
history.

Poland became Christian in 966 A.D. during the rule of Prince
Mieszko who accepted Catholicism from the Czechs by Mieszko's mar-

riage to the Czech princess Dobrawa in order to avoid getting pros-
elytized by the Germans. The Czech origin of Polish Christianity
became more appreciated during the Reformation and the partitions
of Poland by the end of the eighteenth and in the nineteenth century
when religion started playing an increasingly political and nationalistic role. Having kept a certain distance from royal power the Roman
Catholic Church became "a sort of moral check on autocratic rulers."[2]
For opposing the king's lawlessness St. Stanisław, a bishop, was killed
in 1079 by King Boleslaw because he pointed out the immoral actions of the king. However, the king lost his authority and crown
and had to go to Rome to ask the pope for absolution. As early as
the twelveth century both Roman Catholics and Eastern Orthodox
were tolerated. By the fourteenth century when Lithuania became
Catholic and joined Poland creating a powerful Polish Lithuanian
empire under the Piast and Jagiellonian dynasties tolerance was extended to the Armenian Apostolic Church, the Muslim Tartars, and
Jewish Karaites.[3] That happened despite the great conflict between
Poland and the Teutonic Knights of Eastern Prussia, the Muslim Tartars, Orthodox Russians, Ukrainians and Byelorussians and later with
Protestant Sweden and Prussia. Only half of the population of the
great Poland-Lithuania was Roman Catholic and the kings, many of
whom were elected from a variety of countries, did not always closely
identify themselves to the Roman Catholic Church and did not try
to impose upon all the subject the doctrines or ethics of the Catholic
Church or interfere massively into religious matters. One of the kings
proclaimed the imperfectly implemented but nevertheless important
notion, "*sum rex populorum non conscienciarum,*" a principle which
was in sharp contrast to the rejected principle "*cuius regio eius religio*" practiced nearly everywhere in Europe. The Roman Catholic
Church had full rights but was not especially privileged, except that
its bishops were members of the Senate. Poland never joined the
crusades nor was the Inquisition ever allowed to function in Poland.

The Protestant Reformation was a time when tolerance in Poland
reached its apex. By the sixteenth century Poland was inhabited
by a great variety of nations and religions, among which one may
mention Lutherans, Calvinists, Socinians (Unitarians, also called Polish Brethren or more popularly Arians)[4], Jews, Anabaptists, Orthodox, Eastern Rite Catholics, and even Muslims. This led to the
expression "Polonia jest nowa Babylonia." The Protestant Reformation was at first moderately successful among the Polish gentry

and the German population. The former were inclined to Calvinism and Socinianism. The Protestant dissident gentry reached the Sandomierz Agreement in 1570 which gave tolerance to the "orthodox" Protestants (not protected was the radical wing, namely the Polish Brethren). The Protestants with the assistance of the tolerant wing of Polish Catholic gentry, (and opposing the intolerant papal wing of the Counter-Reformation), succeeded to issue the *magna charta* of Polish tolerance, the Warsaw Confederacy of 1573. It was the first act of toleration in the world that covered all religions. Despite much agitation against it and the gradual decline of its enforcement the Warsaw Confederacy was not formally revoked until 1791. The Confederacy amounted to interdenominational peace so that the multinational, multireligious state could survive.[5] In the interest of politics they showed a remarkable religious tolerance, of course, not tolerance in the modern sense of the word.

Poland, a royal republic or perhaps more accurately a republic of the nobility, developed a system of gentry democracy, who comprised about 10 percent of the population and who controlled the election of the Polish kings. The nobility remained mostly Roman Catholic (a minority were Polish Brethren, Reformed or other Protestants). Due to the nobility's interest in expansion toward the east and their alliance with Austria-Hungary and France, both Catholic countries, the gentry's Catholicism was reinforced. Since the Polish Catholic gentry did not experience a political threat from the Jewish and German bourgeoisie or the Ukrainian and Russian peasants they provided a significant degree of toleration. Each community was mostly closed and the primary attitude toward other communities was mostly indifference, which they regarded as "tolerance." According to Prof. Waldemar Chrostowski, the Poles are not speculative theologians but rather interested in a theology rooted in history. When history was "quiet" then the theological relationship between the religious communities was quiet, while when there was trouble in history then theology was used as an instrument of 'ideological' tensions.[6]

Polish nationals gradually solidified their adherence to Catholicism mostly due to the numerous political conflicts with their neighbors of other faiths. The conflicts caused them not to be significantly enticed to join the religion of their rivals, as religion and politics were intertwined. For instance, the grand master of the Teutonic Knights had become Lutheran and so did East Prussia and Prussia that dissuaded the Poles from linking themselves to the German branch of the magisterial Reformation, though the Germans living in Polish lands did. On the other hand, since Poles had not been at war with the Czechs the Czech Brethren had some influence in the urban centers of Poland in the form of Polish Brethren.

Since custom prevented the gentry from engaging in industry the bourgeoisie was mostly not Polish; the only honorable occupations for the gentry were landholding, soldiering, or serving the church. When toward the end of the end of the nineteeth century the nobility became impoverished, they joined the ranks of the intelligentsia thereby creating a vigorous Catholic intellectual tradition. The bourgeoisie were mostly German or Jewish and tended to live in compact settlements, the *shtetls*, where they had complete cultural, ethnic, and religious freedom and were governed by their own religious authorities. While they had economic power they had no political power.[7] Problems of intolerance arose when the owner of the town would sell the rights to a town charter to either the Jews or the Christians which meant that in some places the Jews were suppressed while in others privileged and the same was the case with Christians.

The Polish peasants remained serfs into the nineteenth century and did not always support the anti-foreign revolts of the Polish nobility because the occupying countries liberated the serfs sooner than the Polish. Yet the Polish peasants were largely untouched by any of the religious dissent and diversity and remained faithfully Catholic.

When the Polish state ceased to exist during the Partition, (1795 to 1918, with some intervening rebellions and autonomous statehoods organized in parts of Poland), both the Roman Catholic Church and the Poles became oppressed. From the perspective of religious and ethnic tolerance the partition was disastrous because Russia, Prussia, and Austria attempted to play one religion and ethnic group against the other thus damaging the cherished tradition of toleration. The Russians to the east favored Orthodoxy and Russification, the Prussians to the west favored Protestantism and Germanization, and the Hapsburgs to the south attempted to promote the Polish-Ukrainian conflict in order to turn the Ukrainians against the Russians and promote the Eastern Rite Catholic Church among the Ukrainian population.[8] The Catholic Hapsburg provided relatively greater freedoms for the Poles than the other two. It is not surprising that in the mind of Poles their enemies were also the enemies of the Church. The church became a national institution but not the institution of the state, a characteristic which would become of

great importance when the Communists took control of the state after World War II. The Roman Catholic Church had become the rock
of Polishness, a Polish folk church, and amassed enormous authority.
The nineteenth century created the equation *Polak=Katolik.*[9] It also
created Polish Messianism which expressed itself in the notion that
the Polish nation is the chosen nation because it had suffered so much
without being guilty of any wrongdoing.[10]

In 1918 Poland became independent and started looking for a national identity. In order to shape its national life people started looking to pre-Partition patterns and thus in the twentieth century Poland
lived in a world different from many Western European countries—a
world of eighteenth century categories. The period between the two
world wars was much too short to find such an identity. It seemed
that each constituent group tried to find it in, against, or beside the
main religious institution, the Roman Catholic Church. The majority wanted to find it in the shelter of that Church and so the Roman
Catholic Church returned to power and privilege as stipulated by the
Constitutions of 1921 and 1935 and the Concordat with the Vatican
of 1925.[11] Yet even then there were frequent tensions between church
and state because the government leadership tended to be anticlerical;
President Jozef Pilsudski even converted to Protestantism for mari-
tal reasons. The Polish intelligentsia, especially educators, tended to
be liberal but not atheist. Many Catholics, including some of the
leadership, supported opposition political parties. Large number of
non-Polish population lived in Poland (only a little over 60 percent
of the population was Roman Catholic) and a variety of religions existed. Some of them were legalized (e.g. Lutherans,[12] Reformed[13]
Byzantine Catholics, Polish National Catholics, Old Catholic, and
even a Polish Orthodox Church was organized in 1924) while the
smaller "free churches" (Methodists, Baptists, Seventh-Day Adventists, Pentecostals) had no legal status.[14] Many Protestants reported
social pressures and discrimination. Sometimes they were treated as
"non-religious" by school (where they had to attend compulsory religious education out of which it was difficult to be exempt) as well as
other authorities. To be an atheist or non-religious was certainly not
fashionable but it was legal. The label Type B–Religious Toleration
would still apply to interwar Poland because while generally tolerant,
certain "sectarians" and atheists or non-religious people suffered discrimination. One should also point out that the Communist Party
of Poland was illegal since the Polish-Soviet War of 1920–1921 to the

end of World War II, because of its pronounced pro-Soviet position. There was a Communist group in the Polish parliament and there was also a Polish Socialist Party that was both revolutionary and nationalist, but the followers of Rosa Luxembourg and Felix Dzierzhinski, who were "internationalists," were not tolerated.

During the German and Russian occupations of Poland during World War II over 3,600 clergy were sent to concentration camps and nearly 2,800 (out of 10,000) Catholic priests perished because the occupational authorities considered them the foundation of Polish elite. The Roman Catholic Church suffered so much and fought back so staunchly that no one was able to accuse them of collaboration with the enemy.

In the Soviet occupied zone situation applying to the USSR (see chapter 5) prevailed, namely according to the Soviet Constitution there was freedom of religion but all the churches and religious people were persecuted and priests were often exiled to remote parts of the Soviet Union.[15] Well over half of the 1.5 million Poles deported into the Soviet Union were destroyed early in the war.

In the German-occupied General Gubernia the rules prevalent in Germany applied.[16] Poland soon became the site of many concentration and extermination camps. The Nazis slated many Poles for destruction. Jews suffered most. Of Poland's 3.2 million Jews 2.9 million were killed.[17] Even some Protestants, including a Lutheran bishop, were killed in German concentration camps. While it is beyond doubt that the extermination of Jews took on genocidal dimensions and that Polish Christian prejudices can be seen as a contributing factor, the suffering and destruction of the Polish people was also horrendous. The Katyn Forest, the Warsaw Ghetto uprising and destruction, Auschwitz, Birkenau, Majdanek, and Treblinka, the uprising and burning down of Warsaw are all among the best known symbols of the horrors of World War II. Under those conditions it is hard to talk of real religious freedom though religious worship and activities were permitted especially to those churches that had links with German churches. Privileged were ethnic Germans who flourished under the German authority.[19] This privilege later harmed religious freedom because in the post-World War II period the Lutherans had difficulty to prove that they are not Germans and the Orthodox that they are not Russians more than being citizens of Poland.

From 1918–1939 Poland practiced Type B–Religious Toleration with some tendencies toward a Type A–Ecclesiastical Absolutism by some overzealous Roman Catholics. During World War II this tradition of tolerance experienced a crisis under the brutal onslaught of basically Type C–Secularistic Absolutism societies of both the Soviet Union and, in a somewhat milder form, Nazi Germany. Only after the end of the war would there be an attempt to rebuild a Type B society. The Soviet presence after WWII did not bode well for such an attempt and the onslaught of the Type C model would soon be experienced until 1989.

BEFORE THE GREAT TRANSFORMATION

If Albania is on one end of the East European spectrum of abolishing religion legally and administratively, closely followed by the Soviet Union's drastic curtailment of religious freedoms, then Poland is distinctly, and in many ways uniquely at the other end of the spectrum. It is hard to find in the contemporary world a nation which is more obviously religious—far more than most nations that had never experienced religious persecutions. The vast majority of the Polish people not only consider themselves religious but visit churches and attend services practically daily. Churches are often crammed with people attentively and devoutly participating in the procedures. It was the only Communist country which had chaplains for the armed services from the end of World War II to the present. It was the only country to allow chaplains to prisons and hospitals and where no state permit was needed for religious processions and other ceremonies away from church premises. It was the only country where young people eagerly display religious symbols in public and are frequently seen in church. It is the only country which had two religious universities, the Catholic University of Lublin and the Academy of Catholic Theology in Warsaw, and where a large number of religious publications circulated, though with some impediments. While the nature of Polish religiosity is frequently debated and analyzed its public presence is not denied even by its sharpest critics. One may judge the overall situation of religious liberty as being distinctly better in Poland than in other Eastern European countries. Yet, the degree of religious liberty oscillated, sometimes frequently. In this chapter only the major fluctuations will be noted.

The period from the end of World War II to the present may be divided into five periods, four of them before the Great Transformation, (1) Relative Freedom for Religion, 1945–1947, (2) Stalinist

Restrictions of Freedom, 1948–1956, (3) "A Caged Freedom," 1956–1970, (4) Greater Freedom Despite Continued Repression, 1970–1989, and one of them after, (5) Religious Liberties Achieved, 1989 onward.

1. Relative Freedom for Religion, 1945–1947

The new eastern and western borders given to Poland after World War II completely re-made the religious make-up of Poland. Now few other ethnic groups but Poles live within its borders. Over 95 percent of the population was at least nominally Roman Catholic and the other religions constituted only 3 percent of the population. The Communists would climb from less than 1 percent when the Soviet Army liberated Poland to a little less than 10 percent in 1980 the majority of whom, however, were not atheists but held membership in the party and the church as compatible.

The Soviet military presence proposed and imposed completely foreign patterns and notions. The Communist ideology was at once perceived as the enemy and people simply did not want to think about Communism; the very word provoked opposition primarily because it had come from Russia about which such bitter memories lingered since the Partition of Poland. One of the reasons why this foreign pattern could be imposed nevertheless was that during the war a very large number of people had been killed, imprisoned, and exiled to Siberia, hence many feared for their lives. The Communist strategy was to instill fear in people, and while they still mourn the loss of their dear one's attack the church, because people where still vulnerable and when the churches came under attack they were silent, because they could not summon strength to respond quickly. They often remained indifferent to the imprisonment of this or that clergy-person because they were so hurt that they could not care about others.

The Provisional Government, which was installed in power by the Soviet liberating armies, was a coalition government heavily dominated by Moscow-trained Communists. The Communist party's name was the Polish Workers Party and after the forced merger with the left-wing of the Socialist Party it was renamed the Polish United Workers' Party [hereafter PUWP].[20] Due to internal weakness of the PUWP and the need for international recognition the period from 1945 to 1947 was characterized by a greater degree of democratic processes, though the Soviets were sufficiently in control to undertake a concentrated bid for complete control. On paper the separation of church and state and the freedom of conscience and religion were proclaimed.[21] Since no Constitution was adopted until 1952 the Constitution of 1921 was in force,[22] though there was uncertainty whether all the articles were in force or only those that the government upheld. Articles 111–116 pertained to religion,

Article 111 – Freedom of conscience and religion shall be guaranteed to all citizens.

No citizen shall, by reason of his faith or religious convictions, be limited in his access to rights enjoyed by other citizens.

Article 112 – Freedom of religion shall not be utilized in a manner contrary to law. No one shall evade performance of his public duties by reason of his religious faith.

No one shall be compelled to participate in religious activities or ritual, unless subject to parental or guardian's care.

Article 113 – Every religious association recognized by the government shall have the right to hold collective and public religious services, to conduct its internal affairs independently, to possess and acquire, to administer and dispose of personal and real property, to hold and utilize its foundation's funds, and also to establish institutions for religious, scientific or philanthropic purposes. A religious association may not, however, remain in opposition to the laws of the state.

Article 114 – The Roman Catholic Church, being the religion of the great majority of the nation, occupies a leading position in the state among other religions, which, however, also enjoy equal rights.

Article 115 – The Churches of religious minorities and other legally recognized religious associations shall be governed by their laws, which the state shall not refuse to recognize provided that they do not contain provisions contrary to law.

Article 116 – Recognition of a new religious denomination or one not hitherto legally recognized shall not be refused to religious organizations whose organization, teachings and structure are not contrary to public order or public morals.[23]

There are two perceptions about the degree of freedom during this period. Non-Catholics reported that they experienced unprecedented religious liberties while Roman Catholics found themselves in a less hospitable climate than before the war. Protestants and other non-Catholics remember it as a period of unfettered freedom for all religions and the ability to maintain contacts with the West.[24] The Methodists, Evangelical, Reformed, Mariavite, Old Catholic, and other churches were recognized by special laws, were allowed to organize a theological school, and experienced friendly relations with the government.

On the contrary the Roman Catholics experienced increasing pressure and hostility, though they were originally allowed to occupy many church properties formerly belonging to other churches, particularly in the Western Territories acquired by the Potsdam Agreement of 1945. The government accused a number of Roman Catholic priests and lay people of having collaborated with the Nazis, of waging terrorist activities, and of spreading hostile propaganda against the new regime.[25] It accused the church of being inimical to the new social order under the guise of protecting religious liberty and asked the clergy for unconditional loyalty to the People's Republic. The Roman Catholic episcopate responded to these attacks by issuing repeated appeals and communiques in 1946 and 1947 about violations of human rights, such as job discriminations, limitations of liberty, censorship, torture of prisoners, and the deprivation of pastoral care to prisoners.[26]

The reason for this discrepancy was that the government was planning an assault upon the Roman Catholic Church and decided to provide more leniency and greater freedom and opportunity to the smaller churches which felt overwhelmed by the Roman Catholic Church and harbored grudges against it. Thereby the government would preserve the illusion that the conflict is not about religious liberty but that it is a political struggle with a church that overstepped its rightful social position.

The increasing conflict between the Communist-dominated government and the Roman Catholic Church concentrated in four areas, (1) political, (2) recognition of the annexation of Western territories, (3) educational, and (4) government intervention in Catholic organizations.

1. In preparations for the 1947 election the Roman Catholic leadership clearly preferred non-Communist options, particularly the Roman Catholic Stanisław Mikolajczyk, leader of the Peasant Party. Appeals were issued to voters not to give support to those parties that are not governed by Christian principles. PUWP naturally in-

terpreted this as ecclesiastic meddling in politics on the side of the bourgeois parties that they were in the process of subduing.

2. The Recovered Western Territories (the new Polish Western borders at the Oder-Neisse line) were a particular problem not so much to the Polish Catholics, but to the Vatican.[27] The Polish Roman Catholics of all hues welcomed the annexation and supported the expulsion of the German population and the relocation of Poles, mostly from the lost eastern territories which had been annexed by the Soviet Union. The Church established an organization, "Caritas," to provide relief for the resettled population, sent priests to help with establishment of religious, cultural, and educational activities. This part of the Church's work was appreciated by the government. The problem turned out to be the Vatican. The Vatican seems to have regarded the situation as provisional and refused to incorporate permanently the dioceses into the regular episcopal structure of the Polish church. Rather the Vatican appointed apostolic administrators. Pius XII also issued some statements about the injustices done to the Germans and combined it with his policies favoring a German ecclesiastic administration in occupied Poland. These were regarded with great apprehension and hostility by the government. Cardinals Augustin Hlond, Adam Sapieha, and later Stefan Wyszynski unsuccessfully pleaded with the Vatican to recognize the permanent nature of these changes but were repeatedly rebuffed which created a strain between the Vatican and the Polish episcopate. The Polish episcopate remained loyal to the Vatican anyhow, thereby foiling attempts to create a Polish national Roman Catholic Church independent of Rome, but showed much autonomy in its dealings with the government. The signing of an agreement or accord between the Roman Catholic episcopate and the Polish government in 1950 without permission from the Vatican irritated the pope and was due in part to the frustrations of the Polish hierarchy with the Vatican's uncooperativeness as well as the national agreement that the Oder-Neisse border be permanent.

3. The pre-war laws made religious education mandatory in all schools and those who did not participate in them experienced pressures. Now the government gradually changed this by first controlling religious education and making it optional, and then eliminating it from the curriculum altogether as Marxist scientific materialism was being introduced as the obligatory view. Religious education was allowed on church premises only. The first part of the process was

welcomed by the Protestants and generally opposed by the Catholics. The hierarchy in particular opposed the replacement of a Christian worldview with an atheist one and argued that Christian parents had the right to expect an education imbued with Christian rather than godless values which, they believed, would ruin the national integrity and morality. They saw the national culture threatened under the generally pro-Soviet reinterpretation of history[28] and the introduction of an atheist philosophy.

4. The government sought to disrupt Catholic unity by promoting the establishment and supporting pro-government Catholic organizations, including "patriotic priests," by abolishing other Catholic organizations (such as youth and "Caritas") and meddling into the Catholic publishing activities by means of censorship, taxes, and closure of many publications.

In order to protect itself the Roman Catholic Church closed ranks behind its hierarchy, especially behind the Primate who continued to play a special historical role. The hierarchy attempted to maintain a great degree of uniformity and a common stance. In order to weaken the Church the government supported the creation in 1945 of a Catholic lay organization called Pax which tended throughout much of its history to be pro-government and to disagree with the conservative positions of the hierarchy. Another organization, Znak, was much closer to the hierarchy. On the other hand the "Caritas" organization was taken over by the government and the distinctive Catholic youth movement was prohibited when all youth were incorporated into a single communist-controlled youth movement. The Roman Catholic journals and weeklies were perhaps Eastern Europe's most independent and vigorous religious press but the government drastically reduced the number of publications and their circulation by allotting small amounts of paper and publishing facilities and carrying out both overt and sophisticated censorship. The journals that were too autonomous were temporarily or permanently taken over.

These four issues that got onto the state-Catholic Church agenda during the first period remained areas of contention and restriction of freedom until 1989 with varying degrees of pressure. The worst pressure was applied in the very next period.

2. Stalinist Restrictions of Freedom, 1948–1956

In terms of the proposed scheme of models, the period from 1948 to 1956 represents an attempt to forcefully impose Secularistic Absolutism–Type C upon a society that has had a long commitment to Religious Tolerance–Type B. Because Type B had such a strong hold in Poland, Type C never gained an uncontested dominance.

Between 1947 and 1949 the Communists consolidated their hold on power by means of electoral victories (possibly rigged), party mergers, and the abolition of political or para-political organizations such as Catholic Action. Stalin saw to it that Poland was firmly added into the camp of People's Democracies with no need for coalition governments with bourgeois parties. The appearance of a multi-party system was retained, like in the GDR by completely dominating such parties as the United Peasant Party and by assigning a set number of seats. The government leadership was Soviet-trained and most of the Poles regarded the socialist system as a Soviet import not of their own choosing. From 1947 to 1989 there were no free elections.

The government sought to gain complete control, declaring total war on the church forcing the Roman Catholic Church to fight for its independence and survival. The struggle was enormously inflamed by the papal threat of excommunication of all Catholics who joined or even supported the Communist party. The government responded by issuing a Decree of August 1949 which on the surface seems to reiterate complete freedom to be religious or irreligious and specifies lengthy imprisonment for those who would want to coerce others into believing or not believing.[20] The hitch was that the Decree was mainly aimed at punishing or threatening the Roman Catholic Church should it wish to implement the excommunications.

Apparently neither the government nor the Vatican expected the Polish Roman Catholic Church, though completely loyal to the pope in ecclesial matters, to strike out on its own and develop its own independent strategy that worked remarkably well in both the short and long haul. The architect of that policy was Stefan Cardinal Wyszynski, the Archbishop of Gniezno and Warsaw, and thereby Primate of Poland from 1948 to 1981. It consisted of confidence in the religious and social strength of the Roman Catholic Church and consisted in timely retreats and assertions of the Church's rights, depending on the relative strength of forces but never surrender and often even stubborn resistance. In the long run that policy gained a great deal of admiration by Poles of practically all hues, except the religious minorities who always feared the Roman Catholic Church and tended to be more satisfied by the gains granted to them by the government.

In 1949 and 1950 the government aggressively closed Catholic schools, social services, youth, and publishing activities, while the bishops responded with loud protestation of restriction of religious freedom, by means of pastoral letters which were read from all pulpits and by complaints to the Vatican and whoever else was willing to listen abroad. But the Roman Catholic Church did not expect much help from abroad; they were convinced that the struggle for Poland has to be won from within. The government responded with arrests of bishops and clergy and by creating groups of "patriotic priests" and lay people who accused the hierarchy of being reactionary and feudal.

The "patriotic priests" cooperated in the deceitful take-over of the Church Association "Caritas," initially a mammoth church sponsored charitable organization with over a thousand educational and charitable institutions. The government engineered an illegal take-over of "Caritas" renaming it "Catholic Association 'Caritas' " which was completely outside of Church control. Yet a very large number of people both in and outside of Poland continued with the assumption that "Caritas" is a church organization. Consequently bishops explicitly and vigorously forbid priests to join this organization, allowing them only to assist in actual charitable work. The Episcopate complained that the priests who were enticed to join "Caritas" did political rather than charitable work, thus becoming a tool in the hands of the state.[30]

When in 1950 the bishops signed an accord with the government without the Vatican's blessing many thought it was a defeat for the Church. To the contrary this accord did not signify any great concessions of the Church to the state. The Church vowed to recognize the existing social order and not to support activities hostile to it, but rather to urge the faithful to work harder on reconstruction of the country. The government agreed that the pope is the supreme head of the Church in matters of faith and church administration and that the Church could continue with religious activities outside church buildings, including religious education in schools, pastoral work in hospitals, publication of religious literature and control clerical appointments, and maintain their higher educational institutions.[31]

In July 1952 the Polish *Sejm* adopted a new Constitution with the following provisions about religion:

Article 69 grants equal rights "irrespective of nationality, race, or religion" the infringements of which are punishable.

Article 70 (1) The Polish People's Republic guarantees freedom of conscience and religion to its citizens. The Church and other religious bodies may freely exercise their religious functions. It is forbidden to prevent citizens by coercion from taking part in religious activities or rites. It is also forbidden to coerce anybody to participate in religious activities or rites.

(2) The Church is separated from the state. The principle of the relationship between Church and State, as well as the legal position and property status of religious bodies, shall be determined by law.

(3) The abuse of freedom of conscience and religion for purposes of endangering the interests of the Polish People's Republic shall be punished.[52]

Except for section 3 of article 70, which is vague enough to suffer arbitrary interpretation at the expense of religious individuals and institutions the Accord of 1950 and the Constitution of 1952 appear to completely normalize the role of religion in Poland and to grant full-fledged religious liberties. Appearances, however, are tricky; the greatest violations of religious liberty were yet to come.

An Office for the Affairs of Religious Denominations [hereafter OARD] was set up in 1950 by a provisional statute to control and restrict church activities. More clergy, including bishops were imprisoned, (some like Bishop Czeslaw Kaczmarek to a term of twelve years on the trumped up charges for "spying" for the U. S. and the Vatican) additional Catholic schools and journals closed, and finally in 1953 the government issued a decree which asserted the government's right to appoint and dismiss bishops and priests. Cardinal Wyszynski was unwilling to condemn Kaczmarek and convened a plenary session of the entire episcopate in Krakow at which they unanimously issued a memorandum stating that they cannot (*non possumus*) accept the government's decree on appointments and dismissals but, despite their desire to be cooperative, would rather have vacant positions than unworthy people in offices. They also listed their complaints about the arrests of clergy and laity, destructions of churches, and confiscation of property. The memorandum is a proclamation of independence of the Roman Catholic Church.

The government response was swift. Wyszynski was placed under arrest in the provincial convents of Rywald, Stoczek, Prudnik, and Komancza (from 1953 to 1956) along with eight bishops and 900 priests, while many others were forced to take an oath of loyalty to the Polish People's Republic.[33] Exorbitant taxes were levied upon churches, a number of theological seminaries were closed, religious instruction in schools curtailed (1955) and other repressive measures activated or increased.

While the Roman Catholic Church was the main target of persecution, other churches were also assaulted. Some ministers, particularly Pentecostals, were imprisoned. No foreign visits were allowed to any churches, which meant inability of episcopal supervision for those churches that were administratively part of a world-wide church. Ministers or priests could not preach where they wanted. Pastoral appointments had to be approved by the state. Many clergy experienced pressures to resign and were restricted in their tasks. The slightest event had to be reported both to the OARD as well as to the secretive special Department IV in the police which dealt with the churches and spied on them.[34] In addition to these two supervisory bodies there was also a special department of the Central Committee of the United Workers' Party which headed the entire mechanism of church surveillance and control. The information was fed by the OARD and the police church department to the church department of the Central Committee. They made the decisions and then sent directives back to the other two departments. Very close cooperation took place between the religious affairs departments of the communist parties of the entire Soviet Bloc so that reports had to be sent to Moscow and the Soviets would send instructions to specific countries. This is the main reason why the action against the religious bodies was so well coordinated and synchronized throughout the Bloc, though slight deviations were allowed due to specific circumstances. Such deviations would become particularly frequent in the case of Poland where the Roman Catholic Church turned out to be a much more formidable opponent to the Communist government than any other church in any other country.

Even though Stalin died in 1953, like in many other East European countries the Stalinist type repressions did not cease, but often escalated for the next three years until Khrushchev's "secret" speech against Stalin's cult of personality at the XXII Congress of the

CPSU(B) in February 1956. That speech had repercussions through-out the Bloc and in Poland brought about a veritable revolt.

Waldemar Chrostowski provides a very interesting explanation of why the all out attack against religion from 1948 to 1956 succeeded fairly well.[36] The Communists proposed a new model of life without God that appeared very humane, providing some liberal attitudes to-ward marriage and sex. Radio has become for the first time a mass media over which the communist party succeeded in providing effec-tive propaganda. A new evaluation of the world was being offered to the people and for about three years or so it stimulated people; only later did they become critical and suspicious about government propaganda. The propaganda was strongly anti-church. History, they claimed, started only in 1944; prior to that were only periods of op-pression and suffering for which the church and the priests were largely responsible. They pointed to the national renewal in 1944 and claimed that the church did not renew itself—it remained Vatican-oriented, traditional, antisocial, and antihuman.

It was difficult during that time to make an apology for the church. Polish intelligentsia had been destroyed during the war or imprisoned after the war, thus there were few who could defend the Church with real authority. For the first twenty years after the war practically no alternative to the Marxist intelligentsia existed. And the Marxist intelligentsia was mostly created by means of three-year crash courses at Party schools.

On top of that no real information about the extent of the perse-cution was available. People both knew and did know about persecu-tions. Since the number of persecuted was relatively small (what were a few people who vanished in comparison to the number of people who perished during the war which was still vividly remembered!) they did not react sharply to the persecutions. But they did not know that there was a qualitative difference. To the people it seemed it was still wartime though it was peacetime. The pain of the Nazi pe-riod had anaesthetized the people. They hoped that the imprisoned people would come back because they did not know that they were already dead. No great show trials had taken place in Poland like in most of the neighboring countries. Thus only in 1956 when the new government publicized it did people realize the extent of persecution. The result was that the churches became feeble and poor.

Yet the Church did respond to the persecution. Szymon Chodak describes a gradual transition in the response of the Roman Catholic

Church to the State,

> At first, the Church was only reacting and defending itself against restrictions. But gradually the Church began to initiate a more systematic action in defence of its principles and activity. Eventually, the leadership of the Church began to raise moral issues important to society, but conflicting with the Party's policy. While getting involved in such activities, which, evidently, contained political implications, the Polish Church refused to act as political opposition in the strictly political sense of the word. Whether this was intended or not, by asserting its religious, cultural, and moral role in society it performed the role of the principal opposition in society. Because it formed the only legally available organization outside the all-embracing state and because it promoted a different morality and different value standards, it was perceived as an alternative to the State. . . . In spite of the fact that the Church continued to cling to its conservative tradition, it was regarded as being progressive and, indeed, had to support the movement for democracy. It was thus transformed into a vehicle of revolt.[37]

3. A Caged Freedom, 1956–1970

The anti-Stalinism erupted in Poland with some violence, swept the old pro-Soviet guard out of office and put a new "nationalist" communist group headed by Wladisław Gomulka into office. In order to quiet the restless population from erupting into a full scale revolution Gomulka and his colleagues needed the Roman Catholic Church. They realized that what they had succeeded to do so far was too shallow and resulted in a kind of catastrophe. So they stated that communism is not bad *per se* but that the individuals who conducted it were bad. The truth about the Stalinist horrors of the previous period started coming out. If they were to quiet down the nation they needed the Church to share some of the responsibility. Therefore Gomulka visited Wyszynski who was still under house-arrest and soon had him released and returned to Warsaw.

The year 1956 has been described by Grazina Sikorska as "a brief lull."[38] Most of the imprisoned bishops and priests were released. The decree of 1953 was revoked and only the right to approve or veto clergy appointments, though not actually making them, was retained. Religious instructions was permitted again but outside the schools. The clergy who taught them were paid by the state for this work. It should be noted that the Polish state, in distinction to Czechoslovakia, never paid regular clergy salaries. Religious journals could be established again. Clubs of Catholic intelligentsia were formed. Small representation in the Parliament was given to Catholic lay organization, such as Znak. Pastoral care in hospitals and prisons and the return of expelled bishops and monastics was permitted. Spontaneous Christian-Marxist dialogue, the first in the world, sprang up.[39] There was an euphoria in regard to prospects of religious liberty, alas a short-lived one.

Already in 1957 the communists felt strong enough to reapply the pressure though the old methods were implemented more subtly. Ideological and internal penetration was attempted because they realized that it is easier to kill than change the identity of a person. So from 1957 a period of strong atheization commenced. Religion was again expelled from the school. Summer camps for children were organized at which children would not be exposed to religious influence. Atheism was also promoted by establishing societies of atheists (the National Association of Atheists and Free Thinkers) and publishing along these lines. Religious people were ridiculed and portrayed as backward. The "new man" of socialism was contrasted to the "old woman" image of religion. Theology was separated from the universities and it was considered unserious to even talk of religious values. This track was fairly successful because people are reluctant to be ridiculed about their faith. The crux of these methods was to confine religion to worship.

To accomplish this severe taxation of churches was imposed. The government interfered with religious education which now took place in churches. An attempt was made to control theological education by subjecting seminaries to the Ministry of Education. No new parishes were permitted to be established particularly in the new industrial cities and when churches were built without permission the government attempted to tear them down. Religious festivals were countered by secular celebrations. The hope was that the Roman Catholic Church could be sufficiently subverted to become a national church rather than a part of an universal church so that it could be more successfully manipulated.[40] Those church leaders, both Catholic and non-Catholic, who were more cooperative were rewarded by preferential treatment and thus the term, "caged freedom" is applicable because there were times when the bird was even allowed to leave the cage and fly around the room, only to be placed into the cage at will.[41]

The Second Vatican Council (1962–1965) took place during this period and the Polish bishops were permitted to attend. Pope John XXIII and later Paul VI gave Cardinal Wyszynski and the Polish bishops a very cordial welcome, unlike the rigidly anti-Communist Pius XII. At the Council the Polish bishops, similarly to other East European bishops, showed little enthusiasm for reform. They tended to be conservative and cautious and gave strong support to papal centralism. This was done because they felt that their own position at home would be strengthened if they could simply claim that they were carrying out papal orders in a strongly hierarchical church. It was obvious at the Council as it had been obvious both previously and subsequently that there was another casualty of religious freedom as a result of the Stalinist persecutions, namely the lack of religious freedom within the Church. In order to defend itself a bastion mentality had been created. Wyszynski ruled ably but autocratically. Divergence and dissent within the Church was unwelcome. Not only were the pro-government "patriotic priests" and members of Pax and Christian Social Association, and at times even of Znak the target of episcopal disapproval, but any kind of pluralism in theology and opinions about Church policy that were not identical to that of the hierarchy, fairly normal among Western Catholics, were considered inimical to the interest of the Church. This problem is encountered in Poland even into the 1990s.

A severe clash took place when the Polish bishops wrote a conciliatory letter to the German bishops saying, "We forgive you and we ask your forgiveness." The government, especially Wladisław Gomulka, and the press jumped on the Church asking them who authorized them to forgive in the name of the people and accused them of attempting to enter the field of foreign policy.[42] To punish the church Pope Paul VI was not given a visa to enter the country for the Millennium of Polish Christianity that took place in 1966. Nor did the Polish bishops attend the Synod in Rome in 1967 because some of the bishops were not given passports. Gomulka's increasing obstinacy in dealing with the Church was noted both by the pope at the Synod as well as an increasing number of people within the country and the party.

The year 1966 turned out to be in many ways a pivotal year.

The Millennium of Polish Christianity was used skillfully by Cardinal Wyszynski by intensive years of religious preparation for this historical milestone. He beckoned the nation to come back to its history, something originally resisted by the government, to roots, to a Christian identity and he proposed a Catholic model for education. Most people liked this model much better than the Communist. So the Church very rapidly organized catechetical education, summer camps (parents were more willing to entrust their children to the Church than to the Communists), the youth renewal movement Oasis, later renamed Light-Life when it also included adults, and various devotional and spiritual practices with special emphasis on the adoration of the Virgin Mary, "the Queen of Poland." Pilgrimages, liturgies, books, brochures, religious art, preaching, were all used despite Communist attempts to stop it. For the first time since 1945 Communists were *reacting* more than acting.

The reactions could still be very unpleasant as for instance the founder of the Oasis/LifeLight movement, Rev. Franciszek Blachnicki, was imprisoned, had his offices raided, was taxed heavily despite episcopal protection of the movement. The rapidly increasing membership was frequently interrogated, blackmailed, intimidated, fined, not allowed to travel, and so forth.[43] Blachnicki courageously complained to the authorities about this harassment. Particularly striking is his letter to the Minister of Internal Affairs where he complains about the passport policy, something all Eastern Europeans can identify with, saying:

> the passport policy of the security police, based on just this type of vaguely worded laws, has been an instrument for the limitation of freedom, the discrimination, vexation and blackmail of citizens, and the violation and deprivation of conscience. This policy has unavoidably given free reign to the mechanisms of bribery and corruption . . .[as] citizens are subject to arbitrary, legally insecurable, unenforceable and binding decisions on the alleged basis of "important state and social considerations" by the security police.[44]

The tide, however, had started turning. No more was government propaganda successful, especially with the younger generation. While there were also many young people who were neither Communists nor religious, there was now an increasing interest in religion and a conviction that the Church possesses a greater moral integrity than the government. After so many broken promises people looked toward an authority they could trust. The people themselves now started pressuring the Catholic Church to become a church of the nation, a place of refuge, safety, and opposition, as "our" place. Other options, religious and non-religious, had been perceived as imported.[45]

In 1968 another of the sporadic dissatisfaction by workers against the government occurred. This one caused an outpouring of anti-Semitism. Already the 1956 revolt focused on those Stalinists who were Jewish, the cliché being that the Communist attack against Polish Christians was spearheaded by Jewish members of the party more so than by Polish. Many Jews lost their positions. In 1968 the anti-Semitism was more vitriolic and large number of Jews lost their jobs having been blamed for the government's rigid policies. Very many emigrated to Israel and elsewhere. Such purges would also take place in 1976 and 1980–81 but not on the scale and severity of the 1968 purges. The total number of Jews left in the country is unclear, between 5,000 and 15,000, of which only a small fraction are practicing Judaism. But Polish-Jewish relations remained problematic and every so often some public figure is identified as having had some hidden Jewish ancestors, a stigma jeopardizing their position. (For more detailed information on Jews see below.)

Ronald Monticone sums up the total impact of this period,

> Although the Gomulka era was a very unstable period for Church-state relations and one which was characterized by numerous ups and downs, the intensity of the ideological struggle between Church and state was much diminished when compared to the period between 1948- 1956. The Gomulka era was one in which the Church and state succeeded to some extent in neutralizing the distrust they had built up toward each other in the previous period.[46]

4.   Greater Freedom Despite Continued Repressions, 1970–1989

Many scholars do not treat this period as single period but break it up into four separate periods, (a) 1970–1980, Gierek's reign, (b) 1980–1981, the ascent of the "Solidarity" labor union, (c) 1981–1982, imposition of Martial Law, and (d) 1983–1989, rapid liberalization in the spirit of *perestroika*. The oscillations between these stages were indeed sharp enough to warrant such periodization, but from a

more long range perspective one can see this entire period from 1970–
1989 as the time when the defeat of Type C–Secularistic Absolutism
became obvious and that the Type B–Religious Tolerance became
prevalent. Here we shall treat it as one period but divide it into
sub-periods, as indicated above.

a. Gierek's Reign, 1970–1980

In another wave of popular unrest that needed armed police and
army intervention leading to bloodshed Gomulka was toppled and
the top leadership position in the party went to Edward Gierek, who
governed till 1980. During this period there was greater freedom
though the restrictive laws continued to exist, but were often not
implemented. The period was characterized then by a very uneven
application of regulations. For instance the appointment of bishops
was controlled by the OARD. Poland seems to have one of the more
lenient approval regulations.[47] The churches would submit the names
of three candidates and if no objection was communicated about any
of the candidates by the Office for Religious Affairs within a month
the church was able to chose among the candidates. Otherwise they
would negotiate. Transfer of clergy from one location to another also
had to be approved by both local offices of religious affairs, one application for permission to leave and another application for permission
to take up position. Either office could deny permission and had to
give no reasons. If queries were made the answer was "because of important state reasons."[48] Such problems could be solved sometimes
by appealing to the Warsaw central OARD. The OARD and the local
offices were now turned over to some individuals who tended to be
more understanding, humane, and helpful, such as Kazimierz Kokol
and Adam Lopatka. Nevertheless, they still viewed the task of their
office to restrict the activities of the churches to purely religious one,
keeping them out of cultural and social life.[49]

The Episcopate of the Roman Catholic Church and particularly
Cardinal Wyszynski contributed much to realization of religious lib-
erties by vigorously asking for it and clearly defining it. In 1975
Wyszynski stated:

> there are rights which do not depend upon political condi-
> tions. They depend upon the Creator, who is our Father. No
> society, however strong, can violate those rights: the right
> to life, the right to a decent standard of living, the right to

freedom [. . .] the right to worship God in accordance with
one's own conscience, [. . .] a believer should not be forced
to create catacombs, but has the right to worship God not
only in private, but also in public, the right to form associations, the right to defend and safeguard his rights
[. . .]

When human rights are not respected, the Church has
to cry out and remind people that man has an ultimate value
in the world. So when we see a violation of human rights
we have to cry out 'That is not right'. We have to listen to
God, not to man.[50]

A price was to be paid for these courageous assertions of human rights
and Wyszynski in a letter to the government itemizes the denial of
freedom and office as well as the frequent accusations and slander
that he was not allowed to answer.[51]

One of the characteristics of the 1970s was the continuation of
strikes and the growth of the dissident movement into a powerful
social force. As the government cracked down, often violently, the
Roman Catholic Church defended not only its own religious liberty
but also everyone in society who was being oppressed and discriminated and thus the Church was seen as the defender of human rights.
The dissidents saw a partner in the Church. Important *samizdats*
appeared in which there was a chance to publish what was not allowed by the censors in the official publications. Thus, for example
the editor of *Tygodnik Powszechny*, Jerzy Turowicz was not allowed
to reply to Mieczyslaw Rakowski's article that appeared in *Polityka*
in his own publication but the answer was published in the *samizdat,
Spotkania.* Turowicz pointed to both quantitative and qualitative restrictions imposed on religious publications. According to Turowicz,
the Office for Control of the Press, Publications and Performances,
has often prevented outstanding Roman Catholics to participate in
discussions. He also pointed out that Rakowski is wrong when he
charges that Roman Catholics would restrict the rights of atheists;
the only thing Roman Catholics object to is the privileged position
of atheism in its anti-religious activities. Catholics and other religious people are frequently discriminated against and many jobs and
promotions are out of their reach while party membership assures
numerous privileges, especially in employment, thus dividing society
into privileged and discriminated citizens along the lines of belief.[52]

The most important psychological turning point in the life of the Polish Christians and the nation was the election in 1978 of Karol Cardinal Wojtyla, archbishop of Krakow, to the papacy under the name John Paul II. In retrospect it is clear that this election tipped the balance in favor of religious liberty and human rights, perhaps even outside of Poland.[53] During his three visits to Poland as the pope (1979, 1983, and 1987) John Paul II who had a profound understanding of Communism having lived under the system, continually stressed human dignity, a term the church used synonymously for human rights. Most Poles, both religious and non-religious, were ecstatic about his election.[54] The papal installation and many subsequent papal activities were televised at length and other media also reported and commented positively about him. Poland had become a more open society with freer travel and a much greater amount of information from abroad which brought about, according to Chrostowski, a keen awareness that they were deprived of freedom; they had the idea of freedom and knew there was a possibility of obtaining it. The Christian message of the Gospel made them aware that one cannot live forever as a slave. The Gospel also made them aware that the human being needs both bread and freedom and that therefore not only economic rights but political and religious rights were essential to human dignity.

The euphoria about the papal election was based on more than simply that a Pole became known throughout the world. People did not see it as an isolated miracle but as a result of a process—the fruit of the suffering of a nation. They expected someone worthy of being born, raised, and educated in Poland to become elected to such a lofty office. They saw it as part of wider appreciation of their own personal values, suffering, and worth. People waited for the moment and saw it as a natural result of what they have done in their country.[55] For over thirty years they had been looking for a symbol and in 1978 this symbol materialized: the Deputy of Christ was born in Wadowice and is now in Rome! This gave the people an assurance that they are now completely safe. As Chrostowski saw it, Communism in Poland was for all practical purposes dead; only the corpse was left.[56] People experienced it as if the victory was on their side and that created an air of unrealistic expectations during the "Solidarity era" of 1980–1981 because they lived in a world of dreams, on a border between this world and the next. They felt that Communism was so much on the margins that in a few weeks it will be done away with. The

Transformation of 1989 could have happened already in 1980, had the geo-political situation of Poland been different.

During his June 1979 visit to Poland John Paul II stressed primarily spiritual values and most observers were surprised how religious the atmosphere of his appearances were. Yet he did not hesitate to insert a few times requests to the government that the "fundamental human rights and the free activity of the Church be respected."[57] The pope also expressed his longing that the mission of the Church in Poland is to help liberate the churches in other parts of Eastern Europe, thus directing the Poles to a broader concern than their own nation.

But the change was not going to be that easy and rapid and, in fact, the situation would become more difficult before it would become easier. The period from 1978 to 1989 displayed many ambiguities, ranging from remarkable instances of cooperation between the government and the Church during papal visits or outspoken Catholic deputies in the parliament to instances of violence to priests.

b. Solidarity Era, 1980–1981

In 1980 Gierek was replaced by Stanisław Kania as head of the Party and during his relatively short tenure (until 1981) the situation for the Church improved considerably. An article in the party newspaper *Trybuna Ludu* of February 1981, suggested that all positions in the government should be open to all regardless of party or church affiliation, based on merit alone.[58] Cardinal Wyszynski's death in 1981 was widely mourned; even many of his opponents lauded his work. His successor, Jozef Cardinal Glemp, was more conciliatory than Wyszynski. Gradually, an era of more openness might have dawned had it not been for the threat that "Solidarity" posed not only to a specific government but to the entire system in Poland and indirectly to the rest of the socialist bloc.

In August 1980 the first independent labor union in all of Eastern Europe was founded in Poland, under the name "Solidarity." Almost instantaneously it became immensely popular; with 10–12 million members it had become the single largest voluntary association in Poland's history. The confrontation between "Solidarity" and the government commenced at once and escalated. "Solidarity leaders and members showed considerable interest in the Roman Catholic Church and frequently sang religious songs, erected crosses, and invited priests to say masses at work or during strikes. Religious symbols, especially the cross, had become also working class symbols.[59]

The Church was sympathetic to "Solidarity" not only because "Solidarity" included among its demands greater access of the Church to public life in general and the media in particular, but also because the Church favored pluralism of political forces. It played a most essential role of mediation between the government and "Solidarity" both during the "Solidarity" era" and during the Martial Law period (1981–1984). Obviously this role increased the area of freedom and influence for the Church. Censorship of religious materials and state supervision of religious education ceased. Religious symbols were proudly displayed in public (e.g crucifixes in schools and statues of St. Barbara, patron saint of miners, in mines). Additional religious journals appeared. Priests blessed "Solidarity" banners and said masses, while other religious programs were broadcast on the radio.[60] Pastoral ministry to prisons, reform schools, welfare institutions, and hospitals were permitted and masses were offered in hospitals.[61] All in all, religion was able to blossom.

c. Imposition of Martial Law, 1981–1982

A Soviet invasion was considered imminent, because socialism in Poland and elsewhere in Eastern Europe seemed threatened. Instead, the new Prime Minister and First Secretary of the PUWP, General Wojciech Jaruzelski, imposed Martial Law on December 13, 1981 which lasted till December 31, 1982 [Some date the end on July 22, 1983].

The bishops at first did not react too sharply realizing that this may have been the price to forestall a Soviet invasion that would have resulted in far more bloodshed than the takeover by the Polish military. It was evident that "a hard-line reaction might well destroy the relative freedom and autonomy which the church and society had up to now enjoyed."[62] The bishops urged moderation, discipline, reconciliation and non-violence upon the population. They and other Catholic leaders appealed to the government for the quick abolition of Martial Law, but their pleas fell on deaf ears and consequently the Church's intervention on behalf of "Solidarity" and other banned organizations became evermore insistent and more sharply worded. While nearly all civic organizations, including Catholic and other religious associations were banned, the Church itself was allowed as much, and in terms of permits for church buildings, even more freedom as prior to the Martial Law. Cardinal Glemp complained that some local authorities pressured the church. Since churches were sometimes used as gathering places for underground groups because they had been forbidden by Martial Law, some priests were harassed and even briefly detained because of their support for such prohibited activities.[63] People's movements were restricted, and that included priests, but priests were allowed to do pastoral work among the interned and to travel at home and abroad. The church was allowed to publish purely religious publications. Thus it is obvious that the Church was the freest institution in Poland during this period, a testimony to its importance for the government's hope to settle the crisis.[64] Since the Church did not merely use the freedom for its own benefit but continued to press for greater general freedoms and human rights it now received the praise of even leftist nonreligious dissenters and political activists.[65]

During the period of the Martial Law it was evident that both the Church and the Communists had become wiser. The Communists realized they could not do open battle with the Church, which was the real power in the country, nor could they simply use the Church, because of John Paul II, so they decided to allow the Church react to events in specified locations and thereby doing damage control. Namely, several places and churches were permitted to display clear symbols of resistance where the opposition to the regime could meet and then place the police there to watch who spoke and what was being said.[66]

d. Rapid Liberalization, 1983–1989

The second visit of John Paul II to Poland took place in 1983. After it was over it seemed that the church-state relations were normalizing since the episcopal leadership displayed constant moderation and did not push for an abandonment of socialism, and tried to keep in check those priests who were radical supporters of the still banned "Solidarity." As early as 1982 two priests, Tadeusz Kurach and Jan Biorowski, were arrested and sentenced for "hooliganism." A number of accidents, seemingly staged, befell others (e.g Bishop Kazimierz Kluz and Rev. Honorius Kowalczyk). Some priests received death threats, others were beaten up by attackers who the authorities said they could not identify.

In October 1984 a priest, Jerzy Popiełuszko, thirty-seven-years-old, known for his impassioned sermons on behalf of "Solidarity"

and his "Masses for the Country," and having been previously in-
dicted for his fairly explicit political references against the government disappeared.[67] A few days later he was found dead in the river,
having been tied, beaten, and drowned execution-style. The national
and world public opinion was outraged. This was one case that could
not be hushed up. The Polish government resorted to an unprecedented move; it revealed the kidnappers and killers, as suspected, as
four highly placed members of the security services. To the credit
of the government, they were tried and four of them received lengthy
prison sentences.[68] During the trial there were hints of involvement of
higher-ups but this was quickly suppressed by the judge so the official
explanation was that the four acted on their own, allegedly respond-
ing to the provocations of the radical anti-government activities of the
murdered priest. It was hinted that the Church was co-responsible
because it did not silence Popiełuszko!

During the trial several little known facts were admitted by the
accused and witnesses. One was that there was, indeed, a Department
IV in the Ministry of Internal Affairs (security service) which dealt
with religious questions; the four officers worked in this department.
The activity of Fr. Popiełuszko and other priests were regularly discussed in this department and a "hit list" had been prepared.[69] Other
priests who were attacked by "unknown assailants" were probably also
victims of the same department.

Jerzy Popiełuszko came to be regarded a martyr, and as was often the case, he became more problematic to his opponents after his
death than while he was alive. The church of St. Stanisław Kostka at
which he preached, is where he was buried. It became a museum of his
activities and, more importantly, a national shrine. Many Catholics
had taken to making crosses out of flowers on the streets where conflicts between the authorities and the people had taken place. The
grave of Fr. Popiełuszko was constantly covered by flowers indicating
that their donors came from all parts of Poland. In most churches
people prominently burned candles for Fr. Popiełuszko. In Warsaw of
the late 1980s there were few overt symbols of Communist rule and
quite a few symbols of religious fervor. According to Chrostowski
both the Church and the Communists "needed" a Popiełuszko. For
the Church Popieluszko was a sign and a proof of solidarity of the
clergy with the masses. For the PUWP it was better to have one
or more Popiełuszkos than to have all priests speak against the government. Thus they allowed him to preach for a long time and only

in 1984 they decided to stop his activity insisting on the Church authorities to take him away from St. Stanisław Kostka parish. The plans for sending him abroad were made, but the Communists did not want him to go to Rome and Western Europe. When such a solution started to be implemented they had to martyr him.[70]

The physical assaults against priests did not entirely stop after the trial (e.g. unknown assailants poured chemicals in 1985 on Tadeusz Zaleski, this not being the only or worst incident that Zaleski experienced)[71] and the episcopate decided to complain ever more sharply about such incidents to the government. While eventually such attacks subsided it is ironic that at the time of these attacks Adam Lopatka, then head of the OARD, declared in the *Sejm* that total freedom of religion and conscience had been achieved.[72] Had Lopatka simply been a politician one could justify the word "total" in the context of Eastern Europe and point out that, indeed, there was more religious liberty in Poland in the middle 1980s than any other country in Eastern Europe. But Lopatka is both a scholar and a lawyer (later he was appointed the chief justice of the supreme court); one would expect a more nuanced claim.

It is obvious that prior to the Great Transformation of 1989 the churches in Poland were definitely not confined to the sanctuary. Huge pilgrimages to Częstochowa took place annually with 400,000–600,000 pilgrims going to the shrine of the Black Madonna.[73] Oasis summer camps involved 60,000 youth in 1985. Students and other "Solidarity" activists were taking up collections at the entrances of churches, displaying "Solidarity" announcements and photos while uniformed policemen stood yards away, obviously aware of this 'clandestine' activity but not intervening.[74]

A new theology of inner freedom was also being developed. Popiełuszko frequently stressed that human beings were created in the image of God, who is free, and therefore freedom was implanted by God. Human beings can be crushed but their yearning for freedom cannot be extinguished by violence, especially not in a nation that existed for a millennium.[75] The main developer of a theology of liberation of the spirit was Franciszek Blachnicki. In an explicit contrast both to the personalistic notions of salvation through Jesus and to the Latin American theology of liberation, Blachnicki pointed out that in the context of a totalitarian power the main problems are falsehood and fear. Hence for the individual and the church it is crucial to find the inner courage, to stand up against terror in order to speak the truth about the higher laws of God, the higher values of morality and religion.[76] This is done non-violently by expanding people's awareness to the values of human dignity and freedom. One becomes willing to suffer and even die for the truth; the victory of the resurrection comes through the cross, according to Blachnicki. Such theology became the underpinning of the non-violent Great Transformation of Poland from totalitarianism to democracy.

The Church's sympathy for "Solidarity" was shown again when the labor union was legalized again in 1989. When "Solidarity" was alleged to run candidates for the election for the Senate their public information booths were frequently set up in front of churches and one could observe nuns and clergy helping out with the effort.[77]

The activities of the "Freedom and Peace" movement, which was inspired by sermons of John Paul II, were also supported by the Church and some of their meetings took place in church buildings. Among the principles of the "Freedom and Peace" movement were that peace must be linked to the guarantee of personal freedom for everyone.

> There is no peace wherever there exists a system of state aggression, of ideological coercion; wherever individuals have been deprived of their right to independent decisions, to initiative, where traditional political freedoms have been eliminated . . .

and they pledge themselves "[to] fight for fundamental human rights and for freedom of thought, freedom of association and prisoners' rights."[78]

On May 17, 1989, three new laws were passed by the *Sejm*, "Concerning the State's Attitude to the Catholic Church in the Polish People's Republic," "Concerning the Guarantees of Freedom of Conscience and Religion," and "Concerning Social Security Insurance of Church Personnel."

The first pertains to the Roman Catholic Church and the other two to all churches. The "Law Concerning the State's Attitude to the Catholic Church" finally removed a colossal absurdity according to which the smaller non-Catholic denominations received legal recognitions between 1945–1947 and the majority Catholic Church had no *de jure* standing until May 1989, which, of course, was a constant source of legal restrictions. Since the draft of the law was prepared by the Joint Episcopal-Government Commission and had been approved by both the PUWP and the Plenary Conference of Catholic Bishops and was introduced to the parliament by Prime Minister Mieczysław Rakowski its passage was assured before hand, and indeed there were only 2 against and 12 abstentions.[79]

The law is a veritable charter of religious liberty and autonomy. Art. 2 allows the church to govern itself by its own laws, and regulates its own affairs. Legal status is granted to papal academies and theological seminaries whose degrees had not been previously recognized by the state. Religious education that has been alternatively restricted and liberalized depending on how the tug of war between church and state determined it, has now, according to articles 18–24 been given over completely to the competence of the Church. Even more revolutionary was the permission for the Church to establish schools and other educational institutions, thereby ending the monopoly of the government on education. The Church will also receive expropriated properties, including schools, hospitals, and social and charitable institutions, or compensation (article 63). Chaplaincy in the army is continued and priests and seminarians are exempt from service, except in times of war when they may serve in non-combatant roles (article 29). The Church is allowed a wide array of social services for the benefit of children, patients, prisoners; every area of social and charitable work is open to the church (articles 30–32 and 38–39). The Church is allowed to form freely associations to carry out its mission, not only associations of Catholics which were sometimes in the past organized without the approval of the church (these are permitted under a separate law of associations, as per article 37) but specifically Catholic associations under the control of the hierarchy (articles 33–35). Another radical departure from usual Communist practice is the full access of the Church to publishing and mass media including the right to organize its own publishing houses, radio and TV stations, theaters, film production and movie houses (articles 46–49). Non-profit activities of the church are exempt from taxation and the church may receive gifts freely and retain them in perpetuity (articles 52-59). The state approval of church appointments and their required pledge of loyalty to the state was rescinded by the next to the last article.

Other churches were given the same rights as the Roman Catholic Church in the law pertaining to them. These laws represent the basis for the government's definite abandonment of attempts to promote the Type C–Secularistic Absolutism, model and minimally returning to Type B–Religiously Toleration model, and maximally entering the Type D–Pluralistic Liberty model. Thus the Spring of 1989 brings to a close one era of attempted restrictions and denial of religious liberty, the phase of Communist dominance, with a complete fiasco of this attempt and its decisive repudiation. It ushers a new, more hopeful period after the Great Transformation.

5. Anti-Semitism and Jews in Poland

The unusually large proportion of Jews who dwelled in Poland as a result of Polish tolerance, their near extinction and a painful memory of anti-Semitism created an ambiguous situation that cannot be treated merely as a part of the overall picture. Hence a shorter separate coverage will be presented in addition to the material presented above. The historical and psychological roots of the complex relationship between Poles and Jews and their firm intertwinement has been frequently described.[80] What concerns us here is the post World War II situation in which the small remnant of Jews who escaped the Holocaust were drastically reduced from about 50,000 to perhaps less than 10,000. Most refused to assimilate and emigrated;[81] those who stayed are generally not religious but assimilated so well that one can hardly tell who is Jewish and who is Polish.[82]

Many people in Poland explain the dislike of Jews and the post-War purges not due to any Polish anti-Semitism but to the prominent role Jews played in the establishment and perpetuation of Communism,[83] while a diametrically opposed charge against Jews was that they are "cosmopolitans" [no allegiance to a home country] or Zionists [pro-Israel]. Those who explain the link between Communism and Jews tend to point out that the Jews of Poland gave help to the KGB in Soviet-occupied Poland early during the war in persecuting Christians and that among the Soviet KGB officers and the Polish secret police who were crucial to the incorporation of Poland into the Soviet orbit there was a large number of Jews, who, allegedly had a hatred for things Christian.[84] It is pointed out that there was a disproportionate number of Jews in Communist leadership positions who were loyal Stalinists which led to their purges when the nationalist Communists took the helm. Robert Donnorummo states:

> The fact that the leadership of the Communist Party used anti-Semitism in an attempt to gain some degree of acceptance for its positions in the late 1940s, in 1968, and even

in 1981 means they have some reason to believe that this
tactic would strike a responsive cord in the populace.[85]

With so few Jews remaining in Poland some have dubbed the current
situation as "anti-Semitism without Jews." Observers have found
strong traces of anti-Semitism in 1990 as Jews continue to be scapegoats not only for the Communist take-over, but for the economic
woes that accompany Poland's attempt to move to a free market
economy.[86]

The 1968 "anti-Zionist" campaign decimated the Jewish presence
in Poland to the point of terminating a thousand years of Jewish history in Poland.[87] A Jewish observer, Zeev Ben-Shlomo, noted with
much bitterness that many of the Polish organizers and speakers of the
45th Anniversary of the Uprising of the Warsaw Ghetto in April 1988
figured prominently in the 1968 Anti-Zionist termination of Jewish
presence in the land. The ambiguities are compounded in the apology of the Polish position vis-à-vis Jews by prominent government
spokespersons who themselves are Jews.

Religious Jews are organized into a "Union of Jewish Religious
Organizations" (or the Religious Association of the Mosaic Faith)
controlled by the Office for Religious Denominations.[88] Only a few
synagogues remained operational in Poland and for many years, until
1989, there was no rabbi in all of Poland, until finally in 1989 one from
Israel was allowed to reside in Warsaw and attend the religious needs
of the tiny Jewish religious community. While the daily prayers are
attended poorly, and the weekly prayers sufficiently to have a *minyan*
[quorum], the services for Rosh Hashanah and Yom Kippur are quite
well attended. Kosher food and other ceremonial needs are available.
The Jewish community provides social services mostly for the elderly.
As of 1982 the military regime made it possible to broadcast Jewish
services, something that was impossible prior to World War II and
during the previous Communist regimes.[89]

There seems to be no deliberate restrictions of worship by Jews
in those locations where there are still operating synagogues. In the
cultural sphere the picture is more mixed. The Jewish Theater in
Warsaw seems to flourish. Museums exist and the study of Jewish
history in Poland has been encouraged as of recently. But some Jewish cultural expressions seem to have suppressed before 1989 seemingly simply because they were Jewish. The former concentration
camps are well preserved, respected, and frequently visited, but there
have been failures to point out the uniqueness of the Jewish suffering.

There was a tendency to include the number of Polish Jews simply into the total figure of Poles who were killed without illumination of the tragic scope of the Jewish destruction. In general there seems to be sometimes an unseemly competition as to who suffered more.

An incident that displayed all the raw feelings of the Jewish-Catholic conflicts was the question of the Carmelite convent at Auschwitz, which festered from 1984 to 1990. The deep misunderstandings and distrust that exist between the Jewish and Polish Catholic communities erupted in a number of ugly incidents and bitter recriminations around the establishment of a convent for Carmelite nuns in a building adjacent to the former Auschwitz concentration camp. An agreement was made to relocate the convent within the building of a Center of Information, Education, Dialogue, and Prayer but the terms of that agreement were interpreted differently by various parties and the old mutual hostilities came to the fore, each side feeling that the other deliberately violates their rights.[90]

The good news is that in February 1990 the above mentioned Center began to be built and that Cardinal Macharski of Krakow and Edgar Bronfman, the president of the Jewish World Congress as well as a representative of Prime Minister Tadeusz Mazowiecki were present for the groundbreaking ceremonies, declaring that the conflict over the Auschwitz convent is over.[91] Even more encouraging is that the Roman Catholic Church of Poland officially sponsors a variety of educational programs and dialogues with Jews in order to come to grips with the painful legacy of anti-Semitism.[92] In November 1990 a book appeared, *Zydzi i judaizm w dokumentach Kosciola i nauczniu Jana Pawla II (1965-1989)* [Jews and Judaism in the Documents of the Church and the Teachings of John Paul II]. One may expect that its significance will be enormous because of the impact and position that the Pope has in his own country.

AFTER THE GREAT TRANSFORMATION, 1989 ONWARD

The Great Transformation from Communist-domination to a pluralistic democracy started in Poland sooner than in other Warsaw Pact countries. Among the immediate causes of the change were the frequent demonstrations, rebellions, and strikes which rocked the country from time to time since 1956 and the lamentable economic situation as well as the aspiration for freedom and independence. A serious possibility that Communist monopoly on power could be terminated occurred already during the "Solidarity era" of 1980–81. No political or economic solution could be found as Poland went from crisis to crisis. Mikhail Gorbachev's ascent to power in 1985 and the concomitant change not only in the Soviet Union's *perestroika* and *glasnost* but in its foreign policy as it pledged itself to non-intervention in the internal affairs of its allies made the Great Transformation of Poland not only possible but likely. The time had come when the PUWP simply could not rule Poland alone, not even with the tacit assistance of the Church. All kinds of ploys had been tried, such as the Patriotic Movement of National Rebirth (PRON) and the wrangling about a convening and make-up of the Round Table, but nothing would suffice except the legalization of the "Solidarity" labor union, its transition into a movement (though not formally a political party), then the first free elections in June 1989. "Solidarity" candidates won 99 out of 100 Senate seats and the one PUWP candidate who won a seat ran on a "Solidarity" platform. The voters have spoken and the logical happened. A prominent Roman Catholic journalist and "Solidarity" activist, Tadeusz Mazowiecki, was offered the prime ministership and given the mandate to put together a new government. This government rapidly introduced a series of measures, not always popular, but nevertheless supported by the general populace to change the economy from a state-owned, centrally planned one to a free market economy. The expected shocks to the economy with the convertibility of the *zloty*, did come, such as high inflation, unemployment, difficulty of converting state-owned enterprises to private ownership, increase in prices, strikes and demonstrations. Internal squabbles among "Solidarity" leaders and the lack of unity increased the pessimism of a population somewhat used to being taken care of and being united.[93] Yet it would appear that Poles are ready to embrace pluralistic democracy as new political parties are formed.

What has changed decisively is that the PUWP no longer decided issues of religious liberty.[94] As Poland is becoming a state of laws and not the party, such issues will from 1989 onward be decided by the elected representatives of the people. With the establishment of Mazowiecki's government there is again a continuity with Poland as it was before World War II; psychologically for many the war had only finished in 1989. Thus Poland is trying to find its identity, having rejected its socialist identity as a Soviet import. But Poland has no clear models or patterns; the U. S. and Western Europe are too different to become models. So the Poles are free though they don't seem to know how to use this freedom.[95] Two or three generations had lived in "prison" and even if they had longed for freedom they had no tradition of it and there are many, often contradictory concepts of freedom.

Two areas of concern about religious liberty have surfaced. One, according to Jan Zaborowski, is freedom within the Roman Catholic Church. The second, according to Adam Kuczma, is the perceived threat to the non-Catholic churches by the giant Roman Catholic Church.

The question of freedom within the Church deals both with the issue of pluralism within the Church but also in the manner in which the Church will carry out its public role. One of the issues which surfaced is the request by church authorities to conduct religious education in schools again. Many of Catholic intelligentsia and the Mazowiecki government (the Minister of Education Mr. Samsonowicz and his deputy Ms. Radziwil) opposed this request. The Church had established a very effective religious education on church premises in which the vast majority of children participated voluntarily and many think it is regrettable that this might be abandoned. The Church may well be concerned whether the large enrollment will continue on a voluntary basis since the church will cease to be a symbol of opposition to the government the church may lose this advantage. In spite of protests and hesitations in September 1990 religious education began to be taught in schools again. The Roman Catholic bishops interpreted this as a sign of justice, bringing to an end the old status quo imposed by the Communists.

Another issue is that Poles see the role of the Church to implement moral rules in public life but tend to be lax about implementing the moral norms into their private lives. When the Church became the rock of Polishness it tended to lessen pure religiosity, i.e. people tend to be more faithful to the Church than to the Lord, according to Zaborowski.[96] The national role of the Church may deter believers from religion in a time when the church has all its rights. Indeed, polls taken in March 1990 show that since November 1989 the popularity of the Roman Catholic Church has fallen from 88 percent to 74 percent and that Tadeusz Mazowiecki has overtaken Cardinal Jozef Glemp in popularity.[97] By the end of the summer 1990 the situation reversed itself and Cardinal Glemp overtook Mazowiecki again.

The second issue are the fears of Catholic dominance by the non-

Catholic churches. Apprehensions of this sort are frequently heard by Protestant leaders voiced often for foreign consumption that they may have been better off under the Communists then under the Catholics because the Polish Catholic Church does not have much experience and need of ecumenism. They wonder whether the Roman Catholic Church will again, like between the two World Wars, though there is no Constitutional provision of its special, privileged position, by its sheer size and authority support measures that place the minority population at the mercy of Catholic views in areas such as education, legalized abortion or the ownership of church properties in the Western territories. For this reason the Protestant churches have sent appeals to the parliament urging the inclusion of religious liberties in the proposed new constitution. It is difficult to evaluate whether these concerns are realistic or whether they are the product of the selective memory from the times of conflict. The size of the Roman Catholic majority is a fact. It is true that these other churches are in the shadow of the Roman Catholic Church; how could it be otherwise? But they have to realize that this shadow also defended them and that some of the preferential treatment they had received from the Communists was done in order to weaken the Catholics. Now the situation is changed and the non-Catholic churches no longer need the Catholic umbrella. The question is how to use the victory and how to take advantage of the proportionality. Already the non-Catholic Churches have benefited from the new situation as the Ukrainian Catholics were able to get their own bishop, as the Baptists have established their own seminary, and as the Lutherans have established a school in Silesia. Jehovah's Witnesses, who had been operating unhindered for a while, were given legal recognition in May 1989. All of this bodes well for the non-Catholic churches. Of course, the challenge for the Roman Catholic Church is to change its attitudes toward the other churches, and become more ecumenical, but the other churches also must stop being suspicious. The cooperation of churches on human rights issues needs to carry over into other areas.

One of the interesting features of the post-Transformation era in Poland is that unlike East Germany, Yugoslavia, Czechoslovakia, Hungary, and Romania, there are no dramatic exposes of secret service files or uncovering of collaborators with the secret police. Seemingly there is a "gentlemen's agreement" that no such soul-searching and digging into the dark recesses of the past should be done, for fear that it would lead to disunity and personal tragedies because not only would there be some unsuspected names found in the files of people who informed on others to the police, but some innocent people who were implicated by others while they were under duress may suffer the consequences of such revelations. The working assumption seems to be that what people did at the time of great repressions does not really reflect their free choice and therefore it is best to let the past stay put. Thus the Poles are dealing with the question of collaboration with the Communist secret police in the same manner as they did with the question of anti-Semitism or those Poles who turned over Jews to Nazis—simply avoid dealing with it for fear of opening too many raw wounds or forcing themselves to a soul searching which would possibly harm national unity—a goal of great importance to Poles who are used to seeing themselves surrounded by enemies out of which encirclement one can escape only by harmonious relations with one another. However, mass graves of victims of Stalinist crimes have been discovered in the Warsaw prison; such discoveries cannot forever be dismissed.

Department IV of the Ministry of Interior was abolished in August 1989. It is believed that the department may have been involved in a murder of a priest, Sylvester Zych, as recently as July 11, 1989.[98] Soon thereafter, in October 1989, the OARD was also abolished as a vestige of the Stalinist regime. Some of the responsibilities of the OARD have been assigned to the chief of the prime minister's office, Jacek Ambroziak, a lawyer with close relationships to the Catholic hierarchy. In July 1989 the Vatican and Poland signed a Concordat and full diplomatic relations were resumed with an Apostolic Nuntio posted in Warsaw.[99] The Roman Catholic Church commenced its first television program in the fall of 1989.

In 1980 this author concluded a section on Poland in his book, *Christian-Marxist Dialogue in Eastern Europe* with the Latin phrase *"quo vadis?"* popularized by the great Polish novelist, Henryk Szienkiewicz. At that time it was not clear where Poland was going. In 1990 the answer seems quite clear, in the direction of pluralist democracy and liberty for all of its citizens, religious and non-religious. Getting there may not be easy but the path is the right one.

Chapter 11

R O M A N I A: STATE CONTROLS ROBUST
RELIGIONS

Interesting parallels may be discerned between Romania and
Poland. In both countries the predominant ethnic group is nearly
monolithic in its religious affiliation, and hence, there is a close correlation between religiosity and nationalism; for Poles, it is Roman
Catholicism, for Romanians, it is Romanian Orthodoxy. Both Poles
and Romanians show a devout folk religiosity easily observable in
many areas of life, particularly in large church attendance. Both
dominant churches had a well-educated theological cadre. Both lived
for a long time under rulers of another ethnic and religious identity. Both showed very little inclination toward Communism until
the arrival of Soviet troops at the end of World War II, and both
had minuscule Communist Parties imported from the Soviet Union.
Both harbor strong anti-Soviet feelings for historical reasons and for
territorial losses to the USSR. But, significantly, the Romanians did
not have the experience of toleration that the Poles had and that,
ultimately, accounted for significant differences.

Historical Factors

The Romanians, a people who speak a Romanesque language and
who see themselves as descendants of the Romans, intermarried with
the native Dacians and Getaes, and embraced Byzantize Christianity, i.e. Eastern Orthodoxy. To it they stuck steadfastly during the
many centuries of Turkish and Hungarian overlordship. Moldavia and
Wallachia, caught in the struggle between the Ottoman and Russian
Empires, achieved independence from Ottoman Turkish vassaldom in
1859 and united in 1877; until then the Romanians were mostly serfs,
oppressed and discriminated against, living in great misery. Their
language and culture was protected primarily by the village priests.

In Transylvania ethnic Romanians fared similarly under Hungarian rule which was supplanted by Turkish rule only to fall under the Hapsburg Austro-Hungarians in 1683. Transylvania was multi-ethnic due to the large Hungarian and German minority. Most of the Hungarians and Germans were Roman Catholics, but the Protestant Reformation was quite successful among the Hungarian nobility in Transylvania, and many of the Hungarians became Reformed (Calvinist) with smaller Lutheran and Unitarian[1] churches while many Germans embraced Lutheranism. Eventually Protestants became more numerous and politically more powerful than the Roman Catholics. Hungarians and Germans of Transylvania were in a privileged position being " 'accepted' nations with 'accepted' religions, while the Romanians and their Orthodox religion were merely 'tolerated.' "[2] Protestant eagerness to evangelize the Orthodox population (for which purpose the Bible and catechism were translated into Romanian) made the Orthodox feel beleaguered and experience Protestantism as something foreign. The Hapsburg emperor Leopold I, who was eager to advance Catholicism, proved to be more successful in weaning some Romanians away from Orthodoxy. He offered equal rights to those enjoyed by Catholics for all the Orthodox who would become Uniate, i.e. acknowledge papal primacy and accept a few other Catholic doctrines while retaining their Byzantine or Greek rite. In 1698 an Orthodox synod accepted the offer thereby creating the Eastern Rite Catholic Church.[3] At first very many of the Romanians Orthodox parishes joined this church, a measure roundly condemned by the Orthodox Church. Thus Catholicism, too, was perceived as an aggressive foreign church whose aim was not only to control but to rob the Romanians of their Orthodox identity. The promise of equality of the Eastern Rite Catholic Church with the Latin Rite Catholic church failed to be fulfilled until 1744 when the Eastern Rite Catholics became a "received" or accepted religion. Only in 1762 were the Orthodox, who had in the meantime been strengthened by numerous defections from Eastern Rite Catholicism, recognized by a Hapsburg imperial charter but only as a "tolerated" religion. While the peasant constituency of both the Orthodox and Eastern Rite Catholic churches did not live in enmity with each other and the leaders were generally cooperative in promoting Romanian national resurgence, the Orthodox did continue to harbor the feeling that members of their church had been lured away by political machinations. After World War II, the Orthodox hierarchy would cooperate in the forcible return of the Eastern Catholic

Churches into the fold of Orthodoxy. One political intervention into religious matters was justified by another political intervention, and the masses of the faithful had little say either time.

When in 1918 Transylvania was added to the 'Old Kingdom' to form Romania, the tables turned. Now the Romanian majority decided to assert its predominance over the formerly dominant Hungarian and German minorities, and one way of doing this was to declare the Romanian Orthodox Church as the privileged national church, the state church, which worked closely with the royal government. Keith Hitchins describes the Orthodox Church's relationship with the Romanian state as follows:

> The Church enjoyed certain privileges as a State Church, and its presence was strongly felt in most spheres of public life. . . . [T]he Church avoided controversy over secular domestic and foreign issues and tended, instead, to follow the lead of the State. It also acquiesced in the rather loose supervision that the State exercised over its legislation and personnel. . . . The State was officially a Christian kingdom and it accepted the teachings of the Church about man and the final judgment and recognized the Church's right to carry out its spiritual responsibilities unhindered.[4]

The pattern of acceptance of the state authority and supervision did not change later when the state became a Communist totalitarianism with inimical intentions because the basic understanding of church-state relations continued into the post-World War II era.

Church politics between the two world wars and after World War II seems to be dominated primarily by the political problem of how to translate the desire of the Romanian majority to dominats in a multi-ethnic[5] and multi-religious[6] state in which minorities had been formerly dominant. Revenge for real and imagined grievances of Magyarization and Germanization was a factor in the process of Romanianization. Originally only the Orthodox bishops were members of the Romanian parliament, but as of 1926, four Eastern Catholic bishops and the heads of the Roman Catholic, Lutheran, Reformed and Unitarian Churches also became members.[7] The Orthodox Church feared the increase of influence of Roman Catholicism and bitterly fought the signing of a Concordat between Romania and the Vatican in 1927 (ratified in 1929) which they saw as giving the Catholics greater rights than they enjoyed. The evangelicals or Neo-Protestants, especially the Baptists and Pentecostalists, who recruited primarily from the Romanian Orthodox population, were greatly hindered in their work in the early 1920s, then enjoyed relative freedom from 1928–1937, only to be severely repressed, and even completely closed down for a brief time (1938–1939).[8]

In Romania the struggle between Type A–Ecclesiastical Absolutism and Type B–Religiously Tolerant models was unresolved and features of both co-existed although the church that benefited from the Type A model now became the Romanian Orthodox Church. The Romanians seized the opportunity to promulgate their national church to a privileged position in the same manner in which the Roman Catholic and Protestant churches sought privilege and dominance in prior eras. The Romanians considered the Orthodox Church as their national church, and when they emerged with a national state after years of foreign dominance, they considered it natural to elevate this church to a special position, assuming correctly that the church would contribute to the more effective governing of the Romanian realm. The traditional Byzantine model of Caesaro-papism became even more suitable as the Romanian Orthodox Church became completely autocephalous and elevated the metropolitan primate of Bucharest to the rank of Patriarch in 1925. These were factors favoring the Ecclesiastic Absolutism, Type A arrangement.

Yet the country that was established in 1918 was in reality a multi-national and multi-religious one, which meant that pressures existed toward establishment of Religious Toleration (Type B), which would give equal rights to all or most of the churches. The Romanians who now for the first time ruled over their former overlords (the Hungarians, Germans, and Ukrainians), however, were simply inclined to replace the reigning religion thereby continuing Ecclesiastic Absolutism (Type A model). This became the particular aim of the extreme right-wing of Romanian Orthodoxy, the "Iron Guard" (The Legion of the Archangel Michael), which had a pronounced anti-Semitic, anti-Bolshevik, and anti-foreign ideology. The "Iron Guard" promoted the identification of Romanianism with Orthodoxy and so did to a lesser extent the much more spiritual renewal movement "The Lord's Army" which sought to use evangelistic Protestant techniques to promote adherence to Orthodox spirituality and morality.

At the outbreak of World War II in 1940 parts of Romania that had been formerly under czarist Russia, namely Northern Bukovina and Bessarabia, were annexed by the Soviet Union. Very quickly the Soviets instituted severe persecution of all religions and formally separated church and state driving the Romanians more firmly into pro-fascist positions. During World War II Romania joined the Axis powers and for a brief period recaptured the Soviet-occupied territories in which they rapidly re-instituted Orthodoxy and even helped an Orthodox revival in areas occupied by Romanian troops beyond the former border (e.g. Odessa). The government of General Antonescu instituted a firm state control of the Romanian Orthodox Church and replaced some bishops with those that had greater loyalty to the "Iron Guard." To this "Iron Guard"[9]-controlled-state the Holy Synod of the Romanian Orthodox Church pledged its loyalty in December 1940.[10] Since the Neo-Protestant "sects" were of Western origin, the government of General Antonescu considered them hostile to the state, confiscated their property, and sentenced their leaders to long imprisonment. The German churches in Transylvania were subjected to Nazi interference in church life similar to the one established in the Third Reich.[11] Parts of Transylvania where Hungarians were particularly numerous were ceded to Hungary so that the Hungarian churches were incorporated into their sister churches in Hungary. With the exception of the persecuted Neo-Protestants, all the churches cooperated closely with the pro-fascist government of Romania and Hungary as well as Nazi Germany, regarding Bolshevism as their real enemy. The anti-Bolshevik propaganda was heftily reinforced with the actual persecution of religion in areas which Stalin annexed in 1940. Collaboration with the Nazis was a charge that could and would be used effectively against the certain clergy in the post-World War II period.

FROM THE END OF WORLD WAR II TO THE REVOLUTION OF 1989

The period after World War II may be divided into two major periods: (1) prior to the Great Transformation, 1944–1989, and (2) after the Great Transformation (1990–onward). One might say that two revolutions mark the perimeters of the first period, the Communist revolution dating from the Communist take-over (from 1944–1947) to the anti-Communist revolution of December 1989. The period before the Great Transformation may be further divided into three periods, (a) the "Popular Front" coalition and gradual imposition of restrictions upon churches, from 1944–1947, (b) Stalinist persecutions, 1948–1961, and (c) firm control of the churches with the Romanian

Orthodox Church in a relatively privileged position, 1962–1989. On the whole there was a remarkable consistency in regard to the manner in which religious liberty was handled by the government from 1944 to 1989.

The main characteristic for the entire post-World War II period is that the Churches were not separated from the state but only from the school. The Romanian situation was fraught with ambiguities that defy easy categorization though they can be explained. Basically what happened was that a miniscule Communist Party, originally consisting mostly of non-Romanians, was imposed by the Soviet Union, which gradually Romanianized totalitarian regimes in Europe. Next to Albania, the Soviet Union, and Bulgaria, no other country showed the same police brutality. The sheer police presence was overwhelming.[12] The power of repression was so great that no effective dissident movement could be sustained, except for very brief periods. Yet Romania could present to the world another picture in the 1970s in which it seemed to be a maverick Communist state, more independent of the Soviet Union than any other Eastern block nation, eager for non-aligned status. Romanians who attended international conferences, religious or secular, were often refreshingly flexible. Ultimately, however, these periods of openness succumbed under the personality cult of Nicolae Ceaușescu, a man hell-bent to make an imprint on his country no matter what the domestic or international cost.

The Romanian Orthodox Church found its niche in the state which was not of its choice but with which it was able to work out an arrangement from which both church and state seemed to benefit. While many would have regarded that *modus vivendi* as a sell-out by the church to a government ultimately hostile to all things religious, the Romanian Orthodox Church, enjoyed a vitality unparalleled in the Orthodox world (with the possible exception of the Greek Orthodox Church) that cannot be ignored. As long as the churches of Romania were willing to give uncritical support of their government they were given a good deal of space for their activities. The state did promote the Communist ideology both in schools and in propaganda, but it realized that the citizens of Romania were so ardently religious that the demise of religion would not come in the near future. Hence it was important to permit the work of the churches but at the same time to completely subjugate them to the state and to infiltrate them thoroughly. By not legally separating church and state it was possible to justify this dominance of the government. The dominance of the state over the churches without the churches' ability to influence the state was reflected in Romanian law rather bluntly. Basically the Romanian government treated the traditional churches as a department of the government and the religious leaders as government employees (though only about a third of their salary was paid by the state)[13] who must swear loyalty to the government and who are completely controlled by the Ministry for Religions.[14] For that reason the Romanian government resorted only briefly, right after the war, to the device of organizing a "patriotic clergy union" because it was successful in controlling entire churches from the top down at which point it was more efficient to control the entire church by dealing with it through the head of the religious communion whereafter loyalty to the church leadership was encouraged. Only the "sectarian" Neo-Protestants proved to be somewhat obstinate in not giving complete allegiance to the system. They caused more trouble for the government and, in return, were troubled more by the government.

a.   Gradual Imposition of Control Upon the Churches, 1944–1947

In August 1944 Romania concluded an armistice with the Allies and came under the Allied Control Commission. The framework for the subsequent dealing with the churches of Romania and the entire Balkans was set by the so-called "Vishinsky Plan"[15] which was issued by the Soviet High Command of the Southeast European front. The Vishinsky Plan called for "controlling the clergy by providing or controlling their salaries,

   • liquidating or compromising undesirable clergy and replacing them with Soviet-trained or sympathetic clergy

   • restricting religious activities to worship except for assisting in government-initiated relief activities, and

   • forming an alliance with Orthodox Churches under the leadership of the Moscow patriarchate.[16]

This plan was implemented during this and the next period; only after Romania showed signs of independence from Moscow were the provisions of the common front with the Russian Orthodox Church eliminated.

At the outset in the fall of 1944 and early 1945 some of the German Lutheran and Eastern Catholic clergy were deported to the Soviet Union. Other clergy were enrolled in the "Patriotic Defense" welfare work which contained a good dose of political indoctrination. Those priests who had been active sympathizers with the "Iron Guard" frequently displayed greater willingness to be cooperative with the new government's measures for fear of being targeted for retribution.

By March of 1945 a Popular Front government, predominantly under Communist control, was organized in which a prominent place was played by Prime Minister Petru Groza, the son of a priest and formerly an active Orthodox layman who never renounced his adherence to Orthodoxy. Several other Orthodox priests were in high government positions. By the summer of 1946, the government shifted imposing censorship of religious publications and mail by the Ministry of Religion and announced that all religious meetings would have to be cleared by the Ministry of the Interior. Subsidies of income were granted to all clergy who gave their allegiance to the government and promises of more substantial support were made if the clergy gave fuller support to the government. Some of the older, less cooperative bishops and priests were dealt with by passing a new law on retirement by the age of seventy; this also eliminated them from becoming potential successors to the aging patriarch. While Orthodox relationship with Moscow was encouraged the opposite was the case with churches that had Western foreign ties, especially with the Vatican and, as of 1948, with the newly established World Council of Churches, (both of which were branded as agents of imperialism). Leaders of the Neo-Protestant churches were declared to be imperialist agents.

By November 1947 a second law of the Ministry of Cults altered the manner in which the Orthodox bishops were to be elected, giving the government a substantially greater role in the process. To show its good will toward the churches the government did not include them in the expropriation of lands during the agrarian reform of 1947. But the schools formerly run by churches, their youth organizations, and all other educational facilities were taken over by the government. It seems that no one interfered with the regular worship. People flocked to the churches in these times of great uncertainty, seeking mutual support and divine protection. Germans and Hungarians were particularly afraid of reprisals, but in the beginning no measures were undertaken against Hungarian churches; to the contrary they seem to have been less the target of government interference than the Romanian. This was to change after the 1960s.

By the end of 1947 the Communists consolidated their power sufficiently to force King Michael to abdicate and establish the People's
Republic of Romania on December 30, 1947. While characterized
by great uncertainty and trouble for many clergy the brunt of the
government's interference was yet to come.

b. Stalinist Persecutions, 1948–1961

When Romania was consolidated as a Soviet Bloc country under
the leadership of Gheorghe Gheorghiu-Dej several decisive measures
took place during the very first year that left a lasting mark on the
manner in which the state dealt with religious liberties. On paper, as
in all other Eastern European countries, things did not look bad.

The Constitution of 1948 proclaimed no discrimination based on
religion (article 16) and guaranteed freedom of conscience and freedom of worship (article 27). The same article stipulated that only
schools for the training of clergy may be operated by the religious denominations and that these denominations are free to organize themselves in a manner to be established by law, provided they are not
acting contrary to the Constitution, public security, and morality.
Special attention was given to the Roman Orthodox Church by stipulating that it is to have its own head and a unitary organization and
that it is to maintain an independent episcopate, though standing in
unity of dogma with other Orthodox churches.[17] Separation of church
and state is not mentioned in the Constitution, as in Czechoslovakia.

The very comprehensive Decree No. 177 ("General Governance
of Religious Cults")[18] was issued on August 4, 1948, signed by the
ministers of religion, education, defense, and justice. The first nine articles deal with religious liberties and freedom of worship and promise
quite ideal guarantees of freedom of conscience and religion (art. 1).
Religious hatred which impedes the free exercise of "recognized religions" [apparently not standing in the way of hating or impeding
non-recognized religions] is prohibited. Discrimination for having or
not having a religion is forbidden. Attendance or non-attendance of
religious services or the upkeep of religions may not be compelled by
state or religious authorities. Having a religion may not prevent a
person for getting or holding political or civil rights or being obligated to abide by the laws. Religious practices, orders, associations,
and congregations, according to each religion's own rules, traditions,
and teachings may be organized freely, with the proviso that they
are not anti-Constitutional, immoral, or threaten security and public

order. Ecclesiastic courts may be maintained to discipline members
of a religion but such regulations must be approved by the Presidium
of the Grand National Assembly.

The relations between the state and the religious bodies is regulated in articles 10–22. These laws stipulate that all religious persons including heads of denominations must obey laws and take oaths
when required by law. Each recognized religion regardless of size must
have a central organization to represent them. [This provision goes
against the practice of groups like the Baptists, Jews, and Muslims
who are normally not hierarchically organized.] One of the significant
provisions that influences religious liberty is the question of government recognition. Article 13 stipulates that in order for a religion to
function, it must be recognized by a decree of the Presidium of the
Grand National Assembly after it is proposed by the government on
the recommendation of the Ministry of Religions, and such recognition may be withdrawn "for good and sufficient reasons." In order
to obtain recognition, each denomination must have its statutes describing its administration, management, and articles of faith examined and approved by the Ministry of Religion. Article 15 explicitly
stipulates that the Romanian Orthodox Church is independent and
unitary. Political parties based on religion are banned by article 16.
Local religious bodies must provide the local governments with the
names of their leadership and their size. The heads of religions, bishops, apostolic administrators, vicars, and all religious personnel who
have an administrative function within a denomination, in addition
to being Romanian citizens, must be approved by the Presidium of
the Grand National Assembly, following the previously mentioned
procedure of recommendation, before they assume function in their
respective posts. Likewise they must first be sworn in by the Minister of Religion, while other clergy must be sworn in by the head of
the denomination. Perhaps the most interesting part of the oath, in
addition to "being true to the People" and defend the Romanian People's Republic against domestic and foreign enemies, requires that all
clergy pledge themselves "to secrecy with regard to all matters connected with the service of the State" (article 21).[19] It is clear from
this provision that clergy are regarded regular state employees and
that enormous discretionary powers are given to the state to decide
what is "true to the people." The heads of the denominations' oath
also include a provision that they shall not allow their subordinates
nor shall they themselves undertake "any action likely to affect public

order and integrity of the Romanian People's Republic." Foreign contacts of the churches had to be carried only through the Ministry of Religion and no financial support could be received from abroad. Articles 44 and 45 stipulate that the curricula of schools for the training of clergy must be approved by the Ministry of Religion and that the teachers in such schools must receive approval prior to their appointment and the Ministry may cancel such approval. Professors in such institutions are paid by the state. Army chaplaincy was discontinued with chaplains with many years of service being retired while others returned to the civilian service of their churches. Clergy salaries are paid from the budget of the Ministry of Religion.

The provisions granting religious liberty notwithstanding it would seem that the clergy of all ranks had their hands tied firmly. It is not surprising that very few dissidents in clergy ranks could emerge with such a tight noose around their necks. The legal basis for massive government intervention and control of religious denominations had been created by Decree 177.

Still more telling was Decree 37 of February 1949 detailing the tasks of the Ministry of Religion.

> The Ministry of Cults is the public service through which the State exercises its right of surveillance and control guaranteeing the use and exercise of freedom of conscience and of religion. To this effect:
>
> It supervises and controls all religious cults and their institutions, communities, associations, orders, congregations, and foundations of a religious nature, whatever their kind may be;
>
> It supervises and controls special religious education for training personnel of all religious denominations;
>
> It approves the founding of new religious communities, parishes, and administrative units, the creation of new personnel posts, and the appointments, whether they are paid by the state or not, in the services of various denominations;
>
> It supervises and controls all funds and possessions, whatever their origin and nature may be, of religious cults;
>
> It assures the task of watching over the relations and correspondence between the cults of the country and those abroad; [and, lest anything may have been overlooked!]

It has various other tasks in connection with religious cults.[20]

In Romania the control of the churches was above ground; at least there was no cause for misunderstanding. Lest it be thought that the churches were unappreciative of such complete surveillance the heads of the Romanian Orthodox, Armenian, Reformed, two Lutheran-Evangelical churches (German and Hungarian), Old-Rite Christians, Muslims and Jews met in Bucharest in June 1949 and passed resolutions praising the government for religious liberty and equality and condemned the Roman Catholic Church for anti-state activity.[21]

The legislation did not affect all religions equally due to concrete historical and personal circumstances. The Romanian Orthodox Church fared much better than the Roman Catholic Church in the ensuing months. Although very closely monitored the Romanian Orthodox Church was not required to submit its statues and be accepted for recognition while the other churches were required to do so. Upon the death of Patriarch Nicodim, Justinian was elected, apparently after some government pressure. Patriarch Justinian's election turned out to be of considerable importance and benefit to the Romanian Orthodox Church. Justinian helped hide the Communist leader Gheorghiu-Dej during the war, and was the son of poor peasants with strong personal preference for socialism. With the cooperation of Prime Minister Petru Groza,[22] he steered the Romanian Orthodox Church in these perilous times by strictly abiding by the rules, closely cooperating with the government, and working on the "re-education" of the priests to adapt themselves to the new socialist conditions. Special "missionary courses" at the Orthodox Theological Institute were established in which clergy were counseled how to cope with the new socialist reality. Depending on how they responded to these socialist indoctrination courses clergy were either upward or downward bound in their careers. Justinian also re-invigorated monasticism by mandating monastic reorganization as self-supporting collective labor units and yet maintaining their reputation as centers of spirituality. Only in 1956, after the death of Petru Groza, would the government seriously restrict monasticism (see below). Hundreds of Orthodox clergy would be imprisoned and tortured and Justinian himself would be placed briefly under house arrest[23] but both the patriarch and the monasteries survived this harshest Stalinist attack upon the Romanian Orthodox Church and the Church continued to flourish.

The Romanian Orthodox Church loyally followed both domestic and international policies of the Romanian regimes through all their modulations. They did so not only because they were *de facto* the state church but because of their understanding that the government was working for the benefit of the Romanian people and the ancient Byzantine formula of the symphonia, i.e. the harmonious division of caring for a nation, the state for its secular needs and the church for its spiritual, each keeping to their own competency, was not threatened by the post-war arrangement. The more nationalistic the Communist government of Romania became in the period after the 1960s the more it was agreeable to the Orthodox.

The Catholics were beset by liabilities not encountered by the Orthodox and they would suffer severe government repressions. The Catholics in Romania were divided into a Latin rite Church and an Eastern (Greek) rite with the former being mostly non-Romanian and further divided into national branches (Hungarian and German) with relatively little cooperation between them. Interest in Romanians gradually increased. The fact that the Roman Catholics were under the jurisdiction of the pope was an infraction of the legislation mentioned above. For a while the government attempted to create a national Romanian Catholic Church and, having failed, settled to sever all contacts of the Catholic leadership with the Vatican which lasted into the 1970s.

A greater blow to Catholicism took place with the abolition of the Eastern rite Catholic Church and its absorption by the Romanian Orthodox Church which formally took place at a synod in Cluj on October 1, 1948, and was later confirmed by a Government Decree 358 of December 1, 1948. The Eastern Catholic Church officially ceased to exist though underground activities continued and some of the dissidents, such as Doina Cornea, came from this church.

The facts about cessation of the Eastern Catholic Church are clear, however, interpretations vary. After intimidation, imprisonment, torture, and blackmail, slightly over 430 of the approximately 1,800 Eastern rite priests "were represented by the symbolic thirty-eight delegates (the same number that had signed the original Act of Union with Rome)"[24] at this canonically invalid synod at Cluj. Some later recanted or claimed that their signatures had been forged. A week later, October 8, 1948, without the presence of a single Catholic bishop the Orthodox Church at a synod in Alba Julia declared the union with Rome for the former Eastern Catholics ended. Six Eastern Catholic bishops, about 600 priests, and 600 lay people were arrested and half of all these died in prison.[25] Janice Broun sees it as primarily a government action with which the Orthodox hierarchy, representing a minority of the Orthodox, shamefully complied.[26] In Alan Scarfe's interpretation,

> [t]he move to abolish the Uniates, masterminded by the Soviets, was carefully orchestrated between the church and the party. The Soviets relied heavily on the Russian Orthodox church to provide a political model to other Orthodox churches. Abolition of the Uniates was one expression of this enforced emulation . . .[27]

The present author recognizes truth in both Broun's and Scarfe's interpretations, namely that the government, in emulation of the Soviet model, took a very active and violent role in the termination of Eastern Catholics. But two other factors need to be highlighted. One is the government's antipathy, or rather fear, of Roman Catholicism and its Vatican center, which it had in common with every other Communist government of Eastern Europe. Even more important was the aspiration of the Orthodox churches in all of Eastern Europe, including Romania, to retrieve the churches and the believers which they believed had been unjustly, forcefully, and deceitfully snatched away from Orthodoxy.[28] Anyone understanding Orthodox-Catholic relations knows that the Uniates (Eastern Catholics) are perceived as a constant bone of contention and most Orthodox argue that no sound solution can be found until the reintegration of the Uniates into the mother church. The enthronement speech of Patriarch Justinian on June 6, 1948, illustrates this:

> At this moment, our thoughts turn to our Greek Catholic brothers, who until 250 years ago, were part of our flock. . . . The grievous spiritual agitations which made the life of Transylvanian Rumanians a great tragedy began with the feudal rule of the Hapsburg dynasty . . . In these conditions part of the Orthodox flock in Transylvania, threatened with death, joined the flock of tyrannical wolves and they have not yet had the courage to return to the Mother Church. . . .[29]

From the Orthodox perspective to be a true Romanian one should be Orthodox. Many of the Orthodox did not entirely trust the Romanian royal family of the German Hohenzollern dynasty who had been Roman Catholic and became Orthodox only for political reasons and they feared that royal inclinations were still toward Catholicism.

This is not the place to discuss Orthodox-Catholic relations in Romania but simply to point out that what was a most severe restriction of religious liberties for those Uniates to whom the loyalty to the papacy was significant meant the expansion, though modest, of liberties of those Uniates and Orthodox who favored the reunification. The Orthodox perceived this as an expansion of their liberties; the Catholics as a denial. In 1956 some of the Eastern Catholics who were released from prison wrote a memorandum to the government asking for re-institution of their Church only to be again thrown into the prisons with unusually long sentences and many died while in prison; only one bishop survived it. A fact not open to various interpretations is that the reunification of the Eastern Catholic parishes into the Romanian Orthodox Church was accompanied by incredible cruelty on part of the state, which cannot be justified. Church reunification and separation should be entirely a matter of free religious decision, if not in the past, then at least now.

The Latin rite branches of the Roman Catholic Church fared a little better. They were not forbidden but the Concordat was unilaterally severed by the government in July 1948, and they did not receive formal recognition for the duration of Communist rule but *de facto* they were tolerated.[30] Bishop Antal Marton did submit the statutes of the Roman Catholic Church for approval to the Ministry but they were rejected in 1949 because of traditional Catholic papal dogmas and administrative jurisdictions, which the Catholics in Romania were naturally unable to alter. Of course, the Latin Rite hierarchy expressed solidarity with the Eastern Catholics strongly protesting government oppression and were subsequently accused of trying to overthrow the government in a show trial in 1951. Their bishops and clergy were repeatedly imprisoned and tortured and the number of dioceses were reduced. Only one of the Roman Catholics, Franz Augustin, a provisional administrator who was never trusted by the Vatican and thus not appointed a bishop, was seated in the parliament,[31] along with all other heads of religious communities. There was an attempt in 1949–1950 to organize a "Democratic Action Committee" among the Catholic clergy and force them to sign the Stockholm Peace Appeal but Monsignor Glaser, an assistant bishop, forbade all Roman Catholic clergy to cooperate on the pain of excommunication. A few days later, in May of 1950, Glaser was arrested and "died of heart failure" in prison.[32] Such was the swift and long hand of the "law."

There is no doubt that the Romanian government increasingly used unusual violence to settle religious issues to its liking. The Lutheran, Reformed, and Unitarian theological seminaries were united into a joint seminary in Cluj in October 1948 which came under government control. The state also mandated that the Protestant churches form a federation in order to relate more uniformly to the government but generally this coerced federation did not prove to be successful. Nevertheless they had to declare that they were grateful to the government for full religious freedom and for government salaries.[33] All the health institutions that were under religious sponsorship were nationalized. The Orthodox lay organization, the "Army of the Lord," was first harassed, then closed down in 1947 but continued to meet openly until the 1950s and then continued its activities under the surface.[34] Religious instruction was removed from the schools, made voluntary, and mostly carried out by parents. Although they had received legal recognition Neo-Protestant 'sects' were declared subversive and many of them, like the clergy of all other denominations, suffered unspeakably in the prisons and concentration camps. Rev. Richard Wurmbrand, a survivor of these tortures who later succeeded in emigrating to the West, described these sufferings dramatically in a series of books.[35] Most people who had gone through the regime of Romanian prisons did not dare to speak about it. Cruelties perpetrated in the Balkan countries of Romania, Bulgaria, Yugoslavia, and Albania seem to have been cruder than elsewhere in the East (though Hungarian and Czechoslovak torturers held their own), matched only by the Soviets.

After breaking down some of the church leaders and intimidating others the Presidium approved the statutes of the Seventh-Day Adventists, Baptists, Pentecostalists, and Gospel Christians in December 1950 declaring that they may not maintain their foreign contacts.[36] What the *Journal of the Moscow Patriarchate* reported of the Romanian Orthodox Church was being applied to all churches, namely that freedom of belief was being "coordinated" (i.e. made to hinge on) with civic rights and duties.[37]

The Romanian Orthodox Church was hit by a wave of persecutions directed mostly against the monasteries between 1958 and 1963 with an estimated 1,500 monks, clergy, and lay people arrested. An additional 2,000 nuns and monks, those under the age of forty and fifty respectively, were compelled to leave the monasteries presumably to engage in socially more useful labor. By this time the Roman

Catholic orders had already been nearly eliminated.

The legislation was in place, the methods of surveillance and control likewise. Now the government simply needed to continue to root out by imprisonment, torture, financial pressure, and emigration all real and potential resistance to its policies. That it did do most effectively as long as it was an obedient follower of Moscow's policies, namely into the early 1960s. The cataloguing of the killings, maimings, and broken health and spirit has been and will continue to be done elsewhere; here it suffices to say that the Stalinist period in Romania produced a docile, fearful, and publicly obedient religious constituency. The picture is that of a Type C–State–Secularist Absolutism, but with the strange anomaly of Romania not being a secular state at all. The population remained massively religious. The government and the party seems to have reconciled themselves that they cannot uproot such religiosity soon so they need to control it. Thus alongside Secularist Absolutism, Type C, there were remnants of Type A–Ecclesiastic Absolutism, and Type B–Religious Toleration practices.

C. Firm Control of Churches with Privileges for the Orthodox, 1962–1989

By the early 1960s the church situation "normalized" insofar as a term such as normalization applies to one of the most repressive governments in Europe. Those imprisoned who had survived the Stalinist period were released, though not always immediately allowed back to their parishes. For the Roman Catholics the 1970s provided an opportunity to rebuild the hierarchy, though some, like Bishop Petru Plesca was reportedly interrogated almost daily by the infamous *Securitate* (secret police). Clergy who were exceptionally effective would be sometimes transferred by the Department of Cults[38] to remote parishes, while those who were particularly loyal to the government would receive bonuses beyond the normal one–third government subsidy of their salaries.[39]

With the rise of Nicolae Ceausescu to the leadership of the Romanian Communist Party in 1965 the country started to shape a very independent international policy which raised hopes for an era of liberalization. These hopes were fuelled by a general amnesty which released 12,000 political prisoners and by Romania's Western orientation. International contacts of Romanian church leaders increased and their position among Eastern European clergy, for instance in the Christian Peace Conference or the World Council of Churches, reflected this distinctly independent course, though always faithfully reflecting the official government policy. There tended to be a quick bonding between Romanians and Westerners on account of common suspicions toward Soviet policies.

The improvements in regard to the general relaxation of the 1960s and 1970s tended to be deceptive because the government continued to maintain a very close scrutiny of the churches and to deal harshly with those who stepped out of line. When church leaders showed independence from the government line the government would remove them. Yet despite the compliance of the leaders, or more accurately because of it, the first signs of dissent emerged by the middle of the 1960s and early 1970s.

The first *samizdat* was in the form of a letter by Rev. Stefan Gavrila, an Orthodox priest from Oltenia, in which he complained about problems which a parish priest encounters with local authorities. He writes of pressures to spend more time sermonizing about "patriotic" concerns rather than preaching the gospel and the lack of support by the hierarchy when a priest is beleaguered by local authorities. It seemed to him that the policy of church-state reconciliation was being followed at all costs by the hierarchy, even though it impeded individuality.[40]

Signs of dissent could also be noted in the vigorous Baptist Union, surprisingly by far the largest Baptist Church in Europe with about 160,000 members.[41] Some of the younger clergy in that Union were becoming restless with the subservience of their leaders, partially due to the influence of the international human rights movement (especially the Helsinki Accords) that started impacting younger clergy who received exposure to the West. One such outspoken Baptist clergyman was Iosif Ton who began his dissident activities as early as 1972. He and a small group of like-minded clergy succeeded to stir vigorous discussion about internal freedom and church's treatment by the state at the Baptist Congress in 1977.

Six Evangelicals circulated an Appeal in 1977 which highlighted "the systematic but masked persecution of believers"[42] pointing out that large church attendance is not a proof of religious liberty, but an expression of longing for greater freedoms. The authors of the Appeal point out that evangelical believers are regarded as subversives, not allowed to hold positions of responsibility or advance in their present positions. Their children are ridiculed and hampered in school. No adequate places of worship may be purchased nor are permissions to repair or build given without much hassle. Pastors are placed under great pressure so that many become spiritually defeated and are subject to involuntary cooperation with the Securitate to whom they must report frequently. On top of that they are humiliated that despite all their lack of freedom they must constantly praise the Party and the government for the supposed blessings of full freedom which they enjoy. They conclude that a spade should be called a spade: religious persecution does take place in Romania.

In 1978 a predominantly Baptist religious rights group, named the Christian Committee for the Defense of Religious Freedom and Freedom of Conscience, known better by its Romanian acronym ALRC[43] created a list of twenty–seven needs, most of them religious liberty issues.[44] The list points to the grave shortcomings in regard to religious liberties. Most of the requests are for carrying out religious activities without official approval. The reestablishment of the Eastern Catholic Church and "The Lord's Army" are sought and the right to establish religious associations and link them freely to international religious associations is requested. A crucial request is

> [t]he right to make church appointments; . . . the end of identity cards and permits for priests and pastors, as well as annulment of the obligation to be 'recognized' or 'approved' before taking up a post . . .[45]

They seek the right for clergy to work in hospitals, prisons, and homes for the aged. Certain property rights are requested such as the unhindered buying or renting of property or building of new churches and to receive material help from co–religionists and others abroad. Free dialogue between Christians and Marxists on mass media is sought. Censorship of the religious press should be discontinued and the religious press should have the right to report on all cases of religious persecutions. Printing presses and duplicating machines should be permitted to denominations. (It should be noted that the Romanian government registered all typewriters and examined the typeface several times a year). The clergy should be able to offer completely unhindered religious education. The opening of additional theological training centers, including some on university level, are needed as is the free ordination of clergy without state permission. Congresses and other gatherings of a denomination should be allowed without government permission. Access to mass media including religious broadcasts, re-opening of closed churches and re-instatement of dismissed clergy, the rights to have religious literature while in the Army, to give financial assistance to persecuted believers, visitation rights by clergy, advertising of religious events, the right to refuse a pledge of loyalty to the Communist Party and the right to refuse atheist indoctrination were among the other requests. The list concludes with an appeal for a complete restructuring of church-state relationships pointing out that the Department of Cults was the source of much abuse and restrictions upon religious life. The appellants also call on Romania to respect all human rights to which it subscribed in international treaties.

By 1981 the Romanian Christian Committee for the Defense of Believers' Rights sent detailed lists of repressions of believers, giving names, dates, and places, detailing police searches, refusal of passports, fining for holding of unapproved worship services, importing religious materials from abroad or trying to take them to the USSR, tortures, confinement to psychiatric hospitals, imprisonments, etc.[46]

The evangelical Neo-Protestants were a source of much aggravation to the government because of their tendency, like the Catholics, particularly of the Eastern rite, to hold underground, unapproved, or unregistered meetings. Many of the dissident Protestants were aided by the desire of the Romanian government to keep its most favored trading status with the U. S. and the International Monetary Fund and were thus, for a while, relatively lenient with such dissidents yet finally forcing many of them to emigrate. The dissident appeals and letters are of significance for establishing the situation in regard to religious liberties because they were able to be more forthcoming than the church hierarchies whose greater concern was the institutional functioning of their churches. Here is the classic dilemma, discretion or valor, so aptly highlighted by Trevor Beeson's book.

More problematic for the government was the case of an Orthodox priest, Gheorghe Calciu, professor of New Testament at the Bucharest Theological School. Having been in prison for sixteen years upon release in 1969 becoming ordained in 1973, he became popular among the seminarians for his fervent sermons. In 1978 he delivered a series of Lenten sermons in which he contrasted Christian and communist ethical approaches and openly criticized Romania's governmental repression of religion. By Spring of 1979 Calciu was arrested and sentenced to ten years, of which he served about five-and-a-half years, frequently tortured, near death and blindness.[47] There is no evidence that his superiors intervened on his behalf, though that may have been done discreetly.[48] In public they tended to attack him and finally defrocked him. Upon release he and his family were constantly trailed by a large number of secret police in a rather obvious manner in order to intimidate him and potential supporters. He became perhaps the best known Romanian dissident. In 1985 he was finally forced to emigrate to the West.

The period from 1962 to 1989 created many ambiguities. On the one hand there was a remarkable vitality in theological studies and publishing. The quality of theological education in the Orthodox and Protestant seminaries in Bucharest, Sibiu, and Cluj was high. Theologians from abroad were allowed to teach, research, and travel in Romania. A number of theological students were allowed to study abroad. More theological journals were published in Romania than in most East European countries, though one could occasionally hear that they could be more easily obtained abroad than in the country. Bibles and other religious literature, both scholarly and popular, were published.[49] Participation in international conferences was high and many conferences took place in Romania. Student groups and professors and even researchers known to be critical of Communist religious policies were allowed to visit and all noted the great hospitality of the people. Filming was permitted showing not only the high degree of religiosity but the ability of many active Orthodox lay people to hold concomitantly important positions on the local level of the Communist Party. Beeson concluded that the Romanian Orthodox Church is "among the most flexible and far-seeing Orthodox churches."[50]

The traditional Protestant churches among the Hungarians and Germans were likewise impressive in vitality and scholarship, though the German minority increasingly resorted to emigration to West Germany. The Hungarians, as the largest minority, became increasingly restless and critical of some of their collaborationist leaders.[51] By the late 1980s the Hungarians started fleeing to Hungary in ever increasing numbers. The Neo-Protestants also grew, though such growth may also have been spurred by hope for emigration to the West in an otherwise very tight country that prohibited travel to the general population, not only to the West but also to other socialist countries. Roman Catholics benefited from Ceausescu's visit to the Vatican in 1973 and permitted the building of some Catholic churches and the improvement of episcopal functioning.

The gradual development of "Ceausescuism" multiplied the ambiguities. Toward the end of his increasingly bloody reign, he brought terrible suffering on the citizens. The stages of Ceausescuism developed by Trond Gilberg in regard to Ceausescu's religious and nationalities policies,[52] may be applied here. Until 1968 Ceausescu followed the previously adopted policy of pluralism and attempted to fortify his position by building coalitions, reflected for instance in his reception in 1968 for all leaders of religious denominations.

From 1969 to 1989 Ceausescu promoted somewhat contradictory notions of creating a socialist nation with him as the great helmsman yet often destroying symbols of the past. He wanted to build it upon the traditions of the Romanian national heritage. This meant that there was, on one hand, an increase in atheist socialist indoctrination but on the other an even greater Romanian nationalism directed against the national minorities. The chief rabbi of Romania's 20,000 Jews, Dr. Moses Rosen, twice protested in 1984 and 1987 the increase in anti-Semitism[53] though it had been declared against the law due to pre-war and wartime anti-Semitic excesses.[54] Germans and Serbians complained about suppression of their cultural activities. But the ethnic group that felt itself to be the main target of attack were the Hungarians, the largest minority. The Hungarian church leaders at first did not dare to speak out in defense of the threatened Hungarian heritage, but with greater repression, Hungarians started asking for greater religious freedom for themselves.[55] More and more Hungarians were fleeing to Hungary until by 1987 the stream became a flood and brought such an outrage in Hungary by both the Communist and church leadership that nearly a state of war existed between the erstwhile Communist allies. The plan which threatened the minorities most was Ceausescu's idea of urbanizing the countryside by destroying ethnically distinct villages and creating 'futuristic' socialist agro-urban centers where all would be melted into a Romanian identity. This plan, if carried out, would have destroyed some 5,000 villages (some say 6,000–7,000), with their churches. The Hungarian complaint was heard in Hungary and in the West as if only Hungarian villages had been threatened; the Romanian villages were primarily destroyed except there was no one to speak out in their behalf.

With the increase of Nicolae and Elena Ceausescu's personality cults and a nepotism unparalleled in modern times, the country fell into increasing misery. Huge international loans spent unproductively that Ceausescu determined to repay back in record time (which he did by Spring 1989) completely impoverished the people. There was no food, no electricity, no medical supplies, no heating, and no adequate clothing or housing. By the late 1980s Romania had slipped well below European standards and resembled more a Third World than an European country. Contributing to the misery was Ceausescu's own grandiose plans to re-make Bucharest and other cities into show-cases of socialist greatness in order to immortalize himself.[56] Much dissatisfaction among religious people was the destruction of numerous historical churches with no consultation or suitable replacement in order to make way for this urban renewal; there was great fear that the Patriarchal Cathedral would be destroyed. During the Christmas Revolution of 1989, it became known not only that incredible expenditures were made for sumptuous palaces but that the underground was crisscrossed by secret tunnels, arm depots, hiding places, and listening posts for the *Securitate*—all while the population starved. The hatred for Ceausescu and his clan increased daily, but there was little that could be done—except to praise him. During the 45th anniversary of liberation from Fascism in the summer of 1989 the leaders of all or nearly all religious denominations gathered at a festivity at which they lauded Ceausescu in a manner more appropriate to God than to a human leader.[57]

International secular and religious pressure (e.g. World Alliance of Reformed Churches) was brought to bear upon the Ceausescu government but with no apparent results. Much of it emanated out of Hungary where religious leaders wrote appeals and raised the question of Romanian repressions in international forums, while at home aiding the refugees to a degree that gained them admiration both by the population and the government. Romanian Orthodox prelates took a very defensive attitude when their country was criticized; Metropolitan Antonie for instance threatened to walk out of an ecumenical meeting at which Bishop Károly Tóth of the Hungarian Reformed Church in Budapest spoke out against these repressions. When representatives of the World Council of Churches and the National Council of Churches of Christ in the U. S. offered to visit Romania in 1989 to review the situation and express their concern, they received no answer and no invitation.[58]

While *perestroika* and *glasnost* influenced an increasing number of East European socialist countries a temporary alliance of hard-liners, Erich Honecker of East Germany, Gustav Husak of Czechoslovakia, and Nicolae Ceausescu, was created praising one another's intransigence. The year 1989 saw the toppling of all three. Romania seemed to be the least likely to change due to it's relatively independent stance toward Moscow, but the revolution occurred just before 1989 expired. A bloody one it was since Ceausescu ruled with an iron and bloody hand. He and his wife were summarily executed by a hastily assembled military court while the secret police loyal to him still fought the population which was joined by the army. It was the costliest of East European revolutions in terms of human lives.

It is ironic that the Christmas Revolution of 1989 was sparked by a minister, László Tökés, of the Hungarian Reformed church in Timişoara, a provincial city near the Yugoslav border. Tökés, like many other clergy, had been frequently harassed by the *Securitate*. He preached sermons encouraging Hungarians to stay true to their heritage and stay firm in face of persecution. The government forced his bishop, László Papp to move him, something the pastor and the church members refused to do. Then the Securitate invaded his apartment and beat him up, urging him to move. In order to prevent future beatings or kidnapping members of his congregation kept guard all night long by his apartment.[59] Later they were joined by an ever larger crowd, not only of Hungarians but also Romanians and others. When the group gathered around the house became large enough, it ventured to start an anti-Ceausescu demonstration marching into the center of the city. The *Securitate* fired into the people who had moved into a church killing perhaps about a hundred people.[60] This sparked unrest in Bucharest and other cities; the rest is fairly well known secular history. It is re-assuring that in addition to many compliant clergy there were still among them people like the thirty–seven years old László Tökés who had courage to speak the truth, who were concerned about religious and civil (personal and ethnic) liberties, and who were respected by the people to the degree of sacrificing their lives to defend them. It was this integrity and courage which sparked the most violent of the East European revolutions which would overnight dramatically increase religious liberties. The general human rights crisis had escalated to the boiling point; some religious leaders and members, as it turned out, were not completely subverted and silenced by the regime and were able to provide the spiritual spark for the revolution.

Ceausescuism appears to be structurally an attempt to simplify ethnic and religious pluralism of Romania by minimizing the presence of the Religious Toleration, Type B model and retaining features of Type A–Ecclesiastic Absolutism, with Type C–Secularist Absolutism, superimposed over it poised for an ultimate monopoly when the "new socialist man and woman" emerges victorious over religious superstition. What saved the Type A model from a frontal attack by Type C protagonists is that the Romanian ethnicity in conflict with the ethnicities of national minorities had such a distinct religious embodiment in Romanian Orthodoxy. One simply could not think of Romanian historical traditions without stumbling into Orthodoxy. Reinforcing Romanianism meant reinforcing Orthodoxy and vice versa. Hence these two, unlike in the Soviet Union, did not collide but coexisted in Ceausescuism, though not without ambivalence.

AFTER THE REVOLUTION, 1990 ONWARD

According to Earl Pope:

> the revolution has made it possible for the first time in more than forty years for the churches to be free, to begin to govern themselves, to set their own agendas, to revise their own structures, and to live out their own lives in the fullest and most complete way. They have an unparalleled opportunity for their ministries and for their service, for which in large measure they were totally unprepared, although they had helped prepare the way for the revolution by keeping alive the spirit of democracy and the belief in the innate dignity of every human being. They have already begun to take steps to use this new religious freedom in a creative way.[61]

The first signs of change after the Revolution were the very public celebrations of Christmas; long-suppressed Christmas decorations could be seen in public and in homes as well as in churches. The old leadership of most churches fled (e.g. Bishop László Papp of the Hungarian Reformed Church went to France), retired, or were being pressured by significant segments of their constituencies to resign. Seminary students in Bucharest demanded the resignation of Patriarch Teoctist for his overly compliant relationship with Ceausescu, which he did, only later to re-instated by the Holy Synod on April 4, 1990, declaring that the retirement had been temporary due to health reasons. Tőkés was elected in April 1990 as a new bishop in his church. A period of openness followed even for the Jehovah's Witnesses, who had not been previously allowed legal activity. Many churches actively participated in the relief efforts to the starving and freezing populace.[62] The Eastern Rite Catholic Church was preliminarily legalized again on December 31, 1989, and then recognized by government decree on April 24, 1990.[63] As one may expect, it soon found itself in contention over ownership of their former church-buildings, some of which had been given to the Orthodox Church and others nationalized. The properties that were nationalized were to be returned to them, but the one's used by the Romanian Orthodox Church since 1946 would lead to great dilemmas as to how to adjudicate ownership.

Invited to a meeting of the World Council of Churches, Tökes bluntly criticized the world body for not helping in the struggle for religious liberties in Romania and elsewhere in Eastern Europe having accepted at face value the false assurances of official church representatives who were beholden to the government.[64] Thereby he reopened at an important forum a much needed discussion on the role of international religious organizations, institutions, and leaders in assisting those who themselves are unable to claim religious liberty and human rights due to overwhelming systems of repression. In Romania the churches had to confront the painful issue of the presence of informers among them even at the highest level; many of the most important representatives of the churches had to report monthly, directly to the *Securitate*. Suspicion and distrust was very strong, particularly against the Romanian Orthodox hierarchs. Many of them did cooperate closely with the Communist Party for which they received comfortable positions and perquisites. Some church leaders did confess their guilt for lacking the courage to stand up to Ceausescu but were forced to make humiliating obeisance to the Great Dictator.

Liberty was on the lips of all citizens of Romania when the dictator was toppled. At first it seemed to be not only liberty from the oppression of Ceausescu and his family but also from Communism. The Romanian Communist coat of arms was spontaneously cut out from all Romanian flags, and for a brief moment in early 1990, it was announced that the Communist Party would be banned. A multiparty democracy was proclaimed; free elections were held in May 1990; some of the relatives of Ceausescu were tried; the *Securitate* was formally dissolved; the press and other mass media became freer, and borders were opened. Outwardly it seemed that Romania might head straight into democracy. But many of the conditions for the establishment of democracy simply did not exist in 1990. Alternative political movements and dissidence did not exist in the late 1980s;

new political parties had to be created from scratch or by relying on pre–1947 revivals. The National Salvation Front consisting mostly of former Communists who ran afoul of Ceausescu handily won the first free election with a large plurality, and Ion Iliescu became the president. Demonstrations continued against him, and he resorted to violence to control them. There was evidence that the new secret police followed some old practices of surveillance over the population.

The Department of Cults was abolished, but an even larger Minister of Cults office was temporarily created to which Prof. Nicolae Stoicescu, an active Orthodox believer, was appointed temporarily. Many of the old bureaucrats were retained in their previous positions, a disturbing sign that at least some of the old restrictions may be continued. Stoicescu showed Western visitors the office with thick padded doors where church leaders were summoned to have their passports revoked or be removed from their parishes. Stoicescu discovered his predecessor's report to Ceausescu in which he wrote, "I *succeeded* in reducing the number of religious publications from 100 to 26 as well as the number of pages per publication."[65] Stoicescu declared his interest in encouraging the publishing of more religious literature, sending clergy to prisons and orphanages as chaplains and promote inter-ethnic and inter-religious dialogue. Robert Lodwick, a representative of the World Council of Churches, reported meeting in the summer of 1990 the new bishop of the Cluj district, Kálmán Csiha, who was imprisoned under Ceausescu for six years and was told that the enrollment in the Protestant seminary used to be restricted to eight students per year but jumped to sixty–two first year students in 1990. Bishop László Tökés, prior to his near-fatal automobile accident in Hungary in August 1990, vigorously pressed for Hungarian ethnic rights and against anti-Semitism and anti-Gypsyism. He also reported a great deal of fear and uncertainty among the population as to whether the National Salvation Front of Prime Minister Iliescu may not be a hold-out for former Communists and whether the renamed *Securitate*, Center for Romanian Information, in which sixty of the former secret service continued to be employed, would be willing to let go of their hold over the country. The question whether the Revolution might be kidnapped or stolen was a concern not easily put to rest. Paranoia and justified fear easily mingle in Romanian society.

The re-instated yet tainted Patriarch Teoctist commemorated a six month anniversary of the revolution against "The Dictator" at which President Iliescu, members of the parliament, and of the opposition attended. Is this a sign of change or an evidence that things did not change much? Was the Romanian Revolution a Great Transformation or a form of violent palace coup? Events like these cause the Baptists and other Neo-Protestants to express concern that the Romanian Orthodox Church will become the state church and repress the other churches.[66] Stoicescu's suggestion of using as a model the 1928 Law on Cults which discriminated against the Neo-Protestants reinforced those anxieties.

New relationships were being created between various religious and political groups. The Evangelical Alliance, though at first denied registration by the Ministry of Cults, was formed by the Neo-Protestants, some of whom became politically active. A Christian Democratic Party was also founded. The most easily discernible clustering of the population was along national lines and the Romanian-Hungarian animosity repeatedly flared up in violence and threat, leading in several cases to beatings and death. Lázsló Tökés received death threats, presumably from Romanian nationalist extremists, prior to his festive installation as bishop. The greater freedom of speech and assembly was misused for national/religious conflicts. Anti-Semitism, directed against the remaining 20,000 Jews was expressed more vocally than before. The threat of nationalistic and confessional strife will require greater efforts for creative transformation of Romania into a democratic state.

In the context of a somewhat chaotic situation it became obvious that Type D–Religious Liberties model would not be a likely alternative in the near future. Rather Type C–Secularistic Absolutism, experienced a total repudiation, though secularization of society will continue. The earlier pre-Communist conflict between Type A–Ecclesiastic Absolutism, and Type B–Religious Tolerance, returned to the scene. Unless Type B finds wider acceptance the national minorities, especially the Hungarians, are likely to break out of the country in one way or another, which is what the government fears the most but seems unable to deal with effectively. Earl Pope sees the possibility of the Reformation Churches, Roman Catholics, and Neo-Protestants forming a common front for fuller religious freedom that will cause both the state and the Romanian Orthodox Church serious problems. How these two inclinations, toward Type A and Type B, will be settled remains unclear.

Chapter 12

Y U G O S L A V I A: A STUDY IN AMBIGUITY

The Heritage of Intolerance

Balkan factionalism, separatism, and intolerance are proverbial. Balkanization is neither recent nor finished. Some of the rivalries are 'home made'; others were unwelcome imports by invaders which found fertile ground to fester vigorously because of the proximity of diverse peoples clamoring for identity and recognition.

The southern Slavic tribes settled on what is now the territory of Yugoslavia in about the seventh century A.D. Francis Dvornik's remark, "The early history of the Slavic nations is full of tragic incidents, of brilliant hopes, and promising possibilities which seldom found realization owing to the various circumstances and events beyond the control of the Slavic rulers,"[1] certainly applies to the southern Slavic people and those of other ethnicity who live intertwined with them even to the most recent times. Religion, which was to play a multifaceted role in the history of the area, became a tool of separation practically from the outset of the conversion from the old Slavic religion to Christianity. The eastern and southern regions of what is now Yugoslavia came under the influence of the Byzantine Empire, which impressed upon its sphere of influence the Eastern Orthodox form of Christianity.[2] The western South Slavic lands came under the impact of neighboring Rome from which it inherited the rival Roman Catholic brand of Christianity.[3] Both Rome and Constantinople aspired to the extension of their variant to the entire area; thus, the two forms of Christianity came into sharp conflict with each other fostering fierce loyalties in the local population, each developing the mentality of 'last outpost of the true faith in face of schismatic threat,' which persists until today. The development of a Bosnian form of Christianity in the central regions, believed to be the Bogumil heresy by both the Orthodox and the Catholics, further complicated this initial state of rivalry.[4] On the territory of contemporary

Yugoslavia not only Eastern Orthodoxy and Roman Catholicism but even the 'heretical' Bosnian Church displayed the characteristics of Type A–Ecclesiastic Absolutist society.

The fourteenth-century conquest of most of the territory by Ottoman Turks introduced another deadly religious conflict, namely between an expanding Islam, also very much a Type A society, and a defensive Christianity. Islam, not only the religion of the conquering new settlers but also of many converts primarily from the ranks of the by-then-defunct Bosnian Church,[5] reinforced the frontier-outpost mentality. Religion was a precious form of identification at times when politics were determined by more powerful neighbors and where increasingly clergy, especially among the conquered people, played the leadership role in the absence of other native governing authorities. The Turkish *milet* system—which divided people not so much into territorial units but into religious communities, granting a certain autonomy and responsibility to their religious leaders, thus maintaining all features of the Type A society—tended to rigidify the traditional European identification of an ethnic group with a single religion, even when an ethnic group did not have its own state. The religious leaders exhibited patriotism even in cases where the center of a religion, as in the case of Catholicism, was outside the country or where the rulers, such as the Austrians and Hungarians, were likewise Catholic. Thus the churches became the staunch supporters of the survival of a threatened identity of their membership, religious affiliation became permanently welded to national consciousness. To this day this ethno-religious unity presents an asset, or a problem, depending on the perspective of the viewer. Features of Type A mentality continue to survive and periodically reassert themselves vigorously to the present day.

Then Protestants came onto the scene, further complicating the rivalries.[6] The Reformation was moderately successful in Slovenia and Croatia, only to be wiped out by the Counter-Reformation. In the nineteenth and twentieth centuries some of the newer Protestant denominations made their appearance,[7] but they, too, added to the combative mood of intolerance. The larger group of Protestants were the folk churches of national minorities as the Hungarians, Slovaks, or Germans.[8] The free churches generally pursued a policy of proselytizing the more inert members of the other churches, which, of necessity, led to sharp conflicts. Protestantism could have contributed to the growth of a Type B, Religious Toleration society but it was too weak, both numerically and in duration, while some of the Neo-Protestants were quite intolerant toward the historical churches.

With the formation of Yugoslavia at the end of World War I, the conflicts and intolerance persisted, changing only the group in power. Now Islam was in retreat, with Orthodox and Catholics receiving legal privileges as the established religions of their respective areas, each aspiring to a final vindication of revival, hoping to absorb within its fold more or less the entire population. Protection of religious groups already had a legal basis in international treaties such as the Treaty of Berlin, 1878, and the Paris Peace Conference in 1918.[9]

The Kingdom of Serbs, Croats, and Slovenes, established in 1918 by the Treaty of Versailles, and renamed in 1929 by King Alexander into the Kingdom of Yugoslavia, passed laws in regard to religious communities which were discriminatory in nature, thus taking only small steps in the direction of a Religiously Tolerant, Type B society. Originally the legal status which the religious communities had in the constituent regions was retained so that there were two state churches, the Eastern Orthodox Church among Serbians, Macedonians, and Montenegrins and the Roman Catholic Church among the Croats and Slovenes. These two churches had an established and privileged status in the Kingdom. The Constitution of 1921 did not proclaim a separation of church and state. But it took cognizance of the heterogenous nature of the country by proclaiming that both the historical and adopted religions were legal,[10] but that other than those listed were not permitted.[11] With the Vatican Yugoslavia signed a Concordat in 1929 which was strenuously objected to by the Serbian Orthodox Church, which had aspirations of its own to be the dominant church and felt threatened by the Concordat. The Constitution of 1929 and of 1931 guaranteed freedom of conscience and religion but only to those which were recognized. Communities such as the Jehovah's Witnesses were not given legal status. The Islamic religious community, the Jewish religious community,[12] the Lutheran Church and the Reformed Church were protected by the law and were authorized to carry out religious customs, including religio-civic acts such as marriages, burials, and recording of births. The so-called "free churches" (Baptists, Methodists, Pentecostals, Salvation Army, Church of the Brethren, Blue Cross, Seventh-Day Adventists, and others) were allowed freedom of worship but were denied the above mentioned religio-civic acts.

The major churches, particularly the Orthodox and Catholics, were rather antagonistic to the small Protestant communities (which heartily returned the favor) and sought to induce the local government to limit their activities and harass them. The severest tensions, however, were the great historic animosities between the Serbian Orthodox, Roman Catholic, and Muslim religious communities, which persisted for the duration of the Kingdom of Yugoslavia, and headed into a disastrous direction with the outbreak of World War II.

During World War II the ethnic and religious rivalries, especially between Serbs (Orthodox), Croats (Roman Catholic) and Muslims resulted in a fratricidal civil war (Type A societies at war with each other) in which many old scores were settled by massacres and in which forcible conversions from Orthodoxy to Roman Catholicism were attempted. Some of the "free churches" lost their legal status in certain parts into which the Yugoslav state had been partitioned by the occupying forces. Total bedlam prevailed. This was compounded by the Communist leadership of one of the guerilla forces, the Partisans, lead by Josip Broz-Tito, who were dogmatic Marxist-Leninists espousing the Type C–Secular Absolutist societal approach, and who harbored animosities and suspicions toward all religions, though they did not declare these attitudes as official during the war for national liberation in order not to alienate their support among the peasantry that was largely religious. The declared policy was rather that within the "People's Front" differences would be tolerated and everything would be subordinated to the paramount goal of driving out the occupying Fascist-Nazi invaders.

The war period damaged the position of religion in society not only by great material and human losses to the various churches, but also to the moral and civil reputation of the churches. No church leadership explicitly condemned the occupation. The church that was targeted by the occupying forces for oppression was the Serbian Orthodox Church. Many of its clergy, including the Patriarch, were imprisoned or killed in massacres or concentration camps. Yet the Serbian Orthodox clergy by and large opposed the final victors, the Partisans, siding mostly with the Serbian nationalist guerrillas, named "*Chetniks*," who perceived the Partisans, i.e. the Communists as ultimately a greater threat than the Germans and their allies. Later it was possible for the Partisans to portray the Serbian Orthodox Church leadership as passive or collaborationist with the occupying forces.

The Roman Catholic Church was even more implicated in collaboration.[13] For instance, the creation of the Independent State of Croatia was naturally welcomed by most of the Roman Catholic clergy who were oblivious to its fascist nature and were enthused by the fulfillment of centuries of longing for an independent state. None of the occupational authorities (German, Italian, Hungarian, and Bulgarian) showed endemic hostility toward churches and played up the Bolshevik threat thereby engaging the churches into a compromised position (unlike the clergy of Poland) so that later the charge of collaborationism, which was not always deserved, would be sufficiently credible to dampen the sympathy of a considerable portion of the population. All of this would eventually contribute to an easy victory of the Secularist Absolutism Type C model over the Ecclesiastic Absolutism Type A model, with the Religious Toleration, Type B model having been far too superficially a part of the Yugoslav experience.

The last to arrive on the scene was the 'religion' or pseudo-religion of Communism, originally in a Leninist-Stalinist totalitarian garb. This drove the most recent wedge into an already hopelessly fragmented population. The Communists did not side with any of the existing religions but quarreled with all of them. They, too, aspired to eliminate all rivals, typical of Type C societies. Nurtured on an intolerant soil, driven by an intolerant secular faith, and guided by an example of the militantly atheistic Soviet Union, the Yugoslav Communists were going to heal the rifts of disunity by bringing the entire country to reconciliation through the process of building socialism based on atheistic "scientific materialism." This, too, made demands upon the body and the soul with the ultimate result of bringing one more divisive loyalty into the region. Plurality is the name, intolerance the game.

Regional and national difference characterized the territory of present-day Yugoslavia from time immemorial. Even casual observation shows that this remains the case even during the short period when the Communists were attempting to impose uniformity. The very attempt to impose uniformity was done in diverse ways in different regions in Yugoslavia, resulting in a range from great rigidity and barbarity in some areas to relative flexibility and leniency in others. The great nationalistic upheavals and tensions of 1988 and 1989 are a continued testimony to the absence of uniformity.

FROM THE END OF WORLD WAR II TO 1989: BEFORE THE GREAT TRANSFORMATION

Communist Policies toward Religion

The Communist Party of Yugoslavia was originally a loyal follower of the Communist Party of the Soviet Union and shared all its ideals and approaches. Two well-known Leninist principles dominated this approach.

One was the legal separation of church and state, declaring religion as the private affair of every citizen. This had the effect of relegating religion out of the public sphere into the private spiritual domiain of individuals. Religious liberty was understood narrowly as the freedom to worship or not to worship.

The second principle was that it is the task of the Marxist party as the avant garde of the working class to assist in what is considered the inevitable fading away of religion, thus assisting the process of individual and social liberation from superstitious and exploitative religious practices which are surviving merely as vestiges of the past.

In theory these two principles can be separated by stating that the government applies the first principle, while the Communist Party advocates the second. That theoretical distinction is a vain one, for in practice the government consists of the leaders of the Communist Party, and the second principle becomes decisive in interpreting the first. This conflict of approaches still colors the present situation despite some efforts to modify it by emphasizing legal aspects of the principles of separation of church and state which would tend to diminish state intevention in religious matters, thereby providing for greater religious liberty.

Several discernible stages mark the period from the Communist takeover in 1944/45 to the present,[14] which broadly correspond to the situation of human rights in general within the state.[15]

1. Radical restriction of religious liberty, 1945–1953.
2. Gradual relaxation of restrictions, 1953–1965.
3. Significant liberalization, 1965–1971.
4. Selective restrictions reimposed, 1972–1982.
5. On the threshold of full freedom; new opportunities, 1982–1989.

The Great Transformation commenced in 1989. It will be treated separately at the end of the chapter.

1. Radical Restriction of Religious Liberty, 1945 to 1953

The government and the party mounted an all-out attack on the churches despite a claim of religious liberty. Marxist scholars and even the government leaders admitted in the 1960s and 1970s that harsh measures were undertaken against religious institutions and individuals, including imprisonment, murder, nationalization and destruction of property, and so forth. From 1945 to 1948 the country was under direct Soviet influence and the government attempted to implement the Soviet model. The Yugoslav Constitution of 1945 was a 'carbon copy' of Stalin's Constitution of 1936. To the Yugoslav Communists it seemed that their own dealing with the multinational, multireligious Yugoslavia should be analogous to Stalin's dealing with the multinational, multireligious Soviet Union.

The government intervened heavily in the internal affairs of the churches. The Secretariat of Internal Affairs had to give its approval for the appointment of the clergy to specific parishes. In order to split up the lower and the higher clergy and to gain closer control of the clergy the government forcefully promoted the creation of unions or associations of clergy in the Orthodox, Catholic, and Muslim communities. Members of these unions would be allowed more easily their appointments while others were hindered. Financial benefits, retirement, medical benefits, and ability to teach religion would be granted only to these unionized clergy. Their superiors objected to this attempt to split the clergy from the hierarchy and from each other.[16]

Compulsory religious education was abolished already in 1945. At a meeting of the *Agitprop* on December 12, 1947, it was decided to destroy private and religious publishing ventures by impoverishing them and then to pressure the graphical workers to demonstratively refuse to print religious publications.[17] Josip Broz-Tito's own views toward freedoms is illustrated by his statement regarding freedom of the press:

> I am against writing what is harmful under the guise of freedom of literary creativity. For instance, I can't possibly agree with what in Western democracies is talked about as a supposed freedom of the press. What kind of freedom is that and what does it consist of? It consists in allowing everyone to write even the worst lies and slander under the excuse that this is freedom and that it is moral. From our perspective this is amoral and such freedom is harmful.[18]

The process of curbing the influence of the churches proceeded with every available tool. The agrarian reform was turned against the largest churches, though in Yugoslavia the churches have never been really large landholders. Church taxes were abolished. Church buildings were expropriated; some were destroyed. Church assets were frozen, monasteries and religious schools were closed, religious processions and public ceremonies were generally forbidden, and clergy were prevented from visiting their charges.[19] Several show trials, the most spectacular against Alojzije Cardinal Stepinac in 1946, were to demonstrate the government's resolve to break any religious opposition.[20] Often no such propaganda or legal procedures were deemed necessary; many religious leaders, clergy and lay, were murdered or imprisoned by executive order or arbitrary local initiative. Some were simply brutally murdered, beaten, mutilated or incarcerated, while others simply vanished, never to be seen again.[21]

The Constitution of 1946 separated the church from the state, guaranteed freedom to worship, allowed but did not decree material support of churches by the government, forbade the abuse of religion for political purposes or for spreading religious hatred and intolerance, and declared all citizens equal regardless of ethnicity, race, sex, and religion.[22] Such constitutional principles were a sound basis for liberty, but there were no means to have recourse to legal protection when the government would violate the Constitution.

Contrary to expectation, after Yugoslavia broke off with the Soviet Union and other Informbureau countries in 1948 and until Stalin's death in 1953 the conflict between the churches and the state and oppression of religious communities by the Yugoslav Communists actually sharpened. On the one hand, it seems that the general pattern in socialist societies was to crack down against religion a few years after gaining power. On the other hand, the Yugoslav Communists were still trying to show to the Soviet leadership that they were still real Marxists-Leninists, by cracking down on the intellectuals, peasantry, and religion.[23] What is paradoxical about the situation is that in other areas of life, especially in the economic sphere, especially since 1952, greater freedom was being achieved under the policy of workers' self-management, but there were simply no political and civil rights.[24] Some of the most well-organized persecutions of religion took place between 1950 and the first part of 1953.

The government thought that the Serbian Orthodox Church had excessive ties to the Serbian royalist or *Chetnik* emigrants. The Roman Catholic Church was controlled by the Vatican, and from the perspective of the Communist leadership, it was not only too closely identified with the Nazis during World War II but now seemed to be potentially influenced by the Anglo-American 'imperialists' and other 'reactionary' forces. Hence strong defensive measures were undertaken, showing little sympathy or tolerance for any kind of autonomy by the churches. For instance, by 1953 about one half of all priests in Slovenia—the republic considered to have the most enlightened Communist leadership—were imprisoned. There were some attempts to mediate the conflict by shifting away from the more radical and denunciatory unions of priests to more moderate unions lead by those priests who had participated in the people liberation struggle but who were not at odds with the hierarchy.[25] Tito, for example, received in 1953 a delegation of the new Slovene priestly union consisting of the prior of the Carthesians, Dr. Edgar Leopold, Dr. Trstvenjak, and Jože Lampert. At this time Tito stated that the Catholic Church should become a people's church and not depend on the Vatican.[26] Canon law, of course, does not allow that, but Tito demonstrated that his model was a Bolshevik one by which the Communists preferred to deal with a liturgically oriented national church such as the Orthodox. Due to the Roman Catholic Church's international institutional connection it continued to present a major problem that Tito's government faced after the political opposition was neutralized. They grappled with the power of the hierarchy by supporting the unions of associations of clergy. Some of the members of these unions may have been secret agents or members of the Communist Party just as the hierarchs suspected, but the vast majority were patriotic and democratically inclined clergy who fought against the occupying forces having joined the Partisans and who had serious grievances against an entrenched, conservative hierarchy. The bishops often reacted by disciplining or even excommunicated such priests. Most of those conflicts were reconciled at the time of Vatican II. The government, likewise, abandoned these attempts to divide and rule by the early 1960s and allowed every church to organize itself in any manner it wanted.

2. Gradual Relaxation of Restrictions, 1953–1965

Since the second half of 1953 the persecutions and harassments slowly abated. One of the landmarks in the changing relations between the government and the religious communities was the passing of "The Basic Law on the Legal Position of Religious Communities." Religious communities had been very apprehensive as to what this new law would mean for them, though they were invited at least *pro forma* to contribute their suggestions to the first draft. This law reflected the 1946 Constitution's separation of church and state. One of the constitutional provisions fostering religious liberty was that it allowed the formation of new religious communities. This was utilized over the years so that the sum total of religious denominations in Yugoslavia grew to about fifty. As Stella Alexander described it, the law "sowed the seeds of a slow—very slow—but nevertheless growing confidence in the possibility of obtaining justice under the law."[27] But while the law formally improved the status of religious communities the Communist Party simultaneously sharpened its ideological attacks against religion. Hence this was a classical case of taking away with one hand what was given with the other. Amidst all these ambiguities a gradual reduction of the pressure against churches and religious individuals continued until 1965. Excesses—such as torture, imprisonment on false charges, and even murder by the secret police—were still practiced from time to time, more in some parts of the country than in others. Regional differences in the treatment of religion but not in theory became even more pronounced, a feature which to this day characterizes Yugoslav church-state relations and which have increasingly been handled by the republican and provincial rather than the federal government. What this means is that in one region of the country, for example, in Slovenia and Croatia, the authorities may show a great deal more tolerance and permissiveness toward religious activities, while in another part, for example, in Macedonia or Kosovo, clergy and believers, especially of certain denominations, are openly harassed and intimidated by the police, and where news of the greater liberties in the other parts of the country rarely reached the public.

The new Constitution of 1963 again proclaimed the freedom and privatization of religion, separation of church and state and the prohibition of the abuse of religion for political purposes. Religious institutions were given the right to own limited amount of real estate and to operate schools for the training of clergy.

In 1965 "The Law on the Legal Status of the Religious Communities" was revised to reflect the Constitution of 1963, bringing still greater security to the religious communities.[28] The most important feature of the revision was to remove the threat of closing seminaries if any staff member or student violated a law. Another positive measure was that infringement of the rights of persons because of their religious affiliation or participation in a religious rite was punishable by imprisonment or fine.[29] This latter provision was not strictly applied especially when the infringement was by the authorities. All in all, gradual relaxation of restrictions was progressively evident as the years passed by.

3. Significant Liberalization, 1965–1971

This was the most liberal period in the treatment of the churches. Some call it the 'golden age' in church-state relations. The system had opened up to such a degree that many religious practices were unobstructed. Government interference in internal church matters was minimalized and in some instances was almost completely removed. The churches were permitted to publish journals and books again; theological schools were allowed to expand; clergy could travel freely in and out of the country; religious education on church premises was sanctioned again; and so forth. A growing concern, however, was expressed by the government and the press at the simultaneous increase of politization of the few larger religions, particularly the Roman Catholic but also the Islamic and Serbian Orthodox. To some degree the government was itself responsible for this politization. The Muslims, previously a religious designation, were proclaimed by the Communist Party as a nationality. Previously the contention was that there were *muslims* who were either Croats, Serbs, or Yugoslavians. But since the nationalistic tensions were exacerbated it seemed that by creating a *Muslim* nationality the rivalry between Serbians and Croatians in regard to the muslim ethnic affiliation would be alleviated. Instead, Islam started functioning as a civil religion. Since the Muslim nation did not have the same secular institutions as the others, the Muslim nationality affirmed itself in the existing muslim religious institutions. Political questions were now raised in mosques, and this led to more open conflicts between the state and Islam than with other churches. This situation will probably continue for a while until other forms of expressing Muslim nationalism can be found.

Another new situation was the creation of the autocephalous Macedonian Orthodox Church by means of a schism from the Serbian Orthodox Church. If one were the query the Macedonian Orthodox clergy and believers, nearly all of them would say that they have enough religious liberties. From their perspective this would be true because this corresponds to their notion of the needed space for self-affirmation as national orthodox Christians. The Macedonian Communists favored and gave privileges to the Macedonian Orthodox Church in their attempts to bolster Macedonian nationalism against the Albanians and the Serbians.[30] Thus, the Macedonian national consciousness articulates itself through this church just as the Muslim did through the mosque. Thus the 1980s brought a revival of the articulation of national consciousness via religion among nearly all nationalities.

Nationalist sentiments became increasingly chauvinistic and led to excesses (demonstrations, riots, and terrorist actions) by the late 1960s and early 1970s. Tito and the other leaders feared that the country and/or the social system might collapse. Measures were undertaken not only to purge the Communist Party from 'anarcholiberals' and 'nationalists' but to tighten the reins on religion as well.

In his doctoral dissertation Gerald Shenk, an American Mennonite who lived nearly ten years in Yugoslavia, pointed out that Yugoslav analysts, particularly Ivan Lazić[31] noted the tension between impulses toward tighter central control and impulses toward greater democracy and regional autonomy."[32] While the religious communities generally benefited from trends toward decentralization and liberalization, it is noted that minority groups, however, found themselves in a more ambiguous situation because on certain "issues resurgent regional powers may be asserted to their disadvantage. Given the historic fragmentation of interests, centralizing forces can often make the claim of protecting smaller groups against others."[33]

After 1968 a significant number of humanistic Marxists became interested in religious issues in a much more objective manner than their predecessors. Many became not only sympathetic to certain religious issues, values, and persons but engaged both publicly and privately, though more in print than in public forums, in a Christian-Marxist dialogue, just when this dialogue was waning in some other European countries. Many of these Marxists were significant contributors, theoretically and practically, for the increased liberties granted by the more cautious bureaucratic Marxists.[34]

The People's Assembly ratified the 1966 Human Rights Convention in 1971 as it had adopted in 1962 the UNESCO conventions against discriminations.[35] Later in 1977, the government went so far as to incorporate into its national legislations all the provisions of the Helsinki Accords and U. N. Human Rights declarations.

4. Selective Restrictions Reimposed, 1972–1982

The fourth period, from 1972 to 1983, was characterized by an attempt to install more controls over church life and the suspension or privatization of the Christian-Marxist dialogue. A complete reversal of the concessions made during the previous period did not take place, however. Certain aspects of church life did not suffer at all, but rather, developed steadily, thereby giving additional weight to certain freedoms (for example, non-interference in the curricula and teaching staff of theological schools, fairly easily obtained permissions for repairs of church buildings). Regression took place in a few areas (for example, longer periods of prior notification of authorities required if a foreign visitor was to preach in a church). The situation altered not qualitatively but quantitatively, but an overall increase of confrontational practices could be felt.

Of great significance during the period was the promulgation of still another constitution of 1974 which still further decentralized the country and created *de facto* eight federal units, namely the six republics and the two autonomous provinces. Article 174 states:

> The profession of religion is free and it is the private affair of each citizen. Religious communities are detached from the state, and are free in the performance of religious affairs and rites. Religious communities may establish only religious schools for the training of clergy. The abuse of religion and religious activity for political purposes is unconstitutional. The community may aid the religious community materially. The religious communities may have, within the limits defined by law, the right to own real estate.[36]

Otto Luchterhandt, a German specialist on religious legislation in Eastern Europe, regards the section on abuse of religion for political purposes as dangerous because the government may stretch its meaning and thereby broaden persecution, but on the other hand it does in principle grant greater freedom for the exercise of purely religious and worldview questions.[37]

Radovan Samardžić, then the secretary of the Commission for Relations with Religious Communities of the Federal Executive Council of Yugoslavia wrote:

> The de-politicization of the church is a condition *sine qua non* for its freedom of activity in the Yugoslav political system. Religion is a non-political element of society and hence

an individual's private affair.

. . . .

Yugoslav society does not impose upon the church any conditions for its freedom except that it does not allow any abuse
of religion for political purposes against the socialist social
community, i.e. the church must respect the constitutional-
ity and legality of the social system. It can even be said that
the church itself determines the dimension of its freedom to
the extent to which it adjusts the interests of believers to all
other interests of Yugoslav self-managing socialist society.[38]

Samardžić pointed out clearly that freedom thus understood is
conditional rather than an inherent right; namely, one will be free to
the degree that one accepts or adjusts to the social system; opposing
the social system would bring a reduction in *religious* freedom. This
causes a real problem in that the boundary lines are rarely sharply
delineated. It is the very nature of religion to live in boundary situations and, as the human spirit soars across intellectual and practical
boundaries, to transcend them. Thus, it would be impossible for
the religious communities to strictly adhere to this limitation, and it
would give rise to countless misunderstanding and criticism by those
who felt that such transgression was a calculated and impermissible
violation of the natural limits of religion. The problem was that people who were ignorant of the nature of religion and were hostile to it
(proponents of Secularist Absolutism, Type C) drew up the legislation
regulating religion.

Religious communities continued to be the focus of the kind of
discontent that could not be expressed in another manner, especially
nationalistic or separatist tendencies. Some people in the churches
welcomed this; others were wary. The political authorities had no
effective way of dealing with this because if they wanted to repress
such threats it would seem that they are repressing religious freedom.
The authorities expressed the willingness to use administrative and
legislative restrictions but on the whole shied away from it[39] as they
had become much more sensitive to the role of world public opinion
and were eager to maintain the reputation of being the most open of
socialist societies.

A segment of the domestic religious press, which was growing by
leaps and bounds (from nearly total absence in 1950s to about 40 religious journals and newspapers in 1977 and nearly 200 by the 1980s)

claimed that there was insufficient religious freedom to which administration officials responded defensively by citing the large number of religious leaders, students, and the total number of publications.[40] It was obvious that religious people were by then able to raise their voice in self-defense more publicly and effectively and that government officials, many of whom did not abandon old attitudes resorted to more verbal (rather than violent) attacks. The humanistic Marxist scholars continued the sociological study of religion which charted the way toward greater tolerance and favored the Christian-Marxist dialogue, but many of them during this period had to lay low because Tito feared the loss of leadership and the demise of socialism and tightened the screws within the Communist Party. Some of the most liberal Communists were repressed and others feared the loss of their positions and decided to bide their time and wait for better times—presumably when Tito—the 'Old Man'—would die. He did in 1980.

5. On the Threshold of Freedom: New Opportunities, 1982–1989

From 1981 the people had to start adjusting to the absence of a charismatic leader acceptable to all Yugoslavs, though for a while the Communist leadership behaved as if he had not died. Confused as to which direction to take after Tito's death, most of them vouched to follow in his path. In fact the country started on a slow process of disintegration that was to lead to near chaos and the need for the reexamination of the very foundations on which the federation rested. There was confusion on all levels of federal and republican (state) leadership and the beleaguered economy went from bad to worse. There was general agreement that the country was experiencing a long and profound crisis. National conflicts increased, leading occasionally even to violent conflict. The large religious groups were implicated in it by virtue of their close identification with ethnicity. National conflicts became again religious conflicts.[41] Religious institutions did not consciously seek to diminish the conflict, perhaps because their new-found popularity among those seeking national affirmation provided broader opportunities for their activities. A new openness was being experienced at least with regard to the freedom to discuss in the press, other media, and at conferences certain formerly taboo subjects pertaining to earlier and present failures of the leadership. This period contained not only possible pitfalls (especially the Communists seeking to divert the attention away from economic problems by attacking the churches as scapegoats) but also new opportunities for the expansion of liberties in a country which is without a long democratic tradition.

By and large, the general trend during these successive stages prior to the Great Transformation was toward an increase in the autonomy and liberty of religion, though oscillations were evident both regionally and chronologically. The government of Yugoslavia consciously attempted to create a system, usually called workers' self-management, which was more open and tolerant than the Soviet model. They accepted the conclusion that religion would not vanish as rapidly as they had originally expected and that, therefore, some accommodations must be made since religion continued to exert a considerable influence over large segments of the population. The increased participation in religious practices was interpreted by them as either a larger number of people 'coming out of the closet' when the repressions eased, or as a genuine religious revival, particularly among the young. This necessitated at least a reassessment of the role of religion in the particular circumstances of Yugoslav history. Many humanistic Marxist scholars advocated a more tolerant attitude toward religion, provided religious people did not spearhead an open revolt against the government. The basic concession asked from the churches was not to oppose the socialist system but rather to recognize it at least tacitly. However, explicit endorsement of the socialist system by the churches was not forthcoming. Therefore, the slogan changed from 'if you are not with us you are against us' to 'if you are not against us you are with us.' This called for a less doctrinaire approach to religion, which became hallmark of the Yugoslav Communist attitude toward religion. Srdjan Vrcan, the well-known sociologist of religion captured the changing role of religion with the title of his book, *From the Crisis of Religion to the Religion of Crisis.* Indeed, many people formerly uninvolved or uninterested, including many young people, became much more active participants in the life of the churches and were generally not stigmatized for doing so. The visions of the Virgin Mary in Medjugorje, Herzegovina, became an international sensation after 1981, with over five million visitors in less than a decade. After some feeble attempts to foil these pilgrimages the government yielded and even tried to take advantage of the commercial windfall created by the phenomenon.

Secularist Absolutism–Type C, was receding rapidly in favor of

Religious Toleration (Type B) but with some ominous signs that Ecclesiastical Absolutism, Type A claims may reappear on the scene if the conflicts between the ethno-religious groups were to get sharper.

Legislation Concerning Religion During the Communist Dominance

This section should be prefaced with some preliminary remarks regarding the Communist understanding of government and law. Theoretically their understanding of the role of the government and the law was that they protect the interest of the ruling class. Whenever the perception of that interest changes, as reality changes, there may be swift changes in the government form and personnel as well as in the law. There was no judicial or legislative independence from the executive branch, which consisted entirely of Communist leaders. The text of any law, and even more so its application, was bent in any direction if this was in their interest. Hence it is highly deceptive to point to the text of the law and regard it as normative for actual practices. The letter of the law may proclaim a variety of freedoms, but it was the executive branch that interpreted and guided its application. The judicial branch carried out the decision that the executive branch made, no matter how much bending of the law that required.

Many observers of the Communist countries have noticed that one of the greatest objective weaknesses of the Marxist form of governance was the problem of 'socialist legality.' Since it was solely the party leaders holding monopoly of governing who determined what was in the interest of the 'working people,' there was really little protection of human rights unless that happened to be interpreted as being of benefit to those in power. The meaning of many human rights was bent out of shape by spurious double-talk.

This is not to say that what was in the laws was totally unimportant. If the laws clearly guaranteed certain rights or prohibited certain actions, rather than being vague or secretive, some pressure could be exerted, at least in principle, to get the government minimally to observe the laws which it created. In Yugoslavia, then, laws were not unimportant, though they were not decisive in the exercise of religious liberties. Yugoslavia simply was not a law state before 1990.

The several post-World War II constitutions (1946, 1956, 1963, and 1974) affirmed the basic freedom of religion and conscience, separation of church and state (including separation of schools from the churches), equal status for all religious institutions and individuals before the law, and the prohibition of the use of religion to incite national hatred and intolerance or to abuse religion for political purposes.[42] Article 174 of the constitution of 1974 maintains that the practice of religion is an individual affair, so that no one could be forced to join or be prevented from joining a church. It recognized religious communities as legal persons that are free to conduct worship services, rites, and religious affairs (the latter was left undefined). The government may provide financial support for specific purposes. Religious communities may own properties within the limit of the law. While the constitution gave the appearance of guaranteeing freedom of religion without any consequences for the citizens' status, this was neither clearly spelled out in theory, nor carried out in practice for it was quite impossible for an explicitly religious person to attain higher ranks in government, education, army, or economic management.[43] The constitution guaranteed equality of all citizens, but religious people have nearly always experienced treatment as second-class citizens. The right to participate in public life was denied to the religious communities, and *de facto* individual believers also were limited in their participation in public life, particularly in major decisions.

As mentioned above, in 1953 the first special legislation on religion was promulgated, called "The Basic Law of the Legal Position of Religious Communities." In it the federal government expanded the constitutional regulations, specifying the rights and obligations of the confessional groups as well as rights and responsibilities of government organs dealing with religion. These laws became well known to the religious communities and gave a modicum of stability to church-state relations because they at least made clear what the norms were upon which the government insisted.

The second attempt to provide the legal framework for the developing church-state relations was different from the first in that the regulations were not on the federal but the state (republican and provincial) level. This not only reflected the decentralization of power in the government that had taken place, but also made it possible for the different religious situations in particular states to be treated in a more diversified way. The laws were submitted to public discussion in 1975 and 1976 and have been enacted subsequently (mostly in 1978).

This comprehensive legislation guaranteed that the religious communities may publish their literature and set the conditions for these publications, with minor variants among the states. Clergy were allowed to visit their members in hospitals and homes for the elderly but not in prisons or in the army. Social and economic, including charitable activities, were forbidden to the religious communities, as well as any recreational and educational activities for children and youth which were not strictly tied to some religious observance. Charitable activities had been occasionally tolerated before, and even after the passage of the 1978 law the authorities in Croatia and Slovenia tolerated some charitable work by the churches. Religious education for the ministry and of children were permitted. Theoretically ministerial candidates and a child under fourteen (in Macedonia under ten) may be compelled to participate in religious education if the parents insist, but generally the consent of both parents and the child were required. In actuality, pressures were brought to bear upon children and believers not to take part in such religious education, but it varied from region to region. The pressure was usually applied in schools or at parents' place of employment, making nearly impossible for members of the League of Communists of Yugoslavia (the Communist Party's altered name since the 1960s) to resist.

All places of worship and real estate had to be registered with the government, as did all religious communities. No special permission was needed for activities within church buildings, but for any out-of-door activities permits had to be sought, and such permits were often denied. There was a ban on topics of a political nature at religious gatherings. No pressures could be exerted on people to participate in any religious activities. New religious denominations were permitted to be established. Fines and some imprisonment have been imposed for violating these laws. While there was a feeling that some of these laws were more restrictive than the ones of 1953, there was also the possibility to appeal for redress against violations of these laws, though in practice religious communities have rarely, if ever, sought to prosecute a government official who may have mistreated them. One of the most dramatic cases of a confrontation between a church and an official whom the church felt to be a threat was the 1985 statement by the Serbian Orthodox Church that a high official of the Commission for Religious Affairs of Serbia, Radovan Samardžić, was a *persona non grata* because of comments he allegedly made, which the Serbian Orthodox Church considered inimical to its interests.

Reports of Mistreatment and Abuse

Even good laws are of no avail if they are not conscientiously applied. Yugoslav laws on religious communities were somewhat restrictive but were among the best sets of laws in socialist Eastern Europe. The nagging issue continued to be the abuses of authority in the implementation or non-application of laws, resulting in the mistreatment of individuals and intimidation of communities. There was considerable arbitrariness in the application of the laws by local officials which was condoned by the higher authorities. There was little effective control exercised by the higher over the local officials. As a rule the one with the less tolerant attitude toward religion would prevail in determining the actual government position toward the local churches. Those who were more tolerant were generally more timid in asserting their views. In regions where the conflicts between church and state were greater the abuses tended to be greater. Abuses also tended to be greater where more authoritarian or doctrinaire officials were in power. For instance, with the fall of Alexandar Ranković in 1965 from the vice-presidency of the country, his hold on the organs of internal security (UDBA–the secret police) was broken and a period of relaxation ensued not only for the churches but also for life in general. Thus, the orientation of a key leader or local official was able to determine to what degree human rights were respected.

The evidence shows that the greatest conflict existed between the government and the Roman Catholic Church, and this was also reflected by the greater number of arrests and trials of Roman Catholic clergy than of other church officials. The following is a list of arrests and other repressive acts reported by AKSA, the Catholic News Service from Zagreb,[44] from October 1982 to September 1985:

1. The three-and-half-year sentence of friar Jože Zovko of Medjugorje, who was accused of inventing and orchestrating the apparitions of the Virgin Mary to several teenagers, which brought about mass pilgrimages from home and abroad, was reduced to one-and-a-half years by an appeal court.[45]

2. Only a section of a mosaic in the church at Straževan containing the likeness of the late Alojzije Cardinal Stepinac (rather than the entire mosaic) will be removed.[46]

3. Željko Slonjsak, a parish priest at Kutina, has been sentenced to three years of imprisonment for spreading false information in a collection of sermons, "Flora of Vinogorsko," that he edited—which was a crime according to Article 187 of the Croatian Criminal Code.[47]

4. Marija Car from Duga Resa was expelled from the League of Communists because her husband, who was not a party member,

had christened their child. Her expulsion was sustained despite her appeal.[48]

5. A representative on the Water and Sewage Board in Split was called upon by her youth organization to give an account of her interest in religion.[49]

6. The municipal council in Split prohibited the completion of work on, and usage of finished sections of, the Church of St. Peter in Split. Frane Cardinal Franić protested that the church did nothing illegal.[50]

7. The Veterans' Association of Gornje Cerniljev disassociated itself from verbal offenses in an argument over building a local church. Apparently this was not the first time where the bigotry of state officials has been moderated by the Veterans' Association.[51]

8. The priest of the Holy Cross Church at Siget (Zagreb), Fr. Emmanuel Hosko, issued denials against the accusation that he organized disco dances and sporting events for the youth, apart from spontaneous singing and play after religious instruction.[52]

9. Ivan Lalić, head of the Commission for Religious Affairs of Croatia, cited examples where Catholics carried Croatian flags without the red star and sang old Croatian patriotic (nationalistic) songs at religious gatherings. Such events were not uniformly punished; in Split such infractions draw fines of fifteen to thirty days' imprisonment, while a Serbian Orthodox priest and a teacher in Bosnia-Herzegovina were sentenced to five years of imprisonment for singing *Chetnik* songs.[53]

10. Andjelka Jagnić was imprisoned fifteen days for claiming to have seen a vision of the Virgin in Gala. A journalist of *Slobodna Dalmacija* criticized authorities for the absence of legal grounds for such a sentence. He quipped, "Would Andjelka Jagnić have been sentenced to a month's imprisonment if she had seen her with the child Jesus in her arms?"[54]

11. Great controversy was caused by a statement attributed to Bishop Zazinović of Krk at the Eucharistic Congress in which he allegedly said that godless materialism must be fought by all honorable means, including the shedding of blood. The secular press accused him of favoring inquisitional methods; he defended himself by saying that he criticized not materialists but materialism and that the shedding of blood was a reference to Christians being willing to shed their own blood. He also complained that attempts had been made to discourage believers from attending the Eucharistic Congress.[55]

12. Ivica Mašturko, a Marxist scholar and later Yugoslavia's ambassador to the Vatican, criticized militant atheization. He pointed out that the Socialist Alliance of the Working People of Yugoslavia, which is supposed to gather people irrespective of their beliefs, is almost completely dominated by Communists and that such monopoly runs counter to self-management.[56]

13. Professor Jože Krasovec of the Theological School in Ljubljana was sentenced to a month's imprisonment for the following passage in his book, *Christians for the Future*:

> Militant atheists and the champions of man's functional role in a collective are particularly aware of how powerful and efficient is the religious faith of a community. Hence they deceive the people with slogans saying that religion is a purely private, individual affair. They know that a man must be isolated then he will become their submissive subject, and element in their system.

The prosecutor maintained that such passage incites bad feelings among citizens, while Krasovec defended himself saying that the passage had been taken out of context.[57]

14. Bishop Kos of Djakovo complained about the Commissions for Relations with Religious Communities of Vojvodina and Sremska Mitrovica because, during the celebration of the elevation of the parish church in Sremska Mitrovica to a pro-cathedral they banned a procession of clergy into the church and withdrew transportation facilities to pilgrims just before the onset of festivities. He complained that these acts were illegal.[58]

15. At a meeting of the secretaries of the Communist organizations of Slovenia several prominent members of the Central Committee admitted that there were still cases of discrimination against believers but that these were cases of arbitrariness which harm both believers and unbelievers. Militant atheism was being superseded by a more moderate revolutionary view.[59]

16. The Coordinating Council of the Regional Committees for Relations with Religious Communities of Serbia sharply attacked the Serbian Orthodox religious press for taking a pastoral attitude toward Serbs outside of Serbia, thereby inciting national and religious intolerance. The writings of Professor Atanasije Jeftić were singled out, stating that "it was unacceptable that a theologian and trainer of students at the theological faculty should treat questions unconnected

with the church."[60]

17. Reporting on the meeting of the Holy Synod of the Serbian Orthodox Church, *Pravoslavlje*, stated that permission to build churches where they were destroyed in World War II had still not been obtained in many places, while church property (including court yards and graveyards) had been seized illegally, pupils harassed by school authorities (they and their parents pressured not to go to church or celebrate holy days), and "attempts are even made to force them to eat forbidden foods on fast days."[61]

18. The inconsistencies of application of the law which was noted by *Pravoslavlje* was also contained in a letter to the editor of *Svijet* by the Orthodox priest Željko Gavrilović who wrote, "One could write a book about the sectarian attitudes toward religion on the part of members of the LCY in different areas."[62]

19. The Archbishop of Ljubljana, Dr. Alojzije Šuštar, stated that there are still many attacks on the church and historical distortions and attacks on the church although there has been a marked improvement with respect to obtaining permissions to build new churches, visit the old and the sick, print new brochures, and obtain social security and health insurance for clergy. However, he stated that church members often complained that the "good relations" between church and state, which the government declared, "are just empty words, because of unfortunate personal experiences."[63]

20. The Franciscan friar Vlado Buntić, assistant pastor at Drinovići, had been imprisoned for two months on a summary conviction, without trial; no written copy of the sentence was sent to the parish officer.[64]

21. The building of a cemetery chapel at Cerci was halted by a building inspector although a permit to build had been received. The local Communists complained that the cross of the chapel would be too high and that a road and a House of Culture should be finished first.[65]

22. At a series of seminars for Communists in Dalmatia, it was reported that "hostile, malevolent of sectarian attitudes towards believers still exist and that divisions between people based on their worldviews are still prevalent intolerance towards believers has become a sort of religious attitude."[66]

23. Armin Prebeg, a priest from Split, was sentenced to fifty days in prison for allegedly forcing a woman in a hospital to go to confession.[67]

24. The secretary of the Central Committee of the League of Communists in Bosnia and Herzegovina, Dr. Ivan Cvitković, otherwise a sociologist of religion, stated in a lecture that there are conflicts of conscience for believers, such as a Catholic physician who must perform abortions in the hospital although his beliefs forbid him or a Muslim serving in the army who is not able to eat everything since no provisions are made for religious dietary regulations.[68]

25. The Franciscan friar Emmanuel Jurić from Tuzla was imprisoned for forty days for "insulting the patriotic feelings of citizens" in a confession.[69]

26. The Macedonian Veterans' Association warned that the spread of religious education in Macedonia is harmful, particularly among Albanian Muslims who sent their children to *medressas* rather than public schools.[70]

27. Several high government officials blamed the Catholic Church for violating the principles of the Protocol between the Vatican and Yugoslavia, saying that a section of the Catholic clergy was misusing their rights for "nationalist, anti-socialist, and anti-Yugoslav ends." (These oft-repeated charges of clericalism were leveled mostly at Catholic, but also at Serbian [not Macedonian, however] Orthodox and Muslim, religious leaders.)[71]

28. Franjo Cardinal Kuharić of Zagreb criticized the attempts to suppress religion and deny religious liberties and rights.[72]

29. A member of the Seventh-Day Adventist Church was sentenced to two-and-half years in prison for refusing to bear arms.[73]

30. Religious activities are increasingly described as nationalist or cleronationalist, according to both Serbian Orthodox and Roman Catholic Croatian sources.[74]

These ample illustrations are not exhaustive, nor are they a particularly investigated account of violations of religious rights but primarily the ones that have been reported in the secular or religious press. Many violations are not reported by the victims (analogous to rape victims) for fear of making their situations worse. This author knows the instances of two young men who served the army between 1980–1985 whose persecution was not publicly reported. One who did his military service in the early 1980s, confided after several months to a 'friend' that he was a Seventh-Day Adventist. He was immediately reprimanded by his commanding officers, sent for psychiatric observation, and later dismissed from the army without any indication of what further steps might be taken against him. He and his sister, a student, both shared their impression with the author that it is best not to admit to anyone that one is a believer because there are unpleasant consequences for one's education or career or one's parents' careers. The other, a young Protestant theologian was constantly interrogated and harassed when he served in the army in the middle 1980s for the sole reason of being a theologian.[75]

The Yugoslav police, security organs, and prison guards are known for their brutal methods of investigation and treatment of those who are arrested.[76] As an illustration, a man imprisoned in the late 1970s on a charge unrelated to religion reported to the author that during preliminary hearings he was tied to a radiator and two masked policemen beat him repeatedly with rubber truncheons until he was ready to "admit." After serving two years in prison in Sremska Mitrovica, he was in such a bad condition that he wet his bed every night for a long time. Although a large, strong man, he admitted that he had cried like a child and begged for mercy when he was beaten.[77] Another illustration is the case of a young worker who attended some Marxist 'dissident' meetings in 1983, was then interrogated by the police, and later found dead. This case has become well known in the West. The police claimed that he committed suicide, but obviously it was a case of police murder.

These two illustrations of police methods were not specifically against believers. The last case of police murder for religious convictions known personally to the author was of a Methodist minister from Macedonia, Asen Palankov, in 1958.[78] If the police was willing to use harsh methods against some "trouble-makers," they were certainly willing to use it against others, including religious offenders. This is not merely a logical inference but is empirically confirmed. Other Methodist clergy in Macedonia have been threatened by the police in the 1980s that their "guts will hang from the rafters just as Palankov's did." The clergy are often summoned by the police for 'friendly discussion' sessions which were secretly tape-recorded. At such sessions they were asked to submit membership lists and inquiries were made about their own and their members' political views; requests for church repairs were denied for decades, and church members' legal appeals were consistently denied.[79] This resulted in a general feeling of helplessness and resignation, since they knew that their rights had much less chance of being defended than those of persons who are not religious. It also brought divisiveness into the ranks of church leaders and laity on how one should respond to such pressure.

Generally those who were more intimidated or conciliatory tended to gain an upper hand and set a tone of timidity and compromise. This, in turn, often alienated younger people who had not been directly exposed to such harsh treatment.

On the Brighter Side

Nevertheless, enormous progress was made in the degree of openness and freedom for religion in the twenty years before the Great Transformation, giving Yugoslavia the reputation of granting greater autonomy to the religious communities than elsewhere in Eastern Europe. There were few if any prisoners for purely religious cases. The length of imprisonment for the mixed religio-political (i.e. abuse of religion for encouraging national chauvinism) cases became shorter than in the past. If international pressure was applied or the church authorities complained vigorously enough the length of sentences was reduced, and in some cases it was admitted that it had been an error to imprison them in the first place.[80]

The sociological studies of religion have become scholarly in nature and have not only discovered inaccuracies in the traditional Marxist notions of religion but have admitted the very significant explicit or latent religiosity of the majority of Yugoslavs. Among these sociologists, the vast number (to mention the most prominent ones, Esad Ćimić, Zdenko Roter, Marko Kerševan, Srdjan Vrcan, Štefica Bahtijarević, Ivan Cvitković, Ivica Mašturko, Nikola Dugandžija, and the philosophers Branko Bošnjak, Andrija Krešić and Nikola Skledar) have pressed for a genuine separation of church and state where the state would not be an advocate and promoter of anti-theism but a truly atheist state which would favor neither non-believers nor believers. Their influence, while not determinative, was significant. The Yugoslav Communists were not at all like-minded on how to deal with religion and a considerable struggle took place in which the moderates gained in influence thereby expanding religious liberty more effectively.

In the decade from 1970 to 1980 five times as many religious as Marxist publications (with a circulation of 15,580,000 against 3,478,000) were reported by the theoretical party journal, *Komunist.*[81] No censorship in advance of publication took place. One copy of each published issue had to be submitted to the justice department and the public prosecutor could seek the banning of distribution of a particular issue if the court agreed that the material was objectionable. On rare occasions individual articles or issues of both religious and secular publications were thus censored but usually only after a certain number of the publication already circulated. While there was no complete freedom of publication, it is astonishing, knowing how restrictive that policy used to be, to see how wide the scope of research, writing, translating, and publishing became in respect to books, journals, and newspapers. Material critical of the government and even of the system has been published, sometimes in the established secular press. The religious press is not among the more outspoken critics, but it has definitely benefited from the enlarged scope of the freedom of the press. It is the religious press, along with the secular press, which monitors cases of abuse against believers. There were few if any restrictions in the number of copies, size, or nature of publications, though the religious press was not supposed to treat solely political or social issues. Yet criticism of government social policies did appear in the religious press (for example, anti-abortion statements in the Catholic press). The Bible, Qur'an, Talmud, and other scriptures have been newly translated, published in Yugoslavia or imported from abroad and have been disseminated even through secular outlets. Many book stores carried them as standard items. In some parts of the country there was no shortage of scriptures, but in other parts the demand outstripped the supply.

While the secular press frequently took pot-shots at religion, such attacks were by no means universal. Often journalists and government officials regarded religion positively and advocated more moderate policies. Sometimes, but not always, letters to editors critical of the paper or of some government policy were printed. Cooperation between believers and non-believers was increasingly regarded as much more desirable than conflict. From time to time, in specific cases, the journalist took the side of a religious group over against an official's or court's action.

Pilgrimages to Rome, Jerusalem, Mecca, Padua, as well as sites in Yugoslavia, such as Marija Bistrica, Medjugorje, and the medieval Serbian monasteries took place in large numbers with the assistance of travel and transportation agencies. Masses and services in native and foreign languages were provided and announced in prominent places.[82]

Travel abroad by all, including clergy, and visits by foreign religious leaders were not impeded since the late 1960s. Such visitors like the Ecumenical (Istanbul) and Moscow Patriarchs, the Vatican

Secretary of State,[83] or other prelates and dignitaries (for example Billy Graham) were allowed to preach, visit with their peers, and were received by government officials. Even more encouraging were visits and public lectures by such noble theologians as Hans Küng and Jürgen Moltmann. Each year an international seminar on the future of religion took place at the Inter-University Center for Post-graduate Studies in Dubrovnik. International learned societies discussing the theme of religion have met in Yugoslavia with no interference, and foreign missionaries or professors were allowed to evangelize, preach, or teach in Yugoslavia.

The youth have shown considerable interest in religion and considerably less interest in state-supported atheism. The weekly *NIN* asked:

> Who attracts young people? Two thousand people attended a talk on religion and mysticism in the Youth Centre and five hundred people stood and listened for hours to a discussion on religion in the Student Centre.[84]

This took place in Serbia, where the interest in religion was not as visible as in Croatia. At the 1984 Eucharistic Congress at Marija Bistrica,[85] the majority seem to have been young, and many walked fifty miles or more to the Congress singing Christian songs.

Christian-Marxist dialogues have taken place both in public and in publications, scholarly or otherwise.[86] The scholarly dialogue did not have a direct impact on the relations between government leaders and higher clergy, however it contributed to the general improvement of the atmosphere in which negotiations between officials of church and state occurred. The fruits of the dialogue rendered negotiations to become more constructive.

After years of being denied permission, the Serbian Orthodox Church received the authorization to continue the construction of the enormous Cathedral of St. Sava in Belgrade (claimed to be the largest Orthodox Church in the world), and the church at the site of the former concentration camp of Jasenovac has been finished, while the Roman Catholic Archbishopric of Split has been granted the right to proceed with the building of its cathedral church. Funds were granted by the government for the repair and restoration of historical religious monuments throughout the country. After the earthquake of Skopje all faiths, especially the Macedonian Orthodox Church, were allocated ground for building churches according to a carefully developed urbanization plan. Financial assistance from abroad for buildings has been allowed. The federal and republican governments became aware of the potential financial benefit of some religious activities, especially during the difficult economic crises, and tended to move pragmatically to share in the benefits. This was particularly true of the pilgrimages to Medjugorje.

No quotas were imposed on theological schools, so that they were able to admit as many students as there were applicants. On the whole, there seemed to be a satisfactory number of clergy, though some churches (e.g. the Serbian Orthodox), mainly for internal reasons, experienced greater problems in recruitment than others. The curricula of these schools were entirely in the hands of the churches. Clergy were allowed to form professional associations, sometimes resented by the respective hierarchies but defended by the governments as consistent with the social system. Since the 1970s there was no evidence that such professional associations (e.g. the Theological Center Christian Contemporaneity in Zagreb) were in any way collaborationist with the government. Social security and health insurance were made available to clergy. The churches were allowed to provide pastoral care for the immigrant communities of Yugoslavs working abroad, though they were occasionally accused of supporting émigré organizations hostile to the government. Among tabus that were eliminated was the raising of the question of religious education in public schools as discussion was allowed by the end of 1988 on how to handle this troubling issue without limiting some people's religious freedom.[87]

Thus the rights exercised by religious communities before the Great Transformation were already considerable. As a rule, the list of permitted activities has expanded steadily.

The Ambivalence of the Situation Prior to the Great Transformation

If one noticed only the bright side, then Yugoslavia's record in religious liberties was exemplary and the future bright. However, if one looked only at the instances of government repression, one would conclude that the situation was bleak—certainly not as bleak as in Albania, the Soviet Union, or Bulgaria, but, nevertheless, bleak. Many believers in Yugoslavia as well as observers dwelled at length on this aspect of the limitations of religious liberties. For instance, Jure Kristo stated:

The relationship between the Roman Catholic Church and the Communist regime in Yugoslavia is almost as bad now as in the immediate postwar period (1945–1953). The Communist Party began its relentless, organized attack on the Catholic Church in 1971 through the media and other channels; this onslaught peaked in 1981. Unreasonable, escalated anti-religious propaganda and imprisonment of a number of priests took place.[88]

Pedro Ramet observed the ambiguity as it applied to the Catholic Church in this perceptive manner.

The Catholic Church certainly enjoys more freedom in Yugoslavia than it does in any other Communist country. But it has to fight to win and maintain that freedom, and there remain distinct limits to what the Communist authorities will tolerate. . . Thus the Church remains a tolerated species, but one destined for extinction in the ripeness of time . . . the Church finds itself being nudged to the periphery of social and cultural life to say nothing of its official banishment from politics to a niche in which it cannot be content. . . Its defense of human rights and of the national aspiration of the Croats is part and parcel of that aspiration. But that aspiration . . . is precisely the LCY's definition of the "mortal sin" of clericalism.[89]

A Roman Catholic theologian from Zagreb, Vjekoslav Bajsić, described the situation as being more or less the same since 1963 with some oscillations (for example, improvement after the signing of the Protocol between Yugoslavia and the Vatican). When the relations between the great power blocks deteriorate, it made an impression on church-state relations, even in neutral Yugoslavia, because there was less room for walking on a tight-rope. The churches were more or less doing what they wanted, but some individuals, especially laity, experienced pressure for instance, if they send their children to religious education or if someone carelessly said something tactless. It was not clear who instigated actions against the believers; it was not always by instructions from above. Since the country was not monolithic many local party officials took the initiative themselves in creating difficulties for believers.[90] It was difficult to say what was official line and what was only a press attack. Inconsistencies in interpretation of religious freedom were marked due to various historical and cultural factors which is natural in such a diverse country but they did result in violations of religious freedom.[91] For instance, in Split nuns were prevented from providing child day-care centers, while in Zagreb they continued to do so. In Slovenia the association of Catholic journalists frequently criticized and accused government officials for their negative attitude toward the church, while in Croatia that could not be done. In Croatia there were local obstructions to the building churches, while this was not the case in Slovenia. In early 1985 there were sharp attacks upon the Roman Catholic church, but at the great festival of Sts. Cyril and Methodius in Djakovo in the summer of 1985 everything went well. Likewise, the great Marian pilgrimage and Eucharistic Congress in Marija Bistrica, the largest religious gathering ever in Yugoslavia (about 200,000 to 300,000 people) experienced no hitches. While religion was generally no longer considered an aberration religious people still felt that they were being discriminated against and being barred from politics and public life, i.e. from organizing themselves politically, if they wished to do so, and from using the public media.[92] Scholars such as Srdjan Vrcan, Esad Ćimić, Ivica Mašturko continued their public advocacy for religious freedoms, and Catholic theologians such as Bono Zvonimir Šagi and Protestant theologians as Peter Kuzmič pleaded not only for group religious liberties but also for individual saying that religions should not attempt to force their beliefs and practices on everyone but accept the fact that in a pluralistic democracy individual differences must be tolerated by religious bodies.[93]

In Bajsić's opinion the relationship between church and state under Communist rule would not significantly change. There were no discernible trends toward either reconciliation or sharper attacks. The government did not want to see an increased role for the churches and realized that if religion remains politically unorganized it would not be dangerous. Thus the great issue was the presence of religion in public life. Since nationalism was the most potent formula for gathering people, the government was most nervous, with good reason, about the linkage between nationalism and religion. In Yugoslavia, religion, indeed, tends to be national, which means that due to nationalism one cannot love one's enemy as one's own group. If there had been Christian solidarity in Yugoslavia, then the Communist Party would have faced a serious rival, but this was not the case. Structurally the Communist Party held the nationalities of Yugoslavia together in a precarious balance until 1989.[94]

A similar assessment was made by Martin Hovan, a Methodist minister from Novi Sad. He stated that respect for religious rights definitively improved since the mid–1960s. The government did not interfere in internal matters of the church, though it sometimes requested information about what is going on. The government completely accepted the internal regulations of churches and regarded those church people who break such rules as having made an error. The officials are informed and may even give church leaders legal advice, but they did not step in to settle an issue (a specific problem in the Skopje Methodist Church was cited as an example). The laws disallowed the churches to do anything that is not strictly religious (such as sports, recreation, dances, excursions, etc.). Importation of literature from abroad was more problematic. Up to three copies were allowed to be received without problems, but a special permit had to be issued by the government for bulk shipments. When a bulk shipment was sent without prior permission, the customs office notified the respective church that it cannot be delivered for lack of permit.

According to Hovan, there was no excessive arbitratariness, but there were regional differences. For instance, in Macedonia there was less objection about an educator who attended church services than in Serbia. In Slovenia and Croatia the overall situation was better than in Serbia. In case of problems the churches could seek redress of grievances from the Commission for Relations with Religious Communities on the federal, state, provincial, or municipal levels.[95]

Possibilities for Transformation into Pluralism

Yugoslavia had the possibility but not the probability of transforming itself into a Type D society. The need was there because of the multi-confessional nature of the country and the history of intolerance. But remnants of Type A and Type C mentality remained strongly entrenched and intertwined. Milovan Djilas warned about the dangers of the conflict between these two monopolistic tendencies. Djilas wrote:

> The evidence is that society itself passes into stagnation and illiberality once the conscience of its individual members—religion, in other words—comes under the control of monopolistic ideologies, with church and state constantly sparring for supremacy.

> Freedom has bounds; but it cannot become a piece of prop-

erty. Any attempt to appropriate freedom for a particular doctrine or social group can only result in a loss of freedom for them too.[96]

The responsibility for the conflicts and ambiguities of the Yugoslav situation in regard to religious liberties rests not only on the government; the churches themselves have frequently initiated or contributed to the tension. To proclaim religious liberty and human rights when until very recently the same institution denied it to others and still shows disrespect for the rights even of some of its own members sounds hollow and hypocritical. The past behavior or misbehavior of many of the religious communities was one of the serious obstacles to a successful affirmation of such rights in recent times. The very narrow scope of the religious concern for human rights weakened the effectiveness of any church's witness. The churches have not shown any great creativeness in broadening the notion of religious liberty. The link with nationalism gave some of the churches the clout to defend their own minimal rights, and, regretfully, most have been satisfied to continue to travel this route. They felt that an ever greater claim of being the defender of a certain nationalism would increase their freedom and influence, possibly to the position of a favorite status. This turned out to be correct from a narrow ethno-religious perspective. Very few churches sought to find in their own religious treasure some creative responses or initiatives which would not at the same time threaten the liberties of other churches and find ways for a constructive cooperation. As long as the government continued to be the guarantor of at least legal equality among the religious groups, the churches continued to be fairly ineffective as authentic embodiments of the proclamation and practice of religious liberties and human rights for all and not only for themselves. A positive step in the right direction was taken when several Orthodox, Catholic, and Muslim theologians were appointed as members of the Yugoslav Commission for the Protection of Human Rights.[97]

The main source of denial of religious liberties, however, lies directly in the attitude of the League of Communists, as implemented by the government. While the League of Communists considerably softened its original extremely intolerant attitude, making the situation much more bearable as time went on, their prevailing view was that religion did not belong in the socialist order. By one means or another, religion was to be limited, isolated, marginalized, attacked, and—in the long run—eliminated. Such views could be detected even

at the end of 1988.[98] As long as this persisted, religious people did
not feel at home in their own country, and Communists continued to
suspect them as an alien nuisance and threat. The secretary of the
Commission for Relations with Religious Communities in Croatia, Dr.
Vitomir Unković admitted that Yugoslav legislation on religion was
negative in approach though it did not violate international norms.[99]
Only a minority of Marxist intellectuals worked at discovering a more
conciliatory formula that would recognize the right of religious people
to full civil liberties; while their views have some impact the power-
wielders were less keen to accept their urging. Thus the transition
from a Type C–Secularistic Absolutism, to a Type D–Pluralistic Liberty society, despite the appearance of some of the features of the
latter, proceeded precariously and incompletely.

AFTER THE GREAT TRANSFORMATION:
1989 ONWARD

Yugoslavia's Great Transformation did not hinge on *perestroika*
and *glasnost* in the Soviet block, though such processes in the neighboring countries encouraged the proponents of change. The processes
known as *perestroika* and *glasnost* in Eastern Europe had taken place
in Yugoslavia much earlier and did bring improvements in religious
liberty analyzed in the previous section. The Great Transformation
took place when it was finally realized that Tito was no longer on
the scene to settle the increasingly acrimonious relationship between
the nations and minorities making up Yugoslavia and the pervasive
recognition, even among Communists, that the Bolshevik model of
socialism (with Titoism also being recognized as a form of Bolshevism or even anti-Stalin Stalinism) had become completely bankrupt
as a model for social progress. This recognition took place already in
1987, if not earlier, but the Communist monopoly of power yielded
to demands for change only in 1989.

The interethnic conflicts approached open warfare and brought
the country and the LCY to the point of disintegration. A constitutional crisis of enormous magnitude resulted as no group was entirely
satisfied with the past constitutional arrangements while there was
great disparity in their visions for the future arrangements. Ethnic
tensions were many and varied. The most severe involved the Serbians, the largest nation, who found themselves in strife with nearly
all other nations.

The most severe and violent ethnic conflict took place in Serbia between Serbians and Albanians in the province of Kosovo where Albanians, due to their high birth rate and emigration by Serbians, constituted 90 percent of the population and naturally sought greater autonomy. Having become the third largest ethnic group in the country, most of the Albanians sought the status of the seventh republic while some even aspired to secession and unification with Albania. The Serbs, on the other hand, consider Kosovo sacred as the location of their medieval kingdom and the seat of the ancient Orthodox patriarchate of Peć. Serbs sought to eliminate the autonomy of Kosovo and to reverse the population trend in Kosovo. For that purpose they employed the police and the army, first putting down an Albanian rebellion in 1981 and then by the late 1980s staging a mass movement, called the "anti-bureaucratic revolution," that sought to remake the constitutional arrangements of 1974 which they felt were made at Serbian expense. Dormant Serbian nationalism exploded as one of the most potent political forces under the leadership of a fairly obscure but uncorrupted Communist bureaucrat, Slobodan Milošević,[100] who skillfully channeled the Serbian grievances and frustrations to re-make Yugoslavia more to Serbian liking. Religion did not play a central role in the Serbian-Albanian conflict. However, since the vast majority of Albanians are Muslim and since the Serbian Orthodox Church consistently defended Serbian interests in Kosovo the Serbians, who are generally more folk-religious than church attending, erupted in an emotional identification with Orthodoxy which even the Serbian Communists respected. The Serbian Communist Party thus found itself in an even closer community of interests with the Serbian Orthodox Church than before and granted full and complete scope of actions to the Church. Thus the Serbian Orthodox Church found itself in a *de facto* though not *de jure* privileged position in Serbia. More important than any legal change was the public vindication of the Church in the media and speeches of politicians as the Serbians portrayed themselves increasingly as victims in the postwar Yugoslav state.[101] Tito, who had been an untouchable idol until 1987/88, came to be seen by the Serbians (but also by others) as one of the culprits for their frustrated national expression.[102] The fall of the last idol was a signal that all formerly repressed or tabu topics, including the role of religious communities and leaders (e.g. Alojzije Cardinal Stepinac or Bishop Nikolaj Velimirović) could now surface into the open by the media freed from Communist control and censorship.

The second major conflict is between Slovenia and Serbia. In Slovenia, the western-most republic, the pro-democratic movement was the strongest and the Slovene Communists were early willing to yield to a multi-party system and free secret elections. These they implemented and by 1989 Slovenia functioned similarly to a Western democracy. The Communist Party of Slovenia renamed itself the Communist League of Slovenia—The Party of Democratic Changes and found itself in such sharp conflict with the Serbian Communists that they permanently walked out of the LCY Congress in 1989 thereby effectively destroying it, the one organization that, in addition to the Army, stood for Yugoslav unity. Now only six Communists parties remained, all of which renamed themselves (e.g. Socialist Party of Serbia, League of Communists of Croatia–The Party for Democratic Renewal, etc.) except the C. P. of Montenegro. These parties were locked in a bitter struggle as to which course the country should follow.

The third major conflict is between Serbians and Croatians, the most dangerous because it is between the two largest, most intertwined nations who are burdened by the most historically bitter antagonism. Mutual recriminations abound and the danger of violence is always present and occasionally erupts under various guises. In a tense atmosphere after 1987 the hatred between the Croats and Serbs escalated. The Catholic heritage of Croats and the Orthodox heritage of Serbs surfaced again and became one of the dominant elements of the rivalry casting off quickly the nascent but never genuine ecumenical dialogue between these two religious and cultural traditions.

In 1990 a number of options were realistically possible. The two most pronounced positive options were a freely renegotiated federation or the adoption of a confederate form of government, the former being promoted mostly by politicians from the southeastern parts of the country and gravitating to Belgrade, while the latter promoted by the northwestern part of the country. Another realistic option was a civil war that would lead to the "Lebanonization" of Yugoslavia. A low intensity civil war has actually commenced, as conflicts in Kosovo and in Krajina in Croatia took place between armed and violence-prone groups that have yielded casualties in the hundreds. The Yugoslav People's Army, staffed as it is mostly by a Serbian officers corps that is deeply steeped in Communist ideology, seemed increasingly poised to carry out a *coup détat* that was a fourth option to keep Yugoslavia together presumably as a democratic socialist country, a move greatly feared in the northwestern republics. The Army's threat seemed to be in response not only to the civil war option but also to the option of the right to secession, especially if the confederate option could not be attained. While a number of groups aspire to secede the trend was most pronounced in Slovenia. This Slovene aspiration was confirmed when 95 percent of Slovenes voted for sovereignty and independence including possible secession in a plebiscite on December 23, 1990. Earlier in the year in the free elections in Slovenia in 1989 the Communists did poorly except that the very popular Milan Kučan, a reform Communist, was elected President. The Communists of Croatia did even more poorly in the free elections in May 1990 which was swept by the Croatian Democratic Union, a national independence party, with Dr. Franjo Tudjman becoming the President. Bosnia, Macedonia, Montenegro, and Serbia held free elections in November and December 1990. In Bosnia and Macedonia no clear winners emerged but in Serbia Milošević was elected President by an overwhelming vote (that was boycotted by the Albanians in Kosovo) and his Socialist Party of Serbia won a clear majority, while the Communist Party of Montenegro also won decisively. The situation had not crystallized though it was clear that Bosnians and Macedonians had not sided with Milošević and his centralist tendencies. Milošević's strong showing should not be ascribed to his socialist views but to his strong Serbian nationalism.

The principle of political pluralism resulting in the establishment of a multi-party system was accepted with a vengeance throughout the country as the number of parties proliferated in the hundreds. Political and religious emigrants of all nationalities and shapes were now permitted to return and engage in the political processes. They had a high appreciation for their respective churches and clergy because these had been their most trusted and helpful connection with the native land.

The situation is far more complex than can be described here. The above illustrates that after 1989 Yugoslavia was not the same country that it had been since 1945 as the search ensued for a "third Yugoslavia"[103] though many called for its dissolution and the creation of independent states that would then gravitate toward a united Europe. In the northwestern parts of the country there was no pretense that socialism survived, though Ante Marković, the federal prime minister in 1989 initially talked of a "new socialism"—a democratic welfare state on the Western European model. Even in the southeastern parts of the country it was clear that communist socialism was dead though some of the slogans were kept in usage. Economically there was a rush to a market economy with strong leanings toward modernization and integration into the Western European market. Severe discrepancies in industrial and economic productivity continued yet even the more advanced of the republics in Yugoslavia faced a dismal economic situation with unemployment, inflation, stagnation, and bankruptcies proliferating at an alarming rate. The poverty and misery naturally aggravated the chaotic political situation and resulted in the blaming of others for one's misery; a natural outcome. Hatred, especially along ethnic and therefore religious lines became widespread and intense—almost all-consuming.

The reason for this brief review of the politics and economics was to point to the changed role of religion. Religion had not only experienced a renewal, especially among the young, but a rehabilitation, a new visibility, and almost at once complete religious liberty, though neither new constitution nor new laws were written to reflect this, indicating, again, that the law does not determine practice until the time comes for a well established law state. Religious institutions welcomed the new politics of democratization and affirmation of national and religious self-identity and committed themselves strongly to the "will of the people" (*vox populi est vox Deo* [?]), i.e. their people. Politicians embraced religion publicly. Politics is the fate of religion in Eastern Europe after all!

In Slovenia the electorate voted to power "Demos," a coalition of political parties including the Christian Democrats, a Catholic party, whose leader Alojze Peterle became the prime minister. This conservative party increased in influence after the elections. They were accused by the otherwise thoughtful observer, Dr. Veljko Rus, of wanting to create a Catholic Slovenia following as illiberal a stance as the Bolsheviks did, when in the name of Catholic morality they want to eliminate the opposition and thereby become a threat to democracy and the law state.[104] Rus discerned dangers of clericalism and pointed out that the Christian Democrats behaved as anti-Communists rather than post-Communists. As a symbol of the rehabilitation of religion Christmas was proclaimed a public holiday in 1989. Archbishop Alojzije Šuštar had been given access to public media first to wish the listeners Merry Christmas and a Happy New Year and then more regular access to public life. The Catholic Church in Slovenia had developed a reputation for defending human rights already under the previous archbishop of Ljubljana, Jože Pogačnik. In July 1987 the Conference of Slovenian Bishops issued a declaration asking for greater civil liberties and democratization.[105]

In Croatia the newly elected *Sabor* [congress] included an inaugural mass and Archbishop Franjo Kuharić was prominently photographed with Franjo Tudjman and other politicians of the HDZ (*Hrvatska Demokratska Zajegnica*/Croatian Democratic Union) and other nationalist parties celebrating what was widely regarded as the true re-emergence of independent Croatian statehood. The joint appearance of Dr. Tudjman, a former Communist army general, now appearing with ever greater frequency piously at masses, with Cardinal Kuharić and the nearly daily media coverage of all kinds of Catholic worship and other religious manifestations raised some concern not only by adherents of other religious groups but also those who would like to see a modern secular rather than religious state. To explicit questions about the future of a Croatian state Cardinal Kuharić replied that he was hoping for a pluralistic rather than secular state, a category that he considered outdated. While it was natural that the Catholic Church preferred the situation after 1989 where the state is positively inclined toward religion rather than the Communist state that was inimical to religion, Kuharić claimed that the Church will know how to maintain a separate and critical stance from the state and daily politics.[106] The radical and speedy nature of changes in regard to church-state relations raised the possibility that the new states were heading into a subservient position toward the church—comparable to a new Canossa[107]—and a far more politically active church or a far more intimate embrace or "love affair" between the Catholic Church and the Croatian state than customary in Western societies.[108] Among Serbs of Croatia the Serbian Orthodox quickly replaced Communism as a rallying force.[109] The danger exists for both Roman Catholic and Serbian Orthodox Churches that they might be identified too strongly with one or another political party and thereby alienate believers who prefer other political options and squander the considerable moral prestige that they acquired by means of suffering under Communism.

The religious press took more explicit positions about politicians and elections,[110] and some of the media of political parties kept portraying their politicians at worship. However, except for some local excesses, for the time being at least, the churches did not exceed their appropriate domain though many in Yugoslavia who had been raised to a very restricted notion of the domain of religion may wonder about the appropriate limits of religious activities.

The decision to re-introduce religious education into schools raised many troublesome questions. No one questioned the desirability of religious institutions increasing their educational activities in church buildings and even starting their own church-related schools. But as to the public schools, and until recently all schools were public, should such education be compulsory, the way Marxist indoctrination had been, and if so what will happen to children of non-believers or of minority religions? Should it be voluntary? Should religion, in addition to religious education by the various churches, be taught as an academic subject with no particular confessional identity? Who would teach such courses, clergy or specially trained teachers? The Jewish community of Zagreb, which welcomed the new regime and was promised the rebuilding of the synagogue and cultural center destroyed by the fascists in 1941 opposed the introduction of courses in religion in schools, while the Catholics, Orthodox, and Muslims seemed to welcome it.[111]

The charitable work of the churches that had been tolerated were now permitted and openly encouraged by the new government. An official report to the government about such charitable work and the Social Service Administration was instructed to financially assist the churches in their charitable activity. New laws were proposed that would explicitly allow such religious activity, exempting them from taxes and custom duties, and offering them choices in regard to serving in the military.[112]

In Bosnia and Herzegovina, after attempts by the Communists when they were still in power to prevent it, some political parties were formed along national lines and therefore the Muslim, Orthodox, and Catholic element became rather pronounced in the Muslim, Serbian, and Croatian parties. It is exactly in this republic where the equation of religion and nationality is the greatest and where, unless reasonable dialogue and compromise takes place the most destructive religious and civil war could ensue.[113] Muslims are the most numerous group, making 40 percent of Bosnia's population and some of them have made repeated calls to make Bosnia a Muslim republic.[114] The major Muslim political party is the Party of Democratic Action went through conflicts between the moderates and a clerical militant wing that emphasizes religious symbols and whose more extremist members issued violent threats against politicians of other religiously oriented parties.[115] The question of Muslim identity was re-opened, some arguing for discontinuing the artificial Muslim nationhood and promoting a Bosnian nationhood that would be religiously Muslim. Muslim fundamentalism, though not widely spread, exists and is perceived as a threat by the other religions. Fundamentalism of all sorts, Orthodox, Catholic, Muslim, and Communist are dangerous particularly for Bosnia where the population is so mixed. Dr. Ramet concluded that Muslim religious leaders tended to be less politicized and involved with the government than the Catholics or Orthodox, though influences from other parts of the Islamic world have given them encouragement for a higher profile since the 1960s.

The Serbian Orthodox Church was restored to prominence after forty years of official supression of even the most innocuous national folk traditions that forced it to take a low profile due to accusations and pressures by the Communists. A nearly "fraternal" embrace took place between the Serbian state and the Church in the interest of unifying and defending Serbian interests that both perceived as threatened.[116] The "Patriarch German Epoch" which commenced in ths 1950s was coming to an end as the octogenarian patriarch German became terminally ill in the late 1980s. Metropolitan John , who became the interim spokesman for the Church, seems to have been far more interested in a close linking of church and state, perhaps along the lines of the pre-war "state church."[117] Surprisingly he was not one of the final candidates for the patriarch. Early in December 1990 the first post-war truly free election (i.e. with no state interference) for the new patriarch took place by an unusual method. Three (elderly) candidates were selected by the Holy Synod and the seventy-six-year-old Paul of Raška-Prizren was selected by lot as the new patriarch, a man known for his asceticism and piety, and an aversion to public involvement in politics. The election appeared to be a retreat from the too close embrace of daily politics in which one wing of the Church opted for Slobodan Milošević, while the other embraced his rival, the author Vuk Drašković, who openly promoted Orthodox Christianity in his bid for the presidency, saying that the electorate had a choice between the cross and the hammer and sickle.[118] The mood to respect and promote Orthodoxy as the historic defender of the Serbian people was unmistakable not only by the growing number of believers but even by its former critics. While in 1988 a number of members of the League of Communists of Serbia were expelled from the party, lost their jobs or punished otherwise simply for celebrating the Or-

thodox New Year in a Serbian nationalist manner in 1990 Orthodox
Christmas and New Year were celebrated publicly with much fanfare,
a liturgy on TV, a visit of the ailing Patriarch German by government
leaders, and so forth—a dramatic turnabout.[119] The rehabilitation of
innocent religious leaders who had been sentenced to prison terms was
undertaken.[120] The question raised by some was whether the years
of repression might not paradoxically boomerang into a demand for
legal and societal institutionalization of *svetosavlje*,[121] the particular
Serbian articulation of Orthodoxy.

The February 1990 issue of *Pravoslavlje* [Orthodoxy] summarized a moderate program in which the Orthodox Church called,
among other principles of a democratic and law state, for a multi-
party democracy, liberation from the rule of ideology and of every
sort of cult of personality, de-ideologization of society, the separation
of legislative, executive, and judicial power, and separation of church
and state, with the [Orthodox] Church being a "constitutive factor of
society."[122] In November the same journal emphasized that it would
not be partial toward specific parties but will support the democratic,
multi-party development of Serbia.

In Kosovo the Serbian Orthodox Church is embattled and perceives itself as the last defense from an aggressive Albanian fundamentalist Islam.[123] The conflict is fundamentally political and economic
but as in other conflict areas, religion exacerbates the problem. The
disbanded Albanian legislators met secretly in the Summer of 1990
and proclaimed Kosovo a republic, but the Serbians declared the
election null and void. Slovenes and Croatians sympathized with the
repressed Albanians (e.g. the Catholic Conference of Bishops issued
a statement in Spring 1989 calling for cessation of hatred and calling
for equal rights and freedoms in Kosovo)[124] while the Serbs charged
that this was malicious anti-Serbianism rather than humanitarianism
at work. The Albanians of Yugoslavia are predominantly Muslim,
with a very effective Roman Catholic minority (Mother Theresa is a
significant part; she visited frequently the country of her birth); as
it happens there are very few Albanian Orthodox in this area. Language and tradition, including religious tradition, were ways by which
Albanians kept their identity. As long as the government of neighboring Albania outlawed and brutally destroyed religion there was little
longing by religious Albanians to link up with Albania. But when in
1990 Albania permitted religion to function again one can presume
that such hesitance may soon disappear.

Macedonians found themselves in need of defending their Macedonian identity from exaggerated Serbian claims that they are merely southern Serbs. Claimed by Bulgarians, Greeks, and Serbs and threatened by an Albanian demographic explosion (25 percent of the population being Albanian and Turkish Muslims), many Macedonians angrily reacted against the Albanians and proposed to speak on behalf of all Macedonians in Greece, Bulgaria, and Yugoslavia to unite them into an independent greater Macedonia, in which the Macedonian Orthodox Church would play a prominent unifying role. The Serbian Orthodox Church has not yet recognized the autocephaly of that Church, and many bitter conflicts rage particularly in the border regions where both Churches claim ownership of monasteries and other church properties and involve the political authorities to adjudicate in their interest.[125] The official Macedonian press supported the Macedonian Orthodox Church, but it attacked the Jehovah's Witnesses for their increased activity.[126]

In Montenegro the religious element was also gaining greater volatility as the conflict between those Montenegrins who see themselves as ethnic Serbs combatted those who were Montenegrin nationalists. The former see the Orthodox Church in Montenegro simply as a province of the Serbian Church while the latter have reopened the issue of an autocephalous Montenegrin Orthodox Church. That the religious element was not divided from the political is illustrated by an embarrassing loud verbal confrontation between the proponents of the two positions during a festive episcopal liturgy in the Cetinje monastery and the later physical attack of the president of Montenegro Dr. Branko Kostić when the disputing groups went from the monastery to the State House.[127] One public manifestation of close church-state relations was the festive church burial given in 1990 to the remnants of the last Montenegrin king Nikola who died in Italy decades ago but the Communists had forbiden all royalty, dead or alive to enter the country.

CONCLUSION

Yugoslavia seemed to have two main alternatives: to break up, perhaps violently, due to ethno-religious-ideological conflict or to learn tolerance and dialogue as a means of creating a modern pluralistic, democratic, and free society. There were obviously also other possibilities indicated above, but by early 1991 the country moved ever closer to the precipice of a civil war. The hope was that the difficulties since the establishment of the country in 1918 are birth-pangs of an order which allows a more satisfactory exercise of freedom for the individuals, nationalities and religious communities than the past. This hope was dashed in June 1991 when the civil war flared up into a major conflagration.

The precariousness of the present situation, fraught with ambiguities and pitfalls, reflects at least for the time being, Yugoslavia's way of handling religious liberties. Since the Eastern European revolution, including the one in Yugoslavia, at least in its early stages is more directed to the past than to the future in order to deal with problems that Communism left behind, the unquestionable aim is to abandon Type C–Secularist Absolutism, but not necessarily to turn towards a genuine Pluaralistic Liberty, Type D society, despite expressed verbal interest in that model. Rather they seem to be returning to competing Type A–Ecclesiastic Absolutist societies each seeking monopoly in its respective region. There is also interest in Type B, "Religious Toleration." Due to the diversity of the population one may expect a a period of great competitiveness between the protagonists of the visions of A, B, and D arrangements.

Chapter 13

UP-DATE AND CONCLUSIONS

This chapter is being written two years after the dramatic events signaling the Great Transformation. The author decided to write this chapter at the last possible moment (November 1991) prior to the publication of the book in order to avoid a sense of time warp at least for the readers who will be reading soon after publication.

Deeply disturbing and contradictory trends are discernible in the murky situation. Events continue to move at fast-forward speed in the Soviet Union and Eastern Europe only rarely bringing greater clarity to the picture of what will emerge after the Great Transformation. Some of the developments bring great joy and hope, at least to some of the affected people. Others bring apprehension and tragedy. No longer is the prevalent feeling one of euphoria and jubilation. Rather pessimism, anxiety, and resignation characterize the situation in most cases.

The dismantlement of the Communist system continued as the hard-liner Communist coup in the USSR of August 1, 1991, failed and as the Bulgarian Socialist Party (formerly Communist) lost a national election in October 1991. Throughout the region, constitutions and laws were written that contained guarantees for human rights and religious liberties, bringing Eastern European states in line with Western democratic civil rights traditions. Otto Luchterhandt, in a review of these legal developments, pointed out that many of them went even beyond the international human rights and religious liberty declarations generally providing a bright future for the legal guarantees of religious freedom.[1] The Soviet law on religious communities of October 1, 1990, was not nearly as favorable to the religious communities as the law of the Russian Federation of October 25, 1991, as the former did not yet proclaim the worldview neutrality of the state and retained certain troublesome restrictions.[2] Regretfully, the new

Ukrainian law on religious communities of April 23, 1991, resembled the Soviet rather than the Russian model.[3] One can anticipate that such laws in various republics will all be liberalized in the aftermath of the coup's failure.

The Albanian legislature failed to agree on a new constitution and passed a "transitional" constitution on April 30, 1991, in which article 7 stated that "Albania is a secular state. The state respects the freedom of religious confessions and creates conditions for its exercise."[4] Implicit is the freedom to organize religious institutions. On June 19, 1991, Albania became the last European state to join the Conference on European Cooperation and Security.

On July 9, 1991, the first non-Communist constitution after World War II was passed by the Bulgarian parliament that was still dominated by an ex-Communist majority formally guaranteeing all human rights.

On July 4, 1991, a new "Law on the Freedom of Religious Life and the Position of Churches and Religious Communities," was passed in Czechoslovakia, which, consistent with its more democratic and pluralistic tradition excludes any legal discrimination against religious communities.[5]

The Roman Catholic Church in Poland opposed the insertion of the separation of church and state into a new Polish constitution and insisted that the church and the state should show mutual respect, sovereignty, independence, and a healthy cooperation. But the non-Roman Catholics complained that the two laws on religion which were passed in 1989, one regulating relations with the Roman Catholic Church and the other regulating all other denominations provided the basis for legal discrimination. Non-Catholics including non-believers were organizing themselves to lessen the impact of the pressure on their children stemming from the near-compulsory religious education.[7]

A draft of a new law on religion was discussed in Romania by representatives of all religious communities with a great deal of tension. The Romanian Orthodox Church consented to the formulation that all religious communities are equal before the law and that the Romanian Orthodox Church is not the state religion. However, it rejected the formula of separation of church and state.[8]

In comparison to the laws that were being replaced, the new legislation was positive and promises to provide a solid ground for the exercise of religious liberty throughout the region. One can expect a great deal of struggle for an even more equitable legal treatment of all religions and worldviews as various groups find it possible to communicate their criticisms of existing legislation which promises to be more than a window dressing.

There were, however, also some deplorable developments which bode ill for freedoms in general and religious liberty in particular. The most dangerous is the very rapid spread of national chauvinism leading to discrimination, intimidation, and even war. The second is a state of anarchy in the economy and sometimes in social life in the wake of the dissolution of the all-pervasive Communist controls. Social pathologies caused by totalitarian oppression manifested themselves in many areas of life often slowing down or thwarting democratic developments. Anarchy, lawlessness, impatience with the slow transition from one form of social formation to another, uncertainties that accompany these processes, the easy willingness to use extra-legal pressure to obtain desired ends, and highly polarized and accentuated differences became rampant. The possibility of the emergence of various dictatorial regimes: populist, military, or national-chauvinistic ones is clearly evident. This would be easily justified as a measure against the unravelling of social unity. One can too easily notice a resignation toward such dictatorship in the phrase, "we have always been ruled by tsars and we shall continue to be ruled by them." Even literally there are monarchist longings reawakened in many countries of Eastern Europe, though one can guess that the non-monarchist emperors are the graver threat to democracy.

A short country by country survey of the crucial developments of 1991 which follows the order of the table of contents will be presented here.

In the **Soviet Union**, the attempted coup d'état of August 19–21, 1991, nearly toppled Mikhail Gorbachev, the man most responsible for allowing and facilitating the Great Transformation. His position appeared shaky from the outset, but since he showed himself to be a master of changing threats into assets to his rule in the Soviet Union, many had expected that he will not be challenged by his hard-line opponents by means of a putsch. But to the consternation of millions, that was exactly what eight hardline Communist leaders undertook when they placed him under house arrest during his vacation in the Crimea.[9]

Due to the leadership of Boris Yeltsin and thousands of Muscovites who had tasted the advantages of the liberation from totalitarianism, the coup d'état unravelled surprisingly quickly and before the astonished world public the events decisively moved in exactly the opposite direction from the hard-liner's expectation. The coup seems to have been the death-blow to the Communist Party of the USSR. Gorbachev seemed to abandon his long cherished hopes to reform the party in the direction of democratic socialism and stepped down from his position of the General Secretary, dismissed the Politbureau, and for all practical purposes dissolved the Party which had so firmly ruled the Soviet Union for over seventy years. An order signed by Yeltsin to confiscate all Communist Party property was implemented, and the fate of this party was forever changed. Prior to the defanging and eventual dismantling of the KGB in October 1991, a number of mysterious murders of priests and religious activists took place leading to suspicions that the state security has not abandoned its interference in church affairs. On the whole, however, church-state relations had improved remarkably as compared to the period prior to 1989.

The events of this fateful week in August were not only crucial for the Soviet Union but for all of Eastern Europe as the inhabitants of the former satellites anxiously waited to see whether there will be an attempt to turn the clock back for all of them. Many feared that Soviet troops and occupation would return to their lands. Some, such as the leadership of the Serbian Socialist Party and the Yugoslav Army generals, joined Sadam Hussein, Fidel Castro, and Muamar Ghadafi in welcoming the coup. Their reason was that they hoped that a return of the iron fist in the Soviet Union would provide a clearer justification for their own attempts at violently settling the Yugoslav crisis. This action eroded the support which they had among the moderate Serbian nationalists.

In the aftermath of the coup, many processes in the Soviet Union became possible which were previously stonewalled. The most dramatic was the granting by decree the complete independence of Lithuania, Latvia, and Estonia, to the joy of their nationals at home and abroad and many others who were hoping and praying that the unjust annexation be reversed. All three countries passed legislation promoting religious liberties.[10] One may expect that in these three countries religious liberties will be promoted, though anti-Russian sentiments may lead to a backlash against the Russian ethnic population living in those countries that may have a negative impact on the life of the Russian Orthodox Church in the three countries.

In what form the Union of Soviet Sovereign Republics might survive is anyone's guess. In rapid progression all of the constituent republics proclaimed sovereignty and independence. The decision-making quickly shifted from the Kremlin to the republics. That the disintegration of the Russian empire will take place is nearly certain, though it is not clear whether it will take place in a relatively orderly manner with at least economic cooperation among the economically devastated units or whether a slew of antagonistic states will enter endless nationalist bickering and warfare destabilizing not only the region but the world due to the presence of awesome military armaments stationed in these territories. That threat forced the world leaders to seek ways to eliminate the possibility of nuclear weapons falling into hands of potential madmen, a scenario not at all unlikely when one observes the emergence of extremist nationalist leaders whose forte does not include moderation and stability. Massively violent outbursts among the various ethnic groups in the USSR is not unthinkable but rather a realistic prospect.

Religious liberty was indeed affected by these events. Religion, now rehabilitated and resurrected, emerged as a potent collaborator of nationalism raising the specter of a possible return in some of the nation states of the former Russian empire of the model A – Ecclesiastic Absolutism. A great deal of apprehensiveness on part of national and religious minorities is caused by the triumphalism of the majority ethno-religious unit. Many minorities, especially when they are a segment of a larger, dominant group from an adjacent area, fear that there will be revenge and retaliation upon them for the former experiences of domination. Thus the Ukrainians and Russians living in the Dniester region of Moldavia vehemently reject Moldavian efforts toward independence or reunion with Romania for they fear Romanian oppression, a fear probably well grounded knowing the oppression by Russians and Ukrainians over Romanians in Moldavia prior to the Great Transformation. There is little doubt that the Armenian Apostolic Church will be the dominant force in Armenia, the Georgian Orthodox Church in Georgia, and Muslims on the territories of Azerbaijan, Turkmenistan, Tadzhikistan, Uzbekistan, Kirghizia, and perhaps even Kazakhstan and that other religious groups are likely to suffer various degrees of practical or even legal restrictions. The political developments in Georgia indicate the possibility or even probability that dictatorial nationalistic leadership may suppress dissent, including minority religions.

For the time being, at least until the writing of this chapter, there are, however, great liberties for a wide variety of religious activities. Religious institutions are allowed to function relatively unimpeded. There are numerous reports of a great influx of Western, especially American-based religious groups, ranging from evangelical to the new religious movements, seizing the opportunity to make themselves and their views known to the Soviet public and to win adherents. This is not the place to judge the rightness of their activities, but it is evident that their activities have caused grave concern in the Russian Orthodox Church and among some ecumenical circles who fear the outbreak of hostilities among contending religious bodies. Particularly ominous are the rivalries between the Russian Orthodox and the Roman Catholic (especially Ukrainian Catholic or Eastern Rite) Churches that can and has led to bloodshed. The conflicts are vicious and the general relationship between the Eastern Orthodox and Roman Catholic Churches throughout Eastern Europe has badly deteriorated. Leaders of both churches expressed hope that the antagonism can be controlled,[11] but the conflict is at least as bitter at the base as it is at the top.

Gorbachev officially acknowledged the depth of both official and unofficial anti-Semitism and blamed it for the massive emigration of Jews who fear that civil unrest in the Soviet Union would inevitably play itself out on their hide. The fear is that with lesser degrees of police control anti-Semitic groups may foment the kind of unrest that leads to pogroms. As Stefan Schreiner, a specialist from Berlin demonstrated in a special emphasis issue of *Glaube in der 2. Welt* on Jews in the Soviet Union and Eastern Europe, anti-Semitism is an old-new problem that is widely spread under the new conditions of openness where old prejudices meet new frustrations in the search for scapegoats to explain diverse phenomena ranging from the victory of the Bolsheviks to food shortage and high prices.[12]

Thus, while Michael Bourdeaux is certainly right that:

> [i]t is no exaggeration to say that, in the formal sense, they [churches in the Soviet Union] have made more progress toward religious liberty and acceptance as an integral part of Soviet society than in the previous three-quarters of a century since the Revolution,[13]

it is also true that there are enormous threats not only to religious liberty but to the very lives of people due to the nationalistic, political, social, and economic conflicts that are developing in the direction of civil and regional wars on what is now the territory of the Soviet Union.

The return of expropriated religious properties is a phenomenon throughout Eastern Europe and the Soviet Union. The governments have shown the willingness to give back a wide range of properties (not only sanctuaries) short of handing back large land-holdings. That process will be both difficult and prolonged because a number of these properties have been put to other use, expanded, altered, and often there is no alternate property to relocate the present dweller or user. In many instances, legal documentation to claim the property is lacking or hard to obtain. By and large the religious institutions have shown patience, restraint, and prudence in the process of claiming such properties.[14] The only cases where none of these virtues are displayed are the angry confrontations over ownership of buildings claimed both by the Orthodox and Eastern Rite Catholics that lead to nasty legal and fist fights.

Albania is the last country to turn away from brutal repression of religious liberties. Alia Ramiz, the Communist leader of the country admitted the error of former repressions and showed willingness to grant institutional religious liberties provided they do not divide the country.[15] Religious services commenced, often with a very large attendance, with the very aged and much suffering religious leaders of the various religious communities emerging from the catacombs. With the help of religious leaders from abroad, there were attempts to rebuild the leadership because all religious communities started at zero. The Roman Catholic priest, Simon Jubani, was widely hailed as a martyr and apostle of religious freedom.[16] The religious communities have shown remarkable cooperation in 1991, but this is likely to be strained after the initial joy subsides and Balkan reality (i.e. balkanization) sets in. In any case, the most important fact is that Albania, albeit belatedly, partook in the Great Transformation.

Bulgaria proceeded slowly but seemingly surely on the path of democratization. Probably the most important event was the defeat of the Communists in the election of October 14 and the emergence of the party of the Turkish Muslim minority, "The Movement for Rights and Freedoms," as a likely power-broker between the winner, Union of Democratic Forces and the Bulgarian Socialist Party.[17] To the consternation of the Turkophobic Bulgarians, the party of Turkish Muslims may become the political protector of rights for Muslims. All fifteen religious communities were legalized, and on January

1, 1991, a new Department for Religious Questions was created at the office of the Council of Ministers. A sign that the new department does not wish to interfere in the internal matters of the churches was that its new director, M. Spasov, ruled the previous imposition of Pavel Ivanov as the minister of Sofia Congregational church as invalid but refused to replace him with his contender Hristo Kulichev saying that each church should follow its own internal statutes in selecting its leadership.[18] Bulgarian Orthodox Patriarch Maxim was strongly pressured by his own priests and followers to withdraw to a monastery because of his close collaboration with Todor Zhivkov's government. According to the Bulgarian Orthodox theologian Stefanka Petrova, the predicament of the churches in Bulgaria is that most of the population lacks even a rudimentary Christian ethical outlook, without which the Transformation may not be sufficiently thoroughgoing.[19]

Czechoslovakia was among the countries that changed most quickly from ubiquitous persecution to freedom in a pluralistic society. The major issues of 1991 in addition to the massive rebuilding of all churches, especially the Catholic monastic female and male orders that were previously forbidden and now made a strong comeback, were national conflicts and self-purging of tainted leaders. The national conflicts were primarily among the Czechs and the Slovaks, potentially leading to the dissolution of the federation but also among the Slovaks and Hungarians. The churches undertook to play a reconciling role pleading for unity. The second process was named "*lustratio*" and had to do with the evidences that certain church leaders worked in the past for the secret police. Some, like Pavel Smetana, the new Synodal Senior of the Church of the Czech Brethren, urged understanding, love, and forgiveness of those thus implicated while others, such as the former dissident pastor Miloš Rejchrt, replied in an open letter saying that they should be loved but nevertheless should step down from leadership position as they have lost the trust of the constituency by secretly spying on their fellow Christians.[20] Some Christians complained that there seems to be evidence that the nomenclature installed by the former Communist regime was striking back and that as long as they are in place, no radical restructuring will be possible as they are of a totalitarian mindset which is incompatible with democratic strivings even though they may have changed their vocabulary. The National Council and the Government of Slovakia also officially apologized to Jews for the suffering that was caused to them during World War II.[21]

East Germany no longer existed in 1991 and thus ceases to be in the purview of this book. Nevertheless one may mention that the process of reunification did not go smoothly in 1991. There were those, in both Germanies, who doubted the wisdom of the rapid reunification and who bitterly complained about the high cost (not only financial) of this process. On June 27, 1991, the Protestant churches of both Germanies reunited by the entering of the eight eastern German *Landeskirchen* into the Evangelical Church of Germany (EKD). Even that process will be much more protracted than the formal reunion because the eastern German churches were unsure about church taxation and their somewhat unequal status economically. Church leaders of eastern German Churches spoke of the difficulty to maintain the middle road between rejection and annexation, for which they had to struggle repeatedly and admitted numerous mistakes in the process which they had named "church in socialism." In eastern Germany the question of former surveillance of the churches and cooperation with the *Stasis* [secret service] also kept reappearing as a painful issue.[22] The rise of Neo-Nazism, especially noticeable in the eastern parts of Germany resulted in riots and mob action against foreigners, which also leads to loss of religious liberty by those targeted by hate groups.

Hungary's major preoccupation about religious rights had to do with the fate of their compatriots abroad, particularly in Romania. At home the issues were primarily the return of property to churches. In a consultation between parliamentarian and church leaders, it was agreed that this process be carried out over a ten-year period and that only those properties needed by the churches should be returned. It was recognized that the inheritance of problems from the Communist period would last for a long time. Priests wrongly accused continued to be rehabilitated but not all as Rev. György Bulányi and his "Bush" basis communities continued to run into opposition, mostly from their own hierarchy.[23] The body of Cardinal Mindszenty was returned from Vienna and interned ceremonially in Estergom.[24] Pope John Paul II visited Hungary in August and contributed to improved relationships between Catholics and Protestants by laying a wreath at the memorial to victims of the Counter-Reformation in Debrecen.[25]

In Poland things were going well for the Roman Catholic Church but not necessarily for non-Catholics. Complaints could be heard, such as Adam Michnik's that the Roman Catholic hierarchy is unable to draw limits for itself and that it has an urge to implements Catholic beliefs into legislative norms for all citizens of the country.[26] The episcopate seemed to prefer Lech Wałesa to Tadeusz Mazowiecki as president and Wałesa, indeed, showed strong leanings toward Catholic interpretations. More problematic for non-Catholics than legal preference of Catholics were strong social pressures by Catholic extremists to limit non-Catholics' rights. Some of them explicitly demanded unequal status for non-Catholics saying that untruth must not have the same status as truth. This led some non-Catholics, such as the new Methodist Superintendent Edward Puslicki, to say that they had greater liberties under the Communists.[27] The Ukrainian Catholics and Orthodox had even greater reasons to complain because in some cities church building upon which they had legal claim were possessed by fanaticized Poles, sometimes even against the will of their clergy, not even willing to share the premises, much less yield them to the Ukrainians.[28] Thus the overwhelming religious liberty issue in Poland in 1991 is the domineering position of the Roman Catholic Church and the fear of the other churches that the Catholics are limiting their freedoms. It is certain that the Roman Catholic Church in Poland does not understand what a pluralistic society is. On the positive side, however, the Catholic episcopate issued a helpful, reconciling statement on Catholic-Jewish relations and has made attempts through theologians to deal constructively with questions of anti-Semitism.[29]

Romania's Transformation was the bloodies which was an omen for troubled times ahead. Strife between nationalities also meant strife between religions. The sharpest conflicts continued to be between the Romanian Orthodox Church and the Eastern Rite and Latin Rite Catholics and between the Romanian Orthodox and Hungarian Reformed Churches. The Romanian Orthodox Church became active in Moldavia, leading to expectations that this Soviet Republic will seek re-union with Romania. The expected inner reformation of the Romanian Orthodox Church did not take place. The Hungarian Reformed bishop László Tökés made an appeal for ecumenical cooperation in solving the nationalities question, but he also pointed out the threats and pressures leveled against him.[30] The dialogue between the Romanian Orthodox and Roman Catholic Church was interrupted, and Patriarch Teoctist called on all Orthodox Churches world-wide to do likewise as he accused the Pope of initiating a proselytizing campaign in all of Eastern Europe at the expense of the Orthodox.[31] Continued economic problems and relapses to police surveillance and violence to solve political problems continued to characterize the Romanian scene. Such tensions may easily erupt into much greater bloodshed. Refugees continue to pour to Hungary.

Yugoslavia was the first of the Eastern European countries to liberalize, the first to deteriorate into a state of civil war, and quite possibly the first to completely dissolve its federation. While the civil war was carried out at a low level intensity for several years, the declaration of independence on part of Slovenia and Croatia at the end of June led to a flare-up that became a full-fledged open civil war, the end of which is not to be foreseen. Subsequently Macedonia and Bosnia and Herzegovina openly declared independence, while the Kosovo Albanians did so clandestinely. Yugoslavia is rapidly becoming another Lebanon, and all have become victims.[32] The worst victimization is over people; thousands were killed between June and November. The second great casualty is truth; there is preciously little truth in the propaganda and declarations of the warring parties. All parties to the conflict have carried out savage atrocities upon the others and have claimed that it is only the enemy engaging in such misdeeds. The religions have become co-victims and usually also co-culprits. A second touching and profoundly Christian joint appeal was issued by Patriarch Paul and Franjo Cardinal Kuharić in Slavonski Brod at the beginning of September but to no avail. Very large numbers of church buildings have been destroyed. About 500,000 people, including clergy, had to flee either to the republic where their ethnic group is in the majority or abroad. Baptist sources reported disrupted communications, cessation of services, and flight from the regions where the fighting is most vicious, along with attempts to minister to the threatened population.[33] The refugee problem is serious enough to have caught the attention of Church World Service and other international relief organizations. Nothing is left of domestic ecumenism. Formally there are no restrictions of religious liberties and Croatian authorities even passed a very liberal law on religious activities. But in reality, when people are killing one another in the name of nation and religion, there can be no religious liberty. Bitterness, hatred, and fear characterize the situation that has destroyed years of hard labor and suffering in the hope of creating impressive religious liberties. Even some priests are jeopardizing the future of religious liberties as they don on uniforms and carry weapons ostensibly in support of their flock thereby seriously endangering the church's position in providing non-political pastoral care.[34] Obviously in war human rights and religious liberties are as savagely destroyed as are lives. The author should have perhaps proposed another category, a model E, a society where hatred and collective lunatic behavior ruthlessly tramples on the rights of both believers and un-believers.

Concluding Observations

It is too early to give a definitive assessment of the status of religious liberties prior to the Great Transformation. The period since the Great Transformation has hardly begun and only the vaguest features are discernible. Nevertheless certain observations are in order resulting out of this study.

1. Generally there is a continuity in a country's approach to religious liberty over an extended historical period, even when there are occasional inconsistencies. The initial hypothesis of this study seems to be borne out. In countries where an absolutistic approach existed, it tended to be retained. Thus Ecclesiastic Absolutism (Type A) more readily turned to Secularistic Absolutism (Type C) and generally did not easily become a tolerant (Type B) or Pluralisticly free (Type D) society but rather tended to revert to an Absolutistic model. On the other hand, those societies that practiced Religious Toleration tended after their interlude with Type C to return to Type B or even show inclinations toward Type D.

Consequently: The Balkans remained balkanized. Russia and associated lands remained 'tsarist' and showed intolerance to alternate ways of thinking and worshiping. On the other hand, those countries that achieved a degree of tolerance during their pre-Communist period, namely Czechoslovakia, Hungary, and East Germany, seemed most easily able to move to a system in which liberties and human rights will be respected.

2. Secularistic Absolutism as a model has been discredited. One cannot predict with certainty that there will never be reversions to this model on account of its recent failure because the same was anticipated about the Ecclesiastic Absolutism model, yet there are those who wish to revert to it. On the whole, the prospects of anyone seriously proposing its reintroduction seems unlikely.

Secularistic Absolutism did not destroy religion, but it did cause great harm to religious people. It is evident that totalitarianism did not damage only religious people and institutions but also those who most ardently supported this process. Societies which have gone through the totalitarian experience show both visible and invisible pathologies which are unlikely to heal in generations. Jakub Trojan of Prague indicates in theological terms the direction that needs to be taken in order to accomplish such healing:

> . . . the sins that have not been overcome will inevitably continue to weigh us down in the future. Only through forgiveness can we completely deal with the problem of guilt. But it is only guilt which has been revealed and acknowledged which can be overcome in this way. It is true that love covers a multitude of sins. However, it is only possible to cover things when they have first been exposed to view.[35]

This study has attempted to expose what has transpired in respect to religious liberties. It is obvious that the main culprit was the Communist ideology and Communists who implemented it at all cost. However, it is also obvious that religious people wittingly or unwittingly contributed to the calamity both prior to the Communist take-over and during the Communist period.

3. Religious liberty is one of the human rights and human rights ought not be artificially separated into civil/political and social/economic. When the latter are promoted at the expense of the former, it is obvious not only that the former are violated but that in the last instance even the socio-economic rights are unprotected and fail when the human spirit is enslaved.

4. Secularistic Absolutism was not only the result of a particular interpretation of the works of Marxist classics but a generally well-coordinated international effort spearheaded by the Soviet Bolsheviks. There was an attempt to implement the Soviet model in all Eastern European countries. The success of that effort varied greatly due to the diverse historic circumstances. Eastern Europe, after all, was not a uniform socialist bloc as both its supporters and detractors claimed, but a rather disparate and conflict-prone area, no more united by the socialist experience than prior to it.

Only after the Great Transformation did it become evident to all and to a fuller extent just how great the devastation of the Communist totalitarianism was. According to Waldemar Chrostowski,

> The destruction is so severe and extensive that it is becoming ever more evident that the removal of communists from power does not automatically lead to a pluralistic society.[36]

5. The euphoria resulting from the self-destruction of Communism lasted less than year, replaced by grave threats to human life and value, despite the sudden unleashing of restraints previously placed

upon religion. Miroslav Volf, in an apt use of the parable of Jesus
about the departure of the unclean spirit only to return with seven
even more wicked demons, wrote:

> Amidst the hubbub of dismantling communist totalitarian-
> ism, three other demons threaten to enter Eastern European
> countries: cold-blooded economism, nationalistic totalitari-
> anism, and political clericalism.

> One of these demons—nationalistic totalitarianism—is by
> itself worse than the first, but if all three enter Eastern Eu-
> ropean countries together, the last state of these countries
> would, no doubt, be worse than the first.[37]

Indeed, national chauvinism appears to be the most wide-spread
ideology replacing the Marxist one.[38] By the end of 1991, it has already caused large loss of life and also loss of religious liberty at least
for the besieged nationalities but often also indiscriminately to all living in affected areas. Limited wars and conflicts can develop into total
wars that could affect enormous areas from Dubrovnik to Vladivos-
tok. The disintegration of the Soviet empire and other multi-national
states can lead to oppression of ethnic and religious minorities or wars
between them. Already many church buildings have been destroyed
by combatants. Refugees as well as those who remain to live in near
empty villages are left without the customary pastoral care or the
possibility to worship.

6. The Great Transformation brought about a nearly instanta-
neous unleashing of religion from its strictures. A religious renewal
took place which included even formerly explicit antagonists of religion. A wide-range of religious activities took place as a result of the
implementation not only of benevolent legislation but also the willingness on part of most authorities to atone for the limitations of the
past and thus facilitate religious activities. Many of these religious
activities seem to benefit not only spiritually but even economically
those areas which were devastated by former socialist practices and
by the transition from the command economy to a market economy.

7. For the time being it seems that most religious communities are willing to grant toleration to other religionists based on their
own experience of restrictions and suffering. Memory, however, seems
short lived and there are already evidence that some religious communities are no longer willing to grant the rights and liberties which they
themselves so eagerly covet. The right religious vision could become

a unitive force enabling various Eastern European people to live in peace and freedom with one another, but the narrow, sectarian vision can aggravate the already severe economic and political crisis.

At the end of 1991 one can see that the road left behind is littered by corpses. The road ahead could either be promising or could lead into another valley of tears unless respect for the worth of every individual and every religious and national group becomes more than a beautiful but empty phrase. There has to be not only a transformation of the social system but a transformation of the human spirit. All great religious founders and leaders spoke of its possibility. The present moment could be the catharsis enabling such transformation. The question is only whether people will have enough wisdom and courage to seize it.

NOTES

Notes to Foreword

1. It is not my aim to violate the unique dimensions of the Holocaust which I personally hold in sacred memory but my colleague, the late Nora Levin, one of the best historians of the Holocaust, taught me that regretfully, for all the uniqueness of the Holocaust there are other holocausts and the destruction of millions under Communism even numerically matches the Holocaust.

2. Paul Ricoeur, "The Memory of Suffering," *Criterion* (Chicago), Vol. 28, No. 2 (Spring 1989), p. 3.

3. Ibid.

Notes to Chapter 1

1. Lukas Vischer, "Europeische Kirchen gemeinsam für die Religionsfreiheit" in *Die Religionsfreiheit in Osteuropa*, Eugen Voss, ed. (Zollikon, Switzerland: GW2-Verlag, 1984), p. 13. Translated from German by Paul Mojzes. Book title hereafter abbreviated to *DRO*.

2. Franz Cardinal Koening, "Vorwort," *DRO* p. 8.

3. Rudolf Stamm, "Tolerance and Human Rights," in *The Churches Human Rights Programme for the Implementation of the Helsinki Final Act* (Geneva: Conference of European Churches, 1986), p. 36.

4. Tamas Földesi, "Mediation on Human Rights," *Occasional Papers on Religion in Eastern Europe*, (hereafter *OPREE*), IX, No. 2 (February 1989), pp. 1–8 and "Thoughts About the Freedom of Conscience and Religion," *OPREE*, Vol. IX, No. 5 (September 1989), pp. 1–14.

5. Zdenko Roter, "Modern Society and Religious Liberties: Contribution to the Christian-Marxist Dialogue," *OPREE*, Vol. VIII, No. 2 (May 1988), pp. 1–24; "The Position of Believers as Second-Class Citizens in Socialist Countries: The Case of Yugoslavia," *OPREE*, Vol. IX, No. 3 (June 1989), pp. 1–17.

6. Eckehart Lorenz, "Religionsfreiheit im Verständniss evangelischer Kirchen," in *DRO*, p. 33.

7. Ibid.

8. Charles Davis, "The Political Use and Misuse of Religious Language," *Journal of Ecumenical Studies*, Vol. 26, No. 3 (Summer 1989), pp. 483–495. See also his *Theology and Political Society*. (Cambridge: Cambridge University Press, 1980), pp. 167–169 for a description of pluralism. I use here Davis' framework but amplify and apply it to the East European situation.

9. Davis, "The Political Use and Misuse of Religious Language," p. 489.

10. Ibid.

11. Davis. *Theology and Political Society*, p. 168.

12. Ibid., pp. 168–169. Quoted from C. Davis, "The Philosophical Foundation of Pluralism," in *Le pluralisme: Symposium interdisciplinary Pluralism: Its Meaning Today* (Montreal: Fides, 1974), p. 247.

13. See Zdenko Roter, "Modern Society and Religious Liberties: A Contribution to the Christian-Marxist Dialogue," in *OPREE*, Vol. VIII, No. 2, pp. 3–5. Roter distingushes Types A, B, C, and D and provides the outline of the major characteristics of each type. The names for each type and their detailed development in this chapter are mine.

14. A very strong case is made, especially in regard to the religious nature of Soviet Communism in the USSR in Giovanni Codevilla, "The Limits of Religious Freedom in the USSR" in *Religion and Communist Society*, Dennis J. Dunn, ed. (Berkeley, CA: Berkeley Slavic Specialisties, 1983), pp. 67–84, esp. 68–74.

15. Ibid., p. 69.

16. Ibid.

17. Dobrica Ćosić, "Zbiva se civilizacijska revolucija," [A Civilizational Revolution is Taking Place], *NIN*, No. 2045, (March 11, 1990), p. 60.

18. Zdenko Roter, "Believers as Second-Class Citizens in Socialist Countries: The Case of Yugoslavia," pp. 1ff. Roter writes of those Marxists who from the outset, and often at the peril of their life, struggled against totalitarian tendencies within the Communist parties.

19. For a fine series of evaluations of the exercise of religious liberty in the U. S. at the point of the Bicentennial of Independence

see Franklin H. Littell, ed.. *Religious Liberty in the Crossfire of Creeds* (Philadelphia, Ecumenical Press, 1978).

20. The Churches' Human Rights Programme. Information No. 5 (Geneva Conference of European Churches, July 1986), p. 37.

21. Ibid., Information No.1 (August 1983), p. 5.

22. Vischer, "Europäische Kirche gemeinsam für die Religionsfreiheit," p. 17.

23. Koenig, *op .cit.*, p. 9. John Paul II holds the same position. His view has been summarized as: "Religious freedom is a radical right, because it directly concerns the essence of the human person in his search for the Absolute." in Marc Reuver, ed., *Human Rights: A Challenge to Theology.* (Rome: CCIA & IDOC International, 1983), p. 24.

24. Reuver, *Human Rights: A Challenge to Theology*, p. 26.

25. Milomir Marić, *Deca komunizma*, [The Children of Communism] (Belgrade: NIRO "Mladost," 1987), p. 142, quoting Ivan Ocek. Translated from Serbian by Paul Mojzes.

26. Ricardo Antoncich, "Evangelization and Human Rights," in Reuver, *op. cit.*, p. 48.

27. *The Churches Human Rights Programme for the Implementation of the Helsinki Final Act.* Information No. 1 , pp. 1–3.

28. Theo Tschuy, *An Ecumenical Experiment in Human Rights* (Geneva: The Churches' Human Right Programme, 1985), pp. 34–35.

29. There are also theoretical arguments which assert that a division of power is fictitious and that only one branch of government is and should be the repository of sovereignty.

30. Interview with Prof. Zdenko Roter of University of Ljubljana in West Chester, PA, December 5, 1987. A number of theoretical insights were gained in conversation with Dr.Roter.

31. Tamas Földesi, "Meditation about Human Rights," *OPREE*, pp. 1ff.

32. Philip Potter, "Religious Liberty—A Global View," in Littell. *op. cit.*, p. 133.

33. Paul Grossrieder, "Religionsfreiheit im Verständniss der katholischen Kirche," in *DRO*, pp. 35–36.

34. The author received a letter from a young Protestant theologian from East Germany in late December 1989 in which she stated that even bad socialism is better than good capitalism.

Notes to Chapter 2

1. Many Marx scholars have pointed out that Marx personally was a-religious. Marx was an atheist and even an anti-theist
since he identified God as a power that necessarily limits human self-
affirmation. Marx had no place for a God concept as he had no place
for a notion of transcendence in his own thinking according to Peter
Ehlen, "Zur Frage nach Gott im Denken von Karl Marx," in Otto
Muck. *Sinngestalten*, (Innsbruck and Vienna: Tyrolia-Verlag, 1989),
pp. 156–173.

2. Peter Ehlen, "Die Kategorie 'Freiheit' im Marxschen Denken,"
Studies in Soviet Thought, No. 37, (1989), p. 323.

3. Ibid., pp. 331, 329.

4. Frederick Bender, ed. *Karl Marx: The Essential Writings*,
(New York: Harper Torchbooks, 1972). This is particularly clear in
a selection from *Deutsch-Französische Jahrbücher* entitled "Political
Rights versus Human Emancipation" in which Marx argues against
the liberal notion of religious freedom and human rights, saying that
"since the existence of religion is the existence of a defect" (p. 56),
therefore, freedom of religion as manifested best in the U. S. simply
manifests a secular, political narrowness of which society needs to
be freed. From such writings it was an easy conclusion for Marx's
followers that there was no need to guarantee religious freedoms.

5. Thomas Sowell, *Marxism: Philosophy and Economics* (New
York: William Morrow & Co., Inc., 1985), p. 46.

6. Ibid.

7. Karl Marx and Friedrich Engels, *The German Ideology* (New
York: International Publishers, 1947), p. 74.

8. K. Marx and F. Engels, *The Holy Family* (Moscow: Foreign
Languages Publishing House, 1956), p. 157.

9. Marcel Reading, *Die Glaubensfreicheit im Marxismus* (Vienna, Frankfurt, Zurich: Europa Verlag, 1967), p. 11.

10. Arthur F. McGovern, *Marxism: An American Christian Perspective* (Maryknoll, NY: Orbis Books, 1980), p. 20.

11. Sowell, *op. cit.*, p. 26.

12. Ehlen, "Zur Frage nach Gott im Denken von Karl Marx," p.
166.

13. K. Marx, *Selected Writings*. ed. by David McLellan (Oxford:
Oxford University Press, 1977), p. 8.

14. David McLellan, *Marxism and Religion: A Description and*

Assessment of the Marxist Critique of Christianity (London: The Macmillan Press, 1987), p. 13.

15. Marx and Engels, *Collected Works*, Vol. 3 (London: Lawrence & Wishart, 1975), p. 176.

16. Marx, "Contribution to the Critique of Hegel's Philosophy of Right," in Marx and Engels, *On Religion* (New York: Schocken Books, c. 1964), p. 41.

17. Marx and Engels, "The Holy Family," in *On Religion*, pp. 67–68.

18. Marx, "The Civil War in France," in Marx and Engels. *Selected Works*, Vol. I (Moscow. Foreign Languages Publishing House, 1955), p. 525.

19. Ibid., p. 519.

20. Marx, "The Leading Article of No. 179 of "Kölnische Zeitung," in *On Religion*, p. 36.

21. Zoran Medved, "Intervju: Dr. Jože Pučnik," *Danas* (Zagreb), Vol. IX, No. 436 (June 26, 1990), p. 13. Prof. Pučnik is a sociologist of University of Ljubljana, president of Demos and the Social-Democratic Party of Slovenia and candidate for the President of Slovenia. He is well acquainted with the materials taught at Communist Party courses in Yugoslavia, which were mostly copies of Soviet manuals.

22. McGovern, *op. cit.*, p. 262.

23. Marx, "Critique of the Gotha Programme," in *On Religion*, p. 144.

24. Engels, "Emigrant Literature," in *On Religion*, p. 143.

25. Engels, "Anti-Duehring," in *On Religion*, p. 1 49.

26. Lecture of Dr. Tamás Földesi, dean of Law School, Eötvöss Lorand University, Budapest, Hungary, at Rosemont College, PA, in April 1988. His statements were based on extensive research and a book on that subject published in Hungary.

27. Krystyna Gorniak-Kocikowska, "Technical Development and Its Role for the Creation of the 'Inter-Traditional' Equivalence of God," unpublished manuscript, (August 1989).

28. Trevor Ling, *Karl Marx and Religion in Europe and India*, (New York: Barnes and Noble Books, 1980), p. 15.

29. Marx and Engels, *Selected Correspondence*, trans. by Dona Torr (New York: International Publishers, 1942), p. 337.

30. Sowell, *op. cit.*, pp. 43 and 52.

31. Ibid., p. 206.

32. Ibid.

33. Ibid., p. 207.

34. Ibid., pp. 208–209.

35. McGovern, p. 262.

36. Walter Muelder, *Foundations of the Responsible Society* (Nashville: Abingdon Press, 1959), p. 24.

Notes to Chapter 3

1. Statement by Fr. Vitaliy Borovoy at the Saltjöbaden (Sweden) Christian-Marxist Symposium on Peace in June 10–16, 1979. Borovoy is regarded by many as the most able Russian Orthodox churchman and theologian today. He maintained that without the Orthodox Christians, who were the majority of the participants on the Bolshevik side, the Revolution and the subsequent achievements would not have been successful. Skillfully he chided the Soviet Marxists at the conference for the subsequent *de facto* disenfranchisement of the Christian population.

2. McLellan, *op. cit.*, p. 93.

3. Ibid., p. 96.

4. Lenin, "To the Rural Poor," *Collected Works* (Moscow: 1972), Vol. 6, p. 402.

5. Ibid., Vol. 10, p. 85.

6. Ibid., Vol. 29, p. 134.

7. Lenin, *Collected Works*, 5th edition. (Moscow: Foreign Languages Publishing House, 1962), Vol. 4, p. 2.

8. Lenin, *Selected Works*. (London: Lawrence and Wishart, 1939), Vol. XI, pp. 664 and 666.

9. McGovern, *op. cit.*, p. 264.

10. "Letters to Maxim Gorki," in ibid., pp. 675–676.

11. Contemporary Soviet Communists, even those with liberal leanings, still have difficulties to depart from their view that Lenin's attitude and legislation toward religion was democratic as can be seen from an interview of Konstantin Kharchev, the former chairman of the Council of Religious Affairs of the USSR Council of Ministers by Alexander Nezhny in *Ogonyok*, No. 50 (December 1988), an abridged translation, "AW and Conscience," *Liberty* (July/August 1989), p. 4.

12. Sowell, *op. cit.*, p. 212.

13. Ibid.

14. This was most consistently done by those Yugoslav Marxists who gathered around the now defunct journal *Praxis* from which they

gained their name "Praxis philosophers." Their application of Marxist critique to socialist conditions caused them a lot of persecution by the Communist Party. More recently Tamás Földesi wrote about these issues, "Thoughts about Freedom of Conscience and Religion," *OPREE*, Vol. IX, No. 5, (September 1989), pp. 1–14.

15. These were called *lishentsy*, i.e. those deprived of rights.

16. Zoran Medved, "Intervju: Dr. Jože Pučnik," *Danas*, Vol. IX, No. 436 (June 26, 1990), p. 13. Pučnik provides this insight to explain the massacres of captured enemy army units after (not during) World War II by the Yugoslav partisan forces as well as the massacre of innocent civilians or later trumped up processes against groups from their own midst. These massacres were often carried out with brutal torture and often simply cutting their throats or bludgoning them with mallets. It has now been established that the communist forces used equally inhumane exterminations as did the Nazis and were equally indiscrimate in selecting victims.

17. Aleksandr Nezhniy, "Das Schicksal von Patriarch Pimen," *G2W*. Vol. 18, No. 9 (1990), p. 24. This is a translation of an article from *Ogonyok* (Moscow). Nezhniy cites Lenin's letter of March 19, 1922, as reported by *Izvestiya* (Moscow), No. 4, 1990, but the letter had been published previously in *Vestnik Studentcheskogo Hristianskogo Dvizhenyiya* (Paris), Vol. 98, No. 4 (1970), pp. 54–57.

18. Lenin's letter to the members of the Politbureau of March 19, 1922, quoted in Gerhard Simon, "Kritik an Lenin's Religionspolitik," *G2W*, Vol. 17, No. 2 (1989), p. 15. Translated from German by P. Mojzes. Simon points out that this quote has not been published in any Soviet edition of the works of Lenin. A slightly different version is "We must engage in a most decisive battle against reactionary clergy and suppress their resistance with such cruelty that they will remember it for several decades to come." According to "No Longer Godless Communism," *Time* (October 15, 1990), p. 70.

19. Nikola Milošević, *Marksizam i jezuitizam.* Third, revised edition. (Belgrade: Biblioteka XX vek, 1989), pp. 96–98. Milošević is a professor at the Philosophical Faculty of Belgrade University.

20. "Taboo on criticism of Lenin broken," *Philadelphia Inquirer*, June 29, 1989, p. 8–A.

21. Ibid.

22. Ibid.

23. Ibid.

Notes to Chapter 4

1. Otto Luchterhandt, *Der Sowietstaat und die Russisch-Orthodoxe Kirche* (Cologne: Verlag Wissenschaft und Politik, 1976), pp. 52–53 where Luchterhandt argues that such an influence existed.

2. Dimitry V. Pospielovsky, *A History of Soviet Atheism in Theory and Practice. and the Believer*, (hereafter *HSATPB*), Vol. 1: *A History of Marxist-Leninist Atheism and Soviet Anti-Religious Policies*, Vol. 2: *Soviet Anti-Religious Campaign and Persecutions* (New York: St. Martin's Press, 1987 and 1988 respectively). The problem with Pospielovsky's periodization is that there are gaps in the periodization and inconsistencies between several versions without clear explanation (e.g. see p. x of Vol. 1 overagainst the periodization reflected in the table of contents of the same volume or gaps reflected in the table of contents of Vol. 2).

3. The manuscript was probably completed before the Gorbachev period as the author does not take adequate cognizance of the changes due to *perestroika*.

4. Bohdan Bociurkiw, "Soviet Religious Policy in the Ukraine in Historical Perspective," *OPREE*, Vol. II, No. 3 (June 1982), p. 2.

5. Ibid., p. 3.

6. Pospielovsky, *HSATPB*,. 2, pp. 1 and 6.

7. For a comprehensive treatment of the legal position of the Orthodox Church under the Communist regime and related issues see Otto Luchterhandt, *Der Sowietstaat und die Russisch-Orthodoxe Kirche*. See also Luchterhandt's *Die Religionsgezetsgebung der Sowietunion* (Berlin: Berlin-Verlag, 1978).

8. Coelestin Patock, "Die rusischen orthodoxen Bischofe der letzten 100 Jahre," in *Tausend Jahre Christentum in Russland*, Karl Christian Felmy, et al., eds. (Göttingen: Vandenhoeck & Ruprecht, 1988), p. 438. Some of the bishops were murdered in exile. Patock points out that the exact situation needs to be researched. The above figures did not include figures of the Renovationist and Grigorevtsi schismatic Orthodox.

9. Pospielovsky quotes extensively an allegedly secret document written by Lenin in which he ordered that ". . . we must wage a merciless battle against reactionary clergy and suppress its resistance with such cruelty that it may remember it for several decades . . ." confiscating church properties at the time of the famine when few if any will come to the defense of the church. This secret memorandum

was published in a *samizdat*. See Pospielovsky, *HSATPB*, Vol. 1, p. 35. See also endnote #18, chapter 3.

10. Walter Sawatsky, *Soviet Evangelicals Since World War II* (Kitchener, Ont. and Scottsdale, PA: Herald Press, 1981), pp.36–37.

11. Pospielovsky, *HSATPB*, p. 16.

12. Ignazio Silone in *The God that Failed*, Richard Crossman, ed. (New York: Bantam Books, 1965), pp. 90–91. For some of the profoundest observations on the nature of the Communist totalitarianism, I urge the reader to consult this book written by former Communists who turned away from Communism partly due to their direct encounter with Soviet Communists written by such authors as André Gide, Arthur Koestler, Louis Fischer, Richard Wright, Stephen Spender, and Silone. In general I find the analyses of former Communists or humanistic Marxists on the nature of Communism, especially in regard to liberty, to be the most profound observations on the subject, since it comes from people who had been deeply immersed in the movement and have reached the moment of truth.

13. Bociurkiw, *op. cit.*, p. 6.

14. Sawatsky, *SESWWII*, p. 37.

15. Pospielovsky, *HSATPB*, pp. 55–56.

16. Ibid., p. 56.

17. Pospielovsky, *HSATPB*, Vol. 1 , pp. 133–134. For a discussion of these laws see William van den Bercken, *Ideology and Atheism in the Soviet Union* (Berlin and New York: Mouton de Guyter, 1989), pp. 90–93.

18. All above legislation is recorded in Pospielovsky, *HSATPB*, 1, pp. 132–135.

19. The disdain for democracy and "bourgeois" rights is evident for instance in excerpts of Lenin's *The State and Revolution* and Leon Trotsky's *The Defence of Terrorism* reprinted in *Modern Socialism*, Massimo Salvadori, ed. (New York: Harper & Row, Publishers, 1968), pp. 191–199 and 203–208. Some of these writings chillingly display a violent intolerance aiming a destruction of all who are perceived to stand in the way, even the innocent.

20. Whether Pot Pol's murder of 3 million Kampucheans is worse on a per capita basis and is a case of greater genocide may be open to discussion. Surely one should not forget Mao Tze Tung, Idi Amin, Papa Doc Duvalier, and other henchmen of the twentieth century, yet in sheer absolute numbers Stalin is the worst mass murderer in history.

21. See recent revelations publicly discussed in the USSR, "Soviets: Stalin toll topped 40 million," "An old massacre in Ukraine raises new questions for Soviets," and "Probe is promised into reports of mass burials of Stalin victims," *The Philadelphia Inquirer.* February 5, March 2, and March 7, 1989. The second article estimates 300,000 in Bykovina, Ukraine, and the last 240,000 in the vicinity of Kiev.

22. This author has difficulty with scholars who judge Stalin by the reversal in his policies toward the churches in the aftermath of World War II, forgetting the previous furor and utter horror of the Great Purge. D. Pospielovsky states: "The numbers of laymen, parish priests, monks and nuns martyred by the Soviets in the 1930s and the 1940s for their faith is just too great and the proportion of the known cases to that of the unknown too small, to be discussed in this study." (Vol. 2, p. 81). Jane Ellis states: "the first of many bishops was murdered while the Council was in session, and increasingly during the 1920s and on a massive scale during the 1930s, nearly all the bishops and clergy and incalculably large number of faithful perished in the labour camps or were shot." in *The Russian Orthodox Church* (Bloomington and Indianapolis: Indiana University Press, 1986). What is missing is specifying that Stalin was the culprit.

23. Philip Walters, "The Russian Orthodox Church," *Eastern Christianity and Politics in the Twentieth Century*, Pedro Ramet, ed. (Durham and London: Duke University Press, 1988), p. 74.

24. Milovan Djilas, *The Unperfect Society: Beyond the New Class*, trans. by Dorian Cooke. (New York: Harcourt, Brace & World, Inc., 1969), p. 71.

25. A typed poem in author's file.

26. Legend has it that Stalin dynamited it personally and intended to have a secular building built on the site though divine intervention kept filling it with water, so that the only thing that could be done is to turn it into a swimming pool, which was on that site until recently. According to reports the pool was drained in 1990 and a new church will be built on that site.

27. Tobias, *op. cit.*, p. 19.

28. Ibid., p. 17.

29. Sawatky, *op. cit.*, p. 48.

30. See excerpts of various legislation of that period in Pospielovsky, *op. cit.*, Vol. 1, pp. 135–138.

31. Summary based on excerpts of the text of legislation provided

in Pospielovsky, *op. cit.*, Vol. 1, pp. 138–146.

32. Gerhard Simon, *Church State and Opposition in the USSR*, trans. by Kathleen Matchett, (Berkeley and Los Angeles: University of California Press, 1974), p. 65.

33. See Pospielovsky, *op. cit.*, for parallel columns of the 1975 amendments.

34. Simon, *op. cit.*, p. 66.

35. Quoted in Robert Conquest, ed., *Religion in the USSR* (New York and Washington: Frederick A. Praeger, Publishers, 1969), p. 27.

36. Luchterhandt, *Der Sowietstaat und die Russisch-Orthodoxe Kirche*, p. 89.

37. Cf. Walter Ciszek, S.J., *With God in Russia* (New York: McGraw-Hill, 1964) describes the horrible experiences of the author who was a Catholic priest in a village in Poland that fell under Soviet rule in 1939.

38. Documentary films of that time vividly testify to the population's welcome of the German troops and their anger against things Bolshevik until the Nazis started the mass murder of the Soviet non-Jewish population. Regretfully, during the early period of the Nazi invasion some of the Slavic population actively assisted in the destruction of the Jews.

39. Wassilij Alexeev and Theofanis G. Stavrou, *The Great Revival: The Russian Church Under German Occupation* (Minneapolis: Burgess Publishing Co., 1976), p. xii.

40. From personal conversation with an older Jew in the Moscow synagogue in March 1988, who told me that his brother, after escaping destruction by the Nazis during the War was simply murdered by Red Army troops in 1946/47 for no apparent reason.

41. Simon, *op. cit.*, pp. 69–70.

42. Simon, *op. cit.*, pp.72–91. Kuroyedov wrote an apologetic book claiming complete freedom of religion, *Religiya i tserkov' v Sovyetskom obshchestve* (Moscow: Izdatelystvo politicheskoy literaturi, 1984), pp. 106–107.

43. Both Simon and Ellis mention this figure. But Ellis points out that the estimates of the number of Orthodox churches in any given period vary drastically, the figures often showing a 100 percent discrepancy. See Ellis, *op. cit.*, pp. 15–17. The present estimates vary between 6,000 (Ellis) and 8,500 (Kuroyedov) Orthodox churches.

44. Simon, *op. cit.*, p. 72.

45. Ellis, *op .cit.*, pp. 53–69.

46. E.g. Michael Bordeaux and Kathleen Matchett, "The Russian Orthodox Church in Council 1945–1971," in Bociurkiw and Strong, eds. *Religion and Atheism*, pp. 41–43; Simon, *op. cit.*, pp. 69–88; Ellis, *op. cit.*, p. 5. Pospielovsky, *op. cit.*, Vol. 1, pp. 98–125 and Vol. 2, pp. 98ff., maintains that after Khrushchev's repression there may have been a reprieve in the administrative pressure from 1965 to the early 1970s followed by another atheist offensive lasting into the 1980s.

47. Sawatsky, *SESWII*, pp. 131–153.

48. Michael Rowe, "Religious Persecution and Discrimination," in *Candle in the Wind: Religion in the Soviet Union*, Eugene B. Shirley, Jr. and Michael Rowe, eds. (Washington, DC: Ethics and Public Policy Center, 1989), pp. 139–172.

49. On the Reform Baptist conflict with the authorities see Michael Bourdeaux, *Faith on Trial in Russia* (New York: Harper & Row, Publishers, 1971). Ellis, *op. cit.*, wrote in great detail about the Russian Orthodox dissenters.

50. The KGB worked within the Councils for Religious Affairs but also spied on the churches through its own separate informers. In 1970 the Fifth Directorate was established in the KGB to deal with dissidents and a separate unit was organized to deal with religious dissidents. John Andreson, "Legislative and Administrative Control of Religious Bodies," *Candle in the Wind*, p. 74.

51. See also Anderson, *op. cit.*, pp. 65–89.

52. Marite Sapiets, "Anti-Religious Propaganda and Education," *Candle in the Wind*, pp. 91–115.

53. Andrey Bessmertniy-Anzimirov, "Freedom of Faith: International Norms and Stalinist Legislation," *OPREE*, Vol. 9, No. 3 (June 1989), p. 23.

54. Otto Luchterhandt, "Staat und Kirche in Russland und in der UDSSR, 1887–1987," in *Tausend Jahre Russische Orthodoxe Kirche*, Wolfgang Kasack, ed. (München: Verlag Otto Sagner in Kommission, 1988), p. 119.

55. Philip Walters, "How Religious Bodies Respond to Church Control," *Candle in the Wind*, pp. 117–137. The classification is based on the Furov report (see below).

56. Kuroyedov wrote a number of books and pamphlets, one of which was published also in English. *Church and Religion in the USSR* (Moscow: Novosti Press Agency, 1977). This pamphlet is a

tendentious apologia for Soviet policies maintaining absolute freedom for the performance of all rites.

57. Sawatsky, *Soviet Evangelicals*, p. 148.

58. The author experienced refusal of an offered small donation in U. S. dollars by a dissident, because he felt that the authorities might claim that this was proof that financing came from the CIA or some other Western interests who are initiating and guiding such effort.

59. Sawatsky, *Soviet Evangelicals*, p. 147. See also Luchterhandt, *Die Religionsgesetzebung der Sowietunion*, pp. 121–123 for the text of the law translated into German.

60. Sawatsky, *Soviet Evangelicals*, p. 147. See also Bessmertniy-Anzimirov. *op. cit.*, p. 23.

61. Sawatsky, *Soviet Evangelicals*, p. 149.

62. To be distinguished from the officially registered All-Union Council of Evangelical Christians Baptists.

63. Thus, for instance, an Armenian Apostolic Church prelate and Georgian Orthodox priest, stated at a meeting in West Chester, PA moderated by this author, that there were no prisoners of faith in the Soviet Union but only those who harassed believers were jailed!

64. One of the earliest dissidents was Anatoli Levitin (pen name A. Krasnov) who started writing *samizdats* in 1958. The Evangelical Christians-Baptists *Initsiativniki* became active in 1961. The most active among them were Georgiy Vins and Gennadi Kriuchkov. In 1965 the Orthodox dissenters emerged in large numbers. Among them the best known are Gleb Yakunin, Nikolai Eshliman, Vladimir Osipov, Alexander Solzhenitsyn, Dimitri Dudko, Yevgeniy Barabanov, Lev Regelson, Alexander Ogorodnikov, Vladimir Poresh, Mikhail Meerson-Aksyonov, Zoya Krakhmalnikova, and Vladimir Rusak. The best and most detailed account of the Russian Orthodox dissidents is Ellis, *op. cit.*, pp. 287–454. In the 1970s dissidents appeared among the Lithuanian Catholics, Nijole Sadunaite, Viktoras Petkus, Balys Gajauskas, Antanas Seskevicius, Juozas Zdebskis, and Prosperas Bubnys. The best known Jewish dissidents were Andrei Sinyavsky, Ida Nudel, Anatoly Shcharansky, Alexander Ginzburg, and Vladimir Slepak. Andrei Sakharov and his wife Ellena Bonner and others were examples of secular dissidents who were willing to embrace the cause of religious dissidents in their human rights campaigns.

65. Sawatsky, *Soviet Evangelicals*, p. 151.

66. For a comprehensive treatment of the Human Rights issue

in Eastern Europe see Georg Brunner, et al., *Before Reforms: Human Rights in the Warsaw Pact States. 1971–1988.* (London: Hurst & Co., 1990. For the legal aspects on religion see especially Otto Luchterhandt, "Freedom of Religion," pp. 281–353. The chapter deals with all Warsaw Pact states.

67. The pressures on the Soviet Union for abuse of religious freedom go back to the Bolshevik Revolution. One particularly interesting case was the pressure during the term of President Franklin D. Roosevelt in 1933 on Soviet Foreign Minister Maxim Litvinov, a non-practicing Jew, to use his influence to diminish persecutions of all religions. See Alan Geyer, *Christianity & the Superpowers* (Nashville: Abingdon Press and Washington: The Churches' Center for Theology and Public Policy, 1990), pp. 97–98.

68. Mojzes, "On a Roller Coaster. Religion and *Perestroika*," *OPREE*, Vol. VIII, No. 5 (October 1988), p. 27.

69. See the perceptive analyses of Tamás Földesi, "Meditation on Human Rights" and "Thoughts About Freedom of Conscience and Religion" in *OPREE*, Vol. IX, Nos. 1 and 5 respectively.

70. Conversations of the author with Alexander Ogorodnikov, Andrey Mironov, Gleb Yakunin, Zoya Krakhmalnikova, Andrey and Irina Krivov, Viktor Popkov, Andrey Bessmertniy-Anzimirov, and Nijole Sadunaite in March and/or October 1988 in Moscow. For a more detailed narrative of the impressions of the March 1988 encounter see Mojzes, "On a Roller Coaster. Religion and *Perestroika*," pp. 22–39. In the account below a composite picture is drawn rather than individual testimonies of dissidents. The account also draws on the following *samizdats* (typescripts) received during the author's trips to the Soviet Union: *Byulyteny Hristianskoy Obshchestvenosti*, (Moscow) No. 5 (January 1988), No. 6 (February 1988), No. 7 (April 1988), No. 8 (August 1988), *Doveriye* (Moscow), No. 2 (February 1988), Initsiativnaya gruppa "Za dukhovnoye i biologicheskoye spaseniye naroda," (July 23, 1988), various appeals and open letters and materials from the Ukraine and Lithuania. The materials are so detailed and extensive that their careful examination exceeds the parameters of this study. An interesting theoretical issue, but one that cannot be answered here, is how much prominence to give the dissident accounts. Symptomatic of the problem is that two prominent scholars who read the draft of this chapter made opposite assessment. One thought there was insufficient dependence upon the dissident sources and the other that there was too much.

71. Many writers have analyzed this, including J. A. Hebly, *Striid om vrede*. ('s-Gravenhage, Holland: Uitgeverij Bokencentrum B.V. 1983) also "The Churches of Eastern Europe and the World Council of Churches," *OPREE*, Vol. VI, No. 3 (1986), as well as Michael Bourdeaux, Jane Ellis, and Eugen Voss.

72. Excerpts of the secret reports of the Council for Religious Affairs for 1968. 1970, and 1974 signed by deputy-chairman Vasiliy G. Furov have found their way to Keston College, England, and have subsequently been reprinted in *Religion in Communist Dominated Areas*, Vol. 19, Nos. 9–11 (1980), pp. 149–161, Vol 20, Nos. 1–3, pp. 4–13 and 4–6, pp. 52–57. They were disseminated widely in the West as they give clear insight into the methods of depriving the churches of their freedom. One may find discussion of the report in Shirley and Rowe, eds., *Candle in the Wind: Religion in the Soviet Union*, pp. 80–81, 84, 118–129. 271, 273. Furov co-authored with N. A. Kolesnik a booklet, *Grazhdanstvennost' i religioznaya vyera* (Kiev: Izdatelystvo politicheskoy literaturi Ukraini, 1985) in which the 'bourgeois' notions of religious liberty are scoffed at as vacuous and deceptive. This was part of the orchestrated response to Western criticisms of the denial of religious liberty in the East.

73. John Anderson, "Soviet Religious Policy Under Brezhnev and After," *RCL*, Vol. 11, No. 1 (Spring 1983), pp. 23–29.

74. Keston College estimate. See Sawatsky, "*Glasnost, Perestroika*, and Religion," *OPREE*, Vol. IX, No. 2 (April 1989), p. 9.

75. Interview with Rev. Uldis Savaljevs, Lutheran pastor from Latvia in West Chester, PA, December 29, 1989.

76. E.g. V.A. Kuroyedov, *Religiya i tserkov v Sovyetskom Obshchestve* [Religion and Church in Soviet Society], (Moscow: Izdatelystvo politicheskoy Literatury, 1984), 255 pp.

77. Walter Sawatsky, "*Glasnost, Perestroika*, and Religion," pp. 13–14.

78. An interview of Konstantin Kharchev by Alexander Nezhniy, in *Ogonyok* (Moscow), No. 30 (December 1988) was translated and printed as "Law and Conscience," in *Liberty* (July–August 1989), pp. 2–6. In it he detailed the many ways in which the Council on Religious Affairs manipulated the churches. The vice president of the Council, Karry-Bek Moldobyev, who was sent to substitute for Kharchev at a conference on promoting religious tolerance held in Warsaw, May 14–18, 1989, was a bitter disappointment. His long speech reflected a pre-"new thinking" approach, a unfeeling bureaucratic approach at

its worst.

79. John Anderson, "Legislative and Administrative Control of Religious Bodies," p. 69.

80. "Razreshena peresylka predmetov rel'igioznovo kul'ta, a tak zhe biblii, korana, i.t.d." [Permission to send object of religious worship and also of Bibles, Qur'ans, etc.], *Izvestiya* (Moscow), No. 85 (evening edition), March 25, 1988, p. 6. Apparently up to three copies of Holy Scriptures could be imported by a person at one time.

81. David Remnick, "Priests hold service in the Kremlin," *Philadelphia Inquirer*, October 14, 1989.

82. For a list of achievements of *perestroika* and demands for increased liberties see "Resolutions of the Second Christian Seminar of the Independent Christian Community," (September 30–October 2, 1988, *OPREE*, Vol. IX, No. 3 (June 1989), pp. 43–47.

83. As late as June 1989 *Literaturnaya Gazeta* stated that there was still abuse of psychiatric hospitalization for healthy non-conformists. See "Journal: Soviet psychiatrists still in control," *The Philadelphia Inquirer* (June 30, 1989), p. 15–B. "67 Religious Prisoners in the USSR," *Keston News Service*, No. 345 (March 8, 1990), p. 1. According to *G2W* there were 59 religious prisoners of conscience in 1990, "Über 200 politische Gefangene," *G2W*, Vol. 18, No. 2 (1990), p. 9.

84. Conversation with Prof. Mikhail Krutogolov, Professor of Constitutional Law at the Soviet Academy of Sciences in Moscow, held at Philadelphia, early April 1989. Krutogolov recounted his own personal experience of being sent to distant parts of the USSR on propaganda missions encountering misunderstanding and traditionalism among the local Communist Party leaders.

85. Walter Sawatsky, "*Glasnost, Perestroika,* and Religion," *OPREE*, Vol. IX, No. 2 (April 1989), pp. 12 and 9.

86. William C. Fletcher, *Soviet Believers: The Religious Sector of the Population* (Lawrence, KS: The Regents Press of Kansas, 1981) was an early American scholar to make extensive use of Soviet sociological scholarship on religion. Despite his awareness of the limitations of those sources he gave it more credence than deserved.

87. William C. Fletcher, *Soviet Believers* used data from Soviet sociologists to establish the degree of religiosity in the country. He maintained that Soviet sociologists started using statistical data which could be used in extrapolating the real degree of religiosity over-against church membership figures. But most of the sources which he

cites were still convinced that it is the duty of the scholar to convert believers to atheism. One need only to examine writings such as A. A. Kuznetsov, *Istina protiv zabluzhdeniy i fal'sifikatsiy* [Truth against errors and falsifications], G. G. Ershov, *Smysl zhiznyi i social'noye besmertiye cheloveka* [The meaning of life and the social immortality of the human being], V. N. Nikitin, *Klub voinstvuyushchih ateistov* [The club of militant atheists], V. K. Gerasimenko, *Budni ateistov* [Alert atheists] and a collection *Argumenty* [Arguments] to see that the scholarly authors saw themselves as propagandists against religion as a task no different than a physician is a propagandists against disease.

88. Viktor I. Garadzha, "Soviet Atheism—The Great Debate," originally in *Nauka i religiya*, No. 1 (1989), pp. 2–5 as translated along with responses to Garadzha in *RCL*, Vol. 18, No. 1 (Spring 1988), pp. 72–89.

89. Bohdan R. Bociurkiw, "Soviet Religious Policy and the Status of Judaism in the USSR," *Bulletin on Soviet and East European Jewish Affairs*, No. 6 (December, 1970), pp. 12–18.

90. Ibid., pp. 14–15.

91. Ibid., p. 18.

92. Cf. L. Hirszowicz, "Jewish Culture in the USSR," *Soviet Jewish Affairs*, Vol. 7, No. 2 (1977), pp. 11–13; Yaacov Ro'i, "Jewish Religious Life in the USSR Some Impressions," *Soviet Jewish Affairs*, Vol. 10, No. 2 (1980), pp. 39–50 and Nora Levin, "The Complex Reality of Soviet Anti-Semitism," *Genesis* 2 (Summer 1987), pp. 13–18. For an article from an semi-official Soviet view which diminishes the problems, see the translation into English from *Nauka i religiya*, Iosif Moiseyevich Shapiro, "Judaism in the USSR," *Soviet Jewish Affairs*, Vol. 11, No. 2 (1981), pp. 62–64.

93. *The Jews in the Soviet Union Since 1919: Paradox of Survival*, (New York and London: New York University Press, 1988).

94. Ibid., pp. 471.

95. Ibid., p. 275.

96. Ibid., pp. 312–224.

97. Ibid., p. 345.

98. Conversation of the author with an old Jewish man at the Central Moscow synagogue in March 1988 who informed him that his brother was shot by Soviet soldiers in 1946. With very evident emotions he said that he still cries daily about this loss and repeated several times "I hate the Russians!"

99. Levin, *The Jews in the Soviet Union Since 1914*, p. 483, quoting Svetlana Alliluyeva [Stalin's daughter], *Only One Year* (New York: Harper & Row, 1969), p. 168.

100. Levin, *op. cit.*, p. 508.

101. Ibid., p. 589.

102. Ibid., p. 589.

103. Ibid., p. 652.

104. Ibid., p. 631.

105. Perhaps the worst was Trofim Kichko's *Judaism Without Embellishment* (Ukrainian Academy of Sciences), which stirred international outrage even among some western Communist parties. Kichko penned several similar books and has not been censured in the USSR.

106. Ibid., p. 622.

107. During my visit to the Moscow Choral Synagogue in 1988 several members of the congregation stated that they were aware of the presence of government informers at the Sabbath prayer and even pointed out a couple of the KGB agents.

108. Otto Luchterhandt, "Die Rechtsstellung der jüdischen Minderheit," *Die Minderheiten in der Sowietunion und das Völkerrecht*, G. Brunner and A. Kagedan, eds. (Köln: Markus Verlag, 1988), pp. 99–102.

109. Also available to many Germans, Armenians, and Pentecostals.

110. Jerry Goodman, "Judaism," *Candles in the Wind*, pp. 247–250 and Jane Ellis, "The Religious Renaissance: Myth or Reality?" in ibid., pp. 266–268.

111. Howard Spier, "Soviet Anti-Semitism Unchained: The Rise of the Historical and Patriotic Association, 'Pamyat'" in *Soviet Jewry in the 1980s*, Robert O. Freedman, ed. (Durham, NC: Duke University Press, 1989), pp. 51–57.

112. Aleksandr Bessmertnyj, "Zum Tode von Vater Aleksandr," Vladimir Zelinskij, "Abschied von Vater Aleksandr," and Gleb Jakunin, "Wir sollten die Wahrheit über diesen Mord erfahren," all in *G2W*, Vol. 18, No. 10 (1990), pp. 15–18.

113. Gerald Nadler, "*Pravda* says Jews are in fear," *Philadelphia Inquirer*, July 23, 1990.

114. Christopher M. Leighton, "Suffering the Difference: Reflections on Russian Anti-Semitism," *OPREE*, Vol. XI, No. 1 (February 1991), pp. 25–31. Leighton provided one of the most perceptive

analyses on the painful dilemma that anti-Semitism provides for the Russian Orthodox Church. Rev. Leonid Kishkovsky, president of the National Council of Churches in the USA who has intimate knowledge of the ROC in the USSR also identified anti-Semitism as a problem in the ROC, but thought that in 1990 it should not be exaggerated beyond what it is really at the moment though there is ground for concern and anxiety.

115. Quoted in ibid., p. 29.

116. Leon Trotsky, "Their Morals and Ours," in George Novak, ed., *Their Morals and Ours*, 4th edition (New York: Pathfinders Press, 1986), pp. 13f.

117. Kosta Čavoški, "Revolucionarni Makijavelizam" *Filozofske Studije* XV (Belgrade), Vol. 14 (1983), p. 111.

118. Ibid., p. 112.

119. According to an interview of Alexander Solzhenitzyn by *Time*, (July 24, 1989),pp. 56–60, translated "Solženjicin: Ja sam rodoljub," *Duga* (Belgrade), No. 403, (August 1989), p. 62.

120. Yuriy Borov, "S pištoljem u ruci," [With a Gun in Hand] *Večernje novine* (Belgrade), January 30, 1991, p. 31.

121. In an unpublished paper the author drew a parallel between the Communist Party hierarchy and that of the Roman Catholic Church. There is evidence that the Communists, for all their dislike of Roman Catholicism admired it for its efficient centralized order in the pre-Vatican II times.

122. Nikola Milošević, "Socijalna psihologija Staljinizma," *Filozofske Studije XV* (Belgrade), Vol. 14 (1983), p. 181.

123. Pedro Ramet, "Hypotheses on the Nationalities Factor in Soviet Religious Policy," *OPREE*, Vol. V, No. 2 (April, 1985), pp. 34–51. As of late 1990 Pedro Ramet changed name to Sabrina P. Ramet.

124. Ibid., pp. 35–36.

125. It should be noted that many Communists lost their lives in the Soviet Union during Stalin's purges. But what is less well known is that the long arm of Stalin reached far outside the Soviet Union and that many Communists were assassinated by their own colleagues on orders from Moscow even during World War II and later. Also a number of Communist leaders suddenly died in the Soviet Union during 'medical treatment.'

126. Ramet, "Gorbachev's Reforms and Religion," in *Candle in the Wind*, pp. 279–295.

127. Richard N. Ostling, *Time*, October 15, 1990, pp. 70–71.

128. Cardinal Vincent Sladkevicius delivered a rousing speech at the theological school in Kaunas to 250 priests on August 3, 1988, in which he openly surveyed the repressions of religious people in the past. His address was entitled, "O polozhenyii i zadachakh tserkvi v usloviyakh segodishnyikh peremen," [On the Status and Tasks of the Church under the Conditions of Contemporary Change]. Russian language typescript given to the author by Sr. Nijole Sadunaite in Moscow, October 1988.

129. Roman Solchanyk and Ivan Hvat, "The Catholic Church in the Soviet Union," in *Catholicism and Politics in Communist Societies*, Pedro Ramet, ed. (Durham and London: Duke University Press, 1990), pp. 85–87. "Verfassungsänderung für Religionsfreiheit," *G2W*, Vol. 18, No. 1 (1990), p. 9. Ivonne Luven, "Litauen im Herbst 1990-ein Schwebezustand," *G2W*, Vol. 18, No. 12 (1990), pp. 18.

130. "Minimale Beschränkungen," *G2W*, Vol 18, No. 3 (1990), p. 9.

131. "Diakonie-Seminar in Riga," *G2W*, Vol. 18, No. 3, p. 9. "Statliche Kirchenkontrolle aufgehoben," *G2W*, Vol. 18, No. 12 (1990), p. 7.

132. "Die Kirche Armeniens vor neuen Aufgaben," *G2W*, Vol. 18, No. 2, p. 10 and "Autokephalie der georgischen Kirche," *G2W*, Vol. 18, No. 5 (1990), p. 10.

133. "Erzbischof für unabhängiges Litauen," *G2W*, Vol. 18, No. 10 (1990), p. 11.

134. For a secular analysis of the tragedy of the Russian Orthodox Church and its leaders see Aleksandr Nezhniy, "Das Schicksal von Patriarch Pimen," *G2W*, Vol. 18, No. 9 (1990), pp. 23–27 as translated from *Ogonyok*. A thoughtful assessment that the strategy of survival was the best under the circumstances was made by the brilliant Archpriest Vitaliy Borovoy. See "Überlebenstrategie war richtig," *G2W*, Vol. 18, No. 3 (1990). p. 7. Gleb Yakunin and participants of a "Church and Perestroika" conference in Moscow, on the other hand, sharply criticized the ROK leadership, "Harsche Kritik an der ROK," *G2W*, Vol. 18, No. 2 (1990), pp. 8–9.

135. "Harsche Kritik an der ROK," *op. cit.*, pp. 8–9.

136. Richard Ostling, "Victory for a Dark Horse," *Time*, (June 18, 1990), and Richard Owen, "Russian welcome for reformist Patriarch," *The Times* (London), June 9, 1990.

137. "Religionsgesetz für Russland," *G2W*, Vol. 18, No.10 (1990), pp. 10–11.

138. Alan Cooperman, "Soviet congress passes law to end religious repression," *Philadelphia Inquirer*, (September 27, 1990) indicates adoption on September 26 or 27. The text of the translated law from *Izvestiya* (Moscow) of October 9, 1990, states October 1, 1990, as the date of adoption by the Supreme Soviet. This is confirmed in "Religionsgesetz verabschiedet," *G2W*, Vol 1 8, No. 11 (1990), pp. 8–9.

139. *Bulletin of Christian Opinion* [English language digest of the *Bvulyteny Hristianskoy Obshchesvenosti*, No. II, (1989), esp. pp. 30-47. Also conversations with Alexander Ogorodnikov and Gleb Yakunin. They and other disidents complained that the work was going on in secrecy with seemingly no religious people consulted in the process and that if the high church authorities were to be consulted they may not make strong demands but settle for what is offered to them.

140. John Anderson, "Further Drafts of New Law on Freedom of Conscience," in Shirley and Rowe, *Candle in the Wind*, pp. 297–300.

141. "The text of the Law Concerning Freedom of Conscience and Religious Organization," based on an English translation by unidentified translator [probably Prof. Paul Steeves of Stetson University] based on the Russian text published in *Izvestiya*, October 9, 1990. All information on the law in this book stems from the above source.

142. Luchterhandt, "Neuere Entwicklungen der Religionsgesetzgebung in Osteuropa," *Zeitschrift für evangelisches Kirchenrecht*, Vol. 35, No. 3 (September 1990), p. 302. Luchterhandt's comment deals with the draft of the law which was later promulgated into law.

143. Lecture by Rev. Leonid Kishkovsky, president of the National Council of Churches of Christ in the USA at the CAREE Annual Meeting, Stony Point, NY, October 6, 1990.

144. *Bulletin of the Christian Community*, Vol. II (1989), pp. 34–35, according to Fr. Alexi Scobey.

145. The data vary widely. Metropolitan Filaret of Minsk in a lecture at San Francisco, CA on August 18, 1990, provided the figure of 4,000. Viktor Popkov, a dissident provides the figure of nearly 3,000 by the end of October 1989, in "Bericht über die Bischofssynode in Moskau," *G2W*, Vol. 18, No. 1 (1990). Leonid Kishkovsky offered

the figure of 4,000–6,000 since 1988. The reason for the uncertainty is that with many buildings it is neither clear to which church they may be returned or whether in fact the local authorities will finally relent and return the buildings that are in good repair.

146. Solchanyk and Hvat, *op. cit.*, pp. 89–90.

147. Jane Ellis, "Hierarchs and Dissidents: Conflict over the Future of the Russian Orthodox Church," *RCL*, Vol. 18, No. 4, pp. 307–318.

148. "Überwachung christlicher Gruppen," *G2W*, Vol. 18, No. 2 (1990), p. 10.

149. For instance, the North American Mennonites set up ambitious mission and assistance both to the Soviet Mennonites and the general population, opening offices in Moscow and a publishing endeavor in Karaganda. "Mennonite Central Committee Canada, Council of USSR Ministries Newsletter #11," (January 1991). The World Council of Churches has also arranged relief work.

150. "Kongress über Altgläubige," *G2W*, Vol. 18, No. 11 (1990), p. 10.

151. Lecture by Kishkovsky, *op. cit.*

152. Ecumenical Press Service, October 1–10, 1990, and Keston News Service, No. 363 (November 22, 1990), p. 13.

153. Anatol Lieven, "Russia and the Patriarch," *The Tablet* (London), August 4, 1990, p. 976. Keston News Service, No. 363 (November 22, 1990), p. 14.

154. Kishkovsky, *op. cit.*

155. Quoted in Lieve, *op. cit.*, p. 977.

156. Gerd Stricker, "Divide et impera? Die Russische Orthodoxe Kirche am End des Jahres 1990," *G2W*, Vol. 18, No. 12 (1990), pp. 11–15.

157. Lieven, *op. cit.*, p. 977 and Kishkovsky, *op. cit.*

158. Dimitry V. Pospielovsky, "Religions Themes in the Soviet Press in 1989," *RCL*, Vol 18, No. 4 (Winter 1990), p. 341. According to Oleg Kalugin, a former KGB major,the secret police is still operating in the churches in the Soviet Union, in "Policije u promjenama," *Danas*, No. 436 (April 26, 1990), p. 53.

160. Cf. John B. Dunlop, "The Russian Orthodox Church and Nationalism After 1988," *RCL*, Vol. 18, No. 4, pp. 292–306.

Notes to Chapter 5

1. Bernhard Tönnes, "Religious Persecution in Albania," *RCL*, Vol. 10, No. 3 (Winter 1982), pp. 242–243. Also Odils Daniel, "Nationality and Religion in Albania," *Albanian Catholic Bulletin*, Vol. XI (1990), pp. 90–96.

2. Peter Prifti, "Albania–Towards an Atheist Society," in *Religion and Atheism in the USSR and Eastern Europe*, Bohdan R. Bociurkiw and John W. Strong, eds. (Toronto: University of Toronto Press, 1975), p. 397.

3. Tönnes, *op. cit.*, p. 244.

4. Prifti, *op. cit.*, p. 396.

5. Gjon Sinishta, "Grave Violation of Religious Rights in Albania," *OPREE*, Vol. III, No. 5 (July, 1983), p. 5.

6. Heinz Gstrein, "Albania: Religion on the Upswing," *OPREE*, Vol. VI, No. 1 (February, 1986), p. 35, transl. by Norman Robinson from *Orientierung* (Zürich), Vol. 21, No. 48 (November 15, 1984), pp. 231–233.

7. Tönnes, *op. cit.*, p. 251.

8. Erich Weingärtner, ed., *Church Within Socialism* (Rome: IDOC International, 1976), p. 243. This book provides articles 14 to 40 of the Constitution of 1946 as revised and amended in 1950, 1953, 1954, 1955, 1958, 1960, and 1963.

9. Vladimir Dedijer, *The Battle Stalin Lost*, (New York: Grosset & Dunlap, 1970), p. 31, (where Dedijer described Stalin's suggestion to Djilas asking him to convey the message that Yugoslavia "should swallow up Albania.") and 33 and 101 (where Stalin's pressures on Bulgarians and Yugoslavs to form the Balkan Federation are described). Similar testimony can be found in Milovan Djilas, *Conversations with Stalin* (New York: Harcourt, Brace and Jovanovich, 1962).

10. Sinishta, *op. cit.*, p. 5. Most of the Albanian Communist leaders were of Muslim background.

11. Ibid., p. 249. Tönnes notes the inconsistency between the government's prohibition that Catholics maintain contact with their headquarters, while the Bektashis, whose international headquarters are located in Albania's capital, Tirana, were urged to maintain contacts with Bektashis living abroad. I presume that the hope was to

gain influence abroad especially if the Bektashi leadership could be infiltrated and controlled.

12. Quoted in Tönnes. *op. cit.*, p. 249.

13. *Drita* [Light], Tirana, February 15, 1976, as quoted by Tönnes. *op. cit.*, p. 249.

14. Weingärtner, *op. cit.*, p. 242.

15. Gjon Sinishta, *op. cit.*, pp. 6–7 lists some of the casualties. A longer list of martyrs including casualties until 1954, which are listed in the text, is provided by *Albanian Catholic Bulletin*, Vol. VI (1985), p. 48.

16. *Albanian Catholic Bulletin*, Vol. VI, p. 48.

17. Ibid., pp. 48–49.

18. *Religion in Communist Lands*, Vol. 9, Nos. 1–2 (Spring 1981), p. 66.

19. Sinishta. *op. cit.*, pp. 9–16, provides the most comprehensive account of the events of these three periods.

20. Tönnes, *op. cit.*, p. 253.

21. Denis R. Janz, "Enver Hoxha's Unfulfilled Dream," *Albanian Catholic Bulletin*, Vol. XI, pp. 104–106.

22. This was reflected in his book *With Stalin: Memoirs* (Tirana: 1971). Second edition in 1981. Professor Finngeir Hiorth of Oslo, Norway, reports having read the book and finding no reference on religion except a phrase attributed to Stalin upon which Hoxha chose not to comment. Letter of Hiorth to Mojzes, Oslo, Nov. 17, 1988. See also Hiorth, "Albania: An .Atheistic State?" *OPREE*, Vol. X, No. 5 (October 1990), pp. 14–21.

23. It is not entirely clear what made Hoxha so anti-religious. The answer probably lies in his own psychological make-up. Some have suggested that he saw religion as an obstacle to progress, especially of women, e.g. Janice Broun, "The Status of Christianity in Albania," *Journal of Church and State*, Vol. 28, No. 1 (Winter 1986), p. 48. Another possibility is that he, like the other Communist leaders who formed the circle of ex-Sunnis had been raised in the spirit of an intolerant Islam. Hoxha later showed some sympathies toward the Iranian fundamentalist Islamic revolution and the Afghanistani *mujahedins*, which is inconsistent with the former and consistent with the latter interpretation. It is, however, most likely that he acted in all these cases entirely on political power grounds, accepting and rejecting depending on what suited the taking and holding of power according to Stalinist tenets.

24. Tönnes, *op. cit.*, p. 250. Weingärtner, *op. cit.*, cites the literary journal *Nendori* (September, 1967) as providing the above figure.

25. Prifti, *op. cit.*, p. 400.

26. Tönnes, *op. cit.*, p. 250.

27. Ibid.

28. A good survey of Albania's attitude toward human rights and religious freedoms as part of international law can be found in Otto Luchterhandt, "Die Religionsfreiheit in Albanien und Jugoslawien," photocopied paper, pp. 1–6.

29. Barbara A. Frey and Carl E.S. Söderbergh, "Violations of the Right to Freedom of Religion in Albania: A Report by the Minnesota Lawyers International Human Rights Committee," May 1989, photocopied manuscript. A somewhat later version of this report was published in *Human Rights in the People's Socialist Republic of Albania* (Minneapolis,MN: Minnesota Lawyers International Human Rights Committee, 1990), pp. 75–99. Another version published under Barbara Frey, "Violations of Freedom of Religion in Albania," *OPREE*, Vol. IX, No. 6 (November, 1989). The first draft of this chapter was finished prior to the publishing of the above report. The two pieces were written without our being aware of each other's concurrent work. Both were presented as papers at the Warsaw (Poland) Conference, "Building Understanding and Respect between People of Diverse Religions or Beliefs," May 14–18, 1989. The two papers were very similar, pointing that the data in this case are so clear and unambiguous that it is hard to arrive at any different conclusion than reached by the respective researchers.

30. See David Tracy, "Traces of Religious Customs in Atheistic Albania," Dan Wooding, "Imagine Albania," and Gegase Belfield, "Super-Patriotism: A Shallow Substitute for Religion," *Albanian Catholic Bulletin*, Vol. VII & VIII (1986–1987), pp. 33, 67–69, and 70–72 respectively. Also Wolfgang Stoppel, "Is There Movement in Albania's Religious Policy?" *Albanian Catholic Bulletin*, Vol. XI, pp. 85–86.

31. Gstrein, *op. cit.*, pp. 29–37.

32. "Priesterschicksale," *Glaube in der 2. Welt*, Vol. 17, No. 2 (1989), p. 4.

33. Hulusi Hako, "Toward the Creation of a Totally Atheistic Society," *Albanian Catholic Bulletin*, Vol. VII & VIII, p. 24. Translated from *Rruga e Partise* [Road of the Party] (Tirana), Vol;. XXXIII

(March 1986), pp. 61–73.

34. Ibid, p. 29.

35. Ibid.

36. Ibid., p. 31.

37. "Priester wegen Taufe in Schauprozess verurteilt," *G2W*, Vol. 10, No. 2 (February 1980), p. 33.

38. "Kirchefeste werden weiterhin begangen," *G2W*, Vol. 11. No. 5, (1983), p. 4.

39. Quoted from *Zerii i Rinise* (July 29, 1987) in Janice Broun, *Conscience and Captivity*, p. 42.

40. "Bekenntnis zum Atheismus," *G2W*, Vol. 17, No. 12 (1989), p. 2.

41. *Zëri i Popullit*, June 27, 1989 as quoted by Stoppel, *op. cit.*, p. 86.

42. "Mutter Teresa in Albanien," *G2W*, Vol. 17, No. 11 (1989), p. 2.

43. Though one need to be cautious in regard to such orchestrated visits the very fact that they took place while in the past they had been prohibited is a sign of relaxation.

44. "Gewissensgefangene geleugnet," *G2W*, Vol. 18, No. 4 (1990), p. 2.

45. "Albania Removes Ban on 'Religious Propaganda' Yet Public Worship Still Forbidden," *Albanian Catholic Bulletin*, Vol. XI, p. 117.

46. Denis R. Janz, "Rooting Out Religion: The Albanian Experiment," *The Christian Century* (July 25–August 1, 1990), p. 702 sees no clear reason for the relaxation.

47. The National Council of Churches of Christ in the USA sent an appeal to the government of Albania on religious freedom but never received even an acknowledgement.

48. Stoppel, *op. cit.*, pp. 83–85.

49. "Priests who Survived Religious Holocaust in Albania," *Albanian Catholic Bulletin*, Vol. XI, p. 116. Interview with Sharon Spiro, Rosemont, PA, November 16, 1990, of her visit to Albania in August 1990 indicates not the slightest evidence of religion in a formerly Orthodox village of Vodica.

50. "Religious Freedom Proposed in Albania," *San Francisco Chronicle*, November 9, 1990.

51. Hiorth letter to Mojzes, Oslo, November 17, 1988, maintains that economic progress has been made but starting with past poverty, with some Soviet and Chinese assistance.

52. Those who know tend to ascribe her work not to her religious motivation but to her nationality, according to Hiorth's letter to Mojzes, November 17, 1988.

Notes to Chapter 6

1. Spas T. Raikin, "Nationalism and the Bulgarian Orthodox Church," in *Religion and Nationalism in Soviet and Eastern European Politics*, Pedro Ramet, ed. (Durham, NC: Duke Press Policy Studies, 1984), p. 187. In addition to Bulgarian Orthodox there are Muslims of Turkish and Slavic origin, and small communities of Roman Catholics, Eastern Rite Catholics, Armenian Apostolic Churches, and small Protestant denominations (Baptists, Congregationalists, Methodists, Pentecostalists, Seventh-Day Adventists, Jehovah's Witnesses, and Brethren-Darbyists) as well as a few Jews.

2. Paul Mojzes, "A History of the Congregational and Methodist Churches in Bulgaria and Yugoslavia," (doctoral dissertation, Boston University, 1964), pp. 69–70.

3. Marin Pundeff, "Churches and Religious Communities," in *Bulgarien*, Klaus-Detlev Grothusen, ed. (Göttingen: Vandenhoeck & Ruprecht, 1990), p. 549.

4. Ibid., p. 557.

5. Tobias, *Communist-Christian Encounter*, p. 355.

6. Also called the Committee for the Affairs of the Bulgarian Orthodox Church and the Religious Cults under the leadership of a chairman with the rank of deputy foreign minister.

7. Raikin, *op. cit.*, p. 191.

8. Tobias, *op. cit.*, p. 366.

9. The Bulgarian People's Agrarian Union was also part of the Fatherland Front with the Communist Party but retained no independence.

10. Tobias, *op. cit.*, p. 367.

11. Pundeff, "Churches and Religious Communities," p. 554.

12. E.g. the public humiliation, torture, and trial of the famous Communist, Traicho Kostov.

13. The data were carefully researched and presented in this author's doctoral dissertation from which larger segments are reproduced here, often verbatim.

14. A copy of the English translation of the "Regulations" is on file at the United Methodist Board of Global Ministries (formerly Foreign Missions) Library in New York.

15. A translation of "The Resolution" is on file at UMBGMLib, from which the author made a photostatic copy kept in his file.

16. A quote from the translation of "The Resolution."

17. Ibid. The Resolution was signed by pastors Yanko Ivanov, Tsvetan Tsvetanov, Nikola Pulev, Vasil Marinov, Spas Miloshev, Simeon Popov, Ilia Iliev, Martin Glouharov, Zdravko Bezlov, Georgi Nalbanatski, Tsvetan Litov, and Alexander Georgiev.

18. Robert Tobias, *Communist-Christian Encounter in Europe* (Indianapolis, Indiana; School of Religion Press, 1956), p. 355.

19. George N. Shuster, *Religion Behind the Iron Curtain* (New York: The MacMillan Company, 1954), p. 220.

20. Paul Neff Garber, *The Methodists of Continental Europe* (New York: Board of Missions and Church Extension, The Methodist Church, 1949), p. 118.

21. Tobias, *op. cit.*, p. 355.

22. Ibid., p. 356.

23. Ibid.

24. *The Trial of the Fifteen Protestant Pastors-Spies* (Sofia: Press Department, Ministry of Foreign Affairs, 1949), p. 5.

25. Vasileff, "Po protsesa na Evangelskite pastiri v Bulgariya," [Concerning the Trial of Protestant Pastors in Bulgaria] (1949?, typewritten), p. 5. The identity of the author is uncertain, with no first name provided but only a handwritten identification by Lloyd Black who provided the paper to the author.

26. Ibid., also Tobias, *op. cit.*, p. 357.

27. Vasileff, *op. cit.*, p. 5.

28. Ibid.

29. J. B. Barron and H. M. Waddams, *Communism and the Churches: A Documentation* (London: SCM Press, Ltd., 1950), pp. 36f.

30. Tobias, *op. cit.*, p. 357.

31. Popordanov, *op. cit.*, p. 2.

32. Ibid.

33. According to Spas Raikin during the dictatorial regimes of 1935–1944 they allowed leftists to use their pulpits as they allowed after September 1944 prominent opposition leaders of impecable democratic credintials to do the same.

34. Ibid., p. 4.

35. Ibid.

36. Ibid.

37. Tobias, *op. cit.*, p. 358.

38. James H. Cockburn, *Religious Freedom in Eastern Europe* (Richmond, VA: John Knox Press, 1953), p. 106.

39. Barron and Waddams, *op. cit.*, pp. 37–38.

40. Tobias, *op. cit.*, p. 371.

41. Ibid., p. 377.

42. Barron and Waddams, *op. cit.*, pp. 39–43 and Tobias. *op. cit.*, pp. 371–376 give the entire law in English taken from which the description of the legal provisions is taken.

43. Quoted in Tobias, *op. cit.*, p. 87.

44. Tobias, *op. cit.*, p. 358.

45. Milovan Djilas, *Conversations with Stalin* (New York: Harcourt, Brace & World, Inc., 1962).

46. Vasileff, *op. cit.*, p. 6.

47. Ibid. Also Haralan Popov, unpublished manuscript without a title about the trial written in Bulgarian longhand. He was one of the accused pastors of the Pentecostal churches in Burgas and Sofia, and was imprisoned for over thireeen years. After his release in 1961 he succeeded in leaving Bulgaria and moved to Sweden.

The first account in English was provided in Paul Mojzes' doctoral dissertation, *A History of the Congregationalist and Methodist Churches in Bulgaria and Yugoslavia* based on the handwritten notes mailed by Haralan Popov upon his release. Popov's account was subsequently published as Haralan Popoff, *I Was a Communist Prisoner* (Grand Rapids, MI: Zondervan Publishing House, 1966). A similar account was Haralan Popov, *Tortured for His Faith* (Grand Rapids, MI: Zondervan Publishing House, 1970). Both books also provide an account of the subsequent prison, i.e. labor camp sentence and activities upon release from prison. Mitko Mateev also provided his account of the events in M. Matheeff, *Document of Darkness* (St. Catherines, Ontario, 1980).

48. The chief defendants were the heads of the four denominations, Vasil Ziapkov (Congregational), Nikola Mihailov (Baptist), Yanko Ivanov (Methodist), and Georgi Chernev (Pentecostal). The other accused were the Methodists Zdravko Bezlov, and Aleksandr Zahariev, the Congregationalists Lambri Mishkov, the Baptist Zahari Raichov, Ivan Stankulov, Georgi Vasev, and Mitko Mateev, and the Pentecostals Haralan and Ladin Popov, Angel Dinev, and Yoncho Drianov.

49. No indictment against Mateev is intended here because the

author is convinced that the methods used to break a person were so effective that nearly no one could have resisted them.

50. The general description of the psychological process, which agrees in general with the views of the Western observers and is corroborated with the statements of Haralan Popov is from Vasileff, *op. cit.*, pp. 21–27.

51. Ibid., p. 22.

52. Ibid., p. 24.

53. For a government view of the trials see *Subversive Activities of the Evangelical Pastors in Bulgaria: Document* (Sofia Press Department, Ministry of Foreign Affairs, 1949) and *The Trial of the Fifteen Protestant Pastors—Spies* (Sofia Press Department, Ministry of Foreign Affairs, 1949). Above material: *The Trial*, p. x.

54. Robert L. Wolff, *The Balkans in Our Times* (Cambridge: Harvard University Press, 1956), p. 564. Also Beeson, *op. cit.*, p. 293 and Pundeff, "Churches and Religious Communities," p. 558.

55. Spas Raikin, "The Bulgarian Orthodox Church," *Eastern Christianity and Politics in the Twentieth Century*, Pedro Ramet, ed. (Durham, NC: Duke University Press, 1988), p. 171.

56. At that time the Bulgarian Orthodox Church was not yet a patriarchate but an exarchate, hence Metropolitan Stefan was the head of the Church.

57. Spas T. Raikin, "The Communists and the Bulgarian Orthodox Church, 1944–48: The Rise and Fall of Exarch Stefan," *RCL*, Vol. 12, No. 3 (Winter 1984), pp. 281–292.

58. Ibid., pp. 171–172.

59. Letter to author by Spas Raikin, November 12, 1990. Note the similarity of the nationalization of the Kievsko-Pecherskaya Lavra in the Soviet Union.

60. Pundeff, "Churches and Religious Communities," p. 558.

61. The radical severing of connections with church bodies outside the country lead to such absurdities as the pastor of the Sofia Methodist Church becoming a self-proclaimed bishop of the Methodist Church in Bulgaria which is a radical departure from world-wide Methodist procedures.

62. "Verbot von Religionsunterrich an Jugendliche unter 16 Jahren," *G2W*, Vol. 10, No. 10 (1982), pp. 335–336.

63. Raikin, *op. cit.*, p. 20.

64. Ibid., p. 201.

65. Marin Pundeff, "Church-State Relations in Bulgaria," *Religion and Atheism in the USSR and Eastern Europe*, p. 342.

66. Raikin, "The Bulgarian Orthodox Church," p. 181.

67. Pundeff, "Church-State Relations in Bulgaria," p. 340.

68. In 1950 the Bulgarian authorities unilaterally placed a large number of Bulgarian Turks into cattle trains and moved them to the border. The Turkish authorities did not want to accept them and the trains were on the border for days until Turkey finally relented and accepted these involuntary emigrants. See Wolff, *op. cit.*, pp. 477–479. Spas Raikin contests Wolff's interpretation and maintains that the Turks fled voluntarily due to the policy of collectivization in Bulgaria.

69. Janice Broun, *Conscience and Captivity*, pp. 57–61.

70. "Turkish Muslims in Bulgaria," *Religion in Communist Lands*, Vol. 15, No. 2, (Summer 1987), pp. 209–212.

71. "Neue bulgarische Religionspolitik?" *G2W*, Vol. 13, No. 6 (1985), p. 4.

72. "Vertreibung der Türken aus Bulgarien," *Kirche in der 2. Welt*, Vol. 17, No. 9 (1989), pp. 3–4. Also "Kirche, Muttersprache und Volksgruppen," *G2W*, Vol. 14, Nos. 7–8 (1986), pp. 26–27.

73. The story of two Turks who finally escaped to Yugoslavia on their way to Turkey is vividly described by Srdja Trifković, "Turci u Bugarskoj: Ljudi koji ne postoje," *Duga* (Belgrade), No. 403 (August 5–18, 1989), pp. 45–47.

74. "Bulgarian Slavs continue protest," *Philadelphia Inquirer*, December 28(?), 1989.

75. "Accord in Bulgaria seeks to reduce ethnic tension," *Philadelphia Inquirer*, January 13, 1990.

76. Perhaps the reason why Bulgaria was the only nation to jam Vatican Radio. Keston News Service, No. 319 (February 16, 1989), p. 17.

77. "Neue bulgarische Religionspolitik?", pp. 3-4.

78. The Bulgarian Adventist Church was legally recognized in April 1988.

79. See for instance Keston News Service Nos. 267 (Jan. 22, 1987), p. 11; 269 (Feb. 19, 1987), pp. 20–21; 272 (Apr. 2, 1987), p. 13; 291 (Jan. 7, 1988), p. 291; 314 (Dec. 1, 1988), pp. 13–14; 323 (Apr. 13, 1989), p. 17; 324 (Apr. 27, 1989), p. 17; and 330 (July 20, 1989), p. 9. One interesting case was the overt government attempt to impose Rev. Pavel Ivanov upon the Congregational Church in

Sofia over the congregation's choice of Rev. Christo Kulichev that lead to the latter's exile from Sofia. See "Gewalt anwendung bei der Amtseinsetzung eines reformierten Pastors," *G2W*, Vol. 13, No. 3 (1985), p. 4. Also "Bedränge Pfingstgemeinden," *G2W*, Vol. 15, No. 5 (1987), p. 3.

80. Ibid., p. 4.

81. *Keston News Service*, No. 335 (October 5, 1989), p. 7.

82. Robert Hoare, "Bulgaria," *RCL*, Vol. 18, No. 2 (Summer 1990), p. 174.

83. Ibid., p. 175.

84. "Orthodoxer Priester verhafted," *G2W*, Vol. 17, No. 9 (1989), p. 3. Also Hoare, *op. cit.*, p. 177.

85. " Synod für Status quo," *G2W*, Vol. 17, Nos.7/8, pp. 3–4.

86. "Protestmarsch der Orthodoxen," *G2W*, Vol. 18, No. 1 (1990), p. 3.

87. Mark Elliott, "A New Day for the Church in Eastern Europe," *Center Line* (Wheaton, IL), Vol. 1 3, No. 2 (Spring 1990), p. 2. Also Hoare, *op. cit.*, p. 177.

88. Hoare, *op. cit.*, pp. 177–178.

89. *Keston News Service*, No. 341 (Jan. ", 1990), p. 11. Yet KNS No. 343 (Feb. 8, 1990), p. 9 reports Bulgarian ethnic Muslim demonstrations in the Yakoruda area due to continued attempts by local Communist Party leaders to deny their rights.

90. Letter of Stefcho Ivanov to Paul Mojzes, Sofia, August 4, 1990.

91. "Bishop Recognized," *The United Methodist Reporter* August 10, 1990.

92. "Legalizirani' redovnici," *Veritas*, Vol. 29, No. 5 (1990), p. 27.

93. "The renamed Communist Party leading in Bulgaria's elections," *Philadelphia Inquirer*, June 11, 1990.

94. The Protestants of Bulgaria reported that the Orthodox Church is putting pressure on the government to prevent the passage of new religious laws that would guarantee equality and freedom to all religious communities. See "East Europeans Concerned About the Role of the Majority Churches," *European Bapist Press Service* 02/90, p. 3.

Notes to Chapter 7

1. Jan Milič Lochman, *Christ and Prometheus?* (Geneva: WCC Publications, 1988), pp. 1–6.

2. Rudolf Bohren, "Abriss der tschechischen Kirchengeschichte," *Glaube in der 2. Welt*, Vol. 18, No. 2 (1990), p. 20. Also Williston Walker, *A History of the Christian Church* (Revised by Cyril Richardson, Wilhelm Pauck and Robert Handy) (New York: Charles Scribner's Sons, 1959), p. 392. Pedro Ramet, *Cross and Commissar* (Bloomington and Indianapolis: Indiana University Press, 1987), p. 74.

4. Bohren, *op. cit.*, p. 21 .

5. August A. Skodaček, *Lutherans in Slovakia* (Pittsburgh, PA: Slavia Printing Co, 1982), p. 210.

6. Jan Ligus, "Historical and Philosophical Aspects for Understanding the Church's Situation in Eastern Europe Immediately After WW II," The Couillard Lecture, Moravian Theological Seminary, 1989 (manuscript), p. 2. For a more extensive analysis of efforts toward unity and toleration among the Protestants and between Catholics and Protestants see *Czech Ecumenical Fellowship* (Prague: Ecumenical Council of Churches in the Czech Socialist Republic, 1981) and a slightly more elaborate German version, *Tschechischer Ökumenismus* published by the same publisher in 1977.

7. Skodaček, *op. cit.*, p. 211.

8. Interview with Dr. Jan Ligus, professor of theology of the Jan Hus Theologjcal Faculty in Prague, in Rosemont, PA, October 1989.

9. For excerpts on the text of the Constitution of February 29, 1920, see Ludvik Nemec, *Church and State in Czechoslovakia* (New York: Vantage Press, Inc., 1955), pp. 132–133.

10. Ibid., pp. 75–76.

11. Lochman, *op. cit.*, p. 1 4.

12. Khruschev's memoirs point out that immediately after the Communist take-over of Czechoslovakia Antonin Novotny on a trip to visit Stalin offered him the full incorporation of his country into the USSR, which Stalin, surprisingly refused. See *Time* (October 1, 1990).

13. It is estimated that 27,000 people were tried in show trials for "crimes against the state" with more death penalties carried out

than in similar processes in Hungary, Bulgaria, Romania, and Poland, according to Dorothea Neumärker, *Josef L. Hromádka: Theologie und Politik im Kontext der Zeitgeschehens* (München, Mainz: Kaiser, Grünewald, 1974), p. 126.

14. As noted in chapter 1, Secularistic Absolutism is much more similar to the Ecclesiastic Absolutism (Type A) model.

15. Karel Kaplan, *The Communist Party in Power: A Profile of Party Politics in Czechoslovakia*, edited and trans. by Fred Eidlin (Boulder, CO and London: Westview Press, 1987), *passim.* Hereafter abbreviated as *CPP.*

16. Fred Eidlin, "Introduction" in ibid., p. 4.

17. Interview with Jan Ligus.

18. Josef Hromádka, "Church-State Relationships in a Changing Society," *OPREE*, Vol. X, No. 7 (December 1990), p. 9.

19. Robert Tobias, *Communist-Christian Encounter in Eastern Europe*, p. 493.

20. "The Church and State in Czechoslovakia from 1948 to 1956," Translated from Czech by Julia Joannou, Part I, *Religion in Communist Lands*, Vol. 14, No. 1 (Spring 1986), pp. 59–72. Part II in Vol. 14, No. 2 (Summer 1986), pp. 180–193, and Part III in Vol. 14, No. 3 (Winter 1986), pp. 273–282. Kaplan restricts his study to the conflict between the Roman Catholic Church and the Communist government/party and is one of the most detailed and documented studies of that relationship. He is an historian who worked in the ideological department of the Czechoslovak Communist Party from 1960 to 1964 and again from 1968 to 1970 where he had access to archives not available to other researchers. He was dismissed twice for political reasons .

21. "*Modus Moriendi* of the Catholic Church in Czechoslovakia," *RCL*, Vol. 10, No. 1 (Spring 1982), pp. 23–39.

22. Kaplan, "Church and State in Czechoslovakia," Part I, *RCL*, Vol. 14, No. 1, pp. 60–61.

23. Kaplan, *op. cit.*, pp. 60–61.

24. Quoted in Kaplan, "Church and State in Czechoslovakia," Part I, *RCL*, Vol. 4, No. 1 , p. 68.

25. See relevant texts excerpted in Tobias, *op. cit.*, p. 515.

26. Peter A. Toma and Milan Reban, "Church-State Schism in Czechoslovakia," in Bociurkiw and Strong, eds, *Religion and Atheism in the USSR and Eastern Europe*, p. 279.

27. Ibid., p. 518.

28. Ibid., p. 520.

29. Ibid., pp. 517–518,

30. Kaplan, *CPP*, pp. 61–62.

31. Ibid.

32. Hruza's successor, Janku was perceived as a more liberal man. Naturally since the "velvet revolution" of 1989 when the Rev. Josef Hromádka, the synodal head of the Evangelical Church of the Czech Brethren became Deputy Prime Minister in charge of culture, education, and church affairs Janku was dismissed and the office ceased to be a means of control of the churches.

33. In Slovakia alone thirty Catholic publications were banned, all Catholic publishing houses expropriated, and not a single Catholic book published from 1948 to 1988 according to Ján C. Korec, "Der Kirche sind die Hände gebunden," *G2W*, Vol. 16, Nos. 7–8, pp. 28, 33.

34. Helen Cameron, "Seventy Years of the Church of the Czech Brethren, 1918–88), *RCL*, Vol 17, No. 3 (Autumn 1989), p. 232.

35. Individuals would be sometimes physically barred from attending specific meetings. If a professor of the Comenius Theological faculty, for example, became distrusted by the State Office, he or she would not even be permitted to visit the offices of the Christian Peace Conference, located in the same building with the faculty offices. (From a conversation with Prof. Milan Opočensky in Prague in the middle 1980s.)

36. Korec, *op. cit.*

37. For a detailed description of Catholic church-state relations see Nemec, *op. cit.*

38. Kaplan, "Church and State in Czechoslovakia," Part II, *RCL,* Vol. 14, No. 2, p. 180.

39. Nemec, *op. cit.*, pp. 376–377.

40. Ibid., pp. 377–378.

41. Rabas, "The Roman Catholic Church in Czechoslovakia," *OPREE*, Vol II, No. 6 (September 1982), p. 8.

42. The Forced Labor Camp Act of 1948 was incorporated into the Penal Code of July 12, 1950. Section 36(1) provides that a person who has not ceased to be hostile to the new people's democratic order after serving their prison sentence is to be placed into a forced labor camp. Over seventy such camps were created most linked to mines, particularly uranium mines, and large construction sites. Nemec, *op. cit.*, p. 393.

43. Nemec, *op. cit.*, p. 399.

44. "Gedenkgottesdienst im Stift," *Glaube in der 2. Welt*, Vol. 18, No. 4 (1990), p. 10.

45. Korec, *op. cit.*, p. 29.

45. On the trials of clergy see Kaplan, "Church and State in Czechoslovakia," Part III, *RCL*, Vol. 14, No. 3, pp. 275–278.

47. Korec, *op. cit.*, p. 29.

48. "Repressive Measures Against the Roman Catholic Church," *OPREE*, Vol. 8, No. 3 (April 1983), pp. 12–14.

49. Andrew Skalicky and Alexandra Moravec, "John Huss, the Catholic Church and Ecumenism," *OPREE*, Vol X, No. 4 (July 1990), pp. 44–49. It may be a significant ecumenical breakthrough that Pope John Paul II during his visit to Czechoslavakia in 1990 stated that John Huss may be rehabilitated and proclaimed a saint.

50. Andrew Sorokowski, "Ukrainian Catholics and Orthodox in Czechoslovakia," *RCL*, Vol. 15, No. 1 (Spring 1987), pp. 54–68.

51. Korec, *op. cit.*, pp. 29, 31.

52. Tobias, *op. cit.*, p. 493.

53. This Josef Hromádka is to be distinguished from his name-sake nephew who rose to prominence in the late 1980s. For easier recognition the elder Hromádka's middle name (Lukl) initial will be used.

54. For two recent interpretations of the role of Josef L. Hromádka see Charles West, "Josef Hromádka and the Witness of the Church in East and West Today," and Károly Tóth, "The Heritage of J. L. Hromádka for the Prophetic Ministry of the Church in East and West, Today and Tomorrow," *OPREE*, Vol. X, No. 2 (March 1990), pp. 13–25 and 26–33 respectively.

55. Cf. Joseph L. Hromádka, *Theology Between Yesterday and Tomorrow* (Philadelphia: Westminister Press, 1957), pp. 60–87. See also Neumärker, *op. cit.*, esp. pp. 123–136.

56. Cameron, *op. cit.*, pp. 231–237.

57. Ingo Roer, *Christian Peace Conference* (Prague: Christian Peace Conference, 1974) and Günther Wirth, *A History of the Christian Peace Conference*. Transl. from German by Rachel Campling (Prague: Christian Peace Conference, 1989).

58. For that reason in 1972 Rev. Miloš Rejchrt urged the Union of Clergy to seek withdrawal of the Evangelical Church of the Czech Brethren Church from the membership of the CPC, a move that was supported by a vote of 80–2. See Cameron, *op. cit.*, p. 235.

59. It is not our task here to analyze the mechanics of the governmental influence in the CPC. The U. S. State department regarded the CPC as a "Communist front organization" but their analysis of the work of the CPC is deeply biased and inadequate. The linkage was far more complex and nuanced than the conservative critique of the CPC suggests.

60. Many observers of Western participation in the CPC were hostile in their assessments. A milder negative criticism is Kent R. Hill, *The Puzzle of the Soviet Church* (Portland, OR: Multnomah Press and Washington, DC: Institute on Religion and Democracy, 1989), pp. 167–169 and 178–179.

61. Author's own impressions during his first visit to Prague in the summer of 1967.

62. Jakub Trojan, "Churches in the Gentle Revolution in Czechoslovakia," *OPREE*, Vol. X, No. 5 (October 1990), p. 1.

63. Toma and Reban, *op. cit.*, p. 282.

64. Beeson, *op. cit.*, p. 193.

65. Rabas, *op. cit.* p. 14.

66. Korec, *op. cit.*, p. 31.

67. Ibid.

68. Mojzes, *Christian-Marxist Dialogue in Eastern Europe*, pp. 121–124.

69. Ludek Pachman, "A New 'Prague Spring': The Problem and the Task," *Kontinent 1* (Garden City, NY: Anchor Books, 1976), p. 45.

70. Ibid., p. 46.

71. Ibid., pp. 46–47.

72. "Repressive Measures Against the Roman Catholic Church," *OPREE*, Vol. III, No. 3 (April, 1983), pp. 12–14.

73. Rabas, *op. cit.*, p. 17.

74. Tomsky, *op.cit.*, p. 27.

75. Cameron, *op. cit,*. p. 236.

76. Jan Šimša, "Vater Kardinal," *Glaube in der 2. Welt*, Vol. 1 8, No. 2 (1990), p. 26.

77. Tomsky, *op. cit.*, p. 31.

78. Toma and Reban, *op. cit.*, p. 287.

79. Yet government representatives continued to explicitly predict the liquidation of religion as did Tomáš Trávníček of the National Front at a meeting with clergy in Olomouc in 1975, according to Korec, *op. cit.*, p. 32.

80. *RCDA*, Nos. 1–3 (1977), p. 5.

81. Ibid. The document was signed by Milan Balabán, Svatopluk Korašek, Alfred Kocáb, Jan Šimsa, Jakub Trojan, Miloš Rejchrt, and Josef Zverina.

82. Ibid., pp. 10–11.

83. Cameron, *op. cit.*, p. 238.

84. Ibid., p. 240.

85. Ibid., p. 240. A letter to the Synodical Council by 26 ECCB members of February 2, 1989, published in *RCL,* Vol. 17, No. 3 (Autumn 1989), pp. 244–246.

86. Albert Rasker, "Protestantism in Czechoslovakia," *OPREE*, Vol. III, No. 4 (May, 1983), p. 10.

87. Ibid., p. 13.

88. Josef Hromádka in conversation with the author at Rosemont College, October 3, 1990, stated that none of his children had been allowed to pursue studies of their choice. Professions that entailed dealing with a large segment of the public were out of reach for Christians.

89. Juerg Tschachili, "Begegnung mit einer tapferen und klugen Kirche," *HEKS* (Zurich), No. 191 (January-February, 1987), p. 4.

90. Alexander Tomsky, "*Spektrum*: A Journal from the Czech Cultural Hinterland," *RCL*, Vol. 8, No. 3 (Autumn 1980), p. 180.

91. Korec, *op. cit.*, pp. 26–35.

92. "Die Kirche in den Augen des Staates," *G2W*, Vol. 15, No. 11 (1987), pp. 19–20.

93. Tomsky, *op. cit.*, p. 38.

94. Cameron, *op. cit.*, p. 242.

95. An examination of the *GW2* "Rundschau" section that provides monthly news from all Eastern European countries shows both the degree of repression and the discontent that is in marked contrast to that of Hungary, Poland, East Germany, and Yugoslavia. Romania would probably parallel Czechoslovakia in the repression but in Romania there was no visible dissident community and therefore the conflicts between the authorities and the clergy were not recorded and in any case were different in nature.

96. "5000 politische Häftlingen," *G2W*, Vol. 15, No. 10 (1987), p. 13.

97. "Kritik an ÖRK und LWB," *G2W*, Vol. 17, No. 12 (1989), p. 10.

98. The Constitution of 1978:

Article 16 requires that the entire cultural policy, including education be done in the spirit of scientific Marxism-Leninism.

Article 20 states that all citizens have the same rights and duties.

Article 24 requires that the entire school system be organized along the scientific worldview.

Article 32 states that Freedom of Conscience is guaranteed. Everyone is permitted to follow or not follow a religious confession and to engage in religious activities as long as it does not violate a law.

From *Die Religionsfreiheit in Osteuropa*, pp. 217–218.

99. "Petition von Gläubigen,"" *G2W*, Vol. 16, No. 2, (1988), p. 10.

100. "Anforderungen and die neue Verfassung," *G2W*, Vol. 18, No. 2 (1990), p. 32.

101. Ibid.

102. Alexander Tomsky replies to Stephen Tunnicliffe, *RCL*, Vol. 14, No. 1 (1986), p. 80.

103. "Grosswallfahrten in der Slowakei," *G2W*, Vol. 15, No. 9 (1987), pp. 18–19.

104. Ibid., p. 19.

105. "The Secret Church in Czechoslovakia," *RCL*, Vol. 10, No. 1 (Spring 1982), pp. 40–42.

106. "Zu unrecht Verfolgte," *G2W*, Vol. 17, No. 2 (1989), p. 12.

107. Interview with Jan Ligus.

108. Trojan, "Churches in the Gentle Revolution in Czechoslovakia," p. 1.

109. Trojan, "Zwischen Sintflut und Regenbogen," *G2W*, Vol. 18, No. 6 (1990), pp. 21–22.

110. Jan Milič Lochman, "Wie ein nie versiegender Bach," *Glaube in der 2. Welt*, Vol. 18, No. 2 (1990), pp. 15–18 and "The Will to Walk Upright: The Prague Autumn 1989," *OPREE*, Vol. 10, No. 3 (June 1990), pp. 41–44.

111. Not to be confused with the late Prof. Josef L. Hromádka, his uncle. He resigned from the office of Synodal President shortly after a visit to the U. S. in November 1990.

112. "Neue Regierung mit Kirchenleuten," and "Revision des StGB," *G2W*, Vol. 18, No. 1 (1990), p. 11.

113. "Anforderungen an die neue Verfassung," *G2W*, Vol. 18, No. 2 (1990), p. 32.

114. "Pro-democracy groups claim victory in Czechoslovakia," *Philadelphia Inquirer*, June 11, 1990.

115. Lochman, "The Will to Walk Upright," pp. 41–44.

116. Joseph Hromádka, "Church-State Relationships in a Changing Society," p. 11.

117. Ibid., pp. 12–18.

118. Trojan, "Churches in the Gentle Revolution in Czechoslovakia," p. 4.

Notes to Chapter 8

1. The author wishes to thank Prof. Dr. Helmut Fritzsche for help in interpreting the situation in Germany both prior to the establishment of the GDR and afterwards in a series of interviews in late September 1987 at Rosemont College, PA.

2. Tobias, *Communist-Christian Encounter in East Europe*, p. 525.

3. They abolished all organizations, except the churches.

4. They gathered secretly in homes, but were later actively persecuted. Their young men served as *Bausoldaten*, i.e. are allowed alternative service which does not include carrying arms. A branch of the Jehovah's Witnesses who separated from the U. S. Headquarters was allowed by the GDR authorities to publish a paper.

5. Richard W. Solberg, *God and Caesar in East Germany: The Conflict of Church and State in East Germany Since 1945* (New York: The Macmillan Co., 1961), p. 30.

6. The EKD church constitution was adopted in 1948 in Eisenach.

7. Tobias, *op. cit.*, p. 525.

8. Wolfgang Heyl, *Christians and Churches in the German Democratic Republic* (Berlin: Panorama DDR, n.d.), pp. 20–21.

9. Horst Dähn, *Konfrontation oder Kooperation?: Das Verhältnis von Staat und Kirche in der SBZ/DDR 1945–1980* (Opladen: Westdeutscher Verlag, 1982).

10. Sam Dahlgren, *Das Verhältnis von Staat und Kirche in der DDR während der Jahre 1949–1958* (Uppsala: CWK Gleerups Foerlag, 1972), pp. 30–37.

11. Tobias, *op. cit.*, pp. 541–542.

12. Dahlgren, *op cit.*, p. 32. It should be noted that Marxist-Leninist theory does not regard constitutions as statement of ideal

principles but as reflections of real social conditions, which need to be changed and adjusted when the social conditions have changed. That explains the frequent amending of constitutions.

13. Dahlgren provides a more complete analysis of similarities and departures from the Weimar Constitution in ibid., pp. 33–37.

14. As cited by Dähn, *op. cit.*, p. 174.

15. *The Roman Catholic Church in Berlin and in the Soviet Zone of Germany* (Berlin: Morus-Verlag, 1959), p. 57.

16. Solberg, *op. cit.*, p. 293.

17. As quoted in Dähn, *op. cit.*, p. 96. Transl. from German by P. Mojzes.

18. Ibid., p. 97.

19. *Christians and the Churches in the GDR* (Berlin: Panorama DDR, 1980), p. 56.

20. Otto Luchterhandt, "Die Religionsfreiheit im Verständnis der sozialistischen Staaten," in *Die Religionsfreiheit in Osteuropa.* Ed. by Eugen Voss (Zollikon: G2W-Verlag, 1984), p. 46.

21. *Bürgerpflicht und Christenpflicht. Grundwerte unseres gesellschaftlichen Lebens—Realität und Auftrag* [Citizen duty and Christian duty], (Berlin East: Christlich-Demokratische Union, 1987).

22. Ibid., pp. 56–57.

23. Quoted in book review of Uwe-Peter Heidingsfeld of Otto Luchterhandt's *Der verstaatlichte Mensch*, p. IX, in *Kirsche im Sozialismus*, Vol. 12 (April 1986), p. 81.

24. Otto Luchterhandt, "The Understanding of Religious Freedom in the Socialist States," *OPREE*, Vol. III, No. 3 (April 1983), p. 24.

25. Peter Wensierski, "Theses on the Role of the Church in the GDR," *OPREE*, Vol. III, No. 4 (May 1983), p. 25. Albrecht Schoenherr, "A Contribution to the Direction of the Evangelical Church in the German Democratic Republic," *OPREE*, Vol. VII, No. 2, (April 1987), p. 21.

26. *The Evangelical Church in Berlin and the Soviet-Zone of Germany*, transl. by Patrick Lynch (Witten and Berlin: Eckart Verlag, 1959).

27. *The Roman Catholic Church in Berlin and in the Soviet Zone of Germany.* Note the unwillingness of both this and the preceding publication to regard East Germany as a state ten years after its foundation.

28. Dähn, *op. cit.*, p. 174.

29. Dahlgren, *op. cit.*, p. 101.

30. State youth initiation ceremony.

31. Arvan Gordon, "Recent Trends in the GDR *Jugendweihe:* State and Church Attitudes," *RCL*, Vol. 13, No. 2 (Summer 1985), p. 157.

32. Some regarded Mitzenheim too friendly to the government, thus appearing to break ranks with the other Protestant bishops who were more reserved toward the government but there is no evidence that he was a non-critical collaborator.

33. Martin N. Walton, "The Evangelical Church in the GDR: A Church in Socialism," *OPREE*, Vol. 4, No. 5 (October 1984), p. 5. For a careful analysis of the organization of the Federation of Evangelical Churches in the GDR see Otto Luchterhandt, "Die Neuordnung der Evangelischen Kirchen in der DDR nach dem Ausscheiden aus der EKD 1969," in *Die Rechtsstellung der Kirchen im geteilten Deutschland* (Cologne, Berlin, Bonn, and Munich: Carl Heymanns Verlag KG, 1987), pp. 91–125.

34. Solberg, *op. cit.*. p. 293.

35. Karl Barth and Johannes Hamel, *How to Serve God in a Marxist Land* (New York: Association Press, 1959), p. 82.

36. Dähn, *op. cit.*, pp. 143–144.

37. Ibid., p. 144.

38. lbid., pp. 144–145.

39. Ibid., p. 160.

40. Albrecht Schoenherr, "Ten Years On: The Church-State Discussions of 6 March 1978 in ths GDR," *Religion in Communist Lands*, Vol. 16, No. 2 (Summer 1988), p. 127.

41. Schoenherr, "A Contribution," pp. 25–34, and "Öffentlichkeitsanspruch einer Minderheit," *Kirche im Sozialismus*, Vol. 12, No. 4 (August 1986), pp. 149–152, and "Ten Years On," pp. 126–134.

42. Schoenherr, "A Contribution," p. 27.

43. "The Church in 1985 and 2000—Gathering, Openness, Sending," *OPREE*, Vol. VIII, No. 2 (May 1988), p. 30.

44. Eckehart Lorenz, "Religionsfreiheit im vertsändnis evangelischer Kirchen," *Die Religionsfreiheit in Osteuropa*, p. 22.

45. Ibid.

46. Konrad Feiereis, "Das Zusammenleben von Christen und Marxisten in der DDR," *Dossier*, p. 579.

47. John P. Burgess, "Church-State Relations in East Germany: The Church as a 'Religious' and 'Political' Force," *Journal of Church*

and State, Vol. 32, No. 1 (Winter 1990), p. 19.

48. Max Stackhouse, "The Religious Situation in the German Democratic Republic," *OPREE*, Vol I, No. 1 (February 1981), p. 3.

49. John Burgess, "The Language of Liberation: State and Church in East Germany Forty Years After the End of World War II," *OPREE*, Vol. VIII, No. 6 (1988), pp. 12–35. Burgess provides a careful comparison of the similarities and differences in the attitudes toward peace and liberation but also foreign policy of the GDR.

50. Interview with Fritzsche on September 25, 1988, at Rosemont College, PA.

51. John P. Burgess, "The Language of Liberation," p. 12.

52. In times of tension the government then issued instructions such as that the church may give performances of Bach, but not of Mozart or Haydn!

53. Marc Reuver (ed), *Human Rights: A Challenge to Theology* (Rome: CCIA & IDOC International, 1983), p. 26.

54. Ibid.

55. *The Churches Human Rights Programme for the Implementation of the Helsinki Final Act* (Geneva Conference of European Churches, 1986), Information No. 4, p. 46.

56. Roger Williamson, "East Germany. The Federation of Protestant Churches," *RCL*, Vol. 9, Nos. 1–2 (Spring 1981), p. 13.

57. "Human Rights in Eastern Europe," (Photocopied paper of the Helsinki Working Group of the Committee of the Church and International Affairs, Canadian Council of Churches, 24 January 1985), p. 5.

58. Heino Falcke, " 'Neues Denken'," *KiS*, Vol. 13, No. 2 (April 1987), p. 63.

59. Ehrhart Neubert, 'Reproduktion von Religion in der DDR-Gesellschaft, *Ausser der Reihe* (mimeographed publication of the East Berlin Theologische Studjenabteilung, April 1985), pp. 4–7.

60. Burgess, *op. cit.*, p. 24.

61. Schoenherr, "A Contribution," pp. 29 and 32.

62. "Major Church Events in the GDR (Summer 1987)," *RCL*, Vol. 15, No. 3, (Winter 1987), pp. 330–332.

63. John Burgess letter to author, Crete, Nebraska, February 19, 1989.

64. "Druck auf Christen in der DDR," *Neue Zürcher Zeitung* (Zürich), April 18, 1985.

65. "Church newspaper censored by GDR," *The Lutheran* (November 23, 1988).

66. Falcke, *op. cit.*, p. 61. Translated, "To learn from the Soviet Union is to learn how to win." into "To learn from the Soviet Union, is to learn how to think."

67. "Es muss erkennbar sein, dass die Schnecke sich bewegt," *KiS*, Vol. 18, No. 5 (October 1988), pp. 173–176.

68. Quoted in Christine Doormann, "Ein Versuch, die DDR zu verstehen," *G2W*, Vol. 16, No. 9 (September 1988), p. 11.

69. "Gespräch mit Landesbischof W. Leich," *G2W*, Vol. 16, No. 10 (October 1988), p. 3.

70. "Bundessynode in Dessau" and "Erneute Zensur," *G2W*, Vol. 16, No. 11 (November 1988), pp. 4–5.

71. Beatus Brenner, "Kurskorrektur," *Material Dienst*, Vol. 38, No. 1 (January-February 1987), pp. 16–17.

72. Reinhard Henkys, "New Perspectives for the Jewish Communities in the GDR," *OPREE*, Vol. VII, No. 3 (June 1987), pp. 23–26.

73. "Human Rights in Eastern Europe," (Photocopied paper prepared by the Helsinki Working Group of the Canadian Council of Churches, April-June 1985), p. 3.

74. John Burgess letter to author, Crete, NE, February 19, 1989.

75. Frederick Bonkovsky, "Sources of East German Revolution and German Unification," *OPREE*, Vol XI, No. 3 (May 1991), p. 26.

76. Bonkovsky, *op. cit.*, p. 35.

77. From a letter of John Burgess to the author, Crete, Nebraska, February 9, 1989.

78. E.g. Martin Nesirsky, "A new dialogue in Dresden, Leipzig," *Philadelphia Inquirer*, October 11, 1989.

79. Luchterhandt, "The Understanding," p. 23.

80. Helmut Zeddies, "Religionsfreiheit als Anspruch und Herausforderung der Kirchen," *Ökumenische Rundschau*, Vol. 35, No. 4 (October 1986), p. 398.

81. Mojzes, *Christian-Marxist Dialogue in Eastern Europe.* pp. 49–61.

82. In September and October 1989 four faculty members of that Institute toured the USA dialoguing with each other and with American partners.

83. Robert Goeckel, "The Evangelical-Lutheran Church and the East German Revolution," *OPREE*, Vol. X, No. 6, (November 1990,

p. 30.

84. The Social Democrats came in second with 22 percent and the Democratic Socialists (former SED) third with 16 percent according to *Focus on Central and Eastern Europe*, No. 20, July 20, 1990.

85. "Kirchen zur Wahl," *G2W*, Vol. 18, No. 3 (1990), p. 3.

86. "Bischof übt Kritik," *G2W*, Vol. 18, No. 3, p. 4.

87. "Neuheit Minister für Kirchenfragen," *G2W*, Vol. 18, No. 1 (1990), p. 4.

88. "De Maizière kritisiert Kirchenpolitik," *G2W*, Vol. 18, No. 2 (1990), p. 3.

89. Ehrhart Neubert, "Die Ekklesiologie des Erich Mielke: Stasi-Dokumente und kirchliche Vergangenheitsbewältigung," *Übergänge* (formerly *Kirche im Sozialismus*), Vol. 16, No. 2 (April 1990), pp. 70–75.

90. Ibid., p. 29.

91. Ehrhart Neubert, "Protestantische Aufklärung," *Übergänge*, Vol. 18, No. 4 (August 1990), p. 144.

92. Günther Krusche, "A New Learning Process has Begun: The Church in a Post-Socialist Society," *OPREE*, Vol. X, No. 6, (November 1990), p. 46.

93. "Chronik," *Übergänge*, Vol. 18, No. 4, p. 169.

94. Statement attributed to Johannes Richter of St. Thomas Lutheran Church in Leipzig in Eric Shafer, "Richter: A Witness to Grace," *The Lutheran*, July 7, 1990.

95. " 'Politische Diakonie' statt Friedensgebet?" *G2W*, Vol. 18, No. 4 (1990), p. 2.

96. Bill Yoder, "Glimpses of East German Church Events in 1990," *OPREE*, Vol. X, No. 5 (October 1990), p. 38.

97. Goeckel, *op. cit.*, p. 32.

98. Otto Luchterhandt, "Neuere Entwicklungen der Religionsgesetzgebung in Osteuropa," *Zeitchrift für evangelisches Kirchenrecht*, Vol. 35, No. 3 (September 1990), p. 287.

99. Hans Kanitz, "Freiwilligen-Kirche oder Staatskirche in der DDR?" *G2W*, Vol. 18, No. 5 (1990), p. 23.

100. The East German churches received voluntary contributions from their members but nearly 50 percent of their budget came from West German church subsidies, that were to be gradually terminated with reunification.

101. "Chronik," *Übergänge*, Vol 16, No. 3 (June 1990), 132.

102. "Jugenweihe richtet unübersehbaren Schaden an," *G2W*, Vol. 18, No. 2 (1990), p. 3. Detlef Urban, "Alter Ritus in neuem Gewand," *Übergänge*, Vol. 18, No. 3 (June 1990), pp. 87–88.

103. Goeckel, *op. cit.*, p. 37.

104. "Katholiken formieren sich," *G2W*, Vol. 18, No. 1 (1990), p. 5.

105. "Kirchliche Einheit beider Konfessionen," *G2W*, Vol. 18, No. 10 (October 1990), p. 5. Karl-Alfred Odin, "Die Einheit ist nie aufgegeben worden: Überlegungen zum Weg der Kirchen im Deutschland," *Übergänge*, Vol. 16, No. 2 (April 1990), pp. 62–65. "Weg zu Einheit," *Übergänge*, Vol. 16, No. 5 (October 1990), pp. 175–176.

106. "Wir haben uns geirrt," *G2W*, Vol. 18, No. 11 (November 1990), p. 4.

107. "Sekten getarnt im Vormarsch," *G2W*, Vol. 18, No. 11, p. 5.

108. G. Krusche, *op. cit.*, pp. 44–45.

109. Bill Yoder, "Will the Face of the German Church Change?," *OPREE*, Vol. XI, No. 1 (February 1991), p. 44.

Notes to Chapter 9

1. Today Roman Catholicism is the majority religion of Hungary with western Hungary nearly solidly Roman Catholic. Eastern Hungary has a large concentration of the Reformed churches while the Lutherans are to be found predominantly in northern Hungary.

2. Joseph Pungur, "Protestantism in Hungary," p. 1, manuscript for a projected book on Protestantism and Politics in Communist Societies, edited by S. P. Ramet (Durham, NC and London: Duke University Press, 1992),

3. Pedro Ramet, *Cross and Commissar*, p. 67.

4. "The Reformation: Our Heritage and Task," *Hungarian Church Press*, Vol. XIX, Special Number (June 1967), p. 20.

5. Joseph Pungur, "Protestantism in Hungary," unpublished paper, p. 1.

6. Robert Tobias, *Communist-Christian Encounter in Eastern Europe*, p. 428.

7. "The Reformation: Our Heritage and Task," p. 22.

8. Ibid., p. 4.

9. Leslie Laszlo, "Religion and Nationality,"in *Religion and Nationalism in Soviet and East European Politics*, Pedro Ramet, ed. (Durham, NC: Duke Press, 1984), p. 141.

10. Ibid.

11. Pungur, "Protestantism in Hungary," p. 8.

12. For a good brief account of the war years in Hungary see Hugh Seton-Watson,. *The East European Revolution* (New York: Frederick A. Praeger, Publisher, 1961), pp. 98–105.

13. "The Reformation: Our Heritage and Task," p. 25.

14. In the first election the communists received 17 percent and in the second 20 percent of the vote though the 1947 election was tainted by alleged Communist manipulation but was still comparatively free.

15. According to Tobias, *op. cit.*, p. 432 the first Soviet law passed was the re-opening of churches and the permission of worship. Radio Moscow proclaimed that the Soviets will not interfere in church life nor bother the clergy.

16. E.g. in 1945 the Roman Catholic Bishop Apor of Györ was killed by Soviets, Lutheran Bishop Turoczy was sentenced to ten years and other clergy were sentenced for alleged anti-Semitism and Nazi collaboration but most of these accusations including the Apor and Turoczy cases were pretexts. Apor was killed by Soviet troups while he was barring their way to women who sought refuge in the episcopal palace. Many of the accused were later freed.

17. Pungur, "Protestantism in Hungary," p. 14.

18. Tobias, *op. cit.*, p. 434.

19. This is not a place for an analysis or evaluation of this remarkable but controversial man, but much has been published about him including his memoirs. His books translated into English are, *Cardinal Mindszenty Speaks: Authorized White Book*, Introduction by Ákos Zombory (New York: Longmans Green, 1949); *Four Years' Struggle of the Church in Hungary*, edited by C. Hollis (London: Longmans Green and Co, '949); and *Memoirs* (New York: Macmillan Publishing Co., 1974).

20. Steven Polgár, "A Summary of the Situation of the Hungarian Catholic Church," *RCL*, Vol. 12, No. 4, (Spring 1984), p. 15

21. János Péter was the most successful of the careerists as he became Hungary's chief representative in the U.N. and later the minister of foreign affairs.

22. István Bibo, "Neue Möglichkeiten für die Reformierte Kirche in Ungarn," *G2W*, Vol. 17, No. 6 (1989), p. 16.

23. Interview with Niels Ehrenström, Boston, MA, Spring 1962.

24. J. B. Barron and H. M. Waddams, *Communists and the Churches: A Documentation* (London: SCM Press, Ltd., 1950), p. 62.

25. Péter Török, "Everything is Conditional in Hungary," *OPREE*, Vol. IX, No. 4 (July 1989), p. 37.

26. Pungur, "Protestantism in Hungary," p. 16.

27. Tobias, *op. cit.*, p. 439.

28. See Gary MacEoin, *The Communist War on Religion* (New York: The Devin-Adair Company, 1951), p. 125 and George N. Shuster, *Religion Behind the Iron Curtain* (New York: The Macmillan Co., 1954), p. 193. Pungur's analysis of this process in "Protestantism in Hungary," pp. 17–35 is particularly useful because Pungur used to work in the Department for Foreign Affairs of the Hungarian Reformed Church and had personal knowledge of some of the processes described below.

29. Interview with Ehrenström who was present at the meeting. Also Gyula Gombos, *The Lean Years: A Study of Hungarian Calvinism in Crisis* (New York: The Kossuth Foundation, 1960), p. 30ff. Gombos's book is an extraordinarily good and detailed account of the travail of the Hungarian Reformed Church in the after war period.

30. This was not implemented because subsidies continued beyond the twenty-year limit. The churches remained dependent on state subsidies and indirectly the clergy were handled as civil servants, while the government which held the purse-strings was able to exert financial pressure on the churches in order to bring them into line.

31. For a good discussion of the process area-wide see Zbigniew Brzezinski, *The Soviet Block: Unity and Conflict* Revised Edition. (New York: Frederick A. Praeger, Publisher, 1961), pp. 71–83.

32. For a complete listing of all valid laws regarding religious liberty see Otto Luchterhandt, "Freedom of Religion," in *op. cit.*, pp. 283–353.

33. Interview with Dr. Tamás Földesi, Philadelphia, October 10, 1990.

34. The reader should note the great chronological proximity of the trials of Ordas and Mindszenty, the fifteen Bulgarian Protestant pastors, trials of priests in Poland and Czechoslovakia, and the trials of Eastern Catholic bishops in Romania. It is likely that this is more than a coincidence in light of what is known about the coordination between departments of religious affairs of Eastern European

countries and the USSR.

35. Joseph Pungur, "Church-State Policy in Communist Hungary, 1948–1990," p. 8. (mimeographed paper for the IVth World Congress for Soviet and East European Studies in Harrogate, England, July 21–26, 1990.) Pungur is a professor and clergyman at University of Alberta, Edmonton, Canada.

Fear may have much to do with the statements of the Hungarian Reformed and Lutheran new leadership distancing themselves from Mindszenty, stating that the "Mindszenty case" has nothing whatsoever to do with the denial of religious liberty, which is experienced fully in Hungary, but that it is a conflict between politicized Catholicism and the state. See the text of these problematic statements in Tobias, *op. cit.*, pp. 474–476. The already imprisoned Lutheran Bishop Ordass was offered immediate release from prison if he were willing to sign a denunciation of Mindszenty, which he refused to do. Thus there were those who did the governments bidding and those who did not.

36. Ibid., p. 9. According to András Szennay, "Ringen ums Überleben," *G2W*, Vol. 18. Nos. 7–8 (1990), p. 22. 3,000 monks and 12,000 nuns were expelled from their monasteries in a single day. This number seems too high.

37. These subsidies were actually not phased out even after 1968.

38. Szennay, *op. cit.*, p. 22.

39. Tobias, *op. cit.*, p. 478.

40. Interviews with Dr. Lóránd Boleratzky in Budapest in August 1985 and Rev. Zoltán Dóka in Hévizgyörk in August 1985 and May 1988. Also conversations with Árpád Fasang in Budapest in August 1985 and Rev. György Kendeh in Budapest, May 1988.

41. For an analysis and criticism of one of these theologies see Vilmos Vajta, "Debatable Theology of Diakonia," *OPREE*, Vol. IV, No. 1 (January 1984), pp. 45–60; Vilmos Vajta, "The Hungarian Lutheran Church and the 'Theology of Diaconia,' " and responses in *RCL*, Vol. 12, No. 2 (Summer 1984), pp. 130–148. László Terray, "Was the Reality Cut Out," and the Documentation on the Zoltán Dóka case in *OPREE*, Vol. V, No. 6 (November, 1985), pp. 1–17 and the rest of the issue.

42. The author is not maintaining that popularity or lack of it determines the validity of a theology, but the willingness to subject the theology to an open forum for criticism does, and this the theologians of service did not seem to be willing to do.

43. Pungur, "Protestants in Hungary," pp. 33–34.

44. Szennay, *op. cit.*, pp. 22–23.

45. On May 25, 1990, a group of seven Roman Catholic priests wrote a strongly worded letter to their bishop Dr. Kornél Pataky, accusing him of having been too ready to comply with every order and praise the government and that he should resign after offering public apologies to priests who were persecuted and whom he threatened to punish. See, "Verzichten Sie auf Ihre Ämter, Herr Bischof," *G2W*, Vol. 18, Nos. 7–8, (1990), p. 25. Similar calls have been made by Protestant clergy.

46. Interview with Dóka in 1985 and 1988.

47. Pungur, "Protestantism in Hungary," p. 35.

48. This was a bizarre imitation of the Bulgarian public trial against the Communist Traicho Kostov in 1949!

49. He was, however, released in 1954 without a revokation of his sentence or pardon which means that technically he was a 'criminal' at the head of the Catholic Church. He was rehabilitated only in 1990.

50. Laszlo, "The Catholic Church in Hungary," pp. 159–160.

51. Polgar, *op. cit.*, p. 16.

52. Gombos, *op. cit.*, pp. 102.

53. *Facts About Hungary*, p. 253.

54. Polgar, *op. cit.*, p. 17.

55. Pungur, "Protestantism in Hungary," p. 40.

56. Mojzes visited László Pap secretly in his apartment in Budapest and interviewed him, July 17, 1967, obtaining an account of personal and collective repression.

57. Interview with Dóka.

58. Gombos, *op. cit.*, p. 109.

59. Bibo, *op. cit.*, p. 17.

60. Ibid.

61. E.g. András Vinnai, " 'Self-Criticism' in a Religious Textbook," translated in *Religion in Communist Dominated Areas*, Vol. II, No. 16 (July 1, 1963), p. 124.

62. László Rózsa, "The Converters," *Religion in Communist Dominated Areas*, Vol. II, No. 19 (August 19, 1963), p. 147.

63. Interview with Földesi, October 12, 1990, Philadelphia.

64. For detailed analysis of the agreement see "The Language of Facts" and "The Situation of the Church in Hungary in 1966" in *Church in Transition: Hungary's Catholic Church from 1945 to 1982*,

Emeric András and Julius Morel, eds. (Vienna: Hungarian Institute
for Sociology of Religion, 1983), pp. 38–49 and 59–85.

65. János Wildmann, "Hungary. From the Ruling Church to the
'Church of the People,' " *RCL*, Vol. 14, No. 2 (Summer 1986), pp.
163–164.

66. Ibid., p. 165.

67. Laszlo, "The Catholic Church in Hungary," p. 162.

68. Polgar, *op. cit.*, pp. 21–22.

69. Erich Weingärtner, ed., *Church within Socialism*, p. 133.

70. Tamás Földesi, "Thoughts About the Freedom of Conscience
and Religion," *OPREE*, Vol. IX, No. 5 (September 1989), p. 1. At
the time that was a breakthrough for a Hungarian Marxist oriented
analysis.

71. Ibid., p. 3.

72. Ibid., p. 5.

73. Ibid., p. 10.

74. Földesi, "Meditation About Human Rights," *OPREE*, Vol.
IX, No. 1 (February 1989), pp. 1–8.

75. The author had the occasion to travel from Moscow to Budapest in 1975 with the high Protestant officials and was the accidental beneficiary of the reception by government officials at the
airport to the returning churchmen (term used advisedly; there were
no church women in the delegation).

76. *Church in Transition*, pp. 47–48.

77. Ibid., pp. 54–55.

78. During an interview by Mojzes of one of the "peace priests"
in Budapest a high school teacher-translator and a non-church-goer
provided by the Hungarian Peace Council was so offended by the
blatant lies regarding the real church situation that she exclaimed
after the interview, "Now I know why my mother distrusted the peace
priests!"

79. Interview with Földesi, October 12, 1990, Philadelphia.

80. Still as late as 1975 the author met an educator in Budapest
with two children in medical school who stated that she would not
dare to go to church for her own job's sake and that of the education
of her children. Yet Budapest was reportedly more free in this way
than some smaller cities. Villagers were by and large more free about
church attendance.

81. Ibid., pp. 68–69.

82. *Church in Transition*, pp. 98–99.

83. József Lukács, "Cooperation and Dialogue," *Journal of Ecumenical Studies*, Vol. 15, No. 1 (Winter 1978), pp. 100–108.

84. Interview with Imre Miklós, head of SOCA, in Budapest summer 1975.

85. György Aczel, "The Socialist State and the Churches," *The New Hungarian Quarterly*, Vol. XVIII, No. 66 (Summer 1977), 49–62 and József Cserháti, "Open Gates, *New Hungarian Quarterly*, Vol. XVIII, No. 67 (Autumn 1977), 48–62.

86. *Church in Transition*, pp. 106–108.

87. Ibid., p. 144.

88. Ibid., pp. 187–188.

89. Ibid., p. 289.

90. Ibid., 293.

91. Ibid., p. 226.

92. George Cushing, "Protestantism in Hungary," *RCL*, Vol. 10, No. 2 (Autumn 1982), p. 127.

93. *Church in Transition*, p. 270. Also Leslie Laszlo, "The Base Community—A Challenge to the Peaceful Co-existence between Church and State in Hungary," *OPREE*, Vol. I, No. 6 (November 1981), pp. 1–9.

94. Lawrence Klippenstein, "Peace Initiatives in Eastern Europe: Conscientious Objectors in the USSR, Hungary, and the GDR," *OPREE*, Vol. V, No. 5 (October 1985), pp. 10–17. About 150 pacifists were in jail in 1986 according to Janice Broun, *Conscience and Captivity*, p. 152.

95. Broun, *op. cit.*, p. 157.

96. This was the equivaient of about a month's individual income, roughly equivalent to U. S. $700, which means that even small expenditures had to be approved.

97. *Church in Transition*, pp. 360–361.

98. Imre Miklós, "Church Policy in Hungary," *New Hungarian Quarterly*, Vol. XXIX, No. 110 (Summer 1988), p. 59. In the article Miklós enumerates the educational and social service institutions run by Catholic, Protestant, and Jewish denominations (see pp. 60–65).

99. *Church in Transition*, pp. 360–361.

100. Ibid., pp. 367–368.

101. Emmerich András, "The Hungarian Catholic Church in Tension between Loyalty and Opposition," *OPREE*, Vol. V, No. 2 (April 1985), p. 6.

102. For a helpful listing and texts of these regulations that were known see Emerich András and Julius Morel, *Hungarian Catholicism Handbook*, (Vienna: The Hungarian Institute for the Sociology of Religion, 1983), pp. 140–191. For a German text see Eugen Voss, ed., *Die Religionsfreiheit in Osteuropa* (Zollikon: G2W Verlag, 1984), pp. 241–268.

103. Károly Tóth, "The Church in Socialism," *OPREE*, Vol. V, No. 2 (April 1985), p. 29.

104. Ibid.

105. Several conversations with Rev. Frigyés Hecker, the Methodist Superindent in Budapest, e.g. in 1975 and 1988.

106. See the "Dóka Case" Documentation in *OPREE*, Vol. V, No. 6 (November 1985), pp. 18–45. Also Joseph Pungur, "The Relationship between the Hungarian State and the Hungarian Reformed Church," *OPREE*, Vol. VI, No. 1 (February 1986), pp. 3–14.

107. Cynics may point out that "blood is thicker than water," namely that this was not primarily a matter of principles but ethnic solidarity, because the Hungarian church leaders were mute or cooperative with the official line about the 1968 Czechoslovak and 1981 Polish events. Be that as it may, this critical posture helped both Hungary and Romania. In Joseph Pungur's opinion it was calculated to speak up for Hungarians in Romania. Besides really helping them the churches actually intended to save themselves by demonstrating how good Hungarian they were. By 1988 one could already sniff the winds of radical political change.

108. For a brief survey of the openings and limitations of religious liberties for Roman Catholics in the late 1980s see "U. S. Catholic Bishops' Statement on Religious Liberty in Eastern Europe and the Soviet Union," *OPREE*, Vol. IX, No. 4 (July 1989), p. 12.

110. "The Role of Religion in Our Society," *RCL*, Vol. 15, No. 3 (Winter 1987), pp. 335–339.

111. "The Religious Policy of the Hungarian Government," *RCL*, Vol. 16, No. 2 (Summer 1988), pp. 179–186.

112. Laszlo, "The Catholic Church in Hungary," p. 173. Statements by the various protagonists of the meeting between the Prime Minister and the members of the Catholic hierarchy can be found in "The Church and the Law in Hungary," *RCL*, Vol. 17, No. 1 (Spring 1989), pp. 70–81.

113. Ibid., p. 175.

114. "The Rule of Law in Hungary," *RCL*, Vol. 17, No. 2 (Summer 1989), p. 140.

115. Laszlo, "The Catholic Church in Hungary," p. 144.

116. Ibid., p. 174.

117. László Lukács, "On the Threshold of a New Era in Hungary," *OPREE*, Vol. IX, No. 4 (July 1989), pp. 30–32.

118. The number of communists dropped from 700,000 to 40,000 in the HSWP and 40,000 in the HSP. At the election the HSP drew 11 percent of the vote and was able to be one of the six parties seated in the parliament while the HSWP drew only 2.5 percent of the vote, too few to get a seat in the parliament.

119. Laszlo, "Church Responses in Eastern Europe to Gorbachev's Reforms: 'The Liberalizing Context Hungary,' " *OPREE*, Vol. X, No. 3 ((June 1990), p. 7.

120. Gyula Bárczay, "Neuer Wein in alten Schläuchen?" *G2W*, Vol. 18, Nos. 7–8 (1990), pp. 26–29.

121. Ibid., pp. 26–27.

122. The story is too complex for this setting but it suffices to say that Harmati was not among the original government-approved list of candidates and was placed as a candidate from below.

123. István Szépfalusi, "Der Weg der stillen Schritte," *G2W*, Vol. 18, No. 7–8 (1990), pp. 30–33. Whether Harmati will be able to function as a bishop in democracy is yet to be seen. When the Lutheran pastor, Rev. Gábor Roszik of Gödölö, a parliament member who was elected in a free election, spoke out against church collaborationists including Harmati, the bishop convened a church trial and accused Roszik of violating his oath as clergyman to obey his bishop and suspended him as a pastor, according to Tódor, "Vallásháború '90," *Aréna*, (October 11, 1990), p. 8. Similar problems are taking place in the Reformed Church.

124. It is the author's opinion that the will of the Lutheran Church was carried out with these elections, although Rev. Dóka continued his harsh criticism of the entire process maintaining that all of these people had been the product of acceptability to the state. This strikes me as a too black or white position.

125. The new bishops are Loránd Hegedüs, Mihály Markus, and István Mészáros.

126. "Amnestie für Géza Németh," *G2W*, Vol. 17, No. 3 (1989), p. 11; "Pfr. Dóka rehabilitiert," *G2W*, Vol. 17, No. 6 (1989), p. 14.

127. Ibid., p. 24.

128. Pungur, "Church-State Policy in Communist Hungary, 1948–1990," p. 20.

129. Péter Török, "Everything is Conditional in Hungary," *OPREE*, Vol. IX, No. 4 (July 1989), p. 35.

130. "Neues Religionsgesetz," *G2W*, Vol. 18, No. 3 (1990), p. 11. The writer points out that despite such declarations the remnants of SOCA on the local level still interfered into religious affairs in a number of localities.

131. Karl Schwarz, "Thesen zum neuen Religionsgesetz," *G2W*, Vol. 18, Nos. 7–8 (1990), pp. 34–37 from which the narrative for the survey of the law draws its information.

132. An especially thoughtful declaration is "Erklärung des Presbyteriums des Süddistriktes der ELKU [Lutheran]," *G2W*, Vol. 18, Nos. 7–8 (1990), pp. 33–34.

133. Bibo, *op. cit.*, p. 19.

Notes to Chapter 10

1. Paul Booth, "Editorial," *Religion in Communist Lands*, Vol. 15, No. 2 (Summer 1987), p. 123.

2. Vincent C. Chrypinski, "The Catholic Church in Poland, 1944–1989," in *Catholicism and Politics in Communist Societies*, Pedro Ramet, ed. (Durham, NC and London: Duke University Press, 1990), p. 117.

3. Miroslaw Korolko, "The Gem of Religious Tolerance," *Christian Life in Poland* (Warsaw), Nos. 9–10 (September-October, 1985), pp. 36–37.

4. Polish Brethren were expelled in 1658 but unlike many other countries the "sectarians" were not burned at the stake or massacred.

5. Janusz Tazbir, "Some Notes on Tolerance," *Christian Life in Poland*, Nos. 9–10 (September-October, 1985), pp. 49–51.

6. Interview with Dr. Waldemar Chrostowski, professor of Biblical exegesis and theology at the Academy of Catholic Theology, in Warsaw, June 29, 1990.

7. Interview with Dr. Krystyna Gorniak, professor of philosophy of University of Poznan, Poland, in Philadelphia, March 9, 1990.

8. Interview with Jan Zaborowski, Roman Catholic journalist, in Warsaw, June 29, 1990.

9. Interview with Zaborowski.

10. Interview with Gorniak.

11. Chrypinski, *op. cit.*, p. 118.

12. There were five Lutheran *Landeskirchen* and all declared themselves as German except the Augsburg Evangelical Church which was half-German and half-Polish.

13. The Reformed Church was mostly Polish and included some important Polish nobility but was rather small, under a million members.

14. Interview with Rev. Adam Kuczma, Methodist minister, in Warsaw, June 29, 1990. For example Methodists could not legally purchase property as a church and had to establish the Southern Trade Corp. to buy property. They were allowed to baptize but not to perform legal marriages. Grazina Sikorska explains that this lack of legal status was due to the unresolved situation of merging three segments of Poland that were for over 123 years under three different legal systems. The legal system of the previous administration continued to function for a while. Yet she admits legal and other difficulties for the Orthodox (destruction of hundreds of their churches in 1938–1939), Eastern Rite Catholics, and the Reformed Church, in Grazina Sikorska, "Poland," in Janice Broun, *Conscience and Captivity: Religion in Eastern Europe* (Washington, DC: Ethics and Public Policy Center, 1988), pp. 165–166 and 170–173.

15. Walter J. Ciszek, *With God in Russia* (New York: McGraw-Hill, 1964). Ciszek was a Polish-American Jesuit who served a parish in eastern Poland. He was imprisoned in 1939 and exiled to many different parts of the USSR and was unable to return to the U. S. until the late 1960s. Also interview with Rev. Kuczma who pointed out that the Methodist superintendent was taken to Siberia never to be seen again.

16. Thus while the established historical churches were allowed to function the Pentecostals were persecuted and the Jehovah's Witnesses were exterminated or had to go underground.

17. After World War II it was suggested that in Auschwitz (Oswiecim) alone 4 million people were killed out of whom 2.5 were Jews. A newer study drastically lowers this figure to a documented 1.1 million dead out of whom 960,000 were Jews, 70,000–75,000 Poles, 21,000 Gypsies. 15,000 Russian POWs and the rest were other nationalities. See "Polish study lowers Auschwitz death toll," *Philadelphia Inquirer*, July 18, 1990. This points out a certain conscious or unconscious underestimation of the proportion of Jewish victims and the truly genocidal nature of the Nazi extermination.

18. Waldemar Chrostowski, "The State and Prospects of the Catholic-Jewish Dialogue in Poland," *OPREE*, Vol. X, No 6, (November 1990), p. 14.

19. Many ethnic Germans prior to the outbreak of the war refused to reconcile themselves to living in a Polish state and sympathized with German aspirations to incorporate them into the Third Reich. That caused both inter-ethnic and interconfessional conflict.

20. The pre-war Communist party was dissolved by the Comintern in 1938 after Stalin summoned the entire leadership to Moscow and ordered their mass execution.

21. Chrypinski, *op. cit.*, p. 119.

22. The Constitution of 1935 was declared fascist and illegal.

23. Quoted in Ronald C. Monticone, *The Catholic Church in Communist Poland 1945-1985: Forty Years of Church-State Relations* (Boulder, CO: East European Monographs, 1986), pp. 10–11.

24. Interview with Kuczma.

25. Tobias, *op. cit.*, pp.386–390.

26. Vincent C. Chrypinski, "Church and Nationality in Post-war Poland," in *Religion and Nationalism in Soviet and East European Politics*, Pedro Ramet,ed. (Durham: Duke Press Policy Studies, 1984), pp. 131–132.

27. Due to the Vatican's reluctance to speedily establish a Polish church administration in the Western Territories the government decided not to recognize the Concordat between Poland and the Vatican of 1925 which meant that the Church lost its formal legal status, though there is some controversy on the continuation of that Concordat as reported by Otto Luchterhandt, "Freedom of Religion" in Georg Brunner, ed. *Before Reforms: Human Rights in the Warsaw Pact States, 1972-1988* (London: C. Hurst & Co., 1990), p. 297.

28. Chrypinski, "Church and Nationality in Postwar Poland," p. 127.

29. For the text of the Decree see Tobias, *op. cit.*, pp. 408–409.

30. "The Polish Roman Catholic Association 'Caritas,' " *RCL*, Vol. 7, No. 2 (Summer 1979), pp. 113–117.

31. Sikorska, *op. cit.*, pp. 178–179. The text of the Accord is on pp. 330–332 and Tobias, *op. cit.*, pp. 410–413.

32. Quoted in Monticone, *op. cit.*, pp. 20–21. Poland and Yugoslavia are the only socialist countries which placed the prohibition of the abuse of religion in the constitution; the others placed these provisions into their criminal laws. Poland is the only Eastern Eu-

ropean country not to limit parental rights in regard to the child's religious upbringing.

33. Sikorska, *op. cit.*, p. 180.

34. Interview with Kuczma.

35. Ibid. Kuczma reports that during an encounter with officials of the Soviet Department for Religious Affairs during a visit to Moscow in 1986 they knew practically everything about him.

36. Interview with Chrostowski.

37. Szymon Chodak, "People and the Church versus the State: The Case of the Roman Catholic Church in Poland," *OPREE*, Vol. II, No. 7 (November 1982), p. 32.

38. Sikorska, *op. cit.*, p. 180.

39. Mojzes, *Christian-Marxist Dialogue in Eastern Europe*, pp. 73–80.

40. Sikorska, *op. cit.*, pp. 181–182.

41. Interview with Kuczma.

42. Monticone, *op. cit.*, pp. 39–45.

43. Grazina Sikorska, "The Life-Light Movement in Poland," *RCL*, Vol. 11, No. 1 (Spring 1983), pp. 49–54. The evangelistic thrust of this movement is described in Paul Keim, "Light-Life: Oases of Renewal," *OPREE*, Vol. III, No. 7 (November 1983), pp. 14–21.

44. Quoted in *RCL*, Vol. 11, No. 1 (Spring 1983), p. 59.

45. Interview with Chrostowski.

46. Monticone, *op. cit.*, p. 51.

47. Luchterhandt, *op. cit.*, p. 309.

48. Interview with Kuczma.

49. Sikorska, *Poland*, p. 186.

50. Quoted in Grazina Sikorska, "Cardinal Wyszynski: A Portrait," *RCL*, Vol. 9, Nos. 3–4 (Autumn 1981), p. 95. The two paragraphs are from two different sermons, the first delivered April 14, 1975, and the second May 9, 1971.

51. Ibid., p. 97.

52. "Poland Dialogue between Church and State?" *RCL*, Vol. 7, No. 4 (Winter 1979), pp. 255–236.

53. Chrypinski's comment "that the election of a Polish pope, while decisively tipping the scale in the church's favor, had no visible impact on the basically adverse state-church relations" (Chrypinski, *op. cit.*, p. 121) seems too pessimistic a conclusion especially in light of his observation which follows immediately in which he states the correlation between the state's policy toward the church with the

popular support of the government. After the election of the pope the little support that the government had seemed to dissipate.

54. For a Marxist evaluation see e.g. Janusz Kuczynski, "To Elevate the World The Potential of John Paul II's Pontificate," in Janusz Kuczynski, *Christian-Marxist Dialogue in Poland* (Warsaw: Interprsss Publishers, 1979), pp. 9–31.

55. Interview with Chrostowski.

56. A view also shared by Monticone, *op. cit.*, p. 87.

57. Quoted in Alexander Tomsky, "John Paul II in Poland: Pilgrim of the Holy Spirit," *RLC*, Vol. 7, No. 3 (Autumn 1979), p. 164.

58. Reported in Monticone, *op. cit.*, p. 119.

59. Chodak, *op. cit.*, p. 29.

60. Sikorska, *op. cit.*, p. 189.

61. "Developments in the Polish Churches During 1981," *RCL*, Vol. 10, No. 1 (Spring 1982), pp. 84.

62. Jonathan Luxmoore, "The Polish Church under Martial Law," *RCL*, Vol. 1 5, No. 2 (Summer 1987), p. 129.

63. Ibid., p. 138.

64. Monticone, *op. cit.*, pp. 134–143.

65. Chrypinski, "Church and Nationality in Post-War Poland," p. 134.

66. Interview with Chrostowski.

67. Irena Korba, "Father Jerzy Popiełuszko," *RCL*, Vol. 13, No. 1 (Spring 1985), pp. 89–90.

68. Two were sentenced to twenty–five years in prison and the other two to fifteen and fourteen years. Monticone, *op. cit.*, p. 194. For a more detailed account of the trial see Grazina Sikorska, " 'Justice seen to be done'—the trial of Fr Jerzy Popieluszko," *RCL*, Vol. 13, No. 2 (Summer 1985), pp. 1–24.

69. Ibid., p. 129.

70. Interview with Chrostowski.

71. Sikorska, *Poland*, p. 194.

72. Monticone, *op. cit.*, p. 199. The claim was made on September 11, 1984.

73. Sikorska, *Poland*, p. 196

74. The author's own observation during a visit to Warsaw, January 1986.

75. Grazina Sikorska, "To Kneel Only Before God: Father Jerzy Popiełuszko," *RCL*, Vol. 12, No. 2 (Summer 1984), pp. 152–153.

76. Franciszek Blachnicki, "A Theology of Liberation—In the Spirit," *RCL*, Vol. 12, No. 2 (Summer 1984), pp. 158– 162.

77. Author's own observation during a visit to Warsaw, May 1989.

78. Quoted in Garteh Davies, "Conscientious Objection and the Freedom and Peace Movement in Poland," *RCL*, Vol. 16, No. 1 (Spring 1988), p. 9.

79. Bogdan Szajkowski, "New Law for the Church in Poland," *RCL*, Vol. 17, No. 3 (Autumn 1989), pp. 196–208. The discussion of the law that follows is based on this source.

80. For example Joseph Marcus, *The Social and Political History of the Jews in Poland. 1919–1939* (Berlin: Mouton Publishers, 1983); Isaac Lewin, *The Jewish Community in Poland: Historical Essays* (New York: Philosophical Library, Inc., 1985); Władysław Bartoszewski and Zofia Lewin, eds., *Righteous Among Nations: How Poles Helped Jews, 1939–1945* (London: Earlscourt Publications, 1969); Nechama Tec, *When Light Pierced Darkness: Christian Rescue of Jews in Nazi-Occupied Poland* (New York: Oxford University Press, 1985) and Celia S. Heller, *On the Edge of Destruction: Jews in Poland Between the Two World Wars* (New York: Columbia University Press, 1977) as well as a large number of articles.

81. Bob Donnorummo, "Bourbon and Vodka: A Comparison of the Southern-Black and Polish-Jewish Questions," *OPREE*, Vol. VII, No. 4 (1987), p. 4.

82. Interview with Gorniak.

83. Jan Zaborowski, "Polish Jews: Memory and Heritage," *OPREE*, Vol. VII, No. 4 (1977), p. 21. Zaborowski believes that the issue has more political ramifications as well as the question of interparty power-struggles than Jewish-Polish implications.

84. Interview with Kuczma.

85. Donnorummo, *op. cit.*, p. 7. Donnorummo points out the eeriness of "an anti-Semitism without Jews" for most Poles have no direct contact with any Jew.

86. Rudy Rubin, "Poles blame Jews who don't exist," *Philadelphia Inquirer*, July 27, 1990.

87. Zeev Ben-Shlomo, "Anniversary of the Warsaw Ghetto Uprising," *RCL*, Vol. 16, No. 3 (Autumn 1968), p. 256.

88. Lukasz Hirszowicz, "Judaism in Poland," *RCL*, Vol. 15, No. 1 (Spring 1987), p. 22.

89. Ibid., p. 26.

90. Waldemar Chrostowski, "Controversy Around the Auschwitz Convent," *OPREE*, Vol. 10, No. 3 (June 1990), pp. 15–29.

91. "Baubeginn in Auschwitz," *G2W*, Vol. 18, No. 4 (1990), p. 4.

92. Waldemar Chrostowski, "The State and Prospects of the Catholic-Jewish Dialogue in Poland," *OPREE*, Vol. X, No. 6, (November 1990), pp. 14–27.

93. Some of these are impressions from conversations during a June 1990 visit to Warsaw.

94. Interview with Gorniak.

95. Interview with Chrostowski.

96. Interview with Zaborowski.

97. "Kirche weniger populär," *G2W*, Vol. 18, No. 6 (1990), p. 6.

98. "Kirchenabteilung auflöst," *G2W*, Vol. 17, No. 9 (1989), p. 7.

99. "Diplomatische Beziehungen normalisiert," *G2W*, Vol 17, No. 9 (1989), p. 7. and Tomasz Mianowicz, "Das 'Polnische Modell'," *G2W*, Vol. 17, No. 11 (1989), p. 18.

Notes to Chapter 11

1. When the Socinians (Unitarians) were driven out from Poland they found refuge in Transylvania and Hungary and established Unitarian churches which survive until the present.

2. Trond Gilberg, "Religion and Nationalism in Romania," *Religion and Nationalism in Soviet and East European Politics*, Pedro Ramet, ed. (Durham, NC: Duke Press Policy Studies, 1984), p. 171.

3. Janice Broun, "The Catholic Church in Romania," *Catholicism and Politics in Communist Societies*, Pedro Ramet, ed. (Durham and London: Duke University Press, 1990), p. 209. A frequent" alternate name is the Greek Catholic Church. Here this will be avoided because the actual ritual was originally in old church Slavonic and it was changed into Romanian at a later date.

4. Keith Hitchins, "The Romanian Orthodox Church and the State," *Religion and Atheism in the USSR and Eastern Europe*, Bociurkiw and Strong, eds., p. 314.

5. In addition to Romanians there are Hungarians, Germans, Serbians, Ukrainians, Jews, Gypsies, Armenians, and other smaller national groups.

6. In addition to the majority Romanian Orthodox, there are Catholics (Latin and Eastern Rites), Hungarian Reformed, Evangelical-Lutherans (German and Hungarian), Unitarian, Jews, Muslims, Armenian Apostolic, Serbian Orthodox, Baptists, Pentecostalists, Seventh-Day Adventists, Evangelical Brethren, and so forth.

7. Alan Scarfe, "The Romanian Orthodox Church," *Eastern Christianity and Politics in the Twentieth Century*, Pedro Ramet, ed. (Durham and London: Duke University Press, 1988), p. 213. According to Earl Pope, there are sources that seem to be inferring that the Eastern Rite Catholics virtually shared the establishment with the Orthodox.

8. Trevor Beeson, *Discretion and Valour*, pp. 304–305.

9. Robert Tobias, *op. cit.*, p. 320.

10. Ibid., p. 321.

11. The author travelled several times in Romania, first in 1965, and found that at night the villages, towns, and cities would be almost deserted except for policemen in several type uniforms patrolling nearly every intersection. One may presume that far larger were the number of plainclothes police, the infamous "*Securitate*" for which it is estimated that between one in ten to one in four citizens worked as spies or denunciators.

12. The Neo-Protestants or Free Churches received no financial subsidies.

13. Since 1957 also called the Department for the Cults. In literature the term Religions and Cults is used interchangeably.

14. Vishinsky was the Minister of Foreign Affairs of the USSR.

15. Tobias, *op. cit.*, p. 321.

16. The full text of the relevant articles in Tobias, *op. cit,.* pp. 338–339.

17. The full text of the law appears in Tobias, *op. cit.*, pp. 340–347.

18. Each oath ends with "So help me God." It makes one wonder what are the implications of this invocation for an atheist government.

19. Quoted in Tobias, *op. cit.*, p. 332.

20. Ibid., p. 334.

21. Beeson, *op. cit.*, p. 308 regards Groza the architect of the relatively more benevolent attitude toward the Orthodox Church than experienced in other countries. In 1948 Groza was reported saying about the Orthodox Church that it "is an institution of permanent

benefit to the life of the nation. She is part of the State and as such seeks to remain in step with the spirit of the time."

22. Scarfe, *op. cit.*, p. 222.

23. Broun, *Conscience and Captivity*, p. 206.

24. Broun, "The Catholic Church in Romania," p. 214. Three out of the six bishops died during the first imprisonment but actually five of the six died in prison, two having been re-imprisoned in the late 1950s.

25. Ibid., pp. 213–214.

26. Scarfe, *op. cit.*, p. 219.

27. Earl A. Pope, "Religious Situation in Romania," in *Religion and Communist Society*, Dennis J. Dunn, ed. (Berkeley: Berkeley Slavic Specialties, 1983), p. 126.

28. Quoted in Tobias, *op. cit.*, p. 326.

29. Beeson, *op. cit.*, p. 304.

30. Broun, "The Catholic Church in Romania," p. 219. Earl Pope, who interviewed Augustine reports that this was a source of great personal anguish for Augustine.

31. Tobias, *op. cit.*, p. 335.

32. Ibid., p. 331.

33. For a narrative detailing the harassment of the "Lord's Army" see "The 'Lord's Army' Movement in the Romanian Orthodox Church," *RCL*, Vol. 8, No. 4 (Winter 1980), pp. 314–317.

34. Richard Wurmbrand published a series of books, such as *Christ in the Communist Prisons*, Charles Foley, ed. (New York: Coward-McCann, 1968), *God's Underground* (London, 1968), *If That Were Christ Would You Give Him Your Blanket?* (London, 1970), *Sermons in Solitary Confinement* (London, 1969), and *Tortured for Christ* (London, 1967). Wurmbrand became a well-known anti-Communist who frequently testified in the U. S. Congress and was well known on the conservative lecture circuit. It is hard to know whether he overdramatized and exploited his suffering, but it is well known that massive inhumanity can easily appear incredible. If a fraction of what Wurmbrand writes is true, then the treatment of prisoners by Romanian authorities was more than bestial.

35. Tobias, *op.cit.*, p. 337.

36. No. IV (1949) quoted in Tobias, *op. cit.*, p. 351.

37. Name changed from Ministry of Cults to Department of Cults.

38. Broun, "The Catholic Church in Romania," p. 221.

39. Scarfe, *op. cit.*, p. 227.

40. Grown to 200,000-300,000 according to Pope, "Religious Situation in Romania," p. 140.

41. An excerpt of the text of the Appeal may be found in Appendix N, Broun, *Conscience and Captivity*, pp. 339–340. The exposition of the content of the Appeal is from this text.

42. In Romanian, "Asociatia pentru Libertatea Religiosa Crestina."

43. "ALRC's Programme of Demands," *RCL*, Vol. 7, No. 3 (1979), pp. 170–173.

44. Ibid.

45. "Truths Which Cannot be Hidden," *RCL*, Vol. 10, No. 2 (Autumn 1982), pp. 218–226.

46. Broun, *Conscience and Captivity*, pp. 212–213 and 235–236. Calciu was denounced as a neo-fascist by a group of Orthodox priests, "Letter from Romanian Orthodox Priests," *RCL*, Vol. 7, No. 3 (Autumn 1979), pp. 175–176 and defended by his admirers in ibid., p. 177.

47. Earl Pope reports a source in the hierarchy saying, "we cheered him quietly but in the end we were powerless to assist."

48. Scarfe, *op. cit.*, p. 223.

49. Beeson, *op. cit.*, p. 320.

50. A reprint of *Kialto Szo samizdat* in *RCL*, Vol. 17, No. 4 (Winter 1989), pp. 357–359 and István Tökés, "The *Ex-lex* Situation in the Reformed Church in Transylvania," in ibid., pp. 359–360.

51. Gilberg, *op. cit.*, pp. 177–182.

52. Broun, *Conscience and Captivity*, pp. 233–234.

53. The policy toward the Jews was fraught with contradiction because Romania remained the only Eastern European country not to cut diplomatic relations with Israel, to maintain flights to Israel, and to allow nearly free contacts of Romanian Jews with world Jewry.

54. Gilberg, *op. cit.*, p. 184.

55. Many regarded the aging Ceausescu insane.

56. *Telegraful Roman*, Nos. 29–30–31–32 and 33–34, 1989 (1st–15th of August and 1st September [numbers and dates provided as printed in the newspaper]. This author wrote in an editorial in *OPREE*, Vol. IX, No. 6 (November, 1989), pp. i–ii about the humiliation which such idolatry must have caused to spiritually sensitive religious leaders.

57. Author's own personal knowledge from being on the Europe/USSR Committee of the NCCC. A WCC delegation was re-

ceived earlier in 1989 whose report to the General Secretary, Emilio Castro, was used to make his recommendation to the WCC meeting in Moscow, July 17–26, 1989.

58. Mark Elliott, "László Tökés, Timisoara and the Romanian Revolution," *OPREE*, Vol. X, No. 5 (October 1990), pp. 22–28.

59. Initial reports of a thousand killed seem vastly exaggerated (later reduced to about a hundred) but at the time it fueled popular furor not only in Timişoara but also in Bucharest where the news spread rapidly. For other narratives of the events see Fiona Tupper-Carey, "Romania," *RCL*, Vol. 18, No. 2 (Summer 1990), pp. 180–183 and Earl A. Pope, "The Church and the Romanian Revolution," photocopied paper delivered at the IVth World Congress for Soviet and East European Studies, Harrogate, England, July 21–26, 1990.

60. Pope, "The Churches and the Romanian Revolution," p. 14.

61. It is estimated that 150,000 people died annually of starvation and freezing. Some reports on the situation are Paul McGinn, "Uncertainty in Romania," *America*, Vol. 163, No. 3 (July 28–August 4, 1990), pp. 54–55 and "Romania Land of Hope," *Conscience: International Edition* (Andijk, Netherlands), No. 1 (January 1990), pp. 1–2.

62. Pope, "The Churches and the Romanian Revolution," pp. 23–24.

63. László Tökes, "The Possible Role of Rumania's Churches in the Social Renewal of the Country," World Council of Churches document, published in *OPREE*, Vol. X, No. 5 (October 1990), pp. 29–32.

64. Robert C. Lodwick, "Romanian Trip Report and Romanian Roundtable Meeting," *Caree Communicator*, No. 33 (Summer 1990), pp. 31–32.

65. "East Europeans Concerned About the Role of the Majority Churches," *European Baptist Press Service*, Bulletin 02/90 (February 10, 1990), p. 3.

Notes to Chapter 12

1. Francis Dvornik, *The Slavs in European History and Civilization* (New Brunswick, NJ: Rutgers University Press, 1962), p. 2.

2. The Eastern Orthodox branch of Christianity is currently organized in two churches, the Serbian Orthodox Church (that comprises all Serbians and Montenegrins) and the Macedonian Ortho-

dox Church, the latter having broken off from the Serbian Orthodox Church after World War II and is regarded schismatic by the Serbian Orthodox Church. An estimated 40 percent of the population is Orthodox, though no official statistic on religious affiliation exists and estimates are notoriously inaccurate.

3. While the Roman Catholic Church is formally a single church in union with Rome there are actually a number of clearly discernible clusters of that church along ethnic lines, i.e. the Church among Croatians, Slovenians (being the two larger) and the Church among Albanians, Hungarians, Italians, and other minorities. There seems to be relatively little mutual interest among those branches of a presumable universal church. There is also an Eastern or Greek Rite Catholic Church in union with Rome as well as various branches of Old Catholics who are not in union with Rome. About 35 percent of the population is Roman Catholic, with the same proviso as for the Orthodox.

4. John V.A. Fine, Jr., *The Bosnian Church: A New Interpretation* (Boulder, CO: East European Quarterly, 1975).

5. Currently there are two main groups of Muslims, the Bosnian Muslims who are of Slavic ethnicity and Albanian Muslims. Most Turkish Muslims emigrated. About 15 percent of the population is Muslim.

6. The total number of Protestants is less than 1 percent. Most of the Reformation churches are also ethnically organized and gather primarily national minorities, thus there is a Hungarian Reformed Church, a Slovak Evangelical Lutheran Church and smaller Lutheran clusters among Hungarians, Croatians, and Slovenes.

7. The Neo-Protestants churches are very numerous and quite small. Among the more notable are the Baptists, Seventh-Day Adventists, Pentecostalists, Methodists, Jehovah's Witnesses, and Free Brethren.

8. Prior to World War II the German minority was significant in the northern regions but after World War II nearly all emigrated to West Germany.

9. Arcot Krishnaswami, *Study of Discrimination in the Matter of Religious Rights and Practices* (New York: United Nations, 1960), p. 11.

10. Listed were Serbian Orthodox, Roman Catholic, Greek Catholic, Old Catholic, Lutheran, Reformed, Baptist, Methodist, Nazarene, Muslim, and Jewish faiths.

11. Josip Horak, "Church and State Relations in Yugoslavia," *Journal of Church and State*, Vol. 28, No. 3 (Autumn 1986), p. 477.

12. Most of the Jews emigrated to Israel in the late 1940s and early 1950s leaving behind a minuscule Jewish religious community and only a slightly larger secularized Jewish community.

13. The degree of Roman Catholic complicity with the leadership and policies of the "*Ustashe*" and the leaders of the Independent State of Croatia is the subject of vehement debates which the author wishes to avoid and leaves this complex matter to other historians to investigate.

14. For a detailed description of church-state relations from 1945 to 1972, see Stella Alexander, *Church and State in Yugoslavia Since 1945* (London, New York, Melbourne: Cambridge University Press, 1979). A more elaborate discussion of the periodization is found in Paul Mojzes, "Christian-Marxist Dialogue in the Context of a Socialist Society," *Journal of Ecumenical Studies*, Vol. 9, No. 4 (Winter 1972), p. 25.

15. Other attempts at periodization have been made by other scholars. See, e.g., Zdenko Roter, "Razvoj odnosov med katoliško cerkvijo in deržavo v socijalistični Jugoslavijii," *Teorija in praksa* No. 7 (September 1970), pp. 1280–1282; and Pedro Ramet, "Catholicism and Politics in Socialist Yugoslavia," *Religion in Communist Lands*, Vol. 10 (Winter 1982), p. 257.

16. These are today simply professional associations which the government ceased to manipulate since the 1960s.

17. Marić, *Deca komunizma*, p. 216.

18. Ibid. Translated from Serbian by Paul Mojzes.

19. J. Hutchinson Cockburn, *Religious Freedom in Eastern Europe* (Richmond, VA: John Knox Press, 1953), pp. 94–96.

20. Alexander, *op. cit.*, pp. 95–120.

21. Such measures were not directed only against religious people. These were violent times when Tito's forces were establishing totalitarian control and the brunt of their suppression was leveled not only at various enemies but even at Communists who stepped out of line or who were scapegoated though innocent of charges levelled against them.

22. Trevor Beeson, *Discretion and Valour* (Glasgow: Collins Fontana Books, 1974), p. 264. There is an error in Beeson's text ". . . declared that all citizens are equal in spite of national, racial or religious hatred and intolerance . . ." which I state in its correct

from in the text.

23. Interview with Zdenko Roter, West Chester, PA, November 19, 1987.

24. One needs to remember that Tito and his cohorts were under great pressure from the Soviet Union and its East European allies, having been expelled from the Informbureau and threatened by an invasion, while the relations with the West were still very bad. So, Tito's elite maintained itself in power against all real and potential threats by summary suspension of all human rights, for which they had little inherent respect in the first place. After all, they had no respect for bourgeois law during old Yugoslavia when they had been declared illegal, nor could they respect orderly procedures under the conditions of Nazi occupation and a civil war during World War II. Certainly they were not about to give up power gained in such a bloody manner so quickly. Hence the notion of respect for human rights was alien to them and the idea would emerge only gradually, mostly by the increasing contacts with various Social Democrats from Western Europe, usually via dissidents like Milovan Djilas and Vladimir Dedijer.

25. Stella Alexander, *Church and State in Yugoslavia* (Cambridge: Cambridge University Press, 1979), (pp. 127–131.

26. Interview with Roter, *op. cit.*

27. Alexander, *op. cit.*, p. 146. For an extensive summary of the law see pp. 221–225.

28. Manojlo Bročić, "The Position and Activities of Religious Communities in Yugoslavia," in *Religion and Atheism in the USSR and Eastern Europe*, p. 357.

29. Alexander, *op. cit.*, p. 225.

30. Interview with Roter, *op. cit.*

31. Ivan Lazić, *Pravno-politološki aspekti odnosa vjerskih zajednica prema našem društvu* [Legal-politological aspects of relations of religious communities toward our society] (Zagreb: Institut za društvena istraživanja, 1976).

32. Gerald Shenk, "The Social Role of Religion in Contemporary Yugoslavia," unpublished doctoral dissertation Northwestern University, Evanston, IL, 1987, p. 102.

33. Ibid., p. 103.

34. Mojzes, *Christian-Marxist Dialogue in Eastern Europe*, pp. 128–158.

35. Luchterhandt, "Die Religionsfreiheit in Albanien und Jugoslawien," (photocopied paper), p. 8.

36. Horak, *op. cit.*, p. 478.

37. Luchterhandt, "Die Religionsfreiheit im Verständniss der sozialistischen Staaten," in *Religionsfreiheit in Osteuropa*, pp. 46–47.

38. Radovan Samardžić, *Religious Communities in Yugoslavia* (Belgrade: Srboštampa, 1981), p. 24 quoted in Horak, *op. cit.*, p. 480.

39. Shenk, *op. cit.*, p. 107.

40. Todo Kurtović, *Crkva i religija u socjialističkom samoupravnom društvu*, (Belgrade: Rad, 1978), pp. 353–354. This book is a collection of essays and speeches written by the author while he was the head of the Bosnia and Herzegovina and later federal commission for religious affairs. The book may well be the worst book on religion published in Yugoslavia. The author is the representative of a self-congratulatory approach by members of the Communist Party of Yugoslavia who see all errors made by the churches and a few 'sectarian' communists but the Party was always on the right path.

41. Zdenko Roter, "Yugoslavia at the Crossroads: A Sociological Discourse," *OPREE*, Vol. VIII, No. 2 (May 1988), p. 20.

42. Most of the information on legislation regarding religion is from Ivan Lazić, "Pravni i činjenični položaj konfesionalnih zajednica u Jugoslaviji," in Zlatko Frid, ed., *Vjerske zajednice u Jugoslaviji* (Zagreb: NIP "Binoza," 1970), pp. 45–77; and Stella Alexander, "Yugoslavia: New Legislation on the Legal Status of Religious Communities," *RCL* 8 (Summer, 1980), pp. 119–124.

43. There was even some discussion as to whether the selector and coach of the national basketball team could be a former star who had become a Mormon during his stay in the U. S. A.

44. As reported in AKSA Bulletin, an English translation made by Stella Alexander and Muriel Heppel, and distributed by Keston College in England, hereafter abbreviated as AB.

45. AB, October 21, 1982, p. 8.

46. Ibid.

47. AB, December 17, 1982, p. 9.

48. AB, August 5, 1983, p. 9.

49. Ibid.

50. AB, September 12, 1983, p. 4.

51. AB, November 22, 1983, p. 8.

52. AB, December, 1983, p. 3.

53. Ibid.
54. AB, February 21, 1984, p. 10.
55. AB, March 29, 1984, pp. 8–9.
56. Ibid., p. 14.
57. AB, May 10, 1984, p. 6.
58. AB, July 6, 1984, p. 5.
59. Ibid., p. 7.
60. Ibid., p. 8.
61. AB, August 23, 1984, pp. 7–8.
62. Ibid., p. 8.
63. AB, October 11, 1984, p. 4.
64. Ibid., p. 5.
65. Ibid., p. 8.
66. AB, November 16, 1984, p. 5.
67. AB, June 20, 1985, p. 7.
68. Ibid., p. 8.
69. AB, July 25, 1985, p. 4. A somewhat different account is given on p. 6, where a Franciscan priest, Branko Jurić, was reportedly sentenced to fourteen days for saying in the confessional that, if his penitents were swearing at God, why not swear at Tito and the state.
70. Ibid., p. 5.
71. Ibid., p. 6.
72. Ibid., p. 7.
73. AB, August 16, 1985, p. 7.
74. Ibid., pp. 5 and 6.
75. Conversation with the Lilić family in Novi Sad, Yugoslavia, summer 1982 and with Dr. Miroslav Volf, Stony Point, NY, October 27, 1990.
76. Broun, *Conscience and Captivity*, p. 265, entitled a section of the chapter on Yugoslavia, "Still a Police State," pointing out that despite its reputation as a liberal Communist country there were more political prisoners according to Amnesty International than in most other Eastern European countries. The Yugoslav press reported in the late 1980s and 1990s horror stories by victims of the state security and police brutalities, including mass murders during the 1940s and 1950s (e.g. Pavle Shosberger, "Stavimo tačku na zlo," *Vjesnik*, December 12, 1990, p. 2; "Stravična svjedočanstva o zločinu," *Vjesnik*, July 2, 1990, p. 1, "Zločin se više ne skriva," *Vecernji list*, July 3, 1990, pp. 1, 5).
77. Conversation with Milenko Popov, summer 1982.

78. Paul Mojzes, "A History of the Congregational and Methodist Churches in Bulgaria and Yugoslavia" (doctoral dissertation at Boston University, 1965), p. 598. Janice Broun, *Conscience and Captivity*, p. 257 incorrectly dates the last murder by the police of a believer in 1956.

79. Interview with Kitan Petreski, West Chester, fall 1985.

80. Broun, *Conscience and Captivity*, pp. 261, 270–271, 274, and 279.

81. AB, November, 1984, p. 5.

82. The authorities even permitted the celebration of a mass at an international nudist assembly, though it did provoke considerable upheaval in the Catholic Church when it was suggested that the officiating priest should be nude.

83. Planned papal visits have been repeatedly postponed due to haggling whether it should be a state or a church visit and the Serbian Orthodox qualms about such a visit.

84. AB, May 19, 1983, p. 9.

85. Christopher Cviic, "An Outburst of Faith," *The Tablet*, October 6, 1984, pp. 964–966.

86. Mojzes, *Christian Marxist Dialogue in Eastern Europe*, pp. 128–158.

87. *Aksa Bulletin*, No. 19, ((March 6, 1989), p. 2.

88. "Relations between the State and Roman Catholic Church in Croatia, Yugoslavia in the 1970's and 1980's." *OPREE*, Vol. 2, No. 3 (June, 1982), p, 22.

89. "Catholicism and Politics," pp. 271–272.

90. *Aksa Bulletin*, No. 22 (July 7, 1989), p. 6.

91. *Aksa Bulletin*, No. 22, p. 7.

92. *Aksa Bulletin*, No. 20 (April 26, 1990), p. 6.

93. *Aksa Bulletin*, No. 20, p. 6.

94. Interview with Vjekoslav Bajsić in Zagreb, Yugoslavia, August 2, 1985.

95. Interview with the Martin Hovan in Novi Sad, Yugoslavia, August 6, 1985.

96. Milovan Djilas, *The Unperfect Society: Beyond the New Class*. Transl. Dorian Cooke (New York: Harcourt, Brace & World, Inc., 1969), p. 39.

97. AB, No. 18 (January 25, 1990), p. 2.

98. Ibid., p. 1.

99. Ibid., p. 6.

100. The role of Milošević in the polarization of Yugoslavia is significant. He is certainly a populist and Serbian nationalist with a dedication to socialist principles, but his opponents ascribe to him pronounced bolshevik tendencies. One thing is sure: he was the first politician to clearly see that Tito is really dead and that therefore power is for grabs. He skillfully used the Serbian "mass movement" which toppled all Serbian and Montenegrin Communist officials who favored autonomy and regionalization and became a symbol of the Serbian aspiration to live in a single country. His enemies charged him with an attempt to place all the republics under Serbian dominance.

101. An interesting phenomenon is that all ethnic groups in Yugoslavia perceive themselves as victims of the policies engineered by their rivals.

102. Momčilo Škoro, "Komunisti ruše Broza," *Yu Novosti*, No. 518, (May 20–June 10, 1990), p. 12.

103. The first was "old" Yugoslavia of 1918–1941, the second was the "new" Titoist Yugoslavia of 1945–1989. Many argued that the entire concept had been a mistake, a kind of "shot-gun" marriage with serious questions as to whether the idea could be salvaged.

104. Zoran Medved, "Hoće li se Demos raspasti," *Danas*, Vol. 9, No. 450 (October 2, 1990), p. 24. Medved reports that the reputable sociologists Veljko Rus issued these warnings.

105. Broun, *Conscience and Captivity*, p. 272.

106. Marinko Čulić, "Nismo u naručju vlasti," *Danas*, Vol. 9, No. 461 , (December 18, 1990), pp. 20–23.

107. Jasmina Kuzmanović, "Država ide u Canossu," *Danas*, (September 18, 1990), pp. 35–37. Henry IV came to acknowledge papal supremacy to Gregory VII at Canossa where he was made to wait barefoot for three days prior to the pope's willingness to accept the emperor's penance.

108. Luka Vincetić, "Ljubav oltara i političara," *Danas*, (September 18, 1990), pp. 22–23.

109. "Povratak pravoslavlju," *Vecernji list*, (July 3, 1990), p. 4.

110. E. g. Špiro Marašović, "Gospodo, pomiluj," *Veritas*, Vol. 29, No. 9 (September 1990), p. 5 and Drago Šimundža, "Stvarnosti i obaveze s kojima se zajednički suočavamo," *Crkva u svijetu*, Vol. 25, No. 2 (1990), pp. 97–102.

111. Kuzmanović, *op. cit.*, p. 37 and Ljubo Weiss, "Neizbrisivi tragovi duha," *Danas*, Vol. 9, No. 456, (November 13, 1990), pp. 39–41.

112. "Promjene u zdravstvu," *Vecernji list,* November 22, 1990, p. 3.

113. Milovan Djilas, "Bosna spona ili razdor," in *Borba* as reprinted in *Vjesnik,* (July 2, 1990), p. 12.

114. S. P. Ramet, "Islam in Yugoslavia Today," *RCL,* Vol. 18, No. 3 (Autumn 1990), p. 227.

115. Manojlo Tomić, "Pod šeširom ili fesom," *Danas,* Vol. 9, No. 449, (September 25, 1990), p. 22.

116. Marinko Čulić, "Zaruke zvijezde i krsta," *Danas,* Vol. 9, No. 436, (June 26, 1990), p. 28. This somewhat tendentious article tainted by anti-Serbian bias claims a symbiotic union between the Serbian Orthodox Church and Milošević's government but contains otherwise useful information.

117. See his rather moderate interview in Rade Peleš, "Mitropolit Gospodin Dr. Jovan Pavlović: Nikad nismo imali krstašku strategiju," *Nedelja* (Sarajevo), June 10, 1990, pp. 5–7.

118. "Patrijarh iz šešira," *Danas,* Vol. 9, No. 460, (December 11, 1990), pp. 32–33.

119. Momčilo Škoro, "Prerano kukurikanje," *Yu-novosti,* No. 515, (February 20–March 20, 1990), p. 9.

120. E. g. the late Bishop Vasilije Kostić according to Voja Blagojević, "Vladika je tamnovao nevin," *Illustrovana Politika,* No. 1680, (January 15, 1991), p. 47.

121. Dragan Lakičević, "Prerušeni svetac," *Osmica,* Vol. 11, No. 533, June 14, 1990, p. 10.

122. Čulić, "Zaruke zvijezde i krsta," pp. 28–29.

123. Cf. Metropolitan John in Peles, *op. cit.,* p. 8.

124. AB, No. 22 (July 7, 1989), p. 7. A similar statement was issued by the Commission "Iustitia et pax."

125. Slobodan Reljić, "Mira još neće biti," *NIN,* No. 2085, December 14, 1990, p. 26.

126. AB, No. 22, p. 20.

127. Luko Brailo, "Progledalo drugo oko u glavi," *Nedeljna Dalmacija,* July 1, 1990, p. 13.

Notes to Chapter 13

1. Otto Luchterhandt, "Durchbruch zur Religionsfreiheit Osteuropa und das KSZE-Folgetreffen von Wien," *G2W*, Vol. 19, No. 1 (January 1991), pp. 19–24.

2. Otto Luchterhandt, "Neue Religionsgesetze Russlands und der Sowjetunion," in *G2W*, Vol. 19, No. 2 (February 1991), pp. 23–25. The same issue contains the German translation of both as on pp. 25–32.

3. "Neues Religionsgesetz," *G2W*, Vol. 19, Nos. 6 (June 1991), p. 11.

4. "Religionsfreiheit," *G2W*, Vol. 19, Nos. 7/8, p. 3. Translation from German by Paul Mojzes.

5. "Neues Religionsgesetz," *G2W*, Vol. 19, Nos. 7/8, p. 16.

6. "Gegen Trennung," *G2W*, Vol. 19, No. 5 (May 1991), pp. 5–6.

7. "Gegner des Religionsunterrichts," *G2W*, Vol. 19, No. 1, p. 4.

8. "Kirchen-spannungen," *G2W*, Vol. 19, No. 5, p. 6.

9. For a perceptive analysis of the effects of the coup see Alan Geyer, "Three Days in August: Reflections on the Soviet Coup and Its Consequences," *OPREE*, Vol. XI, No. 6 (December 1991), pp. 1–11.

10. The author received in May 1991 from Prof. Janis Vejš of Riga an English language typescript of a draft of the "Law of the Republic of Latvia: 'On Religious Organizations.' " The law provided greater religious liberty than the Soviet federal law of October 1990.

11. Patricia Lefevere, "Orthodox-Catholic Relations in the Soviet Union," *OPREE*, Vol. XI, No. 6 (November 1991), pp. 39–43.

12. Stefan Schreiner, "Im Strudel von Glasnost und Perestroika," and six additional articles all in *G2W*, Vol. 19, Nos. 7/8, pp. 24–42.

13. In "Foreword," *The Soviet Union on the Brink: An Inside Look at Christianity & Glasnost* by Kent R. Hill (Portland, OR: Multnomah and Institute on Religion and Democracy, 1991), p. 13.

14. In May 1991 during a conference on "The Role of Religion in Newly Pluralistic Societies: The Case of Eastern Europe," in Budapest, Hungary, the participants were told by several members of the parliament who belonged to diverse political parties that they all felt

there was justification to pass enabling legislation for the reclaiming of lost properties, including schools, by religious denomination. Church leaders on the other hand expressed caution not to rush the project because they often lack the financial means to properly maintain such real estate.

15. "Religionsverbot—ein Fehler," *G2W*, Vol. 19, No. 5, p. 9.

16. Probably the richest source of information on developments affecting religious liberty in 1991 is the annual *Albanian Catholic Bulletin*, Vol. XII, 1991.

17. Dan Stets, "Bulgaria communists likely out," *Philadelphia Inquirer*, October 15, 1991, p. 3.

18. "Keine Umgehung des Gesetzes," *G2W*, Vol. 19, No. 5, p. 25. This is a special issue highlighting Bulgaria's religions.

19. S. Popov, "Perestroika Without Christ?" *OPREE*, Vol. XI, No. 5 (October 1991), pp. 15–17.

20. Pavel Smetana, "Die Liebe deckt die meisten Sünden zu," and Miloš Rejchrt, "Ich kann ihnen nicht trauen," in *G2W*, Vol. 19, No. 6, p. 21 and pp. 22–23 respectively. It should be pointed out that in Poland the situation with the files of the secret police were dealt with by allegedly destroying them so that such conflicts would not take place. The above mentioned issue of *G2W* is a special emphasis issue on Czechoslovakia.

21. "Slowakei entschuldigt sich bei Juden," *G2W*, Vol. 19, No. 2, pp. 13–14.

22. "Alle waren 'feindlich-negativ': Zur Stasi-Überwachung der Kirchen," *G2W*, Vol. 19, No. 3, (March 1991), pp. 23–26.

23. "P. Bulányi fordert Rehabilitierung," *G2W*, Vol. 19, No. 1, p. 12.

24. "Kardinal Mindszenty in Estergom beigesetzt," *G2W*, Vol. 19, No. 6, p. 12.

25. During a conference in Budapest in May 1991 , the author heard a lecture by the newly-elected Hungarian Reform Bishop Lóránt Hegedüs, a former dissident pastor who had been exiled to a remote village pastorate. I got the impression that such an isolation did not contribute to an ecumenical vision but rather to a somewhat inflexible and self-righteous attitude toward others. This points that many of the new leaders will have a clear moral vision but perhaps a limited experience in encountering diverse traditions and viewpoints. He also expressed his opinion that the Protestants cannot forgive the Catholics for the past injuries unless the pope lays the wreath at the

monument to the victims of the Counter-Reformation.

26. "A. Michnik über die Lage in Polen," *G2W*, Vol. 19, No.5, p. 5.

27. "Methodisten in Polen," *G2W*, Vol. 19, No. 6, pp. 4–5. Also Bogdan Tranda, "The Situation of Protestants in Today's Poland," *RCL*, Vol. 19, Nos. 1–2 (Summer 1991), pp. 37–44.

28. "Kathedralenstreit geht weiter," *G2W*, Vol. 19, Vol. 5, p. 6.

29. Waldemar Chrostowski, "III Theological Symposium 'The Church, Jews and Judaism,' " manuscript accepted for publication in *OPREE*, Vol. XII (1992).

30. "Ökumenischer Appell," *G2W*, Vol. 19, No. 1, p. 5.

31. "Kirchendialog abgebrochen," *G2W*, Vol. 19, No. 6, p. 5.

32. For a fuller treatment of the subject matter see the author's "Nationalism, Religion, and Peace in Eastern Europe with Special Reference to Yugoslavia," *OPREE*, Vol. XI, No. 6 (December 1991), pp. 12–31.

33. *European Baptist Press Service*, Bulletin No. 11 (July 5, 1991), p. 1.

34. Darko Pavičić, "Svećenik nije komesar," *Danas*, October 8, 1991, p. 28. The reference is to a Franciscan, Fra Duka, who has not been disciplined either by his order or the bishop, though Franjo Cardinal Kuharić, expressed disagreement with this form of ministering to the faithful. He did not condemn it, however.

35. Jakub Trojan, "The Role of Religion in Newly Pluralistic Societies of Eastern Europe: A Protestant Perspective," *OPREE*, Vol. XI, No. 5, p. 1.

36. Waldemar Chrostowski, "Poland: Pluralism After the Experience of the Desert: A Roman Catholic Perspective," *OPREE*, Vol. XI, No. 5, p. 18.

37. M. Volf, "When the Unclean Spirit Leaves: Tasks of Eastern European Churches after the 1989 Revolution," *Cross Currents*, Vol. 41, No. 1 (Spring 1991), p. 83.

38. For a perceptive analysis of the Marxist legacy after the demise of socialism in Eastern Europe see Charles West, "Christian Ethics and the Future of Eastern Europe," *OPREE*, Vol. XI, No. 6, pp. 32–38.